Networking
Self-Teaching Guide

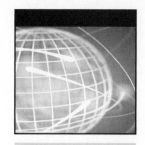

Networking
Self-Teaching Guide

OSI, TCP/IP, LANs, MANs, WANs, Implementation, Management, and Maintenance

James Edwards
Richard Bramante

WILEY

Wiley Publishing, Inc.

Networking Self-Teaching Guide

Published by
Wiley Publishing, Inc.
10475 Crosspoint Boulevard
Indianapolis, IN 46256
www.wiley.com

ISBN: 978-0-470-40238-2

Manufactured in the United States of America

10 9 8 7 6 5 4 3 2 1

Library of Congress Cataloging-in-Publication Data:

Edwards, James, 1962-
  Networking self-teaching guide : OSI, TCP/IP, LANs, MANs, WANs, implementation, management, and maintenance / James Edwards, Richard Bramante.
      p. cm.
Includes index.
ISBN 978-0-470-40238-2 (pbk.)
1. Computer networks. 2. Computer network protocols. 3. Computer network architectures. I. Bramante, Richard, 1944- II. Title.
TK5105.5.E28 2009
004.6'5 — dc22

                    2009004168

This book is dedicated to my brother, Joel, for all that he has done for so many over the years. I sincerely hope that he will forever be able to enjoy all of the good things that life has to offer. Whether he knows it or not, he has always been a source of inspiration for me and his encouragement has kept me going whenever a challenge was thrown my way. The best brother in the world! That's my brother, Joel.

— Jim Edwards

This book is dedicated to those who have supported me, not just during the writing of this book, but throughout my life. There have been many and too numerous to mention, but to all who have been there for me, I am deeply grateful. Deserving special mention are: My son, Rich; his wife, Michelle; my three grandchildren, Vanessa, Ethan, and Olivia; my parents; my siblings, Margaret, Mary, Josephine, Frank, and Salvatore; and the person who believed in me, unfailingly, even through all my blunders, my deceased wife, Barbara.

— Rich Bramante

About the Authors

Jim Edwards has more than 10 years of experience supporting data networks as a Premium Support Engineer. He has authored four books pertaining to data networking, as well as served as a technical editor.

Rich Bramante earned both a bachelor's and master's degree in electrical engineering from the University of Massachusetts – Lowell. He has worked in the technology industry for more than 40 years. For the past 11 years, he has worked for a major telecommunications equipment manufacturer, primarily within the VPN technology area.

Credits

Executive Editor
Carol Long

Development Editor
John Sleeva

Technical Editor
Don Thoreson

Production Editor
Angela Smith

Copy Editor
Lunaea Weatherstone

Editorial Manager
Mary Beth Wakefield

Production Manager
Tim Tate

Vice President and Executive Group Publisher
Richard Swadley

Vice President and Executive Publisher
Barry Pruett

Associate Publisher
Jim Minatel

Project Coordinator, Cover
Lynsey Stanford

Proofreader
Publication Services, Inc.

Indexer
Jack Lewis

Cover Image
© Chad Baker/Photodisc/Getty Images

Cover Designer
Michael Trent

Acknowledgments

First and foremost, Jim wants to thank Rich for being such a great co-author to work with. Rich and Jim had the opportunity to work together on a previous book and we make a great team. Jim is a bit of a pain in the neck,[1] so Rich may have other opinions on this whole team thing.

We would also like to send out a huge word of thanks for all of the individuals involved in the development of this book. To Carol Long, thank you for bringing the idea to us and trusting us to see it through. We really enjoyed it as much as we all thought we would. We also want to send a word of thanks to the development editor, John Sleeva, for keeping us in line. It was a pleasure working with you, sir. To Angela Smith, thank you for all the assistance you gave us during the production phase. It is always nice to work with people who are as friendly and helpful as everyone we have had the pleasure of working with at Wiley. Additionally, thank you to Don Thorenson for being our technical guinea pig and to Lunaea Weatherstone for catching all of our mistakes. Finally, to all the people who work behind the scenes, thank you for your support of this project.

---

[1] There are times when a bit of a pain in the neck is a good thing. Rich would like to thank Jim for his enduring good nature and understanding of the predicaments Rich finds himself involved with from time to time. We do make a good team because we have come to understand that although we work together each has his own methods when it comes to his work. Overall, mutual respect and understanding have helped us endure some trials and tribulations, and at the end of the day we can open a beer and still find a good laugh to share.

Contents

Introduction

The tremendous growth of local area networks (LANs) into the organizational, corporate, and home networks in the last 20 years has shown that there is a need for individuals with networking experience, and that need will remain for a long time coming. The U.S. Department of Labor forecasts an increase of 58 percent in the network and system support job market by 2016. With that growth comes opportunities for individuals with networking knowledge to secure their future.

There are very few instances where a business is run without a network of some sort. Retail environments maintain inventory, report income, transfer personnel information, and many other functions are handled within a LAN. LAN-to-LAN communication, secure tunneling, encryption and authentication, and many other functions are now handled by specific nodes and application programs that are part of the network.

In the beginning, most LANs were created around a shared data communication channel. Although not very reliable, these networks laid the foundation for the LANs of today. In the late 1980s, LANs migrated from a shared medium to more standardized and reliable media. These were twisted pair cabling and the use of a node called a hub. End-user needs were also a driving force in some of the advancements made in all facets of networking technology. Today, the advancements made in areas related to networking are far superior than what one would have dreamed possible back in the days of punch card coding and computers that filled huge rooms.

We have written this book to serve as a self-study guide for individuals looking to move into a networking career. Written as a basic networking guide, the book covers networking technologies, including the hardware, software, transmission media, and data transfer processes, along with operating systems and systems software; LANs, WANs, and MANs; and the interactions of network components.

How this Book Is Organized

The book is divided into four sections.

Part I: Networking Nuts and Bolts

The first part of the book teaches the essentials of networking. It is made up of seven chapters. The information covered in this part is a basic overview of many technologies used in networking today.

- Chapter 1, "Introduction to Networking," provides a review of basic networking concepts, including network types, relationships, topologies, protocols, history of networking, networking topologies, and standards and standards organizations. This chapter is intended as a primer for the target reader of the book. It can also be a great refresher chapter for those of us who like to get back to the basics from time to time. This chapter sets the framework for the rest of the book. Some important insights are provided into the relationship between network architecture and implementation, along with a lot of the history behind the development of modern LAN technology and the relevant standards.

- Chapter 2, "LANs, MANs, and WANs," explains the details of area networks, including the practices, standards, and standards organizations that operate at each level.

- Chapter 3, "Network Hardware and Transmission Media," takes a glance at the hardware and cabling that make up a network. Additionally, there is an introduction to binary numbering, IP addressing, and Ethernet concepts that provides an introduction to the in-depth coverage of these topics throughout this book.

- Chapter 4, "Operating Systems and Networking Software," covers the programs that are involved in a given network. The chapter shows how the operating systems interact with the components within a node and some of the basic services that are provided because of these interactions. Details are provided on how peer-to-peer networking operates, and the services and standards that allow this to happen. Finally, an overview of the more popular operating standards that are found in networks around the world is provided.

- Chapter 5, "The TCP/IP Protocol Suite," explains how the suite allows data communication to take place. No matter where a device is located, if it has a connection to the Internet and the device supports TCP/IP, you have a connection to the world. The chapter also covers the more popular TCP/IP protocols and what these technologies and standards do.

- Chapter 6, "Ethernet Concepts," explains the term *Ethernet* and how it is used to describe the most common network architecture used in a majority of today's networks. Beginning from the development of Ethernet all the way to current Ethernet technology, you will gain insight in the predominant LAN technology of today.

- Chapter 7, "Not to Be Forgotten," provides a basic overview of the most commonly deployed standards and technologies in networking today. From standards that are the tried and true technologies to the up-and-coming standards, this chapter will provide you with the understanding of the protocol and how it is used.

Part II: The OSI Layers

The second part of the book builds on the fundamentals discussed earlier to explore advanced features and capabilities offered in many of the standards that we discussed in the first part of the book. We provide an overview of the individual layers of the OSI model, and explain how the layers work with one another to communicate.

- Chapter 8, "The Upper Layers," covers the upper layers of the OSI reference model: the Application layer, Presentation layer, and Session layer. The chapter also provides information relating to the "translators" used so that information can flow smoothly and without error between these layers and eventually be sent over the network medium to another network node and the device servicing that node.

- Chapter 9, "The Transport Layer," explains how the Transport layer interacts with the Network layer and the Session layer. This layer is responsible for the end-to-end connection and datagram delivery, as well as congestion control and flow control. How connections are set up, monitored, and taken down is discussed. Operations of connection-oriented and connectionless protocols are also explained, with some further exploration of some protocols that operate at this layer.

- Chapter 10, "The Network Layer," looks at the Network layer and explains how it interfaces with the Data Link and Transport layers in communication processes.

- Chapter 11, "The Data Link Layer," discusses the Data Link layer and how it is used to allow for direct communication between network nodes over a physical channel. Covered are topics such as one-to-one communication as well as one-to-many. We cover concerns that are experienced in a LAN, as well as some of the mechanisms that are in place to recover from problems. In addition to the operations of this layer, we discuss the use of Layer 2 switches and bridges in a LAN.

Part III: Network Design and Implementation

The third part of the book takes the information that was covered in the first two parts and uses it to show provide practical insight into how thought processes work in network design.

- Chapter 12, "Design Methodologies," covers every facet of networking design, from inception to rollout. More of a guide that can be followed, the information that is provided will allow you to understand (and possibly develop) design concepts for a given network.

- Chapter 13, "Implementation," expands on the information in Chapter 12 and walks you through the process of implementing your design. At the end of the chapter is an exercise that will allow you to test all that you covered in this part of the book.

Part IV: Managing and Maintaining the Network

The last part of the book wraps up our journey to learning networking and covers the important tasks of securing, managing, and troubleshooting issues within a given network.

- Chapter 14, "Network Security," details the security concerns that those who manage networks need to be aware of and what you can do to assist in preventing attacks.

- Chapter 15, "Network Management," considers the extra functionality that allows nodes to be configured and managed and also allows for traffic monitoring and analysis. The chapter explains the Simple Network Management Protocol (SNMP), along with the structure and content of the management database. Special consideration is given to network operations, including software, staffing and support types, and network management and monitoring tools.

- Chapter 16, "Troubleshooting" details the top troubleshooting strategies for any network. The chapter covers the frequent issues that may arise and outlines some troubleshooting strategies. It also gives an overview of the troubleshooting process from beginning to end.

This book also includes the following four appendixes:

- Appendix A, "Additional Exercises" contains 265 additional questions, broken down by the chapters in which the answers can be found.

- Appendix B, "Exercise Answers" provides an answer to all of the questions that were asked throughout the book. It's up to you (or your instructor) how these can be used. We suggest you try to answer the questions before peeking ... they are really quite simple.

- Appendix C, "Glossary" provides gives definitions for the technical terms that are used throughout the book.

- Appendix D, "Acronyms" contains a multitude of common networking abbreviations and acronyms.

Who Should Read This Book

This book is a self-study guide that is geared toward individuals who have a background in information technology and want to migrate into a networking career, and individuals who are working for a certification or a degree in a networking field of study. Some of these career fields include

- Computer engineering
- Network sales and marketing
- Networking engineering
- Networking support
- Network field service engineering
- Network planning
- Network design
- Network administration
- Network security
- Network operations

The reader is assumed to be at least casually familiar with computers and information technology. It is not necessary to understand any networking concepts, as we cover networks from very basic concepts to more advanced protocols and standards that mandate today's technology, as well as future growth.

There is no attempt on our part to provide a complete, from-the-ground-up tutorial that will make you a professional in networking. That would be a task requiring several volumes of work. Our focus was to provide you with the information you need to have some experience for any popular standard in use in networking today.

The readers of this book can expect to learn everything they need to understand the concepts of networking. We have also provided addresses of websites you can explore to better understand the specifics of a standard that you have an interest in learning more about. Upon completion of this guide, you will have a knowledge of the more popular technologies out there and in the process you will learn about why things work and get some insight into the reasons why things in networking are the way it is.

NOTE If you are interested, we have provided two course syllabi on our website (www.wiley.com/compbooks). One syllabus is formatted for a quarter and the other will fit with an 18-week course schedule.

A Few Words from the Authors

We hope that you enjoy reading this book as much as we enjoyed writing it. We attempted to tie it all together, while providing details to some current and up and coming practices that you will come across at some point in your career.

As you start reading the book, you will notice that we have included a few extras throughout each chapter. Some of these will show up as an Acronym Alert or a Random Bonus Definition. Here are a couple of examples:

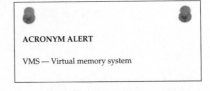

ACRONYM ALERT

VMS — Virtual memory system

Don't get confused when you come across these. The definitions and acronyms are random and do not necessarily apply to the subject in the particular chapter. We did this on purpose. One reason is that it helps break the monotony that one

RANDOM BONUS DEFINITION

10BASE5 — A baseband Ethernet system operating at 10 Mbps over thick coaxial cable.

may experience when reading through these darn technical books. The other reason is that it will hopefully help you to remember the terms as you progress through the book.

Another extra that we have included are our pop quizzes, which do apply to material that has been covered in that particular chapter. Here is an example:

At the end of each chapter are the answers to the pop quiz questions in that particular chapter. This should serve as a quick reference for you as you progress through the book. Additionally, each chapter will

POP QUIZ

Name 10 issues that you might have on the LAN.

have questions that pertain to information contained within the chapter. The answers to these questions are in Appendix B, but try to answer them without looking — you have more to gain that way.

We tried to spice up this book with some jokes and remarks that will hopefully make this enjoyable as well as informative. There are also some secret bonuses that we won't mention here (don't want to ruin the surprise).

Contact the Authors

We welcome your feedback, both on the usefulness (or not) of this, the second edition of this book, as well as any additions or corrections that should be made in future editions. Good network-related stories, jokes, and puns are always welcome. Please feel free to contact us:

```
NetworkingST@gmail.com
```

Networking Nuts and Bolts

In This Part

Introduction
to Networking

What, exactly, is the Internet? Basically it is a global network exchanging digitized data in such a way that any computer, anywhere, that is equipped with a node called a "modem" can make a noise like a duck choking on a kazoo.

— Dave Barry

Most of us would be lost without data networks.[1] Just a few short years ago, when computers were first starting to make their way into the business world, data sharing would normally have to be done by copying and then carrying the data from one PC to the next.[2] Today, the data is transferred from one user to the next in a fraction of a second. The growth that networking has undergone is remarkable. And it doesn't stop there. Every day there are new standards being proposed, new innovations being developed, and updates and changes to these being addressed.

Advances in technology are a fact of life. What needs to be considered is that any advance that requires the movement of data from one point to the next will need the services of a network to do so. This is why the world of networking has grown so much (and will continue to do so). With users transferring large amounts of data and the amount of that data growing at a exponential rate, there seems to be no end to the opportunities networks offer.

This chapter provides an introduction to networking. The intention is to provide you with a good foundation before we dive into the "nitty-gritty" of networking. In this chapter, we cover the history of networking, the TCP/IP and OSI reference models, standards organizations, as well as some discussions and definitions. The approach we took with the first chapter will hopefully be

---

[1] As a matter of fact, everyone would be affected in one way or another.
[2] A.k.a. sneakernet.

an enjoyable read, as well as set the tone for the rest of this book. We tried to make this an interesting base chapter, splitting up the boring parts as much as possible.

So, without further ado, welcome to our introduction to networking.

1.1   Networking: A Brief Introduction

```
Main Entry: net·work·ing3
Function: noun
1: the exchange of information or services among individuals, groups, or
institutions; specifically: the cultivation of productive relationships
for employment or business
2: the establishment or use of a computer network
```

A *data network* is a group of computers connected to one another by communication paths, as well as the standards that allow communication. A network can connect to other networks, allowing virtually worldwide communication between two endpoints. Many networks share information among one another, creating larger networks. Figure 1-1 is an example of a segment of a network.

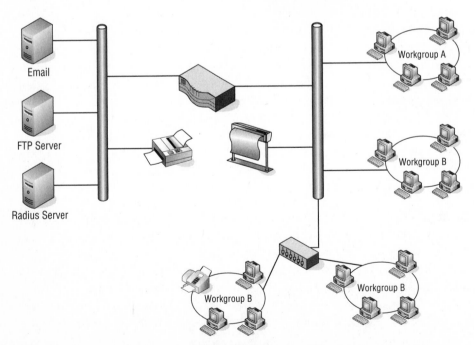

Figure 1-1 A computer network sharing applications as well as hardware

---

[3]*Dictionary.com Unabridged (v 1.1).* Random House, Inc., accessed April 18, 2008.

Many things are shared on a network. Corporate business is conducted nearly exclusively on the network. Networks allow users to share applications that are stored on servers in the network (e-mail applications, word-processing applications, databases, and many others). They allow communication between end users. Data can be shared between companies or individuals for business or personal purposes. Many websites provide opportunities that would have not existed if networks had never been developed. Not to mention the entire file sharing that is enabled by a network. The possibilities are endless, and you can be sure that someone is working on a new, cutting-edge service even as you read this sentence.

Typically, networks are identified by their size. They range from small local area networks (LANs) to larger wide area networks (WANs).[4] Many networks remain isolated from others. They are there to perform tasks that fit the specific needs of the group or organization the network supports. These networks have in place networking standards that support the needs of their organization, without regard to anything outside of the network boundaries. This is due largely to the fact that upgrading (updating) the network can be a cost that the organization has not justified. If an organization does not need a high-speed LAN, why spend the money to upgrade to one?

ACRONYM ALERT

VPN — Virtual private networking

There are many other networks that have taken advantage of the tremendous technology breakthroughs in the past 25 years that enable these networks to share data securely. Vendors can connect to their clients' LAN to exchange business data in an instant. Internet service providers (ISPs) provide the gateway to the Internet for their customers to share information. We discuss many networking advancements throughout this book.

1.1.1   Internetworking

The ability to share information over dissimilar[5] networks is known as *internetworking*. By using a set of standards, nodes in two (or more) data networks can share information reliably between one another. In a bridged network,[6] the term does not really apply[7] as the data is not shared with multiple segments and no internetworking protocol is required to transfer the data.

Internetworking was designed for the specific purpose of providing an avenue for sharing data among different nodes on the network and among

---

[4]These are both discussed in depth in Chapter 2, "LANs, MANs, and WANs."
[5]By dissimilar, we mean networks that are running with different node types and/or standards.
[6]A collection of networks that are interconnected at the data link layer using network bridges.
[7]Although there are some people out there who insist the term does apply.

different system software and operating systems. Consider how data can be shared by the medical profession. Lab work can be returned more quickly, allowing for a more immediate diagnosis. Many hospitals are now allowing x-rays and other data to be viewed over a network. Remote offices are able to access this data in an instant, decreasing the time for a diagnosis to a level not even dreamed of 15 years ago. The possibilities are endless.[8]

Networking terminology can be a bit tricky, but it's really not as confusing as it may appear at first. Following are some of the more common terms[9] used to define networks of various purposes.

> **RANDOM BONUS DEFINITION**
>
> network application — A process or software program that runs on a node within a network.

1.1.1.1   [10] An internet

An internet (lowercase *i*) is a group of distinct networks connected to one another via a gateway.[11] "An internet" is often confused with "the Internet" (uppercase *I*), but an internet is not necessarily part of the Internet.

Basically, any network that conforms to the standards defined in the TCP/IP protocol suite (see Section 1.4) is an internet.

1.1.1.2   The Internet

"A journey of a thousand sites begins with a single click."
— Author unknown

The Internet is what most people think of when they hear the term (upper- and lowercases aside). The Web, WWW, the Information Super Highway, and

---

[8] As a matter of fact, there is work ongoing that may allow a surgeon to log in from home and conduct an operation. Think how many lives can be saved because of this.

[9] As well as one that is outdated, but Jim just loves the word.

[10] Take a note of this number (not the section, the number). By the end of this book, you will know the significance of *all 1's*.

[11] As with many other networking terms, a gateway can mean many things. We are referring to a node capable of relaying user application information among networks employing different architectures and/or protocol suites.
Following are a few other definitions for the term *gateway* (for those of you who are interested):
(1) An internetworking node operating at the transport layer or above.
(2) An old term for an IP router.
(3) A marketing term for anything that connects anything to anything else.

many other terms define the network of networks. The Internet was developed mainly upon its predecessor, the Advanced Research Projects Agency Network (ARPANET). In addition to the Web, it encompasses a worldwide collection of networks, including academic institutions, government organizations, various public networks, as well as private networks (hopefully with the appropriate security measures in place).

SOMETHING YOU JUST HAVE TO KNOW

The Internet Protocol (IP) is the dominant standard used in networking to make sure that information is delivered from a source to a destination. We will talk about IP throughout this book, so it is not necessary to go into an in-depth definition at this point. You just have to understand that IP gets the data there.

1.1.1.3   Intranets (Give Me an "A", Remove My "E", Now Flip the "R" and the "A")

An *intranet* is an IP-based[12] network that is administered and controlled by a single entity. An intranet is a controlled network, with only users who have authorization to be on the network granted access to it (both remotely and physically onsite). A corporate LAN is an example of an intranet.

ACRONYM ALERT

LAN — Local area network

Although intranets are based on (and operate like) the Internet, they are not widely available to just anyone who needs to access them. Security is in place (firewalls, encryption and authentication measures, etc.) that will restrict access to only those who need the access. This allows remote users to access work applications over the Internet, while preventing unauthorized users from gaining access.

1.1.1.4   Extranets

An *extranet* is an intranet that is opened up to allow outside users (e.g., vendors, suppliers, employees, customers) access to the intranet (or any portion thereof). The access normally is provided by a server, which clients access over the Internet. An extranet operates securely to ensure that only authorized users are

---

[12]See! We told you that you would need to know what IP meant.

entitled access to the intranet. An extranet may comprise any of the following for security and privacy purposes[13]:

- **Firewall** — Network hardware and/or software that captures data passing through it and determines whether to pass or drop the data. Firewalls are configurable, and filters can be applied to provide the appropriate security for the LAN.

- **Public key certificate** — An electronic document that can verify and authorize an individual by public key cryptography. Public key cryptography uses two keys[14] (one public key and one private key) to encrypt and then decrypt data to ensure that a message can be transported securely.

- **Authentication encryption (AE)** — A system that is able to protect both the secrecy and the integrity of data communication.

- **Virtual private network (VPN)** — A network that is created when one network connects to another by a secure tunnel.

> **RANDOM BONUS DEFINITION**
>
> Tunneling is a method of securing access to an intranet. Another popular form is through a web server, where registered users can be authenticated after logging in through a web browser login page.

1.1.1.5 *Virtual Private Networks*

A virtual private network (VPN) is an extranet that securely connects separate networks to one another, as well as individuals to networks. VPNs updated[15] the use of dedicated lines that could only be used by one entity at a time. VPN technology is a much more proficient and cost-effective solution than the use of dedicated lines.

VPN technology uses a public network (normally the Internet) to connect users and networks to one another in what are known as *tunnels*. Data integrity is ensured by the use of security measures as well as tunneling protocols that set the rules for the tunnel.

VPN tunneling protocols include:

- Generic Routing Encapsulation (GRE)

- IP Security (IPSec)

---

[13]It's important to note that the technologies listed are not exclusive to extranets, but they are important technologies within extranets.

[14]A *key* is information used to determine an algorithm's output.

[15]Although many organizations now use VPNs (or some other extranet type) for remote access, some networks still utilize the dedicated lines (both owned and leased) when network access is required.

- Layer 2 Tunneling Protocol (L2TP)

- Point-to-Point Tunneling Protocol (PPTP)

Tunneling protocols ensure that the data is encrypted on the sending end of the tunnel and is decrypted appropriately at the receiving end of the tunnel. In addition to the data encryption, security is established to ensure that endpoint addresses are encrypted as well.

> **RANDOM BONUS DEFINITION**
>
> network node — Any device that participates in data communication within a network.

1.1.1.6 Catenet

The term *catenet* stands for "catenated network." A catenet is simply a group of networks that are connected to one another via a gateway. It is an obsolete term that was replaced by some more up-to-date terms (i.e., internet) that we discuss in the pages that follow.

> **AND NOW, A MOMENT OF THOUGHT**
>
> Maybe someone will propose a standard to replace the word *internet* (lowercase *i*) with *catenet* and save us all that darn confusion. I mean, it really would make sense, right? However, should this ever happen, I would bet $20 that it wouldn't be long before "the Internet" became "the Catenet" and then we would be right back where we were before.

What it boils down to is that it would be nice to see the term *catenet* return. It's kind of catchy.

1.1.1.7 Area Networks

Chapter 2, "LANs, MANs, and WANs," discusses area networks in depth. However, for those who may not have heard these terms, it is appropriate to have a brief introduction to area networks in this first chapter.

An *area network* is simply a network that spans a specific geographic area and serves a specific purpose. Any time you communicate over a network (wired or wireless), you are using an area network (or even various area networks and network types). In a nutshell, a LAN, a WAN, and a MAN are basically all the same. The differences are the geographical area that each covers, as well as some of the communication protocols that are in use.

The main three area networks you will probably hear about are the local area network, the metropolitan area network, and the wide area network. There are a few other area network

POP QUIZ

What is a public key certificate?

terms in use at the time of this writing, but they are not referred to as often as the aforementioned. These less common area networks are the personal area network (PAN), the campus area network (CAN), and the global area network (GAN).[16]

1.1.1.7.1 Campus Area Networks

A network that spans a limited geographic area specific to academics is considered a campus area network (CAN). A CAN is nothing more than a MAN that connects university buildings and provides services for the staff of the university and its students.

Some CANs provide additional services such as classroom updates, labs, e-mail, and other necessary services for the students via iPod, cell phone, and other wireless technologies. You may or may not ever have to be involved in a CAN, but at least now you can share your CAN knowledge should the opportunity present itself.[17]

1.1.1.7.2 Global Area Networks

A global area network (GAN) is any network that connects two or more WANS and covers an unlimited geographical area. The entire network connected together would be considered a GAN. GANs are becoming increasingly popular as so many companies are opening offices and operating business on a global scale.

1.1.1.7.3 Local Area Network

A local area network (LAN) is a data network that covers a small geographical area, typically ranging from just a few PCs to an area about the size of an office building or a group of buildings. Unlike WANs, LANs don't require a leased line to operate. LANs also maintain higher data rates than do some of the larger area networks, due mainly to the smaller area of coverage.

Nodes that are members of a LAN communicate with other LAN nodes by sharing some form of channel (e.g., a wireless access point, twisted cable, fiber optic cable). PC users on a LAN often use a shared server to access and work with certain applications used by the organization.

---

[16]In the near future, you might see this one used a lot more. The use of the word *global* has increased over the past few years, so it stands to reason that a GAN is right around the corner.
[17]Or you can just sit on your CAN, er, knowledge and keep it to yourself.

The three major LAN technologies in use today are Token Ring (discussed in Chapter 7, "Not to Be Forgotten"), Ethernet[18] (discussed in Chapter 6, "Ethernet Concepts"), and Fiber Distributed Data Interface (FDDI), also discussed in Chapter 7.

1.1.1.7.4 Metropolitan Area Networks

A metropolitan area network (MAN) is a network that physically covers an area larger than a LAN and smaller than a WAN. The network is normally maintained by a single operating entity, such as government offices, healthcare systems, and any other type of large organization or corporation.

MANs allow communication over a large geographical area, utilizing protocols such as ATM, FDDI, Fast Ethernet, or Gigabit Ethernet.[19] This is a better solution than communication between LANs over a WAN, which relies on routing to decipher and allow communication of different protocol types between various area networks. Communication over a WAN is also slower and more expensive than what is offered by a MAN. MANs also provide control of the transmission of data from endpoint to endpoint, whereas the WAN solution requires that you rely on the service provider for a portion of the data flow control.

1.1.1.7.5 Personal Area Networks

A personal area network (PAN) is a network that is established for an individual user within a range of around 30 feet — for instance, a person has a PDA or cell phone and connects to a PC or other node for the purposes of exchanging data. This is done wirelessly, although wired PANs are feasible in this day and age. A pure wireless PAN is termed a WPAN, although most PANs would likely be made predominately of wireless devices. Although a PAN or WPAN might be considered a LAN or WLAN, the defined area outlined by the terms certainly does help in isolating network segments.

Some examples of devices that might make up part of a PAN include:

- iPhone
- Personal digital assistants (PDAs)
- Cellular phones

---

[18]Ethernet is by far the most popular and widely used LAN technology. As a matter of fact, many LANs are now migrating to Ethernet when they begin replacing legacy nodes in their LANs. Chapter 6, *Ethernet Concepts*, is dedicated to this technology.

[19]Although many MANs still utilize a lot of these various protocols (e.g., FDDI, ATM), Ethernet-based MANs are rapidly becoming the preferred standard. Most new MANs are Ethernet-based, and many MANs are migrating to the Ethernet-based solution as their MAN standard.

- Video gaming systems
- Pagers
- Personal computers or laptops
- Printers
- Most portable peripherals

1.1.1.7.6   Wide Area Networks

A wide area network (WAN) is a network that covers a large geographical area.[20] Most people think of a WAN as a public shared network, which is partly the case, but a lot of privately owned as well as leased WANs are currently in existence.[21] A WAN links other area networks to one another, providing a way to transmit data to and from users in other places. If you think about it, the WAN is the king of the area networks (although this might not hold true for much longer, as the GAN is quickly gaining speed to become the big daddy of them all).

WANs use networking protocols (e.g., TCP/IP) to deliver data from endpoint to endpoint. A WAN also ensures that addressing of endpoints is maintained so it knows where data needs to go to reach its intended destination. Some communication protocols that are used on WANs to handle the transmission of data include:

- Asynchronous Transfer Mode (ATM)
- Frame relay
- Packet over SONET (POS)[22]
- X.25[23]

1.1.1.7.7   Wireless Local Area Networks

A wireless local area network (WLAN) is an LAN without wires. WLANs use modulation technologies that are based on radio wave technology to allow communication with other wireless nodes within a limited geographical area.

Many businesses now offer WLANs for use by their customers (many at no charge). Additionally, many cities in the United States are implementing WLANS throughout their city to allow free access to users within the wireless area.

---

[20]You can consider a network a WAN if the network boundaries exceed the size of a large metropolitan area. But hey, one man's MAN is another man's WAN.

[21]These will not be going away. As a matter of fact, no one knows what the future holds. The possibilities seem endless.

[22]Here is another fun acronym to consider. Instead of Packet over SONET (POS), why not SONET under Packet (SUP)? Then when you greet your fellow networking professionals you could say, "Hey! What's SUP?"

[23]X.25 is an oldie but goodie. It has long been replaced by other protocols. Still, it was one of the earliest WAN protocols and it deserved a mention.

1.1.2   Network Relationships and Topologies[24]

Network relationships refer to the communication that takes place between two nodes over a network. When a relationship is formed, the nodes are able to utilize resources between one another in order to share data. There are two network relationship types that define the foundation

> **RANDOM BONUS DEFINITION**
>
> packet — The encapsulated data that is transmitted and received at the Network layer (see Section 1.4.2.5).

of any network. A *peer-to-peer* network relationship is where both nodes treat each others as equals, whereas a *client/server* network relationship is one in which one node (the server) handles storing and sharing information and the other node (the client) accesses the stored data.

The manner is which nodes in a network connect to a communication line in order to exchange data is an example of a *physical topology*. Another topology type would be a *logical topology*, which defines the way data is passed from endpoint to endpoint throughout the network. The logical topology does not give any regard to the way the nodes are physically laid out. Its concern is to get the data where it is supposed to go.

1.1.2.1   Network Relationship Types

The main difference between the two network relationship types are whether you want to have every user share resources with each other or have a central node that handles all the processing while serving the needs of the clients. This means that pretty much everything else is the same between

ACRONYM ALERT

TCP — Transmission Control Protocol

the relationships. They both use the same protocols and physical connections to the network. Which one is appropriate for an organization depends on the needs, wants, and demands of the users of the network (cost factors, data speed concerns, etc.).

1.1.2.1.1   Client/Server Network Relationship

In a client/server[25] network relationship, one node acts as a server and the other nodes are clients that utilize the resources of the server to access an

---

[24]*Relationships and Topologies (RAT)*. Now, that acronym has a certain ring to it. Or maybe we should have written this heading to read *Network Relationships or Topologies (ROT)*. The former has a better ring, in our opinion, so *RAT* it is!

[25]A client/server network relationship is different from a client/server database system. In both cases, the server provides the data requested by a client, but in a database system, the client node has to use its own resources to format and view the data retrieved.

application or service. In a client/server network relationship, the server stores data (e.g., e-mail applications, encryption and authorization services, printers, VPN network access, and many more) that is used by the users of the organizational LAN. Most servers are Unix based, or a derivative of Unix, such as Linux or SunOS, all of which are discussed in depth in Chapter 4, "Operating Systems and Networking Software." The users interface with the network through a PC or Mac (or whatever device is necessary at that time[26]). The PCs will have an application that contains the information necessary to connect to and share data with the server. Figure 1-2 shows an example of the client/server relationship.

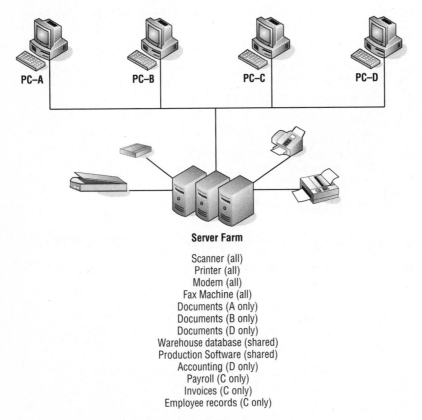

Server Farm

Scanner (all)
Printer (all)
Modem (all)
Fax Machine (all)
Documents (A only)
Documents (B only)
Documents (D only)
Warehouse database (shared)
Production Software (shared)
Accounting (D only)
Payroll (C only)
Invoices (C only)
Employee records (C only)

Figure 1-2 A client/server network relationship

No clients share resources with any other client in the client/server network relationship. They are simply users of the resources that are made available by

---

[26]For the remainder of the book, when a reference is made to a network user, it is assumed that the user is a PC end user. Otherwise, we will specify the type of user that is being referenced. Don't worry, Mac fans. Chapter 4, "Operating Systems and Networking Software" talks about the Mac OS.

the server. The servers maintain and provide shared resources to a specified number[27] of clients.

Advantages of a client/server network relationship include:

- It is a secure way to share data over a network. Because all the accessed resources are on the server, the server is able to control and maintain the security of sessions. Also, instead of multiple nodes in various locations, the server is a single entity and can be secured away from unauthorized visitors.

- Because most servers have more built-in redundancy than a single user's PC, the servers are very reliable in doing their job. Normally, there are backup drives (or other servers) that can be failed over[28] to if there is a problem with the primary drive or server.

- It is easier to back up data that is on the server than to do so with many nodes. Most organizations perform backups at night when the server is not as busy. Having only one node to back up makes it a very simple, time-saving process.

- Servers are fast because they have to serve multiple end users at the same time. The performance standards set for a server are far higher than the standards for a PC.

Of course, it's not all peaches and cream in client/server land. Disadvantages of a client/server network relationship include:

- Administrators of the server have to be trained and experienced. There is a lot to know, and the potential for failure is very high without a trained professional (therefore, be prepared to pay).

> **POP QUIZ**
>
> Encapsulated data that is transmitted and received at the Network layer is called a _____.

- Servers require more physical resources in order to do the job. This makes the price to operate a bit higher than in a peer-to-peer environment.

1.1.2.1.2 Peer-to-Peer Network Relationship

A peer-to-peer network relationship is exactly that: all the users are peers (equals) and they share resources that are necessary to be shared. Each

---

[27]The total number would depend on the capabilities of both the server hardware and the software that it is running on the node.

[28]In a redundant configuration, a failover occurs when the primary has a failure and the backup has to take over as the primary. A failover is transparent to the end users.

computer is required to determine what is to be shared and then ensures that resources are made available to the nodes that need to access the resources. Figure 1-3 shows an example of how this works.

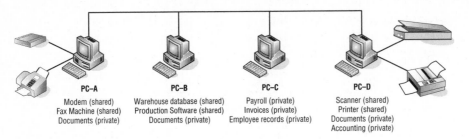

PC–A
Modem (shared)
Fax Machine (shared)
Documents (private)

PC–B
Warehouse database (shared)
Production Software (shared)
Documents (private)

PC–C
Payroll (private)
Invoices (private)
Employee records (private)

PC–D
Scanner (shared)
Printer (shared)
Documents (private)
Accounting (private)

Figure 1-3 A peer-to-peer network relationship

Note that in the example, PC-C does not have any shared resources, but it may have a need to use some of the shared resources in the peer-to-peer network. Therefore, PC-C will be a part of the peer-to-peer topology as a user of the other resources made available by the other peers.

Some examples of shared resources include:

- Printers
- Modems
- Scanners
- Data files
- Applications
- Storage devices

A peer can share any of these in any combination that makes the best use of resources to meet the needs of the users in the network. One computer can provide access to the office printer and scanner, while another computer can have the modem connected to it. By sharing resources, you save the expense of having to have one of everything for every computer in the organization. Security for the shared resources is the responsibility of the peer that controls them. Each node will implement and maintain security policies for the resources and ultimately ensures that only those that have a need can use the resources. Each peer in a peer-to-peer network is responsible for knowing how to reach another peer, what resources are shared where, and what security policies are in place.

Advantages of a peer-to-peer network relationship include:

- It is cheaper to implement and maintain. You don't have to buy multiple peripherals for each computer. You also don't have the cost of purchasing and maintaining a server. Because each peer uses its own resources, there is no stress on only one node to do all the serving.

- A peer-to-peer network does not require a special operating system. A peer-to-peer network can be built on operating systems that are currently running on most PCs.

- There are more redundancy options available in a peer-to-peer network. Because multiple clients are sharing resources, it is a good idea to design a way to have a process failover to a backup peer should the master peer have a failure.

- A peer-to-peer network is easier to maintain than a client/server network, and the job of keeping up with the network can be assigned to multiple people.[29]

Disadvantages of a peer-to-peer network relationship include:

- If a lot of people are trying to use a shared resource, computer performance may be adversely affected.

- Because multiple peers are performing different tasks, it is harder to back up data in a peer-to-peer network.

- Security is not as good as in a client/server network. Because each peer is responsible for maintaining security for the resources it controls, the potential exists that an end user may accidentally or maliciously change the security parameters, causing a security lapse on that particular node. Also, each node is physically available to multiple people (possibly even people who work in the same building but whom you don't know). In a client/server environment, the administrator maintains security and the server is physically set apart from the clients.

1.1.2.2 Network Topology Types

A network *topology* is basically the way all the nodes in the network are connected. There are five primary topologies (bus, mesh, ring, star, and tree) that are installed in various networks. When designing a network, knowing which topology to use is determined by several factors:

- Is speed a concern?
- How reliable does the network need to be?
- How much money are you willing to spend to set it up?
- How much are you willing to spend to maintain the network?

---

[29] And where exactly does the buck stop?

Data is carried in the network by a detailed cabling scheme. How the network performs depends on whether the cabling is set up correctly.[30] Miss a port here or there and you can really cause a network some problems. If there is a cable that is longer than specifications, you are going to have other problems. Once you complete this section, you will come to realize that networking is more than just "plugging it in."

1.1.2.2.1 Bus Topology

The bus topology is probably the easiest one to understand and to implement. It is simply a topology in which all the nodes are connected to a single shared cable (called a *bus*). The cable is terminated at each end to prevent an open loop condition. Figure 1-4 shows an example of a bus topology.

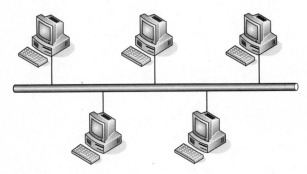

Figure 1-4 A bus topology

As with any of the topology types, the bus topology has benefits as well as drawbacks. The advantages of a bus topology include:

- It's easy to install and maintain.
- Adding new nodes is rather simple.
- Less cabling is required than with some of the other topology types.
- It's inexpensive to implement.

The disadvantages include:

- If the cable breaks at any point, network access is lost to all nodes on the segment.
- It can be expensive to maintain over a period of time.
- Data communication is slower than with some of the other topologies.

[30]When designing a network, the placement of the cabling is the first thing that you need to consider and then you expand from that. Of course, wireless networking is an option, but you still begin planning the wireless network by determining where the access points should be.

- The network segment traffic flow is affected each time a node is added.

- There is a limit to the number of nodes that can be added to the segment.

When a node that is connected to a shared bus needs to pass data on to the network, it has to have a mechanism for detecting whether other nodes are transmitting data at the same time. It must do this to prevent a collision on the bus (see Figure 1-5) or have a set of rules to follow when a collision occurs. In the example, you see that node C is trying to send data to node D. At the same time, node A is sending data to node E. Because there is no way to determine whether the other node was passing data, a collision occurs on the bus. This is not the worst part — because there was no mechanism within the bus topology to detect collisions, both of the sending nodes assume that the data reached the intended recipients and they relax, thinking they successfully sent the data.

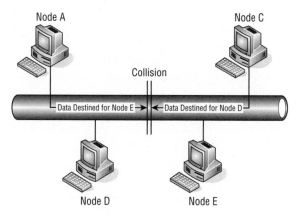

Figure 1-5 The dreaded collision

Collision avoidance can be handled in the following ways in a bus topology:

- **Carrier Sense Multiple Access with Collision Detection (CSMA/CD) protocol**[31] — This is a method of determining if another node is sending data by listening on the bus first. If it senses that the channel is being used by another node, the node will delay transmitting its data until the channel is available. CSMA is used to avoid collisions, while CD will detect

> **RANDOM BONUS DEFINITION**
>
> physical port — A physical interface that resides on a network node. Not to be confused with a TCP/UDP port.

[31]Protocols are discussed in Section 1.1.3.

when a collision occurs and will stop transmitting data. Once a set period of time has lapsed, the sending node will send the data again. Take note that if CSMA is used without the CD, each sending node will send the entire *datagram*,[32] even when a collision occurs.

■ **A bus master** — A bus master is an application running on one of the nodes within the segment or a separate node known as an *input/output (I/O) controller*. The bus master is the master node and all other nodes are referred to as slave nodes. The master controls the transmission of data to and from all nodes within the bus topology.

> **RANDOM BONUS DEFINITION**
>
> TCP/IP port — A number in the data packet header that maps to a process running on a node. Not to be confused with a physical port.

1.1.2.2.2 Mesh Topology

There are two types of mesh topologies that can be used. A full mesh topology (Figure 1-6) is a configuration where all the nodes within the network segment are connected to one another. A partial mesh topology (Figure 1-7) is where some nodes are connected to all the others, and some only connect to the ones they need to communicate with.

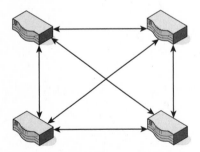

Figure 1-6 A full mesh topology

As with almost any topology, there are some advantages and some disadvantages to the mesh topology. One advantage of the mesh topology is that you have a lot of redundancy. If one node is down, the others are virtually unaffected. There is always a route around broken or blocked paths.

---

[32] A *datagram* is a self-contained entity of data that is transmitted from one endpoint to another within a network. Layer 3 packets and Layer 2 frames are two examples of datagrams. As a matter of fact, many network professionals use the three terms interchangeably.

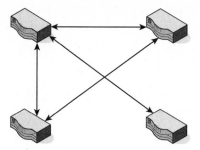

Figure 1-7 A partial mesh topology

One major disadvantage of the mesh topology is that it is expensive to implement. Also, as the network grows, so does the complexity of the mesh topology. In Figure 1-6, there are four nodes within the mesh topology. Imagine what a nightmare it would be to maintain a mesh that included 100 nodes.

ACRONYM ALERT

FTP — File Transfer Protocol

1.1.2.2.3   Star Topology

The star network is one of the more popular network types used by organizational LANs. In the star topology, all nodes in the network connect to a central node that handles the passing of datagrams between the nodes. Figure 1-8 shows an example of the star topology.

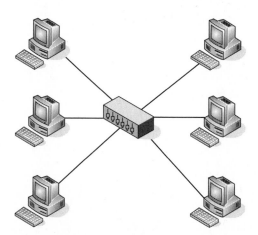

Figure 1-8 A star topology

The central node receives a datagram and then broadcasts the data to all the nodes it connects to. The connecting nodes can communicate with each other by sending data to and receiving data from the central node. Should one of the connecting nodes go offline, the central hub will discontinue communication to the one node only and the other connecting nodes will continue to operate.

The advantages of a star topology include:

- It allows for direct communication between two nodes.
- It's simple to implement and maintain
- It helps to narrow down problematic network segments.
- It's easy to troubleshoot and allows for quick recovery.[33]

The disadvantages include:

- If the central node fails, all the other nodes are affected.
- If there is an increase in network traffic, the central node may become "sluggish," affecting the performance of some, if not all, of the connecting nodes.
- Scalability within the network is limited to the capabilities of the central node.

1.1.2.2.4   Ring Topology

The ring topology can be a bit confusing, as the term *ring* defines the logical topology rather than the physical topology. As shown in Figure 1-9, the ring passes data logically from station to station until the data reaches its destination.

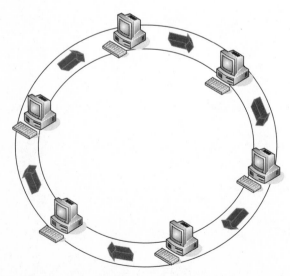

Figure 1-9 A ring (logical) topology

[33]When the problematic link is discovered, all you have to do is pull out the cable to prevent the issue from propagating to the rest of the nodes within the star.

Each node handles each datagram that is passed, verifying whether the datagram is destined for it and, if not, passing it along to the next node. In the ring topology, there is a single path from one node to the next. Should there be a break along the way, all nodes on the ring will no longer be able to communicate on the network. To overcome this, many ring topology networks employ a dual ring, with data passing in the opposite direction on a redundant ring (see Figure 1-10).

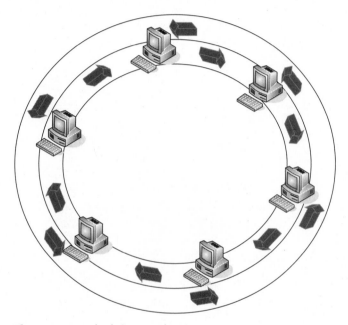

Figure 1-10 A dual-ring topology

Advantages of a ring topology include:

- There's no need to have a mechanism to ensure collision-free datagram passing.
- It can expand to cover a greater number of nodes than some of the other topology types.
- It's fairly simple to maintain.

Disadvantages of a ring topology include:

- A failure with one node on the ring may cause an outage to all connected nodes.
- Any maintenance (e.g., adding a node, making a change to a node, removing a node) would affect all the nodes that connect to the ring.
- Some of the hardware required to implement a ring is more expensive than Ethernet network cards and nodes.

- Under normal traffic load, a ring is much slower than other topologies.

- There are not many of this type of network, as most networks are migrating to Ethernet.

1.1.2.2.5   Hierarchical Topology (a.k.a. Tree Topology)

A hierarchical[34] topology is very similar to a star topology. Like the star topology, the hierarchical topology has a central node that connects multiple nodes to one another. However, in the hierarchical topology, each node could potentially act as a central node to a group of other nodes. Figure 1-11 shows the physical layout of a hierarchical topology.

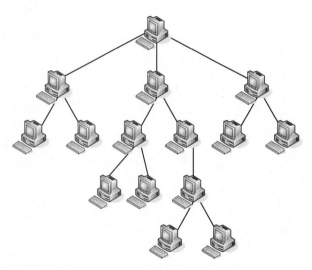

Figure 1-11 A hierarchical topology

Notice how a hierarchical topology is similar to an organizational structure. The mainframe computer would be the single node at the top of the chart, and then the lower levels would be other minicomputers and PCs. The hierarchical topology is quite effective in smaller areas, where a central mainframe can connect to different minicomputers, and the minicomputers can provide a central connection for the PCs in the departments they serve.

1.1.3   Protocols

Simply put, a *protocol* is a standard (or set of standards) that governs the rules for setting up a data connection, communicating between endpoints once the connection is set, and transferring data between those endpoints. There are

---

[34]Jim used to have a colleague who could never get the pronunciation right for the word "hierarchical." He would pronounce the word "harr-arrr-cul-cul." No matter how hard he tried, he never could get the word down. It was pretty funny.

protocols set for both hardware and software, and sometimes for the combination of the two.

Network protocols vary in purpose and complexity. They are usually used to detect the physical properties of both the

> **POP QUIZ**
>
> What is the difference between a physical port and a TCP port?

sending and the target nodes, as well as whether the target node is available. Once the connection endpoints are determined, a protocol will handle the initial communication[35] between the endpoints as well as the rules for the connection. The protocol will identify how each end will know where a data stream starts and stops, what format it will be sent and received in, and what to do with the data if there are any problems with the transfer.

The Internet would not be what it is if it were not for the protocols, especially the Internet Protocol (IP) and the Transmission Control Protocol (TCP), used in combination with each other and referred to as TCP/IP or the TCP/IP protocol suite.

TCP/IP and many other protocols are discussed throughout this book, but here is a short list of a few of the more common protocols:

- **File Transfer Protocol (FTP)** — FTP is used to transfer large amounts of data from one node to another. The FTP protocol uses an FTP server to serve files to an FTP client.

- **Hypertext Transfer Protocol (HTTP)** — HTTP is a communications protocol that allows for data transmissions within data networks as well as the World Wide Web (WWW). HTTP uses a server (e.g., a website) to serve the clients (end users) data the clients have requested via a web browser.

- **Hypertext Transfer Protocol over Secure Socket Layer (HTTPS)** — HTTPS is an enhancement to HTTP that allows secure sessions over SSL. These sessions provide adequate security for private transactions on the WWW.

- **Internet Message Access Protocol version 4 (IMAP4)** — IMAP4 is a protocol that allows a client to connect to and retrieve e-mail from an e-mail server.

- **Internet Protocol (IP)** — IP is a standard that allows for the transfer of data between nodes that are connected on a network. Each node within an IP network has a unique address that identifies it for the purpose of locating and sharing data between nodes. The latest version of IP that has been released is IPv6.

---

[35]The initial conversation between the two endpoints is commonly referred to as a *handshake*.

- **Post Office Protocol version 3 (POP3)** — POP3 is a protocol that allows an e-mail client to connect to an e-mail server and retrieve mail that is destined for that client.

- **Simple Mail Transfer Protocol (SMTP)** — SMTP is a protocol that allows a network user to send and receive e-mail.

- **Simple Network Management Protocol (SNMP)** — SNMP is a protocol that allows for the sharing of management data on a network. SNMP allows network administrators the ability to quickly access network nodes to monitor performance, troubleshoot, baseline, and ensure that the network is capable of addressing the needs of the organization.

- **Transmission Control Protocol (TCP)** — TCP is a protocol that connects end users with one another and ensures the integrity of the exchanged data.

- **Trivial File Transfer Protocol (TFTP)** — TFTP is a protocol that is a simpler form of FTP.

- **User Datagram Protocol (UDP)** — UDP is a protocol that connects end users to one another and transfers datagrams, but does not ensure the integrity of the datagrams.

1.1.3.1 *Transmission Control Protocol*

The Transmission Control Protocol (TCP) ensures that data is transmitted from endpoint to endpoint in a reliable manner. TCP operates at the Transport layer of the OSI reference model (more on this in Section 1.4). TCP is normally associated with the TCP/IP protocol suite; however, it is its own entity. It is a protocol that can adapt to a variety of data delivery standards, providing reliable data delivery.

TCP is the reliable[36] transport protocol that controls the flow of data between hosts. TCP divides messages into smaller segments and ensures the data arrives error-free and is presented by the target node in the correct order. TCP manages the flow of data and makes adjustments to the size and the speed in which the data is transported. TCP is used by most of today's more popular networking services and applications, including the World Wide Web (WWW), e-mail, and Secure Shell (SSH).

---

[36] The key word here is "reliable." This does not imply that TCP can provide the quickest delivery available. TCP is designed to offer reliable and accurate delivery, but it does not guarantee timely delivery and is not used when speed is needed to transmit data. The Real-time Transport Protocol (RTP) is normally used in these instances.

TCP is a connection-oriented protocol. This means that there is a connection between two endpoints before any data is sent. A connection-oriented protocol also ensures that once the data arrives at a destination, it is put back together in the proper order. A connection-oriented protocol cannot promise that data won't get dropped, but if it is received, it will be sequenced appropriately.

1.1.3.2 User Datagram Protocol

The User Datagram Protocol (UDP) provides a method for transmitting datagrams between endpoints, but no guarantee of the delivery is made. This means that a datagram may be duplicated, can go missing, and may not arrive in the order in which it was sent. This also means that UDP is a faster transmission standard than TCP.

UDP is preferred in situations where you need data to be transmitted quickly. There is simply more processing power to get the data to the destination because there is no error checking. UDP supports broadcasting[37] and multicasting,[38] so messages can get to destinations within a network segment as well as to everyone within the network.

UDP is a connectionless protocol, which means there is no guarantee that the intended destination is available. There is no checking the communication line prior to transmitting data, it is just transmitted.

1.1.3.3 Internet Protocol

The Internet Protocol (IP) is the protocol that defines how data is transmitted between two nodes. Datagrams are forwarded to a destination endpoint based on the IP address that is assigned to the endpoint. When data is transmitted, the data is encap-

> **POP QUIZ**
>
> Because IP does not establish a connection before sending data to an endpoint, it would be considered a _____ protocol.

sulated into datagrams and multiple datagrams may be required to transmit a single message. Each datagram is treated as its own entity without regard to any of the other datagrams that make up the message. Each datagram can choose whatever path it wishes to take to reach a destination. That is IP's job: to get the datagram to the destination by the quickest route possible.[39]

---

[37]Sending data to everyone connected to the network segment.
[38]Sending data to a select group of nodes.
[39]It is TCP's job to put them back together again.

1.2   History of Networking

On April 3, 1860, the Pony Express officially opened for business. Covering 250 miles in each 24-hour period, the riders would travel at full gallop from one Pony Express station to the next. At each stop, they would change horses, exchange mail, and head on to the next stop. After 100 miles or so, the rider would be relieved by a fresh rider to continue the journey. What an accomplishment this was. Only 15 years prior to that, it would take six months to get a message from the east coast to the west coast. The Pony Express could do it in about 11 days. The Pony Express dissolved in October 1861, when the first transcontinental telegraph was transmitted.

Now look where we are today. In milliseconds, we can send a letter from Hong Kong to New York, or talk over the Internet with a loved one on the other side of the planet. We can get trip directions, listen to a radio station anywhere in the world, work, and play games — all at the same time. It is amazing how far communication has come.

It might surprise you to know that the concept of connecting nodes to one another was developed as a way for research organizations and educational institutions to share resources. There was one significant event that occurred that opened the doors for a lot of various research, some of which eventually introduced the network concept. What exactly was this event? It was the race to space.

The Soviet Union launched the Sputnik satellite on October 4, 1957. This alarmed many American citizens and was an embarrassment to many people in the United States because of a few failed attempts prior to that date. The launch of the Sputnik satellite is said to have ushered in the Space Age, but that is not all it changed. It changed the attitude of those who were involved in the United States space program, as well as the attitude of U.S. citizens. After Sputnik launched, funds began flooding to research agencies and institutions. The National Defense Education Act was signed to promote studies in math, science, and foreign languages. One of the agencies formed was the Advanced Research Projects Agency (ARPA) in 1958.

ARPA was formed as an agency that would be tasked by the United States Department of Defense (DoD) to research and develop projects. ARPA was not required to focus on only projects of military concern, and it was quickly determined that a focus on computers would be a worthwhile investment. In 1962, ARPA chose Dr. J.C.R. Licklider to lead the computer research effort.

WHAT'S IN A WORD?

If you think that the whole catenet/internet/Internet terming conventions seem a little confusing, you haven't seen anything yet. Check this out:

(continued)

WHAT'S IN A WORD? *(continued)*

The Advanced Research Projects Agency (ARPA) was formed in 1958. In 1972, ARPA was replaced by the Defense Advanced Research Projects Agency (DARPA). DARPA did the same job that ARPA did, but DARPA was established as a separate defense agency (still under the Secretary of Defense).

In 1993, DARPA became ARPA and was put back as it was when it was first formed. In 1996, the name was officially changed to DARPA again.

Licklider realized even before his appointment the potential of connecting nodes to one another to share resources. He had developed what he called a *galactic network* concept, and he was able to convince other researchers (including those who took over when he left) how important his concept was. He outlined his plan to accomplish this concept and the very first large network research team was formed. This team, known as the *ARPA community*, was a group of universities across the United States. It is important to note that Licklider left his position before his concepts became a reality, but his successors moved ahead in their development.

ARPA formed a subgroup called the Information Processing Techniques Office (IPTO) to focus on research pertaining to anything related to computing. It was funding from ARPA/IPTO that assisted in the ARPA community of educational and scientific institutions to investigate time and resource sharing possibilities.

> **POP QUIZ**
>
> What is the difference between a WAN and a LAN?

Many people today still feel that the Internet was developed to provide a fallback mechanism in the event of a nuclear attack. This is probably due to the fact that there was so much funding poured into development after the launch of the Sputnik satellite. The official reason that was given for the concept of networking nodes together was simply to share files and resources among investigative agencies and groups.

In 1968, ARPA allowed contractors to bid on the plan they had been working on, and BBN Technologies was brought in. In 1969, ARPANET was born. The original ARPANET was a network with several small computers referred to as *interface message processors* (IMPs), which were nodes that performed packet-switching and were used to connect to each other by modems and to users on host computers.[40] The IMPs were configured with 24 Kb[41] of memory,

---

[40]Don't think of these hosts as PCs. These hosts were huge computers, sometimes occupying a whole floor of a building.

[41]Kb = kilobits

supported up to four host computers, and were able to connect to a maximum of six other IMPs. The IMPs communicated with one another over leased communication lines. The original ARPANET was made up of four IMPs that were established at the following locations:

- Stanford Research Institute
- University of California, Los Angeles
- University of California, Santa Barbara
- University of Utah

BBN Technologies developed the first communications protocol, known as the *BBN Report 1822*, which later became known as the *1822 protocol*. The 1822 protocol simply specified the manner in which a host communicated with the IMP. The 1822 protocol predated the OSI reference model (see

ACRONYM ALERT

DoS — Denial of service

Section 1.4) and did not really follow the layering process we use today.[42] The 1822 protocol was eventually replaced by the Network Control Protocol (NCP), which incorporated a transport function. The NCP remained the main communication protocol until 1983, when it was replaced by the TCP/IP protocol suite. The TCP/IP protocol suite was more resilient than the NCP, and its introduction was the birth of communication networks as we have known them to date.

Eventually, ARPA got out of the networking business to focus on research in other areas. The Defense Department retained the military portion of the ARPANET and named it the MILNET. The remainder of ARPANET remained with research and educational organizations, and BBN Technologies continued to maintain these networks. Because of the split of ARPANET, many of the resources available to the institutions and organizations were severed in the interest of security required by the MILNET. In response to this, the National Science Foundation funded the development of the Computer Science Network (CSNET), which provided access to shared resources for these groups. Eventually, the network grew and was transformed into the National Science Foundation Network (NSFNET), which was developed originally to allow researchers access to five supercomputers at the following locations:

- Cornell University
- Pittsburgh Supercomputing Center

---

[42]It can be said that the 1822 protocol used the physical, data link, and network layers as the host system packaged data and sent it to the address of the IMP (directly connected). The IMP, in turn, routed the data to the destination IMP, which sent it to the destination host.

- Princeton University
- University of Illinois
- University of California, San Diego

The NSFNET used the TCP/IP protocol suite as a communications protocol and was completely compatible with the ARPANET. In the early 1990s, more and more organizations started accessing what was now called the Internet, but permissions had to be obtained from the NSFNET to use many of the services that were offered. The main supercomputer centers maintained and monitored the Internet's growth.

Today networks are defined by the way they get information from point to point. The nodes used and the standards deployed are integral parts of any network, defining the very basis for that network's existence. Networks are commonplace and growing on a global level. Only the future can tell what new advances will be made for this global communication vehicle.

INTERNET TIMELINE TRIVIA

1957: The Advanced Research Projects Agency (AARPA) is formed.

1961: The Massachusetts Institute of Technology (MIT) began researching data-sharing potential. There are fewer than 9,500 computers in the world.

1966: ARPANET is under development, packet-switching technology is launched.

1969: ARPANET is launched.

1971: The number of nodes on the ARPANET is 15.

1973: London and Norway join ARPANET. Global communications are launched.

1974: TCP is launched. Data communication speeds increase and the reliability of data transmission improves.

1975: The first ARPANET mailing list is launched. TCP tests are run successfully from the U.S. mainland to Hawaii as well as to the U.K., via satellite links.

1976: Unix is developed.

1978: TCP and IP split into two separate protocols.

1982: TCP/IP becomes the standard used by the Department of Defense for data communication within the U.S. military's network.

1984: The number of nodes on the Internet is over 1,000. Domain Name Service is launched.

(continued)

INTERNET TIMELINE TRIVIA *(continued)*

1987: The number of nodes on the Internet is over 10,000.

1988: The Internet experiences its first Internet worm.

1989: The number of nodes on the Internet is over 100,000.

1990: ARPANET is disbanded. The first commercial Internet service provider (ISP) is launched.

1991: The first Internet connection is made (at 9600 baud). The World Wide Web is launched.

1992: The number of nodes on the Internet is over 1,000,000.

1994: The WWW becomes the most popular service on the Internet. Some radio stations start broadcasting over the Internet.

1995: Internet streaming technology is introduced.

1996: Web browser software vendors begin a "browser war."

1997: Over 70,000 mailing lists are now registered.

1998: The 2,000,000th domain name is registered.

2000: The first major denial-of-service (DoS) attack is launched. Most major websites are affected.

2002: Blogs become cool.

2003: Flash mobs are born. Flash mobs are groups of people who gather online and plan a meeting in a public place. Once they assemble, they perform a predetermined action, ranging from pillow fights to zombie walks. The participants leave as soon as the meeting is over. (Wikipedia has a good article about flash mobs: www.wikipedia.org/wiki/Flash_mob.)

2005: The Microsoft Network (MSN) reports that there are over 200 million active Hotmail accounts.

2006: Joost is launched, allowing for the sharing of TV shows and video using peer-to-peer technology.

2008: Online search engine Technorati reported that they are now tracking and indexing over 112 million online blogs.

1.3   Standards and Standards Organizations

As we have discussed already, the standards that are put in place to ensure that data communication can be shared between nodes on a network are an essential part of the network. Without a standard way of doing things, networks would not be able to operate nearly as efficient as they do today.[43] So it is fair to say that based on what we have discussed so far, we can all be in agreement that standards are required in order for data communication to be shared on a network. Standards serve the following purposes:

- Set up and maintain rules to be followed in the network
- Define how network hardware interfaces operate
- Maintain all communication protocols that are in use in a network
- Offer the ability of utilizing the hardware and software available from multiple vendors and ensure that these are interoperable with like resources from other vendors

Standards begin when an individual or organization has an idea. A proposal is put forth and a committee reviews it to determine if the proposal has any merit. If the proposal is accepted, the idea will be transferred to a development committee, which will outline the scope of the proposed standard and submit a draft to a committee that will vote on whether the standard is to be approved. If the standard is passed for approval, the final draft is written and then published as a new standard.

There are three main types of networking-related standards. It important that you understand the differences, as it is virtually a guarantee that you will need to know this at some point.

- **De facto standards** — A de facto standard is a standard that began as a proprietary standard and then grew to a standard that is used by pretty much everyone. As a matter of fact, it is widely assumed that many proprietary standards are developed with the hopes that they will become de facto standards.[44] A de facto standard is similar to an open standard in that it is universally used by multiple vendors, but it is never approved as a formal open standard.

- **Proprietary standards** — A proprietary standard is a standard that is developed and owned by a specific vendor. When PCs first started coming out, most vendors tried to avoid admitting the importance of a cooperative standard that could be used between different vendors. The technology was starting to boom, and corporate confidentiality was a huge concern, so it was important to keep their standards to themselves. As a matter of fact, it really made sense that having control of a standard

---

[43]That is assuming that they would work at all without standards.
[44]Why would they do this? To become the industry leader for whatever the standard covers. Think about it this way. If you want to purchase a computer that supports the widget standard, you might have more faith in the company that introduced and has supported the standard for years, as opposed to purchasing a PC from "Mom and Pop's PC shop," which only recently started supporting the widget standard.

as it would be beneficial to the future of the company. To take this even further, companies saw no real value in supporting the proprietary standard of the competition (why have to pay them for the rights to use the standard?), so instead they developed something close to what the competition had, and then encouraged the consumer to move to what they had to offer, as they did "xyz"[45] more than the competitor. Proprietary standards still exist, but they are not as common as they once were.

- **Open standards** — An open standard is a standard that is used by almost everyone. Most vendors involved in networking resources now realize that they can be just as competitive while developing cooperative standards that are agreed upon by other

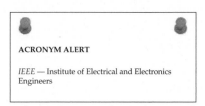

ACRONYM ALERT

IEEE — Institute of Electrical and Electronics Engineers

vendors. This quickly became evident as consumer demand grew. Consumers wanted to be able to choose from multiple vendors, and expected the nodes to communicate well with one another. There are some companies that still prefer to work with mostly proprietary standards, but there is a larger customer base for devices that use open standards.

This section discusses some of the standards organizations and what purpose each one serves. These organizations develop formal standards for the area of networking they are applicable to. Most standards committees operate as nonprofit organizations and are made up of researchers, educators, specific vendors, and industry professionals. In turn, vendors model the development of their products based on the agreed standard.

1.3.1 American National Standards Institute

The American National Standards Institute (ANSI) is the organization responsible for ensuring that guidelines are established for every type of business you can imagine. From construction standards to agricultural standards, ANSI is responsible for outlining and

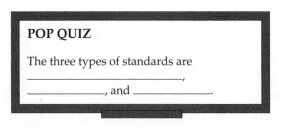

POP QUIZ

The three types of standards are
_____,
_____, and _____.

accrediting these standards. The mission of ANSI is to ensure that standards are defined and followed in order to protect and ensure global competitiveness

---

[45]This could be anything from a true advance over the competitor to a "prettier" package.

for American business and ultimately improve life standards for the American consumer.

ANSI is the organization that represents the United States in working with the global community on issues relating to two important global standards organizations. These are:

- International Organization for Standardization (ISO)
- International Electrotechnical Commission (IEC)

It is important to note that ANSI is not the developer of standards; rather, it oversees the development of standards by accrediting the standards once they have been set up and proposed by what are known as Standards Development Organizations (SDOs). It is the responsibility of the SDOs to develop and maintain standards that represent the users for their group.[46]

Examples of some of the SDOs that have had standards accredited by ANSI[47]:

- American Dental Association (ADA)
- North American Die Casting Association (NADCA)
- Standards Australia (SAI)
- Institute of Electrical and Electronics Engineers (IEEE)
- Chinese Standards (SPC)

RANDOM BONUS DEFINITION

working group — A group formed by interested members of an organization. The working group can have open meetings, as well as communication through Internet forums and mailing lists. The working group works on issues relating to standards and standards development.

1.3.2 International Organization for Standardization

Founded in 1947, the International Organization for Standardization (ISO)[48] is an organization that is tasked with standardizing international standards for various interests. Based in Switzerland, the ISO is made up of members

[46]By "group," we mean the individuals outside of the SDO for whom the developing standards will apply.

[47]This list is provided as an example of the broad range of communities that are ANSI accredited. That being said, some of these have nothing to do with networking. If you are interested in further reading, you can go to the ANSI website (www.ansi.org), or there is a search engine you can use to locate standards and SDOs (www.nssn.org).

[48]You might wonder why the acronym is not IOS for the International Organization for Standardization. Being an international organization, the acronym would be different depending on which country you were in (English would be IOS, but the French acronym would be OIN, which stands for Organisation Internationale de Normalisation). The forming members of the organization agreed upon ISO, which came from the Greek word *isos*, meaning "equal." This provided a globally standard acronym for the organization.

from 157 nations. In addition to the development of international standards, the ISO also is responsible for publishing an assortment of technical reports, specifications, and guides. Following is a list of some of the available ISO standards:

- **ISO/IEC 9541 –Information Technology** — Font information interchange
- **ISO 9000** — Quality management system in production environments
- **ISO 9141** — Network interconnection of computers in a vehicle
- **ISO 15930** — Portable Document Format (PDF)

The preceding is only a short example of the many standards maintained by the ISO. For further reading, visit the ISO website at `www.iso.org`.

1.3.3 International Electrotechnical Commission

The International Electrotechnical Commission (IEC) is responsible for standards that relate to electrotechnology (electronics and related technology). The strict standards developed by the IEC are used by its members as references when standardizing electrotechnical resources and contracts. Products that are manufactured to these standards can be used regardless of where in the world you live. The IEC is credited for promoting trade and technical efficiency on a global scale. This ensures that the end user can operate the IEC-supported device without having to understand the complexities that may be involved in the technology itself.

In addition to international standards, the IEC also produces various publications that outline specifications and guidelines for areas that may not be considered standards. Many of these publications are revisions to existing standards or draft standards that are under review.

1.3.4 Telecommunications Industry Association

The Telecommunications Industry Association (TIA) develops standards that apply to telecommunications technologies. TIA has over 70 formulation groups, each of which manages different subcommittees composed of industry professionals, manufacturers, service providers, and even government representatives.

These subcommittees and formulation groups devise and de-

> **RANDOM BONUS DEFINITION**
>
> birds of a feather (BoF) — A BoF is an informal discussion group that consists of members who share a common interest or concern.

velop standards that are submitted to ANSI for accreditation. TIA committees write and maintain standards and specifications for the telecommunications industry. TIA also participates within various international telecommunications groups representing the interests of the United States on a global forum.

1.3.5 Electronic Industries Alliance

The Electronic Industries Alliance (EIA) is an association made up of technical and electronic manufacturers from the United States that cooperatively work with each other to ensure that the development and competitiveness of these companies are represented on a global scale. The issues the EIA addresses are of interest to the common good of these companies as a whole, ensuring that the companies are able to achieve the success they deserve. The EIA focuses on the following areas:

- Cyber security
- The environment
- Information technology reform
- Telecommunications reform
- Global competitiveness
- Global trade and market access

1.3.6 International Telecommunication Union

Dedicated to bringing worldwide communication to everyone, the International Telecommunication Union (ITU) is an organization that works to facilitate telecommunications and data network development and continued growth on a global scale. The ITU is striving to enable individuals everywhere to have access to benefits that are available with the information community and the global economy.

In 2007, the ITU launched the Global Cybersecurity Agenda (GCA), envisioning the future assurance of cybersecurity as well as cyber peace throughout the Internet. Another goal of the ITU is to strengthen communications to assist in disaster recovery and prevention efforts in major countries as well as developing countries that lack resources and economies to support the Information Age.

ACRONYM ALERT

RIP — Routing Information Protocol

1.3.7 IEEE

Originally, IEEE was the acronym for the Institute of Electrical and Electronics Engineers. Over time, the scope and mission of the IEEE grew into other related fields, and now the name of the organization is simply IEEE (that's I-triple-E). The IEEE develops[49] global standards applicable to information technology, telecommunications, power generation, and other related services. The IEEE has developed and maintains more than 900 standards that are active and in use. Additionally, more than 400 draft standards are in development.

The IEEE membership is made up of scientists, engineers, and other leaders in the fields of computer science, electronics, engineering, and related professions. Membership in the IEEE provides access to the latest developments in technology, assists in career development, provides access to technical information, and many other benefits.

In additional to the standards that are developed and maintained by the IEEE, the organization publishes almost a third of the world's technical literature for the fields of computer science, electrical engineering, and electronics. They also maintain an online digital library, sponsor conferences, offer educational and special-purpose grants, and bestow recognition awards.

One of the largest family of standards maintained by the IEEE is IEEE 802. The IEEE 802 organization is made up of 22 working groups (see Section 1.3.7.1) that work to develop standards applicable to LAN, MAN, and some WAN technologies. This section introduces some of the IEEE LAN standards. For more information about the IEEE, go to their website, `www.ieee.org`.

1.3.7.1 IEEE 802 Working Groups

A *working group* is a team of professionals who are brought together to work on new research activities. Usually these are formed when an individual or a group presents a suggestion for a resolution to a current standard or on the behalf of a new technology that is being mainstreamed. Working groups are often referred to as a task force, task group, study group, advisory group, and many others. Following is a list of IEEE 802 working groups and their current status:

- ▪ **Active groups**
  - ▪ 802.1 Higher Layer LAN Protocols Working Group
  - ▪ 802.3 Ethernet Working Group
  - ▪ 802.11 Wireless LAN Working Group

---

[49] As a matter of fact, at the time of this writing, IEEE touted that they were the leading developer of international standards.

- 802.15 Wireless Personal Area Network (WPAN) Working Group
- 802.16 Broadband Wireless Access Working Group
- 802.17 Resilient Packet Ring Working Group
- 802.18 Radio Regulatory Technical Advisory Group
- 802.19 Coexistence Technical Advisory Group
- 802.20 Mobile Broadband Wireless Access (MBWA) Working Group
- 802.21 Media Independent Handoff Working Group
- 802.22 Wireless Regional Area Networks
- **Inactive groups**[50]
  - 802.2 Logical Link Control Working Group
  - 802.5 Token Ring Working Group
- **Disbanded groups**
  - 802.4 Token Bus Working Group
  - 802.6 Metropolitan Area Network Working Group
  - 802.7 Broadband TAG
  - 802.8 Fiber Optic TAG
  - 802.9 Integrated Services LAN Working Group
  - 802.10 Security Working Group
  - 802.12 Demand Priority Working Group
  - 802.14 Cable Modem Working Group
  - QOS/FC Executive Committee Study Group

The remainder of this section lists some of the standards that have been developed by the IEEE working groups that deal with subject matter common in most LANs and MANs.[51] These working groups are IEEE 802.1, IEEE 802.3, IEEE 802.5, and IEEE 802.11.

1.3.7.2 IEEE 802.1

IEEE 802.1 is responsible for the development of numerous standards, as well as providing recommendations for the following areas: 802 LAN architecture, 802

---

[50]"Inactive" does not mean the technology is not out there; it just means there are no updates being worked on at this time.

[51]These are also the main working groups within the IEEE 802 family that sets standards for the material covered in this book.

MAN architecture, 802 WAN architecture, 802 overall network management, protocol layers above the MAC and LLC sublayers (see Section 1.4), and 802 Security. Following is a list of IEEE 802.1 standards:

- **IEEE 802.1AB** — This standard defines how to use the Link Layer Discovery Protocol (LLDP) as well as identifying node access points for network and device management.

- **IEEE 802.1AD** — This standard sets the rules used by service providers to use bridges, so they can basically provide the equivalent of a separate catenet to their customers.

- **IEEE 802.1AE** — This standard defines the MAC security guidelines for the purpose of data security.

- **IEEE 802.1B** — This standard defines the rules for remote management of IEEE 802 LANs.[52]

- **IEEE 802.1D** — Of all the 802.1 standards, this is the one that is the most well known. It is also the most used standard and outlines the rules followed by LAN bridges and switches.

- **IEEE 802.1E** — This standard outlines the rules for using multicast to reliably transfer large amounts of data to multiple network nodes.

- **IEEE 802.1F**[53] — This standard outlines some common definitions used for system management information common through the series of IEEE 802 standards.

- **IEEE 802.1G** — This standard outlines the rules that allow bridges in LANs to communication using WAN technology.

- **IEEE 802.1H** — This is more of a recommendation than a standard. It provides a way for end stations and bridges in an Ethernet LAN to communicate with end stations and bridges in other LANs that use a non-native encapsulation type.

- **IEEE 802.1Q** — This standard outlines the requirements and rules for nodes operating in an virtual LAN (VLAN). Like the 802.1D standard, this is one of the more widely used and implemented 802.1 standards.

- **IEEE 802.1X** — This standard outlines the rules that allow a way of authenticating devices attached to a LAN port at the Data Link layer (see Section 1.4).

---

[52]The Simple Network Management Protocol (SNMP) is the de facto standard, used by pretty much everyone. Because of this, the IEEE 802.1B standard is not used very often.
[53]SNMP has pretty much taken over. 802.1F has joined 802.1B on the not used often list.

1.3.7.3 *IEEE 802.3*

IEEE 802.3 is the standard for Ethernet-based LANs. It defines the rules for the Media Access Control (MAC) sublayer and the Physical sublayer of the Data Link layer (Layer 2 of the OSI reference model, which is discussed in Section 1.4) in an Ethernet LAN. IEEE 802.3 is one document maintained by the IEEE 802.3 working group — the IEEE 802.3 standard. Supplements to the standards are identified by letter designations at the end (for instance, 802.3a, 802.3c, etc.). The following is a list of some of the supplements that have been part of the 802.3 standard:

- **IEEE 802.3a** — Thin coaxial cable, 10BASE2
- **IEEE 802.3c** — Specifications for repeaters
- **IEEE 802.3d** — Fiber optic inter-repeater link
- **IEEE 802.3i** — UTP cable, 10BASE-T
- **IEEE 802.3j** — Fiber optic LAN, 10BASE-F
- **IEEE 802.3u** — Fast Ethernet, 100BASE-T
- **IEEE 802.3x** — Full duplex operation and flow control
- **IEEE 802.3z** — Gigabit Ethernet over optical fiber
- **IEEE 802.3ab** — Gigabit Ethernet over UTP cable, 1000BASE-T
- **IEEE 802.3ac** — Frame extensions for VLAN-tagging
- **IEEE 802.3ad** — Link aggregation
- **IEEE 802.3ae** — 10 Gbit/s Ethernet over fiber
- **IEEE 802.3af** — Power over Ethernet
- **IEEE 802.3ah** — Ethernet in the First Mile
- **IEEE 802.3ak** — Ethernet over Twinaxial
- **IEEE 802.3an** — 10GBASE-T
- **IEEE 802.3ap** — Backplane Ethernet
- **IEEE 802.3aq** — 10GBASE-LRM
- **IEEE 802.3as** — Frame expansion

1.3.7.4 *IEEE 802.5*

IEEE 802.5 is the standard for Token Ring–based LANs. I t defines the rules for the Media Access Control (MAC) sublayer and the physical sublayer of the Data Link layer (Layer 2 of the OSI reference model, which is discussed in Section 1.4) in an Token Ring LAN. IEEE 802.5 is one document that was maintained by the IEEE 802.5 working group (now inactive) — the IEEE 802.5 standard. Supplements to the standards are identified by letter designations at the end (for instance, 802.5c, 802.5j, etc.). The following is a list of some of the supplements that have been part of the 802.5 standard:

- **IEEE 802.5c** — Dual-ring redundant configuration
- **IEEE 802.5j** — Optical fiber media
- **IEEE 802.5r** — Dedicated Token Ring/full duplex operation
- **IEEE 802.5t** — 100 Mb/s High Speed Token Ring
- **IEEE 802.5v** — Gigabit Token Ring

1.3.7.5   IEEE 802.11

IEEE 802.11 is the standard for wireless LAN technology. All the supplements to 802.11 follow the basic protocol, with the difference being the frequency, speed, and distance supported. The original 802.11 standard supported an operating frequency of 2.4 Ghz.[54] The maximum supported data rate is 2 Mbit/s, with an indoor range of 20 meters and an outdoor range of 100 meters.[55]

- **IEEE 802.11a** — The 802.11a standard supports an operating frequency of 5 GHz. The maximum data rate for 802.11a is 54 Mbit/s and the average data rate is approximately 23 Mbit/s. 802.11a reaches a maximum indoor range of 35 meters and an outdoor range of 120 meters.

- **IEEE 802.11b** — The 802.11b standard supports an operating frequency of 2.4 GHz. The maximum data rate for 802.11b is 11 Mbit/s. 802.11b reaches a maximum indoor range of 38 meters and an outdoor range of 140 meters.

- **IEEE 802.11g** — The 802.11g standard supports an operating frequency of 2.4 GHz. The maximum data rate for 802.11g is 54 Mbit/s. 802.11g reaches a maximum indoor range of 38 meters and an outdoor range of 140 meters.

- **IEEE 802.11n** — The 802.11n standard supports an operating frequency of 2.4GHz and 5 GHz. The maximum data rate for 802.11n is 248 Mbit/s. 802.11n reaches a maximum indoor range of 70 meters and an outdoor range of 250 meters.

---

[54]In this section, operating frequencies are listed in accordance with the industrial, scientific, and medical (ISM) radio bands.
[55]Any guesses on why the outdoor range is higher? Two words: NO WALLS.

- **IEEE 802.11y** — The 802.11y standard supports an operating frequency of 3.7 GHz. The maximum data rate for
802.11y is 54 Mbit/s. 802.11y reaches a maximum indoor
range of 50 meters and an outdoor range of 5000 meters.

1.3.8 Internet Society (ISOC)

The Internet Society (ISOC) was formed in 1992 as an organization dedicated
to structuring the development process of Internet standards. ISOC maintains
a global focus, striving to ensure that the ongoing development and growth of
the Internet provides benefits to users all over the world.

ISOC has more than 27,000 members split into groups and chapters throughout the world. The main offices are in Washington, D.C., and Geneva,
Switzerland. ISOC has several organizations that assist in its purpose, including the Internet Architecture Board (IAB), the Internet Research Task Force
(IRTF), and others. There are three main goals that ISOC works to achieve.
They support the Internet Engineering Task Force (IETF) in standards development. They also work with organizations, institutions, and other groups
to form public policy to promote global equality for all global users of the
Internet. Finally, ISOC is dedicated to technical education by providing training, educational grants for experts in the field in developing countries, and
conferences pertaining to issues that affect the Internet.

More information can be found on the ISOC website: www.isoc.org.

1.3.9 Internet Engineering Task Force

The Internet Engineering Task
Force (IETF) develops and maintains the standards pertaining
to the TCP/IP protocol suite.
Membership is open to anyone, and the committees are
composed solely of volunteers
(although sometimes employers and sponsors may fund
research). The IETF is a task force within ISOC.

> **RANDOM BONUS DEFINITION**
>
> IP address — An address assigned to
> network nodes in order to transmit data at
> the Network layer.

The IETF has both working groups and birds of a feather (BoF) discussion
groups. Regardless of the group type, each has a charter that explains the goals
of the group. Decisions are determined by an open consensus, rather than a
vote. Once a BoF or working group completes its goals, the group dissolves[56]

---

[56]Some working groups have it written into their charter that the working group can continue to
take on new tasks that pertain to the working group.

and the members usually go on to other tasks. Following are some important terms that pertain to the standards process within the IETF:

- **Internet Architecture Board (IAB)** — The IAB is a committee within the IETF. It is responsible for defining and managing the rules for the Internet's architecture. As an IETF committee, the IAB provides oversight and direction to the IETF and is an advisory group for the ISOC.

- **Internet Assigned Numbers Authority (IANA)** — The IANA is responsible for three very important Internet technical functions. The first function is the assignment of protocol name and number registers for many Internet protocols. The second function is maintaining the top-level domain names (a.k.a. the *DNS root*), the .int domain, the .ARPA domain, as well as maintaining the Internationalized Domain Name (IDN) registry. The third service provided by the IANA is the coordination of IP addresses and Autonomous System (AS) numbering used for routing data on the Internet.

- **Internet Engineering Steering Group (IESG)** — The IESG manages the activities of the IETF and is also responsible for reviewing and monitoring Internet standards development and, ultimately, the approval of the standards.

- **Internet-Drafts** — Internet-Drafts are documents that are being worked on by the IETF or one of its working groups, BoFs, members, etc. Internet-Drafts are not approved standards and should not be treated as such. An Internet-Draft must have some revision or edit every six months, or it must be either removed or transformed into an approved standard. An Internet-Draft is also referred to as a *draft standard* (DS).

- **Request for Comments (RFCs)** — RFCs are documents that provide new technology information, updates to standards, better ways of doing things, R and D, and other miscellaneous information[57] dealing with network technologies. The IETF reviews RFCs and takes up some of ideas and proposals in the RFCs as an Internet standard. Some people confuse RFCs with Internet standards, but they are not the same thing. If the IETF decides to adopt an RFC for consideration to be a standard, it starts the RFC on a *standards track*. Initially, the RFC will be a proposed standard (PS). If the RFC makes it past the approval process, it then becomes a draft standard (DS). Finally, if the RFC gets approval through the draft process, it becomes an Internet standard (STD).

---

[57]You can even find some funny RFCs, such as RFC 1438, "Internet Engineering Task Force Statements Of Boredom (SOBs), or RFC 1097, "TELNET Subliminal-Message Option." There are quite a few out there; see how many you can find. Read a couple and then write to Jim or Rich and tell them which one is your favorite. Or better yet, write your own and submit it. See if it gets published.

Interested in reading more? You can get more information about the IETF on the IETF website (www.ietf.org).

1.4   An Introduction to the OSI Reference Model

In 1977, ANSI began work on what eventually became known as the OSI reference model.[58] A working group was formed, and the proposal was submitted to the ISO to begin working on a networking suite to develop a layer model for network architecture in an attempt to standardize. ISO and the International Telecommunication Union –Telecommunication Standardization Sector (ITU-T) participated in a joint effort to standardize networking. The joint effort became known as the Open Systems Interconnection (OSI). OSI was an effort to establish some commonality among communication protocols. Through the efforts of the OSI, the OSI protocol suite and the OSI reference model were born.

Since its inception, the OSI reference model has been the model that most networking professionals first learn about.[59] It still remains an excellent model to learn networking architecture from. It's important to note that the reference model is only a guide and not the rules

> **RANDOM BONUS DEFINITION**
>
> MAC address — The physical (hardware or adaptor) address that identifies a network node

for networking. It serves as a tool for vendors to follow if they want their product to be available for use in multivendor environments. It is important to note that many of the protocols on the market today are modeled after the TCP/IP reference model (see Section 1.6), and may not fit into any particular layer of the OSI reference model.

The OSI reference model is a standard reference model for data communication between network nodes. From a user's perspective, it is used as a reference to define and understand a network. From a vendor's perspective, it is used when developing a product that you expect to be able to operate with products from other vendors.

The OSI reference model divides data communication into seven layers, as shown in Figure 1-12. The lower three layers are used to pass data between

---

[58]The OSI reference model is also known as the OSI Basic Reference Model, the seven-layer model, and the OSI model. For the purposes of standardization, we will refer to this as the OSI reference model throughout this book. This does not infer that the other names are not appropriate, only that it is preferred by the authors.

[59]The OSI reference model has been largely superseded by publications that have been developed since it first came out.

network nodes, whereas the upper four layers are used when user data is passed between end users.

Layer 7	Application
Layer 6	Presentation
Layer 5	Session
Layer 4	Transport
Layer 3	Network
Layer 2	Data Link
Layer 1	Physical

Figure 1-12 The OSI reference model

1.4.1   All People Seem to Need Data Processing— A Mnemonic Device

You might think that this is silly, but no self-respecting self-teaching guide would hold back from sharing information that might be of a benefit to the reader. You need to know the layers of the reference model and what each layer does. It will not only make you sound like you know what you're doing, it will also help you understand what others are talking about. It is also about an 80 percent certainty that you are going to be asked to name the layers, so here is a quick tip on how you can remember them. Simply take the first letter of each name in the model, in order, and replace it with a word that fits into a sentence. For instance:

Application–Presentation–Session–Transport–Network– Data link–Physical

becomes

All–People–Seem–To–Need–Data–Processing

You can also do this in reverse order:

Physical–Data link–Network–Transport–Session–Presentation– Application

becomes

Please–Do–Not–Throw–Sausage–Pizza–Away[60]

Figure 1-13 has an example of these two mnemonic devices, set next to the layers in the OSI model. Many other mnemonic devices have been made up for the purposes of memorizing the layers, and you're certainly welcome to create your own. Hey, if it works, don't knock it!

ACRONYM ALERT

OSPF — Open Shortest Path First

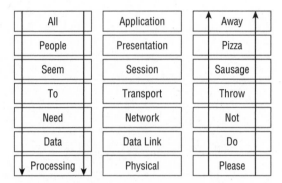

Figure 1-13 Using a mnemonic device as a memory aid

1.4.2 A Layered Approach

The OSI reference model is a systematic approach to outlining the services of protocols that define network architecture. Each layer within the model works with the layers above and/or below them to serve a data transmission purpose. In most networks, the theory of the OSI model may not represent the entire network, and that is why it is a reference model, not a required set of rules.

The OSI reference model breaks down the services within a network into seven layers. Each layer represents protocols that perform a certain purpose or method for allowing data communication within the network. Data is transmitted from a user on the network to another user. It is an application that begins and ends the network connection process. As shown in Figure 1-14,

[60]Jim actually once interviewed an individual who when asked to name the layers of the OSI model actually said, "Please do not throw sausage pizza away" out loud to remember the layer names. His intention wasn't to say it out loud, but he did. He also ended up getting the job.

data flows from Layer 7 to Layer 1, is transmitted to the destination, where it travels up the layers to the end user. So what exactly is going on in these layers? Let's talk about that for a while.

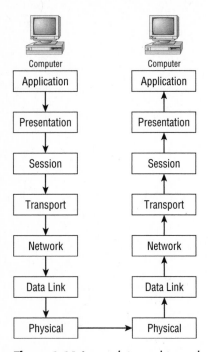

Figure 1-14 A complete, end-to-end network connection

1.4.2.1   Layer 7 – The Application Layer

The name *application* might confuse you at first. The Application layer contains the operating systems that enable application programs to interface with the network. This layer serves application processes that the network uses, but not the applications that interface with the user. Let's look at a couple of examples.

- **Example 1: Sending an e-mail** — The Application layer defines the protocols used in an e-mail transmission, but not the interface that the end user has to initiate in order to send the e-mail.

- **Example 2: Initiating an FTP session** — The Application layer defines the protocol used for a file transfer, but the end user has to initiate an interface with an FTP application to perform the file transfer.

Keep in mind that the OSI reference model is for the architecture of networks and network nodes. Therefore, the Presentation layer does not define end users and the interfaces they have with a PC (and the applications running on the

PC). Not only does the Application layer serve the applications process, it also sends service requests to the Presentation layer. Examples of some common, and a few uncommon, Application layer protocols and services include:

- Association Control Service Element (ACSE)
- Common Management Information Protocol (CMIP)
- Common Management Information Service (CMIS)
- CMIP over TCP/IP (CMOT)
- Dynamic Host Configuration Protocol (DHCP)
- File Transfer Access and Management (FTAM)
- File Transfer Protocol (FTP)
- Hypertext Transfer Protocol (HTTP)
- Internet Relay Chat (IRC)
- Network File System (NFS)
- Post Office Protocol 3 (POP3)
- Remote Operation Service Element (ROSE)
- Reliable Transfer Service Element (RTSE)
- Simple Mail Transfer Protocol (SMTP)
- Simple Network Management Protocol (SNMP)
- Telecommunications Network (Telnet)
- Virtual Terminal Protocol (VSP)
- X.400 –Message Handling Service Protocols
- X.500 –Directory Access Service Protocol (DAP)

1.4.2.2   Layer 6 – The Presentation Layer

The Presentation layer responds to service requests from the Application layer, and sends service requests to the Session layer. The Presentation layer also is responsible for accepting data from the lower layers and then presenting the data to the Application layer, and, ultimately, to the destination. The following functions operate at the Presentation layer:

- Encryption services
- Decryption services
- Data compression services
- Data decompression services
- Translation services

The Presentation layer takes care of translating data from lower layers so the data is understood at the Application layer. This saves the Application layer the headache of having to translate the data itself. The translation also occurs at the Presentation layer when data is being passed down the stack from the Application layer. Note that the Presentation layer is not always needed[61] and that the Application layer may actually work with the Session layer and keep the Presentation layer out of the loop. Here are some examples of the data formats that are defined at the Presentation layer:

- American Standard Code for Information Interchange (ASCII)
- Binary
- Extended Binary Coded Decimal Interchange Code (EBCDIC)
- Joint Photographic Experts Group (JPEG)
- Musical Instrument Digital Interface (MIDI)

1.4.2.3 Layer 5 – The Session Layer

The Session layer is responsible for setting up communication between nodes. The Session layer responds to service requests from the Presentation layer[62] as well as sending service requests to the Transport layer. The Session layer may also provide access control services, authentication, data synchronization, and other services.

The Session layer establishes a communication session, manages the session, and then terminates the session between endpoints. The Session layer is able to gather data streams that are coming from multiple originators and can ensure that the data is synchronized correctly for the destination.[63]

Here are some examples of the data formats defined at the Session layer:

- Network Basic Input/Output System (NetBIOS)
- Network File System (NFS)
- Secure Shell (SSH)
- Structured Query Language (SQL)

1.4.2.4 Layer 4 – The Transport Layer

The Transport layer takes care of getting data from endpoint to endpoint. As long as there is an open communications path, the Transport layer can do its job. The Transport layer receives requests from the Session layer and sends

---

[61]This is due to the fact that encryption/decryption and compression/decompression are not always used.

[62]As mentioned previously, the session layer can also respond to the application layer if the presentation layer is not necessary for a session.

[63]Imagine how much fun we would all have if the destination had to just figure it out on its own.

requests on to the Network layer. The Transport layer ensures end-to-end delivery of data, allowing communication to occur between various endpoint nodes within a network.

The Transport layer utilizes various standards to ensure that data arrives in the right order and that its integrity is maintained. To do this, several functions occur at the Transport layer, including:

- Ensuring that a connection is established
- Disassembling and then reassembling large data streams
- Flow control
- Error recovery
- Data sequencing

The Transport layer is similar to a delivery service, such as the U.S. Postal Service, UPS, or Fed-Ex. They sort, separate, and distribute packages, and have different priorities and classifications. Without caring what is in the package, they get the package where it is supposed to go.[64]

Some examples of Transport layer protocols include:

- AppleTalk Transaction Protocol (ATP)
- Transmission Control Protocol (TCP)
- User Datagram Protocol (UDP)
- Sequenced Packet Exchange (SPX)

1.4.2.5 Layer 3 – The Network Layer

The Network layer is responsible for exchanging data between nodes across several data paths. The Network layer uses nodes called routers to route packets from endpoint to endpoint. The Network layer allows the packet to pass through various network topologies, choosing from multiple paths until it reaches its destination.

The Network layer is able to transfer variable amounts of data between endpoints over one or more networks. The Network layer breaks data into smaller packets and then reassembles the data once it arrives at its destination. The Network layer is also responsible for identifying when an error in data transmission occurs.

IP is the most well-known and widely used Network layer protocol. Remember, IP is connectionless and is not required to regulate and ensure reliable data delivery. It does, however, identify errors in transmission, ensuring that bad packets are dropped. Also, it is IP that fragments data into packets that the next node on the network can support.

---

[64]Hopefully in the condition it is expected to arrive in.

Some examples of Network layer protocols include:

- Internet Protocol (IP)
- Internetwork Packet Exchange protocol (IPX)
- Routing Information Protocol (RIP)
- Internet Control Message Protocol (ICMP)
- Address Resolution Protocol (ARP)
- Reverse Address Resolution Protocol (RARP)
- Open Shortest Path First (OSPF)
- Internet Group Management Protocol (IGMP)

1.4.2.6   Layer 2 — The Data Link Layer

For the most part, LAN communication is handled at the Data Link layer and the Physical layer. At the Data Link layer, network nodes known as *switches* or *bridges* pass frames between nodes in the LAN. Data communication at the Data Link layer can be between two nodes (point-to-point) or between a single endpoint node to many endpoint nodes (point-to-multipoint).

The Data Link layer ensures data delivery between nodes, using the physical addresses of the nodes. It is important that considerations are made for the physical topology of the network segment for the data link traffic. The Data Link layer provides for data flow control, which is used to prevent a node from receiving more data than it can handle at any particular time. The Data Link layer also provides for error notification to the upper layers when a data transmission error occurs.

> **RANDOM BONUS DEFINITION**
>
> multiplexing — The act of combining multiple data streams into a single signal and then transmitting the data over a shared medium. Also known as *muxing*.

Some examples of Data Link layer protocols include:

- High-level Data Link Control (HDLC)
- Serial Line Internet Protocol (SLIP)
- Point-to-Point Protocol (PPP)

The IEEE divides the Data Link layer into two sublayers: the Logical Link Control (LLC) sublayer and the Media Access Control (MAC) sublayer. The LLC sublayer is referred to as the *upper sublayer* of the Data Link layer, whereas the MAC sublayer is the *lower sublayer*. The LLC sublayer multiplexes and demultiplexes data transmitted over the MAC sublayer. The IEEE standard that encompasses the LLC sublayer is IEEE 802.2. The MAC sublayer acts as an interface between the LLC sublayer and the Physical layer. The MAC sublayer makes it possible for network nodes to communication within a multipoint network (such as a LAN or a MAN), by providing address and access control services.

1.4.2.7 Layer 1 – The Physical Layer

The Physical layer serves the Data Link layer. The Physical layer provides a way for the data to be transmitted in a network. Data is converted into a signal which is passed to an endpoint over a physical connection. The Physical layer is responsible for the procedures, mechanics, and the electricity required for operating.

Examples of network nodes that are Physical layer nodes include network adaptors (NIC cards), network hubs, and modems.

1.5 TCP/IP, Please (and Don't Be Stingy with the IP)

TCP/IP is the main protocol used by the Internet and most other network types. If you are a node that connects directly to the Internet, then you will use the TCP/IP protocol to communicate with other nodes. Earlier you learned that TCP and IP are two separate protocols that work with one another. TCP handles breaking down data into small packages, known as *packets*, and then puts the data back together when the data arrives at its destination. IP knows how to get the data there. In this section, we introduce TCP/IP. In Chapter 2, "The TCP/IP Protocol Suite," we will discuss it more in depth. This introduction is required, however, because you will need to have a basic understanding for some of the material covered in Chapters 2 through 4.

A network is simply nodes that are connected to one another to pass data. For data to arrive intact and at the right destination, you must have the protocols that can make sure this happens. This combination of protocols is the TCP/IP protocol suite. TCP/IP was brought about to standardize communications protocols, as there were a lot of proprietary protocols when networking was in its infancy.

> **POP QUIZ**
>
> What is ARPANET? (Note: If you don't know the answer to this one, go back and reread Section 1.2. The next paragraph is where that information starts to come in handy.)

If you are reading this, that means you remember what ARPANET was. This is important, because you probably remember when those supercomputers from different geographical areas first talked to

POP QUIZ

Name the four IMPs that made up the original ARPANET.

each other. Well, the ARPANET protocols that made that happen are what is now known as TCP/IP. The name TCP/IP somewhat implies that these two protocols are what makes TCP/IP what it is. Actually, TCP/IP is a collection of several protocols that work with one another to accomplish data transmission. TCP/IP has its own reference model (see Section 1.5.3) that basically follows the OSI reference model. The protocols that make up TCP/IP use the TCP/IP reference model to map out where they are to function.

Over the years, other protocols have been used to provide upper-layer functionality to transmit data. There are still a few of these out there, but most people support and utilize the TCP/IP protocol. Why use TCP/IP? The answer is simple: because everyone uses TCP/IP. Besides the fact that everyone uses it in some fashion or another, there are several other reasons why TCP/IP has grown into the "method of choice." Some of these are:

- **Routing** — TCP/IP was designed to route data from node to node of networks of variable sizes and complexities. TCP/IP is not worried about the status of nodes in the network; it is concerned about the networks that it should know about. Various protocols within the TCP/IP protocol suite manage data flow between networks.

- **Addressing** — And guess what is built into TCP/IP? That's right, IP. IP provides a way for a node to identify other nodes within a network and deliver data to any endpoint node it has been made aware of.

- **Name resolution** — TCP/IP provides a way to map an IP address (10.10.10.10) to an actual name (networkz.org). Can you imagine how tough it would be to remember the IP addresses of all the websites you needed to know about? Name resolution really helps.

- **Doesn't discount the lower layers** — Although TCP/IP operates at the upper layers (Layer 3 and above), it does have the ability to operate at the lower levels as well. This means that for most LANs and WLANs, and some MANs and WANs, TCP/IP is able to work with multiple networks of these types and connect them to each other.

- **Open standards** — TCP/IP was mainstreamed to enable different nodes to communicate with one another. The open standards that TCP/IP contains are available to anyone. These standards are determined through the RFC process discussed in Section 1.3.9.

- **Talking endpoint to endpoint** — TCP/IP provides a way for one endpoint to speak directly with another endpoint, regardless of any nodes that are in between. It is as if the endpoints were directly connected to one another, even when they are not physically connected to the same local network. Thanks to TCP/IP, both the originating and the destination nodes can exchange connection acknowledgements directly with one another.

- **Application support** — TCP/IP provides protocols that provide a commonality among end user applications. Often when an application that utilizes TCP/IP is developed, many of the functions required for the application are already common with any node supporting TCP/IP.

There are some basic Network layer services provided by any network. All user applications that utilize TCP/IP rely on these standard services to assist in data transport. The first of these standards is that TCP/IP supports connectionless datagram delivery. The TCP/IP network is able to route data from node to node based on the address of the source and destination nodes, but is not concerned about the order in which the data is sent. Having connectionless datagram delivery gives TCP/IP the flexibility to support a wide range of hardware through the network. The other basic service that is used by TCP/IP applications is a reliable transport service. Endpoints establish a connection prior to exchanging data. This allows a temporary connection to appear, from a user's perspective, as a direct connection. The connection remains while the endpoints exchange data (regardless of the amount of data that is transported).

1.5.1   TCP/IP Applications

End users are able to navigate networks by using applications based on the TCP/IP protocol suite. They are able to do so without having any understanding of exactly what it takes to get information shared with destination nodes. The only details the average user needs to know is how the actual interface works. Users rely on the software and technology to get the data to an endpoint.

Numerous TCP/IP-based applications are in deployment within networks worldwide. The following list contains some of the more popular applications that are widely used today:

- Electronic mail (e-mail)
- File transfer
- IP address allocation
- Remote login
- Web browser

1.5.2 TCP/IP Utilities

In addition to application support, TCP/IP also provides some helpful utilities that are available in any node that supports TCP/IP. These utilities provide a variety of information that can be used to help maintain the network. These utilities will be discussed in detail throughout the book. It is important to be aware of these, and no good networking introduction would be complete without a summary of the utilities and the purpose they serve. There are three main categories of TCP/IP utilities:

- ▪ **Diagnostic utilities** — These utilities assist in troubleshooting issues within the network.

- ▪ **General purpose utilities** — These utilities are used to connect to other TCP/IP nodes to perform a specific action, to exchange data, or to allow remote management and related services.

- ▪ **Services utilities** — These utilities are software applications that are offered by a TCP/IP-based server to TCP/IP clients.

Table 1-1 contains a list of some commonly used TCP/IP utilities.

Table 1-1 TCP/IP utilities

DIAGNOSTIC UTILITIES	GENERAL PURPOSE UTILITIES	SERVICES UTILITIES
Address Resolution Protocol (ARP)	File Transfer Protocol (FTP)	TCP/IP print server
IPConfig	Line Printer Daemon (LPD)	Web server
Line Printer Daemon (LPD)	Remote Copy Protocol (RCP)	File Transfer Protocol server
netstat	Remote Shell (RSH)	E-mail server
nslookup	Telnet	
ping	Trivial File Transfer Protocol (TFTP)	
route		
tracert (Windows) Traceroute (other operating systems, such as Linux, Unix, and others)		

1.5.3   The TCP/IP Reference Model

The TCP/IP reference model, the specification established by DARPA[65] to set the rules for ARPANET (and now maintained by the IETF), was developed long before the OSI reference

POP QUIZ

What is the Post Office Protocol?

model. Rather than the seven-layer OSI reference model, the TCP/IP reference model has only five[66] layers, as shown in Figure 1-15.

Layer 5	Application
Layer 4	Transport
Layer 3	Network
Layer 2	Data Link
Layer 1	Physical

Figure 1-15 The TCP/IP reference model

An important thing to note is that the TCP/IP reference model, although represented in layers, does not really operate in a layered manner as the OSI reference model does. There is not a lot of agreement where the layers really fall, though you will often hear about the upper and lower layers in the TCP/IP reference model. The main point is that regardless of whether you follow the OSI reference model or the TCP/IP reference model, the functionality of the network is, for the most part, the same.

As mentioned previously, Chapter 2 discusses the TCP/IP reference model in depth. For the purposes of this introductory chapter, it is important to have only an introduction to the model. The TCP/IP reference model layers are:

■ **Application layer (Layer 5)** — The Application layer in the TCP/IP reference model assumes most of the functions performed by the Session and Presentation layers of the OSI reference model. All upper-layer protocols are handled at this layer.

---

[65] At least we think it was DARPA ... or was it ARPA? Okay, enough funning around — it was DARPA at the time.

[66] A lot of people don't consider the physical layer to be part of the TCP/IP reference model. For the purposes of this book, we have decided to include the physical layer. We don't want you to be confused in the future when someone mentions the four-layer TCP/IP model.

- **Transport layer (Layer 4)** — The Transport layer functions the same in both reference models. The two major protocols that operate at this layer are TCP and UDP. TCP is a connection-oriented protocol and therefore provides reliable delivery. UDP, on the other hand, is connectionless and provides unreliable data delivery.

- **Network layer or Internet layer (Layer 3)** — This layer performs the same functions as Layer 3 of the OSI reference model. The network layer is responsible for routing a packet from a source to a destination. It can do this within a LAN as well as over multiple LANs, MANs, and WANs.

- **Data Link layer (Layer 2)** — This layer is often combined with the Physical layer and is referred to as the host to Network layer. The TCP/IP reference model largely ignores these lower layers. All it cares about it that there is a connection to pass data on.

- **Physical layer (Layer 1)** — This layer is often combined with the Data Link layer and is largely ignored as well, although it does provide the connections to get data passed to a destination. Make no mistake, however: If the Physical layer isn't working, you will miss it real quick. It's like that old saying, "You don't know what you've got until it's gone."

1.6   Chapter Exercises

1. The network used exclusively by the University of Texas is an example of a _____ area network.

2. What are the names of the layers in the OSI reference model?

   Layer 7 _____

   Layer 6 _____

   Layer 5 _____

   Layer 4 _____

   Layer 3 _____

   Layer 2 _____

   Layer 1 _____

3. List at least five applications and/or utilities that use TCP/IP.

   _____

   _____

   _____

_____

_____

4. What are the two types of network relationships?

_____

_____

5. Explain the difference between a client/server network relationship and a client/server database system.

_____

_____

_____

_____

_____

6. What is the 1822 protocol?

_____

_____

_____

_____

_____

7. What are the three types of standards? Do a search on the Internet to see if you can find at least one of each standard type.

_____

_____

_____

8. The 802.11n standard supports an operating frequency of _____ and _____. The maximum data rate for 802.11n is _____. 802.11n reaches a maximum indoor range of 7 _____ and an outdoor range of 250 meters.

9. T or F: The application layer of the OSI model concerns itself with the application/user interface on a PC. _____

10. In this chapter, we listed seven reasons why TCP/IP has grown to be the method of choice. What are these seven reasons?

_____

_____

_____

_____

_____

_____

_____

_____

1.7   Pop Quiz Answers

1. What is a public key certificate?

   Public key certificates are electronic documents that can verify and authorize an individual by public key cryptography. In public key cryptography, two keys (one public key and one private key) are used to encrypt and then decrypt data to ensure that a message can be transported securely.

2. Encapsulated data that is transmitted and received at the network layer is called a _packet_.

3. What is the difference between a physical port and a TCP port?

   A _physical port_ is an interface that resides on a network node. A _TCP/IP port_ is a number that is in the data packet header that maps to a process running on a node.

4. Because IP does not establish a connection before sending data to an endpoint, it would be considered a _connectionless_ protocol.

5. What is the difference between a WAN and a LAN?

   The main difference between a _LAN_ and a _WAN_ is the size of the geographical area that is covered. A _LAN_ covers a small geographical area whereas a _WAN_ covers a large geographical area.

6. The three types of standards are called a _de facto_ standard, a _proprietary_ standard, and an _open_ standard.

7. What is ARPANET?

   ARPANET stands for the Advanced Research Projects Agency Network and was the first packet-switching network ever. The Internet was developed from the ARPANET.

8. Name the four IMPs that made up the original ARPANET.

   ▪ Stanford Research Institute
   ▪ University of California, Los Angeles

- University of California, Santa Barbara
- University of Utah

9. What is the Post Office Protocol?

   Post Office Protocol (POP) is a protocol that allows an e-mail client to connect to an e-mail server and retrieve mail that is destined for that client.

LANs, MANs, and WANs

This is my LAN; that is your LAN; we are joined at the MAN, but I am also connected to a WAN ... from sea to shining sea.
— The authors

Digital data communications has changed rapidly and continues to evolve due to the demand of many types of "data consumers." High-speed data communications is no longer the preferred network of only large companies; everyday consumers use these networks for various forms of communication — voice, text, video, and teleconferencing. The past decade has seen a convergence of a wide range of services utilizing the public network simply referred to as the Internet.

The term *Internet* covers a wide range of network devices and services offered by a wide range of companies commonly referred to as the *telecommunications industry*. This chapter discusses local area networks (LANs), metropolitan area networks (MANs), and wide area networks (WANs). The topics will be discussed in this order, but it is not meant to imply that this was the evolutionary process in networking technology. In reality, it is perhaps more like WANs, LANs, and then MANs. However, there have been areas of overlap where the evolution of all three occurred simultaneously.

The quote above is trying to give a sense of the relationship between LAN, MAN, and WAN. Some LAN networks are a personal thing, like my LAN at home. It is mine, all mine, and not to be shared with others.[1] Strategically speaking, a LAN is owned by a person or small group, but it is fairly local

---

[1]Rich gets a little over-possessive at times. He is a giving soul and does go out of his way to share with others, but his LAN is his LAN.

geographically no matter how many network nodes it may have. MANs may comprise many LAN networks spread about a geographical region whereas WANs can be global. However, the purpose of the MAN or WAN is so that users on LANs, no matter where they may be located geographically, can communicate with each other in the sharing of data and network resources.

2.1   Local Area Networks

A LAN may consist of computers, printers, storage devices, and other shared devices or services available to a group of users within a "local" geographical area. These devices are interconnected either via copper wire, optical wire (fiber), or wireless media. Information passing over the LAN is controlled by a set of network protocols that allows for the orderly sharing of data between applications and devices, even though these may come from many different companies and manufacturers.

ACRONYM ALERT

PAN — Personal area network

2.1.1   LAN Standards

As discussed in Chapter 1, the IEEE recognized that standards had to be developed in order for LAN devices from differing manufacturers to be able to communicate with one another. The IEEE 802 Overview and Architecture standard heading described how these devices are to be interconnected on both LANs and MANs.

For the purposes of this chapter, the standards that will be primarily discussed as far as LAN networks go are:

- 802.2 Logical Link Control
- 802.3 CSMA/CD Access Method and Physical Layer Specifications
- 802.5 Token Ring Access Method and Physical Layer Specifications

2.1.1.1   802.2 Logical Link Control

The lower two layers of the Open Systems Interconnection (OSI) reference model, Data Link and Physical, are addressed within the IEEE 802.2 standard. It further divides the Data Link layer into two sublayers, Logical Link Control (LLC) and Media Access Control (MAC). This allows for ease in mapping between different LAN Physical layers throughout the 802 family of LAN/MAN standards.

The 802.2 implementation uses a strategy of having the LLC sublayer as a common interface between the upper layers and the Physical layer no matter what type of media is being used in the construction

RANDOM BONUS DEFINITION

hop count — A measure of the number of routers that a packet has passed through.

of the LAN. Figure 2-1 shows the LLC structure.

Destination Service Access Point DSAP 8 bits	Source Service Access Point SSAP 8 bits	Control 8 to 16 bits	Data Variable Length

Figure 2-1 The IEEE 802.2 LLC structure

- **Destination service access point** — The type of service that is to receive the packet based on assigned SAP numbers, which are independent from the type of network being used.

- **Source service access point** — The type of service sending the packet based on assigned SAP numbers, which are independent from the network type being used.

- **Control** — Used for flow control and contains the send and receive sequence numbers ensuring packets are being received in the proper sequence.

- **Data** — A variable length field containing the information being carried within the packet.

The Media Access Control sublayer provides addressing and channel control. The MAC address, considered the physical address of the device, is a unique value that allows multiple devices to share the same LAN no matter what the physical medium being used for its implementation. Examples of shared medium networks are those utilizing bus, ring, or wireless topologies. Figure 2-2 illustrates the format of the 48-bit MAC address.

As illustrated, the address is split into two sections. The most significant three octets make up the portion of the address that is referred to as the *organizationally unique identifier* (OUI). These identify the organization that issued the identifier. The NIC specific portion of the address assigned and the serialization of the assigned numbers are under the control of the organization that owns the assigned OUI. With 24 bits of address, an organization can assign 16,777,216 unique addresses to devices they have manufactured. Assigned OUI addresses are maintained by the IEEE and can be found at http://standards.ieee.org/regauth/oui/oui.txt.

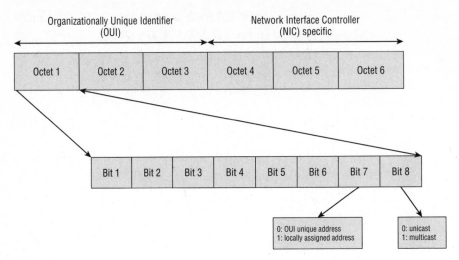

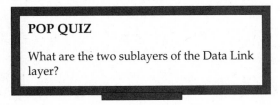

Figure 2-2 The IEEE 802 MAC address format

Bit B8 determines if the packet is either a unicast addressed packet, meaning it is directed to a single network node address, or broadcast, which is directed to all network nodes within a subnet.

MAC addresses are usually written with either hyphens or colons separating the hexadecimal numbers representing each of the octets. A MAC address annotated with the use of hyphens would look like 00-04-54-AA-B1-C2. If using colons, it would be presented as 00:04:54:AA:B1:C2.

POP QUIZ

What are the two sublayers of the Data Link layer?

There is provision for network administrators to locally assign MAC addresses to network interface controllers. If the NIC has been manufactured to allow modification of the factory-assigned MAC address, the administrator can set the bit to indicate that the MAC address has been locally assigned. The NIC portion of the address can be a number for the interface that is of administrator's choosing. Locally assigned addresses do not contain values representative of assigned OUI values. An example of a typical locally assigned MAC address would be:

```
02-00-00-01-00--F4
```

2.1.1.2 802.3 CSMA/CD Access Method and Physical Layer

The IEEE 802.3 standard contains a group of standards that addresses the unique characteristics of the network Physical layer being used on the network.

These standards were evolutionary and were issued as new types of media with differing characteristics were developed.

This standard defined the MAC structure for CSMA/CD,[2] as shown in Figure 2-3.

Start Frame Delimiter	Destination Address	Source Address	Length	802.2 LLC Structure	Frame Check Sequence

Figure 2-3 The CSMA/CD MAC structure

When first introduced, IEEE 802.3 dealt with the use of data networking on a bus type network architecture using thick coax cable. This coax cable carried the designation of 10BASE5 and was more commonly referred to as *thicknet*. This type of cabling was rigid

> **RANDOM BONUS DEFINITION**
>
> multicast address — A method of identifying a set of one or more stations as the destination for transmitted data.

and difficult to work with. It required a transceiver that would tap[3] the cable to form a node on the network. A cable constructed with a 15-pin D style connector was needed to connect the transceiver to the device residing on a node of the network.

To circumvent the difficulties with 10BASE5 cabling, a new standard was developed, IEEE 802.3a, which still is bus network architecture but utilized thin coax, commonly referred to as *thinnet*.[4] The cable used was referred to as *10BASE2*, with RG-58 coax cable being the popular choice. RG-58 cable being thinner offered more flexibility over the RG-8 cable that was used in a 10BASE5 network. The network was formed by using lengths of RG-58 cable terminated with a BNC connector on each end. A BNC T connector formed the network node at the back of each workstation. The network was terminated on each end with a 50 ohm terminator. Figure 2-4 illustrates a simple 10BASE2 network with three workstations connected to the network using a BNC T connector to connect to the network interface card.

[2]Carrier Sense Multiple Access with Collision Detection is necessary in a bus architecture where any workstation may transmit randomly at any given time. The bus segment these workstations reside on is sometimes referred to as a *collision domain*.

[3]This type of tap was also referred to as a vampire tap since it had a pointed probe that pierced the protective layer of the cable insulation to strike the "vein" at its core, which was the center copper conductor. The bits would be allowed to flow like the life's blood of the network was being sucked out. OK, getting a little too dramatic with the class B horror movie genre references.

[4]Thinnet was also referred to as cheapernet since the cost factor was a mere fraction of the cost of 10BASE5 cabling, being more readily available at many electrical supply houses. There really is something to that supply and demand theory that I learned in my economics classes.

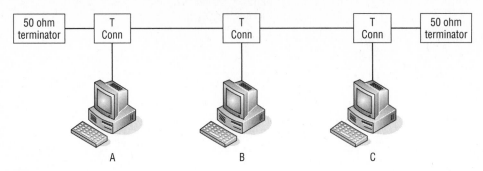

Figure 2-4 A simple 10BASE2 network

The BNC T connector on workstation B has a coax cable connected to it going to workstation A and another going to workstation C. Workstations A and C, having only one cable connected to their BNC T connector and being at each end of the network, require that the open connection on each BNC T connector be terminated with a 50 ohm BNC terminator. Although this is an improvement over 10BASE5 cabling, the one drawback is that workstations not on the end of the network required two cables to be terminated at the workstation's BNC T connector.

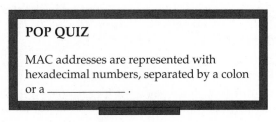

POP QUIZ

MAC addresses are represented with hexadecimal numbers, separated by a colon or a _____ .

Bus-based network architectures have inherent problems with cabling that don't exist in star-based networks. The development of IEEE 802.3i (a bus network that allows for wiring to have the appearance that it is physically a star-based topology while maintaining the CSMA/CD bus network architecture) provided for network cabling that uses unshielded twisted pair (UTP) and is commonly referred to as 10BASE-T. This allows for the use of Category 5 cable, which contained four twisted pairs contained within an unshielded jacket. Each end of the cable is terminated with an RJ-45 plug for short lengths of cable. Larger installations may terminate at wall jacks for workstation areas and to a patch panel at a central location. Since these appear to be spokes out to the workstations, the central location would require a device to concentrate these network nodes on a CSMA/CD network. The devices that accomplish this are appropriately called *hubs*. Figure 2-5 shows a hub and workstations in a CSMA/CD network.

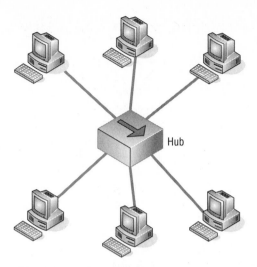

Figure 2-5 A CSMA/CD network using UTP cabling and a hub

Each workstation can be located at varying lengths from the hub. The maximum length of cable between a workstation and a hub is 100 meters.[5] This topology allows for the easy reconfiguration of the workstation. If a workstation is removed, there are no special considerations as there are with a 10BASE2 network topology.

The maximum transmission speed of the IEEE 802.3 networks discussed in this section is 10 Mbps. Subsequent standards have been added to the IEEE 802.3 standard that provide for 100 Mbps Fast Ethernet and 1Gbits/s over twisted pair wire.

> **RANDOM BONUS DEFINITION**
>
> nibble — A 4-bit unit of data (half of a byte).

A QUICK REMEDIAL LESSON

Mega represents a million of something. In decimal number notation, it is 1,000,000. This number can be represented in shorthand notation as 1M.

(continued)

[5]Meters are a metric measurement of distance. A quick calculation would be there are roughly 3 feet to the meter. Therefore, 100 meters is about 300 feet. But to be more precise, it's 328.08 feet.

A QUICK REMEDIAL LESSON *(continued)*

Giga represents a billion of something. In decimal number notation, it is 1,000,000,000. This number can be represented in shorthand notation as 1G.

Now, we have millions and billions of bits, but what exactly is a bit, you ask? It is a single binary number represented by a 1 or a 0. Even if the value is 0, it still requires a signal on the wire, so this is one place where exactly zero does truly represent something.

Ten million bits per second (10 Mbps) is 10 million binary numbers having a value of either 0 or 1 being sent over some medium in a one-second interval. With giga rapidly becoming the new standard in Ethernet transmission speed, which is the equivalent of a billion bits per second (bps) hitting the wire, data that is normally referenced in bytes containing 8 bits of data would equate to 125 MBps (125,000,00 bytes per second) as the maximum number of bytes that can be sent within a second. Note that lowercase "b" signifies bits and that uppercase "B" signifies bytes in the notation used to reference these quantities. Make sure you keep your bits and bytes straight because you can be off by a factor of 8 in your calculations — usually not a problem when you overestimate but you can really feel some heat if you underestimate a network's throughput capability.

2.1.1.3 802.5 Token Ring Access Method and Physical Layer

The IEEE 802.5 standard defines a Token Ring protocol that is much different from that of a CSMA/CD protocol. With CSMA/CD, multiple workstations can transmit onto the wire at the same time, potentially causing collisions. When a collision occurs, they remedy the situation by backing off and retransmitting. With Token Ring, only one workstation is permitted to transmit onto the wire, that being the workstation currently in possession of the token.

Transmission onto the wire is sequential in a fixed pattern. After a workstation possessing the token has completed its transmission onto the wire, it passes the token to the next workstation. This is an advantage over CSMA/CD when the network has fewer workstations. As the number of workstations increases, the advantage is lost and the chattier CSMA/CD finally wins out.

POP QUIZ

What is the maximum length of a cable between a workstation and a hub?

When Token Ring was first introduced by IBM, it possessed a speed of 4 Mbps, thus not offering any advantage over CSMA/CD networks. With the introduction of 16 Mbps Token Ring, it was a toss-up between it and CSMA/CD networks far as performance when the total number of workstations is lower. Figure 2-6 illustrates the IEEE 802.5 frame structure.

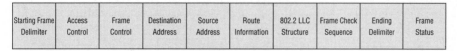

Starting Frame Delimiter	Access Control	Frame Control	Destination Address	Source Address	Route Information	802.2 LLC Structure	Frame Check Sequence	Ending Delimiter	Frame Status

Figure 2-6 The IEEE 802.5 Token Ring frame structure

There are two minor differences between the IBM and IEEE 802.5 standards for Token Ring:

- The number of nodes on a ring is up to 260 nodes per IBM specification, and the IEEE 802.5 standard limits it to a maximum of 250 nodes.

- IBM allows up to 8 fields for route designation when source routing is employed, whereas the IEEE 802.5 standard allows for a maximum of 14 fields.

The frame format for IBM/IEEE 802.5 is as follows:

- The **Starting Frame Delimiter** and **Ending Delimiter** fields are each a single byte with deliberate breaches in certain positions of the Manchester Code[6] so that the start or end of a frame can never be recognized from any other portion of data on the wire.

- **Access Control** is a single-byte field serving to signal control and maintenance functions. The fourth bit position in this field is the token bit. If it is set to 1, this frame is a token and only consists of the Starting Frame Delimiter, Access Control, and Ending Delimiter. A token frame is only 3 bytes long.

- **Frame Control** is a single-byte field that indicates if the frame is control information or data.

- The **Destination Address** field contains either 2 or 6 bytes of addressing information, depending on whether the frame is addressed to a single node or a group of nodes.

- The **Source Address** field contains either 2 or 6 bytes of addressing information that indicates the address of the sending node.

- The **Route Information** field is present only when source routing has been enabled. It defines routing control, a route descriptor, and type of routing information contained within the packet.

---

[6]The Manchester Code is Phase Encoding used within telecommunications where each data bit has a minimum of one voltage transition within a fixed time slot, making it self clocking since the clocking signal can be extracted directly from the encoded data stream.

With source routing enabled there is a minimum of two fields that will be present. The 2-byte route designator field defines a ring number and the bridge number that the frame is to pass through. The last route designator will contain the ring number of the receiving node and a bridge number that is set to zero.

- **802.2 LLC Information Structure** is a variable-length field that, surprise, contains 802.2 LLC information.

- **Frame Check Sequence** is a 4-byte field containing the checksum information verifying the integrity of the frame starting from the Frame Control field through the 802.2 LLC/Data field.

- **Ending Delimiter** is an 8-bit field that indicates the end of the frame.

- **Frame Status** is a 1-byte field indicating that the intended recipient has received the frame.

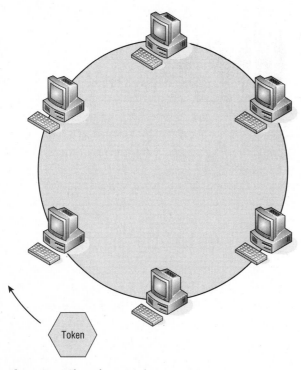

Figure 2-7 The token-passing sequence

Figure 2-7 is a logical visualization of a Token Ring network. The token is a frame type that is transmitted sequentially around the ring network. When a workstation needs to transmit on the ring, it keeps the token and modifies it with address and data information, and then transmits it onto the ring. The receiving station the data frame was intended for accepts the frame and sets a flag in the frame to acknowledge proper receipt of the frame. The receiving station then retransmits the frame with the flag set back onto the ring network. On receipt of the frame with the flag set, the transmitting workstation transmits a new token frame onto the ring network and forwards it, allowing any of the following sequential workstations an opportunity to transmit onto the network.

In a Token Ring network, one of the workstations becomes the active ring monitor. Any workstation can be an active monitor, but only one workstation at a time. It is the role of the active monitor to detect data frames that have traveled around the ring more than once. Once a frame that traveled around the ring more than once is detected, the active monitor will remove the frame from the network and discard it. If the active monitor determines that a token frame is missing from the ring network, it purges the ring network of any frames and then transmits a new token onto the ring network. The active monitor workstation is responsible for the timing and clocking on the ring network. All workstations on the ring network use the timing from the active monitor to ensure that the same timing is being used to receive and send data.

A workstation becomes an active monitor by an election process when the absence of a ring monitor is detected. Upon detection of this message, a workstation transmits a claim token onto the ring network. Any subsequent workstation with a higher address that wishes to participate as the active monitor initiates a new claim token and transmits it onto the ring network. Through this election process the workstation with the highest address and participating in the claim token process is elected as the active monitor.

Although Token Ring is a logical ring, its topology appears as a star-based network. This is accomplished by cabling and connectors designed by IBM. The cabling consists of IBM type 1 shielded twisted pair (STP) cable and a unique connector design which is bulky, giving it a distinct space disadvantage compared to other cable connectors. To complete the ring, these connectors are plugged into a media access unit (MAU), as illustrated in Figure 2-8.

The cable is constructed with a receive pair and a transmit pair. When the Token Ring connector is inserted into the MAU,[7] the receive pair is connected to the transmit pair of the preceding workstation. The transmit pair is connected to the receive pair of the following workstation, and the MAU completes the ring. Multiple MAU units can be combined to form a larger single ring network, as needed.

2.1.1.4 The Collision Domain Battle

Both IEEE 802.3 and Ethernet are CSMA/CD network standards; however, the two are not fully compatible with each other. Although both 802.3 and

---

[7]MAU (media access unit) allows multiple units connected in a star topology to form a logical Token Ring. These devices are sometimes referred to as a "ring in a box."

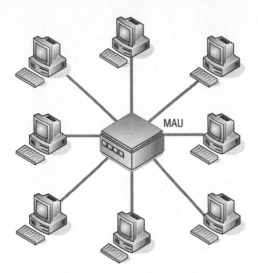

Figure 2-8 A Token Ring network using MAUs

Ethernet devices can coexist within the same LAN network, there are important differences. The major difference between IEEE 802.3 and Ethernet is the frame format. For them to coexist in the same LAN, the network software must be able to differentiate between the different frame types.

Figure 2-9 illustrates the IEEE 802.3 frame.

7 Bytes	1 Byte	6 Bytes	6 Bytes	2 Bytes	1 Byte	1 Byte	1 or 2 Bytes	Variable Length	4 Bytes
Preamble	Start Frame Delimiter	Destination Address	Source Address	Length	Destination Service Access Point	Source Service Access Point	Control	Information (Data and Padding)	Frame Check Sequence

Figure 2-9 The 802.3 frame structure

The IEEE 802.3 frame contains the following fields:

▪ **Preamble** — A 7-byte binary pattern used to establish frame synchronization.

▪ **Start Frame Delimiter** — A single byte used to denote the start of a frame.

▪ **Destination Address** — The address the frame is being sent to. Although the standard allows this field to be anywhere between 2 to 6 bytes in length, the implementation in common use consists of 6 bytes.

▪ **Source Address** — This field contains the address of the device sending the frame. The standard allows this to be anywhere between 2 to 6 bytes in length, but most implementations use 6 bytes in defining this field.

- **Length** — A 2-byte field used to denote the size of the IEEE 802.2 structure, including header and data.

- **Destination Service Access Point** — A 1-byte field that indicates which network protocol the receiving device should use in interpreting the frame.

- **Source Service Access Point** — A 1-byte field indicating which network protocol was used to create the frame. Normally this field contains the same information as the Destination Service Access Point.

- **Control** — This field may be either 2 or 6 bytes long, where the length of the field is indicated by the first 2 bits of the field. It is used for indicating various commands such as exchange identification, test, connect, disconnect or frame rejection.

- An information field containing data and any number of required padding bytes.

  - **Data** — A variable length field that contains the actual information that is being transmitted within the frame.

  - **Pad Bytes** — An optional field that contains no information but is added to ensure that the frame meets the minimum length requirement.

- **Frame Check Sequence** — A 4-byte field that contains the checksum of the fields starting with the Destination Address through the Data field.

Figure 2-10 illustrates the Ethernet frame.

7 Bytes	1 Byte	6 Bytes	6 Bytes	2 Bytes	Variable Length	4 Bytes
Preamble	Start Frame Delimiter	Destination Address	Source Address	Type	Information (Data and Padding)	Frame Check Sequence

Figure 2-10 The Ethernet frame

The Ethernet Frame contains the following fields:

- **Preamble** — A 7-byte binary pattern used to establish frame synchronization.

- **Start Frame Delimiter** — A single byte used to denote the start of a frame.

- **Destination Address** — The address the frame is being sent to. Although the standard allows this field to be anywhere between 2 to 6 bytes in length, the implementation in common use consists of 6 bytes.

- **Source Address** — This field contains the address of the device sending the frame. The standard allows this to be anywhere between 2 to 6 bytes in length, but most implementations use 6 bytes in defining this field.

- **Type** — This is a 2-byte field that indicates the network protocol or the protocol service contained within the frame.

- **Information** — This is a variable length field that contains the actual data being carried by the frame and any number of bytes of padding to ensure the minimum frame size.

- **Frame Check Sequence** — A 4-byte field that contains the checksum of the fields starting with the Destination Address through the Data field.

The key difference between the IEEE 802.3 frame and the Ethernet frame is Ethernet's Type field. The IEEE 802.3 frame uses the IEEE 802.2 Source Service Access Point and Destination Service Access Point fields to indicate which network the frame is coming from and which network it is going to.

A list of registered Ethernet types can be found at `http://standards.ieee .org/regauth/ethertype/eth.txt`.

2.1.1.5 *The Most Common Wireless Standards*

As covered in Chapter 1, the IEEE 802.11 is a group of standards defining the operation of network communications using radio frequencies. These standards are loosely interchanged with the term Wi-Fi, but do have some differences with the standards of the Wi-Fi Alliance. With the proliferation of wireless network products into the marketplace, the Wi-Fi Alliance is in the process of certifying these products before amendments to the 802.11 are completed. Today's wireless products are being sold under the following standards:

ACRONYM ALERT

STE — Spanning tree explorer

- **802.11** — This is the legacy base standard for wireless networking

- **802.11a** — This standard's advantage is the use of the less crowded 5 GHz band, but its chief disadvantage is that its signals are more easily absorbed and dampen the signal quality as the signal travels through solid objects along its path.

- **802.11b** — Introduced in 1999, this standard uses the 2.4 GHz broadcast band providing a typical data rate of 4.5 Mbps with a maximum data rate of 11 Mbps. Its major disadvantage is that it can receive interference from other devices that also share the 2.4 GHz frequency band such as microwaves, cordless telephones, and a wide variety of Bluetooth devices. The substantial increase of data rate throughput and the reduction of product cost have led to the rapid acceptance of this standard as the definitive standard for wireless LAN networks.

■ **802.11g** — Consumer demand for higher data rate products led to the introduction of products that supported the older IEEE 802.11a and b standards as well as this standard, which made these products capable of supporting all three standards within a single device. However, an 802.11g standard wireless LAN network can reduce the overall speed of the network if one device participating in the wireless network is only capable of supporting the IEEE 802.11b standard. As with 802.11b, this standard also falls prey to the same interference from other devices sharing the same frequency band.

■ **802.11-2007** — This is a standard that was released to be all-inclusive of the amendments to 802.11 since its introduction. To date this is the most conclusive standard document that defines wireless LAN network operation.

■ **802.11n** — With a proposed release date of 2009, this is an amendment that will add additional features to the 802.11 standard and will include multiple input/multiple output (MIMO) technology. MIMO will use multiple antennas for both transmission and receiving, which would offer significant increases in range and data rate throughput without the need for increased bandwidth of transmission power. Although it is still in draft, many vendors are beginning to sell products labeled under the 802.11n standard. To avoid any interoperability problems between differing vendors, it is recommended to purchase routers and access points from the same manufacturer.

The standards listed above are not all-inclusive of the IEEE 802.11 standard. They are the most commonly known and discussed standards when there is a discussion on wireless LAN networks. Additional information can be found at the IEEE 802.11 group's website at `http://ieee802.org/11/`.

2.1.2   LAN Topologies

Chapter 1 presented a variety of network topologies. In this chapter, we will attempt to provide further information concerning the implementation and use of these topologies in the creation of a LAN.

Figure 2-11 illustrates a very basic network map. The purpose is to demonstrate that even a simple network can and probably will use a variety of media, protocols, and network devices. The media shown on this network topology is a combination of wired systems, which include both ring and bus network topologies, along with a network segment that is connected using wireless network technology. Users are connected to the network either hard-wired to a bus or ring LAN segment or through a wireless LAN access point.

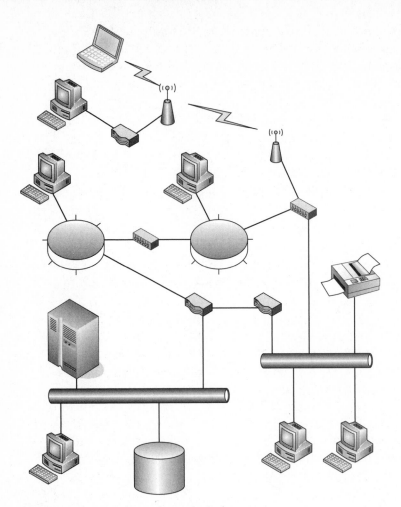

Figure 2-11 A sample LAN's topological map

The network allows for the access of users to network resources such as mainframe computers, network storage devices, network printers, and other shared resources connected to the network. The LAN segment illustrated in this figure has no access to the outside world via the Internet and is self-contained. Most of today's LAN networks ultimately do connect to the Internet and will be discussed further in the "Metropolitan Area Networks" and "Wide Area Networks" sections of this chapter. So the focus of this section is solely on the LAN. This is the section that deals with "this is my LAN and that is your LAN" area of networking.

A LAN can contain a single network segment of any media type, or it may be a collection of two or more of the network media currently in use today. So, if a LAN is a combination of different media types, how do they interconnect? This is where devices called gateways, bridges, and routers come into play. They are depicted in Figure 2-11 as boxes between LAN segments. How you plan to implement your network and the networking address schemes that are to be used will determine which type of these devices would need to be used for these network nodes. These devices will be covered in depth in Chapter 3, "Network Hardware and Transmission Media." For the purpose of this chapter, it will be generally accepted that these devices do allow for communications between LAN segments with different media and network protocols.

2.1.2.1 Token Ring Network Topologies

Wired Token Ring networks are still around, but the number of new installations is declining as more new network installations opt toward wired bus network implementations. The need to discuss the wired Token Ring network architecture is due to the fact that there are a number of these networks still deployed in the field today even though they are considered legacy[8] networks.

The original design of a Token Ring network was literally a ring where each node of the network was daisy-chained to the next node until the network came back around to the first node in the ring. There was a ring-in (RI) port and a ring-out (RO) port, with the RO of one station connecting to the RI of the next upstream station on the ring. This would continue until all the network nodes had been connected. The major disadvantage of this network design was that the disruption or disconnection of any one node on the ring brought the whole network down. Newer Token Ring networks were designed using hubs or media access units (MAUs), which allowed for ease in cabling while maintaining the logical ring of the Token Ring network architecture. Figure 2-12 illustrates the construction of a Token Ring network with two nodes with the use of a two-port MAU.

Figure 2-12 A simple Token Ring network

Obviously, a network of this construction has a limited use. To overcome this limitation, an eight-port MAU was designed with the ability to extend the Token Ring by daisy-chaining multiple eight-port MAU units together using the RI and RO ports on the eight-port MAU. Figure 2-13 illustrates this more complex Token Ring network.

---

[8] A legacy network is one that is installed and operational although its technology has been superseded by other network technologies. Networks in large organizations are mostly evolutionary. It is not uncommon to find some networks still operational although they are no longer sold and supported by the original manufacturer. A lot of companies work on the "if it ain't broke, don't fix it" mentality when it comes to their internal LAN networks.

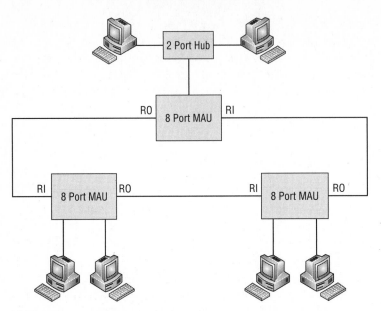

Figure 2-13 A typical Token Ring network

Up to a maximum of 33 MAU units can be interconnected to form the ring network. The distance between MAU units is determined by the cable used to interconnect them. With the use of Type 1 cable, MAU units can be placed up to a maximum of 100 meters apart. If greater distances are needed, a repeater is required. Repeaters used for copper wire network segments can increase this distance up to 740 meters. If even greater distances are

ACRONYM ALERT

UDP — User Datagram Protocol

required, the network segment can be further extended up to four kilometers with the use of a fiber optic repeater and fiber optic cable.

Workstations and hubs connected to the MAU by cable are referred to as lobes. Normally a lobe connects a workstation to a MAU, but if multiple workstations in the same area need to be connected to the ring network, this is accomplished with the use of a lobe access unit (LAU). A LAU unit splits the lobe into two or more lobes. A LAU can be placed at the end of a cable to allow for the connection of multiple workstations in that area. Although LAU units sound as if they are the same as MAU units, there is a major difference. Unlike a MAU, a LAU cannot be used to create a standalone ring. So LAU units are basically used as hubs.

Although the difference between LAU and MAU units has become obscured because some manufacturers market products called LAU units, in reality they are functionally MAU units. However, the primary use of both MAU and

LAU units is in maintaining the functioning of the ring network as devices are disconnected from the network.

A MAU or LAU allows a lobe on the ring to be opened for the insertion of a new workstation, and it closes the ring when a workstation is removed from the network. This allows for flexibility of network construction and any necessary network reconfiguration without the problem of interruption of ring network function.

2.1.2.1.1   Token Ring Cabling

The physical layout of a Token Ring network depends not only on the placement of MAU, LAU, and hub units, but also on the cabling being used in its construction. It has been previously mentioned that the cable construction can be either STP or UTP cable.

2.1.2.1.1.1   Shielded Twisted Pair Cable   STP Token Ring cable, also known as *IBM Type 1 cable*, is constructed with twisted pair wires that are shielded. The use of this cable allows for Token Ring lobe connections to be a maximum of 100 meters apart. STP cables are terminated with either DB9 connectors or patch connectors. Generally, patch connectors are used to connect to MAU units, whereas DB9 male connectors are used to connect to workstations or LAU units. DB9 female connectors are used to daisy-chain one LAU unit to another.

The signals carried by the cable are transmit and receive. Two shielded pairs are needed for these differential[9] signals. Table 2-1 lists the DB9 pin assignments.

Table 2-1 DB9 Pin Assignments

SIGNAL	PIN
Receive +	1
Receive −	6
Transmit +	9
Transmit −	5

2.1.2.1.1.2   Unshielded Twisted Pair Cable   UTP Token Ring cable, also known as *IBM Type 3 cable*, is constructed with unshielded twisted pair wire similar to telephone cable. These cables are terminated with RJ-45 modular

---

[9]Differential Manchester encoding is used for the transmission and reception of data in the use of either STP or UTP Token Ring cabling. The balanced signals for both the send and receive data signals allow for data integrity and greater noise immunity.

plugs. This style of Token Ring cabling is dependent on the operating environment the network segment is in and the speed of the LAN itself. This cabling is used to form lobe segments that do not exceed 45 meters. Typically these cables[10] are constructed using 10BASE-T UTP cable terminated on each end with RJ-45 plugs. The RJ-45 pin assignments are listed in Table 2-2.

Table 2-2 RJ-45 Pin Assignments

SIGNAL	PIN	WIRE COLOR
Receive +	4	White with orange stripe
Receive −	5	Orange with white stripe
Transmit +	6	White with blue stripe
Transmit −	3	Blue with white stripe

2.1.2.1.1.3 Other Variations of Token Ring Cabling   For special environments or applications, IBM also uses cabling that consists of Type 2, Type 5, Type 6, Type 8, and Type 9 cables.

- **Type 2** — Consists of two STPs as can be found in Type 1 cable and four UTPs as can be found in Type 3 cable.
- **Type 5** — Consists of multimode fiber optic cable used to extend the Token Ring network and to interconnect optical repeaters.
- **Type 6** — Consists of two STPs. It is considered a low cost, short distance cable with a maximum length of 45 meters and is often used for MAU-to-MAU connection.
- **Type 8** — Consists of two parallel pairs. The wires in this cable are untwisted and have a maximum length of 50 meters. The primary purpose of this wire is in installations requiring the cable to run under carpeting.
- **Type 9** — A lower cost alternative to Type 1 cable with a maximum length of 65 meters. It consists of two pairs of STPs.

2.1.2.1.2 High-Speed Token Ring

There have been efforts made to push the speed of Token Ring networks beyond the standard 16 Mbps. High-speed Token Ring has not been fully deployed with the decline in newer Token Ring installations. However, it is

---

[10]Although these cables appear to be similar to those used for Ethernet 10BASE-T patch cables, they are not the same. Ethernet 10BASE-T cables are constructed to use pins 1 and 2, and 3 and 6, for their twisted pair combinations.

worth mentioning since there is a high likelihood of it being encountered in the remaining legacy Token Ring networks.

- **32 Mbps Token Ring** — Both IBM and other vendors of Token Ring components and devices attempted to push Token Ring operation to a higher speed.

- **Token Ring switches** — These are in the form of switching bridges capable of speeding up how messages travel between network rings.

- **Fiber distributed data interface (FDDI)** — Although closely related to Token Ring, it is not officially considered as part of the Token Ring family. They both use a token-passing protocol.

2.1.2.2 Bus Networks Topologies

Bus networks initially were designed as a physical bus allowing devices to be connected to nodes along the bus. Figure 2-14 shows a typical bus network.

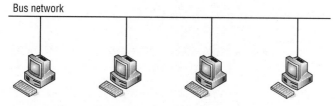

Figure 2-14 A typical bus network

In this illustration, workstations are connected to the bus with the use of transceivers. With 10BASE5 cabling being used to form the bus network, external transceivers were typically used to connect a workstation to the network. In later bus implementations using 10BASE2 cabling in the form of RG-58 coax cable to form the bus network, the transceiver was integrated into the network adapter card that was installed within the workstation.

The transceiver not only converted the digital data generated by the workstation into the appropriate data signals, it performed other functions useful to both 802.3 and Ethernet LAN networks.

- **Collision detection** — Provided by circuitry designed to detect collisions on the bus network. If a collision is detected, the transceiver notifies the transmitting function that a collision has occurred and then broadcasts a jamming signal on the network to notify other systems connected to the bus network. The LAN is then allowed to settle before the resumption of transmissions on to the bus.

- **Heartbeat** — Generation of a short signal to inform the main adapter that the transmission is successful and collision free. Although specified in the 802.3 standard and the Ethernet standard, it is rarely used because many adapters confuse this signal with the signal that signifies a collision has occurred.

- **Jabber** — The function that allows the transceiver to cease transmission if the frame being transmitted exceeds the specified limit of 1518 bytes. This helps prevent a malfunctioning system or adapter from flooding the LAN with inappropriate data.

- **Monitor** — This function monitors LAN traffic by prohibiting transmit functions while receive and collision functions are enabled. It does not generate any traffic onto the LAN.

A bus network created using 10BASE5 or thick coax cable can have a maximum overall segment length of 500 meters. Each node on the segment is created with the use of a transceiver. Nodes on a thick coax cable are to be spaced no closer than 2.5 meters with a maximum number of 100 nodes per segment. The impedance for thick coax is 50 ohms. With the use of repeaters, the overall length of the combined segments is not to exceed 2,500 meters.

Generally, bus networks that are formed by using 10BASE2 cabling use adapters that have the transceiver function built in. The network is formed using a BNC coax T connector connected to the workstation's BNC coax connector. Workstations are then daisy-chained together

> **RANDOM BONUS DEFINITION**
>
> twisted pair — A communications medium consisting of two copper conductors twisted together.

using lengths of coax cable terminated at both ends with coax plugs. These interconnecting cables should not be less than 0.5 meters in length with a maximum of 30 nodes and a total length of 185 meters per network segment. The BNC T connector on each end of the network segment requires a 50 ohm terminator to be attached to the open end of the T connector to maintain the cable impedance. This is essential to maintain signal integrity and the dampening of any signal reflections on the cable. With the use of repeaters, the overall length of the combined segments is not to exceed 925 meters.

The maximum frame size for both IEEE 802.3 and Ethernet frames is 1518 bytes. 802.3 provides for a maximum data segment size of 1460 bytes while Ethernet allows for a maximum data size of 1500 bytes. The original speed for Ethernet was 10 Mbps.

There are two other implementations of logical bus networks: the star topology and the tree topology.

2.1.2.2.1 Star Network Topology

A star topology is implemented with the use of hubs and UTP cables terminated with RJ-45 plugs. Hubs maintain the logic of the bus network while the UTP cables radiate out in a star pattern. Figure 2-15 illustrates a star network formed with the use of a single hub and UTP cables that are no longer than 100 meters in length.

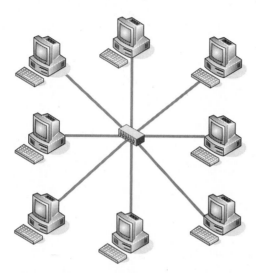

Figure 2-15 A star network

The simplicity of this type of network is the ease in which devices may be added or removed from the network. The only limiting factor for this type of network with a single hub is the number of ports contained on the hub. This type of network is only useful for a small self-contained work group with no requirement of connecting to other network segments located elsewhere.

2.1.2.2.2 Tree Network Topologies

Tree network topologies consist of network segments connected by hubs and other devices in various combinations to create the network. Network segments can either be geographically close or remote. Many networks fall into the tree network architecture. This is especially true for very large networks with many nodes. Figure 2-16 illustrates a simple logical diagram showing a series of user nodes.

This could be considered a top level drawing where the later drawings show more detail of how the segments are to be connected and the media that make up the network segments. Figure 2-17 illustrates what one of the network segments might look like. It is a combination of devices using both wired and wireless media to connect nodes within that network segment.

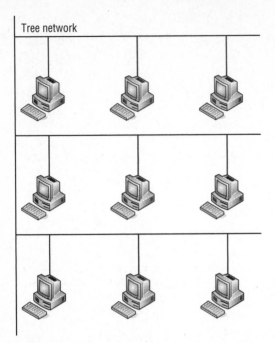

Figure 2-16 A logical drawing of tree network topology

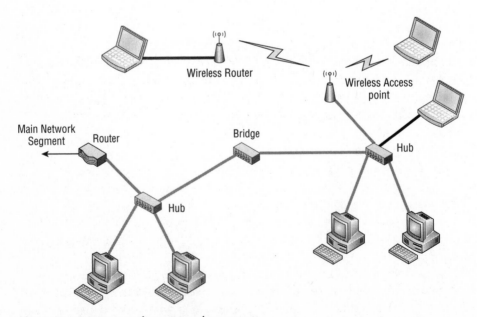

Figure 2-17 A tree topology network segment

Laptop users with wireless enabled laptops can communicate directly from their laptop to a wireless access point to gain access to the network. Laptops that are not wireless enabled can be directly connected to the wired network segment using the network interface card, which is internal to the laptop. Another option, if needed, is to connect the laptop to a wireless router that is able to communicate to the wireless access point to gain access to the network. Workstations on the network segment are connected to the network with the use of a hub. Separate local network segments are connected with the use of a bridge. This whole network segment is connected to other network segments with the use of a router.

2.1.2.2.3   Devices that Make Up a Network

True bus networks[11] can still be found, but they are considered legacy networks by today's standards. Most newly deployed networks, although they are bus networks, logically make use of devices to maintain the bus while nodes are placed in either a star or tree network topology or, in many cases, a combination of both. The majority of cabling used is 10BASE-T UTP cable connected to the bus network devices with the use of RJ-45 plugs.

The following devices may be found in a variety of network topologies:

- **Hubs** — Considered to be passive network devices.[12] Passive hubs allow the connection of multiple nodes to the network. They can be stand-alone or daisy-chained to other hubs to form a larger network segment.

- **Repeaters** — Used to extend network segments beyond the recommended distance over wire cabling by performing signal regeneration to ensure that data integrity is maintained over the long network segment.

- **Bridges** — Used to divide a network into smaller segments to reduce the number of network devices contending on the network segment for network access. The bridge only passes network traffic that is specifically intended for the other network segment that it is connected to.

- **Ethernet switches** — These are more predominately used today in LAN networks to perform the role of bridges in dividing a network into smaller segments to reduce network contention between network devices. A single Ethernet switch is capable of having multiple network segments contained within it. This is accomplished by programmable ports, which may be dedicated to virtual LAN (VLAN)

---

[11]The term *true bus network* refers to networks that are physically constructed as a bus. They consist of either thick or thin coax cable. These networks use 10BASE5 and 10BASE2 cabling to form the network segment.

[12]Passive network devices such as hubs are designed to maintain the electrical characteristics of a bus network while physically giving the appearance that they are interconnected in either a star or tree network topology.

segments on that device. They usually contain multiple ports and are similar in appearance to hubs but differ in that hubs are not able to reduce network contention on the network segment they are being used on. Some Ethernet switches provide the ability to gang multiple devices together to form a larger network segment.

- **Routers** — Used to connect multiple network segments but differ vastly from bridge devices. Bridges operate solely on the information contained within the 802.3 data frame and are not effected by the routing protocols being run over the network. Routers operate at the network protocol level and forward network traffic based upon the network protocol information contained within the data frame being forwarded from one network segment to another.

- **Network interface cards (NIC)** — A term used predominately to refer to the cards contained within devices connected to the network. However, the devices that fall under this category are wide and diverse, from cards meant to fit into a PC slot to other devices intended to connect via a USB port. Some NIC devices fit into a PCMCIA card slot on a laptop and allow it to gain network access via a wireless link. They all serve the same purpose: to allow a device to connect to a LAN.

The devices briefly described in this section are covered in further depth in Chapter 3.

2.1.2.2.4 Bus Network Cabling

This section discusses the following bus wire types: 10BASE5 coax (thicknet), 10BASE2 (thinnet), and 10BASE-T (UTP). The predominant wiring used in today's network is 10BASE-T, which is commonly referred to as *Ethernet cabling*. The characteristics and limitations of each cable type will be discussed in this section.

2.1.2.2.4.1 10BASE5 Thicknet This cable type was the initial introduction to CSMA/CD bus network topology. The network segment is formed using this thick coax cable, which has a maximum segment length of 500 meters. Being thick and heavy, the cable is difficult to handle when routing the cable throughout a building. A network node is formed with the use of what is commonly referred to as a *vampire tap*. This device pierces the jacket of the coax cable to make contact to the center conductor of the coax cable and provide the signal to the network node with the use of a transceiver. The physical construction of the transceiver appears the same for both Ethernet and IEEE 802.3, both using a DB15 connector style. However, where they differ is in the circuit assignment for each pin. Table 2-3 shows the DB15 pin assignments for both Ethernet and IEEE 802.3.

Table 2-3 DB15 Pin Assignments

PIN	ETHERNET	IEEE 802.3
1	Ground	Ground control in
2	Collision detected +	Control in A
3	Transmit +	Data out A
4	Ground	Data in
5	Receive +	Data in A
6	Voltage	Common
7	Control	Out A
8	Ground	Control out
9	Collision detected −	Control in B
10	Transmit −	Data out B
11	Ground	Data out
12	Receive −	Data in B
13	Power	
14	Power ground	
15	Control	Out B

The Ethernet transceiver specifies the pinout for three signals, transmit, receive, and collision detect, whereas the IEEE 802.3 standard provides for an added signal of control out (which is not used). Although the pin assignments are such that a cable manufactured for either standard would work with the other standard's transceiver, it is not recommended due to differences used in signal grounding.

Vampire taps may not be located any closer together than 2.5 meters with a maximum of 100 taps per network segment. Network segments can be combined with the use of repeaters to increase the overall combined network length to 2,500 meters. The characteristic impedance of 10BASE5 cable is 50 ohms.

2.1.2.2.4.2 *10BASE2 Thinnet* 10BASE2 networks are constructed mostly with the use of RG-58 coax cable, which has a characteristic impedance of 50 ohms. This cabling is more desirable for use in network segments due to its lower cost and greater flexibility than that of 10BASE5 cable. Network nodes are easily formed with lower cost BNC T connectors, whereas 10BASE5 cabling requires a more expensive vampire tap transceiver. However, 10BASE5 cable is capable of far greater network segment length than 10BASE2, which makes it more suitable for a network backbone. The 10BASE2 network, with its lower cost and ease of reconfiguration if needed, is more suited for a work group environment clustered in a smaller geographical area. To properly terminate a 10BASE2 network to maintain the characteristic 50 ohm impedance across the network and reduce signal reflections on the wire, the last BNC T connector on each end of the network segment must have a 50 ohm BNC terminating plug connected to the open tap on that BNC T connector.

The overall segment length for a 10BASE2 cabled network is 185 meters with a maximum of 30 network nodes per segment. The minimum distance between network nodes is 0.5 meter. The overall network length that can be achieved with the use of repeaters for 10BASE2 is 925 meters.

2.1.2.2.4.3 10BASE-T UTP Cabling These days, 10BASE-T cable and Ethernet UTP cable are simply synonymously called *Ethernet cable*. Although logically it is considered as bus topology cable, it is point-to-point between a network node device and a device that completes the logical bus. Cable construction is similar to telephone cable, which makes it easily routable through a building. Similar to telephone cable in larger installation sites, patch panels are used to terminate cables from differing locations throughout the facility.

Ethernet cables of various lengths terminated with RJ-45 plugs on both ends are usually referred to as *patch cables* or *straight-through cables*. These cables are used to connect a network node device to a network device that completes the logical bus. Table 2-4 shows the pinout for an RJ-45 plug on an Ethernet cable.

Table 2-4 RJ-45 Pin Assignments

PIN	SIGNAL
1	Transmit +
2	Transmit −
3	Receive +
4	
5	
6	Receive −
7	
8	

It can be seen that a patch cable or straight-through cable carries the same signal from one end to the other on the same pin if both RJ-45 jacks are wired exactly alike. However, there is another cable that appears physically identical but is wired differently, called a crossover cable. These cables do literally just that — they cross over the transmit signals to the receive signals. The purpose of these cables is to connect two network devices whose connectors are wired exactly the same. A simple example of this would be two computers connected by a crossover cable to use the network cable to transfer files between them.

Many of today's network devices such as hubs and switches use auto-sensing, auto-switching ports to sense the cable and dynamically configure the port to ensure that the transmit signal from another network device is connected to its receive signal input. This was not always the case, so in order to expand a network segment, crossover cables were necessary to daisy-chain multiple hubs together. Figure 2-18 illustrates how hubs can be daisy-chained to form a larger network segment.

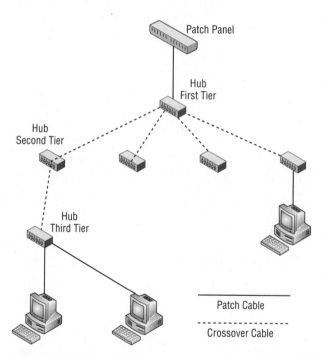

Figure 2-18 Daisy-chaining for an expanded network segment

In Figure 2-18, a local geographical area is serviced by a series of hubs to allow network devices in that location to gain access to the network. The feed for this network is from a patch panel over a patch cable to the first tier hub device. This device with the use of crossover cables is attached to a number of second tier hubs. In this illustration, one of the second tier hubs is connected using a crossover cable to a third tier hub, which services some computers attached to the network. This appears at first to be an unlimited geometric progression, but in reality it is a bus network, so network devices do contend for network bandwidth. It can be readily seen that all devices on this network segment that send traffic to other network segments need to have it pass over the single cable between the patch panel and the first tier hub device. This is often referred to as a single point of access.[13]

Hub manufacturers saw the inconvenience of having two cable types and began to design and sell hubs with a mechanical switch on one of the ports so that a patch cable could be used between hubs in place of a crossover cable. More recent Ethernet port designs have led to the development of a port device using electronic auto-sensing, auto-switching to configure the port to match transmit and receive signals no matter if a patch or crossover cable is connected to the port.

Any segment of the network shown in Figure 2-18 may not have a cable linking two network devices that exceeds 100 meters. The overall combined length of the entire segment with the use of hubs and repeaters may not exceed 2,500 meters. For smaller local networks, these lengths are more than adequate. For much larger installations, special considerations will be required to ensure data integrity on the network.

2.1.2.2.4.4 So What about Speed and Duplex? The initial speed standard for CSMA/CD bus networks over UTP cable was 10 Mbps. Since the initial introduction, devices that can pass network traffic at 100 Mbps (100BASE-TX) are now fairly common. Many of today's installations make use of gigabit speeds (1000BASE-T), which sometimes is referred to as *gig-E*. These advances in technology have allowed for the attainment of greater network speeds without the need for changing the current wiring infrastructure. Devices capable of any of the speeds listed are able to do so over existing Category 5 cabling.

> **RANDOM BONUS DEFINITION**
>
> ping — A utility program used to test for network connectivity by using the echo request and echo response mechanisms of ICMP.

Duplex is either half-duplex or full-duplex. The difference between the two is that full-duplex devices are capable of transmitting and receiving at the same time, whereas half-duplex devices are either in transmit or receive mode but never both simultaneously.

Since UTP cabling is connected in a point-to-point fashion, the ports connected to each end of the cable must be able to transmit and receive at the same speed. On some devices, these are only manually configurable. Some devices

---

[13]Single point of access is also a single point of network failure. Depending on the number of devices in a local area or how critical network availability is to those users, some thought should be given to network segmentation and redundancy. There will be further discussions and examples of this throughout this book.

are able to negotiate speed and duplex with their peer port to set the speed and duplex to be used over the link.[14] This mode of operation is referred to as auto-negotiation.

Careful attention must be paid to the speed and duplex of an interface. If there is a mismatch between the devices, network performance will be degraded and full network speed cannot be realized. This is a small detail that's often overlooked but has major implications in overall network performance.

2.2   Metropolitan Area Networks

The term *metropolitan area network* is a bit nebulous and embraces a variety of differing network scenarios. The common denominator in all these networks is that they cover areas that are much larger than a conventional LAN is capable of, as discussed in Chapter 1.

The technological development of fiber optic network devices has facilitated the growth of both private and public MAN networks. Fiber optics allowed the network to stretch to over several kilometers, which made extended networks more feasible. Fiber distributed data interface (FDDI) is used for the backbone that interconnects distant portions of the MAN. So what exactly is an FDDI?

2.2.1   Fiber Distributed Data Interface

Fiber optic cabling presents several advantages over conventional copper wiring. It is lighter in weight than copper, weighing in at roughly 10 percent of a copper cable of the same length. It is capable of driving data signals much further with less loss and is immune to crosstalk and noise caused by electromagnetic interference (EMI). Fiber optic cable, being electrically inert, aids in the elimination of ground loops between sending and receiving nodes.

Since fiber optic cable does not emit any radio frequency interference (RFI) when data is transmitted on the cable, it cannot be snooped using radio frequency detectors as copper wire can. The only way data can be eavesdropped on is by actually breaking the cable and placing a receiver in the line. Since this action would not go undetected, fiber optic cabling offers greater security over copper.

All this stuff about fiber optic cable is great, but how is it used in a network, you ask? Well, knowing you read the section on Token Ring LAN segments, the authors feel we do not have to review the concept of token passing. If we are wrong, you should go back and read the Token Ring section about how a token is passed about a ring. Although the token-passing concept is

---

[14]*Link* is a reference to a cable connecting (linking) two network devices' ports. Many interface connectors on network devices have an LED indicator to indicate the presence of link. Link on an interface indicates that the transmit and receive signals are properly connected and the two devices are capable of communicating over the cable (link).

similar, FDDI is not the same as the IEEE 802.5 Token Ring standard. FDDI was standardized under ANSI standard X3T9.

From the previous paragraph, you are already aware that FDDI is implemented using token passing over a ring topology consisting of fiber optic cable. Construction of the network consists of dual rings, a primary ring and a secondary ring. Both rings are capable of passing data, but usually the counter-rotating secondary ring, which can carry data in the opposite direction, is reserved to be used as a backup in case of ring failure. Figure 2-19 shows a logical representation of an FDDI network.

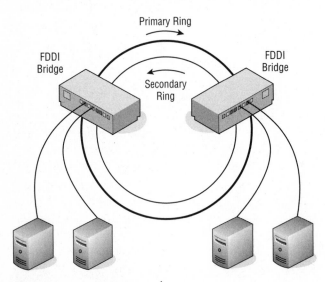

Figure 2-19 An FDDI network

Although this network is shown logically as a ring, it is physically deployed in a star topology similar to that of wired Token Ring networks. FDDI bridge/concentrators complete the logical ring while also providing the optical to electrical signal conversion to allow data to be transferred from an optical network segment to a wired network segment and in the reverse direction.

To facilitate the star physical topology, fiber optic cable is dual strand cable. There is one fiber optic strand carrying intelligent light information to the FDDI bridge concentrator while the other strand allows for the transmission of data from that FDDI concentrator to the next. These fiber optic network cables are sometime called *light pipes*.[15]

---

[15]Don't confuse fiber optic data cables with those fiber strands you see at the mall emitting all those wild colors. Although similar in terms of light being transmitted through an optical fiber, the quality and construction are far different. After all, it is for the purpose of sending intelligent data.

FDDI networks are capable of transmitting data at 100 Mbps for a maximum ring circumference of 100 kilometers. If both the primary and secondary rings are used, an effective data rate of 200 Mbps can be achieved. This is what makes FDDI the preferred choice for backbones on large LAN networks and for deploying a MAN over a wide geographical area.

To pass data from either an Ethernet or Token Ring LAN segment requires a bridge to transform electrical signals into intelligent light impulses. These bridges fall into two categories, encapsulating bridges and translating bridges. Encapsulating bridges encapsulate Ethernet frames into FDDI frames, and translating bridges translate the received frame source and destination MAC addresses into FDDI addresses. The maximum FDDI frame size is 4500 bytes.

A dual ring FDDI network can connect up to a maximum of 500 stations. Since FDDI requires a repeater every 2 kilometers, it is unsuitable for a WAN network deployment. FDDI lends itself easily within existing metropolitan infrastructures where cabling is routed in hostile environments under streets and overhead lines. It is impervious to EMI, so no special shielding is required other than having the fiber jacketed to withstand the environment it is to be placed in. Since fiber cable depends on a continuous, undistorted fiber to transmit data without degradation, care must be taken to maintain a minimum bending radius for the type of fiber cable being used, to prevent a possible crimp in the fiber. A distortion of the fiber can cause light reflections that could render the total cable length unusable for the transmission of data.

Fault tolerance is built into the dual ring FDDI network. When an interruption on the primary ring is detected, beaconing is used to determine where the break occurred. Beaconing is also used to monitor the health of the ring network token-passing process. Each station on the ring is responsible for checking the token-passing status of the ring. If a fault is detected by a station, it transmits a beacon onto the ring. The upstream station receives the beacon and begins to transmit its own beacon. The downstream station ceases beaconing after receiving a beacon from its upstream station. The process keeps moving to the next upstream station around the ring until the beaconing station does not detect a beacon from its upstream station. The fault has been isolated between the beaconing station and its upstream station. The secondary ring can then be placed into service by allowing for data traffic flow in the opposite direction. When the beaconing station detects its own beacon being received on the primary ring, it is notified that the fault has been isolated and repaired. Upon receipt of its own beacon, the station shuts off beaconing and returns to normal service.

2.2.2   A MAN Example

Anytown, USA, considers itself a happening place. Not wanting to miss out on being part of the "connected" age, the city fathers have launched a plan to provide computer services to all city departments. In order for the local citizenry to see their tax dollars at work, they decided as part of the overall project they would provide Internet access to the general populace. The greater Anytown metropolitan area spans several miles, with some buildings as far as five miles away from city hall.

The mayor called in the heads of Anytown's IS department, told them of his great vision, and asked how they would go about implementing his great plan. The IS department managers went away scratching their heads and wondered how they were to pull this one off. The general thought within the group was that, since the mayor's vision was pie in the sky, they would draw up a proposal that would be doable while still maintaining their control over the administration of Anytown's information services.

After several weeks of thrashing about among the IS department's staff, the plan was devised and drawn up. The big night arrived, and the chief of Anytown's IS department wore his Sunday best for the presentation of the devised plan to the mayor and the city counselors.

When the slide was placed on the overhead projector, the mayor and counselors saw what is shown in Figure 2-20.

The IS chief's explanation went as follows. The main departments within Anytown's government already had LAN technology deployed within the areas they were responsible for. General communication and the passing of data between departments was being done via e-mail. By implementing a citywide FDDI network, each department's LAN would be able to send data directly from station to station over the newly connected LAN networks. He went on to explain that servers located on each individual LAN would be centrally located within the IS department at city hall. Each department location would be connected directly to city hall via high-speed fiber optic cable, shown as dashed lines on the MAN network diagram.

He went on to further explain that each department currently was responsible for its own Internet access. With the proposed high-speed fiber optic network, this could be consolidated under the control of the city hall IS staff. A single high-speed network connection would give Internet access to not only all city departments but also the general public. It was stated that there would be

POP QUIZ

IEEE 802.5 limits the number of nodes on a ring to _____ nodes.

security precautions put in place to prevent unauthorized access to servers maintained by the city.

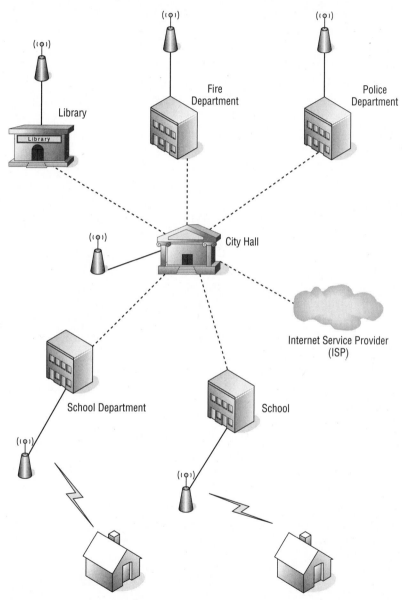

Figure 2-20 Anytown's MAN

The local telephone company would be contracted to run the dedicated fiber optic cable from city hall to the remote buildings over their current cableways and overhead lines. The general public would have access over wireless links to access points located throughout the city to ensure that all of Anytown's citizenry would have equal access to the Internet service provided by the city. For those without personal computers or unable to connect to the citywide wireless network, public access computers would be located at schools and libraries.

With his presentation completed, the IS chief asked if there were any questions. The mayor seemed pensive at first and then asked, "Can you explain why there is only wireless Internet for the public?" The IS chief said, "Yes, sir, I can." He went on to explain that the infrastructure cost to bring a wired Internet alternative to all of the city inhabitants would drive costs for the project beyond reach of the city's budget. Also, some of the expenses for the FDDI network could be recouped over time from consolidation of common services utilized by each city department. Providing a citywide wired public network would be cost-prohibitive. The IS chief went on to explain that there were already a few Internet providers servicing the Anytown greater metropolitan area, and those citizens desiring a wired Internet access were more likely to already be subscribed to their service or would do so in the future.

The mayor thanked the IS chief for his presentation. The counselors all voted their approval, and the mayor began drawing up his new campaign speech on how he was instrumental in getting Anytown connected.

This example of how a MAN might come about is largely tongue-in-cheek. However, it does demonstrate that the basic definition of a MAN is a network that covers a wide geographical area that can be either a city or include the greater metropolitan area of a city. The feasibility of MAN networks would not be possible without the availability of high-speed networks such as Metro Ethernet or FDDI optical networks.

The chief piece of information that the student should take from this section is the awareness that a high-speed data link is required when connecting LAN networks located some distance apart. When users and services on both ends of the link are contending for use of the link, the speed at which the link is able to pass traffic will be the determining factor of the performance of the interconnected LAN networks over that link. A safe rule of thumb is the more bandwidth the better. It gives better performance and allows for future growth and expansion of the connected LAN networks.

2.3   Wide Area Networks

As discussed in Chapter 1, the main use of a WAN is to provide a high-speed data network between two geographically distant networks. This chapter will discuss a few WAN telecommunications services most used in the makeup of a WAN network.

WAN networks are constructed from a wide range of service levels that can be obtained from the telephone companies. These can range from slow, low-grade analog circuits to high-speed digital signal services. The most widely used and available WAN standards are POTS, ISDN, and frame relay.

ACRONYM ALERT

QoS — Quality of service

2.3.1 Whose POTS?

POTS stands for plain old telephone service. It refers to the use of voice-grade telephone lines to form a point-to-point data connection. Because these voice lines can be found in many places around the world, it is possible to create a WAN connection between two LAN networks that are far apart. Figure 2-21 illustrates a dialup modem[16] connection between two offices.

This figure shows two LAN networks, one located in Boston and the other in Santa Fe. This is a manual WAN connection operation. Each modem can be set to auto-answer so that when another modem dials in, it will answer the call and allow the connection to be completed. This is a very rudimentary WAN network. It works and is still the only available WAN-type connection that can be made from some very rural areas of the country.

The speed of the WAN connection is determined by the type of modem and the signal quality of the telephone line it is connected to. Customary speeds that can be attained are between 28.8 and 57.6 Kbps. There are devices in the marketplace that automate the dialing process. These are considered to be dial-on-demand routers. These devices reside on the LAN and will automatically dial a preprogrammed number when they detect that the data received from the network is destined for a LAN at the other end of the dialup WAN connection.

With a clear line and the use of compression, some modem-based devices are capable of throughput of 115 Kbps. As other access technologies have rolled out, such as DSL and Internet access over cable and fiber to the home, modem use has fallen off. These newer technologies can provide higher speed access to the Internet, but they are unable to provide a point-to-point WAN connection, which some organizations require. Later in this section we will discuss how these technologies can be used to provide a virtual point-to-point WAN connection.

---

[16]Modem takes its name from modulate/demodulate. It is a device able to both modulate and demodulate a digital signal into an analog signal that can be sent across standard voice-grade telephone lines.

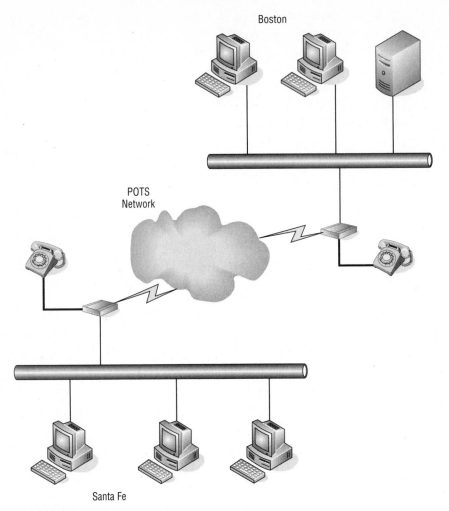

Figure 2-21 A POTS WAN connection

2.3.2   Integrated Services Digital Network

Integrated services digital network (ISDN) is a set of standards to provide voice, data, and video transmission over a digital telephone network. It is similar to a POTS line and modem in that it is able to use existing premises wiring to make a called connection to another ISDN subscriber. However, it can only call another ISDN subscriber, whereas a POTS setup can call any number

POP QUIZ

What is the major difference between Ethernet and IEEE 802.3?

that has an analog telephone connection to it. By integrating analog and digital signal transmissions using a digital network, ISDN is capable of delivering an improved data rate over typical modem connections. Unlike POTS, ISDN service is mostly concentrated in major metropolitan areas.

Taking advantage of LAN-to-LAN connectivity with ISDN providing the link can best be accomplished with the use of ISDN routers. They are typically configured for on-demand dialing. When there is data to be sent from one LAN to a remote LAN, the router will dial the remote ISDN router. When the remote ISDN router answers the call, data can be sent across the link. Since most ISDN service usage is typically billed by the number of calls and total minutes connected, ISDN routers may utilize an idle timer. This timer determines when there is no traffic being passed across the link. When the idle time interval has been reached, the call is terminated. These timers need to be set properly to eliminate excessive dialing and increased telephone charges. It is recommended that you understand how your local ISDN provider bills for this service. It could be by connected minutes, number of calls, or a combination of both. The only advantage that ISDN has over leased lines is that for low usage data connections it is cheaper than paying for a point-to-point leased line connection. ISDN is at a cost disadvantage in situations where the line is up for great periods of time. In those circumstances, it is best to look into using a leased line.

The two most commonly found ISDN services are:

▪ **Basic rate** — Provides two B channels of 64 Kbps and a single D channel of 16 Kbps.

▪ **Primary rate** — Provides 23 B channels of 64 Kbps and a single D channel of 64 Kbps for U.S.- and Japan-based subscribers. Subscribers in Europe and Australia are provided with 30 B channels.

An advantage that ISDN has over other WAN connection types when connecting to sites located in other countries is the service levels have been standardized by the International Telegraph and Telephone Consultative Committee (CCITT), so subscribers with ISDN service around the globe are able to interconnect to form a WAN network.

2.3.3 Point-to-Point WANs

In reality, all the WAN connections we spoke of in the two previous sections are also point-to-point WAN connections even though they require a manual or automated dial from a modem-based router. For the most part, when people refer to a point-to-point connection in the telecommunications arena, the first thought that comes to mind is directly connected point-to-point leased line connections. Figure 2-22 illustrates an organization with three major offices located in New York, Los Angeles, and Miami. The amount of data traffic between these locations warrants dedicated point-to-point WAN connections. The lines in use are considered to be of the T class variety.

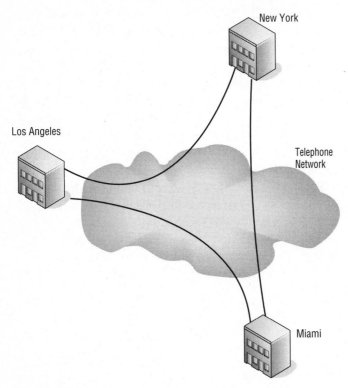

Figure 2-22 A point-to-point WAN network

Organizations do not only use these lines for data transmission. The lines can also be used for telephone, teleconferencing, and other forms of communications. The most common services used for these T class connections are T1, fractional T1, and T3. T1 can provide 1.544 Mbps of speed while T3 can deliver 44.736 Mbps.

> **RANDOM BONUS DEFINITION**
>
> preamble — A frame field used to allow a receiver to properly synchronize its clock before decoding incoming data.

A full T1 line provides 24 channels, each with 64 Kbps of bandwidth. When an organization leases a dedicated full T1 line, they are responsible for the T1 multiplexer equipment located at each endpoint. They can then dedicate the channels in any manner they choose. An example of this would be 6 channels dedicated to telephone service, 2 channels for teleconferencing, and the remaining 16 channels dedicated to moving data between locations. For organizations with demands for more bandwidth, the option would be to move up to T3 service. These services are point-to-point through the telephone network, but the service level is guaranteed by the telecommunications company. The lease cost is determined by the required bandwidth and distance between locations.

Organizations that require guaranteed throughput between organizations but do not need the speed of a full T1 can purchase a number of channels split out from an existing trunk circuit. This does provide a cost advantage, but it has its downside — the organization does not have control over where that circuit is routed. Cost is determined by the number of channels required and the distance between the locations. As the number of channels begins to increase, the cost advantage of fractional T1 is lost.

2.3.4 Frame Relay

So far, we have talked about WAN circuits being directly connected endpoint to endpoint, although traveling through a switched telephone network. Those connections were dedicated to creating a full-time fixed bandwidth connection. Frame relay[17] is designed for data traffic that tends to move in bursts. This is accomplished by using packet switching in a switched cloud provided by the telecommunications companies.

Because frame relay lends itself to burst-oriented traffic, it is not suitable for real-time applications such as telephones or teleconferencing. As information is moved in packets, the service is provided as a committed information rate (CIR). It is

> **POP QUIZ**
>
> What are the two most common ISDN services?

listed as a bandwidth number, but that does not necessarily mean you have continuous access at that bandwidth.

The level of service is measured for frame relay using a formula that includes committed burst size (CBS) over an interval of time. The basic formula is as follows:

```
Time = Committed Burst Size (CBS) / Committed Information Rate (CIR)
```

---

[17]Frame relay is based on X.25 packet-switching technology, which was developed to move data signals that were primarily analog, such as voice conversations. X.25 works in Layers 1, 2, and 3 of the OSI model. Frame relay only uses Layers 1 and 2, giving it greater speed that is about a factor of 20 over X.25. This is accomplished by dropping packets that are found to be in error and relying on the endpoints to process packet-drop detection and request retransmission of packets.

To illustrate this further, a customer has chosen a service that provides a CIR of 64 Kbps and a CBS of 256 Kbps. At first glance, it appears that traffic can burst up to 256 Kbps, but that is not the case. If CBS is divided by CIR, the resulting value is four seconds. This means the circuit needs to be capable of moving 256 Kbps in any four-second interval. This is far different from what most people think burst rate means. So the CIR and CBS need to be carefully looked at when subscribing to a frame relay service. If the network burst rate begins to exceed the CBS, network congestion will occur and data traffic will be affected. When selecting a frame relay service, it is best to have a good knowledge of the networks to be interconnected over frame relay. Figure 2-23 illustrates how a frame relay network may be implemented.

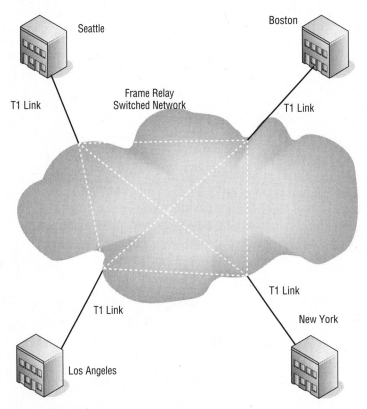

Figure 2-23 A frame relay network

This figure shows an organization with offices in Boston, New York, Seattle, and Los Angeles. Each has a T1 connection to the frame relay switched network. In this figure, each office is connected to every other office within the frame relay switched network using a private virtual circuit (PVC), which is illustrated by the dashed lines between each of the nodes connected to the switched network. This does have an advantage over pure point-to-point

WAN implementations, but it is best suited for burst type traffic and not traffic requiring a continuous guaranteed rate.

2.3.5 Using the Internet for Your WAN

The Internet is a network mesh that covers most of the globe. So it is possible to connect remote LAN networks over the Internet. However, the Internet is really a best-attempt-possible service. It is not guaranteed far as performance and is open to the public, which makes security a major concern. The chief advantage of using the Internet over other subscriber services is cost. Other than local Internet access fees, there are no other charges involved such as can be found when using a dedicated long line solution. Unlike dedicated point-to-point services, it is inconsequential how these devices connect to the Internet. The type of connection to the Internet is not a factor in the creation of the virtual point-to-point connection. Factors that can affect performance include the speed of the connection and its reliability where connectivity is concerned. Although electrons move at the speed of light, intelligent electrical signals are also subject to latency problems the greater the distance is between two endpoints of a network.

The solution of using virtual private networks (VPN)[18] is only viable in scenarios that require a remote office to connect to a central office. It is not intended to replace dedicated high-speed point-to-point network connections. Data integrity and security are maintained and ensured using encryption and encapsulation of the data packets that are transmitted over the Internet. Authentication is used to confirm that an endpoint device or user is fully authorized to send and receive data from the VPN connection. Figure 2-24 illustrates how VPN connections may be used as a substitute for a dedicated WAN network connection.

A remote office in Boston is connected to the corporate office in New York using the Internet to form its VPN tunnel. This is a peer-to-peer tunnel where each endpoint knows the other and is part of the security as the peers are known to each other. Authentication security is increased with the use of preshared keys (PSK), and other authentication methods such as certificates and tokens may also be added. Once the VPN

> **POP QUIZ**
>
> True or false: Virtual private networking is networking that does not require any hardware at all.

---

[18]For further information on how to use VPN tunnels, check out *Nortel Guide to VPN Routing for Security and VoIP*, by James Edwards, Richard Bramante, and Al Martin (Wiley Publishing, Inc., 2006).

tunnel is formed, traffic destined for either LAN is passed through the tunnel as if it were a dedicated link. The end-user workstations only need to be concerned with the address of the device on the other LAN. The VPN routers are the only devices that need to be aware of the endpoint address of its peer VPN routers. So for this purpose, the peer-to-peer tunnel functions as if a dedicated point-to-point link is in place between the two LAN networks.

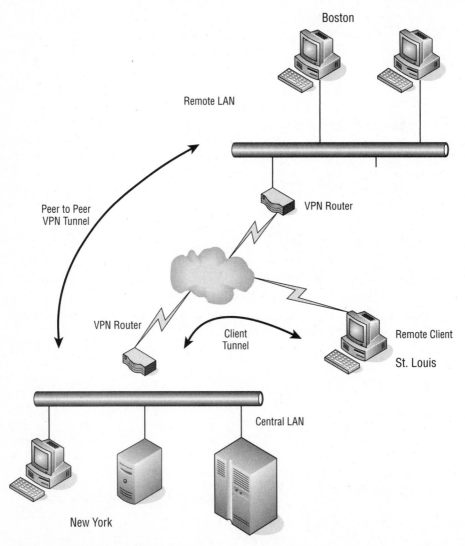

Figure 2-24 A VPN as a WAN

VPN routers are also able to accommodate end-user tunnel connections. For this example in Figure 2-24, a user in St. Louis is able to connect to the central office in New York to gain access to the network and use the services on that network. Since remote users can contact the central office from almost anywhere, their endpoint addresses would not be previously known. However, users are required to be authenticated in the same manner as a peer-to-peer tunnel, which may include multiple forms of authentication processes. Once authorized, a user is able to access the services they are authorized to use. Many installations require additional authentication to access internal servers. Access to the network does not necessarily mean access to all devices. VPN routers are capable of applying security policies on both peer-to-peer and end-user client tunnel connections.

The protocols used for VPN tunneling are Point-to-Point Tunneling Protocol (PPTP), Layer 2 Tunneling Protocol (L2TP), and IPSec (IP Security).

2.4   Chapter Exercises

1. The term *modem* is short for _____ .

2. A _____ is a network where network devices are located within close proximity to each other.

3. CSMA/CD is an acronym for _____ and is associated with a network using a _____ network topology.

4. Which network topology allows for orderly network access for the stations connected to that network?

5. What two standards define a CSMA/CD network?

   _____

   _____

6. Name three media types that can be used to connect devices located on a LAN?

   _____

   _____

   _____

7. The major characteristic of 10BASE-T cable is:

   _____

8. A personal computer (PC) requires a _____ to be connected to a local area network (LAN).

9. FDDI is an acronym for _____, which is often used to construct citywide networks called _____ .

10. POTS is an acronym for _____ .

11. A dialup service that connects to a digital network is _____ .

12. What technology can be used to create a point-to-point network connection over the Internet?

2.5   Pop Quiz Answers

1. What are the 2 sublayers of the Data Link layer?

    Logical Link Control (LLC) and Media Access Control (MAC)

2. MAC addresses are represented with hexadecimal numbers, separated by a colon or a *hyphen*.

3. What is the maximum length of a cable between a workstation and a hub?

    100 meters

4. IEEE 802.5 limits the number of nodes on a ring to *250* nodes.

5. What is the major difference between Ethernet and IEEE 802.3?

    Frame format

6. What are the two most common ISDN services?

    Primary rate and basic rate

7. True or false: Virtual private networking is networking that does not require any hardware at all.

    False

CHAPTER 3

Network Hardware and Transmission Media

Men have become the tools of their tools.
— **Henry David Thoreau**

Most Internet users don't understand the hardware and media used to give them the freedom they enjoy on the WWW. There are a lot of different types of nodes that serve specific purposes, as well as different transmission media types that connect network nodes together. The average Internet user is mainly concerned that they are able to send that important e-mail and have it get there, or that they are able to download the new episode of *Survivor*. For the average user, the Internet simply is there, and that is fine for them.

The same holds true in today's workplace. Almost every business uses a network in some form and in some capacity. Even if a worker does not interface with a computer, they are probably working off a printout that was generated electronically and often from a database that connects to ... you got it — a network. As long as they have what they need to perform the functions they need to do, they don't care what it takes to get the data passed from one point to the next.

The fact that you are reading this book means you have a reason for learning how data is transmitted. That means you need to know the information in this chapter intimately.[1] In later chapters, when we refer to a router, you need to recognize that name and know what it does.[2] This chapter provides an explanation for most of the network hardware that is in use in networks today. Network traffic and traffic patterns, as well as the cables (or lack of) used to pass the traffic, are also discussed. After reading this chapter, when

---

[1]This in no way implies that you don't need to know the rest of the information in this book.
[2]Besides that, if we kept saying "node" through this whole book, we would all get pretty bored and probably a little confused. Maybe that is why they got rid of the term "network" — people simple got bored and confused.

someone asks you to explain what *"10 half or 100 full"* means, you will be able to explain what they mean, define the difference between the two, and list a few pros and cons of each.

3.1 Stuff You Just Need to Know

There are a few things you need to have a basic understanding of before we jump into this chapter. First, you need to know what bits and bytes are. Even if you know what bits and bytes are, take a quick skim through this section. We also provide an overview of network addressing, encapsulation types, and other technologies we will

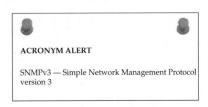

ACRONYM ALERT

SNMPv3 — Simple Network Management Protocol version 3

be discussing throughout this chapter. If everything seems familiar to you, please feel free to skip to Section 3.2. If further discussion is required for any of the information in this section, it will be introduced when appropriate.[3] If you decide to skip to Section 3.2 and later get to a point in this chapter where you are not sure about something, check back to see if it was explained in this section.

3.1.1 Bits, Bytes, and Binary

A binary number is a system of numbering used in data communications. Sometimes referred to as the *base-2 number system*, the binary numeral system represents numeric values by a 0 or a 1. The numeral system that we are all most familiar with is the base-10 number system, often referred to as the *decimal numeral system*. The decimal numeral system represents numeric values by a 0, 1, 2, 3, 4, 5, 6, 7, 8, or 9. Table 3-1 shows a comparison of the decimal and binary systems.

You can see that the decimal representation of the number ten is 10, whereas the binary representation is 1010. In the binary system, the numbers are counted just like they are in the decimal system. Numeric symbols count incrementally one at a time and when the highest symbol is reached (a 1 in binary, a 9 in decimal), the number resets to 0 and carries one to the left.

For example, if you count from zero through ten in decimal, it looks like this: 0, 1, 2, 3, 4, 5, 6, 7, 8, 9, 10. When the highest symbol (9) is reached, the number carries over a 1 symbol to the left and then resets the first symbol to 0. If you count zero through ten in binary, it looks like this: 0, 1, 10, 11, 100, 101, 110, 111, 1000, 1001, 1010. In binary, when the highest symbol (1) is reached, it carries a number to the left and resets, just like in decimal.

---

[3]In fact, this is information you are probably familiar with. We won't dwell too much on this section; that way we can have more room to talk about the beefier hardware that moves data in any given network.

Table 3-2 shows some examples of converting decimal numbers to binary.

Table 3-1 Decimal Numbers and Their Binary Number Equivalents

DECIMAL	BINARY
0	0000
1	0001
2	0010
3	0011
4	0100
5	0101
6	0110
7	0111
8	1000
9	1001
10	1010

Table 3-2 Decimal/Binary Conversions

DECIMAL	128	64	32	16	8	4	2	1
BINARY	0	0	0	0	0	0	1	1

Starting from the right of the table, you can reference the decimal symbols with the binary symbol. The decimal number 3 is equal to (2+1). The binary symbols that correspond with the decimal symbols being referenced are then set to 1 and all others are set to 0.

DECIMAL	128	64	32	16	8	4	2	1
BINARY	1	0	0	0	1	0	0	1

Starting from the right of the table, you can reference the decimal symbols with the binary symbol. The decimal number 137 is equal to (128+8+1). The binary symbols that correspond with the decimal symbols being referenced are then set to 1 and all others are set to 0.

The symbols that are used in the binary system are known as *binary digits*, or *bits*. The single digit in the binary number is 1 bit (which is a 1 or a 0). For example, binary number 0100 is 4 bits long. The bit is the basic unit of information in data communication. It is much like a toggle switch with only two settings, on (1) or off (0). In data communications, the bit is set based on electrical levels. A 1 is set if voltage is received, and a 0 is set if there is no voltage.

There are other terms you will come across that you need to understand when referencing a group of bits. Eight bits are equal to 1 byte, 1,024 bits are equal to 1 kilobit (Kbit or Kb), 125,000 bytes are equal to 1 megabit (Mb), and so on (see Table 3-3).

Table 3-3 Grouping of Bits

SI NAME	BINARY VALUE IN BITS	BINARY NAME (IEC)
Kilobit (Kbit)	2^{10}	Kibibit (Kbit)
Megabit (Mbit)	2^{20}	Mebibit (Mibit)
Gigabit (Gbit)	2^{30}	Gibibit (Bibit)
Terabit (Tbit)	2^{40}	Tebibit (Tibit)
Petabit (Pbit)	2^{50}	Pebibit (Pibit)
Exabit (Ebit)	2^{60}	Exbibit (Ebit)
Zettabit (Zbit)	2^{70}	Zebibit (Zibit)
YottaBit (Ybit)	2^{80}	Yobibit (Yibit)

We have already determined that 8 bits are referred to as 1 byte. To continue, 1,024 *bytes* is equal to 1 *kilobyte* (*KB* or *kB*), 1,048,576 *bytes* is equal to 1 *megabyte* (*MB* or *Mbyte*), and so on (see Table 3-4).

3.1.2 Non-human Resources

There is a vast array of resources in use in a network. Anything that is used within the network to provide data to the end users (e.g., applications, operating systems, servers, memory, storage devices, etc.) is considered a network resource. All the hardware and media discussed throughout this chapter are network resources. In this section, we refer to the processing and storage resources used by the nodes in a network.

Table 3-4 Grouping of Bytes

SI NAME	BINARY VALUE IN BYTES	BINARY NAME (IEC)
Kilobyte (KB, kB)	2^{10}	Kibibyte (KiB)
Mebibyte (Mbyte)	2^{20}	Mebibyte (MiB)
Gigabyte (Gbyte)	2^{30}	Gibibyte (GiB)
Terabyte (Tbyte)	2^{40}	Tebibyte (TiB)
Petabyte (Pbyte)	2^{50}	Pebibyte (PiB)
Exabyte (Ebyte)	2^{60}	Exbibyte (EiB)
Zettabyte (Zbyte)	2^{70}	Zebibyte (ZiB)
Yottabyte (Ybyte)	2^{80}	Yobibyte (YiB)

Network resources can be classified as volatile or nonvolatile.

```
vol·a·tile4
adjective
1: readily vaporizable at a relatively low temperature
2: flying or having the power to fly
3: a: lighthearted
b: easily aroused <volatile suspicions>
c: tending to erupt into violence
4: a: unable to hold the attention fixed because of an inherent lightness
 or fickleness of disposition
b: characterized by or subject to rapid or unexpected change
5: difficult to capture or hold permanently
non·vol·a·tile5
1: not volatile:
a: not vaporizing readily
b: of a computer memory : retaining data when power is shut off
```

[4]volatile. (2008). In *Merriam-Webster Online Dictionary*. Retrieved May 14, 2008, from www.merriam-webster.com/dictionary/volatile

[5]nonvolatile. (2008). In *Merriam-Webster Online Dictionary*. Retrieved May 14, 2008, from www.merriam-webster.com/dictionary/nonvolatile

3.1.2.1   Volatile Memory

Data storage is performed by a storage device or memory that is set aside for the storage of data for a nonpermanent period of time. In other words, a device receives and reviews data, processes it, and then moves on to the next data process. It uses

> **POP QUIZ**
>
> The decimal number 211 is equal to what binary number?

volatile memory or storage in order to perform this action. Once the data is no longer needed, it can be removed and new data can take its place. When power is removed, volatile memory does not retain its data.

3.1.2.1.1   Random Access Memory

Random access memory (RAM)[6] is the most well known form of memory in the data environments. It is called random access memory because it is memory that is available for data storage and access, regardless of the order in which it is stored. Information stored in RAM is accessible until

> **RANDOM BONUS DEFINITION**
>
> data storage density — The quantity of data that can be stored within a data storage medium.

it is cleared out or the device it is being used on is shut down.

Computers store OS and system data in RAM when the computer boots up. The remaining space that is not used by the system software is utilized as programs are accessed and used on the computer. Data access is quicker with data that is stored in RAM than any of the other storage devices a computer may use.

3.1.2.1.2   Dynamic Random Access Memory

Dynamic random access memory (DRAM) is the type of RAM that is used as the main memory by most PCs. DRAM has to have a little jolt of electricity every couple of milliseconds in order to operate. DRAM uses a transistor and a capacitor for each storage cell it contains. Each received bit is stored in a cell. As the capacitor loses its charge, an electronic charge refreshes the capacitor.

---

[6]A lot of companies are working on a nonvolatile form of RAM. This will speed up the boot-up and shutdown times of a device, and will save energy as well. As more and more companies are releasing "green"-friendly devices, this technology may debut soon (maybe even before this book is released).

DRAM is considered high density because it is able to store more data than other memory types. This is because each storage cell only requires one capacitor and transistor. Examples of DRAM modules include:

- Dual inline memory module (DIMM) — Designed for use in personal computers, miscellaneous workstations, and servers.

- Single inline memory module (SIMM) — Used in personal computers prior to the late 1990s.

- Single inline pin package (SIPP) — Used in older computers that had the Intel 80286 processor.

- Synchronous dynamic random access memory (SDRAM) — DRAM with a serial interface, which allows the memory to accept new instructions while it is still processing previous instructions. Used in computers, workstations, and servers.

3.1.2.1.3 Static Random Access Memory

Static random access memory (SRAM) uses electronic circuitry to store bits in memory. SRAM does not need to be charged, as there are no capacitors being used to store the bits. SRAM cells maintain one of two states, either a 0 or a 1. SRAM is most commonly used as the cache memory for most microprocessors, storing up to several MBs of data. Device system registers will also often use SRAM as the mode of memory.

> **POP QUIZ**
>
> The binary number 01011100 is equal to what decimal number?

3.1.2.2 Nonvolatile Memory

Memory that can retain data even when it is not receiving power is known as *nonvolatile memory*. Nonvolatile memory is used as a secondary storage device. This is where data that needs to be stored for long periods of time is located, such as configuration files, OS software, and systems software. For the most part, nonvolatile memory is slower in moving data than volatile memory. This is the main reason that nonvolatile memory is used for storage.

3.1.2.2.1 Magnetic Storage Media

You might use magnetic storage a lot more than you are aware of. Not only are computer hard disk drives and backup tape drives (and a few other storage devices) magnetized data storage devices, magnetic storage is used in the audio and video world as well. As a matter of fact, the strip on the back of your debit and credit cards is magnetic storage for identification data that communicates with the card reader used when you purchase something.[7]

Data stored on electronic media can be removed and the space that it was occupying can be reused for other data. Data is written onto the medium with electrical impulses that set a bit to either positive or negative polarity. When data is accessed, the polarity of the bit is read, and the setting of the bit (1 or 0) is determined.

3.1.2.2.2 Read-Only Memory

Memory used to store information that is not intended to be modified is known as read-only memory (ROM). ROM is often referred to as *firmware*, which is the software required for hardware-specific operations. ROM chips can retain this data even without electricity applied to the device. There are arrays of different ROM chip types; among these are:

- **Read-only memory (ROM)** — Memory that is configured and set by the manufacturer. It contains device systems software necessary for the proper operation of the device.

- **Programmable read-only memory (PROM)** — A memory chip that can be written to only once. This will allow someone other than the manufacturer to write data onto the PROM. Just like ROM, the data is there forever. A device known as a PROM programmer (PROM burner) is used to write the data onto the chip.

- **Erasable programmable read-only memory (EPROM)** — A memory chip that can store data that may need to be overwritten at some point. The data on the EPROM is erased by UV light and can then be reprogrammed with a PROM burner.

ACRONYM ALERT

PCMCIA — Personal Computer Memory Card International Association

- **Electrically erasable programmable read-only memory (EEPROM)**[8] — A memory chip that can store data that may need to be overwritten at some point. The data on the EEPROM is erased by an electrical charge and can then be reprogrammed with a PROM burner.

---

[7]You can now "pay at the pump," thanks to magnetic storage.
[8]Say that five times real fast!

3.1.2.2.3 Flash Memory

Flash memory is a form of EEPROM that is used by a device for specific storage purposes. Digital cameras, video gaming systems, laptops, many network devices, and PCs all use flash memory. Examples of flash memory are:

- Memory cards for cell phones
- Memory cards for digital cameras
- Memory cards for video game systems
- PCMCIA[9] type 1 memory cards (3.3 mm thick)
- PCMCIA type 2 memory cards (5.0 mm thick)
- PCMCIA type 3 memory cards (10.5 mm thick)
- Personal computer system BIOS chip

PC BIOS memory chips are the most commonly used fixed type of flash memory. The other types of flash memory are removable and can hold a lot of data. When feasible, flash memory is preferred over hard disk drive memory because it is

> **POP QUIZ**
>
> What is the binary name for the binary value of 2^{50}?

faster, smaller, lighter, and does not have any moving parts. On the downside, flash memory is more expensive when comparing the cost of an equal amount of storage space on a hard drive.

3.1.3 Encapsulation

Encapsulation is the act of including data from an upper-layer protocol within a structure in order to transmit the data. As we discussed in Chapter 1, most applications use either TCP or UDP. If data is transmitted from the Application layer, the data that needs to be transmitted is passed to the Transport layer. Let's say that TCP is the protocol that is used. TCP adds a TCP header to the datagram and then the datagram is passed to the Network layer where it is encapsulated into an IP packet. The packet is then passed to the Data Link layer where it is encapsulated into a frame (Ethernet, Token ring, etc.) and then transmitted over the physical media to a destination. Figure 3-1 shows an example of this.

---

[9]Many people still refer to this type of memory card as a *PCMCIA card*. This is actually no longer the appropriate term. PCMCIA memory cards are now simply called PC cards.

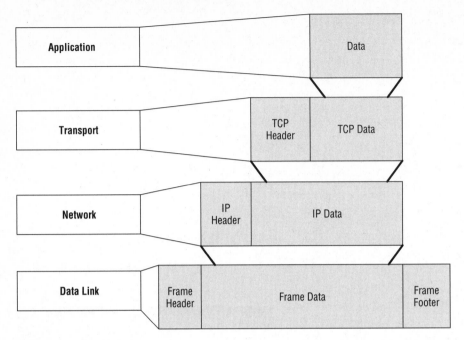

Figure 3-1 Encapsulation

Information passed from layer to layer is called service data units (SDUs) or protocol data units (PDUs). The difference between an SDU and a PDU is that the PDU specifies the data that is to be transmitted to the peer layer at the receiving end. The SDU can be considered the PDU payload. Recall from the paragraph above, data is transmitted from Layer 7 to Layer 4, from Layer 4 to Layer 3, and so on. The data that is put together to be passed from Layer 7 to Layer 4 is the PDU. The SDU is what it becomes when it is encapsulated into the PDU of the lower layer. Figure 3-2 shows an example of what PDU is used at each layer in the OSI reference model.

Each layer within the OSI reference model creates a PDU for any data that needs to be transmitted to the next lower level. In addition to the data in the PDU, each layer assigns a header to the PDU as well. Refer now to Figure 3-3. Data is being transmitted from Layer 7 to Layer 1, across a medium to the Physical layer on the opposite end, and then up each layer until it reaches Layer 7. Notice that each layer appears to communicate directly to the layer on the opposite end. When each layer passes data to the layer below it, the data (including the higher layer header) becomes an SDU. When the layer attaches its header to the SDU, it becomes the PDU that is transmitted to the next lower layer.

Layer	PDU
Application	Data
Presentation	Data
Session	Data
Transport	Segment
Network	Packet
Data Link	Frame
Physical	Bit

Figure 3-2 PDUs used at each layer in the OSI reference model

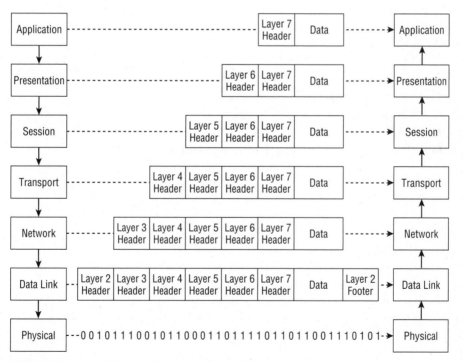

Figure 3-3 Layer-by-layer encapsulation

3.1.4   Data Communication Equipment and Data Terminal Equipment

Data communication predominately takes place between nodes that are known as either data communication equipment (DCE)[10] or data terminal equipment (DTE). In order for communication to take place between nodes, one end of the connection must be a DCE and the other a DTE. If you have to connect a DCE to a DCE or a

> **RANDOM BONUS DEFINITION**
>
> straight-through cable — A twisted pair cable that is wired for normal DTE to DCE communications.
> crossover cable — A twisted pair cable that is reverse-wired for DCE-to-DCE or DTE-to-DTE communications.

DTE to a DTE, a null modem[11] or a crossover cable[12] must be used. The plug connector of a hub (see Section 3.3.4) or a modem would be an example of a DCE, whereas the plug connector on an NIC card (see Section 3.3.2.2) would be an example of a DTE.

In data communications, synchronization between nodes is known as clocking. The DCE is responsible for providing the clock signal while the DTE is responsible for synchronizing its clock based on the signal received. The DCE uses what is called *internal clocking*, setting the clocking without any outside influence. The DTE uses *external clocking*, which requires a signal in order to set and synchronize its clocking.

3.1.5   All Your Base Are Belong to Us[13]

We don't want to jump into Ethernet signaling at this point (Chapter 6, "Ethernet Concepts," will cover this in depth). We do want to introduce some terms that you will come across in this chapter (10BASE-T, 100BASE-TX, etc.), so you will understand what they mean.

Baseband simply refers to the way data is transported on the wire. A baseband signal is data that transported as digital data on an unmultiplexed channel over the transmission medium. The BASE in the term 10BASE-T stands for broadband. The number preceding BASE is the speed (for instance, 10BASE means that the transmission medium can support Ethernet transmission at a

---

[10]DCEs are also often called *data carrier equipment*.

[11]Serial cables that crosslink the transmit and receive wires. Also can be an adapter that is used to cross the signals.

[12]Normally a crossover cable is an Ethernet cable that is reverse-wired on each end. This will put all output signals on one end of the cable to be the input signals on the other, and vice versa. This is appropriate for other technologies, but is most common in Ethernet.

[13]If you are an Internet gamer, you are probably familiar with this slogan. This broken English translation appeared in a European release of the Japanese video game *Zero Wing*.

speed of 10 Mbps over baseband). All symbols following BASE identify either a distance of transmission or a medium type (5 for 500 meters, T for twisted pair, F for fiber optic).

3.1.6   Computer Buses[14]

Computers can be modified and any hardware that is added to the computer is known as a *peripheral*. New peripherals come with software, known as a *driver*, that is loaded on your PC and provides the instructions the computer will use to learn what it needs to communicate and coexist with the

ACRONYM ALERT

PCI — Peripheral component interconnect

peripheral. Within the computer, there is a system that can logically connect multiple peripherals within the same set of wires. This system is known as the *computer bus*. Computer buses are also used to connect computer internal components (more on this in a minute[15]).

A computer bus can operate as both a *parallel* bus and a *serial* bus. What's the difference? Glad you asked. Parallel buses transmit several bits of data at the same time, in parallel on the bus, whereas serial buses transmit data one bit at a time, sequentially to the destination. The main types of computer buses are an *internal* bus and an *external* bus. The internal bus is the bus that is contained within the computer and connects internal components to the shared bus; an external bus is a bus that connects peripherals to the motherboard.

3.1.7   IP Addressing

Nodes in a TCP/IP network are assigned a numeric value, known as an *IP address*. We will be discussing IP addressing throughout this book, so this is a short overview. The IP address usually is unique and provides a network identify for the node. Although there are new versions of IP that are growing in popularity, currently[16] IP version four (IPv4) is still what the majority of networks are using.

An IPv4 address is a 32-bit number that is divided into four fields, called *octets*, separated by dots. Each octet represents 8 bits of the total 32-bit number. This is known as *dotted decimal notation*. An example of dotted decimal

---

[14]Not to be confused with a commuter bus.

[15]Disclaimer: This actually may take more or less than a minute. It depends on how fast you can read and how many breaks you take.

[16]IPv4 is popular at the time of this writing, although this may change in the near future, as a lot of new vendor implementations are using IPv6.

notation would be the IP address 192.168.1.1.[17] The meaning of the octet that is represented by each number depends upon what *network class* the IP address belongs to. The entire IP address is separated into two parts: the network part and the host part. Figure 3-4 shows an example of the difference in network classes.

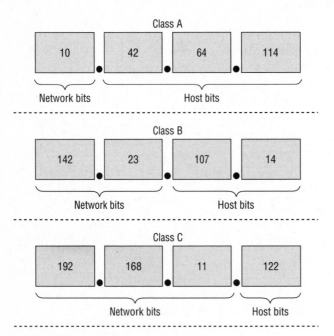

Figure 3-4 IP address network classes

The four[18] network classes are as follows:

- **Class A** — Class A addresses are identified by a number from 1 to 126 in the first octet. In Class A addresses, the first octet identifies the network and the remaining three octets identify the host. These addresses are normally assigned to larger networks.

- **Class B** — Class B addresses are identified by a number from 128 to 191 in the first octet. In Class B addresses, the first two octets identify the network and the last two identify the host. These addresses are normally assigned to medium-sized networks.

- **Class C** — Class C addresses are identified by a number from 192 to 223 in the first octet. In Class C addresses, the first three octets

---

[17]IP addresses are identified in decimal (dotted decimal notation, to be specific). If converted to binary, this number is 11000000.10101000.00000001.00000001 (note that there are 8 bits in each field).

[18]There is also a Class E network class, but it is not an approved standard and is experimental.

identify the network while the last octet identifies the host. These addresses are normally assigned to small to medium-sized networks

▪ **Class D** — Class D addresses are a little different than the other classes. Class D addresses are used for multicasting. These addresses always begin with the first 4 bits being 1110 and the remaining 28 bits identifying the network in which the multicast message is to be sent.

DID YOU JUST NOTICE THAT?

If you were paying attention during the previous discussion of IP network classes, you may have noticed that the number 127 is skipped in the transition from Class A (first octet containing 1–126) to Class B (first octet containing 128–191). This is because the number 127 in the first octet represents a special type of IP address called a loopback address. Used mainly for troubleshooting, the loopback IP simply loops datagrams back to the sender.
Some other special IP addresses include:

◆ **0.0.0.0 — Default network (where packets go when the router doesn't know where a host is)**

◆ **1.1.1.1 — Broadcast to all on a specified network**

3.2   Transmission Media

Transmission media refers to the modes and materials by which the data is transferred in a network. Network cables, light waves, and so on are all considered transmission media. (If you are referring to more than

> **POP QUIZ**
>
> Define *RAM*.

one medium, it is called media.[19]) Transmission media provide a way for data to be passed from one endpoint to another. The medium does not guarantee delivery nor is it concerned with what information is contained in the datagram; it simply provides the path for the data.

In the United States, there are two forms of transmission media in data communications. The first type, *bounded* or *guided*, is a communication line (or any other type of solid medium) that transports waves from one endpoint to another. The second type, *unguided* or *wireless*, is where data is passed wirelessly from one access point (antenna) to another.

---

[19] Another one of those terms that is often misused but always understood.

3.2.1 Network Cabling

Wireless communication as a transmission medium is becoming more and more popular, but network cabling is still the backbone of any network. There are many different types of cabling, each serving a specific purpose to meet the needs of the network. Often you will find different types of cabling running side by side between nodes in the network. It's important to understand the cabling types that are in use on any network you configure and how to maintain them. The major cable types are:

- Twisted pair
- Coaxial
- Fiber optic

The type of cabling that is used depends on the network. Data traffic requirements, the size of the network, the topology of the network, the protocols in use, the nodes in place, cost considerations, and many other things need to be taken into account when designing and/or maintaining a network. In this section, we will discuss the more popular cable types and how they work.

TIPS FOR INSTALLING AND REPLACING CABLES

Whenever you need to replace cables, or are tasked with designing and implementing a cable run, there are a few hints you should be aware of that will save you headaches in the future.

1. Use cable ties to keep cables grouped together. Do not use tape, staples, glue, rubber bands, etc. The cable ties are easy to work with and easy to remove when you need to.

2. Make sure to label the cables on each end of the link. It can be very time consuming to try to track down a problem if the cables are not labeled. Tape, glue, and even rubber bands work well for this task. Staples or tacks do not.

3. Keep the cable off the floor. If you do not have a choice, then make sure you cover the cable with a cable protector.

4. Stay away from anything that may cause electrical interference.

5. Cut your cables too long on purpose — leave some excess (on both ends) to work with in the future.

6. Make a detailed drawing of the cables that are installed in the building. The drawing needs to be easy to understand when tracking cable routes and endpoint connections.

(continued)

TIPS FOR INSTALLING AND REPLACING CABLES *(continued)*

7. **Implement a "hands-off" policy for end users. Make sure you know who is touching the cables and interfaces attaching end-user nodes to the network. This is especially important in coaxial runs. One glitch and all the users go down.**

3.2.1.1   Twisted Pair Cable

Twisted pair cabling consists of two or more pairs of conductors that are twisted together within the cable. The conductors are wrapped in plastic and then all of the pairs are wrapped within the cable, making them less susceptible to outside electrical interference. Twisted pair cables are used primarily in areas with short to medium distances between nodes. Twisted pair is less expensive than coaxial cable or fiber cable, and is often used as a consideration in network design.

There are four pairs of twisted wires in a network Ethernet cable. These are color coded in blue, brown, green, and orange. Each twisted pair has one solid and one striped wire. Here is a list of the wires that are within a normal twisted pair cable:

- Blue
- Blue/white
- Brown
- Brown/white
- Green
- Green/white
- Orange
- Orange/white

> **POP QUIZ**
>
> Define *encapsulation*.

There are two main types of twisted pair cabling in use in LANs. Unshielded twisted pair (UTP) is the most popular copper cable type. Shielded twisted pair (STP) is the other type. Ethernet and Token Ring both use twisted pair cabling.

- **Unshielded twisted pair** — UTP cabling is the type of copper cabling that is used the most in networks today. UTP cables consist of two or more pairs of conductors that are grouped within an outer sleeve. Figure 3-5 shows an example of a UTP cable.

Figure 3-5 UTP cable

UTP cable is often referred to as *Ethernet cable*, because Ethernet is the predominate technology that uses UTP cable. UTP cabling is cheap, but does not offer protection from electrical interference. Additionally, bandwidth is limited with UTP in comparison with some of the other cable types.

■ **Shielded twisted pair** — STP cabling is a type of copper cabling that is used in networks where fast data rates are required. STP cables consist of two or more pairs of conductors that are grouped together and then an additional metal shield wraps around the twisted pairs, forming an additional barrier to help protect the cabling. Finally, all of the cables are grouped together and a final outer sleeve is placed over the wiring. Figure 3-6 shows an example of an STP cable.

Figure 3-6 STP cable

STP cables are also referred to as Ethernet cables. STP cables provide additional protection to the internal copper, thus data rates are increased and more reliable. The conductors that are grouped together can be shielded as individual pairs (in other words, each pair will have its own shield), or all pairs can be shielded as a group.

The ANSI/TIA/EIA-568-B standard, *Commercial Building Telecommunications Standard*, is the standard that defines the requirements for installing and maintaining cabling systems, component, and data transmissions in commercial buildings. In the standard, the categories (Cat) of twisted pair cabling are outlined. As of the release of the ANSI/TIA/EIA-568-B standard, the only categories that are recognized by the standards are Cat 5e and above.[20] Table 3-5 lists all the categories, but you need only to know they exist. You should focus on Cat 5e and above, as this is the direction the data world is heading.

Table 3-5 ANSI/TIA/EIA-568-B Standard Categories

CATEGORY	ANSI/TIA/EIA-568-B STATUS	USED FOR	PERFORMANCE
Cat 1	Unrecognized	ISDN, ISDN basic rate interface (BRI), doorbell wiring, POTS voice communication	Less than or equal to 1 Mbps
Cat 2	Unrecognized	Token Ring	4 Mbps
Cat 3	Unrecognized	10BASE-T Ethernet	16 MHz
Cat 4	Unrecognized	Token Ring	20 Mbps
Cat 5	Unrecognized	100BASE-T Ethernet	Less than or equal to 100 MHz
Cat 5e	Recognized	100BASE-T and 1000BASE-T Ethernet	Less than or equal to 100 MHz
Cat 6	Recognized	Backward compatible to Cat 3, Cat 5, and Cat 5e cabling; 10BASE-T, 100BASE-TX, and 1000BASE-T Ethernet	Less than or equal to 250 MHz
Cat 6a	Recognized	10GBASE-T Ethernet	Less than or equal to 500 MHz
Cat 6e	Recognized	10GBASE-T Ethernet	Less than or equal to 625 MHz

Twisted pair cables can be hard-wired to endpoints or attached to a registered jack (RJ) connector. The most common connector is often referred to as an *RJ45 connector*. The RJ45 connector resembles the connector for land-based telephones, only larger. If you have plugged your PC into a network, then you plugged in an RJ45 (see Figure 3-7).

---

[20]This does not mean that other categories are no longer in use. They probably are and will be in networks that never change (which are rare). It simply means there are no plans to advance the category (and you can bet there are not a lot of vendors out there that will continue to build based on Cat 5 and below technology).

Figure 3-7 An 8P8C plug (RJ45)

STUFF YOU JUST HAVE TO KNOW

Let's take a moment to talk a little about registered jacks. A registered jack (the *RJ* in *RJ45*) is simply a standardized network interface. The pattern of the wiring, as well as the construction of the jack itself, is based on the standard for which the jack was developed. Although we have written mostly about the RJ45 in this chapter, this does not imply that the RJ45 is the only type of interface you will come across. So we have provided the following handy-dandy reference list for your information.

◆ RJ11 — Used for telephone wires. If you pick up a phone (land line, of course) and look at the wire that plugs into the phone, you are most likely looking at an RJ11 connector.

◆ RJ14 — Same as above, but for two lines instead of one.

◆ RJ25 — For three lines.

◆ RJ61 — For four lines.

◆ RJ48 — For T1 and ISDN lines.

◆ RJ49 — For ISDN BRI lines.

◆ RJ61 — For twisted pair cables.

The term *RJ45* refers to what is normally attached to any 8 Position 8 Contact (8P8C) jacks and plugs, but the true RJ45 standard defines the mechanics of the interface as well as a wiring scheme that does not match the ANSI/TIA/EIA-568-B standard. There are two parts to the 8P8C: the plug and the jack. The plug is what was referred to in

ACRONYM ALERT

HDLC — High-Level Data Link Control

Figure 3-7 and is often called the *male connector* or *male plug*. The *jack* is the interface that the plug goes into and is called the *female connector* or *female jack*.

There are eight pins, numbered 1 through 8 in an RJ45 connector. Sometimes these are labeled on the plug. If they are not labeled, you can identify the pin numbers by holding the connector in your hand with connector pins facing upward and outward. The pin that is closest to you will be pin number 1 and then they are sequentially numbered through pin number 8. (See Figure 3-8.)

Pin 1-

Pin 8-

Figure 3-8 RJ45 pin numbering

ANSI/TIA/EIA-568-B defines the pin to twisted pair definitions for pin assignments when connecting the twisted pair to the 8P8C connector. The definition of the pin/pair assignment[21] is named T568A and T568B.[22] The standard to use depends on the 8-pin cabling system that is in use. T568A and T568B define the order in which twisted pairs should be attached to the 8P8C adapter. Table 3-6 shows an example of the cable pin-outs for a T568A straight-through cable.

The difference between the T568B pin-out definitions and the T568A pin-out definitions is that the green pair and the orange pair are reversed. Table 3-7 shows the pin-outs for T568B.

3.2.1.2 *Coaxial Cable*

Coaxial cabling is not as popular as twisted pair cabling, but there still are some networks that use it.[23] Figure 3-9 shows an example of a coaxial cable. Within the cable, there is either a single inner conductor or group of conductors that are twisted together to form one. The conductor is then wrapped in a plastic sleeve, which is wrapped in a metallic conducting shield. Finally, these are all wrapped in an insulating sleeve. There may be a slight variation between cable vendors, but the functions of the coaxial cable remain the same.

[21] The pin/pair assignment is often referred to as the *cable pin-outs*.
[22] T568B is not to be confused with the standard ANSI/TIA/EIA-568-B.
[23] Most of these were networks that were built in the late 1980s and early 1990s. Most new deployments use twisted pair.

Table 3-6 T568A Straight-Through Pin-Outs

8P8C PIN NUMBER	WIRE COLOR	10BASE-T 100BASE-T SIGNALING	1000BASE-T SIGNALING
1	Green/white	Transmit+	Bidirectional data A+ (BI_DA+)
2	Green	Transmit−	Bidirectional data A− (BI_DA−)
3	Orange/white	Receive+	Bidirectional data B+ (BI_DB+)
4	Blue	Not used	Bidirectional data C+ (BI_DC+)
5	Blue/white	Not used	Bidirectional data C− (BI_DC−)
6	Orange	Receive−	Bidirectional data B− (BI_DB−)
7	Brown/white	Not used	Bidirectional data D+ (BI_DD+)
8	Brown	Not used	Bidirectional data D− (BI_DD−)

Table 3-7 T568B Straight-Through Pin-Outs

8P8C PIN NUMBER	WIRE COLOR	10BASE-T 10BASE-T SIGNALING	100BASE-T SIGNALING
1	Orange/white	Transmit+	(BI_DA+)
2	Orange	Transmit−	(BI_DA−)
3	Green/white	Receive+	(BI_DB+)
4	Blue	Not used	(BI_DC+)
5	Blue/white	Not used	(BI_DC−)
6	Green	Receive−	(BI_DB−)
7	Brown/white	Not used	(BI_DD+)
8	Brown	Not used	(BI_DD−)

Figure 3-9 An example of coaxial cable

The inner conductor and the conducting shield work on the same *axis* and work together to pass data — hence the name *co* (cooperative) and *axial* (running on the same axis). Data is transmitted in the space between the inner conductor and the outer conducting shield. Coaxial cables are best suited for high-frequency or broadband signaling.

The connectors that are used to connect coaxial cable runs are known as *bayonet Neill-Concelman (BNC) connectors*. There are two main types of coaxial cabling, *thin coaxial* and *thick coaxial*, often referred to as *thinnet* and *thicknet*. When used for Ethernet, they are called *thin Ethernet* (10BASE2) and *thick Ethernet* (10BASE5).

Thin coaxial cabling, known as *RG-58*, is used for connections that use a low power signal. In Ethernet, the maximum distance that data can be transmitted is 185 meters. A node must be placed within that distance, or data corruption and deletion may occur. Thick coaxial cabling, known as *RG-8*, is used for connections that require a higher power signal. The maximum travel distance between nodes using thick coaxial cables is 500 meters.

3.2.1.3 Fiber Optic Cable

When used in data networking, fiber optic cables are groups of thin strands of glass or transparent plastic that is able to carry data for long distances. The fibers are grouped together to form the *core* of the cable. The core is wrapped in a *cladding*, which is denser glass material that reflects light back to the core. Surrounding the cladding is a buffer. Finally, there is an outer wrap called a *jacket* that helps protect the core from damage. Fiber optic cable has helped make a lot of the advances in networking over the last few years. The use of fiber cables provides for an increase in the distance data can travel between nodes, as well as speeds that are, well, as fast as light.[24] Optical signaling is not hampered by electronic interference, so data loss is not seen as often as with twisted pair or coaxial.

Fiber optic cabling works by sending reflections of light from one endpoint to another. The light travels between the core and the cladding and back again. The cladding reflects the light back to the core, much like a mirror does if you shine a light into it. This is known as *total internal reflection* (see Figure 3-10).

---

[24]Light signals can be transmitted at speeds of up to 40 Gbps.

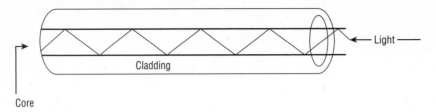

Figure 3-10 Total internal reflection in a fiber optic cable

Fiber optic cables are advantageous as a transmission medium for fast data exchange over long distances. Fiber optic cabling can also save space in a LAN as it requires less space than copper cables. There are two main types, or modes, of fiber optic cabling used for data communications: *single-mode fiber* (SMF) and *multi-mode fiber* (MMF).

▪ **Single-mode fiber optical cabling** — SMF cables are thinner than MMF cables. This is because SMF cables are designed to carry a single beam of light. Because there are not multiple beams involved, the SMF cable is more reliable and supports a much higher bandwidth and longer distances than MMF cables. The bulk cost of SMF cabling is much less expensive than MMF cabling. Figure 3-11 shows an example of an SMF cable.

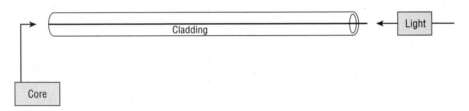

Figure 3-11 Single-mode signaling

▪ **Multi-mode fiber optical cabling** — MMF cabling is made for shorter distances. Unlike SMF, there are multiple beams of light, so the distance and speed are less. Granted, supporting data rates of up to 10 Gbps for distances as far as 300 meters is nothing to sneeze at. Because of the additional modes, MMF cabling is able to carry much more data at any given time. Figure 3-12 shows an example of MMF cabling.

POP QUIZ

What is IEEE Standard 802.11?

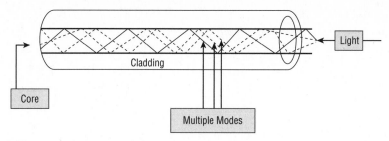

Figure 3-12 Multi-mode signaling

3.2.2 Wireless Communication

Wireless communication has really grown in the past few years. Many businesses, universities, and even some cities have now implemented wireless access for anyone to use. There is nothing like being able to sit in a bookstore or a coffee shop and being able to connect to the Internet and all that it offers. Signals in wireless communication are sent via antennas, microwave stations, satellite, or infrared light.

Wireless communication enables data to be transferred through the air via a communication signal. Communication is normally handled by infrared light or high-frequency radio waves. Infrared communication normally takes place between nodes. The wireless signal between a PDA and a PC is an example of nodes that use an infrared signal. Data communications, radio, and cellular phones are all examples of nodes that use radio waves for data communication. Section 3.3.3.9.3 covers the hardware that makes wireless communication as a transmission medium a reality.

3.3 Network Hardware

A lot of different types of network hardware work together[25] to issue, pass, respond, receive, and otherwise transmit data in a network. Network hardware performs the operations necessary to receive and forward data that it is responsible for. Not all network hardware is created equal. Keep in mind, however, the hardware is built to support the available standards that the particular node should be able to support. Most of the hardware in networks is nothing more than a big paperweight without the software loaded on the device to teach it what to do and sometimes how to do it. To take this a bit further, the hardware and software are useless without someone to configure

---

[25]There are also times when the network hardware does not work well together, but we will save that discussion until Chapter 16, "Troubleshooting."

it. Until computers are able to think for themselves, it is always going to take human intervention to get a node to operate correctly in a LAN.

The following sections list network hardware common in networks today. Not all the devices listed are in place in every network. They are available to anyone who needs the device in order to support implemented or planned standards within a network.

3.3.1   End-User Interface Hardware Types

A network exists to serve the needs of the end users. The network administrator (head honcho, big daddy, C-3PO, or whatever else the person is called) plans very carefully to ensure that the right equipment is purchased and brought into the network. The hardware has to be able to support data traffic needs as well as the necessary standards and protocols. Look at it this way: it wouldn't do you any good to buy a cell phone from one vendor and then order the cell phone plan from another vendor. Most likely, the cell phone would never work.[26]

The end users interface with some specific hardware devices that they need to do their job. In Figure 3-13, you can see an example of some of the many hardware devices that an end user may actually interface with. At the very least, an Internet user will have a PC or laptop and an adapter of some sort that will allow the PC to connect to a network. In many office environments, multiple users will share the services of a printer, fax machine, or copy machine. The network is what allows them to do this. For the purposes of this chapter, we will not discuss the end-user direct access hardware. It would be information that you are most likely familiar with.

3.3.2   Connecting End Users

Although there are many different user interface types out there, we are going to focus on the PC or laptop as the user interface type for the remainder of this book. If we enter into discussions of other user network interfaces, we will define these as they come up.

> **RANDOM BONUS DEFINITION**
>
> wireless fidelity (Wi-Fi) — A term that describes certain types of 802.11 WLANs.

---

[26]Jim heard on the news the other day that a cell phone vendor out there claims its service will work with any other vendor's plan. Looks like maybe we can all get along.

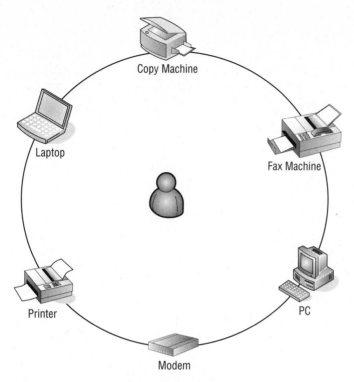

Figure 3-13 End-user hardware types

The user interface is the device, software application, software program, or other tool the user uses to complete a network transmission. The network interface is the physical interface that allows the network node to connect to the network.

It's important to note the distinction between a network interface and a user interface. Take a look at Figure 3-14. Really, you couldn't tell a user to go interface with a router and send an e-mail to 192.168.2.2. Now look at Figure 3-15. The opposite holds true, as well: you can't tell a router to send an e-mail to your brother Joel in Abilene.

End users interface with cell phones, telephones, PDAs, PCs, e-mail programs, word processing programs, and a variety of other software and hardware tools. They may go as far as installing a network adapter so they can connect to the network, but the adapter really is not a user interface; it's a way for a PC (or other node) to pass and receive data to and from a network.

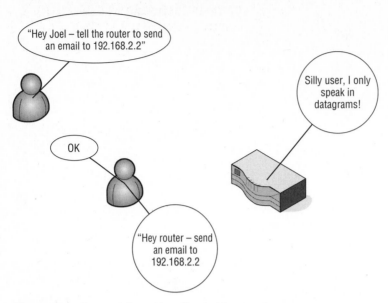

Figure 3-14 A user trying to interface with a router

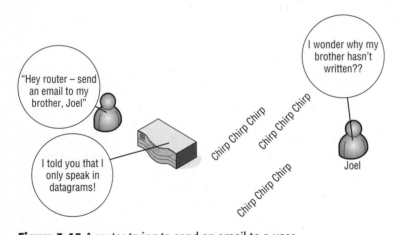

Figure 3-15 A router trying to send an email to a user

3.3.2.1   Network Interfaces and Adapters

Like many other things in networking, the terms *interface* and *adapter* can have various meanings (and sometimes they mean the same thing).

We already discussed user interfaces and the types that are associated in that group. We are now
going to discuss network interfaces and network adapters.
Before we do that, take a look at
how Merriam-Webster defines
an interface and an adapter.

> **RANDOM BONUS DEFINITION**
>
> Worldwide Interoperability for Microwave
> Access (WiMAX [IEEE 802.16]) — A task
> force responsible for the IEEE 802.16
> standards for broadband wireless access
> (BWA) networks

```
in·ter·face[27]
noun
1: a surface forming a common boundary of two bodies, spaces, or phases
  (an oil-water interface)
2 a: the place at which independent and often unrelated systems meet and
  act on or communicate with each other (the man-machine interface)
b: the means by which interaction or communication is achieved at an
  interface transitive verb
1: to connect by means of an interface (interface a machine with a
  computer)
2: to serve as an interface for
adapt·or[28]
also adap·ter
noun
1: one that adapts
2 a: a device for connecting two parts (as of different diameters) of an
  apparatus
b: an attachment for adapting apparatus for uses not originally intended
```

A network interface is any device or method that serves as an access point
to a data path among various network nodes within a network. A network
interface is also the point that connects users with a network that is outside
the boundaries of their LAN. Network interfaces provide a way for a node to
speak to other nodes, regardless of the standards that are in place along the
data path.

There is more to a network interface than simply installing it and then
plugging in a cable. The network interface is also able to convert data from
proprietary or noncommon standards to one that is shared, thus allowing
nodes to communicate with another one even if they don't have the same
protocols implemented. A network interface connects end-user devices to a
network. The network interface controller (NIC) that is in a standard desktop
computer is a type of network interface. The point at the boundary of a LAN,

[27]*Merriam-Webster Online Dictionary.* Retrieved May 9, 2008, from www.merriam-webster.
com/dictionary/interface.
[28]*Merriam-Webster Online Dictionary.* Retrieved May 9, 2008, from www.merriam-webster.
com/dictionary/interface.

which connects the LAN to an outside network, is another type of network interface. In Layer 3 environments, *interface* is often the term used to describe a network connection and really isn't considered hardware.

Network adapter is usually the term given to the hardware interface to the network. Previously we said that an NIC card is a network interface that a computer uses. An NIC card is also referred to as a network adapter.[29] The NIC card adapts to the computer, allowing it to have an interface to the network. Confused yet? Wait — there's more. There is also what is known as a *virtual network adapter*, which is an application that assists a computer to connect to the Internet without a physical adapter. This is usually done over WiFi or WiMAX.

We really shouldn't dwell on this much longer. With practice, you will learn how to *adapt* to your fellow networking gurus and can *interface* with one another while talking about how great this book is and how much you enjoyed reading it.[30] You will get a better feel for adapters and interfaces throughout the remainder of this book. It's not as difficult as it may seem, we promise.

3.3.2.2   *Network Interface Controllers*

The network interface controller (NIC)[31] is a hardware card that allows a PC to participate in passing and receiving data on a network. An NIC is commonly referred to as an *NIC card*, *LAN card*, *LAN adapter*, *network card*, *network adapter*, *Ethernet adapter*, and a few other names. Often the name may be a reference to technology the NIC is supporting (i.e., an Ethernet card). All are entirely acceptable and, regardless of what term you use, generally understood by whoever is participating in the discussion.[32] Figure 3-16 shows an example of an NIC card.

NIC cards operate at Layers 1 and 2 of the OSI reference model. Because NIC is a physical connecting device, providing a user with network access, it is a Layer 1 device. However, because it uses a system for addressing nodes, it is also a Layer 2 device. NIC cards[33] have a 48-bit serial number assigned to them, which is the MAC address. NIC cards normally take one of two forms; they can be an expansion card that has to be physically inserted into the bus on the PC motherboard or they can be integrated into the motherboard. You may also have interfaces that have a difference connector type, such as a USB interface.

---

[29] A good portion of the time if someone says "network adapter," they are talking about an NIC card. Or the adapter at the end of a cable (serial adapter, Ethernet adapter, etc.).

[30] It seemed like a good time for a shameless plug.

[31] Some people assume that NIC stands for network interface card. This is not correct, although the term NIC card is accepted by most. If NIC were network interface card, then an NIC card would be a network interface card card.

[32] If you are ever unsure, just ask someone.

[33] Okay. We said that it was a funny term, but it's one we are comfortable with. It is less awkward to ask someone, "Who do you buy the NIC card from?" than "Where did you get that NIC?"

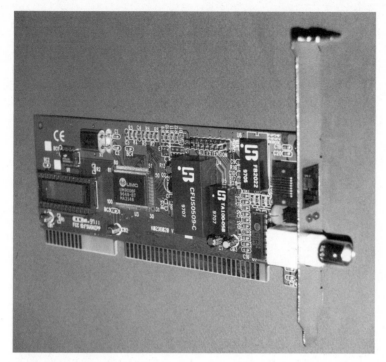

Figure 3-16 An NIC card

3.3.3   To Boldly Go Where Data Needs to Flow (or, How Does that E-mail Get to Brother Joel?)

We have our cables, computers, NIC cards, buses, and all the things we need to get our bits to hit the NIC card and travel across our UTP to a destination on the other side of the LAN. As you can see in Figure 3-17, our bits just are not going to go very far. The application sends the data to our NIC card, who forwards it on to the medium, who just cannot figure out where the bits should go.

We all know that the example in the preceding paragraph is simplistic, but if you think about it, that is about all we have covered so far. Well, folks, it's time now for us to talk about the nodes in the network. Some of these nodes you may not ever come across in real life, and others you will become very familiar with. There are a lot of different nodes in a network, and often equipment from many different vendors of node types is implemented within the same network.[34] When designing a network, it is important to put the right node in place to perform the right job. You really don't need a router

---

[34]Don't put all of your eggs in one basket.

in a bridged network, nor would you try to use a repeater to connect to your Internet service provider (ISP).

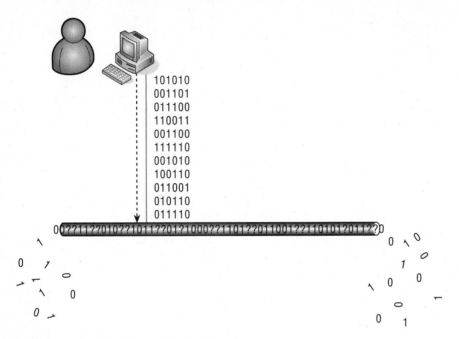

Figure 3-17 Sending data to the pseudo-net

This section does not provide an in-depth discussion of the standards involved with and the modus operandi of any individual node. Most of these will be covered in upcoming chapters. This section is more of an introduction to networking hardware. Where does the data go when it leaves your computer? What other nodes might you be using and not even realize it? These are the types of questions you will be able to answer when you are done with this section. The next time you hear someone say, "Hey, what's all the hubbub?" you may be able to come up with a witty quip in response.

3.3.3.1 Concentrators

A network *concentrator* is a node that is able to multiplex signals and then transmit them over a single transmission medium. Most concentrators support multiple asynchronous[35] channels and one high-speed synchronous channel. The term *concentrator* is often used generically when referring to some nodes

---

[35]In data communication, an *asynchronous* process is one that does not require a clocking mechanism in order to work. A *synchronous* process does require clocking — in other words, it has to be synchronized in order to work.

known as hubs (see next section). A concentrator usually provides *point of presence (POP)* access for remote users, as well as performing other functions.[36]

3.3.3.2 *Hubs*

Hubs are commonly used to connect devices within network segments[37] to one another. Figure 3-18 shows an example of a typical hub deployment in a network segment. Notice in the figure, the hub actually supports data rates of both 10 Mbps and 100 Mbps. There are a lot of different types of hubs, with varying numbers of hosts supported. Some support multiple data rates while some only support a single data rate. The hub that is appropriate for your environment should be chosen based on the needs of the network and the end users.

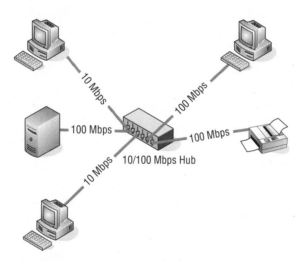

Figure 3-18 Hub deployment

When data is received by a hub, the hub forwards the received data to all the nodes that connect to it. All ports see datagrams received on any other ports within the hub. Hubs are considered *shared media*, as there are multiple hosts sharing a common transmission medium. If a hub is made aware of a collision (data that collides when two or more hosts try to pass data at the same time), it will signal the other ports to stop transmitting until the collision is resolved. Hubs also

ACRONYM ALERT

FPGA — Field-programmable gate array

---

[36]Some concentrators are also able to perform high-layer functions, such as routing.
[37]Segments are areas of a LAN that are contained within a boundary with the boundary termination node being a router, switch, or a bridge.

typically determine if one of the ports is having problems (excessive collisions, corrupted data, etc.). If so, the hub can react and shut the port off from the rest of the shared media. Hubs are considered Layer 1 nodes.

Hubs have largely been replaced in recent years, due to the popularity and cost reduction of network switches, though they are still in use for many home and small business networks. Additionally, hubs can be used to copy datagrams that are sent to or received by a specific node and have that information forwarded to one or more network monitoring connections.

3.3.3.3 *Media Access Units*

Media access units (MAUs), also referred to as *multi-station access units*,[38] function similarly to hubs, but for Token Ring networks. Data flows through the MAU in a logical ring topology, although the physical topology is a star topology configuration. The MAU can recognize any hosts that are inactive and disable the port the host is on so as not to disrupt the operation of the logical ring. MAUs are considered Layer 1 nodes.

Take a look at Figure 3-19. You see that all hosts are physically connected to the MAU in a star topology, while communication between the hosts is still performed as if the hosts were physically connected in a ring.

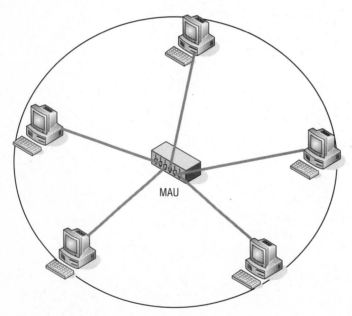

Figure 3-19 An MAU — physical star, logical ring

---

[38]There are two acronyms that are common when referring to the multi-service access unit, MAU and MSAU.

3.3.3.4 Repeaters

Repeaters are used to give data the extra push it needs to reach an endpoint. Transmission media has distance limitations before the signal experiences degradation, known as *attenuation* or *signal loss*. When the distance limit has been reached, instead of placing another switch, hub, or router in the path, a repeater is used.

> **POP QUIZ**
>
> What does MAU stand for?

The role of the repeater is simple: it accepts data and then retransmits it to the other side. Copper and fiber optic cabling are both supported by repeaters geared for the cabling type. Additionally, there are repeaters available for networks that use wireless as a transmission medium.

3.3.3.5 Bridges and Switches

Functionally, bridges and switches are pretty much interchangeable. Both are Layer 2 devices that support and perform the same basic function of joining network segments within the LAN (see Figure 3-20). Bridges traditionally were very small (some had only two port interfaces). When sold on the market, some bridges fetched a very expensive price, especially if they could support data rates that matched the rates supported by the transmission media in place.

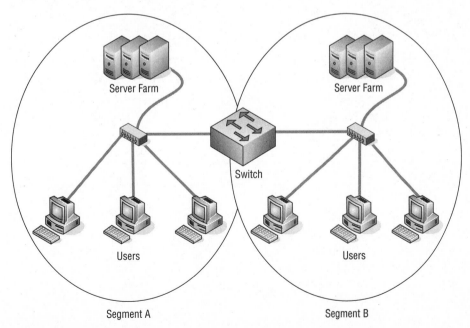

Figure 3-20 An example of a switch bridging two LAN segments to one another

In the late 1980s and the early 1990s, the demand started growing for faster systems and faster networks. LANs were expanding to the point where a shared media network was no longer able to handle the demand. Advancements in technology paved the way for system resource (processor and memory) advancements, which allowed vendors to build nodes with more flexibility in the number of ports than traditional bridges could support, all at the speed supported by the connected transmission medium. These nodes were termed *switches*, but their functions remained the same as what a bridge did — the switch just was able to do more of it. The term *switch* is more of a marketing term, used to separate the legacy nodes from the new and improved version.[39] For the most part, a bridge is a switch and a switch is a bridge and both do more than a hub.

AN UNRELATED MOMENT OF PAUSE

Too bad they didn't think of these:

- ◆ AMIGA — A Merely Insignificant Game Addiction
- ◆ BASIC — Bill's Attempt to Seize Industry Control
- ◆ CD-ROM — Consumer Device, Rendered Obsolete in Months
- ◆ COBOL — Completely Obsolete Business-Oriented Language
- ◆ DOS — Defective Operating System
- ◆ ISDN — It Still Does Nothing
- ◆ LISP — Lots of Infuriating and Silly Parentheses
- ◆ MIPS — Meaningless Indication of Processor Speed
- ◆ PCMCIA — People Can't Memorize Computer Industry Acronyms
- ◆ PENTIUM — Produces Erroneous Numbers Through Incorrect Understanding of Mathematics
- ◆ SCSI — System Can't See It
- ◆ WWW — World Wide Wait

Switches have almost completely replaced hubs in today's networks. The prices of switches and hubs are fairly close when taking into account the number of supported hosts. Some reasons why switches are preferred over hubs are that switches are configurable, support more hosts within a single node, and perform faster and more reliably than a hub.

---

[39]The sales and marketing folks continue to do this today. In Sections 3.3.3.7 and 3.3.3.8, we will discuss upper-layer switching (Layer 3 switching, web switching, application switching, etc.), which is nothing like traditional switching, but it sounds good and it sells.

Switches are deployed in various locations in a network. Switches are able to determine the best path to a network segment through the use of the *Spanning Tree Protocol (STP)*. STP allows a network to be

> **RANDOM BONUS DEFINITION**
>
> buffer — A block of memory used to store data temporarily.

designed to include redundant links, which ensures that data gets to its destination if the primary link fails. STP also ensures that there are no loops in the network, which might be introduced with the addition of the redundant links. Spanning Tree has had many improvements made in the past few years. We will discuss the Spanning Tree Protocol further in Chapter 11, "The Data Link Layer."

Switches are also capable of being configured with multiple *virtual LANs (VLANs)*, which allow nodes to communicate as if they were all connected within the same LAN segment, regardless of where the nodes physically reside. In a VLAN environment, broadcast messages are only sent to the interfaces that are members of the VLAN, leaving the remainder of the switch the opportunity to serve other areas. Figure 3-21 shows an example of the logical topology of a fully meshed switched network.

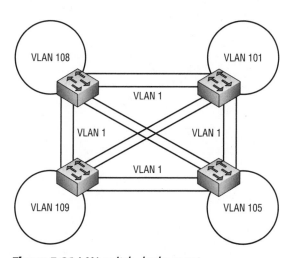

Figure 3-21 LAN switch deployment

Take note of all the available links and let's take a moment to discuss what problems may occur if there were no way to control the flow of data. Keep in mind that switches forward data in the direction of the node that knows where the MAC address of the destination is. In the example, if a host in VLAN 108 needs to get data to a host in VLAN 105, and there is nothing configured on the switch to assist in forwarding decisions, which path would the data take?

Each switch would flood the data out all other switches and would continue to do so at an alarming rate. Keep in mind that there are other nodes in other VLANs doing the same thing. A basic example, but enough for you to see that there are problems. That is what makes switches special — all the tools available today to address these issues and many more that may arise. We will discuss switching in more detail in Chapter 11.

3.3.3.6 *Routers*

Routers make it possible for our e-mails to make it to their destination. They make the decisions that are necessary to get data from one user to another. It would be virtually impossible to meet the demands of users today without a router in the mix, helping make decisions on how to get data from point A to point B.

Routers are advanced network nodes that connect networks of different types. Routers are intelligent enough to know how to get data from a Token Ring subnet to an Ethernet subnet, without data corruption of any kind. Routers support many protocols and standards that allow much more flexibility in their deployment. A router can be placed in the network to join two or more LANs together, two or more WANs, a LAN to an ISP, and so on. Figure 3-22 shows a router joining two networks to one another and joining both of them to the Internet.

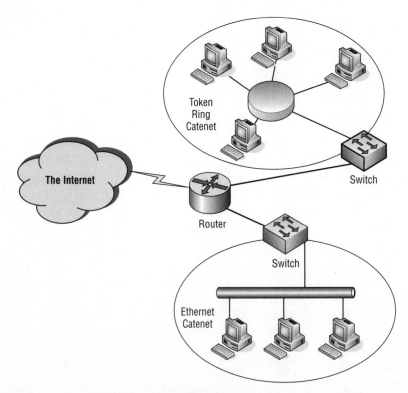

Figure 3-22 An example of a router deployment

Routers operate at Layer 3 of the OSI reference model and use IP addresses for data delivery. Routers also are able to communicate with other routers and share path information, so when a packet is received, it can be

> **POP QUIZ**
>
> At which layer of the OSI model does a switch operate?

sent toward its destination over the best path possible. Routers run algorithms to assist in determining the best path, and they share information with one another, so every router can be on the same page. Routers ensure that data gets to where it is supposed to go.

Routers maintain routing tables that help determine where the best path is to a destination. The routing table includes information that shows what subnets the router has learned and the path to the next node (next hop) that leads to the destination IP address. The routing table is able to place a metric or cost to a destination to assist in routing decisions. The entries in the routing table can be configured (static) or learned via a routing protocol such as RIP or OSPF. Following is an example of a routing table:

```
Active Routes:
Network Destination Netmask Gateway Interface Metric
  0.0.0.0 0.0.0.0 192.168.1.1 192.168.1.104 1
  127.0.0.0 255.0.0.0 127.0.0.1 127.0.0.1 1
  192.168.1.0 255.255.255.0 192.168.1.104 192.168.1.104 1
  192.168.1.104 255.255.255.255 127.0.0.1 127.0.0.1 1
  192.168.1.255 255.255.255.255 192.168.1.104 192.168.1.104 1
  224.0.0.0 224.0.0.0 192.168.1.104 192.168.1.104 1
  255.255.255.255 255.255.255.255 192.168.1.104 192.168.1.104 1
Default Gateway: 192.168.1.1
```

In the example, you can see that the routing table has information on the destination addresses that it is aware of, the subnet mask that is assigned to the destination IP address, the *gateway* (next hop to destination), the interface through which the data needs to go in order to reach the gateway, and the metric assigned to the destination. The metric is the number of hops to a destination. If there is only one route, the metric is ignored. If there are multiple routes to a destination, the one with the lowest metric is used.

Routers can be as simple as a router in a home office to as complex as an Internet backbone router. Routers support multiple protocols and interfaces, which allows them to be operated and translate data coming from multiple network types. Routers are discussed in greater detail in Chapter 10, "The Network Layer."

3.3.3.7 *Layer 3 Switches*

Section 3.3.3.5 discussed traditional Layer 2 switches and the functions they perform. Layer 3 switches can operate at Layer 2, as well as function like a router. Layer 3 switches can be config-

> **RANDOM BONUS DEFINITION**
>
> bit — A unit of data that is either a 0 or a 1.

ured to make routing decisions to send data to a destination. Routers use software to perform logic decisions for operation and use a microprocessor to perform packet switching. Layer 3 switches have replaced the need for software logic decisions and some hardware that routers rely on with integrated circuitry to perform these tasks. The circuitry that is used is known as *application-specific integrated circuits (ASICs)*.

Layer 3 switches combine the wire speed technologies used by Layer 2 switches and the tools necessary to route packets as a router. Layer 3 switches make routing decisions based on the same routing table information as a traditional router does. As far as the hardware design, a Layer 3 switch and a router look a lot alike in many cases. Both are configurable and the higher end ones have slots where different types of modules can be inserted, increasing the protocols that are supported by the node.

Layer 3 switches are predominately developed for larger corporate LANs. The Internet still utilizes routers in the core to get data to a destination. Most Layer 3 switches are not able to support the WAN interfaces required for routing Internet data. Layer 3 switches are often referred to as *routing switches* or *Ethernet routing switches*.

Layer 3 switches also have the ability to control the flow of data by implementing what is known as *class of service* (CoS), which provides for packet queuing into classes of service to ensure that data with a higher priority is attended to before data with a lower priority.

3.3.3.8 *Upper-Layer Switch Types*

There are nodes that perform functions at Layer 4 and above of the OSI reference model. The term *switch* is more of a marketing term, as these nodes are nothing like traditional Layer 2 switches. Some of the terms that are assigned to switches that fall in the upper-layer category include:

- Multilayer switches
- Server load balancer switches
- Web switches
- Layer 7 switches
- Application switches
- Layer 3 switches
- Layer 4 switches

- Layer 4–7 switches

- Content switches

The previous section discussed the Layer 3 switch. The Layer 3 switch is able to route data much like a router at wire speed, as well as function as traditional Layer 2 switches. Layer 3 switches are also sometimes referred to as multilayer switches.

POP QUIZ

At which layer of the OSI model does a router operate?

A Layer 4 switch operates at the Transport layer and expands the functions that are performed by Layer 2 and Layer 3 switches. Layer 4 switches prioritize data based on applications that are in use. A Layer 4 switch provides for CoS to be deployed throughout the LAN (not just within the switch). An example of providing priority for applications would be in a LAN where e-mail traffic takes precedence over Telnet traffic. These parameters can be configured so if there are some users who need Telnet more than e-mail, it can be configured to allow for this. Layer 4 switches are also referred to as multilayer switches.

Server load balancers (SLBs) distribute traffic destined for a server. They share the load for requests between multiple servers, without the end user even being aware that there is any node between them and the server. Figure 3-23 shows an example of a switch performing load balancing for HTTP requested to a website.

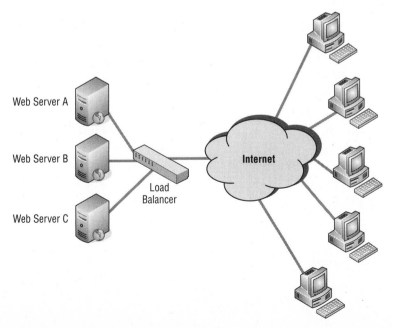

Figure 3-23 Deployment of a server load balancer

Load balancers also spoof the IP address of the server, which helps secure the servers from attack. Load balancers divide requests destined for the server among all the servers that are attached to the load balancer. If a load balancing solution is not in place, all traffic hits the same server, which could potentially cause latency and rejecting of requests to the server.

Some of the upper-layer switches are also able to cache data for speedy access. These functions are known as *data acceleration*. Some also support cryptographic protocols — for instance, Secure Sockets Layer (SSL) and Transport Layer Security (TLS). Load balancing, data acceleration, cryptographic protocols, and many more things.[40] Who could ask for anything more?[41]

3.3.3.9 *Remote Access*

Network nodes that are used to provide remote users the capability of accessing a computer or network from a remote location are known as *remote access nodes*. Many corporate LANs utilize VPN technology to allow users into the LAN from any location, as long as they have access to the Internet. Some users may not have access to the Internet, and in those cases, they can use a modem to connect to the remote location.

Home users also have modems that allow them to connect to the service provider. Once connected, the users can digitally travel to almost anywhere in the world. They can also use VPN client software to connect to the VPN server (or rather, to the node that is running the server software). Remote access technology, like

> **RANDOM BONUS DEFINITION**
>
> modulation — The process of manipulating a waveform to create a signal that sends a message. In data communications, modulation is performed by a node that converts a digital signal to an analog signal, in order to be communicated over a phone line.

many other networking technologies, has grown by leaps and bounds in the last decade. Remote access (with the necessary applications) allows people to telecommute and work from remote locations as often as necessary.[42] Additionally, remote access gives small offices the capability to connect to the corporate LAN to conduct business. This is a much cheaper option than what was provided in the 1980s to early 1990s.

---

[40]That's what Layer 4–7 switches are made of.
[41]We assure you: someone is always asking for more.
[42]Or as long as the boss will allow them to do so.

Remote access gives clients, vendors, and partners the capability to connect to the corporate LAN. The system administrator controls who gets to go where once they are on the LAN. In this section, we discuss the hardware nodes that provide an avenue for these technologies to exist.

3.3.3.9.1 Modems

The term *modem* is derived from its two main functions. A modem modulates and demodulates. This means that a modem converts digital data to an analog signal and then converts it back again when the data reaches the modem that is connected to the destination node. Figure 3-24 is an example of remote users accessing a corporate network segment via a modem.

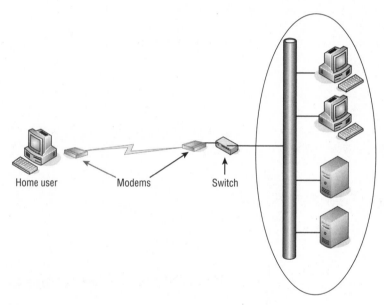

Home user   Modems   Switch

Figure 3-24 Modem remote access

Data that is sent and received by a modem is measured in *bits per second (bps)* or by its *baud rate*. Bps is a measure of the amount of data (number of bits) that can be sent in one second. Baud rate is determined by the type of modulation used and represents the number of times that a signal is changed in one second. The baud rate and the bps rate are not the same number.

Modems that connect a user's PC to a phone line are called dialup modems. Dialup modems are not the only modem type that is available. Internet access is now available to most people in the United States and other parts of the world at very high data rate speeds. There are different types of modems available to the average user as well as businesses and other organizational types. Here is a list of a few of these:

- Cable modem
- Asymmetric digital subscriber line (ADSL) modem
- Digital subscriber line (DSL)
- Microwave modem
- Optical modem
- Wi-Fi modem

The type of modem to use really depends on the needs of the user(s). A person who plays video games online would be much happier with a cable or DSL modem over the traditional dialup modem. Someone who goes online to send and receive e-mail once a week can probably survive with a dialup modem.[43]

3.3.3.9.2 VPNs

VPN technology provides a way for a remote user or branch office to connect virtually to a remote LAN over the Internet. A VPN supporting node has three main functions:

- Provide remote access for individual users
- Provide remote access for a branch office or other LAN
- Ensure that only authorized individuals are able to access the LAN

There are many different types of nodes that support VPN technology. Some are called *VPN routers, VPN switches, extranet routers,* and *extranet switches.* As long as the node in question's predominate jobs are

> **POP QUIZ**
>
> What is the common name for a modulator/demodulator?

remote access, authentication, and encryption, the node is VPN-compatible. VPN hardware supports enhanced security, load-balancing methodologies, and the capability to support an increased number of clients that can be connected at the same time, based on the processing power of the node.

---

[43]But good luck with opening some of those attachments.

3.3.3.9.3 Wireless

Wireless remote access is a growing technology. Many business and companies are providing access to the Internet and/or the LAN for their customers and employees. There are two main nodes that are needed for wireless remote access. You need to have an end user with a wireless NIC (WNIC) and an access point for them to connect to. The end user is known as the wireless client. Access points are the boundary nodes for the network. A wireless client would be any node that is used to connect to the network without a solid communication path. Figure 3-25 shows an example of wireless remote access.

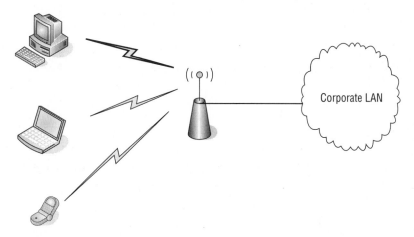

Figure 3-25 Wireless remote access

Some examples of these client node types would be:

- Cellular phones
- IP phones
- Laptops
- Workstations
- Computers

Notice that a wireless client does not have to be a portable device. It can be a stationary device as well, as long as it has an interface that supports wireless technology. There are many access point nodes; some are integrated into other network node types. Within networks that are completely wireless there are wireless bridges, switches, routers, and so on, just as there would be in any wired LAN.

3.3.3.10 Servers

Network servers are nodes that manage the resources available to the users of the network. There are many different types of servers, normally named for the function they perform. A few examples include:

- **Print servers** — Manage traffic destined to a network printer.
- **File servers** — Store files for network users.
- **Network servers** — Manage the traffic on the network.
- **FTP servers** — Manage file transfer.
- **Mail servers** — Manage e-mail traffic.
- **Fax servers** — Manage incoming and outgoing fax messages.
- **List servers** — Manage mailing lists.
- **Proxy servers** — A node that resides between a client and a server, whose purpose is to manage requests destined to the server. Proxy servers allow for shared connections and free the server up so the performance of the server from a end-user perspective is greatly improved.

Network servers are nodes that are dedicated to the technology they are configured to support. These nodes have nothing else to worry about but that specific function. Some servers can have multiple applications running and therefore have the resources necessary to support each of those. Even if the node is running multiple applications, the application itself is the server and is still referenced by the function it is set to do.

> **RANDOM BONUS DEFINITION**
>
> AppleTalk — A protocol suite developed by Apple Computer.

3.4 Chapter Exercises

1. Explain what "10 half or 100 full?"[44] means to you, what the difference is between 10 half and 100 full, and list pros and cons of each.

2. List three types of interfaces and three types of adapters.

3. Why is an NIC card considered both an interface and an adapter?

---

[44]We told you that someone would ask this someday.

4. List three examples of flash memory.

5. List the PDU for each of the OSI layers:

Layer	PDU
Application	_____
Presentation	_____
Session	_____
Transport	_____
Network	_____
Data Link	_____
Physical	_____

6. What is the difference between volatile and nonvolatile memory?

7. What is the difference between STP and UTP cabling?

8. Explain when you would want to use MMF cables instead of SMF cables. Next, explain in what instances SMF cabling would be preferred over MMF cabling.

9. Define *modulation*.

10. What is the main difference between a Layer 3 switch and a router?

3.5   Pop Quiz Answers

1. The decimal number 211 is equal to what binary number?

   11010011

2. The binary number 01011100 is equal to what decimal number?

   92

3. What is the binary name for the binary value of 2^{50}?

   Pebibit (Pibit)

4. Define *RAM*.

   Volatile memory that is available for data storage and access, regardless of the order in which it was received.

5. Define *encapsulation*.

   Encapsulation is the act of including data from an upper-layer protocol within a structure in order to transmit the data.

6. What is IEEE Standard 802.11?

   IEEE 802.11 is the standard that is maintained by the IEEE outlining WLAN communications. Sometimes, IEEE802.11 is also referred to as Wi-Fi, although traditional Wi-Fi standards are not included in IEEE 802.11.

7. What does MAU stand for?

   Media access unit

8. At which layer of the OSI model does a switch operate?

   Layer 2

9. At which layer of the OSI model does a router operate?

   Layer 3

10. What is the common name for a modulator/demodulator?

    Modem

Operating Systems and Networking Software

Part of the inhumanity of the computer is that, once it is competently programmed and working smoothly, it is completely honest.

— Isaac Asimov

This quote by Isaac Asimov points out the basic difference between human intelligence and that which is attributed to computers. True computers can be designed and built to calculate, retain, and retrieve vast amounts of data in microseconds and display it in graphics and color beyond what human language is able to relate.[1] However, computers are programmed devices that are only able to operate on a set of rules designed by humans.

True, there are programs that attempt to give computers a form of artificial intelligence, but being only machines that work within a defined rule set, they can only respond in a completely honest manner. On the other hand, humans are capable of lying at any time and often do. We will not get into the philosophical or psychological reasons for why humans have a tendency toward lying. Whatever their reason may be, humans can be whimsical, whereas when a computer acts in that manner, it usually gets its guts torn out. So, now aren't you happy you are not a computer?

The essential piece of software each computer requires is an operating system. Without it, a computer would just sit and not do a meaningful piece of work, just like some humans we know. It is the basic process that operates on human requests and responds accordingly, if programmed to act in that manner. The network drivers embedded in the operating system communicate with the portions of a computer that interact with the network. The operating system assists other application programs to communicate with a server that

---

[1] Try to tell the average human to produce a fancy graph on the fly!

is located remotely and can only be reached over the network. There are other programs involved in the network arena, but the purpose of this chapter is to cover the basic computer operating system and how it interacts with network components. There will also be discussion on network operating systems (NOS) and their place in the network.

4.1   Computer Operating System Basics

To understand computer operating systems and their place in the universe, it is essential to first discuss some computer design basics. Everyone by now has heard the acronym CPU (central processing unit). Some may say it means the computer itself, such as a personal computer, without any peripherals attached to it. In days gone by,

ACRONYM ALERT

ARE — All routes explorer

a CPU could have taken up some serious floor space, filling a large room or many rooms with racks of equipment. Today, a desktop computer has roughly a footprint of one square foot. This represents a significant difference in floor space, but today's CPU also has major advantages in speed, storage, processing power, and energy consumption. Even though modern computers are far more capable than their early predecessors, they still operate pretty similarly when it comes to handling data.

4.1.1   CPU Basics

The CPU is the heart of any computer. Data and instructions flow into it so the data can be manipulated and acted upon in a controlled manner. Data and instructions are stored within the memory system of the computer. Figure 4-1 shows a block diagram of a basic CPU.

The memory storage area can be constructed of various storage devices ranging from semiconductor to magnetic media. For this section, all you need to know is this is where the instructions of a program and the data that program is to operate on reside. The memory interface contains circuitry that provides addressing information to the memory storage devices so that data may be retrieved. Once the data is received, it is passed to circuits that decode the retrieved data to determine if it is an instruction or data that needs to be operated on. If the latter, the appropriate input registers are loaded with the data. If it is determined that the retrieved data is an instruction, the arithmetic logic unit (ALU) is given the instruction. Depending on the instruction the ALU receives, it performs an operation on the data contained in the input registers and places the result of that operation in the output registers so that data can be moved back to the memory system for storage.

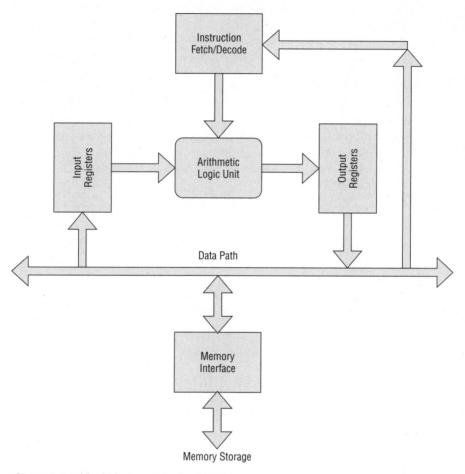

Figure 4-1 A block diagram of a basic CPU

The ALU is the device that performs mathematical operations on the data it is presented with. These are not only the basic functions of addition, subtraction, multiplication, and division, but also Boolean logic[2] such as or, and, and their negated logical functions. The ALU is solely responsible for actual mathematical manipulation of the data it is presented with. The remainder of the CPU functional blocks is solely for the purpose of retrieving data and seeing that it is returned to the memory system properly so it can be easily accessed if needed.

[2]A system of logical operations. The term *Boolean* comes from the name of the inventor of Boolean algebra, George Boole.

QUICK REVIEW

The Boolean algebra or function is usually indicated by a + sign between variables, such as A+B=C. A variable is usually true when its value is equal to 1 and false when its value is equal to 0. An or function result is true if any of the variables making up the function is true. A negated or function is usually referred to as a nor function and its value is false if any of the variables making up the function is true.

The Boolean algebra and function is indicated with a "." sign between variables, such as A·B=C. An and function result is only true if all of the variables making up the function are true. A negated and function is usually referred to as a nand function and its value is only false if all the variables making up the function are true.

The following table shows two variables and the resultants of the or, nor, and, and nand functions.

A	B	OR	NOR	AND	NAND
0	0	0	1	0	1
0	1	1	0	0	1
1	0	1	0	0	1
1	1	1	0	1	0

This discussion is a simplification of what a CPU is. However, what once took racks of equipment is now contained on a single microprocessor chip. Current microprocessors are magnitudes more powerful than those early computers and use much more sophisticated designs that take advantage of bigger data paths, larger addressing capabilities, caching, look-ahead memory fetch,[3] parallel and multiple processor technologies — to name a few.

POP QUIZ

What function does an arithmetic logic unit provide?

The next section discusses the overall computer architecture and how the CPU interacts with those other computer subsystems.

---

[3]A memory fetch grabs the immediate contents of a memory location. Look ahead memory fetch is intuitively retrieving data from memory using the idea that memory fetching is mostly sequential and to save time memory contents would be retrieved in blocks of sequential memory addresses.

4.1.2 Computer Basics

A computer is a collection of subsystems under the control of the operating system, which is the driving intelligence behind the electrical circuits it runs over. Without an operating system, a computer is just a pile of chips, boards, wires, and circuits that would not do any useful thing. But, then again, an operating system is just a collection of ones and zeroes, which is just a bunch of useless information without a computer to execute those commands and instructions. So computers and their operating systems need each other to make a complete package.

In this section, we will be discussing a generic computer system. Most computers have the subsystems being discussed or at least some compatible variation of those subsystems. Figure 4-2 illustrates a block diagram of a basic computer system.

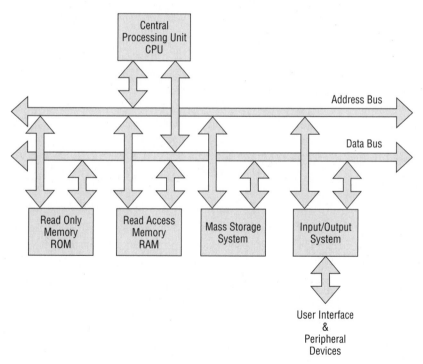

Figure 4-2 A block diagram of a basic computer

We already discussed the CPU portion of a computer. You know that it executes instructions and operates on data, but where is that data obtained? In Figure 4-2, the memory system is distributed across the ROM (read-only memory), RAM (random-access memory), and mass storage System. Why the need for different memory systems? Each has its own purpose within a computer system.

4.1.2.1   Read-Only Memory

When power is first applied[4] to a computer, commands must be inputted into the CPU to initialize the computer system. A CPU is designed to output an initial address to the address bus to retrieve the first instructions from the ROM. The ROM is a fixed storage subsystem that has the initial boot-up instructions to initialize the system. Most boot-up programs perform both an initialization of the computer and a check of the subsystems to ensure they are functional. The ROM may consist of semiconductor devices that contain bits of the data making up the instructions to be executed that are not alterable by the user. However, current personal computer systems do allow for updates to the ROM software program for bug fixes or feature enhancements. ROM devices in this category are usually called *electrically alterable read-only memory devices.*[5]

ACRONYM ALERT

CRC — Cyclic redundancy check

This means the device can be written to if necessary using special sequences under control of the operating system. The boot-up code is critical for computer initialization. If this code becomes corrupted for any reason, the computer may not be usable and may require profes-

POP QUIZ

Would it be advisable to cycle power to the computer while a ROM upgrade is in process?

sional maintenance to restore it back to operation. For this reason, many computers flash warning messages and precautions when the ROM is being accessed under user control. ROMs can be upgraded safely, but do not attempt an upgrade without fully understanding the upgrade process. Typically, once the process has been initiated, it cannot be interrupted until it has completed and the computer has rebooted. If you ever have any questions about upgrading ROM, consult your computer documentation and, if necessary, contact the support staff of the computer's manufacturer.

4.1.2.2   Random-Access Memory

Random-access memory (RAM) consists of semiconductor devices that are used for temporary storage of program instructions and data. The usual design is

---

[4]Technically, you have power within the PC as soon as the battery is plugged in — in other words, when you press the "on" button on the node.

[5]The actual devices used in today's computers are called EEPROM (electrically erasable programmable read-only memory).

an array of these devices residing in the address space of the CPU. As their name implies, they can be accessed randomly no matter what address the information to be retrieved is residing at. This also means the CPU under program control may write data to locations within its address space and store the information for later retrieval. RAM space is usually controlled by the operating system, which designates locations for fixed buffer space for functions under its control and for use by the application programs that may be running at the time. Modern operating systems are capable of running multiple processes at the same time. Each of these processes require operational memory space, so it is critical that memory management be handled properly and as efficiently as possible.

All programs running under the control of the operating system must be well behaved and adhere to the memory space allocation given. When a program violates its memory space allotment, it may overwrite locations being used by other applications or the operating system. If a rogue application overwrites memory used by the operating system for control of the computer, there is a strong likelihood that machine control will be lost and the user will no longer be able to operate the computer under normal conditions. It is in these times that a computer may need to be rebooted to restore operation.

The amount of memory space a computer may contain is determined by how large an address a CPU is able to generate. In the early microprocessor-based PCs, the number of bits of address was only 16, which would allow for a maximum of 65,536 discrete memory addresses. You can determine the address space of a device by taking the number 2 and raising it to the power of the number of address bits that are generated by the CPU. For example:

- $2^{16} = 65,536$ for 16 address bits

- $2^{20} = 1,048,576$ for 20 address bits

- $2^{24} = 16,777,216$ for 24 address bits

- $2^{32} = 4,294,967,296$ for 32 address bits

RANDOM BONUS DEFINITION

active monitor — A node in a Token Ring LAN that is responsible for handling many boundary conditions and housekeeping functions, including generation of a common clock, elastic buffering, and removal of circulating high-priority tokens.

Earlier PCs were mostly character-based computers. Programs were smaller and not as memory-intensive as the visually oriented operating systems of today. As processor capabilities expanded with increased processing speeds and greater addressing ability, software became more sophisticated by taking advantage of these increased capabilities. In the early days, there was a constant battle between hardware designers and their software counterparts. The standing joke used to be that software is like a gas; it will occupy the space that is provided. This is still pretty much true, but to the software developers' credit, they have done some totally marvelous things with the space they filled.

The real battle lines were drawn on the lines of cost. Hardware had fixed costs and increased rapidly as memory needed to be expanded. Those lines have been obliterated somewhat by the advances in chip design, with increased densities and lower power con-

> **POP QUIZ**
>
> True or false: The information contained within RAM is saved when the computer is powered off.

sumption of newer processor and memory chips. Costs dropped dramatically and the capabilities of PCs expanded exponentially. This leads to the conclusion that there is a direct correlation between memory size and computer performance. A general rule of thumb is to buy as much memory as you can afford. However, it is really application-dependant. Applications such as gaming software require much more memory and processor speed, whereas someone who just wants to type a few reports can get by on a relatively smaller amount of memory and decreased processor speed. The marketplace puts PCs on the cutting edge of technology as consumers become more sophisticated. It can only keep pushing the demands on memory and processors to increase their abilities, and this is the driving force for today's technology.

4.1.2.3   Mass Storage System

The mass storage system is comprised of a collection of multiple devices storing programs and information either in magnetic or optical media formats. The very earliest PCs used floppy disks to write and retrieve information in a somewhat nonvolatile manner when the computer was powered off. The "somewhat nonvolatile" comment is for anyone who had to suffer through the loss of information due to a flaw in the magnetic media or the electronics of the device controlling this media. If it can be easily written, it can be easily removed or erased.

Just as memory chips underwent improvement, so did magnetic media devices. Floppy disks went from single-sided to double-sided and higher densities. The last floppy disks were high-density 3.5-inch plastic-encased disks that were more reliable than their predecessors but still could suffer similar data losses. The highest

ACRONYM ALERT

BOOTP — Bootstrap Protocol

density obtained with floppy disks was 1.44 MB, which is a lot for a typewritten document but far from having the capacity to store some of today's programs. Programmers had to develop schemes to distribute their software using multiple floppy disks. A user had to sit by the computer during the installation of such a program and wait for the message to load the next disk. The process was tedious and time-consuming.

The development of optical storage devices, such as CD-ROM, increased storage capacities in a movable media format from just over 1 MB to the vicinity of 700 MB. This was a boon to both software developers and computer users. DVD devices, with their higher capacity for data storage, increased what CD-ROM could store by a factor of 10 — or roughly the ability to store 7 GB of information. Current day computers are shipped with optical drives that can read and write both CD-ROM and DVD media formats. Optical media now has read-write capability, but the process is slower than that of magnetic media. However, as a removable media storage system, it has many advantages over its magnetic predecessors. Even though optical disks are more robust as far as data retention, they still can be rendered unusable by physical damage. A severe scratch can make an optical disk unreadable.

Nonremovable disk storage systems are referred to as *hard disks*. They are "hard" because the magnetic media was originally sprayed on the surface of rigid aluminum disks, which were mounted within an enclosed airtight container to eliminate data corruption due to dust and other contaminants.

> **POP QUIZ**
>
> When a computer is first powered on, the first device it is most likely to read its initial set of instructions from is the
>
> _____.

Magnetic media was bonded to a soft pliable Mylar surface, thus the name "floppy disk." The advantages of hard disks are their ability to store vast amounts of information and its fast retrieval times. Initially, hard drives were commercially available only to users of large mainframe computers, but as development progressed on these devices, the pricing was such that it was commercially feasible to sell them to the PC market. The first PCs shipped with a whopping hard disk storage capacity of 5 MB. Many of today's graphics-intensive programs would not be able to load onto the drive, let alone the operating system or any other user data. It is not uncommon today to see laptops with 200 GB hard drives and desktops with 500 GB[6] storage capacities. Hard drives are usually mounted within a computer's case, but many drives are sold as external drives communicating between the drive and computer over the USB port.

---

[6]This really is an amazing amount of data storage. Can you imagine what increases will be made within the next decade?

4.1.2.4   Input/Output System

A computer is not very useful if information cannot be entered into it or retrieved from it. The *input/output system* is a collection of circuits that allow for information to be entered by the user via a keyboard, pointing device, scanner, etc. It also provides a method for information to be displayed to the user. This can be in the form of video screens, teletype, printers, plotters, etc. These are the most common methods of input and output from a computer system. There are many specialized input/output devices for data entry and retrieval not mentioned in this section, but the idea is always the same: move information into the computer and retrieve it from the computer after it has operated on it.

Because input/output devices interacting with other physical devices and humans may experience timing differences with the CPU, there needs to be a way of storing the information and notifying the CPU when the data is present. Generally two schemes were devised to accomplish this. One is where the input/output devices are mapped to dedicated memory addresses and the CPU polls these locations to see if there is information that needs to be acted on. This is referred to as *memory-mapped I/O*. The other scheme is *interrupt-driven I/O*, where a device writes information into a dedicated register at a fixed port location and sets an interrupt requesting service from the CPU.

> **RANDOM BONUS DEFINITION**
>
> bit stuffing — A technique that provides a unique frame delimiter pattern yet maintains payload data transparency by inserting an extra 0 bit after every occurrence of five 1 bits in the payload data stream.

In a memory-mapped I/O system, the CPU determines which location it should poll under operating system control. In an interrupt-driven I/O system, the CPU responds to interrupts (and there may be many, depending on the number of I/O ports to be serviced). Interrupts adhere to a fixed interrupt priority scheme, which is hierarchal. The CPU can be processing an interrupt request and be preempted by a higher priority interrupt request.

Regardless of which I/O scheme is used in a computer, the operating system must be able to deal with input/output data requests. It must be able to determine when a device is acting unresponsive and either notify the user or take other action as determined by the program. Generally the operating system is responsible for data movement between the various systems within the computer. However, a user may be running an application, such as a word processor, which is running over the operating system. When a user depresses a key on the keyboard, the operating system reads the key and presents that information to the word processor program, which may request that it also be displayed on the video screen.

On PCs, input/output connections are in the form of ports dedicated to either serial or parallel data communications. *Serial communications* refers to the information being passed one bit for each time interval, which is determined by the speed of the port. Generally serial devices are slow data rate devices such as keyboards, modems, pointing devices, scanners, etc. However, with the development of Universal Serial Bus (USB), high-speed serial ports, devices such as hard disk drives and printers can be used due to the increased data rates on these ports. Parallel ports on older PCs were mostly relegated as printer ports. *Parallel data communications* means that data is sent a whole byte at a time for each cycle of the port. USB has become today's de facto standard for peripheral ports.

> **POP QUIZ**
>
> Name a device that you might find connected to a serial port.

4.1.3   Operating System Basics

Operating systems in one form or another have been around since the inception of the first computer. Of course, the first computers were of the mainframe variety with character-oriented terminals.[7] Users entered commands and data in the form of alphanumeric characters that could be found on any typewriter. Data retrieved from the computer could be displayed on the terminal screen for small queries, or, for larger reports, outputted to a printer.

The most basic form of an operating system is a file manager. It is able to create new files on the storage medium being used. It is also able to catalog the files for easy retrieval and has some sort of indexing ability similar to that of a filing cabinet. Computers and their operating systems were first designed to adopt systems that were similar to the business practices of those days. The earlier computers were a high-speed filing system able to store, index, and retrieve data faster than a filing clerk.

ACRONYM ALERT

DMA — Direct memory access

Operating systems underwent some dramatic revisions with the introduction of the PC. Initially, these operating systems were similar to those found

---

[7]The first terminals were alpha-character-oriented. They were merely an electronic form of a typewriter. Graphic terminals that could display some sort of graphic (usually at low resolution by today's standards) were a later innovation in terminal design. Terminals connected to the computer via serial cable.

on the larger computers. They too were character-oriented. The major early PCs initially ran on proprietary operating systems such as Apple's DOS (Disk Operating System) and Tandy Radio Shack's TRS-DOS (usually phonetically pronounced *tris-dos*). The first cross-platform PC operating system to gain popularity was Digital Research's CP/M (Control Program for Microcomputers), originally designed to run on Intel 8080/8085 microprocessor-based computers. It migrated to the Zilog Z80 which was capable of executing the Intel 8080-based instruction set and was a mainstay of the Z80-based PCs for a number of years.

The major limitation of CP/M was that it was designed for 8-bit microprocessors and was only capable of addressing 64 KB of memory. As microprocessors moved up in capability, CP/M began to lose ground to other operating systems, mainly Microsoft's MS-DOS. Digital Research did finally release a 16-bit version as CP/M86, but it was not able to compete against the IBM/Microsoft juggernaut.

Initially, MS-DOS was locked up by IBM and was sold with the IBM PC as IBM DOS. Other PC manufacturers were on the outside looking in and attempted to adopt CP/M86, but the popularity of the IBM PC running MS-DOS left them far behind on the number of PCs being sold. The off-brand manufacturers eventually developed clone PCs that were able to run MS-DOS, thus boosting their PC sales. The developer of CP/M and CP/M86, Digital Research, also developed a clone to MS-DOS called DR-DOS to compete with Microsoft. The number of PCs now running MS-DOS caused IBM to lose their competitive edge and to eventually give up on the PC market.

Although CP/M was a cross-platform operating system, the hardware it was running over could have major differences. As a result, a CP/M program on one computer could not run on another computer from a different manufacturer. The portability of CP/M was the core operating system (sometimes referred to as the *kernel*). The CP/M kernel provided a common interface for user input and application programs that would run over different computer platforms. The computer manufacturers had their own software designer teams that would write the software code needed to allow the kernel to communicate with other hardware systems of the computer system. These pieces of code were referred to as *hardware drivers*.[8] Each subsystem in a computer system could have its own driver if needed. An example of this is the mass storage subsystem. The kernel would call for a file and the driver would cause the floppy drive to seek the track and sector where the beginning of the file was located. The point is, although there was commonality as far as user interfaces and the applications able to run on CP/M, they could have been

---

[8]Hardware drivers are synonymous with device drivers. It is the code that is designed to allow the kernel of the operating system to properly communicate with the device/hardware no matter how different in design they may be. The device driver acts as a translator to allow for the correct operation of the device/hardware.

operating on computers whose hardware had substantial differences from one manufacturer to the next.

Soon after the IBM PC was introduced and its hardware specifications were published, clone PCs began to enter the marketplace. Since IBM opened its architecture, it was not able to legally protect its design, and the PC marketplace ballooned overnight with clones from a number of hardware manufacturers. This phenomenon led to a PC base that not only was able to have the same operating system but also had hardware commonality, which was a boon to the peripheral manufacturers.

RANDOM BONUS DEFINITION

byte — A unit of data that is equal to 8 bits.

With the consolidation of today's PC marketplace, there are really only two variations of PCs. Today's PC users are either in the Apple Mac domain or the PC domain (PCs from various manufacturers able to run the various iterations of Microsoft DOS). Today, Apple

POP QUIZ

What is the acronym for a user interface that uses a point-and-click method of executing computer commands?

manufactures and markets laptops and desktop PCs based on its Macintosh family of computers. Macs were the first PCs that took advantage of a point-and-click–based operating system.[9]

Today's PC world is divided between the Mac operating system and Microsoft Windows operating system. Both are GUI (graphical user interface) based and use a graphical display screen and some sort of pointing device. However, even with the whiz-bang colorful interfaces, the operating system is basically performing the same functions as its predecessors. The only difference is that instead of parsing text instructions, the user input interpreter uses positional information, and if a mouse is used, a right, left, or double-click will cause the operating system to act on the object that is being pointed at on the video graphical display screen.

4.2 Network Operating System Basics

As the need grew for PCs to interconnect and share data and common resources, the opportunity arose for the design and marketing of network

---

[9]If this had caught on before Windows came out, it might have been a much different world today.

operating systems. The most common design of network operating systems was the client/server implementation. PCs were clustered for individual users (clients) to share files on the file server or print data files on printers under the control of a print server. Figure 4-3 illustrates an example of network running a network operating system (NOS).

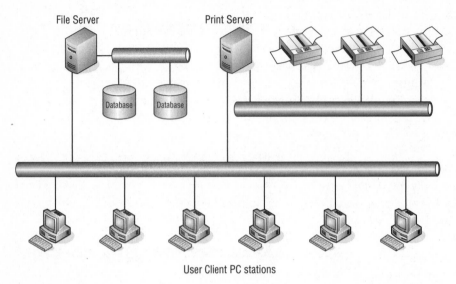

User Client PC stations

Figure 4-3 A computer network under the control of a network operating system

Actually, "network operating system" is a bit of a misnomer in that the NOS really runs on computers that are servers placed in the network. Figure 4-3 shows a single[10] file server and a single[11] print server. In reality, on large networks there could be multiple servers in use. Also, for a small office, the functionalities of both the file server and print server can be combined in a single server. Being a client/server application, the responsibility for authentication of clients with the authority to connect to the server depends on the server to verify that clients have the necessary valid security credentials. In larger networks with many clients, that function can be placed in entirely separate servers solely responsible for granting network access as well as the permission levels a user will have while logged into the network.

There are networks where the software that is being run on a local PC is actually an application located on the server. An example of this is a word processor program that has a fixed number of network licenses. The theory is that not all users would use the program simultaneously, so a company could save some costs by sharing applications over the network. Once all the licenses

---

[10]Just because they are single does not mean they are available.
[11]See footnote 7.

are occupied, subsequent users would need to wait until another user logged out of the program, thus releasing the license. Users could be prevented from loading a program from a server if the network or the server is being heavily worked. Once the program is downloaded to the local PC, there is no further network interaction required until the application is released by the user. This interaction was called the *file services* portion of the NOS.

Print services were also an important piece of NOS. Printer requests would be queued to the print server servicing that portion of the network. A print server could have one or many printers under its control. As print job requests arrived at the print server, it would determine the printer the print job was to be outputted to. The print server queued the print jobs on a first-come, first-served basis. Print jobs were stored on the print server and parceled out to the printer as fast as the printer was able to take the data. Today's network-ready printers are basically their own print server with the intelligence and storage capacity required to queue print jobs from a large user base.

ACRONYM ALERT

FIFO — First in, first out.

There were many networking operating systems, but the most popular were Novell NetWare and Microsoft Networking. Novell utilized an IPX/SPX protocol stack to provide communications over its network. Both Novell and Microsoft have since migrated to supporting the TCP/IP protocol suite over their networks. TCP/IP is not a NOS; it is a protocol that controls communications between peers. A client/server application can be run over a network that uses TCP/IP protocol for communicating over the network, but the actual client/server application is independent on the protocol itself.

The majority of today's networks are TCP/IP-based networks that have a wide range of applications running over them. A workstation may have multiple sessions to various servers on the network simultaneously. Most people use e-mail and may be logged into a corporate mail server while running other applications to other servers over the same network. The need for a network server running a NOS is not required when running the TCP/IP protocol over a network.

4.2.1 Peer-to-Peer Networking

When discussing network operating systems, the context of the discussion is usually based around client/server networks. To perform peer-to-peer networking, where one computer can share data and resources with another computer, requires some sort of application program. The earlier versions of peer-to-peer networking were crude and cumbersome to configure and use. However, as Microsoft evolved its Windows operating system, they added peer-to-peer as well as workgroup network capabilities. Windows was the first GUI-based operating system that was able to support this type of networking.

Windows users are able to share drive space and locally attached printers with other users on the same network using what is commonly referred to as *Windows networking*. Windows networking depends on the host names of each computer to be different if they reside within the same network. This was first accomplished with NetBIOS API (application programming interface) running on each Windows computer on the network. In today's networks, NetBIOS is usually run over the TCP/IP protocol. In this scenario, each computer has both a unique computer name and an IP address. The services NetBIOS provides are related to the Session layer of the OSI model.

On smaller networks, the computer broadcasts the name of the computer that it wants to establish a session with. On large networks, broadcasts can become intrusive and affect network throughput speeds. Large Windows networks will utilize a WINS (Windows Internet Name Service) server for computer name resolution. It maps computer host names to network addresses, thus eliminating multiple broadcasts on the network. WINS can be thought of as the name service for NetBIOS networks and is similar to a DNS (Domain Name Service) server in operation on a TCP/IP network.

Figure 4-4 shows a small peer-to-peer Windows-based network.

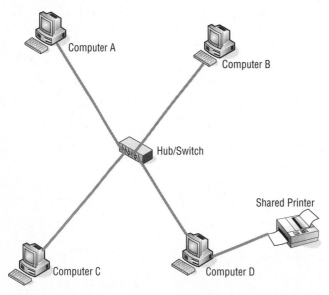

Figure 4-4 A small, Windows-based peer-to-peer network

In this figure, the PCs are labeled Computer A, B, C, and D. However, they may be named in any manner a user or network administrator chooses. It is a good idea to select meaningful names such as joes_pc, jims_pc, and so on, to give a frame of reference for the PC. In larger companies, the computers may be named by department and function. Naming is purely arbitrary, but knowing what each PC is named can be helpful, especially when trying to troubleshoot network issues.

Within this network, Net-BIOS provides computer name registration and resolution, a connection-oriented communi-cation session service, and a con-nectionless communication for datagram distribution service.

> **RANDOM BONUS DEFINITION**
>
> cheapernet — Another name for 10BASE2.

Before a computer can either start a session or distribute datagrams on the network, it must use the NetBIOS name service to register its name. Net-BIOS utilizes UDP port 137 for the name service. The NetBIOS name service functions are to add a name or group name, delete a name or group name, or find a name on the network.

Since in today's networks NetBIOS is run over TCP/IP, NBT (NetBIOS over TCP/IP) utilizes TCP port 139 for the session service. The session mode of NBT allows two computers to establish a connection to pass communications between them. The NetBIOS primitives[12] associated with the session service are as follows:

- **Call** — Opens a session to a remote computer using its NetBIOS name.

- **Listen** — Listens for session requests using NetBIOS name.

- **Hang Up** — Ends a session that had been previously established.

- **Send** — Sends a packet to the computer that a session has been estab-lished with.

- **Send No ACK** — Similar to Send but does not require a returned acknowledgement that the packet was received.

- **Receive** — Waits for the arrival of a packet from a computer a session has been established with.

The *datagram distribution service* is a connectionless service where messages are sent without regard to error detection or remediation. It is incumbent upon the application using this service to provide the necessary data error detection and recovery when needed. UDP port 138 is used by NBT for this datagram distribution service.

---

[12]This list is almost the same responses that one can expect from the family teenager. However, for a NetBIOS session these are the root terms used to describe a particular sequence within the session.

The primitives used for datagram distribution by NetBIOS are as follows:

- **Send Datagram** — Sends a datagram to a remote computer using its NetBIOS name.

- **Send Broadcast Datagram** — Sends a datagram to all the NetBIOS names that are registered on the network.

- **Receive Datagram** — Waits for the arrival of a packet from a Send Datagram process.

- **Receive Broadcast Datagram** — Waits for the arrival of a packet from a Send Broadcast Datagram process.

Fortunately, setting up a small Windows-based local network is easy to do. The previous discussion in this section gives you an appreciation of what is going on under that colorful GUI screen. The unfortunate part is that Windows, with all its various generations, had added twists and bends to the methods used to configure networking on a PC using the Windows operating system for its OS. It is the author's recommendation to review the documentation for your particular version of Windows before attempting to configure your PC for networking. The configuration overview as well as the screenshots in the remainder of this section are based on Windows XP.

Most of the PCs purchased within the last couple of years come pretty much network-ready. Many desktops come with an Ethernet NIC card[13] installed, and many laptops not only have a hard-wired NIC for Ethernet connectivity but also have some sort of wireless connection interface. However, if you have an older PC that you would like to add to your network and it does not have a NIC installed, you have choices available to you to make your PC network-ready. Desktop computer models may either use an internal card, if there is an interface card slot available, or some sort of external solution. There are network interfaces available that will plug into the USB port. If you are not all that computer savvy, I recommend taking down as much information you have about your PC and visiting your local computer store. The sales clerk or computer support staff should be able to assist you in purchasing the appropriate solution to make your computer network-capable.

Older laptops can be easily made network-ready with the addition of a network PCMCIA card. The usual choice is either a card that supports a hard-wired Ethernet solution or a WLAN PCMCIA card, which enables you to connect to your local network wirelessly. The choice is solely dependent upon the current installed network. If this is an initial setup, I strongly suggest investigating a wireless solution. The beauty of a laptop is its mobility, and to have it tethered by an Ethernet cable may not be the ultimate network solution.

[13] Keep in mind, NIC = network interface controller.

NICs require drivers to be able to interoperate with the operating system. Windows has moved to the plug-and-play philosophy where the Windows operating system detects when new hardware has been installed. In most cases, with interface cards

ACRONYM ALERT

IP — Internet Protocol

from larger manufacturers there is a high probability that Windows will have and load the appropriate driver. If your card is one that Windows is unable to auto-detect, the Windows wizard may request that you load a driver disk to complete the installation of the card. In most cases, there is usually a disk in the box with the card or documentation that will point you to a website or FTP server where the appropriate driver[14] can be downloaded.[15] You can use that downloaded file to complete the installation of the card.

With your wired Ethernet Interface installed, you can navigate to your local area connections properties. On Windows XP, click Start ≻ Control Panel. On the Control Panel screen, select Network Connections for the classic view, or if using category view, select Network and Internet Connections. Select the Local Area Connection that is associated with the NIC card you have installed. With the icon for the interface selected, right-click and scroll to Properties. A window should appear labeled Local Area Connection Properties, similar to Figure 4-5.

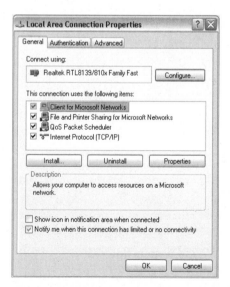

Figure 4-5 Windows XP Local Area Connection Properties

---

[14]Not to be confused with diver, one who deliberately jumps headfirst into water.
[15]Assuming that you have another computer that has network capability and is able to reach the Internet to get the file to download.

On this PC, Client for Microsoft Networks is already installed and enabled. If it is not yet installed on your PC, select the Install button and a new window will open labeled Select Network Compo-

RANDOM BONUS DEFINITION

flooding — The process of sending a frame to all of a switch's ports, with the exception of the port the frame came in on.

nent Type. Select the Client component and click on the Add button. The Select Network Client window will open. Select Client for Microsoft Networks and click OK. If you want to share parts of your file system or locally attached printers, you must enable File and Print Sharing. In the Local Area Connection Properties window, click the Install button. When the Select Network Component type window appears, select Service and click on the Add button. The Select Network Service window will appear. Select File and Printer Sharing for Microsoft Networks, and then click OK. You now have Microsoft Networking enabled with file and printer services enabled. We will revisit both file and printer sharing in a bit. For now, it's on to how we get TCP/IP on this puppy.

If you do not see Internet Protocol (TCP/IP) in the Local Area Connection Properties window, the protocol must be added. Click on the Install button in the Local Area Connection Properties window. When the Select Network Component window appears, select Protocol and click on the Add button. On the Select Network Protocol window, select Internet Protocol (TCP/IP) and click OK. The protocol has now been installed but must be configured.

Before getting into the configuration of TCP/IP on this Windows PC, a brief description is in order of the difference between a statically assigned IP address and an IP address that has been assigned by a server acting as a DHCP server. This topic will be covered and mentioned in other chapters, and by the time this book

ACRONYM ALERT

MIB — Management information base

is finished there will be no question that you will know the differences and how they come to be assigned. First, a statically assigned IP address is pretty obvious. It is an IP address that is assigned to the PC by a user or administrator and is the same IP address the computer will have assigned to it each time the PC is booted up.[16] The only things that have to be known prior to assigning the static IP address is that the IP address is unique and not assigned to another computer on the same network segment, that the address to be assigned fits into the addressing scheme being used on that network segment, and, lastly, that the subnet mask assigned with the IP address is compatible with the IP

---

[16]What it is *not* is an address that is applied via a static charge.

address and is the subnet mask assigned to that network segment. Static IP address assignment is not difficult in a small network, but it can become rather unwieldy in a large network. And if a network redesign is required with a change in IP address assignment for that network, it can become a support nightmare in very short order. If it can be avoided on the network you are setting up, it is recommended to do so and use a DHCP server for IP address assignment.

So, how does one come up with a DHCP server for their network? Of course, you could have an actual server running a DHCP service, but for a small network, such as that shown in Figure 4-5, it would be a waste of resources. There are many newer network devices that do run a DHCP service if configured to do so. Most routers, both wired and wireless, are capable of running a DHCP service. If the hub/switch shown in Figure 4-5 were replaced by a mini-router like those used for cable/DSL Internet access, you could have a DHCP service running on that network. The beauty of having a local DHCP server is that if there is ever a need to change a network's addressing scheme, default gateway, or the DNS servers being used, there is just a single point that requires configuration change. So there is a major support advantage of running a DHCP service on your network. It is easy to see the advantages of having such a service on large networks with many PCs. One reason to consider DHCP even for a small network is if there are laptops being used. The advantage of using a laptop for a PC is its portability and its mobility of moving from one network to another. Although it is doable, having to configure your TCP/IP setting each time you move from one network to another can grow old very quickly.

To set the IP properties of the installed NIC, click on Start ≻ Settings ≻ Control Panel. On the Control Panel, select Network Connections. Right-click on the Local Area Connection you are going to configure IP addressing on, and then select Properties. Select Internet Protocol (TCP/IP) and click on the Properties button. The window where properties can be configured will appear and look similar to that shown in Figure 4-6.

Notice that this interface is configured for obtaining an address dynamically from a DHCP server somewhere on the existing network. To do this, only the two radio buttons to automatically select these addresses need be selected. However, if you select to statically assign the IP address, each of the grayed fields needs to filled in with the appropriate information.

- **IP address** — A unique IP address that is not currently used on the network segment where the computer is to be connected

RANDOM BONUS DEFINITION

host — Any node in an IP network.

- **Subnet mask** — The subnet address assigned to the network segment that the computer is to connected to.
- **Default gateway**[17] — The IP address of the node that acts as the default gateway for the network segment the computer is connected to.

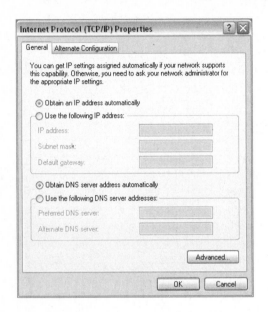

Figure 4-6 Windows XP Internet Protocol (TCP/IP) Properties screen

The DNS (Domain Name Service) server is required if the computer is going to attempt to connect to remote computers by using a domain name.[18] In Figures 4-3 and 4-4 the networks are self-contained and it is assumed that someone is keeping track of IP addresses that have been assigned. In those situations, there is no need for a DNS server to reach the other PCs on the network. Each user will need a list of what those IP addresses are for all computers and other network resources, such as printers. However, in

ACRONYM ALERT

ns — Nanoseconds.

---

[17] A quick definition of a default gateway is that it is the IP address of a node that is used when a computer needs to start a session with a computer that is not resident on the same network.

[18] A domain name server is a computer residing on the Internet providing requested services. For example, a web server may have a name like www.mywebsite.com. Since the IP protocol is dependent upon finding an address using numerical addresses, someone needs to resolve the name to a numeric address. This is the role of a DNS server and it gets its information from the authoritative service on the Internet where the name has been registered.

this current interconnected world the need for DNS is paramount. Figure 4-7 shows a small local network connected to the Internet using a router with a high-speed connection.

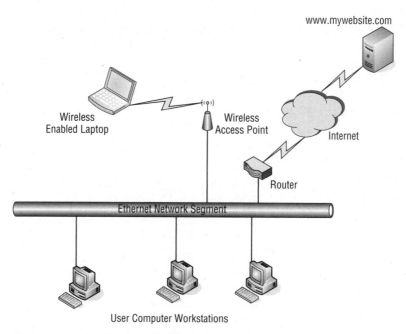

Figure 4-7 A small local network connected to the Internet

Usually when a user or company signs up with an Internet service provider (ISP), they are provided information such as the public IP address that is to be used on the router and its default gateway's IP address. The ISP also provides local DNS service located within the ISP's network, which can be pointed to for DNS name resolution. In a statically assigned IP scheme, these addresses would need to be entered in the appropriate fields of the Internet Protocols (TCP/IP) Properties window to enable the computer to query the provided DNS servers for name resolution when needed. This will need to be done for every computer on the network if they are to be able to connect to computers by IP host name. Most ISPs provide two DNS server addresses. Normally these would be called a *primary DNS address* and a *secondary DNS address*. The primary DNS address is entered in the Preferred DNS server box, whereas the secondary DNS address is entered in the Alternate DNS server box. The PC is now configured to communicate with other PCs on the local network and other computers that may be found on the Internet.

QUICK TIP

There are a couple of quick tests you may want to perform to verify the operation of the NIC card and the connectivity to the local network and the Internet.

1. Click on the Start button in the lower-left portion of your Windows screen.

2. Select Run.

3. In the Run window, enter **cmd** and click OK. A DOS window will open where DOS commands can be entered.

4. Type the command **ping 127.0.0.1**. You should receive back four messages stating "reply from 127.0.0.1." This indicates that your NIC card is working properly with Ethernet and TCP/IP. If you receive "Request timed out" messages, your card has not been properly configured.

5. To verify your network connectivity, attempt to ping the local default gateway[19] for your network. If you get "Request timed out" messages, verify your physical connection to the LAN.

6. If you get good responses back from the local default gateway, you may want to also check your connection to the Internet.

7. Ping the IP address of the router's default gateway. If you get good responses, you are able to reach the Internet. If you receive "Request timed out messages" and you own the whole network, you will need to troubleshoot further. If you are on a company network, contact your network administrator.

8. DNS name resolution can be quickly checked if the Internet connectivity test passed successfully. Ping an Internet connected computer by its host name. For example, **ping www.mywebsite.com**. Receiving "Request timed out" messages may not be an indication of a problem with DNS. Some sites drop ping requests in order to combat denial-of-service attacks of their site. What you would want to see is that the name has been resolved to a numeric IP address. If so, then DNS appears to be working properly and you should be able to connect to the site using your web browser.

9. If DNS resolution does not appear to be working, verify the address you had entered on the Internet Protocol (TCP/IP) Properties. If there are no typos, you may want to attempt to ping the IP address of the DNS server. If there are no replies, you may want to attempt to ping the secondary DNS IP address. If you get a reply there, you may want to place the secondary DNS IP address in the preferred DNS server address field and test again, pinging by Internet host name. If problem persists, contact your ISP or your network administrator.

---

[19]This is the IP address inserted in the Internet Protocol (TCP/IP) Properties for the Default Gateway field. A default gateway is normally the IP address of a router located on your network that has access to the Internet.

> **POP QUIZ**
>
> Name two network operating systems that are prominent in today's networking world.

This section configures a Windows-based PC not only for use on a Microsoft network but also for any TCP/IP-based network, which includes the Internet as we know it today. There will be changes coming such as IPv6,[20] but the basics will remain the basics. What is learned here is scalable to any new nuances that may be coming into the world of networking.

4.2.1.1 File Sharing on a Peer-to-Peer Network

When we configured the NIC card on the PC to permit file sharing, we did not expound on how this is accomplished in a Microsoft Windows world. The strategy is to first determine what is needed to be shared between users. Whole drives, including hard drives, floppy drives, CD-ROM drives, and DVD drives, can be shared. However, any portion of the file system can be shared down to the lowest subdirectory within a directory structure. So this allows for drive, directory, and subdirectory file sharing, all of which can be accomplished over the local network.

From My Computer, right-click on the drive that you are willing to share. From the drop-down menu, select Sharing and Security. A new window will open showing the properties for the drive (see Figure 4-8).

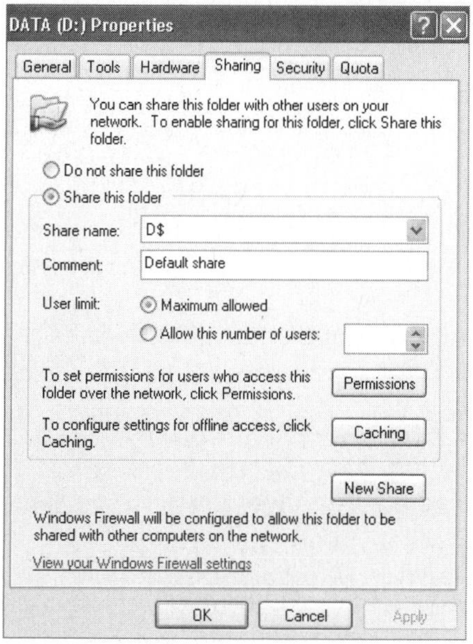

Figure 4-8 Windows XP drive properties

[20] We will cover this in Chapter 10, "The Network Layer."

Notice the message about the security risk that is involved in sharing a whole hard drive. You can proceed if you wish or you can back off to the directory you want to share. Multiple directories can be shared on a hard drive.

QUICK TIP

Proper planning can simplify sharing of directories over the network. Create a single folder that you want to share. Under that folder you can create other folders (subdirectories) that will be shared with the parent folder. The whole directory tree under the shared folder will be shared when you allow sharing on this folder.

One instance where it makes sense to share an entire drive is where removable media is concerned. Floppy drives, CD drives, and DVD drives can be both read and written to, as needed. The floppy drive is nowhere to be found on today's newer laptops, so if you need to generate a floppy disk with information from your laptop, share the drive on the desktop to accomplish that task. Granted, it may not be as fast as a directly connected floppy drive, but it can get you by in a pinch.

Enabling file sharing is only half of the task. You may want to create user accounts on the PC. This can be accomplished under the User Accounts section of the Control Panel. For other computers to use the shared folder, they will need to map a network

RANDOM BONUS DEFINITION

router — A network node that operates at the Network layer.

drive. This can be done from My Computer by selecting the Tools drop-down menu and then Map Network Drive. This window is illustrated in Figure 4-9.

The format shown on this window is \\server, which would be the NetBIOS computer name of the computer where the shared directory is located. An example would be \\joe_pc. However, with TCP/IP enabled on the network connection, this

POP QUIZ

What can be shared using Windows file sharing?

also may be an IP address of the computer where the shared directory is located. The command format would be similar but with the IP address of the computer is placed where the computer name had been. An example would be \\192.168.5.154. The \share is the name assigned to the shared entity, whether it is a drive or directory on the hard drive. The naming is fairly arbitrary and the owner of the computer can use any name he or she pleases. However, the owner must play nice and give the name to the user who would be sharing the data contained in that directory. Without the proper shared name, the share cannot be established. If a guest account or user account has been created for that user, they will be prompted for the account prior to gaining access to the shared data. However, for file sharing to work properly, the computer with the shared directory must be powered on and connected to the network before its shared resources can be accessed.

Figure 4-9 Windows XP Map Network Drive screen

4.2.1.2   *Printer Sharing on a Peer-to-Peer Network*

In today's networking world there are network-ready printers that act as their own print server. They can obtain a network IP address, be given a name, and will allow themselves to be mapped to from other computers connected to the network. This section does not deal with those printers but with the printers that are locally connected to computer on the network.

These printers may be locally connected to a network PC with a parallel port, serial port, or USB port.[21] To share a locally connected printer, select Printers and Faxes from the Control Panel. Select the printer to be shared by pointing to it and clicking the right-mouse button. In the drop-down menu, select Sharing. A new window similar to the window in Figure 4-10 will appear on the screen.

ACRONYM ALERT

RAM — Random-Access Memory

---

[21]Extra credit: What is the benefit and the disadvantage for each of the port types? (This is a question that you will have to research — unless you already know).

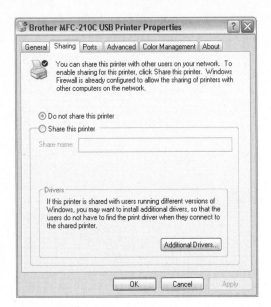

Figure 4-10 Windows XP Printer Sharing screen

Select the radio button to share this printer and enter a share name in the box provided. Windows will attempt to enter a name that is being used locally, but this can be changed as needed. For this example, it a high-speed laser printer connected to Flo the secretary's computer, and other users in the department would like access to that print resource, so a share name may be something like `flo_printer`. Other computer users on the network can then go to Control Panel and select Printers and Faxes and then Add a Printer. They may either browse the network for Flo's printer or enter the name directly, as discussed in the file sharing section. For the sake of this example, the name may appear as `\\flo_pc\flo_printer`, where `flo_pc` is the server name of the computer and `flo_printer` is the share name for the laser printer sitting by her computer. If needed, the IP address assigned to Flo's computer can be used in place of a server name.

QUICK TIP

The use of IP addresses in place of server names is indicative of static IP address assignment. If the network is designed to use dynamic IP address assignment, this could cause problems for users on the network since a computer's assigned IP address could theoretically change each time it is booted up.

Remember that a shared resource in a peer-to-peer network
environment assumes that the
resource is available on the network. The computer providing
the source must be powered on
and connected to the network
for the resource to be shared.

POP QUIZ

Which printers connected to a
network-connected computer can be shared
with other users on the network?

4.3   Other Operating Systems

So far in this chapter, we have concentrated on the client aspect of networks
and the Internet. However, many computers on the Internet and within
the corporate environment are large computers running a wide range of
applications. Although there are many similar applications that can run on a
PC and offer the same type of service, they may not be equally able to handle
many users at the same time. Large computers were initially designed and
used to service multiuser environments, whereas the small computer or PC
was initially designed with the single user in mind. As a result, the operating
systems that control these large machines are much more robust when it comes
to handling a large number of simultaneous users.

This section will concentrate on the network aspects of these operating
systems and how they are used within both the corporate network environment
and the Internet.

4.3.1   Unix

Unix was first developed by AT&T Bell Labs as a multiuser operating system. It
was initially designed to handle many users connected simultaneously and all
sitting in front of character-based terminals. These terminals were connected
to terminal concentrators that were able to aggregate a number of users for
ease of communications with the computer the Unix operating system was
running on. TCP/IP had not been implemented and the Internet was in its
earliest planning stages.

Since its inception, Unix, because of its kernel design was able to be ported
to a number of different computer platforms from a variety of computer
manufacturers. Later, the operating system program was emulated and offered
by other software vendors and computer manufacturers. The discussion
in this section will cover the basics to get a Unix-based computer onto a

TCP/IP network. Since these are usually specialized computers from many manufacturers, it would be difficult to get into specifics for all the variations and iterations, so consider this a familiarization with the requirements to make a Unix-based computer network-able.

Unix is a flat file operating system, which basically means that most of the configuration files are in readable text. Configuration is accomplished using one of the resident text processor programs that are part of the utilities that come with the operating system. The appropri-

> **RANDOM BONUS DEFINITION**
>
> trap — A message that originates from a network management client to a network management server to notify the server of a notable event.

ate files can be edited as needed to configure the TCP/IP settings on the computer. Usually, systems of this vintage have system administrators who maintain and update the /etc/hosts[22] file. The information that needs to be modified includes the following:

- The host name
- The IP address assigned to the interface
- The subnet mask being used for the network segment the computer resides on
- The IP address of the DNS server that is going to be used
- The default gateway that is residing on the same network segment as the computer

The version of Unix you are working with will determine which files and syntax of commands will need to be used. Luckily, most iterations of Unix have resident help in the form of the *man pages*. These pages are an online manual and the common syntax is man <command>, where <command> is the command you need help with. You will be informed if the command does not exist. When in doubt, issue the man command and you will get a complete description of the command along with the various switches that are used by the command.

Newer versions of Unix come with configuration utility programs that assist with the network settings and configuration. Edits of the related network files are automated for ease of use, but essentially it performs the same edits that an administrator can do with a text editor.

---

[22]The Unix /etc directory contains configuration files for devices connected to the computer. The hosts file aids in host name to IP address resolution. For further information on the Unix directory structure, including the full contents of the /etc directory, consult the operating manual supplied with your Unix system.

The following are a few useful commands for troubleshooting network issues on a Unix computer:

- `arp` — Displays a table that shows the IP address to physical MAC address relation for nodes on the same subnet with the Unix computer. This is useful when there are connectivity issues between the Unix computer and that host. If there is an `arp` entry for the problem node, there is a possible Physical layer issue.

  ```
  arp -a
  ```

- `ping` — An important troubleshooting command that helps to determine that the TCP/IP stack is configured properly on the Unix computer, that the network interface is configured properly, that the default gateway is reachable, and that domain name services are configured properly.

  ```
  ping 127.0.0.1
  ```

  If no response is received, you need to verify that TCP/IP services have been loaded and are running on the Unix computer.

  ```
  ping <address of default gateway>
  ```

  If no response is received, verify that TCP/IP has been bound to the NIC. Check that the operating system has been configured properly as far as the NIC's hardware address and the proper interrupt request number. If the operating system is configured properly, check for a Physical layer issue.

  ```
  ping <address on another subnet>
  ```

  This verifies that the subnet mask has been properly set in the TCP/IP configuration and that the request is sent to the default gateway correctly. If no response it received, check set-

ACRONYM ALERT

SMTP — Simple Mail Transport Protocol

  tings to verify that the default gateway is set correctly in the TCP/IP parameters after you were successful in pinging the default gateway.

  ```
  ping <Internet hostname>[23]
  ```

  This will verify that the DNS service is correctly configured on the TCP/IP stack. If no response is received, attempt to ping the configured DNS server using its IP address. If no reply is received, there may be a connectivity issue. Repeat the ping test to the default gateway. If that passes, verify the settings in the TCP/IP configuration.

---

[23]Internet host name is the fully qualified domain name (FQDN) of the host server you are attempting to reach. An example of a FQDN for a host name would be www.google.com.

- `netstat` — A network status command that will display status and information on the network interfaces[24] configured on the Unix computer.

  The following are some switches that can be used with the `netstat` command:

  - `-a` — Displays information on all interfaces.

  - `-i` — Displays configuration information.

  - `-n` — Displays IP addresses.

  - `-r` — Displays routing table information.

- `ifconfig` — Used to display information on the interfaces that are found on the Unix computer. These interfaces can be Ethernet or other types of interfaces.

- `route` — Used to add static routes to the Unix computer's routing table.

- `traceroute` — A useful tool to show the nodes an echo request[25] needs to pass through to reach its intended target. The target address may be either a numeric address or an alphanumeric Internet host name.

> **POP QUIZ**
>
> Which command can be used to verify the TCP/IP stack has been properly configured on a Unix computer?

```
traceroute <address>
```

4.3.2 Linux

Linux[26] has many similarities and commonalities to Unix. However, it was designed more for the desktop environment even though it will run on larger computers. The number of Linux variations is too many to mention, and each has its own piece of window dressing when it comes to configuration. Similar to Unix, Linux can be configured with a text editor, if necessary.

The variables that are configured are part of a script that is loaded each time a Linux computer is booted. Therefore, changes in network configuration would require a reboot so that these scripts can be executed with the new variables

---

[24]Network interfaces on a computer can be of the LAN variety (NICs) or interfaces for WANs, such as a WAN card for a T1 line.

[25]Echo request is part of the ICMP protocol primarily utilized by the `ping` command. The ICMP components of a `ping` command are `echo request` (the ping to a target IP address) and `echo reply` (a successful response from that target). `traceroute` uses these components to verify the path by receiving and logging the network nodes that the `echo` request passed through on its way to the target IP address.

[26]One of the Unix-like operating systems.

in place. The Linux distribution being used will determine the name of the script. In some distributions, the script responsible for initializing the kernel for networking may have the name `rc.inet1`, whereas the script that starts the networking services may be named `rc.inet2`. Again, the distribution and vintage of Linux being used may cause these file names to be totally different. You should consult the documentation for your Linux version prior to configuring or making network changes on the Linux computer.

The networking information for the kernel runtime can be accessed and displayed through the `/proc` file system. The `/proc` file system is usually mounted when the computer is first booted. If it is not mounted, there will be a message stating that `procfs` is not supported by the kernel. If this is the case, the kernel will need to be recompiled with `procfs` support enabled.

Most Linux distributions come with a set of binaries[27] containing all the applications and utilities needed for networking support. These applications and utilities may change from time to time with updates to the kernel and the networking utilities. These updates and applications need to be recompiled in order to be used as part of the Linux operating system.

The following are a few of the basic networking configuration and monitoring commands:

- `hostname` — Sets the name of the computer entered in the `/etc/hosts` file.

  `hostname <name of the computer>`

- `ifconfig` — Allows the interface to be available to the kernel networking layer. This command is normally a portion of the network initialization script that is executed at system boot-up.

  `ifconfig <interface> <assigned IP address>`

- The first interface required to be activated is the loopback interface.[28] The following `ifconfig` command configures this interface:

  `ifconfig lo 127.0.0.1`

---

[27]Binary files are programs that have already been compiled for the system the program is to be executed on. Since Linux can run over many various platforms, application programs need to be compiled on the computer to execute properly. To save users time, many Linux OS providers have already compiled these programs for the platform they are and are considered to be included binaries with the operating system. An example of different platforms would be those that are built around the Intel family of microprocessors versus those computers that have been designed and built using the Motorola 68000 microprocessor family.

[28]The loopback interface on a computer is a logical network interface which will allow for testing of applications requiring network connectivity. Using this adapter permits the testing of those applications even though the computer is not connected to a network. An example of this would be a computer that is running as a web server testing itself by launching a web browser and navigating to the loopback IP address of 127.0.0.1. The web browser will bring up the server's own home page. A less sophisticated use is in checking the IP stack of the computer by pinging the IP address 127.0.0.1. If no response is returned, there is a problem with the IP stack of that computer.

The following entry in the host table is inserted upon execution of this command:

```
localhost 127.0.0.1
```

> **RANDOM BONUS DEFINITION**
>
> wire speed — The maximum frame and data rate that is supported on a given interface.

Configuration of an Ethernet interface is accomplished using the following command:

```
ifconfig eth0 <interface address> netmask <interface subnet mask>
```

Status of an Ethernet interface can be obtained by executing the following command:

```
ifconfig eth0
```

- route — Used to add or delete routes from the kernel's routing table.

```
route [add | del] [-net | -host] target [if]
```

  - add — Adds a route.
  - del — Removes a route.
  - -net — Specifies it is a network route.
  - -host — Specifies a host address.
  - target — Specifies the address of either the network or host.
  - if — Specifies the network interface the route should be directed to (optional).

  To add a default gateway, execute the following command:

```
route add default gw <address of gateway node>
```

- netstat — As in Unix, a useful command to verify the operation and status of the Linux network components.

```
netstat [-nr, -i, -ta]
```

  - -nr — Displays the kernel's route table with IP addresses displayed in dotted numerical notation.
  - -i — Displays interface statistics for currently configured network interfaces.
  - -ta — Displays a list of both active and passive TCP sockets. This command option can also be modified to also show UDP (-u), RAW (-w), and Unix sockets (-x).

- arp — Displays the kernel's ARP table.

```
arp -a
```

Linux is a very robust and feature-rich operating system that is under constant development and improvement. The commands in this section are just a beginning when it comes

> **POP QUIZ**
>
> True or false: The name Linux is a derivative of the words Unix lite.

to Linux. Much more investigation is required, and the information that is available from a wide range of sources is beyond the scope of this section and book.

4.3.3   Sun Solaris

Sun Microsystems initially developed the Solaris operating system for their Sun SPARC workstations. It has been ported to X86 Intel-based computers and is distributed and supported by Sun Microsystems. Like Linux, it has similarities and commonalities with the Unix operating system. The latest release of Sun's operating system is Solaris 10.

Although Solaris-based workstations are capable of operating in a standalone (not networked) environment, the operating system provides strong networking tools to allow it to be interconnected not only to the local LAN but the Internet.

Solaris does provide a number of installation programs that will configure the built-in installations.

Enabling a network interface on a Solaris computer requires the following actions:

1. Install device drivers.
2. Reboot to reconfigure the system.
3. Assign an IP address on the interface.
4. Create a hosts file entry to map the IP address to the host name.
5. Configure the interface to pass traffic.

The IP address is assigned to an interface when the IP address is entered into the hostname file located in the `/etc` directory. As with Unix and Linux, this can be accomplished with the use of a text editor.

An interface is configured to allow IP traffic with the use of the `ifconfig` command. The command can also be issued to verify the operation of an interface and to monitor its health. Issuing the `ifconfig -a` command displays all active interfaces on the computer. Incorrect configuration of an interface will result in an error message being returned stating "no such interface." To enable an interface, issue the following command:

```
/usr/bin/ifconfig eri0 up
```

To verify connectivity over TCP/IP with other hosts on the network, issue the following command, which will display the kernel's ARP table:

```
arp -a
```

The flags that can be returned in the ARP table are as follows:

- P — Indicates a published address
- s — Indicates a static address
- U — Indicates an unresolved address
- M — Indicates a mapped address for multicast

Solaris allows for manual tuning of protocol transmission parameters for increased performance. This can be accomplished with the use of the ndd command. Using ndd parameter options for TCP, UDP, IP, and ARP will display a list of parameter values related to that particular protocol. An example of this would be the issuing of the command ndd /dev/tcp \? to display a list of all the parameters that are currently related to TCP.

ACRONYM ALERT

SRT — Source route/transparent bridge

Like Unix and Linux, Solaris uses the netstat command to display network statistics and to verify the operational status of network interfaces.

netstat is capable of displaying the following statistics:

- Data collection by protocol type
- Statistics grouped by node address, which may be IPv4, IPv6, or Unix-based
- Data related to DHCP
- Multicast grouped interface data
- Details of the routing table
- Data associated to STREAMS[29]
- State and status of all IP interfaces
- State of all active logical and physical interfaces, routes, and sockets

netstat can display protocol statistics for packets of the following types: TCP, UDP, RAWIP, IPv4, IPv6, ICMPv4, ICMPv6, and IGMP. Each of these

---

[29]STREAMS is a flexible programming model used for Unix communications services. It allows for the definition of standard interfaces for character input and output both within the kernel and between the kernel and the rest of the Unix system. It is a collection of system calls, kernel resources, and kernel routines.

packet types has specific parameters associated with it. Generally they display the total number of packets in and out and those that are in error. When monitored, these counters can be used to point out possible problem areas.

Issuing a `netstat -m` command will display the system calls, standard libraries, and kernel associated with writing network applications that use the STREAMS package. Additional details on this function can be obtained by reading the man page for the `streamio` command.

Sun Solaris version 10 can be obtained free of charge from the download section of the Sun Microsystems web page. A version with documentation can be ordered directly from Sun for a nominal charge. If you are interested in learning more about the configuration and maintenance of a Sun system, the X86 version can be loaded on any i86 Intel microprocessor-based computer.

> **POP QUIZ**
>
> List some of the Solaris network commands that are similar to those found in Unix and Linux.

4.4   Chapter Exercises

1. If you have a network-capable PC, try using a few of the network utilities discussed in this chapter.

2. Open a DOS window by running `cmd` from Start, Run. Enter the command `ipconfig` and note what is displayed.

3. Issue the command `ipconfig /all` and note what is displayed.

4. If your network allows your PC to access the Internet, execute this command `tracert <insert your favorite website URL>` and hit the Return key. Note the results. You may want to repeat this with other Internet addresses.

5. To display information about all the interfaces on a Unix computer, which command would need to be issued?

6. What is used on the Internet to find the numeric address of a computer host that resides on the Internet?

7. True or false: Floppy disks are the fastest form of magnetic media.

8. True or false: AT&T is the sole provider for the Unix operating system.

9. Can you name at least one Linux distribution?

10. If a microprocessor designer wanted to allow his newest chip design to access a greater amount of memory space, what might he do to accomplish this?

4.5   Pop Quiz Answers

1. What function does an arithmetic logic unit (ALU) provide?

    The ALU performs mathematical operations on the data it is presented with.

2. Would it be advisable to cycle power to the computer while a ROM upgrade is in process?

    No.

3. True or false: The information contained within RAM is saved when the computer is powered off.

    False.

4. When a computer is first powered on, the first device it is most likely to read its initial instructions from is the *ROM*.

5. Name a device that you may find connected to a serial port.

    Generally serial devices are slow data rate devices such as keyboards, modems, pointing devices, scanners, etc. However, with the development of Universal Serial Bus (USB) high-speed serial ports, devices such as hard disk drives and printers can be used due to the increased data rates on these ports.

6. What is the acronym for a user interface that uses a point-and-click method of executing computer commands?

    Graphical user interface (GUI)

7. Name two network operating systems that are prominent in today's networking world.
    - Novell Netware
    - Microsoft Windows networking

8. What can be shared using Windows file sharing?
    - Drives
    - Directories
    - Subdirectories

9. Which printers connected to a network-connected computer can be shared with other users on the network?

    All of the ones designated for sharing.

10. Which command can be used to verify the TCP/IP stack has been properly configured on a Unix computer?

    ```
    ping 127.0.0.1
    ```

11. True or false: The name Linux is a derivative of the words Unix lite.

    False — The correct answer is Unix-like.

12. List some of the Solaris network commands that are similar to those found in Unix and Linux.

    - `netstat`

    - `ping`

    - `traceroute`

The TCP/IP Protocol Suite

I dwell in Possibility.
Emily Dickinson

TCP/IP is the name that refers to the group of protocols that it encompasses. This group of protocols is known as the *TCP/IP protocol suite*. It's called TCP/IP because of the two main protocols that are part of the group: TCP and IP. The TCP/IP protocol suite is also known as the *Internet protocol suite*, as TCP/IP is pretty much the backbone of the Internet (and the majority of all networks out there).

There are many good books that cover the TCP/IP protocol suite. Some of these are multivolume, so that might give you an idea of the amount of information that is covered in the standard. TCP/IP can be considered the most widely used standard of the Internet, much as Ethernet is the dominant LAN standard. In addition to multiple standards, TCP/IP also includes any applications, tools, and transmission media used in the network to pass datagrams. As a matter of fact, RFC 1180, "A TCP/IP Tutorial," states that the term *internet technology* is more appropriate than *TCP/IP* when defining the purpose of the standard.

As we discussed in Chapter 1, "Introduction to Networking," the processes and standards contained in the TCP/IP protocol suite are mapped to one of four layers.[1] These layers are based on the four-layer model of DARPA. Every layer within the TCP/IP reference model is cross-referenced to the seven-layer OSI reference model.

The TCP/IP protocol suite allows data communication to take place. No matter what the node is, who it was made by, which operating system software

---

[1] Or five layers, depending on what school of thought one follows.

is running, and where the node is located, TCP/IP makes it work. TCP/IP has kept up with the tremendous growth that the Internet (as well as networks in general) has experienced. The possibilities seem endless and may very well be. The quote we selected for this chapter really is appropriate for the TCP/IP protocol suite because anyone involved with any facet of the TCP/IP protocol suite should always dwell in the possibilities.

This chapter covers the more well-known protocols and functions that make up TCP/IP. What do these technologies and standards do? What layer of the TCP/IP reference model does each fall into and why? What are the differences among IPv4, IPv6, and IPng? These are just a few questions that will be answered in the pages to come.

5.1   The TCP/IP Layers

Developers of networking protocols adhere to a layered approach. Each layer is responsible for a different portion of the data communication that is occurring at any time. There are many protocols that are part of the TCP/IP protocol suite. Each protocol functions within a layer of the TCP/IP model, depending on its function. Figure 5-1 shows an example of the TCP/IP model, how it corresponds to the OSI model, and some of the more well-known protocols that are served at each layer.

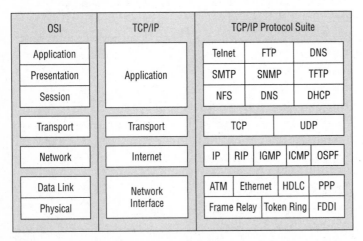

Figure 5-1 TCP/IP reference model layering

The layers in the TCP/IP reference model roughly correspond to one or more layers of the OSI reference model. Protocols of the upper layers can focus on the layer they are a member of, without concerning themselves with the functions performed by the lower levels. This is huge during the development of the protocol, as it enables developers to focus on the development at each layer, rather than worrying about an all-encompassing standard. The layers of the TCP/IP reference model and their responsibilities are as follows:

- **Network Interface layer** — The Network Interface layer corresponds to the Physical and Data Link layers of the OSI reference model. This layer is also often referred to as the *Link* layer or the *Data Link* layer. The Network Interface layer is responsible for the device drivers and hardware interfaces that connect a node to the transmission media.

- **Internet layer** — The Internet layer corresponds to the Network layer of the OSI reference model. This layer is also known as the *Network layer*. The Internet layer is responsi-

> **RANDOM BONUS DEFINITION**
>
> uplink port — Any switch port that is designed to connect to a backbone switch or network.

ble for the delivery of packets through a network. All routing protocols (RIP, OSPF, IP, etc.) are members of this layer. Nodes that perform functions at this layer are responsible for receiving a datagram, determining where to send it to,[2] and then forwarding it toward the destination. When a node receives a datagram that is destined for the node, this layer is responsible for determining the forwarding method for information in the packet. Finally, this layer contains protocols that will send and receive error messages and control messages as required.

- **Transport layer** — The Transport layer corresponds to the Transport layer of the OSI reference model. Two primary protocols operate at this layer: Transmission Control Protocol (TCP), and the User Datagram Protocol (UDP). This layer serves the Application layer and is responsible for data flow between two or more nodes within a network.

- **Application layer** — The Application layer corresponds to the Application, Presentation, and Session layers of the OSI reference model. Users initiate a process that will use an application to access network services. Applications work with protocols at the Transport layer in order to pass data in the form needed by the transport protocol chosen. On the receiving end, the data is received by the lower layers and passed up to the application for processing for the destination end user. This layer concerns itself with the details of the application and its process, and not so much about the movement of data. This is what separates this upper layer from the lower three layers.

---

[2]Based on the IP address that is assigned to the destination network or node.

The design of the TCP/IP model was based on the original Department of Defense network model. The act of layering network protocols is known as *protocol layering*. Protocol layering ensures that data sent by one layer on the source side is the same data received at that layer on the destination side. This layered principle allows focus to remain on the functions of protocols at the layer and ensure that the data matches on each end.

Most applications will use the client/server method of communication. One of the host nodes will act as the server, and the other as a client. Each layer will use a protocol or a group of protocols to transfer readable data from the source layer to the peer layer on the destination side.

Figure 5-2 shows an example of which protocols would be involved to transfer an e-mail message from a source to a destination.

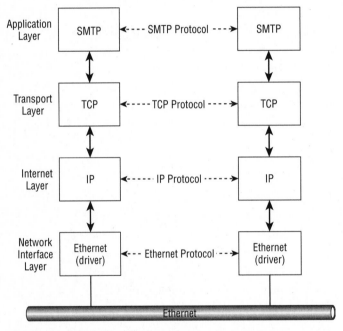

Figure 5-2 TCP/IP layering in action

As you can see, a user on one side of a communication session initiates an e-mail to be sent to the user on the destination side of the session. The Application layer protocol that is used in this process is the *Simple Mail Transfer Protocol (SMTP)*. SMTP will use TCP as the Transport layer protocol, IP as the Internet layer protocol, and then use the Ethernet interfaces at the Network Interface layer to send the data to the media for transport to the other end. This works exactly the same way when there are multiple networks in the mix (see Figure 5-3).

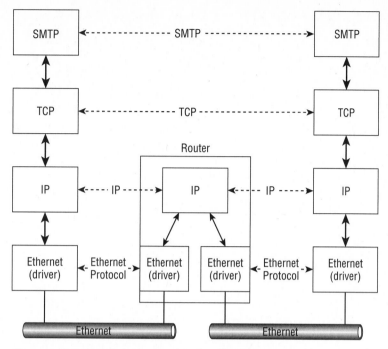

Figure 5-3 TCP/IP layering in multiple networks

In this example, a router is connecting two different networks.[3] Notice that the layers on each end, even though they are not local, are still able to recognize information from their respective peers, as though they are on the same segment. There you have it. That is how the layered model works. The next section discusses many of the protocols that make up the TCP/IP protocol suite.

5.2   Popular TCP/IP Protocols

Now that you know the principles of protocol layering and how it relates to the TCP/IP protocol suite, it's time to discuss the various protocols that operate at each layer. There are many more protocols that are part of the TCP/IP protocol suite. This section covers some of the more widely known (and used) protocols in use in many networks today.

---

[3]That's the really nice thing about a router. It does not care what type of network it connects to. It can be Token Ring, Ethernet, or many others. The layers don't realize any of this as long as they can talk to their peer.

5.2.1   The Application Layer

A lot of applications are supported by nodes that run TCP/IP. Many of these are commonly included with the operating system software running on the node. If they are not built into an operating system, these applications can readily be found on the Internet, often free of charge. The Application layer is not concerned with the movement of data from one point to another on a network. Its only concern is the details of the application to ensure that what goes out is what is interpreted on the other end. The following protocols are discussed in this section:

- Domain Name System
- Simple Network Management Protocol
- File Transfer Protocol
- Trivial File Transfer Protocol
- Simple Mail Transfer Protocol
- Network File System
- Telecommunications Network Protocol
- Secure Shell

5.2.1.1   Domain Name System

A domain name is simply the name assigned to a node on a network. It is also the name that is assigned as a host name for a given URL on the Internet. For example, if you want to go to the Cable News Network (CNN) website, you would open a web browser application (for example, Firefox, Internet Explorer, etc.) and initiate an HTTP session for the domain name that is assigned to CNN:[4]

```
http://www.cnn.com
```

In the example, cnn.com is the domain name that you want to reach because you know that is the domain name for the CNN website. So, why is DNS important? Well, instead of a direct answer to that question, let's answer it this way: What is the IP address for the CNN website? If you know

ACRONYM ALERT

AFP — AppleTalk Filing Protocol

---

[4]This example was probably too simple, so don't get fooled into thinking that any website you want to go to will have a domain name that matches the site. It depends whether that domain name is owned by someone else and, if it is, whether the owner is willing to sell the domain name. During the initial Internet boom, a lot of people had the foresight to buy popular domain names and later sold them for a lot of money.

that one, you really are doing well, but most likely you do not know the CNN website's IP address. If you have access to a computer that supports TCP/IP, you can find out what the address is. Open up a command-line session and initiate a `ping` to the domain name, and you will be able to see the IP address assigned to the domain name. Here is a `ping` that was run to the `cnn.com` domain name and the IP address that was returned:

```
C:\>ping cnn.com

Pinging cnn.com [64.236.16.20] with 32 bytes of data:

Reply from 64.236.16.20: bytes=32 time=88ms TTL=51
Reply from 64.236.16.20: bytes=32 time=88ms TTL=51
Reply from 64.236.16.20: bytes=32 time=87ms TTL=51
Reply from 64.236.16.20: bytes=32 time=87ms TTL=51

Ping statistics for 64.236.16.20:
    Packets: Sent = 4, Received = 4, Lost = 0 (0% loss),
Approximate round trip times in milli-seconds:
    Minimum = 87ms, Maximum =  88ms, Average =  87ms
```

As you can see in the example, the IP address assigned to the CNN website is 64.236.16.20. Once you know the IP address, you can put that number where you would normally enter the URL in your web browser, and it should bring up the site.

The need for DNS is simple. Humans speak in words, whereas computers speak in numbers. Bits and bytes are all the computers understand. This is why a node has to be assigned a number.[5] Sure, humans can learn numbers and use them as well, but it would probably take a lot of conditioning to remember all the numbers in IP addresses that are assigned to nodes in networks worldwide.[6]

DNS is a database that maps host names to IP addresses. The database is referred to as a *distributed database*, as DNS information is distributed among several servers. Each server will maintain the DNS information that is assigned the server to serve to clients within its own network. DNS uses the client/server model, and the protocol itself provides the facility for the servers to share this information with authorized clients.

> **RANDOM BONUS DEFINITION**
>
> store-and-forward — A mode of switch operation where frames are completely received before they are forwarded onto any of the output ports of the device.

---

[5]Remember back when we couldn't send an e-mail to Brother Joel?

[6]Are you kidding? Jim has a hard enough time just remembering how old he is.

DNS names are organized hierarchically,[7] with an unnamed root at the top, then what are known as *top-level domain* (TLD) names next, followed by *second-level domain,* and, finally, one or more subdomains. The names assigned to nodes in the DNS hierarchical tree are often referred to as *labels.* This organized hierarchy is known as the *DNS namespace.* The DNS namespace sets the rules for how the labels are organized in the domain name. Figure 5-4 shows an example of the DNS namespace.

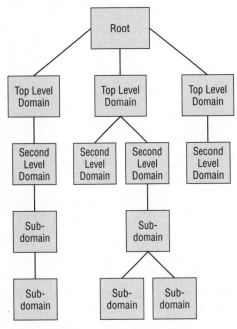

Figure 5-4 DNS namespace hierarchy

The DNS namespace hierarchy requires a different administrator on each level. This ensures that the administration of a particular branch in the DNS tree does not become too cumbersome. At each level of the namespace, there is an administrative authority that provides updates to the database. The delegation of authority should ensure that no level of the namespace becomes too hard to manage.

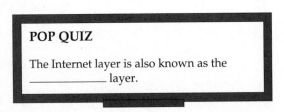

POP QUIZ

The Internet layer is also known as the _____ layer.

---

[7]There is that word again.

Authorities at each level must ensure the DNS server is updated as required. Whenever there is a new node added into the network, the authority adds this to the database. Any removed nodes are required to be updated as well. Not keeping up with these can cause real headaches to end users as well as additional traffic on the network. DNS servers are normally installed in a redundant fashion. Updates are made to the primary server and then are synchronized with the secondary server.[8] This ensures there is not a complete failure of DNS services should the primary server fail.

So, let's see this in action, shall we? We are going to assume there is a company that sells widgets and has decided to use DNS resolution so that end users don't have to remember all of the IP addresses they have to access. DNS name syntax for this company could be:

```
widgets.co
```

In this example, `co` is the top-level domain name, and `widgets` is the second-level domain name. Notice that in between `widgets` and `co` is a period (.), which is called a *dot*. The DNS name `widgets.co` would be pronounced *widjits-dot-see-oh*. Pay attention to the dot that separates the levels within the domain name structure. In any name, the dot separates the levels. You can quickly identify the TLD when you run out of dots.

ACRONYM ALERT

μs — Microseconds

Now, let's assume there is an additional subdomain level, and an authority has been assigned to assign names to nodes within the particular department (Payroll, Production, Planning, and Sales) nodes. The namespace would be updated to reflect this (see Figure 5-5), and the name syntax for each could be[9] as follows:

```
payroll.widgets.co
production.widgets.co
planning.widgets.co
sales.widgets.co
```

The Internet Assigned Numbers Authority (IANA) is responsible for maintaining the DNS *root zone* and is the authority for domain names, IP addresses, and other parameters as well as appointing the authorities that sponsor them.

---

[8]The synchronization is handled by the secondary server. The secondary server will query the primary periodically to see if there are any updates and, if so, will perform the update to its record.

[9]The authority for the level can assign almost anything that he wants. Normally the name would reflect some identification that reflects the users it serves. The name must be 63 characters or less; other than that, the sky is the limit.

Sometimes the top-level domain names are specific for a particular group or organization. For instance, the top-level domain name for the country of France is .fr.[10]

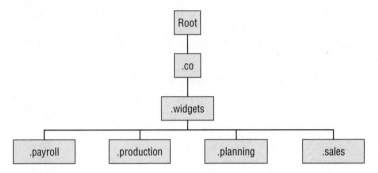

Figure 5-5 An example of the hierarchical tree structure for the widgets.co domain

Sometimes the top-level domain is not really assigned to a particular purpose and therefore is generic in nature. These types of domain names are called *generic top-level domains* (gTLD). Some of the more well-known gTLDs are

- **.biz** — restricted for use by businesses
- **.com** — intended for use by commercial organizations
- **.edu** — postsecondary educational institutions
- **.gov** — restricted for use by the United States federal, state, and local governments.
- **.jobs** — for sites related to employment
- **.mil** — the United States Military
- **.net** — miscellaneous[11]
- **.org** — miscellaneous organizations

5.2.1.2   Simple Network Management Protocol

Today's networks are no longer the shared media environments they once were. As you learned in Chapter 3, "Network Hardware and Transmission Media," a lot of different nodes are deployed in the networks of today. More often than not, there is traffic sharing between nodes and multiple protocols that regulate the flow of data in the network. All this growth requires a way to keep track of what is going on within the network.

[10]Which is basically the country code.
[11]This domain was originally intended for large network infrastructure support centers.

Determining traffic patterns to ensure that the network keeps up with end-user demands is not an option; it is a necessity if the network is to live to its full potential. Having the ability to monitor the network[12] for any problems that may occur and

---

RANDOM BONUS DEFINITION

protocol — A set of algorithms, communication formats, and processes used in the process of data transmission in a network.

---

getting notification when a problem has arisen is just as (if not more so) important.

Once again, the technology opened up for the development of a protocol that would do these things. That protocol is the Simple Network Management Protocol (SNMP). SNMP is a protocol that runs between an SNMP *manager* and an SNMP *client*, also known as an SNMP *managed system*, for the purpose of sharing management information pertaining to the managed system. Software that runs on the managed system used to communicate system information with the SNMP manager is known as the *SNMP agent*. The information that is shared is determined by the information (known as *managed objects*) set in the management information base (MIB).[13]

Communication between an SNMP manager and an SNMP agent is handled in two directions. The SNMP manager can query the SNMP agent for system information, or the SNMP agent can report information to the SNMP manager. There are five Protocol Data Unit (PDU) types that are exchanged between an SNMP manager and an SNMP agent.[14] These are the GetRequest, GetNextRequest, SetRequest, GetResponse, and Trap. The GetRequest, GetNextRequest, and SetRequest are all PDUs that are sent from the SNMP manager to the SNMP agent. The GetResponse and Trap are sent from the SNMP agent to the SNMP manager (see Figure 5-6).

We discuss these in more detail in Sections 5.2.1.2.1 and 5.2.1.2.3.

5.2.1.2.1   SNMP Managers

The SNMP manager is a workstation that is running SNMP manager software. In some environments, the SNMP manager function is shared by more than one manager, so the resources of one device are not completely consumed trying to monitor the nodes in its charge. System failover is another reason why you may want to have multiple managers in your network.

---

[12]In a proactive manner.

[13]You will often hear people refer to the management information base as "the MIBs."

[14]An easy way to remember who is responsible to send what message type is to remember that the *requests* are sent by the SNMP manager to the SNMP agent, *requesting* information. That leaves only the SNMP response, which are the responses by the SNMP agent to requests that were sent by the SNMP manager, and a trap, which is notification of a problem.

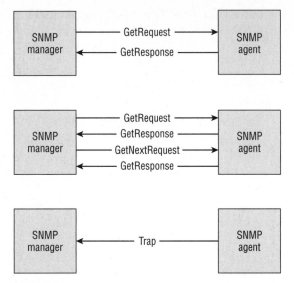

Figure 5-6 An example of SNMP's five PDUs in action

SNMP managers normally output audible alarms and also color-coded reporting in real time. SNMP managers enable you set the protocols and nodes that you want to keep an eye on.

Information that is sent from the SNMP manager to the SNMP agents can be one of three message types:

- **GetRequest** — This message type is a request by the SNMP manager for information pertaining to a variable within a particular managed object.

- **GetNextRequest** — This message type is used to retrieve information that is contained in subsequent requests for information pertaining to a managed object. This helps speed up the retrieval process as the SNMP manager does not have to send a GetRequest for each variable needed.

- **SetRequest** — This message type is used by the SNMP manager to make a change to a variable within a managed object.

5.2.1.2.2 SNMP Managed Devices

An SNMP managed device is any network node that has SNMP agent software running on it for the purposes of network management.

ACRONYM ALERT

UTP — Unshielded twisted pair

5.2.1.2.3 SNMP Agents

The SNMP agent is the software that runs on the SNMP managed device. This software is what allows the managed device to release system information to the SNMP manager. The information to be monitored is set by the SNMP manager and is known as the *managed objects*. Some of the information that can be gathered is port failure, traffic patterns, network unreachable, protocol failures, and many other things.

Information that is sent from the SNMP agent to the SNMP manager can be one of two message types:

- **GetResponse** — This message type is a response to the requests that are sent by the SNMP manager. This can be anything from a value of a variable for a managed object to an error response (for example, if there is no value or if the SNMP agent does not recognize the managed object that the SNMP manager is requesting information about).

- **Trap** — This message type is used by the SNMP agent to report a change of state for a managed object, as well as reporting errors. Some examples of errors that may be reported by the SNMP agent include

  - Link up — The link is up and operational.

  - Link down — The link is down.

  - Cold start — To start a node from the beginning (i.e., a reboot).

  - Warm start — To resume from where a process had left off.

  - OSPF neighbor state changes — In IP routing, the process of learning OSPF topology changes.

  - Authentication failures — Data that is received that cannot be authenticated or verified.

  - Hardware failures — The issue is caused by a problem with hardware.

  - Traffic bursts — The transfer of large amounts of data, without interruption, to a destination node.

5.2.1.2.4   Management Information Base

A management information base (MIB) is a database that contains manageable objects and variables of these objects pertaining to a network node, for the purpose of node management within a network. SNMP itself is not able to define details for the information it retrieves; that is what a MIB is there for.

The reason to keep MIBs and SNMP as separate standards is simple. This allows the management station to monitor multiple nodes, many with a different set of MIBs specific to the node. A MIB is configurable and can be updated. If a node is upgraded to support new and/or approved standards, the MIBs can be updated on the manager to match what is available on the agent.

The formal language used by SNMP is *Abstract Syntax Notation 1* (ASN.1, pronounced *A-S-N-dot-one*). ASN.1 specifies how information can be mapped so it can be readable by humans and data nodes as well. The purpose of this encoding of data is

RANDOM BONUS DEFINITION

half duplex — A communication mode where a device can either transmit or receive data across a communications channel, but not at the same time.

to assign names and variables contained within a MIB to a standard so they can be precisely read and recorded by administrators as well as SNMP supported nodes. A subset of ASN.1 is the Structure Management Information (SMI) standards, which define the relationship of MIB objects.

The MIB structure is similar to the structure that is used by DNS. It is a hierarchical tree structure with an unnamed root at the top of the tree and then levels of *object identifiers* (OID). An OID is a series of sequential integers separated by dots. The OID defines the path to the sought object. Figure 5-7 shows an example of the OID for the MIB variables.

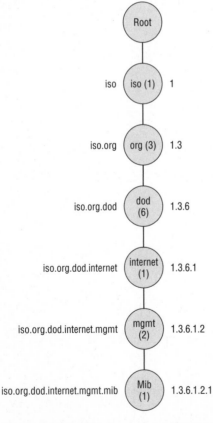

Figure 5-7 The OID structure for SNMP MIB variables

In Figure 5-7, you can see the OID string on the right side of the tree and the corresponding names for each level. All MIB variables will start with `1.3.6.1.2.1`, which is assigned the named value of `iso.org.dod.internet.mgmt.mib`.

5.2.1.2.5   SNMP version 2

The Simple Network Management Protocol version 2 (SNMPv2) introduced improvements and additions to some of the areas in the original SNMP standard. These improvements include

- Improved security
- SNMP-manager-to-SNMP-manager communication
- Improved performance
- Confidential sessions
- Additional protocol support
- Improvements in the way Trap PDUs are handled

SNMPv2 also introduced two new types of PDUs. The first one is called *GetBulk-Request*, which improved on the *GetNext-Request* PDU by giving the SNMP manager the ability to retrieve all of that consecutive data in one request instead of one request in between responses. In other words, everything is handled in one request and return

ACRONYM ALERT

TAG — Technical action group

response. The second PDU type that was introduced by SNMPv2 is *Inform*, which allows an SNMP manager to receive and reply to traps sent to and from another SNMP manager.

SNMP and SNMPv2 are not completely compatible. They use different message formats as well as handle protocols differently. There are some optional configuration strategies that will help these versions coexist within the same network. One of these optional strategies is called a *bilingual network management system*, where an SNMP manager will determine what version an agent is using and then will speak with that agent in the version the agent understands. The other strategy is through the use of a *proxy agent*, where an SNMPv2 agent can act as a middleman and translate communications between an SNMPv2 manager and an SNMP agent.

5.2.1.2.6   SNMP version 3

The Simple Network Management Protocol version 3 (SNMPv3) is considered the official standard and is the one that will be developed upon if there are any updates or enhancements needed at some point in the future.

SNMPv3 introduces some very important support for securing the access to nodes in the network and also offers remote node configuration support. SNMPv3 ensures message integrity, authentication, and encryption to assist in preventing unwanted individuals from accessing important information from traffic between the managers and the agents.

5.2.1.3   *File Transfer Protocol*

The File Transfer Protocol (FTP) provides the ability for users to access an FTP server and transfer files to and from the server. FTP is used by network nodes as well as end users for file transfer of large amounts of data.[15] FTP is a really easy protocol to use. It provides an interactive interface for end users, authenticates and provides access controls based on the authorizations that have been given to the users, and enables the system administrator to determine the format of the stored data.

The only thing that is required for file access with the FTP protocol is a node that is running FTP server software, and the users must have some sort of a client software application running on their workstations.[16] The server needs to know the user credential information. The user needs know their user ID and password, as well as the name or IP address of the FTP server.

Nodes that participate in an FTP session can be in the same building or across the world from one another. To connect to the FTP server, all you have to do is issue an `ftp` command. The following example opens an FTP session between a workstation and the widgetsinc.com FTP server. Once connected, the FTP server will print any messages that are configured on the server and then will request the login credentials.

```
% ftp widgetsinc.co
Connected to widgetsinc.co
220-FTP server ready
230- Have a great day!
230-
230-Access to this network and the information on it are the lawful
230-property of widgets.co and its employees. If you
230-are not an authorized user then you are not authorized
230-on this server.
230-User (widgetsinc.co:(none)):
```

Previously we said that FTP provides an interactive interface for end users, provides user access control, and that the format of the data stored can be of various types. Now, let's take a look at some of these functions. For the examples in the following sections, we used a Microsoft Windows PC via

---

[15]Sure, you can e-mail files too, but try to e-mail a 100 MB file.
[16]If the node is TCP/IP compliant, the utility should already be available.

the cmd.exe[17] window for all command-line operations. Additionally, there is a freeware FTP server application (Cerebus FTP server) that is available for download and supported by most Windows-based PCs. This application can be downloaded

> **RANDOM BONUS DEFINITION**
>
> full duplex — A communication mode where a device has the ability to simultaneously transmit and receive data across a communications channel.

at www.cerberusftp.com. We recommend that you use this application if you are interested in replicating some of the examples.

End users can use an FTP client application to access a node that is running the FTP server software for the purpose of either placing files on the server (with the put command), or getting files from the server (with the get command).

The directories on an FTP server can also be manipulated by the end user, provided the user had the appropriate credentials when they log in. We will talk more about user access in the next section; for now, all you need to know is that you can perform the following functions with FTP:

- Retrieve files
- Store files
- Create directories
- Remove directories
- Rename directories
- View hidden files and directories
- Issue miscellaneous commands to navigate the directory tree

ACRONYM ALERT

SA — Source address

As with any command-line structure you may come across, FTP utilizes several commands to perform tasks while in an FTP session. The command structure can vary from operating system to operating system, but the function of the command remains the same. Table 5-1 lists some of the more common FTP commands.

Keeping track of whether you are here or there is important when you are in an FTP session. Keep in mind that you will be working with files and directories on two nodes. If you are *getting* a file, you are pulling it off of the remote node and filing it away on your local node. Likewise, if you are *putting* a file, you are getting a copy of the file on your local node and saving it on the remote node.[18]

---

[17]cmd.exe is a command-line interpreter for most Windows-based systems that are in use today. It is the command that allows a user to communicate with the OS.

[18]This sounds straightforward, and it really is. It does get confusing at times when you have been working on an issue for a while and sleep deprivation sets in.

Table 5-1 Common FTP Commands

COMMAND	FUNCTION
ascii	Sets the file transfer mode to ASCII.
binary	Sets the file transfer mode to binary.
cd	Changes to another directory.
close	Terminates a connection.
delete	Removes a file.
get	Places a copy of a file on the remote node into a specified directory on the local node.
hash	Used to monitor the file transfer process. For every 1028 bytes received, a # will be placed on the screen.
help	Lists available FTP commands.
?	Gets information about commands.
ls	Lists the names of the files in the current directory.
mget	Used to copy more than one file from the remote node to the local node.
mkdir	Makes a new directory.
mput	Used to copy more than one file from the local node to the remote node.
put	Used to copy a file from the local node to the remote node.
pwd	Determine the directory path to the current directory.
quit	Terminates the FTP session.
rename	Renames a file or directory.
rmdir	Removes a directory and any subdirectories, if applicable.

Now it's time for a special treat. The following walks through the process of putting a file from the local node onto the remote node.

1. Once you have the name or IP address of the remote node (the FTP server), open up a session with the server, using an FTP client (in our case, we are using the command line). You should see some confirmation that you have connected, then the banner (if there is one) is printed, and you will be prompted to log in.

```
C:\>ftp 192.168.1.104
Connected to 192.168.1.104.
```

```
220-Access to this network and the information on it are the
220-lawful property of widgets.co and its employees. If you are
220-not an employee or an authorized user, then you are not
220-authorized to be on this server.
220
User (192.168.1.104:(none)):
```

2. Log in using the credentials that have been provided to you. Some users may have more rights on the server than other users. Most FTP server administrators also allow for anonymous logins. Anonymous logins are beneficial if you have customers, vendors, and partners you may want to share files with, but not give them full access, only access to the directories they have a need to connect to. Once you have logged in and provided the password, you will receive confirmation that you have been authorized on the server.

```
User (192.168.1.104:(none)): jedwards
331 User jedwards, password please
Password:
230 Password Ok, User logged in
```

3. Use the `ls` command to see what directories and files the current directory possesses. In the following example, note that there are two directories: ftproot and widgets.

```
ftp> ls
200 Port command received
150 Opening data connection
ftproot
widgets
226 Transfer complete
```

4. If you determine that you want to change to the widgets directory, use the `cd` command.

```
ftp> cd widgets
250 Change directory ok
```

ACRONYM ALERT

LLC — Logical Link Control

5. Use the `ls` command to see if there are any subdirectories; note the customers directory. Assume that you want change to that directory (with the `cd` command) and prepare to copy a file from our workstation to the remote node.[19]

```
ftp> ls
200 Port command received
150 Opening data connection
ftproot
```

---

[19]If you know the path name for the destination directory, you can change to that directory by listing the path (cd widgets/customers).

```
ftp> cd customers
250 Change directory ok
```

6. To verify your current directory, you can issue the pwd command.

```
ftp> pwd
257 "/widgets/customers" is the current directory
```

7. You can set the transfer mode to ASCII.[20]

```
ftp> ascii
200 Type ASCII
```

8. You can set the transfer mode to binary.

```
ftp> binary
200 Type Binary
```

9. Now put the file in the directory on the remote node. In this example, you will transfer two files: transfer.doc and transfer2.doc.

> **POP QUIZ**
>
> What is the function of the FTP command ascii?

```
ftp> put c:\transfer.doc
200 Port command received
150 Opening data connection
226 Transfer complete
ftp: 24064 bytes sent in 0.01Seconds 2406.40Kbytes/sec.

ftp> put transfer2.doc
200 Port command received
150 Opening data connection
226 Transfer complete
ftp: 24064 bytes sent in 0.00Seconds 24064000.00Kbytes/sec.
```

10. Since you transferred multiple files, you can also do this with the mput command. Take note that there is a confirmation required between files.

```
ftp> mput c:\trans*.*
mput c:\transfer.doc?
200 Port command received
150 Opening data connection
226 Transfer complete
ftp: 24064 bytes sent in 0.01Seconds 2406.40Kbytes/sec.

mput c:\transfer2.doc?
200 Port command received
150 Opening data connection
226 Transfer complete
ftp: 24064 bytes sent in 0.01Seconds 2406.40Kbytes/sec.
```

[20]ASCII is the default mode.

11. Finally, log out of the session with the `quit` command. This will close the session and display any messages, if configured.

```
ftp> quit
221 Have a great day
```

TIME FOR SOMETHING NICE TO KNOW

The `?` command and the `help` command do not require an FTP session to be established in order to run. If you type the command `ftp`, you initiate the FTP client. Once you have the FTP prompt, you can issue the `help` or `?` command to see a list of FTP commands. You can also connect to the remote node using the `open <destination name or IP address>` command. Here is an example of both these commands, and the output:

```
C:\>ftp
ftp> ?
Commands may be abbreviated. Commands are:

!            delete        literal       prompt        send
?            debug         ls            put           status
append       dir           mdelete       pwd           trace
ascii        disconnect    mdir          quit          type
bell         get           mget          quote         user
binary       glob          mkdir         recv          verbose
bye          hash          mls           remotehelp
cd           help          mput          rename
close        lcd           open          rmdir

ftp> open 192.168.1.104
Connected to 192.168.1.104.
```

5.2.1.4   Trivial File Transfer Protocol

Why waste time with a protocol that is so *trivial?*[21]

The Trivial File Transfer Protocol (TFTP)[22] is another popular file transfer program. Since the protocol uses UDP (see Section 5.2.2.2), there is less chatter than with the FTP protocol, which uses TCP (see Section 5.2.2.1). TFTP is mainly used

> **RANDOM BONUS DEFINITION**
>
> Session layer — Layer 5 of the seven-layer OSI model, responsible for process-to-process communication.

---

[21]Okay, it's a lame joke, but we could not resist.
[22]Note that not all nodes support TFTP. If a network is performing file transfer in a controlled environment, it is likely that TFTP is not used at all.

with the Bootstrap Protocol (see Section 5.3.4) to transfer node configuration files for nodes that do not have hard disk storage.[23] TFTP is also utilized to transfer files to and from network nodes for the purpose of troubleshooting, configuring, upgrading, and so on.

TFTP is a simple protocol that is small enough to be stored in a node's ROM. It requires a TFTP client and a TFTP server in order to function. Since UDP is a connectionless protocol, the TFTP server allocates different ports in order to support multiple TFTP clients at any given time. Security parameters are limited with the TFTP protocol. A system administrator can provide user access to only certain directories, but there is a potential for a security problem in the network if the TFTP sessions are not monitored and maintained.

TFTP does not have all the functions that are available with FTP. To understand why, keep in mind that TFTP is a simple file transfer protocol designed to transfer boot-up files for diskless nodes. You won't be able to browse directories, make directory changes, list files or directories, and you will be limited to the files you have been assigned.

TFTP commands are very similar to the FTP commands (keeping in mind that there are fewer options with TFTP). Table 5-2 contains a list of the most often used commands.

Table 5-2 Common TFTP Commands

COMMAND	FUNCTION
connect	Sets the remote node and/or ports for file transfer.
get	Places a copy of a file on the remote node onto a specified directory on the local node.
hash	Displays hash marks (#) to monitor file transfer progress.
mode ascii	Sets the file transfer mode to ASCII.
mode binary	Sets the file transfer mode to binary.
put	Copies a file from the local node to the remote node.
quit	Terminates the TFTP session.
rate	Displays the transfer rate information.
status	Displays relevant information about the transfer.

TFTP is connectionless. This means that a connection is not established prior to the transfer of data. When a user issues the tftp <hostname or ip

---

[23] Also known as diskless nodes or diskless systems.

address> command or the connect command, the client does not actually make a connection; rather, it buffers the information to use when it initiates the file transfer process. Following are a few TFTP command examples from a cmd.exe window:

1. To view the commands that are available in the cmd.exe command line for TFTP, you simply initiate the tftp command.

```
C:\>tftp

Transfers files to and from a remote computer running the TFTP service.

TFTP [-i] host [GET | PUT] source [destination]
```

-i	Specifies binary image transfer mode (also called octet). In binary image mode the file is moved literally, byte by byte. Use this mode when transferring binary files.
host	Specifies the local or remote host.
GET	Transfers the file destination on the remote host to the file source on the local host.
PUT	Transfers the file source on the local host to the file destination on the remote host.
source	Specifies the file to transfer.
destination	Specifies where to transfer the file.

2. To retrieve a file from the remote node and save a copy on the local node, use the get command.

```
C:\>tftp 192.168.1.104 get /widgets/Users/dns.doc
Transfer successful: 20480 bytes in 1 second, 20480 bytes/s
```

3. Finally, to place a copy of a file that is stored on a local node onto the remote node, use the put command.

```
C:\>tftp 192.168.1.104 put c:\dns.doc /widgets/Users/dns2.doc
Transfer successful: 6 bytes in 1 second, 6 bytes/s
```

It's as simple as that. Note that you have to know the full path for the file that you want to get and place on the remote node. This is because the TFTP protocol does not support directory path browsing. This makes it a little less simple than FTP, but if used mainly for transfer of files for diskless systems and system modification, it should easily serve the purpose of most networks.

5.2.1.5 *Simple Mail Transfer Protocol*

The Simple Mail Transfer Protocol (SMTP) is a protocol used for the transfers of electronic mail (e-mail) between network nodes. SMTP sets the format of e-mail from the client running on one node to a server running on another.

SMTP is not involved with the way an end user interfaces with an e-mail application or stores e-mail messages, when to check for new messages, or when to send messages, nor is it involved in determining what e-mail messages to accept or not accept on the destination node. SMTP is concerned only with how the e-mail messages are transferred across the shared medium.

SMTP works with the Post Office Protocol version 3 (POP3) and/or the Internet Message Access Protocol (IMAP), which enables e-mail messages to be stored (queued) on a server. The client periodically queries the server to check for and retrieve new messages. Without POP3 or IMAP, some messages might have a hard time reaching a destination due to the limited ability to queue data on the receiving node. In summary, POP3 and IMAP receive e-mail messages, and SMTP sends them. Many SMTP server applications include POP3 support in the same package.

Communication in SMTP is initiated by the client. The server will respond to a client query with a response code and an explanation. The server will also respond to other servers with response codes. Response codes can be used when troubleshooting e-mail transfer problems. Table 5-3 lists the server response codes and their meanings.

The client also has a set of messages that it will send to the server. There are a total of five messages used by a client to send an e-mail message. These are

- **HELO** — Used by the client to identify itself to the server

> **RANDOM BONUS DEFINITION**
>
> collision — When simultaneous transmission is attempted by two or more nodes on a shared Ethernet LAN

- **MAIL** — Identifies the end user sending the message

- **RCPT** — Identifies the end user the message is being sent to

- **DATA** — Identifies the contents of the message
- **QUIT** — Terminates the session

Table 5-3 SMTP Server Response Codes

SERVER RESPONSE CODE	EXPLANATION
220	Ready to receive mail from the client
221	Server is closing the session
250	Message sent from the server to the client informing the client that a requested action has been completed
251	Message sent from one server to another that it is forwarding mail for a user whom the server does not recognize
354	Message sent to a remote server in response to a query from that remote server about whether it can send mail
421	Server is unavailable
450	Message sent by the server to inform the client that a message could not be sent because the destination mailbox was not available
451	Message sent by the server when there is an error in processing a request; when this occurs, the request is terminated
452	Server has run out of storage space and cannot accept the message
500	Syntax error with a command
501	Syntax error with a function of a command
502	Server is not configured to support the request
503	Requests from the client are out of sequence and cannot be understood
550	Message cannot be delivered to the remote server or mailbox; if local, the mailbox is not available
551	The mailbox is not local, and the server cannot forward the message due to configuration constraints
552	User has run out of storage
553	SMTP address format is not correct
554	Request failed — no specification as to why

Following is a cleartext example of an SMTP session. We will assume that the client has already set up a connection request and is waiting for the response from the server (which is the response code 220 in the first line of the following example). The lines that begin with S: are messages from the server, and the lines that begin with a C: are messages from the client.

```
S: 220 smtp.widgets.com SMTP Service ready
C: HELO smtp.example.org
S: 250 Hello smtp.example.org, I am glad to meet you

C: MAIL FROM:<slick@example.org>
S: 250 Ok

C: RCPT TO:<blah@widgets.com>
S: 250 Ok
C: RCPT TO:<halb@widgets.com>
S: 550 That is not a valid user

C: DATA
S: 354 Input mail.  End data with <CR><LF>.<CR><LF>
C: From: "Slick Johnson" <slick@example.org>
C: To: Blah Blah Blah <blah@widgets.com>
C: Date: Thurs, 15 Jun 2008 08:02:11 -0500
C: Subject: Example
C:
C: Hey Blah!
C: I need 20,000 widgets.  Please send ASAP.
C: Sincerely,
C: Slick
C: <CR><LF>.<CR><LF>
S: 250 Ok

C: QUIT
S: 221 Bye
```

Notice how the five messages are organized in the SMTP transfer. Also, note that one of the intended recipients is not a valid user.

5.2.1.6   *Network File System*

Developed originally by Sun Microsystems, the Network File System (NFS) protocol allows end users access to files that are stored remotely as if the files were local to the end user's workstation. The original version of NFS used UDP as a transport protocol; however, with the release of NFS version 3 (NFSv3) in 1995, the protocol included transport via TCP. This made it more feasible to use NFS over a WAN, thus increasing the options available for networks that had implemented and utilized NFS.

Like all the Application layer protocols discussed so far, NFS is a client/server application. Using NFS, end users are able to view, store, update, and manage files on a remote server. All that is required is that the originating node has an *NFS client* application running and the remote node has an *NFS server* application running.

Files that are shared on the server node are *mounted*, or set as accessible, for the users in the network. Access is controlled based on the permissions or privileges that have been set for an individual user. Permissions are set based on what directories the user is authorized to access. Privileges can be read/write (user can modify the file) or read-only (user can view the file but cannot modify the file).

ACRONYM ALERT

CPU — Central processing unit

An NFS server must have some background applications running, known as *daemons*,[24] in order for the client to be able to connect to and utilize the services that are provided through the NFS protocol. Following are the daemons that need to run on the NFS server:

- **nfsd** — This is the NFS daemon, which receives and processes requests from the NFS client(s).

- **mountd** — This is the NFS mount daemon, which receives requests from nfsd and processes them.

- **rpcbind** — This is a daemon that provides a way for the NFS clients to see what ports the NFS server is using.

MORE UNIX DAEMONS

Here is a handy-dandy reference list of common Unix daemons and their functions.

◆ **dcpd** – The DHCP daemon, which allows for the dynamic configuration of TCP/IP data for nodes running the appropriate client application.

◆ **fingerd** – The finger daemon, which provides finger protocol access to the server.

◆ **ftpd** – The FTP daemon, which supports and services FTP requests from a node running the client application.

◆ **httpd** – The HTTP daemon, which provides web server support.

(continued)

---

[24]When you look at a node's file system, you can usually tell which processes are daemons. Most of these are identified with a "d" at the end of the name of the process. For instance, the *http* daemon is labeled *httpd*.

MORE UNIX DAEMONS *(continued)*

♦ **lpd** — The line printer daemon, which manages the spooling of print jobs.

♦ **nfsd** — The NFS daemon, which receives and processes requests from the NFS client(s).

♦ **ntpd** — The NTP daemon, which manages node clock synchronization.

♦ **rpcbind** — The RPC daemon, which takes care of remote call procedure conversions.

♦ **sshd** — The SSH daemon, which monitors for SSH request from an SSH client.

♦ **sendmail** — The SMTP daemon, which handles e-mail transport.

♦ **syslogd** — The system logging daemon, which logs system processes and system log messages.

♦ **syncd** — The synchronization daemon, which synchronizes file systems with system memory.

NFS is more commonly used with nodes that are running a *Unix-like*[25] operating system; however, there are many other operating systems that can use and implement NFS in an environment where it is feasible to do so.

> **RANDOM BONUS DEFINITION**
>
> hub — A central interconnection device used in a star-wired topology

Users working in an NFS environment are able to access their home directories that are stored on the NFS server from any workstation that has access to the server. This is a huge benefit, especially for users who may migrate from workstation to workstation. Another benefit of NFS implementation is workstation resource sharing (not having to fit every workstation with the entire same storage medium and software requirements).

5.2.1.7 Telecommunications Network

The Telecommunications Network (Telnet) protocol gives a user the ability to access and manage a remote node. Almost all nodes that are running TCP/IP will support the Telnet protocol. The *Telnet client* initiates a session with a node that is running the *Telnet server* application.

---

[25]Unix-like is a term that is used to identify an operating system that is similar to the original Unix operating system.

The server runs `telnetd`, which listens for a Telnet client request. Telnet is used mostly for system administration, management, and troubleshooting, but can also be used to check the status of other server types in the network.

> **POP QUIZ**
>
> What does an SMTP server response code 421 mean?

To initiate a Telnet session, issue the following command:

```
telnet <ip address or dns name>
```

If you are successful, you will either be prompted with a login prompt or you will be at the user interface for the node. It depends on the settings of the remote node. Optionally, you can initiate a Telnet session in a Windows environment by issuing the `telnet` command. This will bring you to the Microsoft Telnet prompt, where you can view a list of commands. You can also initiate your session with the `open <ip address or dns name>` command. Following is the Windows Telnet client interface:

```
C:\>telnet

Microsoft (R) Windows 2000 (TM) Version 5.00 (Build 2195)
Welcome to Microsoft Telnet Client
Telnet Client Build 5.00.99206.1

Escape Character is 'CTRL+]'

Microsoft Telnet> ?

Commands may be abbreviated. Supported commands are:

close           close current connection
display         display operating parameters
open            connect to a site
quit            exit telnet
set             set options (type 'set ?' for a list)
status          print status information
unset           unset options (type 'unset ?' for a list)
?/help          print help information
```

5.2.1.7.1   Network Virtual Terminal

Because there are so many different operating systems, it's important that a client and server can participate in a Telnet session regardless of which operating system they are running. This is done through the use of a virtual node known as a *network virtual terminal* (NVT). The NVT basically provides a way for the client to provide a mapping to the interface the end user is using, and the server will map to a terminal type that it supports. Data in the NVT environment is input to a *keyboard* and then output to a *printer*. Figure 5-8 is an example of an NVT.

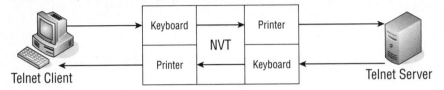

Figure 5-8 An NVT example

5.2.1.7.2 Options and Option Negotiation

If a Telnet client supports it, the client and server have the ability to negotiate the use of features known as *options* for the session. Options can be negotiated before a Telnet session is set up or at any time during the session. The following four control characters are used for option negotiation:

- **WILL** — Used when the sender wants to enable an option

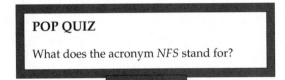

- **WONT** — Used when the sender wants to disable an option

- **DO** — Used when the sender wants the receiver to enable an option

- **DON'T** — Used when the sender wants the receiver to disable an option

Table 5-4 lists some Telnet option codes.[26]

Option negotiation can be initiated by the server and the client. Some options are specifically for a client (that is, the server doesn't have a need to request), and some are for the server.

5.2.1.7.3 Modes of Operation

Telnet servers and clients comply with one of three modes of operation:

- **Half-duplex mode** (the default) means that communication takes place in half-duplex. This in and of itself is why this mode is for the most part never used. Most nodes now support full-duplex, which means that communication cannot be handled in half-duplex

---

[26]Currently there are more than 50 option codes.

mode. In this mode, echoing is performed by the client, and the client will not transmit new data until the line that was sent previously is complete and has been received by the remote node.

Table 5-4 Option Codes

OPTION CODE	OPTION	EXPLANATION
0	Binary	Assumes that transmission is binary
1	Echo	Repeats information received
3	Suppress go ahead	Suppresses go ahead signaling
5	Status	Lists the Telnet status
6	Timing mark	Sets the timing mark
24	Terminal type	Sets the terminal type
31	Window size	Sets the window size
32	Terminal speed	Sets the terminal speed
33	Remote flow control	Sets the remote flow control
34	Line mode	Sets to line mode

- **Character mode** is a mode where only O-N-E_C-H-A-R-A-C-T-E-R at a time is transmitted. The server will provide an acknowledgment when it receives each character and the echoing is performed by the server. The client, in turn, will send an acknowledgment to the server as well.

- **Line mode** is the mode where full-duplex transmission occurs with data being transmitted a line at a time. In line mode, text that is entered by the user is echoed locally and only full lines of data are transmitted to the server. This greatly reduces the number of packets that are required to be transmitted across the network.

5.2.1.8 Secure Shell Protocol

The Secure Shell (SSH) Protocol provides a very important function that Telnet lacks: the ability to protect the integrity of the data being transmitted by supporting encrypted connections between network nodes.

SSH utilizes *public key cryptography*, which provides cryptographic keys to authenticate remote nodes and users. In public key cryptography, two keys are involved in the encryption/decryption process: the *public key*, which can be shared by multiple remote nodes, and a *private key*, which is a secret used to decrypt a corresponding public key.

Nodes that support SSH have both a public and a private key assigned to them. The private key is protected by a password, which is entered by the user. The private key corresponds with the public key, which matches

---
POP QUIZ

What is the purpose of Telnet option code 32?

---

the public key on the remote end. The remote node has a private key as well that will decrypt the information sent to a readable form for the remote user.

SSH is used primarily as an encrypted form of Telnet. With SSH, you can log in and be authenticated so the session is less vulnerable to attack than is the Telnet session. SSH also provides other functions, which makes it a very appeasable application to support in a network.

SSH servers listen for requests coming from an SSH client. The SSH daemon runs on the server node. There are many SSH variations in today's networks. The most popular ones are OpenSSH and Putty.[27] The most recent version of the SSH protocol itself is SSH version 2 (SSH-2), which has been submitted as a proposed Internet standard.

5.2.2   The Transport Layer

The next layer of the TCP/IP reference model is the Transport layer. It is the layer that accepts requests from the Application layer, and it sends requests to the Network layer. Transport protocols operate at the Transport layer. The two most popular of these protocols are the User Datagram Protocol (UDP) and the Transmission Control Protocol (TCP) at the Transport layer, both of which we introduce in this section. Chapter 9, "The Transport Layer," will discuss these in more depth.

5.2.2.1   Transmission Control Protocol

We bet you are thinking to yourself that you must have heard about this protocol before. Well, you have heard of it. At the very least you have heard it mentioned in this book, and it's a good possibility that you have heard of it if you have ever configured your computer to be

---
RANDOM BONUS DEFINITION

Media Access Control — The entity or algorithm used to arbitrate for access to a shared communications channel.

---

[27]These and many others are open source applications, which can be downloaded from many different websites. An Internet search will point you to where you can download these.

connected to a network. You may not have known what it does, but you have heard of it.

TCP is used to transport data. It ensures that data is placed in sequence (the order that it was sent in), that data arrives at its destination (or will force a retransmission if it didn't), and it helps cut down on over-traffic in the network. To give you an idea of why TCP is important, take a look at Figure 5-9.

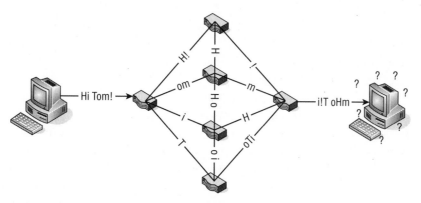

Figure 5-9 An example that proves why TCP is very helpful

In the figure, you can see that a node wants to send the message "Hi Tom!" to a remote node.[28] There are many different paths that data can take to get from the originating node to the remote node. Assuming that we are sending one character at a time, each character will take whatever path the routers tell it to take. Because the originating and the destination nodes do not know which path the data is taking, the destination node will have no way to put the data back together when it receives it, and therefore will most likely receive a jumbled mess. Note that the destination node receives all the data, but the message received is "i!T oHm," which is nothing like the originating message.[29]

TCP is a connection-oriented protocol, which means that a TCP session must be established between a TCP server and a TCP client before any data transmission occurs. Most professionals use the analogy of a telephone when explaining the meaning of connection-oriented. When you make a phone call, you wait until someone answers the other end before you say hello, hey, how's it going, or anything else that you called to say.[30] This is exactly how TCP works. An originating node will contact a destination node to make sure they

---

[28]For this example, it really does not matter what application is being used to send the message. All that is important is that you understand that the information is coming from the Application layer and is being sent to the Network layer.

[29]Can you imagine what Brother Joel might think about this message?

[30]Some phrases can be uttered that we can't mention in this book.

are available to get the message. Once confirmation is received that it is okay to send data, the transmission begins.

TCP is also considered a *reliable* protocol because there are functions built into TCP that provide for various checks and balances to ensure the integrity of the data being transmitted. Some of the reliability functions are

- TCP is able to break down data that is received from the Application layer into *segments*.

- TCP places an acknowledgment timer on sent segments. When the timer expires, if the originating node does not receive confirmation from the remote node that the segment was received, the originating node will resend the segment.

- TCP maintains a checksum (within the TCP header and within the actual data payload) that is set on each end of the connection. The checksum is used to ensure that data arrives exactly as it was sent. If the receiving node notices that the checksum does not match (invalid checksum), the receiving node will throw the segment away. In throwing the segment away, the receiver does not receive the segment. This means that the receiving node does not send an acknowledgment, which causes the originator to send it again.

- TCP datagrams are not sent in order. They traverse the network over the best path possible (based on calculations made by nodes, which we discuss in several places throughout this book). TCP supports the ability for the receiving node to put all of the datagrams back into the correct order, once they have been received.

- TCP can recognize duplicate datagrams and can discard them when received.

- TCP supports what is known as flow control. Flow control is a way for each node to know how much buffer space

> **POP QUIZ**
>
> What does the acronym *SSH* stand for?

they have available to receive data. This way no node will overwhelm the other node with more data than it can handle.

Examples of applications[31] that use TCP would be

- FTP
- Telnet

---

[31] Notice that some protocols use both TCP and UDP (DNS, for instance).

- SMTP

- DNS

- POP3

- HTTP

- DNS

- IMAP

5.2.2.2 *User Datagram Protocol*

Here is a bonus question for you. The User Datagram Protocol (UDP) is part of the Transport layer and is used to do what to data?

That's right! Just like TCP is used to transport data between nodes, UDP is also used to transport data within a network. That is about the only thing (at least functionally) that the two have in common. UDP does not guarantee that data is going to be delivered to a destination. Basically, UDP throws the data toward the destination and then moves on to its next task. This makes UDP a connectionless protocol.

UDP is usually used to send short bursts of datagrams between nodes where reliability is not a big concern. UDP can get data to a destination quicker, as it avoids all of the overhead required when all the checks and balances are occurring within TCP. Also, because UDP is connectionless, it can support *broadcasting* (sending messages to all nodes within a broadcast domain) and *multicasting* (sending messages to all nodes that are subscribed to the network).

> **RANDOM BONUS DEFINITION**
>
> operating system — The application software responsible for the proper operation of a given node.

UDP provides an optional checksum that can be assigned to the UDP header as well as the data payload. This ensures that if any data that is sent over UDP requires a header and data payload checksum, the destination is able to do so. If any error checking is required, it will normally be performed by the application, not via UDP.

Most voice and video applications transmit over UDP. If you have ever watched a video online that cut out or got choppy at times, this is because data was not being received. Recovery from these choppy moments can go unnoticed for the most part. If TCP were used in these instances, there would be delays that last much longer when packet loss is requiring retransmission of the data. Keep in mind that speed is the consideration when going with UDP, not reliability.[32]

---

[32]You can always reload that video if you want to watch it again.

Examples of protocols that use UDP include

- DNS
- BOOTP/DHCP
- TFTP
- SNMP
- RIP
- NFS

UDP accepts data (the payload) from the Application layer. It then adds a UDP header and passes the header and the payload to the Internet layer, where it is encapsulated into an IP packet and is passed on to the Network Interface layer and over the transmission medium to the destination, where it makes its way up to the Application layer on the destination end of the connection.

5.2.3   The Internet Layer

The final layer that we will be discussing in this chapter is the Internet layer. Although we will discuss this layer in detail in Chapter 10, we wanted to provide a quick overview of some Internet layer protocols.

> **POP QUIZ**
>
> Name the two popular transport protocols that we discussed in this chapter.

This layer is responsible for ensuring that there is a path to a destination. It receives information from the Transport layer and ensures transmission to the destination node. Some examples of protocols that operate at this layer include

- Internet Protocol (IP)
- Internet Group Multicast Protocol (IGMP)
- Internet Control Message Protocol (ICMP)
- Address Resolution Protocol (ARP)
- Routing Information Protocol (RIP)
- Open Shortest Path First (OSPF)
- Border Gateway Protocol (BGP)
- Internet Protocol Security (IPSec)

Although all layers of the TCP/IP reference model are important in their own right, the Internet layer is probably the most important one. It provides the ability to route data to a destination based on an IP address. It manages the IP addressing structure for a network, and it also defines the datagrams that are transported to a remote node.

5.2.3.1 *Internet Protocol*

The Internet Protocol (IP) is the most important protocol that exists within the Internet layer. IP receives data from one of the Transport layer protocols, packages it into a datagram, and then transports it to and from a given set of nodes. IP is a connectionless protocol, which means it does not establish a line of communication prior to transmitting.[33] IP is also responsible for the IP addressing for network nodes.

The network node that is responsible for getting data between different networks is a router. The router is responsible for receiving a datagram known as a *packet* and pointing the packet in the direction it needs to go, based on the IP address the packet is looking for. IP addresses are learned by the router based on information from another router or information that it has discovered as it was passing packets to and fro. The information received for the purpose of routing packets is determined, calculated, and provided for by a routing protocol. IP addresses can also be configured and set statically (hard coded), but this is a tedious task to maintain. The dynamic option is a preferred method.[34]

ACRONYM ALERT

FCS — Frame Check Sequence

Since IP is connectionless, the upper layers are responsible for any error checking. The most IP will do is drop a packet and then send a message to the source IP address telling them that the packet didn't make it to where it was supposed to go. There are many protocols that work with IP and are placed into an IP packet for transmission. Some of these include

- TCP
- UDP
- ICMP

There are a few versions of IP in use today. IP version 4 (IPv4) is the most commonly used version, but a proposed standard, IP version 6 (IPv6), is in use and

POP QUIZ

Which layer of the TCP/IP reference model is probably the most important one?

---

[33]Here is more of that repetition that we mentioned in the front matter of this book.

[34]You will find that there are times when static routes make the most sense. They can also help you get a route back up when you are troubleshooting an issue. Static routes can be your friend.

is intended to eventually be the successor to IPv4. The main difference between IPv4 and IPv6 is the addressing. IPv6 allows for more addressing flexibility, as there is room for a larger address space. Both versions will probably be around for a long time, and there are ways to ensure that they can coexist, but eventually you will probably see a migration to IPv6.

Have you ever heard of *IP Next Generation (IPng)?* IPng is nothing more than the unofficial name for IPv6. The name was coined early and replaced when the proposed standard was submitted.

5.2.3.2 *Internet Group Multicast Protocol*

The Internet Group Multicast Protocol (IGMP) is a protocol that provides support for IP multicasting. IGMP provides a way for messages to be sent to multiple nodes. Nodes are grouped into multicast groups, so when a multicast message is destined for a group, only that group will receive the message.

IGMP messages are transmitted in an IP datagram. Multicast routers (that is, routers that can support multicasting) use IGMP messages to keep track of what groups are connected to what interfaces on the router. When the operating system of the originating node initiates a program process that requires IGMP support, the node will send a report out of an interface in which the process joins the group. Processes can join groups over multiple interfaces. When there are no other processes running in a group, the node will no longer report the group.

IGMP queries are sent out by a multicast router periodically to see if anyone has a process that might belong to a multicast group. This query is sent out of every router interface. When a remote node receives an IGMP query, it will respond with one report for each group that it recognizes as having a running process.

There may be many remote nodes running processes that are tied to a multicast group. Each node is responsible for reporting process and group information. The times that these reports are sent are staggered so there are not too many nodes responding at the same time. For a router to acknowledge a multicast group, there must be at least one node that is a member of the group.

5.2.3.3 *Internet Control Message Protocol*

The Internet Control Message Protocol (ICMP) is responsible for reporting conditions that need attention. When something goes wrong with IP, TCP, or UDP transmission, ICMP is there to let you know about it. Like ICMP, TCP, and UDP, ICMP messages are transmitted within an IP datagram.

Two versions of ICMP are in use today: *ICMP version 4* (ICMPv4)[35] and *ICMP version 6* (ICMPv6). ICMPv4 was developed to work with IPv4, so with the release of IPv6 updates were required and ICMPv6 was born.[36]

The functions of each version are basically the same. ICMP*vwhatever* is there to pass messages. Following are the main reporting functions performed by ICMP:

- Error reporting
- Testing and troubleshooting
- Informational reporting

IP and ICMP work very well together. As a matter of fact, you can consider ICMP the "right-hand man" of IP. While IP is busy packing up data and routing that data to a destination, ICMP is taking care of all the busywork. ICMP passes messages that help ensure IP can perform its job well.

Many consider ICMP one of the simplest protocols there is. If you think about it, this is true. ICMP doesn't have to give a lot of thought or calculation to do its job. All it has to do is pass messages.

5.2.3.4   *Routing Information Protocol*

The Routing Information Protocol (RIP) is a dynamic routing protocol that is used in many networks. It is a *distance-vector* protocol, which means that each router will advertise the destinations it is aware of and the distance to each destination to neighboring routers.

> **POP QUIZ**
>
> What is the difference between *IPng* and *IPv6*?

Many different implementations of RIP were in place when the protocol became an Internet standard. Although there were a few differences between RIP implementations in different networks, the differences didn't cause many interoperability issues in production. A second version of RIP (RIPv2, or RIP2) was introduced and offered a few improvements over the original version of RIP. The most notable of these improvements was the support of variable length subnet masking (VLSM)[37] and support for authentication.

[35] ICMPv4 wasn't always called that. It was called simply ICMP since its inception. The v4 was added later to separate it from ICMPv6.

[36] ICMPng in and of itself is a pretty cool acronym. Not too many adopted the term, but at least one of the authors of this book would have adopted it (yes, we are talking about that author who thinks *catenet* is a cool term).

[37] VLSM increases the efficiency of the utilization of IP addresses in a given network by allowing different subnet masks to be used for each subnet. This will be discussed in Chapter 10, "The Internet Layer."

RIP determines distances to a destination based on what is known as a *hop count*, which is the number of devices a packet must pass through on the way to a destination. The hop count increases each time a packet reaches a node along the path to its destination. The link taken by the packet from one node to another node is the actual hop. Figure 5-10 shows an example of hops[38] in a network.

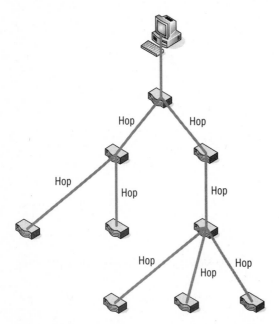

Figure 5-10 Hops in a RIP-routed environment

Now, let's quickly review the operation of RIP. When a router first boots up, one of the first things it will do (once connectivity is established) is send a packet out of each interface requesting routing tables from each of the neighboring routers. In turn, each router will send the routing table to the router that requested it. As the router receives the routing table from the neighboring routers, it will send a response telling the neighbors it has received the requested routing table. The neighbors will respond with any updates they may have since they last sent the routing table. If there are no updates, the neighbors will validate that they know of the originating router.

Once the preliminary routing table updates are performed, the routing table of each router will be broadcast to all other neighbor routers. This update occurs every 30 seconds. Updates known as *triggered updates* will occur whenever

---

[38]This is not to be confused with the flower hops, which is a key ingredient in beer. There is a shortage of hops at the time of this writing, which makes the hobby of home brewing a bit more expensive than in years past.

there is a change with the hop count to a destination. When triggered updates occur, only the information that has changed is sent.

5.2.3.5   *Open Shortest Path First*

The Open Shortest Path First (OSPF) protocol is a dynamic routing protocol that uses the *link state* between nodes to determine routing paths for packets. The link state is simply the state of the link to the next router (the neighbor). Routers in an OSPF environment do not check the distance from one point to another in a network. Instead, the routers monitor the state of a link to each of its neighbor routers (the router next door). The link states are logged into the *link state database* (LSDB), which is then shared with all the neighbors. LSDB information that is received is used to build the routing table for the router and then the information is shared with its neighbors.

Although an OSPF system can be a single autonomous system, most often OSPF routers are assigned as members of OSPF areas. Each area is identified by a 32-bit identifier, much like an IP address. Routers in the OSPF environment are also assigned tasks they need to perform to ensure that the routing domain runs smoothly. Following are a few important terms you will need to know:

- **Backbone area** — The core of the entire OSPF network. The identifier that is assigned to the backbone area is 0.0.0.0. All areas are connected to the backbone area.

- **Stub area** — An autonomous system that only receives LSDB updates from routers within the same area. The stub area only receives external routes through the default route.

- **Not so stubby area (NSSA)** — A stub area that contains no external routes. The NSSA can retrieve external updates and send them to the backbone.

- **Internal router** — Any router that only shares information with routers in the same area.

- **Backbone router** — Any router that participates in the backbone area. Most backbone routers are ABRs as they share information between areas. There may be some routers in the backbone that are not ABRs, but these are still backbone routers as they are in the backbone area.

- **Area border router (ABR)** — Any router that is a member of more than one area.

- **Autonomous system boundary router (ASBR)** — Any router that shares link state with a router in another area is called an ASBR. Note that any router within the area can be an ASBR; this includes area border routers, backbone routers, and internal routers.

- **Designated router (DR)** — Any router that handles advertisements on multi-access networks. The DR is elected by a process among other routers. It is responsible for being the representative for the multi-access network to the rest of the network. It is also in place to ensure that data is not flooded due to the multi-access environment.

- **Backup designated router (BDR)** — Any router that takes over the responsibilities of the DR if the DR should fail.

5.2.3.6 *Border Gateway Protocol*

The Border Gateway Protocol (BGP) provides for IP data communication between routers that are in different autonomous systems (AS). BGP routers share information with one another, providing paths that can be used to reach an AS. To prevent routing loops, BGP routers make a determination of the best path and any possible loops are pruned from the decision tree.

An AS can be classified much as areas are in OSPF, including

- **Multihomed AS** — An AS that connects to more than one other AS. A multihomed AS does not participate in transit traffic.

- **Stub AS** — An AS that connects to only one other AS. A stub AS does not participate in transit traffic.

- **Transit AS** — An AS that connects to more than one other AS. A transit AS participates in local and transit traffic.

Data traffic within an AS is either *transit* traffic (just passing through) or *local* traffic (traffic that starts or ends[39] within the AS).

Like RIP, BGP is a distance-vector protocol. However, instead of counting hops to a destination, BGP counts the number of autonomous systems it takes to get to a destination. BGP also supports policy-based routing. In other words, policy specifications are set by the system administrator and are used to allow BGP to determine the best route to a destination, ensuring all policies are strictly enforced. This means that even though there may be a quicker path to take to a destination, policies may prevent a datagram from going on that path.

BGP sends what are known as *keepalive messages* to its neighbors to ensure that the neighbors are reachable. If they are not reachable, BGP will recognize this as a link failure.

5.2.3.7 *Internet Protocol Security*

Internet Protocol Security (IPSec) is a suite of protocols that allow for security and encryption for IP datagrams. IPSec is designed to provide endpoint to

---

[39]The alpha and omega of BGP traffic types.

endpoint datagram security (*transport mode*) for nodes that do not support security protocols.[40] IPSec is also used in VPN environments (*tunnel mode*), which allows the gateway to the network to provide security and authentication services for the users and networks the node supports.

IPSec provides several types of security for networks and the users of the networks. One of the biggest functions that came from IPSec is the ability to encrypt datagrams so that only the destination can read and understand them.[41] IPSec also provides checks of datgrams to ensure that they have not been tampered with in transit. Finally, IPSec provides for the authentication of users, to ensure that anyone that should not have access doesn't.

AN UNRELATED MOMENT OF PAUSE

Three friends were out driving one day. One was a network sales engineer, one was a network hardware engineer, and one was a network software engineer. All of the sudden the right rear tire blew out, and the car rolled to a stop. Since the car was full of problem solvers, the three friends jumped out of the car to survey the situation.

The network sales engineer proclaimed, "The car just won't do anymore; it is time to buy a new one!"

The network hardware engineer gave it some thought and then said, "We need to try swapping the left tires with the right tires. If that does not fix it, then we need to swap the front tires with the rear tires. If we are still having problems at that point, we will have to replace the tires."

The network software engineer then piped in, "You guys are just wasting time. We need to get back in the car and drive some more to see if the problem will just work itself out."

5.3   End of Chapter Hodgepodge

We hope that you now have a better understanding of the TCP/IP reference model, some of the protocols that operate in each layer, and how each layer interfaces with each of the other layers. As you continue through the pages of this book, we will be revisiting a lot of these protocols and discussing some of the details that make each one tick.

In this section, we will discuss some of the other processes that operate in a TCP/IP environment. Like many of the other functions and specifications that we have discussed in this chapter, we will be revisiting some of these in upcoming chapters.

---

[40]These nodes may support security, but not at the level that a network needs the node to.
[41]Remember when we were talking about key exchange?

5.3.1 There Is Hope for Diskless Nodes

The Bootstrap Protocol (BOOTP) manages IP parameters on a given network. It assigns IP addresses for a *pool* of users. Not only that, it also provides for operating system initiation for remote diskless nodes.

BOOTP is a network protocol that uses UDP for transport. When a node is booting up, there is a bootstrap process that initiates the execution of the node's operating system. If a node is running a *BOOTP client*, the node will send a request to a *BOOTP server* for assignment of an IP address, along with any other startup assistance that the client node requires (and the BOOTP server supports). BOOTP is normally integrated into the node's motherboard or NIC card.

The *Dynamic Host Configuration Protocol* (DHCP) evolved from BOOTP. Several enhancements were provided with DHCP, although BOOTP is simpler to implement and maintain. A single *DHCP server* can provide IP addresses, subnet masks, gateway information, and more. When a node connects to the network, the DHCP client will broadcast a request for information from the DHCP server. The server will then send the requested information so the node can connect and operate in the network.

BOOTP and DHCP are called *communication management protocols*. They can work separately or together (together is the most often implemented). DHCP can serve the requests that come from a BOOTP client.

5.3.2 A Little More Information on Routing

Just when you thought we had finished with our discussion about routers, here we are back on the subject.[42] Following are a few terms that we wanted to quickly touch on. Why not? We have to discuss them somewhere.

- **Routing protocol** — The protocol that performs functions that allow the routing of packets between routers. RIP, OSPF, and BGP are examples of routing protocols. Sometimes confused with a *routed protocol*, which is not the same thing.

- **Routed protocol** — A protocol that participates in transmitting data between nodes within a network. Telnet, SNMP, and IP are all examples of a routed protocol. Routed protocols are sometimes incorrectly termed *routing protocols*.

- **Gateway** — The entry point for an entity. A computer that provides access to a network area is a gateway. A network that provides access to another network is a gateway. Many applications have gateways that allow information sharing. The node that connects the LAN to the Internet (or any other network type) is a gateway.

---

[42]We are far from finished with our discussion on routers.

- **Interior Gateway Protocol (IGP)** — A routing protocol that operates within an AS. RIP and OSPF are IGPs.

- **Exterior Gateway Protocol (EGP)** — BGP is often called an EGP, although the EGP protocol was the predecessor to BGP for IP routing between autonomous systems.

- **Static routing** — IP routing information that is manually configured on a node by a system administrator.

- **Dynamic routing** — IP routing information that is learned by the node through a routing protocol, such as RIP.

> **POP QUIZ**
>
> What are the two IGPs that we discussed in this chapter?

This concludes our discussion of routers for this chapter.

5.3.3 Sockets and Ports Are Not the Same Thing

A couple of important terms that often get confused are *socket*[43] and *port*. Note that we are referring to TCP and/or UDP ports, not to the physical interface of the node. A TCP or UDP port is a number assigned to the datagram header that is mapped to a particular process or application on a given node. A socket is the end-point of data communication flow on a network.

TCP and UDP ports are basically an extension of addressing used by TCP/IP to ensure that data communication is tied to the correct running process. Each packet header that is transported over TCP or UDP has a source and destination port logged in it. The port number can range from 0 to 65535. Port numbers are divided into three sections. These are *well-known ports* (0 through 1023), registered ports (1024 through 49151), and dynamic and/or private ports (49152 through 65535).

TCP/UDP WELL-KNOWN PORT NUMBERS

Following is an example list of many popular well-known TCP and UDP port numbers. TCP well-known port numbers are identified by an assignment of 0 through 1023. This list is only an example to provide the port numbers for many of the protocols we have covered, along with a few that are just darn interesting.

(continued)

---

[43]Sockets are also often called TCP or UDP sockets (depending on the transport protocol), Internet sockets, or network sockets.

TCP/UDP WELL-KNOWN PORT NUMBERS *(continued)*

For a complete and current list, go to `www.iana.org/assignments/port-numbers`.

Port Number	Description	Applicable Protocol
0	Reserved	TCP and UDP
1	TCP port service multiplexer	TCP and UDP
5	Remote job entry	TCP and UDP
7	Echo	TCP and UDP
20	FTP – data	TCP
21	FTP – control	TCP
22	SSH	TCP and UDP
23	Telnet	TCP and UDP
25	SMTP	TCP and UDP
53	DNS	TCP and UDP
67	BOOTP/DHCP – server	TCP and UDP
68	BOOTP/DHCP - client	TCP and UDP
69	TFTP	TCP and UDP
80	HTTP	TCP and UDP
101	NIC host name server	TCP and UDP
107	Remote Telnet service	TCP and UDP
109	POP2	TCP and UDP
110	POP3	TCP and UDP
115	SFTP	TCP and UDP
118	SQL	TCP and UDP
123	NTP	TCP and UDP
135	DCE endpoint	TCP and UDP
143	IMAP	TCP and UDP
161	SNMP	TCP and UDP
162	SNMP trap	TCP and UDP
166	Sirius	TCP and UDP
179	BGP	TCP and UDP
213	IPX	TCP and UDP
220	IMAPv3	TCP and UDP

(continued)

TCP/UDP WELL-KNOWN PORT NUMBERS (continued)

Port Number	Description	Applicable Protocol
389	LDAP	TCP and UDP
401	UPS	TCP and UDP
500	ISAKMP	UDP
513	Login	TCP
513	Who	UDP
515	Lpd	TCP
520	RIP	UDP
546	DHCPv6 client	TCP and UDP
547	DHCPv6 server	TCP and UDP
647	DHCP failover	TCP
666	Doom (video game)	UDP
989	FTP data over TLS/SSL	TCP and UDP
990	FTP control over TLS/SSL	TCP and UDP
992	Telnet over TLS/SSL	TCP and UDP
1023	Reserved	TCP and UDP

Any application that provides a common and well-known service (SMTP, FTP, Telnet, etc.) will monitor for incoming requests on the well-known ports. Firewalls can be configured to allow or deny specific ports, thus enhancing network security. If a request comes in with a port that is not defined, the server will assign a port number for the duration of the application process.

ACRONYM ALERT

CRC — Cyclic redundancy check

The socket is the combination of an IP address or node name and a port number. The syntax of a socket would be

```
<ip address> :< port number>
```

An example of this would be the Telnet protocol, which uses port number 23 (for both TCP and UDP). If the host that is running the Telnet server has an IP of 10.10.10.10, the Telnet client would send a request to that IP for port number 23. The syntax would look like this:

```
10.10.10.10:23
```

Any given port can have a single passive socket, which monitors for incoming requests, but can serve multiple active sockets, each serving a request from a different client.

5.4   Chapter Exercises

1. What are the four layers of the TCP/IP reference model?

   _____

   _____

   _____

   _____

2. Name four Application layer protocols that we discussed in this chapter.

   _____

   _____

   _____

   _____

3. Explain the structure of the DNS hierarchy.

4. What are the five PDU types that are used by SNMP?

   _____

   _____

   _____

   _____

5. What is the purpose of FTP?

6. Why does TFTP not perform many of the functions that FTP does?

7. What is a daemon?

8. What are the four control characters used by Telnet for option negotiation and their meanings?

   _____

   _____

   _____

   _____

9. TCP is a _____-oriented protocol, whereas UDP is a _____ protocol

10. What are the three main reporting functions that we said are performed by ICMP?

    _____

    _____

    _____

5.5   Pop Quiz Answers

1. The Internet layer is also known as the _Network_ layer.
2. What is the function of the FTP command `ascii`?

   Sets the file transfer mode to ASCII.
3. What does an SMTP server response code `421` mean?

   Server is unavailable.
4. What does the acronym NFS stand for?

   Network File System
5. What is the purpose of Telnet option code `32`?

   Used to set the terminal speed.
6. What does the acronym SSH stand for?

   Secure Shell
7. Name the two popular transport protocols that we discussed in this chapter.

   TCP and UDP
8. Which layer of the TCP/IP reference model is probably the most important one?

   The Internet layer
9. What is the difference between IPng and IPv6?

   None. Other than the names, they are the same protocol.
10. What are the two IGPs that we discussed in this chapter?

    RIP and OSPF

Ethernet Concepts

The system of nature, of which man is a part, tends to be self-balancing, self-adjusting, self-cleansing. Not so with technology.
— **E.F. Schumacher**

The term *Ethernet* is a catchall word used to describe the most common network architecture used in a majority of today's networks worldwide. If you were to say to someone, "Describe an Ethernet cable," 99 out of 100 would probably respond that it consists of unshielded twisted pair (UTP) cable that is terminated on each end with RJ45 plugs. That is mostly true in today's network, but Ethernet technology has evolved from its early coaxial cable days to what it is today.

All Ethernet networks, no matter the type of cable that is in use, are Carrier Sense Multiple Access with Collision Detection (CSMA/CD) networks that adhere to the standards described in IEEE 802.3. This is true for either coaxial or UTP cable Ethernet networks. Let's review how Ethernet came about and how it evolved to its current emanation of Ethernet cable technology.

NOTE The term *Ethernet* is derived from two words: *ether* and *net*. Ether is a medium that can be made from pretty much anything. This is evident in today's network environment, where network signals can be carried over wire, fiber (fiber optic), or air (wireless). The word *net* may be short for *network*, but one of the authors likes the idea of visualizing a fishing net, where each node is tied to adjoining nodes, and there are multiple paths from one to the other.

6.1   The Beginning of Ethernet Technology

From 1973 to 1975, Ethernet had its start at the Xerox Palo Alto Research Center (PARC). Xerox filed a patent application in 1975 with the U.S. Patent Office for a Multipoint Data Communication System with Collision Detection. Patent 4,063,220 described how multiple data processing stations distributed along a branched cable segment would be able to communicate with each other. It included descriptions of the cable the devices needed to send and receive data on that cable. It also included a packet description outlining both source and destination addresses along with data and error fields.

In the experimental implementation of Ethernet, data rates were 3 Mbps, and the source and destination address fields were only provided 8 bits for addressing, which limited the number of devices that could be addressed on the network. There were 16 bits allocated for the packet type, which would be used to define a packet type that would be used within a particular protocol.

> **NOTE** Mbps means "megabits per second," where mega is the value of a million. So 100 Mbps is 100 million bits per second. Remember that a bit is a single binary digit of either zero or one. Even if only one stream of zeros was being generated, there are still 100 million of them in a second. It may represent a whole lot of nothing, but in the network world they truly have value.

One of the original inventors on the Xerox patent, Robert Metcalfe, left Xerox in 1979 to form 3Com to promote LAN development and the use of PCs as nodes on the Ethernet network. He was instrumental in convincing Digital Equipment Corporation (DEC), Intel, and Xerox to work together to promote Ethernet as a LAN standard. This standard came to be known as the *DIX standard*, after the companies (DEC, Intel, Xerox) who came together to create the standard.

The DIX or Ethernet II standard describes a frame format that provides 48 bits each for destination and source addresses, along with 16 bits for the packet type. The standard also set the data rate at 10 Mbps. Figure 6-1 illustrates a DIX/Ethernet II frame.

Destination MAC Address (6 bytes)	Source MAC Address (6 bytes)	Ethernet Type (2 bytes)	Data Payload (46 to 1500 bytes)	CRC Checksum (4 bytes)

Figure 6-1 A DIX/Ethernet II frame

The Destination and Source Address fields are 6 bytes in length and are usually presented as a group of 12 hexadecimal numbers. These addresses are called the *Media Access Control (MAC) addresses* and are a unique Ethernet hardware address assigned to a network interface card (NIC). The DIX/Ethernet II standard has been superseded by IEEE 802.3.

> **NOTE** Hexadecimal number system is an easy way of illustrating 4 binary bits, which can have values from 0 to 15. The values 0 through 9 are presented as their actual value, while the units 10 through 15 are represented by the alpha characters A through F, respectively. The 16 (the root *hexadeca* means 16) values that can be contained in a hexadecimal number are 0, 1, 2, 3, 4, 5, 6, 7, 8, 9, A, B, C, D, E and F.

Although Ethernet was originally designed to allow computers to communicate with each other over a coaxial cable as the broadcast transmission medium, twisted pair Ethernet cable systems have been under development since as early as the mid-1980s. The first network topology using UTP cable was StarLAN, and it was introduced with a data rate of 1 Mbps. However, StarLAN would eventually evolve into what became known as *10BASE-T*, which is the predominant UTP cable in use today.

Since the publication of IEEE 802.3 in 1985, there have been several amendments that provide for increased Ethernet rates. Table 6-1 lists the data rates that can be found in use today.

Table 6-1 Ethernet Types and Speeds

ETHERNET TYPE	SPEED
10BASE-T	10 Mbps
Fast	100 Mbps
Gigabit	1000 Mbps

Ethernet has emerged as the de facto network standard worldwide. It has withstood challenges from other networking protocols over time, and as a result, large numbers of products from a wide range of manufacturers are readily available

> **POP QUIZ**
>
> What was the first type of cable used to form an Ethernet network?

and are able to successfully interconnect based on this standard. Due to the economies of scale, networking products have decreased in price while performance has increased. Ethernet allows for flexibility in network implementation that is easy to maintain and manage. The installed base for Ethernet networks is huge, guaranteeing that Ethernet will be around for some time to come. There will always be improvements inserted into existing networks, but they will not cause a total dumping of the current Ethernet network.

6.2   Ethernet Components

We discussed how UTP cable evolved from UTP telephone wire used to create the StarLAN networks. It would stand to reason that some of the concepts would be carried over from the Telco influence in setting Ethernet standards. Ethernet components using UTP cabling fall into two categories:

- Data terminal equipment (DTE)
- Data communications equipment (DCE)

This nomenclature is part of the long-standing serial communications standard EIA RS-232. Much like that standard, the Ethernet standard uses this framework as the basis in developing standards for the electrical signal characteristics for

> **RANDOM BONUS DEFINITION**
>
> bridge port — A network interface on a bridge.

Ethernet cabling and signals. Figure 6-2 illustrates a DCE and DTE device connected with UTP cable.

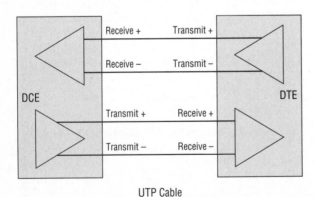

Figure 6-2 Interconnection of DCE and DTE Ethernet devices

This figure represents the conceptual interconnection of two Ethernet devices using UTP Ethernet cable. You will notice that the cable appears to be straight across, although physically the + and − wires are twisted together within the jacket of the cable. This type of Ethernet cable is often referred to as a *patch cable* or a *straight-through cable* because there is no crossover from receive to transmit circuits.

> **NOTE** Twisted pair wire does have a purpose. The pair of wires are twisted together in a uniform manner with a fixed number of twists per foot. Why should the cable be twisted in the first place? To look pretty? To keep the wires from drifting apart? Okay, the answer is: to combat the effects of electromagnetic interference (EMI). Electrical waves are all about us, now more so than ever with the plethora of cell phones and other mobile devices. When these waves intersect wire, they can induce minute fluctuations in voltage. No big deal, right? Just a little static on the line. Wrong! These signals could cause erroneous data to be read, so signal integrity is an absolute necessity. (How would you like it if your ATM card was swallowed before you could get your money out?) Now, do not go adding extra twists to your Ethernet cable thinking this is going to increase your immunity. In reality, you will alter the electrical characteristics of the wire and cause reflections within the cable, which is bad as EMI. Leave the cables alone and go pop some bubble wrap if you need to keep those idle hands busy.

So, we have DCE and DTE Ethernet devices, but which is which? A good way to remember this is by recalling the early days of RS-232. The term *data terminal equipment* often referred to teletypewriters, whereas *data communication equipment* most often referred to modems. When PCs were introduced, the majority of telecommunications was accomplished via a modem. (Yes, we recall those days — the 300 baud handset devices where you squeezed your phone's handset into the foam cuffs so it could receive the actual audio signals through the telephone.)

> **NOTE** A *handset* refers to a standard telephone like we had back in the olden days. The telephone wire was connected to the base, and the handset portion had a spiraled wire, which always managed to get so twisted that you found you could not talk on the phone unless your head was about a foot off the table where the base rested. The base contained the actual dialing mechanism, which allowed you to dial the number you wished to connect to. Yes, "dial" — where do you think the word originated? Surely, not from punching those minute buttons on the latest whiz-bang cell phone, which has given us a new set of human ailments such as "texting thumb."

As telephone technology evolved from mechanical dialing mechanisms to touch-tone dialing, modems also implemented those technologies. Even today's modems — whether external or

> **RANDOM BONUS DEFINITION**
>
> bandwidth — The data-carrying capacity of a device or communications channel.

internal modems embedded in a laptop, PCMCIA modem card, or PCI modem card in a desktop computer — all support both dial and touch-tone dialing methodologies in their designs.

> **NOTE** What is meant by mechanical dialing? The old rotary phones had a dial with numbers and letters assigned around a dial mechanism shaped like a wheel with finger holes assigned the numbers 1 through 9 and 0 for either the number zero or Operator if that number was dialed first and by itself. A number was dialed by placing one's index finger in the hole with the corresponding number that was desired and then in a circular motion moving the dial to the stationery finger-stop and releasing the dial to allow it to step back. As it stepped back, it sent a pulse on the wire to the home office, where stepping relays would increment to set up the circuit corresponding to that number. Switching theory was developed and used by the telephone companies in order to eliminate human operators who would actually make the circuit connection for the caller. The number selected would determine the number of pulses, which stepped the home office stepping relay to that number. You can just imagine how many relays were required to set up those switching offices. Today's modems use a relay to pulse line the number of times required for the number to be dialed, and that is what is meant by the pulse setting on the modem.
>
> Touch-tone dialing was devised by the telephone companies to accomplish pretty much the same thing as pulse dialing. However, it uses a more modern technique of using distinct audio tones for each discrete number. If you ever listened to a modem dial with tone dialing, you know it sounds like automatons in sci-fi movies.

PCs pretty much replaced teletypewriters as the device to use for telecommunications. They were supplied with RS-232 serial ports. With a terminal emulation program, these PCs became the modern-day teletypewriter. We said that teletypewriters were DTE devices,

> **POP QUIZ**
>
> An Ethernet network device that forwards data on the network would be considered what type of Ethernet device?

so the PC with an Ethernet NIC is an Ethernet DTE device. Modems are DCE devices, and since they pass data along the network, devices like Ethernet hubs, routers, and switches are also considered to be DCE Ethernet devices.

6.2.1 DCE and DTE Cabling Considerations

We mentioned that a straight-through cable was one where the wire from pin 1 would be connected to pin 1 on the other connector. Let's discuss the RJ-45 modular plug that is used on any UTP Ethernet cable. Figure 6-3 represents how an RJ-45 plug would look if you held the plug with its gold contacts facing you. Pin 1 of the plug will be on your left, with pin numbers incrementing until pin 8 on your right is reached. The pin numbering is sequential.[1]

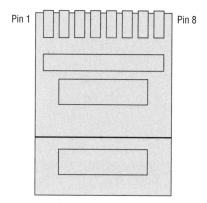

Pin 1   Pin 8

Figure 6-3 An RJ-45 modular plug

UTP Ethernet cable consists of four twisted pairs,[2] for a total of eight wires contained within an unshielded jacket. The wires are colored with four solid colored wires, each of which is twisted together with its mate, which is mostly white with a colored stripe that matches the color of its solid colored mate. How and to what pin these wires connect to on the RJ-45 plug adhere to old telephone company standards and are contained within the TIA/EIA-568-A and TIA/EIA-568-B standards. Table 6-2 lists the wiring scheme for T568A wiring, and Table 6-3 lists the wiring scheme for T568B wiring.

ACRONYM ALERT

AFP — AppleTalk Filing Protocol

---

[1]Sequential is derived from the word *sequence*, which means one after the other. For those in the reading audience who find it difficult to grasp this concept, we shall be more precise in the pin numbering definition. Starting on the left with pin 1, the pin numbers increment in sequence: 2, 3, 4, 5, 6, 7, and pin 8, which is the last pin on the right. Now, if you tell us you can't count, then we have a major problem here, and you need additional help, which is beyond the scope of this book.

[2]Pair refers to the number two. So a twisted pair of wire would consist of two discrete wires which have been twisted together for . . . what? Noise immunity, good answer.

Table 6-2 T568A Wiring Pin-out

PIN	PAIR	WIRE	COLOR	ETHERNET SIGNAL
1	3	Tip	White/green	Transmit +
2	3	Ring	Green	Transmit −
3	2	Tip	White/orange	Receive +
4	1	Ring	Blue	
5	1	Tip	White/blue	
6	2	Ring	Orange	Receive −
7	4	Tip	White/brown	
8	4	Ring	Brown	

Table 6-3 T568B Wiring Pin-out

PIN	PAIR	WIRE	COLOR	ETHERNET SIGNAL
1	2	Tip	White/orange	Transmit +
2	2	Ring	Orange	Transmit −
3	3	Tip	White/green	Receive +
4	1	Ring	Blue	
5	1	Tip	White/blue	
6	3	Ring	Green	Receive −
7	4	Tip	White/brown	
8	4	Ring	Brown	

A straight-through cable can be wired with either the T568A or T568B wiring scheme as long as both ends of the cable are wired exactly the same using the same wiring pin-out.

A crossover Ethernet cable must have one plug wired with the T568A wiring scheme and the other plug wired following the T568B wiring pin-out. The purpose of a crossover cable is to interconnect to like devices, regardless of whether they are

---

RANDOM BONUS DEFINITION

Application layer — The highest layer of the seven-layer OSI model.

DCE or DTE devices. The crossover is to have the transmit signals from one device terminate on the receive signals of the other device so they can pass data between them. A quick analogy is connecting two microphones together; the two parties could scream into them but neither could hear the other. Now, if we take one microphone and crossed over to a speaker and did the same for the other microphone, then parties would be able communicate without a problem.[3] The same goes for Ethernet devices — just because there is some sort of Ethernet UTP cable strung between them does not mean they are "supposed" to communicate.

So, when you are having problems getting two Ethernet devices to communicate, the first place to look is at the Physical layer (such as the cable being used).

HELPFUL HINT

Since for the most part Ethernet cables use RJ-45 jacks, which are mostly clear plastic, it is fairly easy to determine if a Ethernet UTP cable is either a straight-through or crossover cable. Take the two connectors on the ends of the cable and hold them against each other with both plugs oriented in the same direction. Scan the colors of each. They should look exactly alike on a straight-through cable. If it is a crossover cable, you will notice that the colored wires on pins 1 and 2 of one plug have moved to pins 3 and 6 of the other, with the reverse also being true.

If for any reason the cables do match as described in this note, there is a likelihood it is a cable used for another purpose or it is supposed to be an Ethernet UTP cable but has been manufactured incorrectly.

Do yourself a favor: if you find cables in your box of goodies that appear different from what has been described in this note, discard them in the nearest wastebasket. Many countless hours have been wasted fighting problems with bad cables, not only by people in general but by network administrators who should know better.

For the frugally minded who cannot bear to toss anything away, our recommendation is to cut the ends off the cables so you will not be tempted to use them in your network. You may want to use them to tie up all those newspapers that have been collecting in the corner and bring them to a recycling drop-off in your community.

6.2.1.1   Interconnecting Like Ethernet Devices

We have already discussed that Ethernet devices fall into two categories, DCE or DTE type devices. It has also been stated that interconnecting to like Ethernet

---

[3]We fully acknowledge that his simple-minded analogy has very little likelihood of succeeding in the real world because there is a whole lot of electronics that needs to be added for it to actually work. The purpose of any analogy is to demonstrate in the simplest terms how something works.

devices requires the use of a crossover cable. For example, two PCs with NIC cards can be directly interconnected with a crossover cable, as illustrated in Figure 6-4.

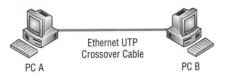

Ethernet UTP
Crossover Cable

PC A   PC B

Figure 6-4 Two PCs interconnected via Ethernet

In this simple figure, the two computers are able to communicate with each other over the crossover cable. There must be some sort of networking protocol running on the PCs, such as TCP/IP, and some sort of application that will allow the sharing of data or devices (which may be

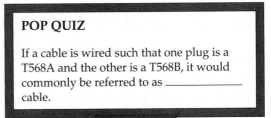

POP QUIZ

If a cable is wired such that one plug is a T568A and the other is a T568B, it would commonly be referred to as _____ cable.

locally connected to either or both of them). Some operating systems, such as Microsoft Windows and Apple Macintosh, are "network-able" and include tools and utilities to facilitate data and device sharing over the network.

The last example showed two Ethernet DTE devices interconnected, but how about DCE devices? We already mentioned that DCE devices are in the form of hubs, switches, and routers, so we know we are dealing with that kind of device. Why would anyone want to connect those types of devices? To illustrate this, we will consider a few simple examples.

ACRONYM ALERT

BER — Bit error rate

The first example is a case where we have a stack of dumb,[4] eight-port, passive hubs and there is a small office with 15 workers who need to be interconnected to a local server to share the resources available on that server. Figure 6-5 illustrates one method of how these passive eight-port hubs may be used to accomplish this.

The three hubs are placed about the office for the ease of cabling between each other and the workstations connected to them. Since these hubs have eight ports, with one

ACRONYM ALERT

TTL — Time to live

---

[4]Dumb means exactly that: dumb. There is no internal intelligence contained within the unit.

port dedicated for linking to the other hub, this leaves seven available ports for workstation connections. As you can see in Figure 6-5, two of the hubs have seven workstations each connected to them. That leaves one workstation and the server to be connected to the LAN. The hub that is used to connect these devices and the other two hubs has only used four of the eight available ports, so if needed there are four ports remaining for future expansion. You can see from the cabling legend that the workstations and the server are connected to the LAN with a patch or straight-through Ethernet UTP cable. The hubs are connected to each other using crossover cables since we are interconnecting like DCE Ethernet devices.

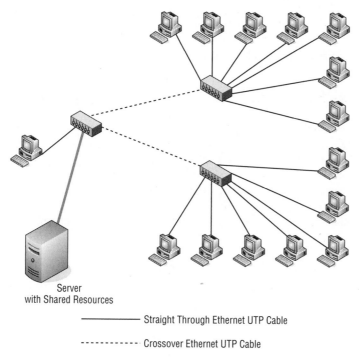

Server
with Shared Resources

————————— Straight Through Ethernet UTP Cable

- - - - - - - - - - - Crossover Ethernet UTP Cable

Figure 6-5 A LAN created with passive hubs

This scenario is not uncommon, and a few of you who may be familiar with cabling hubs today may be scratching your head. We remember the day when this was standard operating procedure for interconnecting passive hubs, so go with us on this one. Yes, there have been improvements in hub technology. One was actually adding what was called an *uplink port*, where a DTE port was added to the device to facilitate it being connected to another hub, with a patch cable eliminating the need to find a crossover cable, in case you forgot to purchase one when you purchased the hub. Another improvement is an uplink port with a switch dedicated to it that switches its receive and transmit circuits to match the cable and the port it was connected to at the other end. The most recent innovation in hub and switch design is that all ports on the hub are now auto-sensing and auto-switching.

NOTE Auto-sensing is accomplished by electronic circuits that determine if the incoming wires to a signal pair of pins are connected to a transmitter or a receiver. Once the "sense" of the wire is determined, this information is passed to the circuits responsible for auto-switching.

Auto-switching is circuitry added to a port to configure the port to which pins receive and transmit circuits should be connected to. If one set of pins is determined to be a receive pair, then the other set of pins must be the transmit pair. Receive and transmit are mutually exclusive in that one set of pins must be the receive circuit and the other must be the transmit circuit. If both sets of pins are the same, either receive or transmit, the device is defective.

HELPFUL HINT

Most Ethernet devices with RJ-45 jacks to accommodate Ethernet UTP cables have LED[5] lights showing the link status. If there is no link indication, the first place to check is the cable. Both devices connected with the same cable should indicate link while connected. If you pull one end of the cable and the other device's link light is still illuminated, you may not be connected to the correct device. In large LAN implementations, many times a cable is pulled to ensure that it loses link so one knows the port assignment is correct on both ends of the cable.

We can see that look on your face. You are thinking that if devices can do auto-sensing and auto-switching, why do you have to learn the differences in cable types? The answer is, you may be correct if you are only doing new implementations and using stock cables you buy already assembled. However, there is a large installed base of legacy systems that have dedicated ports wired as either a DTE or DCE, so cable knowledge is essential.

Let's continue with another example. Remember, it still is not yet an auto-sensing/auto-switching world. Figure 6-6 shows a part of a larger installation at a corporate office. There are many user workstations, but for sake of illustration there

ACRONYM ALERT

HTTP — Hypertext Transfer Protocol

[5]LED is the acronym for light emitting diode. It is actually a semiconductor device that will illuminate when a current is passed through it. Some are single colored while others are able to change color depending on how the device is electrically driven.

are only a few in the figure drawing. This figure may represent a floor or department location within a building.

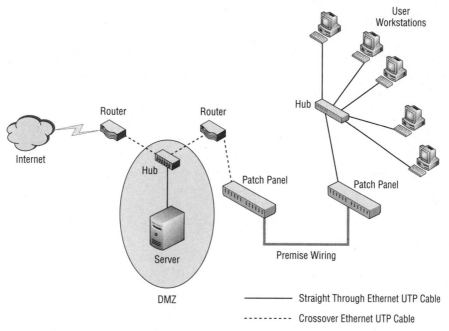

Figure 6-6 A larger LAN implementation

There are three DCE devices in this drawing, two routers and a hub that are interconnected using crossover cables. Off the hub there is a server connected with a patch cable/ straight-through Ethernet UTP

RANDOM BONUS DEFINITION

multimode fiber — An optical fiber that allows signals to propagate in multiple transmission modes simultaneously.

---

cable. The placement of the hub and server is considered a DMZ (demilitarized zone). The purpose of a DMZ is to regulate access to the networks it is connected to. In this scenario, there is a network of corporate user workstations that have access to a corporate server and the Internet. The routers within the DMZ have been programmed with policies that allow approved users from the Internet to have access to the corporate server but not to pass to any other networks connected to the DMZ. These routers and other equipment may be located in a data center on another floor from the users who need access to the server and the Internet. This is where premise[6] wiring comes in.

[6]*Premise* is the term used to represent a given locale like a home or building. Thus, premise wiring is the wiring contained within the building.

Cable needs to be run from the data center to the floor where the user workstations are located. This is done by running Ethernet-grade[7] cable, which is terminated on patch panels[8] located in the data center and the wiring closet on the floor where the user workstations are located.

HELPFUL HINT

We have seen wiring closets that are neat and orderly, and others with wire strung everywhere and piled on the floor like a large bowl of my mother's spaghetti and meatballs. (For more information on my mother's secret recipe, read the note on it.)

If you are a network administrator and want to do yourself a favor, please try to keep your wiring closets orderly and well labeled. You do not want to be called at all hours of the night or on vacation or even on your weekends off, and that will be the case each time someone is troubleshooting a problem and has no clue as to which cables go where. Do it right up front and you can truly have peace of mind. If not, your ears will be burning each time someone curses you for making their job harder.

The patch panels are wired with Category 5e or Category 6 cable from panel to panel as straight-through cables. There is no crossover taking place within the long-run cables. If a crossover is needed, it will be taken care of from the patch panel to the device using an Ethernet UTP crossover cable. This is illustrated in Figure 6-6 with the router that is connected to the patch panel. Notice on the other patch panel that although the switch is a DCE Ethernet device, it is connected with a patch cable. This is because it connects to the router at the other end, which is connected to the patch panel with a crossover cable, so that only a single crossover is required. Double crossover[9] cables will basically negate the crossover function, and the device link lights will not illuminate.

---

[7]Ethernet using UTP cable was initially designed on the idea of using existing premise wiring that was in place for telephone communications. With improvements in speed on Ethernet circuits, a higher quality cable was necessary to support these new requirements. Today's new cable installations should be using Category 5e or Category 6 cable, especially if Gigabit Ethernet is to be used.

[8]Patch panels are an old holdover from the telephone company days. However, remember the basis of Ethernet over UTP was to use existing premise wiring, which was telephone UTP cable. It stood to reason if those cables are attached to patch panels, then patch panels would become part of the Ethernet UTP connectivity equation.

[9]Double crossover is like a double negative: two negatives make a positive, so you don't have the crossover. It may come in handy sometime when you find yourself up to the armpits in crossover cables but are unable to find that one badly needed patch cable. Now, how would you connect them?

The server and all the user workstations are DTE devices connecting to other DTE devices, so the cables used are straight-through (patch) Ethernet UTP cables. With the right routing protocols and security policies in place, users at the

POP QUIZ

You are interconnecting two Ethernet devices, but neither device is showing a link light on the assigned port. List in order of likelihood where the problem might be.

user workstations are able to access the local corporate server as well as the Internet, while the corporate LAN is protected from unauthorized users from the Internet.

AN UNRELATED MOMENT OF PAUSE – MAMA BRAMANTE'S SECRET SPAGHETTI AND MEATBALLS RECIPE

The thought of all of the cables in a wiring closet made Rich think of his mother's spaghetti and meatballs. Rich decided to share the recipe with you all: Well, the recipe is not under lock and key like you see in some of those commercials on TV, and no, the dog doesn't know it either. The reason it is so secret is that my mother had the knack of making it without measuring ingredients other than with her watchful eye. I always said she could cook for five or fifty and it would always be the same, and it was. There is nothing like a mother's cooking, eh?

So, I am going to give you a list of ingredients, and you can mix up a batch. You may surprise yourself and it could be almost as good as my mom's. My mother always started the sauce before the meatballs. (For you Italian readers out there, "sauce" is "gravy.")

◆ Sauce Steps:

1. Using a large pot, pour a liberal amount of olive oil to a depth of about a quarter of an inch and heat to a temperature that would fry whatever you place in it.

2. Slice up (slice, not dice) a medium-sized onion. Add the onion to the oil and brown to a dark crisp. Remove the onion from the oil and set aside.

3. Take some garlic cloves and slice them so you have these tiny garlic slabs. Add them to the oil and just brown (do not cook as long as the onions).

4. Once the garlic is brown, add two cans of peeled Roma tomatoes into the olive oil/garlic mix. Be careful that the oil does not splatter back.

(continued)

AN UNRELATED MOMENT OF PAUSE — MAMA BRAMANTE'S SECRET SPAGHETTI AND MEATBALLS RECIPE *(continued)*

5. Stir in one can of tomato paste and the fried onions. Stir for consistency and let simmer while making the meatballs.

◆ Meatball Steps:

1. Put about a pound or pound and a half of fresh ground beef into a large mixing bowl.

2. Grate in an amount of bread crumbs that is about a third of the hamburger volume. (Stale Italian bread allowed to thoroughly dry to a rock was used to make the bread crumbs. Not much was wasted when feeding six kids.)

3. Finely dice two garlic cloves and add to the mix.

4. Finely chop two or three sprigs of fresh parsley and add to the mix.

5. Grate in some fresh Parmesan or Romano cheese — about half a cup or slightly more.

6. Add salt (not too much, as the cheese is salty) and some ground black pepper.

7. Create a cavity in the mix and add three whole eggs into the mix.

8. Mix all the ingredients thoroughly so that the whole batch is consistent throughout.

9. In a large skillet, preheat olive oil to fry the meatballs in. Scoop up enough of the beef mixture to make a golf ball size meatball. Roll the meatball in the palm of your hand (wash your hands before and after this process) to form a firm ball that can withstand frying without falling apart.

10. Fry the meatballs to a deep brown crust on all sides before dropping them into the sauce.

◆ Spaghetti Steps:

1. Once everything is simmering in the large sauce pot, it is time to boil the water for the spaghetti.

2. Add a half teaspoon of salt to the spaghetti water and bring to a rapid boil.

3. Add a pound of spaghetti (smaller amount for a smaller gathering) to the water and stir in.

4. Keep an eye on the pot since rapidly boiling spaghetti has a tendency to foam up and overflow the pot.

(continued)

AN UNRELATED MOMENT OF PAUSE – MAMA BRAMANTE'S SECRET SPAGHETTI AND MEATBALLS RECIPE *(continued)*

5. Once the spaghetti is cooked and is soft but firm to the bite (al dente), strain it in a colander.[10] Make sure the spaghetti is well drained.

◆ Serving Steps:

1. Dump the colander of spaghetti into a large serving bowl.

2. Add some of the sauce (no meatballs) to the spaghetti and mix thoroughly to where the spaghetti has sauce on it but not is swimming in the sauce. I know there is a fine line to this, so add sauce slowly.

3. Once you are satisfied the spaghetti has sufficient sauce on it, fish out two meatballs for each diner and place in the bowl on top of the spaghetti.

4. Serve with freshly grated cheese on the side, a little vino, good company, and conversation.

Congratulations! You have just served up Mama Bramante's favorite dish to *la famiglia*.

6.3 Ethernet and IEEE 802.3's Relationship to the OSI Model

There is a close similarity between the ISO OSI model and IEEE 802.3 model, with the difference being at the Data Link layer of the OSI model, as illustrated in Figure 6-7.

The Physical layer is the same in both models and is dependent upon the media[11] being used. This layer deals with parameters such as cable pin-out, signal electrical characteristics, modulation encoding of the data being modulated on carrier signals, and data synchronization.[12] Once it has been determined that the receive buffer has received a complete frame, the Data Link layer is signaled and the frame is passed up to that layer.

ACRONYM ALERT

MAN — Metropolitan area network

---

[10]For those of you who are uninformed about cooking utensils, a *colander* looks kind of like a leaky bucket or a hemispherical pot shot full of buckshot holes. Not useful for holding water, but it sure comes in handy when draining spaghetti.

[11]Media is in reference to the method of delivery of the data. Obviously in a wired network it depends on the type of cable and the NIC cards being used. However, other methods of delivery such as wireless and optical can be used. So media for the most part is how the data moves between data points.

[12]Data synchronization refers to the capability to detect the start of a data frame from a stream of data bits and the fact that the binary pattern is a complete frame.

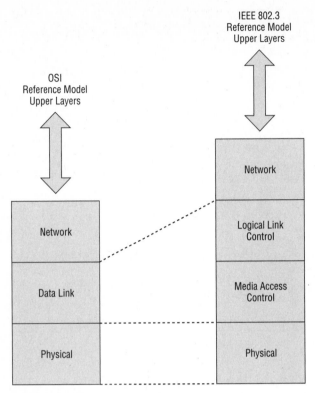

Figure 6-7 OSI's relationship to IEEE 802.3

In the OSI reference model, the Data Link layer accepts service requests from the Network layer and sends service to the Physical layer. It is the layer responsible for data transfer between adjacent network nodes and has the capability to detect and correct errors that may occur on the Physical layer. Although the Data Link layer is responsible for data transfer over the Physical link, many data link protocols do not provide acknowledgments of a successful receipt and acceptance of a frame. Some data link protocols do not even provide for a checksum to detect errors in transmission. In these cases, frames received depend on higher-level protocols for frame flow control, acknowledgments, retransmission, and error checking.

The IEEE 802.3 reference model divides the OSI model's Data Link layer into two sublayers, the Logical Link Control sublayer and the Media Access Control sublayer. The Logical Link Control sublayer resides in the upper layer of the OSI Data

POP QUIZ

Into which two sublayers of the IEEE 802 reference model is the OSI reference model Data Link layer divided?

Link layer, whereas the Media Access Control sublayer is in the lower portion and provides the interface to the Physical layer.

6.3.1 Logical Link Control

The IEEE 802 standard for the Logical Link Control resides in the upper portion of the OSI reference model's Data Link layer and provides the same functions no matter what media is being used. The Physical layer can be Ethernet, Token Ring, or wireless LAN, of which the Logical Link Control sublayer is primarily concerned with providing flow control, error control, and what multiplexing protocols are being used over the Media Access Control sublayer.

Logical Link Control flow control manages the data transmission rate between two network nodes to prevent one node sending faster than the speed of the receiving node. If one node is receiving data from multiple network nodes, it may not be able to receive as quickly as the sending node would like to transmit. Flow control depends on feedback from the receiving node to the sending node signaling possible congestion and its inability to receive data at higher speeds. In an Ethernet network, a receiving node that is unable to keep up with a sending node will transmit a PAUSE frame to halt transmission for a given period of time. The PAUSE frame for flow control can be used only on network segments that are running at full-duplex.[13]

POP QUIZ

With which functions is the Logical Link Control sublayer mainly concerned?

6.3.2 Media Access Control

The Media Access Control sublayer provides the interface between the Physical layer and the Logical Link Control sublayer. The Media Access Control sublayer is responsible for data encapsulation and frame assembly for sending frames, and de-encapsulation and error checking of received frames. It also provides addressing and a channel access control mechanism, which allows multiple nodes on a local area network to communicate.

The Media Access Control address, or the physical address of the node device, is commonly referred to as the *MAC address*. It is an industry standardized unique address assigned to each network adapter at the time of manufacture. Although highly unlikely, there is a possibility of duplicate

---

[13]We previously defined full duplex as the capability to send and receive simultaneously. It is logical that if a half-duplex node is currently receiving, it is unable to transmit until all the data is received. This makes a PAUSE frame unusable in half-duplex network segment.

MAC addresses on a network segment due to the capability to overwrite a manufacturer's previously assigned MAC addresses.

HELPFUL HINT

Although I have seen only one case of a duplicate MAC address on a LAN segment, I know it is possible. Depending on the network size, it can be a real nightmare. (Unfortunately, for the case I worked, it was a large network.)

For whatever reason, the site in the case I worked decided that they would assign their own MAC addresses for every device in their network. Although they had full control and well-documented logging of MAC addresses, it took a while to find the offending node.

Ultimately, knowing the MAC address of the device that was being adversely affected was helpful. Using a process of elimination that allowed for a digit being entered into a MAC address incorrectly aided in locating the culprit. If the site had not properly documented their MAC addresses and where they were assigned, the other option would have been to assign a new MAC address (which they preferred not doing) to the device that had not been previously assigned.

I am sure they had good reasons to use their own MAC address scheme, and they attempted to document it well, which is a major plus. However, it is best to leave well alone and use the already assigned MAC address to identify the device on the LAN segment.

Because Ethernet is a CSMA/CD (Carrier Sense Multiple Access with Collision Detection) network protocol, not only are all the network nodes on a network segment required to have unique physical hardware addresses, but there must be a provision for the control of the multiple access of more than one node at a time. The Media Access Control sublayer provides channel access control to allow multiple access.[14]

When multiple network nodes are connected to the same physical media, there is a high likelihood of collisions occurring. The multiple access protocol is used to detect and avoid packet collisions where multiple nodes contend for access to the same physical media. Ethernet and IEEE 802.3 are the most common standards used for CSMA/CD networks.

CSMA/CD utilizes a carrier-sensing scheme. If a transmitting node detects another signal on the media while it is transmitting a frame, it ceases transmittal of that frame and immediately transmits a jam signal onto the media. All nodes on the network are aware a collision on the media has taken place and will

---

[14]Multiple access allows more than one data stream to share the same Physical layer media. Examples of shared media networks are bus topology networks, ring topology networks, wireless networks, and Ethernet point-to-point links running at half duplex.

back off and not transmit for a period of time, which is calculated using a back-off delay algorithm. After the back-off delay has elapsed, the node will attempt to retransmit the frame, giving it a higher probability of success.

The methods used for collision detection depend on the media being used. On a wired Ethernet bus, it is accomplished by comparing the transmitted data with the data being received off the wire. If it is

> **POP QUIZ**
>
> When a collision occurs on the media, what does the transmitting network node do?

determined that they differ, the transmitting station on that node recognizes that another node is transmitting at the same time and a collision has occurred. All transmitting nodes then cease transmission and use the calculated back-off interval before attempting to transmit again. The back-off algorithm is a calculation that randomizes the back-off interval for each transmitting node so that the probability of another collision is very low.

HELPFUL HINT

CSMA/CD is required in a half-duplex network environment. Although the protocol works well if all network node devices remain well behaved, a single "chattering" network node can cause all data flow on a network segment to cease. Of course, this is a malfunction, but it is within the realm of possibility. A quick sniffer trace[15] of that network segment should out the culprit pretty quickly.

With the movement to higher-speed full-duplex Ethernet devices, the need for CSMA/CD is diminishing, although it must be maintained for legacy network segments and devices.

6.4   Ethernet Frame Format

Figure 6-8 illustrates the basic Ethernet frame format.

Preamble	Start of Frame Delimiter	Destination Address	Source Address	Frame Length/ Type	Data	Frame Check Sequence

Figure 6-8 The basic Ethernet frame format

---

[15]Sniffer trace is a technical colloquialism referring to a packet capture. There are dedicated pieces of equipment to capture and display packets or you can load packet-capture software on a laptop. The sniffer trace will permit you to see the traffic that is on a network segment.

The basic frame format illustrated in Figure 6-8 is required for all MAC implementations of the IEEE 802.3 standard. Some additional optional formats also are used to widen the basic capability of the protocol. Following is a list of the basic frame fields:

ACRONYM ALERT

OUI — Organizationally unique identifier

- **Preamble** — A 7-byte field consisting of alternating 1s and 0s to alert a receiving station that a frame is being received. It is a method used to aid synchronization between the Physical layer receiving circuits and the incoming data stream.

- **Start of Frame Delimiter** — A 1-byte field consisting of a field of alternating 1s and 0s ending with two consecutive 1 bits to signal that the next bit is the leftmost bit in the leftmost byte of the destination address.

- **Destination Address** — A 6-byte field that contains the address of the node that is to receive the frame. The leftmost bit in this field indicates if the frame is destined for a individual node address (0) or a group address (1). The second from the leftmost bit is an indicator if the address is a globally assigned address[16] (0) or a locally administered address[17] (1). The remaining 46 bits of this field contain the address value of the unique node address, a group of network nodes, or all nodes on the network.

- **Source Address** — A 6-byte field that contains the hardware address of the transmitting node, which is always a unique individual address where the leftmost bit of the field is always set to 0.

- **Frame Length/Type** — A 2-byte field that indicates either the number of bytes contained within the Data field of the frame or an alternate frame format type. If the Frame Length/Type has a value of 1500 or less, this value indicates the number of bytes contained within the frame's Data field. If the field value is 1536 or greater, it is used to indicate the

[16] A globally assigned address is the address assigned to the network interface at time of manufacture. These addresses are assigned in blocks to manufacturers and can be used to distinguish which device is from which manufacturer by the hardware address used on that network segment. This can be a valuable troubleshooting tool where large network installations are concerned.

[17] A locally administered address is a MAC address that has been locally assigned by a network administrator. It overrides the default MAC address assigned to the network interface by the manufacturer. Without extreme care, there is a distinct possibility that duplicate addresses could appear on the local network. Duplicate addresses are a big no-no in the networking world. So, if you need to do this, be very careful or you could be in a lot of hot water.

alternate frame type that is being used for either a received or transmitted frame. Table 6-4 lists a handful of the common frame types.

Table 6-4 A Few Common Frame Types

FRAME TYPE	PROTOCOL
0x0800	Internet Protocol Version 4 (IPv4)
0x0806	Address Resolution Protocol (ARP)
0x8035	Reverse Address Resolution Protocol (RARP)
0x809b	AppleTalk
0x80f3	AppleTalk Address Resolution Protocol (AARP)
0x8100	IEEE 802.1Q Tagged Frame
0x8137	Novell IPX
0x86dd	Internet Protocol Version 6 (IPv6)

■ **Data** — This field contains the data that is being sent within the frame. It can be any number of bytes of information up to and equaling the maximum number

> **RANDOM BONUS DEFINITION**
>
> network management — The process of configuring, monitoring, controlling, and administering a network's operation.

of 1500 bytes that is allowed for this field. However, if the number of bytes is less than 46, a number of bytes must be added to pad the field to reach its minimum length of 46 bytes. The minimum frame size, per the IEEE 802.3 standard, which does not include the preamble, is 64 bytes. Frames of less than 64 bytes are discarded as frames from collisions, faulty NICs, or software-caused under-runs.

■ **Frame Check Sequence** — A 4-byte field that contains a 32-bit CRC (cyclical redundancy check) checksum value, which is calculated and inserted by

> **POP QUIZ**
>
> What is the maximum number of bytes that can be contained in the Data field of an Ethernet frame?

the sending network node and used by the receiving network node to validate the received frame. Both the sending and receiving nodes calculate the CRC value by using the data contained within the Destination Address, Source Address, Frame Length/Type, and Data fields.

6.4.1   Transmitting a Frame

When a frame request is received by the Media Access Control sublayer from the Logical Link Control sublayer, it is accompanied by the data to be sent and the destination address where the data is to be delivered. The Media Access Control sublayer starts the transmission process by loading the data and address information into the frame buffer. The preamble of alternating ones and zeros, along with the start of frame delimiter, are inserted into their appropriate fields. Destination address and source address information is then added to the fields to which it is assigned. The data bytes received from the Logical Link Control sublayer are counted, and the number of bytes to be contained within the Data field is added to the Frame Length/Type field. The data from the Logical Link Control sublayer is inserted into the Data field, and, if the total number of data bytes is less than 46, a number of pad bytes are added until the number of data bytes is equal to 46. A CRC calculation is performed on the data contained within the Destination Address, Source Address, Frame Length/Type, and Data fields, and then appended to the end of the Data field.

Once the whole frame is assembled and ready for transmission, the Media Access Control sublayer's next operation depends on whether it is operating in half-duplex mode or full-duplex mode. If it is oper-

> **POP QUIZ**
>
> What does the Frame Check Sequence field of an Ethernet frame contain?

ating in half-duplex mode, it cannot transmit and receive simultaneously. Since IEEE 802.3 requires that all Ethernet Media Access Control sublayers support half-duplex, if the Media Access Control sublayer is operating in that mode, it is unable to transmit until any incoming frame is completely received. In full-duplex mode, this is not an issue, and the frame can be transmitted immediately.

6.4.1.1   Half-Duplex Transmission

With the development of the CSMA/CD protocol, multiple network nodes are able to share a common media without the need for a centrally located bus arbiter, tokens, or dedicated transmission time slots to determine when they would be allowed to transmit on the media.

NOTE Time division multiplexing (TDM) is a form of digital multiplexing where two or more bit streams are transmitted on a common communications medium. Although it appears as if they are simultaneous, they are actually sharing the time domain. The time domain is divided into a number of fixed time slots. Each data stream is dedicated to a fixed time slot or channel. Although the same media is being shared, it is not the most efficient use of the media if all or some of the channels are not transmitting. If no data is being streamed on a channel for a particular time slot, it is still using up part of the bandwidth dedicated to it and cannot be used by other channels.

Each portion of the CSMA/CD protocol can be summarized as follows:

- **Carrier Sense** — All network nodes continuously listen on the network media to determine if there are gaps in frame transmission on the media.

- **Multiple Access** — All network nodes are able to transmit anytime they determine that the network media is quiet.

- **Collision Detection** — When two network nodes transmit at the same time, the data streams from both nodes will interfere and a collision occurs. The network nodes involved must be capable of detecting that a collision has occurred while they were attempting to transmit a frame. Upon detecting that the collision has occurred, both nodes cease transmission of the frame and wait a period of time determined by the back-off algorithm before again attempting to transmit the frame.

Although bit signals are propagated on a shared network medium at the same rate, the amount of time it takes to transmit a whole frame is inversely proportional to the speed the interface is capable of transmitting it. This means that the time

> **POP QUIZ**
>
> What is the name of the transmission mode that allows either transmitting or receiving at different time intervals but never within the same time interval?

it takes to actually transmit a frame onto the network medium is less. By analyzing this, you can see that a worst-case scenario would be if two network nodes were at two extreme ends of the network media. Electrical signals travel at the same rate, but the amount of time to put a whole frame on the media is much less at higher interface speeds. In order to detect that a collision has taken place, time is needed to travel to the far end of the

> **ACRONYM ALERT**
>
> RTMP — Routing Table Maintenance Protocol

network segment and back. To allow collision detection to occur within the transmission window of a sending network node, limitations were established for cable lengths and minimum frame length as higher interface speeds were developed. Table 6-5 lists these limitations.

Table 6-5 Half-Duplex Operational Limitations

PARAMETERS	10 MBPS	100 MBPS	1000 MBPS
Minimum frame size	64 bytes	64 bytes	520 bytes
Maximum collision diameter[18] UTP cable	100 meters	100 meters	100 meters
Maximum collision diameter with Repeaters	2500 meters	205 meters	200 meters
Maximum number of repeaters in network path	5	2	1

6.4.1.1.1   Gigabit Ethernet Considerations

Although the Gigabit Ethernet frame is similar to the standard Ethernet frame, it is slightly different in minimum frame length. As you can see in Table 6-5, the minimum frame size expanded from 64 bytes to 520 bytes for a 1000BASE-T frame. The Gigabit Ethernet[19] frame is illustrated in Figure 6-9.

Preamble	Start of Frame Delimiter	Destination Address	Source Address	Frame Length/Type	Data	Frame Check Sequence	Gigabit Carrier Extension

Figure 6-9 The Gigabit Ethernet frame

In order to maintain the same collision domain diameter, the developers opted to increase the minimum frame length to 520 bytes. The longer frame was obtained by adding an extension to the frame after the Frame Check Sequence field. The Carrier Extension field is automatically removed by the receiving network node. The added frame length makes it possible for a frame collision to be detected because of the added time it takes to transmit a minimum-sized gigabit frame

ACRONYM ALERT

SRB — Source routing bridging

---

[18]Maximum collision diameter refers to the network media length from one transmitting network node to a receiving network node. Worst case is that each node is at the extreme end of a network segment. In wired network media, this equates to cable length and is linear, whereas in a wireless environment, it truly can represent a circle, where the diameter is the maximum distance from transmitter to receiver.

[19]Gigabit per second capability is the capability to pass a billion bits per second on an interface. Remember, a bit is either a single binary 0 or a 1. Whatever the bit value is, there is a lot of stuff coming at you all at once.

onto the network media. The time is close to that of a 64-byte minimum-sized frame being transmitted on the network medium by a 10/100 half-duplex NIC.

The standard for CSMA/CD Gigabit Ethernet added *frame bursting*, the capability of a Gigabit Ethernet NIC's Media Access Control sublayer to transmit a burst of frames without releasing the access to the network media. This is possible since the time needed to place a minimum-sized frame on the network media is much less than the total propagation delay round-trip time of the frame traveling over the network media.

Bursting is accomplished by allowing the transmission of a burst of frames within a time interval slightly greater than that needed for transmitting five maximum-sized frames. The media is kept occupied for the transmitting node by inserting frame carrier extension bits between the frames in the burst. Figure 6-10 illustrates a burst frame sequence.

In Figure 6-10 you will notice that the first frame may have a carrier extension added to it if it does not meet with the minimum frame size of 520 bytes. Between frames or the frame gap periods, the network media is kept busy with a continuous carrier by inserting carrier extension bits. For subsequent frames within a frame burst that do not meet the minimum frame size, a Frame Carrier Extension field is not needed since the frame gaps are being filled with extension bits while in the frame burst transmission mode. Frames will continue to be sent in burst mode until the burst frame limit has been reached. If there is a frame in the process of transmission when the burst frame limit has been reached, the frame is allowed to complete its transmission before the transmitting node releases the network media. Burst frame mode is only supported in Gigabit Ethernet.

> **POP QUIZ**
>
> What name is applied to the transmission mode that allows multiple frames to be sent without the need to release the network media between frames?

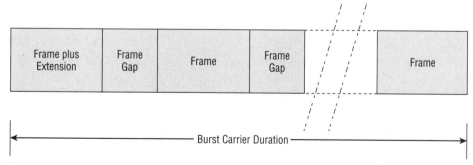

| Frame plus Extension | Frame Gap | Frame | Frame Gap | | Frame |

← Burst Carrier Duration →

Figure 6-10 The Gigabit Ethernet burst frame sequence

HELPFUL HINT

Since frame burst mode is not supported in 10 Mbps or 100 Mbps Ethernet, it is not a good idea to add these types of network devices to a network segment that is running at gigabit speeds. If you need to mix these devices on the same network segment, you should not use burst mode on that network segment.

6.4.1.2 Full-Duplex Transmission

Full-duplex transmission is the capability of a network node to transmit and receive simultaneously. It is a simpler method of communications than half-duplex since the need for collision detection is eliminated. However, it can only be attained in UTP networks or fiber optic networks, where transmit and receive circuits remain separated. The capability to send and receive at the same time effectually doubles the bandwidth of the network link between network nodes.

The first cabling used for Ethernet networks was coaxial. Because this wired medium was being used for both transmission and reception, the CSMA/CD protocol was developed to permit a sending and receiving network node to communicate over the same cable. Moving from the coaxial wire network media to the UTP cable media, the half-duplicity of the coaxial cable was maintained with the use of hubs that simulated the coaxial cable. So the need to maintain the CSMA/CD protocol was carried forward from the coaxial wire network environment to the UTP cable environment using a half-duplex mode of communications.

Full-duplex is a point-to-point method of communication, where the transmit circuit of one network node is directly connected to the receive circuit of another node, and vice versa. This is fine in a network where two network devices are connected directly to each other, but this is far from the capability to connect many network nodes together over a LAN. If hubs force network nodes into using half-duplex communications, how does one build a multinode network where the devices communicate using a full-duplex communications method?

With the advent of Layer 2 network switches, full-duplex communications are possible on a multinode network. There is a difference between a "dumb"[20] hub and an "intelligent" switch. Hubs are actually considered part of the Physical layer because they are not decision-making devices. They basically provide the interconnectivity on the physical level for network nodes.

---

[20]Hubs are sometimes called dumb or passive since they do not have any intrinsic intelligence to make a decision on how two nodes are to connect. They are *always* connected in half-duplex mode.

HELPFUL HINT

Do not confuse terms such as *switching hub* or *intelligent hub* with true Layer 2 network switches. What is often being referred to in those terms for a hub is the capability to sense the pins for transmit and receive signals and configure the hub accordingly to accommodate the cable connecting the network node to the hub. Once the hub is configured, it still supports half-duplex communications. To run full-duplex on your local network segment, make sure the device you have selected is a true Layer 2 network switch. Layer 2 switches are more expensive than hubs, so there is a cost consideration.

The name *Layer 2 switch* means exactly what it implies: it is a network device that operates within the first two layers of the OSI reference model. Of course, Layer 1 is the Physical layer, which implies that the construction of the ports of an Ethernet Layer 2 switch is designed with sockets that will accommodate UTP cables terminated with RJ-45 plugs. This physical attribute is no different from that of an Ethernet hub's; they look almost alike but operate very differently. As the name implies, the Layer 2 portion is the Data Link layer of the OSI model, and that is the major difference between a hub and a switch. Hubs do not know or care about the hardware addresses of the devices that are connected to them. In a hub-interconnected network, the endpoint network nodes are responsible for knowing and deciphering the messages on the network media to determine if a frame is addressed to them. The Layer 2 switch uses this very information to electronically interconnect the ports that are connected to it using hardware source and destination addresses. The Layer 2 switch is not concerned with any other aspect of the frame other than being able to direct it to a port that corresponds to the hardware address of the device connected to it. In setting up this connection, the switch is able to maintain the network nodes connected to it to be able to communicate in full-duplex mode.

In full-duplex mode, a frame can be transmitted as soon as it is assembled. However, there is a requirement that the gap between successive transmitted frames be long enough for frame synchronization. Each transmitted frame that is transmitted must still adhere to Ethernet framing standards.

> **POP QUIZ**
>
> What does the term *full-duplex* mean?

6.4.1.2.1 Full-Duplex Flow Control

In the half-duplex mode of operation, a network node does not transmit unless the network medium is silent. It then transmits and while doing so attempts to detect any network collisions that may have occurred within its transmit interval. Since in full-duplex mode the transmit circuit is separate from the receive circuit, there is no need for collision detection. But how will a transmitting network node know when there is a need for a delay in transmission?

A method of signaling between Media Access Control sublayers was devised to allow a receiving network to signal a transmitting network node that there is network congestion and to cease frame transmission for a period of time. This is referred to as *flow control*. To cause the cessation of frame transmission from a transmitting network node, the receiving network sends a PAUSE frame with a set delay time for the transmitting network node to wait before transmitting the next frame.

If congestion is relieved after a PAUSE frame with a set interval is sent, the receiving network node may transmit another PAUSE frame with the time-to-wait value set to zero. Upon receiving this PAUSE frame, the transmitting network node may begin transmission once again.

PAUSE frames are Media Access Control sublayer frames that have the Frame Length/Type field set to 0x0001 hexadecimal. The destination MAC address that is contained within the transmitted PAUSE frame is set to 01-80-C2-00-00-01. This reserved multicast[21] address is a signal to the receiving switch that the frame is a PAUSE frame for a particular port and will not forward the frame to the other ports that are on the switch. A network node receiving a PAUSE frame will not pass the frame beyond the Media Access Control sublayer.

ACRONYM ALERT

UI — User interface

The time-to-wait interval within a PAUSE frame is contained within a 2-byte unsigned integer with a value between zero and all bits of the 2 bytes set to ones.[22] Each unit of delay

POP QUIZ

What is flow control used for?

is equivalent to 512 bit times. In a 10 Mbps network, the bit time is equivalent to 0.0000001 seconds or a tenth of a microsecond. You can imagine how small these times are by factors of 10 in 100 Mbps and Gigabit Ethernet networks. In

---

[21]Multicast is the capability to transmit a frame to all network nodes on the network. Upon seeing that the address is set for a multicast broadcast, a node on the network will receive the frame since it was intended to be received by all network nodes on the network.

[22]Two bytes or 16 bits of ones are represented by 1111111111111111 binary, FFFF hexadecimal, or 65,535 decimal. These are all equivalents. However, there will be times in networking or digital circuits where the bit position carries a different connotation than simply a value. Usually these values are represented by a binary bit stream and are more an indication of position or time than just a value.

a 10 Mbps network, the minimum delay would be 51.2 microseconds, which is quicker than you can blink an eye. So you can see that for major congestion, the wait to send delay will have a greater value than the minimum of one.

HELPFUL HINT

Full-duplex and flow control are available for all network speeds of 10 Mbps, 100 Mbps and 1 Gbps. However, on any one particular link between a network node device and a switch, the transmission speed, duplex mode, and flow control all need to match. This is on a link-per-link basis. so it is possible that there can be links of various speeds, duplex, and flow control on differing ports within the same switch. Unless you are certain you know the configuration on a switch, it is not a good idea to swap ports blindly unless you are certain the ports are set identically. If switch ports are set to autonegotiate, they *should* be able to self-configure and settle on the method of communication to be used over the network link.

6.4.1.3 *Autonegotiation*

Autonegotiation is the capability of a NIC to negotiate the communication parameters that are to be used between it and the port it's connected to. The negotiation between peers only happens on a direct link between the two network nodes. The two devices can have different capabilities but will negotiate upon the duplex and the highest transmission speed the two network interfaces are capable of. Devices of 10 Mbps, 100 Mbps and gigabit speed can be matched on the same network link if needed.

The maximum speed that can be attained on any one network link would be the maximum speed of the slowest network interface. An example of this would be if a 10 Mbs interface set to half-duplex is plugged into a switch port that is set to autonegotiate. Assuming that the switch has the capability to perform at 100 Mbs at full-duplex, it would negotiate the port settings down to 10 Mbs at half-duplex, which is below its rated capability. This allows for flexibility within the network environment where the switch has been placed, but is not really beneficial for network performance. Autonegotiation has its place and at times can be very beneficial, so that network administrators do not have to configure each port every time they want to swap a port.

Another example would be if one end of a network link has a 100 Mbps network interface and the other end has a gigabit interface connected to it. If both interfaces were set to autonegotiate, they would ideally settle

RANDOM BONUS DEFINITION

Physical layer — The lowest layer of the seven-layer OSI model.

upon 100 Mbps at full duplex. However, this is assuming that the two network node devices play nice and can settle on that speed and duplex. Depending on manufacturer and the network interface being used, a link may need to be set permanently to a speed and duplex due to the inability of the two devices to negotiate a speed and duplex that works for both of them.

There may be instances where both interfaces do negotiate a speed but for some reason one interface settles upon half-duplex while the other settles upon full-duplex. On the surface everything may appear to be working as planned. However, performance over the link may be affected and communications seem slow. Mismatch in duplex is not uncommon and at times goes unnoticed until major network degradation is noted.

It is possible when two network node ports are interconnected that it appears that one network interface may have failed. The two devices will not bring up the link. There are a couple of ways to attack this problem. One is to hard-set both ends to a speed and duplex that you know they are capable of and see if you can send data across the link. The other method is to have a third network node device that you know is reliable connect to each to see if the link will come up with either device connected. This test is not conclusive, but if both devices can link with the known device, the culprit may be that autonegotiation between the two network interfaces is not working.

There is a possibility that two network node interfaces may appear to autonegotiate properly and can operate for an extended period of time without any problems. Then it is noticed that some network performance

> **POP QUIZ**
>
> What is autonegotiation?

problems have arisen. Traffic over a particular link seems to degrade, comes back, and then degrades again. This can be an indication that the autonegotiation between the two network node interfaces may be flapping.[23] If these network ports are set to autonegotiate, it would be best to manually configure them for the highest common speed and duplex and then monitor the link to see if performance picks up. If not, it can be an indication of bad cabling or possibly one network node interface may be having problems.

---

[23]Flapping (or flopping or flipping) generally describes an unstable network interface link. This is perhaps an offshoot of the old digital design days when flip-flops were used to maintain a particular state. Flip-flopping has wiggled its way into our society to mean something that is either indecisive or changes state whimsically. A good example of this would be today's politicians.

HELPFUL HINT

Some devices indicate link status and/or speed, but few indicate whether the link is running half- or full-duplex. You may want to become familiar with the network devices being used in that network segment. This will allow you to use monitoring tools to determine if speed and duplex for the link are set properly for the two network node interfaces that are connected on the link. Many network node devices do provide software tools for monitoring and measuring performance of the ports on the device. These software tools are usually a part of the software suite that came with the network device and can be used not only for configuration but also for troubleshooting.

6.4.2   Receiving a Frame

The receiving of a frame is the same no matter what type of network interface is in use. The electrical signals are received from the network media and loaded into a frame receive buffer. The major difference is between half-duplex network interfaces and full-duplex interfaces. A network interface that is strictly a half-duplex interface can use the same frame buffer for both transmitting and receiving a frame. However, full-duplex interfaces need to be capable of both transmitting and receiving at the same time, so a receive frame buffer is needed as well as a transmit frame buffer.

When a frame is received by a network interface, it is loaded into the receive frame buffer and the destination address is compared to see if it matches the unique MAC address of the network interface or network group address or if the frame is a broadcast frame. If there is an address match, the frame length is checked along with the Frame Check Sequence field. The Frame Check Sequence field is checked against the checksum, which was calculated as the frame was received from the Physical layer. If this matches, the Frame Length/Type field is checked to determine the frame type of the frame that was received so it can be properly be parsed and passed to the appropriate upper layer.

Once the frame has been unloaded from the receive buffer and passed up the ISO reference model to the upper layers, the network interface is then ready to receive another frame from the Physical layer. If

POP QUIZ

When a frame is received, what is the first criteria that is checked?

a frame does not pass the proper framing criteria, it is discarded and the interface is readied to receive the next network frame.

6.5   Traffic Optimization

What exactly is traffic optimization? It connotes a lot of various things, but the gist of the term is overall improvement in network performance. In the earlier sections of this chapter, we discussed speed and duplex and how they can affect the performance on a particular network link. We can see that there are advantages of having certain network paths being faster than others. Links going between devices that aggregate numerous network nodes need to be faster and more reliable than those of a single workstation to a hub or network switch. Figure 6-11 illustrates a network consisting of many user network nodes interconnected with high-speed switches that have high-speed gigabit interfaces between them.

The high-speed switches in this figure are to aggregate the multiple workstations and allow them to stream network data unimpeded by congestion caused if the data links between the switches were of the same speed as those between the workstation and the switches. In this example, the workstations are connected to the switches using a 100 Mbps full-duplex link. The switches are interconnected with high-speed gigabit full-duplex links and provide a redundant path if needed.

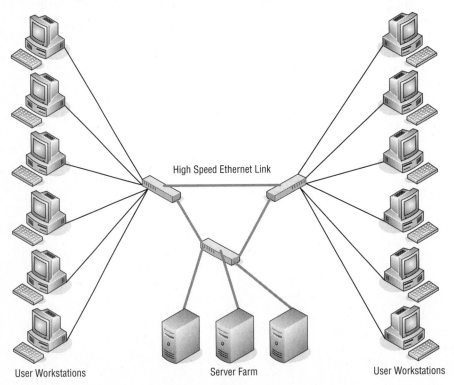

High Speed Ethernet Link

User Workstations   Server Farm   User Workstations

Figure 6-11 A network segment with high-speed links

The redundant[24] path shown in this figure allows for any of the high-speed links to go down and still have workstations on both network switches to which they are connected be able to access the server farm. These servers can provide various services such as e-mail, mass data storage, and client/server applications The servers are interconnected over a high-speed data link with a gigabit NIC to eliminate congestion on any one server. This increases the likelihood that there would be less congestion on these data links but does not totally eliminate the possibility that congestion could occur.

ACRONYM ALERT

SNAP — Sub-network Access Protocol

When administering large network installations it is important to understand the traffic patterns that are present on the network. Network efficiency can be increased where needed. The idea is to balance the need

POP QUIZ

What is the first step you should perform before implementing a network?

versus what it will cost since there can be areas of overkill where the investment in network resources is underutilized and thus is not a wise decision. Careful planning can greatly aid in determining where more network resources are required and limit the amount of waste of underutilized network segments. Know the business environment in which the network you are administering is installed. A carefully thought-out network is easier to install, maintain, and troubleshoot and runs efficiently with higher reliability.

6.5.1 Traffic Shaping

In the previous section, we discussed planning where high-speed links would be required. This approach is best-effort, and there is no differentiation of the type of traffic or if it is more important traffic than that of another transmitting network node. With real-time applications such as Voice over IP and videoconferencing, there is a need to give priority to these frames so they can be delivered in a timely fashion.

What if there was a way to tag a frame so it would be given a priority over another frame that need not be delivered as quickly? If frames are marked, they can be queued so the frames with priority will be forwarded on to the next segment. A simplified diagram illustrates this in Figure 6-12.

---

[24]Redundant path or redundancy in a network is the capability to provide multiple paths to various network resources to add fault tolerance. If one or more high-speed links go down, the network will either be unaffected or, at worst, be partially affected. It may not be able to have all of the network resources available to all of network users, but there will be areas of unimpeded network operation.

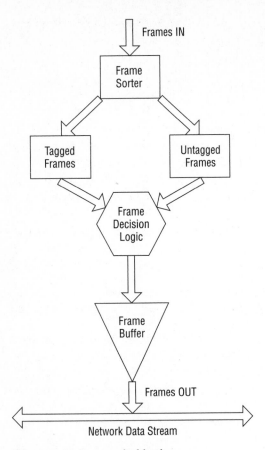

Figure 6-12 Frame prioritization

Frames are tagged to identify them as frames that should be transmitted over the network with priority. As frames enter into a network node that is to transmit tagged frames with priority, they are checked for a priority tag. A queuing system is used to keep both tagged and untagged frames in

the same order as they are received. When the network node device is ready to transmit the next frame, a check is made by frame decision logic to see if there are any tagged frames to be sent with priority. If there are tagged frames, they will continue to be transmitted until there are no remaining tagged frames that need to be transmitted. When the tagged frames bin is empty, untagged frames will be transmitted until the next tagged frame arrives in the tagged frame bin. All frames are sent in the order they are received, with the tagged frames being transmitted before any untagged frames.

We have discussed the Layer 2 switch, but tagging requires a higher level than that. Routers are capable of operating at Layer 3 and can make decisions on tagged packets. However, there

is a more recent development in the switching area — the Layer 3 switch (sometimes called the *routing switch*). Routing switches perform many of the same functions as routers, except they operate much faster. Conventional routers depend on software for the routing protocols and decision making. Routing switches implement the routing decision process in hardware, allowing higher throughput of frames. These network devices may be faster than routers as far as forwarding frames, but they are not as flexible or as programmable as a conventional router.

6.5.1.1   VLAN Tagging

VLAN[25] tagging was standardized in IEEE 802.1Q. The standard allows for 4 bytes used for tagging purposes to be inserted between the Source MAC Address and the Frame Length/Type fields. Any modification of a frame will destroy the Frame Check Sequence checksum, so after the frame is assembled with the 802.1Q tagging the checksum is recalculated and placed in the Frame Check Sequence field. Figure 6-13 illustrates the 802.1Q VLAN header.

Tag Protocol Identifier (TPID)	Priority Code Point (PCP)	Canonical Format Indicator (CFI)	VLAN Identifier (VID)
16 Bits	3 Bits	1 Bit	12 Bits

Figure 6-13 The IEEE 802.1Q VLAN header

- **TPID** — The Tag Protocol Identifier is a 16-bit field containing the hexadecimal value of 0x8100 as an indicator that the frame is an 802.1Q tagged frame.

- **PCP** — The Priority Code Point is a 3-bit field[26] that contains a value from 0 to 7 and is used to indicate the priority level of the frame. Zero is the lowest priority and 7 is the highest.

[25]VLAN is an acronym for virtual local area network. Normally, a LAN is localized within a network segment. However, in a switched network environment, the member network nodes of a VLAN do not need to be located within the same local vicinity. They are identified as a group belonging to a particular VLAN.

[26]The maximum value of 3 binary bits is 7: 111(binary) = 7 (decimal). The binary value positions are 4+2+1, which equals 7. This little exercise is for those readers who may find themselves "base-2 challenged."

- **CFI** — The Canonical Format Indicator is a 1-bit field when set to the value 0 to indicate that the MAC address is in canonical format, which is always set

  to 0 for Ethernet switches. If a frame is received with the CFI set to the value 1, it should not be bridged to an untagged port.

- **VID** — The VLAN Identifier is a 12-bit field that specifies which VLAN the incoming frame belongs to. If this field is set to the value of 0, it indicates that the frame does not belong to a VLAN and that it is only a priority tag.

The advantage of having network node devices that are part of a VLAN group equipped with VLAN tagging is primarily the capability to tag outgoing frames with a priority. This means that frames that require

POP QUIZ

What does the acronym VLAN stand for?

timely delivery are expedited over the network before less critical or best delivery frames. Another advantage is that network node devices can be grouped and are allowed to communicate across multiple LAN networks as if they were all on a single LAN network. The destination address is filtered by the switches and bridges in the network path and only forwards the frames to the ports that service the VLAN the frame belongs to. Because of the configurability of these switches, network management is made simpler, allowing for easy addition, removal, movement, or other configuration changes required on a VLAN port.

HELPFUL HINT

Layer 3 (or routing) switches seem so easy to manage and configure. We will again caution about the need for documenting your network well, unless you prefer to go through a multitude of switch configurations, port by port. It is even more imperative because of configurations where ports can be moved and juggled without physically going out and moving a cable on a port. Switch networking issues can be daunting on a large network, so there is no substitute for good network documentation.

(continued)

HELPFUL HINT *(continued)*

If you need to call for support on a problem, remember that the support engineer does not have a crystal ball[27] to look into your network. He is going to rely on your ability to know your network and know it well. Support engineers do not like playing guessing games. It is a waste of their time and will add to your frustration level as your boss blows his hot breath on the back of your neck.

Want to be a good network administrator? Document, document, document!

6.6   Chapter Exercises

1. What does the acronym CSMA/CD stand for?
2. What form of communications eliminates the need for collision detection?
3. When you choose not to configure an Ethernet port for speed and duplex mode, what are you relying on?
4. What is needed when setting up VLAN networking?
5. What is a source address? What is a destination address?
6. What is the maximum number of bytes the Data field can contain in an Ethernet frame? What is the minimum number of data bytes?

6.7   Pop Quiz Answers

1. What was the first type of cable used to form an Ethernet network?

   Coaxial cable

2. An Ethernet network device that forwards data on the network would be considered what type of Ethernet device?

   DCE (data communications equipment)

---

[27] A crystal ball is a device a network administrator hopes the support engineer at the other end of the hotline has when he frantically calls for support. Alas, he does not possess one, so drop to your knees and start praying. Or you can take the easy way out and start documenting your network from initial installation through configuration changes, additions, and anything that modifies the network.

3. If a cable is wired such that one plug is a T568A and the other is a T568B, it would commonly be referred to as _____ cable.

   Crossover

4. You are interconnecting two Ethernet devices, but neither device is showing a link light on the assigned port. List in order of likelihood where the problem might be.

   ▪ Cable type

   ▪ Defective cable

   ▪ Bad network interface

5. Into which two sublayers of the IEEE 802 reference model is the OSI reference model Data Link layer divided?

   ▪ LLC (Logical Link Control)

   ▪ MAC (Media Access Control)

6. With which functions is the Logical Link Control sublayer mainly concerned?

   ▪ Flow control

   ▪ Error control

   ▪ Multiplexing protocols

7. When a collision occurs on the media, what does the transmitting network node do?

   Stops transmitting

8. What is the maximum number of bytes that can be contained in the Data field of an Ethernet frame?

   1500 bytes

9. What does the Frame Check Sequence field of an Ethernet frame contain?

   CRC calculation using the bytes of the Destination Address, Source Address, Frame Length/Type, and Data fields.

10. What is the name of the transmission mode that allows either transmitting or receiving at different time intervals but never within the same time interval?

    Half-duplex

11. What name is applied to the transmission mode that allows multiple frames to be sent without the need to release the network media between frames?

    Burst mode

12. What does the term *full-duplex* mean?

    The capability to transmit and receive at the same time.

13. What is flow control used for?

    To stop a transmitting node from sending when congestion is detected.

14. What is autonegotiation?

    The capability of two network node peers to negotiate the speed and duplex used on the link they are connected to.

15. When a frame is received, what is the first criteria that is checked?

    Destination address

16. What is the first step you should perform before implementing a network?

    Carefully plan out the network.

17. How is a frame given priority?

    Tagging

18. What does the acronym VLAN stand for?

    Virtual local area network

CHAPTER 7

Not to Be Forgotten

*If you would not be forgotten as soon as you are dead and rotten, either write
things worth reading or do things worth the writing.*

— Benjamin Franklin

We are now at the end of the "Networking Nuts and Bolts" part of this
book. So far we have discussed most of the predominate standards that are
implemented in the majority of networks. We have discussed the popular
LAN and WAN standards that you will most likely be involved with should
you continue in your quest of network knowledge. What you have seen in
this section of the book is only a portion of the technologies that are available
and/or implemented in many networks.

This chapter is going to provide an overview of some of the other standards
and processes that are available and, for the most part, in use (if only in a
small percentage of networks). The way we see it, it just wouldn't be a good
networking book if these weren't at least mentioned.[1] Some of the technologies
in the following pages are of a dying breed, whereas others are just starting
to grow. Whatever their status, these are standards that have been replaced
by other standards, enhanced by revisions to the original standard, developed
to support proprietary hardware and/or software products, or developed to
support a new technology.

When a standard is placed on the road to becoming obsolete,[2] it is normally
due to technology advancements that the standard cannot support. This does
not mean you cannot use the standard, but it does mean there will be no further
advancements to the standard and, for the most part, what you see is what

---

[1] Although there are many good networking books out there that deal with even a single protocol.
[2] The process of retiring a standard is known as placing it into an "end-of-life" status.

you get (WYSIWYG).[3] Some of the standards we will discuss are proprietary but are often implemented as the standard of choice, and some are newer technologies that are just experiencing "startup growth" and will probably prove themselves to be a major part of networks in the next decade.

At the end of the chapter, we have provided an introduction to the structure of a datagram — what it is, how it works, and why it is important. This is to ensure that we keep that network knowledge flowing.

7.1 Can't Get Enough of Those LAN Technologies

In the last chapter, we discussed Ethernet, which is the most popular of LAN protocols in use today. Because of the advancements and cost savings offered by Ethernet, many other protocols have been retired (or are not as commonly used as Ethernet).

> **RANDOM BONUS DEFINITION**
>
> 100BASE-T — The term used to describe baseband Ethernet transmission of 100 Mbps.

In this section, we discuss a few LAN protocols that were once on the cutting edge, and may still be out there serving in some capacity.

7.1.1 Attached Resource Computer Network

In Chapter 1, we defined a LAN as a data network that covers a small geographical area. This normally ranges from an area with just a few PCs to an area about the size of an office building or a group of buildings. Attached Resource Computer Network (ARCnet) is a protocol that was once very popular in LANs, and has even found a purpose in today's Ethernet world. ARCnet is now used as an embedded standard to serve networks that control automation services, transportation, robotics, gaming, and other similar network types.

Developed by the Datapoint Corporation in the late 1970s, ARCnet was designed to use token-passing bus technology over coaxial cabling. The physical topology of ARCnet is a star/bus topology (see Figure 7-1). ARCnet touted speeds of up to 2.5 Mbps[4] and distances of up to four miles. ARCnet is considered the first truly commercially available LAN. Due to the low cost of the infrastructure and the simplicity in implementation and maintenance, ARCnet was very popular when it first arrived.

---

[3]Pronounced "wizzy-wig."

[4]A later version of ARCnet was released in the early 1990s and was called ARCnet plus. It could operate at speeds of up to 20 Mbps. By the time ARCnet plus had come out, however, Ethernet was quickly becoming the standard of choice.

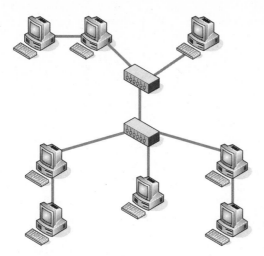

Figure 7-1 An example of an ARCnet topology

ARCnet doesn't have all the bells and whistles that are offered in networks today. It is a very simple technology that is easy to implement and run. A big drawback with ARCnet is that when an interface is brought into the network, the address of the interface has to be set by whoever is installing it. Most of the time, the address is set by jumpers or switches on the resource interface module (RIM)[5] itself.

ARCnet was designed to give Datapoint nodes the capability to share resources over the token bus, thus increasing the overall power of the attached nodes. Datapoint had originally intended to keep what became known as ARCnet fully proprietary because if the public bought their gear, they could tout resource sharing as a selling point.

Datapoint had some problems with the design of the RIM chip, so they eventually contracted with Standard Microsystems Corporation (SMSC). SMSC successfully built the chip specifically for Datapoint, and in the final negotiations got the approval to sell a version of the chip to other vendors — and ARCnet was born.

7.1.2   StarLAN

StarLAN technology is, for the most part, the predecessor to what we all know as Ethernet. Often referred to as *1BASE5* and developed in the early 1980s by AT&T, StarLAN provided a way

> **POP QUIZ**
>
> What was the name of the company that developed ARCnet?

---

[5]The RIM is basically the ARCnet-supported NIC card.

for nodes to communicate with one another over a telephone line. StarLAN operated at 1 Mbps and eventually supported speeds of 10 Mbps.[6] 1BASE5 actually came out after coaxial cabling came out supporting 10 Mbps. This is part of the reason that StarLAN never really got deployed in most LANs. Once 10BASE-T came out, the only time StarLAN was used was when someone needed a low cost infrastructure and speed was not a concern. Figure 7-2 shows an example of the StarLAN topology.

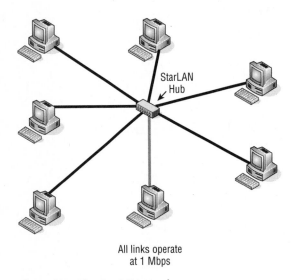

StarLAN
Hub

All links operate
at 1 Mbps

Figure 7-2 The StarLAN topology

StarLAN networks used UTP as a transmission medium and typically connected nodes to one another through at least one hub. StarLAN was able to also connect to multiple nodes without a hub by daisy-chaining them one by one upon the shared medium. The maximum number of nodes in a daisy-chain configuration was 10. Figure 7-3 shows an example of daisy-chaining.

7.1.3 Token Ring

Token Ring network technology was developed by IBM in the late 1970s. IBM submitted the proposed standard to the IEEE LAN standards committee, which adopted the proposal and used the standard as the basis for the IEEE 802.5 standard. Token Ring topologies are a star physical topology and a ring logical topology, as shown in Figure 7-4.

[6]By this time, however, 10BASE-T was out, which rendered this advancement moot.

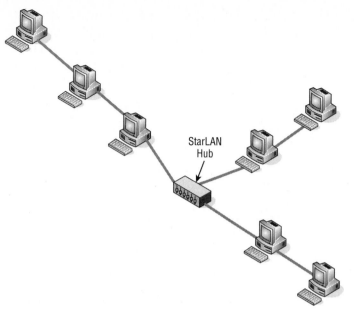

Figure 7-3 Including a daisy chain in a StarLAN configuration

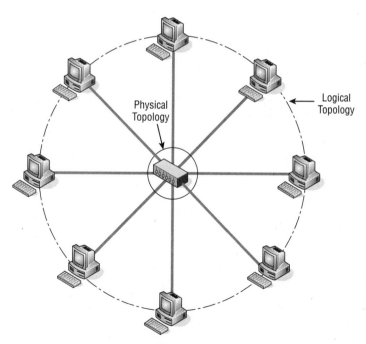

Figure 7-4 A Token Ring topology

Token Ring networks pass a signal, known as a *token*, from one node to the next. The node that you receive the token from is the *upstream neighbor*. The node that you pass the token to is the *downstream neighbor*. Each node receives the token, takes action, and then passes the token to the downstream neighbor (see Figure 7-5).

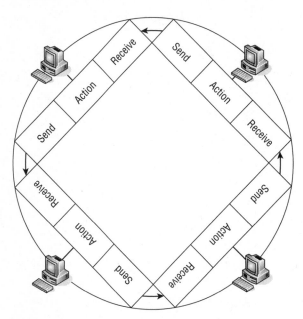

Figure 7-5 Token Ring operations

The actions that are taken are determined by whether the node has control of the token. If a node controls the token, it transmits the token onto the ring to the downstream neighbor, which receives the token and then passes it on the ring to its downstream neighbor. The data is captured by each node, and once the token has made it back to the originating node, that node will remove it from the ring, thus freeing the ring up for the next token to be passed.

> **POP QUIZ**
>
> What technology is also known as 1BASE5?

The original Token Ring supported speeds of 4 Mbps and later came to support 16 Mbps. It didn't take long for networks to upgrade to support the higher speed, especially as the demands on the LAN grew. There is an 802.5 approved standard for Token Ring, allowing up to 100 Mbps speeds, but this never really became popular.[7]

---

[7] Anyone care to guess why?

7.1.3.1   Token Ring's Modus Operandi

In a Token Ring environment, only one node can transmit data from itself at a time. The originating node is given the token in order to pass it on to the network. The node sets the Token bit from a 0 to a 1, which transforms the Token into a datagram known as a *frame*. The data is passed from node to node around the ring. Each node inspects the frame and forwards it to the downstream neighbor.

Once a node inspects the data frame and recognizes its own address as a destination address, the node retains a copy of the data and sends the data on to the next node in line. The data continues around the ring, inspected by all nodes, and then returns to the originating node, which retrieves the

ACRONYM ALERT

TTL — Time to live

frame from the token and sends a new token[8] on to the next node. Once the token arrives at a node that wants to send data, the process begins again.

7.1.3.2   Token Ring Media

Token Ring originally operated on STP cabling but converted to UTP cabling in the 1990s. This was greatly appreciated by the networking community, as it offered a cheaper and less bulky medium.

MMF[9] cabling was supported officially in 1998 when an approved amendment was written into IEEE 802.5, although in actuality a lot of networks were using it already. Token Ring 100 Mbps operation is conducted on the exact twisted pair specification that is used for 100 Mbps Ethernet.

7.1.3.3   The Format of the Token Ring Frame

Token Ring uses one of three frame types. *Token frames* have the token bit set to 0 and have no data. *Token data frames*[10] have the data payload contained within the frame (the token bit is set to 1). The abort frame carries no data and is used to stop its own transmission of data, or used to clear up data that is on the line.

The fields contained within the token frame are fairly simple to understand, as shown in Figure 7-6.

---

[8]Sending a "new" token simply means that the token bit is set back to 0, indicating an available token.

[9]Quick refresher: In Section 3.2.1.3 we discussed the two types of optical fiber, multi-mode fiber (MMF) and single-mode fiber (SMF).

[10]Also known as a token command frame.

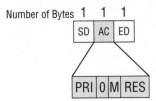

Figure 7-6 An empty Token frame

- **SD** (start of frame delimiter) — This field lets the receiving node know when the frame begins.[11]

- **AC** (access control) — There are four subfields in the access control field, all used to transmit information to the access control process within Token Ring.

  - **PRI** (priority bits) — The priority bits show the priority level of the frame.

  - **0** (token bit) — This bit differentiates the frame type. In Figure 7-6, the token bit is set to 0, identifying it as a token frame.

  - **M** (monitor bit) — The monitor bit is used by a node that is known as an active monitor node. This bit is used to detect various errors.

  - **RES** (reservation bits) — The reservation bits are used by a node to announce that it has data to send and needs to use the token as soon as it is available. Reservations are based on the priority level that has been set.

- **ED** (end of frame delimiter) — This field lets the receiving node know when the frame ends.[12]

The token data frame format is pretty much an extension of the token frame format. The first two fields are identical, but the third field is moved to the end of the frame (where it belongs). Several fields are in between that contain the data and the information that a node will need to send and receive frames on the Token Ring.

> **POP QUIZ**
>
> What is the signal called that is passed in Token Ring from one node to the next?

---

[11] There has to be something identifying the beginning of the frame.

[12] When you have to be clued in when the frame starts, there has to be some way to let you know that the frame is complete.

Figure 7-7 shows the fields contained within the token data frame.

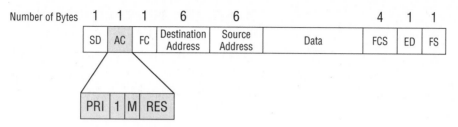

Figure 7-7 Token frame with data attached

- **SD** (start of frame delimiter) — This field lets the receiving node know when the frame begins.
- **AC** (access control) — There are four subfields in the access control field, all used to transmit information to the access control process within Token Ring.
  - **PRI** (priority bits) — The priority bits show the priority level of the frame.
  - **1** (token bit) — This bit differentiates the frame type. In Figure 7-7, the token bit is set to 1, identifying it as a token data frame.
  - **M** (monitor bit) — The monitor bit is used by a node that is known as an active monitor node. This bit is used to detect various errors.
  - **RES** (reservation bits) — The reservation bits are used by a node to announce that it has data to send and needs to use the Token as soon as it is available. Reservations are based on the priority level that has been set.
- **FC** (frame control) — The frame control field is used to separate network management data frames from user data frames.
- **Destination Address** — This field contains the 6-byte network address of the node the frame is destined for.
- **Source Address** — This field contains the 6-byte network address of the node the frame originated from.
- **Data** — This field contains the data from the upper layer protocol that is being transmitted. There is a certain limit on the amount of data that can be included in the frame. At 4 Mbps, the limit is 4,528 bytes. At 16 Mbps, the limit is 18,173 bytes. At 100 Mbps, the limit is 18,173 bytes.
- **FCS** (frame check sequence) — This field is a checksum algorithm that checksums the frame from the FC field to the end of the Data field.

- **ED** (end of frame delimiter) — This field lets the receiving node know when the frame ends.
- **FS** (frame status) — This field is used by the originating node to detect whether there were any errors during transmission. This includes: if the destination node copied the data; if there were any errors encountered; and even if the destination node recognized itself as the destination node.

> **RANDOM BONUS DEFINITION**
>
> trunk — A name defining a bundle of links, also known as *aggregate links*.

7.1.4 Fiber Distributed Data Interface

The *Fiber Distributed Data Interface (FDDI)* is a LAN[13] and/or MAN technology. FDDI[14] was the first such technology that could operate at 100 Mbps. FDDI is an ISO standard and is fully compatible with the IEEE 802 standards.

Although FDDI could function as a LAN technology, it is cheaper and easier to use 100 Mbps Ethernet. When FDDI was developed, it was intended to provide higher speeds in LANs than the quickest rate that was available at the time: 16 Mbps Token Ring or Ethernet. FDDI is sometimes used to connect server farms and multiprocessors to the network. Most often you will find FDDI deployed within the backbone of the network, providing quick connectivity between other networks.

7.1.4.1 FDDI Does What FDDI Does

FDDI was designed to operate over shared fiber media. The fiber connected nodes in a ring similar to the IEEE 802.5 Token Ring standard configuration. The difference is that FDDI uses a dual-ring topology over a shared fiber medium.[15] Data traffic on a FDDI ring flows in a counter-rotating manner. This means that data on one of the rings goes in one direction while the other ring carries traffic in the opposite direction. The ring that actively carries data is the primary ring

> **POP QUIZ**
>
> What information is contained in the Destination Address field in a Token Ring frame?

---

[13]Most networks use FDDI at the MAN levels.
[14]Pronounced "fiddy."
[15]There is a newer standard for FDDI that allows the use of twisted pair cabling instead of fiber. This is called the *Copper Distributed Data Interface (CDDI)*, discussed in Section 7.1.4.1.2.

and the other is the secondary ring, which remains in an inactive status until needed. Figure 7-8 shows an example of the FDDI topology.

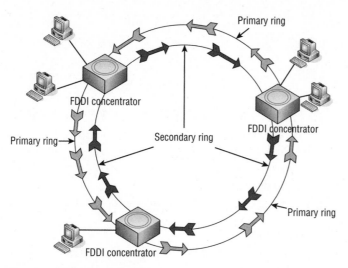

Figure 7-8 FDDI topology

Notice that unlike Token Ring, which connects to a central MAU, there are concentrators[16] that connect nodes to the FDDI topology. We will discuss the different concentrator types in Section 7.1.4.2. Other nodes that can be used within a FDDI ring are servers, routers, switches, and so on. As long as the node is able to support FDDI, it can be used for its intended purpose on the FDDI ring.

The FDDI protocol supports optical fiber (FDDI) as well as copper cables (CDDI)[17] as a shared medium. The operations provide the FDDI functions, with the difference being the medium type used. Both have advantages and disadvantages, which we will discuss in the next two sections.

7.1.4.1.1 Fiber Distributed Data Interface

FDDI is the FDDI protocol over fiber optic cabling. Both MMF and SMF optical fiber medium types are supported in a FDDI environment.

---

[16]Refer to Section 3.3.3.1 if you do not remember what purpose the concentrator serves in a network.

[17]The official name is *twisted pair physical medium dependent (TP-PMD)*; however, CDDI seems to be gaining in popularity. CDDI is a Cisco term, while TP-PMD is the ISO term. It seemed to us that it is easier to refer to this as CDDI for the purposes of this book, but you may need to know both acronyms when working in a professional environment (you don't want to get caught saying, "Huh?" when someone asks you if your TP-PMD is running). As has occurred many times in the history of networking, terms come and go. What is important is that you understand what they are referring to.

There are advantages in using optical fiber as the primary transmission medium:

- Performance
  - Greater distances
  - Faster transmission speed
- Reliability
- Data security

Each advantage is due to the actual medium itself. Optical fiber uses light instead of electricity to carry data. This prevents the leaking of electrical signals, thus improving performance and the reliability of the transmission of data. This also increases security as there is no way to tap into the fiber optic cable. This ensures that, for the most part, only the individuals that are intended to see the data will see the data.

7.1.4.1.2 Copper Distributed Data Interface

Copper Distributed Data Interface (CDDI) is the FDDI protocol over twisted pair media instead of fiber. CDDI is officially known as *twisted pair physical medium dependent (TP-PMD)* and is also known as *twisted pair distributed data interface (TP-DDI)*. CD*TP-PMD*DI uses both STP and UTP cable types.

The main advantage with copper is that it is cheaper and easier to install and maintain than fiber. Because copper cannot transmit the distances that fiber can, it is often used to connect nodes to the concentrator in the FDDI environment. Figure 7-9 shows an example of this.

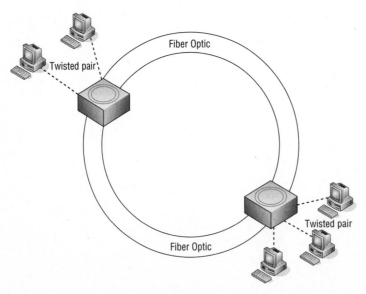

Figure 7-9 FDDI and CDDI together

7.1.4.2 FDDI Node Types

One of the really neat things about FDDI is there are options for how you can configure it. Will you use fiber or copper? How many nodes and concentrators should be supported? What types of concentrators should you use? FDDI offers a lot of choices for you.

The four main node types in the FDDI environment are:

- **Single attachment station (SAS)** — Connects to the FDDI ring through a single connector. The connector has an input port and an output port. Data is received on the input port and is sent to the downstream neighbor via the output port. The SAS connects to a concentrator and then to the primary ring only.

- **Single attached concentrator (SAC)** — Like the SAS, the SAC concentrator connects to only the primary ring. The connection is made through another concentrator.

- **Dual attachment station (DAS)** — Connects to the FDDI ring through two connectors (each with an input and an output port). Can connect directly to the ring or through a concentrator.

POP QUIZ

What does the acronym *FDDI* stand for?

- **Dual attached concentrator (DAC)** — A concentrator that connects to both rings.

7.1.4.3 The FDDI Frame Format

The FDDI frame format is very similar to the format of a Token Ring frame. FDDI uses either token frames or token data frames. Figure 7-10 shows an example of a token frame.

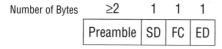

Figure 7-10 An empty token frame

- **Preamble** — Provides a vehicle to ensure the receiving node is synchronized to receive the frame.

- **SD** (start of frame delimiter) — This field lets the receiving node know when the frame begins.

- **FC** (frame control) — This field is used to separate network management data frames from user data frames.

- **ED** (end of frame delimiter) — This field lets the receiving node know when the frame ends.

The token data frame format is pretty much an extension of the token frame format. The first two fields are identical, but the third field is moved to the end of the frame (where it belongs). There are several fields in between that contain the data and the information a node needs to send and receive frames on the Token Ring.

Figure 7-11 shows the fields contained within the token data frame.

Number of Bytes	≥2	1	1	6	6		4	1	1
	Preamble	SD	FC	Destination Address	Source Address	Data	FCS	ED	FS

Figure 7-11 A token frame with data attached

- **Preamble** — Provides a vehicle to ensure the receiving node is synchronized to receive the frame.

- **SD** (start of frame delimiter) — This field lets the receiving node know when the frame begins.

- **FC** (frame control) — This field is used to separate network management data frames from user data frames.

- **Destination Address** — This field contains the 6-byte network address of the node the frame is destined for.

- **Source Address** — This field contains the 6-byte network address of the node the frame originated from.

- **Data** — This field contains the data from the upper layer protocol that is being transmitted. There is a certain limit on the amount of data that can be included in the frame. At 4 Mbps, the limit is 4,528 bytes. At 16 Mbps, the limit is 18,173 bytes. At 100 Mbps, the limit is 18,173 bytes.

- **FCS** (frame check sequence) — This field is a checksum algorithm that checksums the frame from the FC field to the end of the Data field.

- **ED** (end of frame delimiter) — This field lets the receiving node know when the frame ends.

POP QUIZ

What are the four main node types in the FDDI environment?

- **FS** (frame status field) — This field is used by the originating node to detect whether there were any errors during transmission. This includes: if the destination node copied the data; if there were any errors encountered; and even if the destination node recognized itself as the destination node.

7.2   As If You Haven't Had Enough of These Sweet Protocols

It was tough to decide what to include in this section. There are a lot of protocols and other services that you will need to know. For one thing, you will probably come across some, if not all, of them at some point. Additionally, many of the protocols were built upon some networking original protocols, so understanding their function and structure is helpful in understanding the more advanced protocols that have come out in recent years.

The information in this section should really help you start piecing out how things are connected in today's networks. It should also help you better understand the next two parts of this book (especially when you will be tasked to design your own network).

This section is fairly long, but it simply made sense to put it all in here. After reading through this chapter, if you like what we did, you can thank author Jim. If you don't like it, it was author Rich's idea.

7.2.1   Digital Equipment Company Network

The Digital Equipment Company (Digital)[18] developed and released the first version of the *Digital Equipment Company Network (DECnet)* protocol in the mid-1970s. For years, Digital had been developing a series of minicomputers that were known as the *programmed data processor (PDP)*[19] series. DECnet was developed to allow two PDP series 11 (PDP-11) nodes to connect to one another over a point-to-point link and share resources.

---

[18]Many people in the industry refer to the Digital Equipment Company as "DEC" (pronounced "deck"), but the official "short name" is Digital.

[19]Digital decided to use the term programmed data processor (PDP) instead of what it truly was — a computer. This is because computers were known to be complicated and very expensive. To thwart the negative press the computer had developed, the term PDP was used and sold to a market that could not afford a computer.

AN UNRELATED MOMENT OF PAUSE

A reporter was given an opportunity to do an exclusive interview with a network engineer who had been sent to the International Space Station to upgrade the network.

Reporter: "So, how do you feel now that you have been there for 3 days?"

Engineer: "Lady, how would you feel if you were stuck in space, floating inside a grouping of about 120,000 parts all bought from the lowest bidder?"

DECnet is not in and of itself a complete single standard; it's a suite of protocols. As with most protocols that continue to have an end-user demand, DECnet has undergone several updates to the original protocols. Following is a brief overview of the DECnet phases:

- **DECnet phase I** — Allowed two PDP-11 series to communicate with one another.

- **DECnet phase II** — Increased support to networks of up to 32 nodes. The nodes did not have to be identical, but were requested to be able to interoperate with each other. Communication between nodes was done via a point-to-point link. File sharing was an important upgrade during this phase.

- **DECnet phase III** — Increased support to networks of up to 255 nodes. Communication was handled via point-to-point link, as well as multidrop links. Support was added to allow DECnet networks to communicate with networks of other types. Routing and network management were also supported at this phase.

- **DECnet phase IV** — Increased support of networks of up to 63 areas, supporting up to 1023 nodes each. Phase IV included Ethernet support as well as some hierarchical routing standards. Also, a client was developed for Microsoft DOS and some Windows platforms that allowed workstation support of the DECnet protocol.

- **DECnet phase V** — IOS standards were rolled into this phase, moving the protocol from a proprietary standard to an open standard. The name phase V was later changed to *DECnet/OSI*, identifying the compatibility with other OSI standards. Eventually, some TCP/IP protocols were added and the name was changed to *DECnet-Plus*.

ACRONYM ALERT

SONET — Synchronous Optical Network

DECnet phase IV introduced a layered network architecture that is similar to the architecture outlined in the OSI reference model. The DECnet layered model is known as the *digital network architecture (DNA)*. In the DNA model, each layer serves the layers above it and requests services from the layer beneath it. The structure and purpose of the DNA model are much like the OSI model, each layer being responsible for a function to support the protocol. Each layer is mostly based on the proprietary protocol, so some of the upper layers share functions within individual substandards.

The DNA changed as well when DECnet phase V came about, due to the multiple open standard support that was now part of the protocol. Most of the upper layers support both the proprietary and the open standards that became part of the protocol suite.

Note that you don't have to know all the proprietary standards in the protocol suite; know only that it operates in a hierarchical manner.

7.2.2   Xerox Network Systems

Xerox Network Systems (XNS), developed by the Xerox Corporation[20] in the late 1970s and early 1980s, was a suite of protocols that supported a variety of functions. Although it was never a true competitor to TCP/IP, XNS was adopted by many vendors to run within their LANs.[21]

XNS also utilized a reference model that roughly matched the OSI reference model. There were a total of five levels[22] in the XNS reference model:

- **Level 0** — Roughly corresponded with the OSI Layers 1 and 2.

- **Level 1** — Roughly corresponded with the OSI Layer 3.

- **Level 2** — Roughly corresponded to the OSI Layers 3 and 4.

- **Level 3** — Roughly corresponded to the OSI Layers 7 and 7.

- **Level 4+** — Roughly corresponded to the OSI Layer 7.

XNS used a routing protocol called the *Internet Datagram Protocol (IDP)*, which was responsible for datagram delivery within a network as well as an addressing scheme for the routing of said datagrams. Because the format of the IDP packet differed[23] from some other routing protocols, we wanted to break down the packet for you in Figure 7-12 so you can see the fields that are contained in the packet.

Number of Bytes	2	2	1	1	4	6	2	4	6	2	
	CS	L	TC	PT	Destination Network #	Destination Host #	DSN	Source Network #	Source Host #	SSN	Data

Figure 7-12 The IDP packet format

[20]That was pretty obvious, wasn't it?
[21]XNS was modified for several of these companies to suit the needs of their particular network.
[22]Not layers.
[23]For one thing, the IDP network address contains the following: a 4-byte network number, a 6-byte host address, and a 2-byte socket field.

- **CS** (checksum) — Used to determine the integrity of the packet upon receipt by the destination.

- **L** (length) — Identifies the length of the packet.

- **TC** (transport control) — This field actually contains two subfields. The first subfield identifies the current hop count for the packet. The other subfield identifies the maximum time the packet can live on the network.

- **PT** (packet type) — Identifies the format of the packet.

- **Destination Network #** (destination network number) — The 4-byte destination network identifier.

- **Destination Host #** (destination host number) — The 6-byte destination host identifier.

- **DSN** (destination socket number) — The 2-byte destination socket identifier.

- **Source Network #** (source network number) — The 4-byte source network number.

- **Source Host #** (source host number) — The 6-byte source host identifier.

- **SSN** (source socket number) — The 2-byte source socket identifier.

- **Data** (data) — The payload!

> **POP QUIZ**
>
> What are DECnet's five phases?

7.2.3 Internetwork Packet Exchange

The *Internetwork Packet Exchange (IPX)* protocol is normally found within networks with nodes running the Novell NetWare operating system. Novell NetWare was built to support the protocols that were a part of the XNS protocol suite. IPX is a datagram protocol used to route packets within a network. It is connectionless-oriented protocol (IP, for example) and therefore does not have to ensure a connection before it puts the packet onto the transport medium.

IPX uses a distance-vector protocol (RIP, for example), making routing decisions based on hop counts. IPX RIP works similarly to RIP, but instead of using a hop count for distance determination it uses what is known as a *tick*. A tick is simply a measure of time ($1/18^{th}$ of a second) delay that is expected for a particular distance on the medium. If there are two routes to the destination and the ticks are the same on each path, the route with the lowest hop count is the one that will be chosen.

IPX uses an IPX address for host/node identification. There are two parts to the IPX address. The first part of the IPX address is the *network* number: the remaining part is known as the *node* number. The network number is 4 bytes long (that's a total of 32 bits for those of you who are counting).[24] The node number is 6 bytes long (48 bits), which happens to match the length of the MAC address of the NIC. Why does it match? Because the MAC (IEEE 802) address is the number that is used for the node number part of the IPX address. Figure 7-13 is an example of the IPX address.

Network–4 bytes	Node–6 bytes

Figure 7-13 The IPX address

Because the node has its own MAC address, the only requirement you need to have an IPX address assigned to the node is to plug it into an interface to the network. The node will send out

> **RANDOM BONUS DEFINITION**
>
> workgroup switch — A switch used within a single department or workgroup.

a broadcast letting the network know it has joined the network. The appropriate router will then assign the network number to the node. The node now has identification and can send and receive IPX datagrams. IPX is simple to implement — it is basically plug and play.

By now you have to be asking if there is anything complicated about IPX. The answer is no, but there is something you need to know about the IPX datagram format: there is not just a single datagram format. Why? Originally, IPX frame formats served well on the early Ethernet networks within a single network. But as networks grew and as LANs began communicating with one another, other standards were introduced and existing standards were improved, and IPX could not support communication with nodes outside of their known network number–which is why four Ethernet frame formats are used.[25]

Novell proprietary frame format — This is the original frame format that was used. It is often referred to as *802.3 raw* (minus the LLC [802.2]). Figure 7-14 is an example of this.

Number of Bytes	6	6	2		4
	DA	SA	LNH	IPX Packet	CRC

Figure 7-14 The 802.3 raw frame format

---

[24]If you are counting, or even thought of counting, then you get extra credit! Great job!
[25]The router is responsible for translating and reformatting different formats so the destination can understand the information within the frame.

- **DA** (destination address) — The 6-byte destination MAC address.
- **SA** (Source address) — The 6-byte source MAC address.
- **LNH** (length) — This field identifies the amount of data contained in the data payload field.
- **IPX Packet** — This is the IPX datagram portion of the frame. The following subfields are part of the IPX packet:

    CS (checksum) — This field is normally not used. If it is used, then it is not compatible with the Novell proprietary format.

    PL (packet length) — The length of the IPX packet.

    TC (transport control) — The hop count (this is an incrementing field).

    PT (packet type) — Identifies the format of the data in the payload portion of the packet.

    DNN (destination network number) — The 4-byte destination network identifier.

    DHN (destination host number) — The 6-byte destination host identifier.

    DSN (destination socket number) — The 2-byte destination socket identifier.

    SNN (source network number) — The 4-byte source network number.

    SHN (source host number) — The 6-byte source host identifier.

    SSN (source socket number) — The 2-byte source socket identifier.

    Data — The payload!

    CRC (cyclic redundancy check) — This is a 4-byte value that is part of the frame check sequence (FCS), used to determine if a frame is intact at the receiving end.

802.3 frame format — This is the same format used by Ethernet, followed by the IPX data payload. Figure 7-15 is an example of this.

POP QUIZ

Which operating system uses IPX?

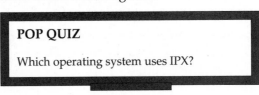

Figure 7-15 The 802.3 frame format

- **DA** (destination address) — The 6-byte destination MAC address.

- **SA** (source address) — The 6-byte source MAC address.

- **LNH** (length) — This field identifies the amount of data contained in the data payload field.

- **IPX Packet** — This is the IPX datagram portion of the frame. The following subfields are part of the IPX packet:

    CS (checksum) — This field is normally not used. If it is used, then it is not compatible with the Novell proprietary format.

    PL (packet length) — The length of the IPX packet.

    TC (transport control) — The hop count (this is an incrementing field).

    PT (packet type) — Identifies the format of the data in the payload portion of the packet.

    DNN (destination network number) — The 4-byte destination network identifier.

    DHN (destination host number) — The 6-byte destination host identifier.

    DSN (destination socket number) — The 2-byte destination socket identifier.

    SNN (source network number) — The 4-byte source network number.

    SHN (source host number) — The 6-byte source host identifier.

    SSN (source socket number) — The 2-byte source socket identifier.

    Data (data) — The payload!

    CRC (cyclic redundancy check) — This is a 4-byte value that is part of the frame check sequence (FCS), used to determine if a frame is intact at the receiving end.

802.3 with 802.2 frame format — The header of this format is the same format used by IEEE 802.3, then comes the LLC header, and finally the IPX data payload. Figure 7-16 is an example of this.

> **RANDOM BONUS DEFINITION**
>
> access priority — The priority used to determine access privileges on a shared LAN segment.

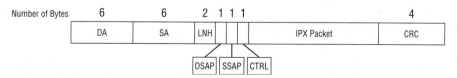

Figure 7-16 The 802.3 with 802.2 frame format

- **DA** (destination address) — The 6-byte destination MAC address.

- **SA** (source address) — The 6-byte source MAC address.

- **LNH** (length) — This field identifies the amount of data contained in the data payload field.

- **DSAP** (destination service access point) — This field identifies which service access points[26] the LLC information should be delivered to.

- **SSAP** (source service access point) — This field identifies the service access point the data originated from.

- **CTRL** (control) — This field contains information used by the LLC on the receiving node that identifies the LLC frame type.

- **IPX Packet** — This is the IPX datagram portion of the frame. The following subfields are part of the IPX packet:

    CS (checksum) — This field is normally not used. If it is used, then it is not compatible with the Novell proprietary format.

    PL (packet length) — The length of the IPX packet.

    TC (transport control) — The hop count (this is an incrementing field).

    PT (packet type) — Identifies the format of the data in the payload portion of the packet.

    DNN (destination network number) — The 4-byte destination network identifier.

    DHN (destination host number) — The 6-byte destination host identifier.

    DSN (destination socket number) — The 2-byte destination socket identifier.

    SNN (source network number) — The 4-byte source network number.

    SHN (source host number) — The 6-byte source host identifier.

    SSN (source socket number) — The 2-byte source socket identifier.

    Data (data) — The payload!

    CRC (cyclic redundancy check) — This is a 4-byte value that is part of the frame check sequence (FCS), used to determine if a frame is intact at the receiving end.

Sub-network Access Protocol (SNAP) frame format — Uses the IEEE 802.3 standard header, LLC header, SNAP header, and finally the IPX data payload. Figure 7-17 is an example of this.

---

[26] A *service access point (SAP)* is a label that is assigned to endpoints in a network.

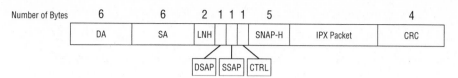

Figure 7-17 The SNAP frame format

- **DA** (destination address) — The 6-byte destination MAC address.

- **SA** (source address) — The 6-byte source MAC address.

- **LNH** (length) — This field identifies the amount of data contained in the data payload field.

- **DSAP** (destination service access point) — This field identifies which service access points that the LLC information should be delivered to.

- **SSAP** (source service access point) — This field identifies the service access point that the data originated from.

- **CTRL** (control) — This field contains information used by the LLC on the receiving node that identifies the LLC frame type.

- **SNAP-H** (Sub-network Access Protocol[27] header) — There are two subfields contained within this):

  VC (vendor code) — This identifies the vendor code of the source.

  ET (ether type) — This identifies the version of Ethernet being used.

- **IPX Packet** — This is the IPX datagram portion of the frame. The following subfields are part of the IPX packet:

  CS (checksum) — This field is normally not used. If it is used, then it is not compatible with the Novell proprietary format.

  PL (packet length) — The length of the IPX packet.

  TC (transport control) — The hop count (this is an incrementing field).

  PT (packet type) — Identifies the format of the data in the payload portion of the packet.

  DNN (destination network number) — The 4-byte destination network identifier.

  DHN (destination host number) — The 6-byte destination host identifier.

  DSN (destination socket number) — The 2-byte destination socket identifier.

---

[27]SNAP is an extension of LLC.

SNN (source network number) — The 4-byte source network number.

SHN (source host number) — The 6-byte source host identifier.

SSN (source socket number) — The 2-byte source socket identifier.

Data (data) — The payload!

- **CRC** (cyclic redundancy check field) — This is a 4-byte value that is part of the frame check sequence (FCS), used to determine if a frame is intact at the receiving end.

All of you Token Ring fans, don't fret. IPX also can be encapsulated and transmitted on a Token Ring network. Figure 7-18 shows the format of the Token Ring frame.

ACRONYM ALERT

ARB — All routes broadcast

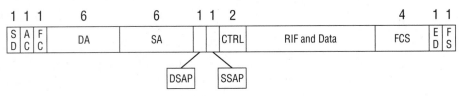

Figure 7-18 The IPX Token Ring frame format

- **SD** (start of frame delimiter) — This field lets the receiving node know when the frame begins.

- **AC** (access control) — There are four subfields in the access control field, all used to transmit information to the access control process within Token Ring.

- **FC** (frame control) — This field is used to separate network management data frames from user data frames.

- **DA** (destination address) — This field contains the 6-byte network address of the node the frame is destined for.

- **SA** (source address) — This field contains the 6-byte network address of the node the frame originated from.

- **DSAP** (destination service access point) — This field identifies which service access points[28] the LLC information should be delivered to.

- **SSAP** (source service access point) — This field identifies the service access point that the data originated from.

- **CTRL** (control) — This field contains information that is used by the LLC on the receiving node that identifies the LLC frame type.

---

[28] A *service access point (SAP)* is a label assigned to endpoints in a network.

- **RIF** (routing information) — This field assists in ensuring the Token Ring frame is sent in the correct direction.

- **Data** — The payload!

- **FCS** (frame check sequence) — This field is a checksum algorithm that checksums the frame from the FC field to the end of the Data field.

- **ED** (end of frame delimiter) — This field lets the receiving node know when the frame ends.

- **FS** (frame status) — This field is used by the originating node to detect whether there were any errors during trans-

> **POP QUIZ**
>
> True or false: IPX is not supported on a Token Ring network.

mission. This includes if the destination node copied the data, if there were any errors encountered, and even if the destination node recognized itself as the destination node.

7.2.4   Point-to-Point Protocol

The *Point-to-Point Protocol (PPP)* is really not a protocol at all; rather, it is a suite of protocols that work to allow IP data exchange over PPP links. Prior to the release of PPP, the standard that was being used for IP serial link transmission was the *Serial Link Internet Protocol (SLIP)*. SLIP did a decent job of transmitting the IP data, but it wasn't reliable, wasn't secure, and really wasn't able to support the performance demands of end users. Additionally, SLIP was used in LANs where the cabling wasn't long at all — SLIP just couldn't support communication over longer distances. PPP was developed to address these issues, as well as support serial communication for many network layer protocols, not just IP.

To support the multiple protocol datagrams, PPP uses the following three main components:

- PPP encapsulation method
- PPP Link Control Protocol (LCP)
- PPP Network Control Protocol (NCP)

7.2.4.1   PPP Encapsulation Method

PPP specifies a frame format that is to be used to encapsulate higher layer data. The format is based on the format used for the *High-level Data Link Control (HDLC) protocol*. HDLC is a synchronous Data Link layer protocol developed by the ISO and used as a reference for the PPP standard.

7.2.4.2   PPP Link Control Protocol

LCP is the foundation protocol of the PPP protocol suite. It is the big kahuna in PPPland, supervising all the other protocols to ensure that they are performing the actions they are responsible for. LCP controls the PPP links. The processes involved in setting up and negotiating the rules for a link, managing the activity on the link, and closing the link when the data transmission is complete are all functions overseen by LCP.

7.2.4.3   PPP Network Control Protocol

ACRONYM ALERT

RFC — Request for Comments

NCP is the control protocol that ensures the correct Layer 3 protocol is being used. NCP establishes which network layer protocol is required and then it sets the parameters needed to ensure that data can be recognized and understood at the endpoint. PPP supports multiple NCPs running on the same link, regardless of the type or which of the Layer 3 protocols is being supported.

7.2.4.4   Please, Tell Us More

PPP has to set up a PPP link in order to communicate to the destination. The first node will test the link by sending an LCP frame. Once LCP has set up the link and all of the session parameters have been negotiated between the endpoints, NCP frames are then sent to set up and configure the parameters for the particular NCP type to be used. Once all these steps have occurred, packets can be sent. The link remains established until it is no longer needed or something external[29] causes link failure.

7.2.4.5   PPP Frame Format

We previously mentioned that PPP was designed based on the HDLC protocol. The frame format is the same for PPP and HDLC; however, PPP does not use all the fields. Therefore, some fields are set to a standard number for PPP.[30] Figure 7-19 depicts the PPP frame format.

- ▪ **Flag** — The PPP Flag field is always set to binary 01111110. This field indicates the start point and end point of the frame.

---

[29]In other words, PPP didn't do it.
[30]Why reinvent the wheel?

- **BA** (broadcast address) — This field is set to binary 11111111.

- **CTRL** (control) — This field is used by HDLC and is used for certain control parameters. The PPP control field is always set to binary 00000011.

- **Protocol** — This field identifies the protocol type for the information contained in the data payload.

- **Data** — The payload!

- **FCS** (frame check sequence) — This field is a checksum algorithm that checksums the frame from the FC field to the end of the Data field.

- **Flag** — The PPP Flag field is always set to binary 01111110. This field indicates the start point and end point of the frame.

> **POP QUIZ**
>
> What serial transmission standard was used before PPP came out?

1	1	1	2		Up to 4	1
Flag	BA	CTRL	Protocol	Data	FCS	Flag

Figure 7-19 The PPP frame format

7.2.5 X.25

X.25 is a Network layer protocol standard that is maintained by the International Telecommunication Union – Telecommunication standardization sector (ITU-T). Used within packet-switched networks, X.25's purpose in networking is to provide the rules on how connections between nodes are set up and maintained. X.25 protocols[31] allow communication between different networks, regardless of what equipment and protocols they are running. Communication between the networks is actually handled through an intermediary (more on this in a little bit) at the Network layer. X.25 is a reliable connection-oriented standard of protocols.

X.25 uses the following three main types of nodes (see Figure 7-20):

- **Data terminal equipment (DTE)** — Nodes that communicate on the X.25 network (these are the computers and nodes that connect the user to a network). Think of the DTE as the user nodes.

---

[31]Did you notice the *s*? Yep — it's a suite of protocols, not really a single protocol.

■ **Data circuit-terminating equipment (DCE)**[32] — A network access point (normally a modem or packet switch that is the interface to the *cloud*).[33] Think of the DCE as the network nodes.

■ **Date switching exchange (DSE)**[34] — The nodes that are in the cloud. These nodes are responsible for passing data from DTE to DTE.

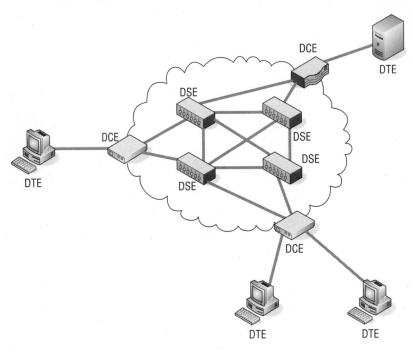

Figure 7-20 Deployments of the X.25 node types

In X.25 data transmission operations, every DTE must have an association with a DCE. Don't confuse DTE and DCE as being single standalone network nodes. DTE and DCE are actually the functions performed. As a matter of fact, a single node can provide multiple functions (for instance, a node can be both a DCE and a DSE.

DCEs and DSEs are the nodes that route the packets through the cloud to a destination. Each and every packet that is transmitted may take a different

---

[32]Also known as data communications equipment and data carrier equipment.

[33]*Cloud* is a term that defines the WAN infrastructure. Normally networks connect using a communication protocol (such as X.25). There is usually a switch that is the interface to the cloud. Once a packet hits the cloud, the provider is responsible for routing data to a destination. What goes on in the cloud stays with the cloud — meaning the endpoint networks don't necessarily care how the provider is getting the data there, just as long as it gets there.

[34]Also known as packet switching exchange (PSE).

path to get to the destination DCE and ultimately the destination DTE. Usually, the DTE connects to the DCE over some type of network, but two nodes can be connected directly. When there is a direct connection between nodes, then one of the nodes has to perform the functions of a DCE.

The DTE is responsible for serving multiple sessions over a single connection to the DCE. Each and every session first needs to be connected to the DCE. Once the connections are established, the transmission of data can occur. Figure 7-21 is a basic diagram that depicts the session setup and processes.

RANDOM BONUS DEFINITION

broadcast address — The well-known multicast address defining all nodes.

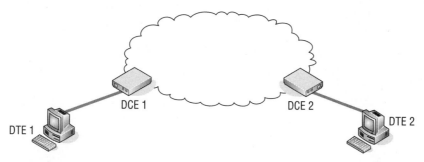

Figure 7-21 A basic X.25 network

A session can be established in one of three ways (refer to Figure 7-21):

- The DTE can send a message to the DCE, letting the DCE know it has data to transmit. For instance, DTE 1 contacts DCE 1 and lets the DCE know it has data to transmit to DTE 2. This is known as a *switched virtual circuit (SVC)*.

- A DCE can receive a message from another DCE, letting the DCE know that a DTE is requesting to send data to another DTE. For instance, DCE1 informs DCE 2 that DTE 1 wishes to pass data to DTE 2.

- The session can be left up at all times. In this scenario, as far as the DTEs are concerned, they can just pass the data to the destination DTE whenever they have data to send. No session setup is required. This is known as a *permanent virtual circuit (PVC)*.

THE X.25 PAD

Some DTEs (for instance, dumb terminals) are not complex enough to understand full X.25 functionality. Therefore, they need a little assistance in communicating with the DCE. X.25 also supports a node type that performs just this function (helping the little guy out).

The packet assembler/disassembler (PAD) is a node between the DCE and the DTE that is used to assemble packets, disassemble packets, and buffer data until the DTE is ready to receive.

X.25 was developed and used before the OSI reference model was developed. To understand the protocol X.25, all you have to know is that (with only a few exceptions) operations can be mapped to the functions of the lower three levels (Physical, Data Link, and Network) of the OSI reference model. The three levels of the X.25 suite are as follows:

1. **Physical level** — This level corresponds to the OSI Physical layer. This includes defining all of the electrical and mechanical functions that are used by the physical medium. Some X.25 protocols operating at this level include:

   - V.35
   - X.21bis
   - RS232

2. **Link level** — This level corresponds to the OSI model's Data Link layer. Functions that are performed at this level are the framing of packets, numbering packets, receipt acknowledgment, flow control, error detection, and recovery, etc. The X.25 protocol that operates at this level is *Link Access Procedure, Balanced (LAPB)*.

3. **Packet level** — At this level, data is exchanged between X.25 nodes. The protocol that is used at this level is the *Packet Layer Protocol (PLP)*.

> **RANDOM BONUS DEFINITION**
>
> routing — The passing of data among various networks.

7.2.5.1 X.25 Operations

When an X.25 session is established, the session is assigned a virtual circuit number that is known to only the DTE and its associated DCE. The virtual circuit number is what is used to route the packets to the destination. The virtual circuit number is normally a shorted number, so the route lookup process is shorted (fewer bits and bytes to look at).

The virtual circuit is nothing more than a path to a destination. A virtual circuit number reinforces the existence of a reliable path from one DTE to another DTE. As mentioned previously, there are two types of virtual circuits: *switched virtual circuits (SVC)* and *permanent virtual circuits (PVC)*. The SVC is a circuit that is established as needed between DTEs. Each time a DTE needs to send data, the SVC will have to be set up before communication occurs and closed when the session terminates. The other type of virtual circuit, the PVC, is set up only once. It is used between DTEs that have a constant need to send data to other DTEs.

Additionally, X.25 supports what is known as *multiplexing*, which means that it can carry multiple sessions over a single physical line. Each session would maintain its own virtual circuit, which will identify the destination DTE. Multiplexing is used when a single DTE has several processes that need to communicate with multiple destinations. Once data arrives at the destination, it is demultiplexed and sent to the appropriate DCE to be passed to the endpoint DTE. Figure 7-22 shows an example of how this works.

ACRONYM ALERT

ATP — AppleTalk Transaction Protocol

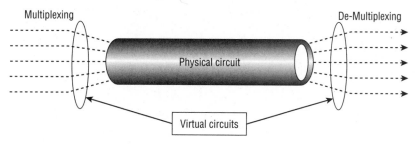

Figure 7-22 A multiplexing example

7.2.5.2 Link Access Procedure, Balanced

The *Link Access Procedure, Balanced (LAPB)* is the X.25 Data Link layer protocol that ensures reliable, error-free packet framing and data communication management. LAPB employs the use of three message frame types:

- **Information frame type** — Frames of this type are known as *I-frames*. I-frames are used to pass upper layer data and some control data. I-frames perform packet sequencing, flow control, and error detection and recovery.

- **Supervisory frame type** — Frames of this type are known as *S-frames*. S-frames are used to pass control data, such as transmission requests, status reporting, I-frame receipt acknowledgements, and termination requests.

- **Unnumbered frame type** — Frames of this type are known as *U-frames*. U-frames are used to pass control data, such as session setup, error reporting, and session termination.

LAPB frames include a header, the PLP data that is being passed to the other end, and a frame trailer. Figure 7-23 shows the format of the LAPB frame.

Number of Bytes | 1 | 1 | 1 | | 2 | 1

| Flag | AD | Ctrl | Data | FCS | Flag |

Figure 7-23 The LAPB frame format

- **Flag** — The LAPB Flag field indicates the start point and end point of the frame.

- **AD** (address) — This field identifies whether the frame is carrying a response or a command.

- **CTRL** (control) — This field details which frame type (I-frame, S-frame, or U-frame) is being used, the frame sequence number, and the frame function.

- **Data** — The payload! In LAPD, this is the PLP packet.

- **FCS** (frame check sequence) — This field is a checksum algorithm that checksums the frame from the FC field to the end of the Data field. This is where error checking and data integrity are monitored.

- **Flag** — The LAPB flag field indicates the start point and end point of the frame.

7.2.5.3 *Packet Layer Protocol*

The *Packet Layer Protocol (PLP)* is the X.25 Network layer protocol that is used to direct the flow of packets between two DTE nodes over a virtual circuit. PLP can run in conjunction with other protocol standards (for instance, ISDN interfaces on a WAN or LLC within a LAN). There are five defined modes of operation for the PLP:

- **Initial session setup mode** — Used to set up an SVC or PVC between DTE nodes.

- **Data transfer mode** — Used to transfer data between DTEs.

- **Idle mode** — Used by SVCs to keep a session active when no data is being transmitted at the time.

- **Session termination mode** — Used to terminate a session and to clear the SVC.

- **Re-initialization mode** — Used to synchronize data transmission between a DTE and its associated DCE.

ACRONYM ALERT

ISP — Internet service provider

7.2.6 Asynchronous Transfer Mode

Asynchronous Transfer Mode (ATM) is a standard maintained by the ITU-U. Its function is to pass fixed-size datagrams known as *cells* over an ATM network. ATM is a connection-oriented standard, which means the connection is up between nodes before data can be transmitted.[35] Unlike pure packet-switched networks (IP, Ethernet, X.25, etc.), where the frames are of variable lengths, ATM provides *cell-relay* (transmission of data that is encapsulated into a fixed length cell) services on a packet-switched network.

ATM uses nodes that are called *ATM switches*[36] for the transfer of cells within a network. An ATM switch is not a switch in the Layer 2 meaning of the term. It is actually more like a router in functionality.

7.2.6.1 ATM Generic Cell Format

ATM cells are a fixed 53 bytes in size (see Figure 7-24). The first portion of the cell is the header information and is 5 bytes long. The remaining 48 bytes are for the data payload. ATM cells are perfect for passing large amounts of data (streaming video, for example). The fixed length cells do not require the delays that can occur in synchronous data transmission because the variable length packets can cause long upload and download times. Asynchronous transmission, on the other hand, is a steady stream of cells.

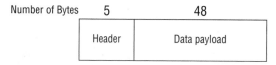

Figure 7-24 The ATM cell format

---

[35]Repetition – repetition - repetition.
[36]Often nodes are tagged with the word *switch* by the marketing folks out there. It's a buzzword that is often used to impress the customer base.

7.2.6.2 An Overview of ATM Operations

ATM is efficient and reliable. It offers transmission delay (there is no time lapse waiting for your turn), guaranteed to serve constant streams of data and patient enough to wait until data is ready to be passed.

ATM networks contain nodes that are called ATM switches, as well as endpoint nodes that support ATM. ATM switches are responsible for passing data traffic to destination ATM switches and/or ATM endpoint nodes. Endpoint nodes are responsible for interfacing other network types to the ATM network. Examples of endpoint nodes include (see Figure 7-25):

- ATM channel service unit/data service unit (CSU/DSU)
- LAN router
- LAN switch
- LAN workstation

> **POP QUIZ**
>
> Which protocol operates at the packet level of the X.25 model?

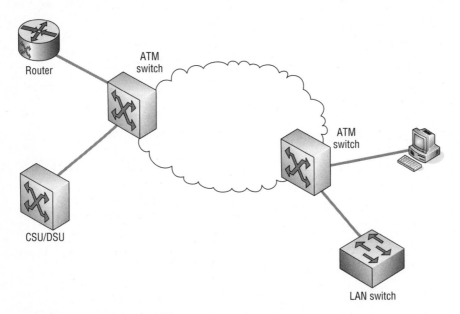

Figure 7-25 An ATM network

7.2.6.2.1 ATM: Virtual Paths, Circuits, and Channels

Closely emulating the virtual circuit concept that is used in X.25, ATM uses what are known as *virtual path identifiers (VPI)* and *virtual circuit identifiers (VCI)*[37] for the routing of cells in an ATM environment. The VPI/VCI pairing

---

[37] Also known as a *virtual channel identifier*. A channel is basically the same thing as a circuit.

is found in the ATM header and is used to map sessions that are active at any given time. The VPI is used by ATM switches to keep track of the paths to a destination. The backbone switches do not care about the VCI; it's the interfacing nodes (nodes that are outside of the backbone) which include that in path definition. When a switch includes the VCI in its switching decisions, it considers the VPI/VCI pair as a single number.

Different types of VPIs and VCIs are used in an ATM network:

Virtual circuit types

- Permanent virtual circuit (PVC) — This is a static virtual circuit.
- Soft permanent virtual circuit (SPVC) — This is a dynamic PVC.
- Switched virtual circuit (SVC) — This is an "as needed"[38] virtual circuit.

Virtual path types

- Permanent virtual path (PVP) — This is a static virtual path.
- Soft permanent virtual path (SPVP) — This is a dynamic PVP.

The VPI and VCI sessions are identified in the header of the ATM cell. THE VPI is a 12-bit identifier[39] and the VCI is a 16-bit identifier. Virtual circuits must be set up before any data transmission can occur. A virtual path is a group of virtual channels, which are bundled together and transmitted across the ATM network over a shared virtual path. Even though there may be multiple virtual circuits between ATM switches, the VPI and VCI pairing is used only by the endpoint nodes that are involved in the session (see Figure 7-26). Notice how this ATM multiplexing is very similar to the multiplexing processes in X.25.

> **RANDOM BONUS DEFINITION**
>
> end of frame delimiter — Used to indicate the end of the Data Link encapsulation.

7.2.6.2.2 ATM: Link Interface Types

There are two primary types of link interfaces used in an ATM environment. *The network-network interface (NNI)* and the *user-network interface (UNI)*. The UNI is the link that connects ATM endpoint nodes to an ATM switch. The NNI is the connection between ATM switches through the cloud.

---

[38]This could also be "on demand."

[39]Four bits of this can be used for *generic flow control (GFC)*, when the communication is taking place between an endpoint node and an ATM switch.

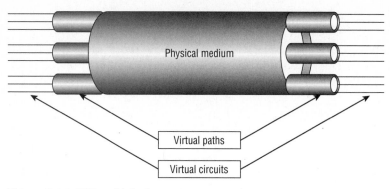

Figure 7-26 ATM multiplexing

Both interface types can be broken up into public UNIs and NNIs or private UNIs and NNIs. Private interface types are used to connect nodes within an ATM topology that is specific to their organization. The public interface types are used to connect nodes on a public network (available to everyone).

7.2.6.2.3   ATM Cell Header Format

The format of the cell header that is used in the ATM cell is determined by the interface type being used. The UNI header (see Figure 7-27) is used for communication between an endpoint node and an ATM switch, while the NNI header (see Figure 7-28) is used for communication between ATM switches.

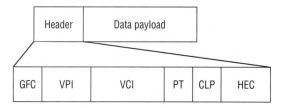

Figure 7-27 The UNI header format

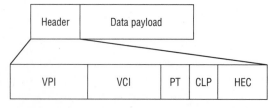

Figure 7-28 The NNI header format

UNI header

- **GFC** (generic flow control; 4 bits) — Used to assist in identifying the nodes that are part of a shared ATM interface.

- **VPI** (virtual path identifier; 8 bits) — Used to identify the VPI portion of the VCI.

- **VCI** (virtual circuit identifier; 16 bits) — The circuit number used to associate the session's virtual circuit.

- **PT** (payload type; 3 bits) — Identifies the data type in the data payload portion of the ATM cell.

- **CLP** (cell loss priority; 1 bit) — Often referred to as the *discard bit*, set by the sending node for cells that can be discarded if link congestion occurs. Also can be sent by nodes if there is a connection that is exceeding the bandwidth allotment for its session.

- **HEC** (header error control; 8 bits) — The checksum algorithm used for the information contained within the header only for error detection and control.

NNI header

- **VPI** (virtual path identifier; 12 bits) — Used to identify the VPI portion of the VCI.

- **VCI** (virtual circuit identifier; 16 bits) — The circuit number that is used to associate the session's virtual circuit.

- **PT** (payload type; 3 bits) — Identifies the data type in the data payload portion of the ATM cell.

- **CLP** (cell loss priority; 1 bit) — Often referred to as the *discard bit*, set by the sending node for cells that can be discarded if link congestion occurs. Also can be sent by nodes if there is a connection that is exceeding the bandwidth allotment for its session.

- **HEC** (header error control; 8 bits) — The checksum algorithm used for the information contained within the header only for error detection and control.

7.2.6.3   *ATM Reference Model*

ATM is a protocol suite whose functions are described by a reference model. The ATM reference model uses layers that correspond to the Physical layer and a portion of the

ACRONYM ALERT

DRAM — Dynamic Random Access Memory

Data Link layer of the OSI reference model. The layers that are part of the ATM reference model are as follows (see Figure 7-29):

- **ATM adaptation layer (AAL)** — Comparable to the functions of the OSI reference model's Data Link layer. This layer is responsible for sorting higher layer data from the ATM processes. This layer combines its services with the service of the ATM layer.

- **ATM layer** — Comparable to the functions of the OSI reference model's Data Link layer. This layer handles the relay of cells through the ATM environment. This layer is also responsible for cell multiplexing.

- **Physical layer** — Responsible for transmission of data on the medium.

> **POP QUIZ**
>
> What are the three virtual circuit types used in ATM?

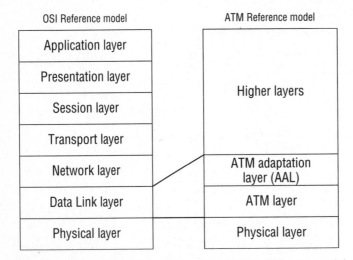

Figure 7-29 A comparison of the OSI and ATM reference models

7.2.6.4 Traffic Management

Several classes of service are defined for user data that is passed within an ATM network. These are as follows:

- **Constant bit rate (CBR)** — Data is passed constantly. The bandwidth required to pass the data is always available.

- **Variable bit rate (VBR)** — Data is passed often. The bandwidth required to pass the data is available, but there are limits on the amount of data that can be passed. The following two types of VBR are used:

  Variable bit rate real-time (VBR-rt) — This is used to pass real-time application data.

  Variable bit rate non-real-time (VBR-nrt) — This is used to temporarily store data in a queue when there is not enough available bandwidth to pass all of the data. It is used with applications that send data, but is not real-time.

- **Available bit rate (ABR)** — Data is passed when bandwidth is available. ABR supports congestion feedback so the sending node will know when there is too much congestion to pass data.

- **Unspecified bit rate (UBR)** — Data is passed if there is bandwidth available, and is dropped if there isn't any available bandwidth. There are no guarantees about delivery.

7.2.6.5 ATM Adaptation Layer Types

The AAL provides interface types that support the service class type that it is assigned to. The type of AAL to be used is determined by the sending node and the type announced when the initial call setup is sent. The AAL types are:

- **AAL1** — Supports CBR transmissions.

- **AAL2** — Supports VBR transmissions.

- **AAL3/4** — Supports both connectionless and connection-oriented data transmission. This AAL type is used to transmit switched multimegabit data services (SMDS)[40] packets.

- **AAL5** — Supports both connectionless and connection-oriented data transmission. This AAL type is used to transmit non-SMDS packets.

  RANDOM BONUS DEFINITION

  network layer — Layer 3 of the OSI reference model.

---

[40]SMDS is a connectionless telco service that supports various protocols and functions needed to transmit data over a high-performance packet-switched network. This protocol is outside of the scope of this book, so this footnote should provide all the information that you will need — a basic definition pertaining to the service.

AN UNRELATED MOMENT OF PAUSE

By now, we felt that you might be in need of a study break. To make your break a bit more enjoyable, here is a great peanut butter cookie recipe. Make a couple of batches to enjoy while you continue on with this book. If you are hyper-motivated, you can reread the section on X.25 while the cookies bake. That section is a good lead-in to the next section, "Frame Relay."

Ingredients:

- 1 cup firmly packed brown sugar
- 1/2 cup peanut butter
- 1/2 cup softened butter
- 1 tsp vanilla
- 1 egg
- 1 cup sugar
- 1 1/2 cups flour
- 1/2 tsp baking powder
- 1/2 tsp baking soda
- 1/2 tsp salt

Preparation steps:

1. Preheat oven to 375°F.
2. Combine brown sugar, butter, and peanut butter in a large bowl. Beat on medium speed until well mixed.
3. Add egg and vanilla; continue beating until well mixed.
4. Reduce speed to low.
5. Add flour, baking powder, baking soda, and salt. Beat until well mixed.
6. Shape dough into 1-inch balls; roll in sugar.
7. Place the balls 2 inches apart onto ungreased cookie sheets; flatten balls in a crisscross pattern with fork dipped in sugar.
8. Bake for 8 to 10 minutes or until edges are lightly browned.

Bon appétit!

7.2.7   Frame Relay

Frame relay is a WAN protocol that operates as a packet-switched network. Like other packet-switched network protocols, frame relay uses the following:

- Multiplexing
- Variable length datagrams

Frame relay is very similar to X.25, and is often considered the upgraded version of X.25. Because frame relay uses various WAN interface types (such as ISDN) to handle Layer 3 functions, and because communication media has improved, frame relay does not have to do the error checking and recovery that X.25 did. Because there is less chatter, frame relay is able to provide quicker and more reliable data transmission, which pretty much renders X.25 obsolete.

Frame relay services operate at the Physical and Data Link layers of the OSI reference model. Originally designed to operate over ISDN interfaces, it now supports transmission over broadband ISDN and ATM.

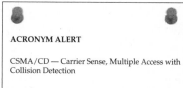

ACRONYM ALERT

CSMA/CD — Carrier Sense, Multiple Access with Collision Detection

7.2.7.1 Frame Relay Node Types

If you reread the section on X.25 while your cookies were baking, you will probably remember the X.25 node types are DTE, DCE, or DSE. In frame relay, you cut out the DSE and have the two node types that are used (see Figure 7-30):

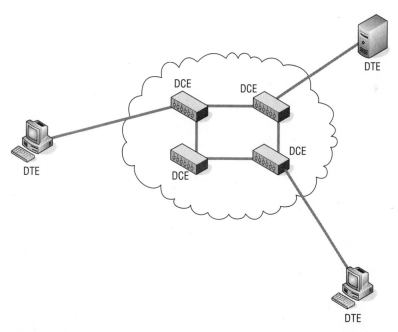

Figure 7-30 DCE and DTE relationship in a frame relay environment

- **DTE** — Nodes that communicate on the frame relay network (these are the computers and endpoint nodes that connect the user to a network). Think of the DTE as the user nodes.

▪ **DCE** — These are the devices that are within the cloud that transports the data over a WAN. Because the DCEs in frame relay are able to handle the clocking and packet-switching services, there is no need for an intermediary device, like the DSE in X.25

7.2.7.2   Virtual Circuits . . . Again?

Frame relay provides a connection-oriented service at the Data Link layer. Before data can be transmitted, the connection has to be up. The connection is associated with a unique data link connection identifier (see the next section). It is the DLCI that defines the virtual circuit between DTEs. Frame relay supports the multiplexing of virtual circuits to be established over a physical circuit. The frame relay virtual circuit types are:

▪ SVC — A temporary connection

▪ PVC — A permanent connection

7.2.7.3   Data Link Connection Identifier

The identifier used to define a circuit is known as the data link connection identifier (DLCI). The DLCI is a value that is normally defined and assigned by the telco provider. The DLCIs are only important to the DTEs. The DCEs normally employ various methods and routes from circuit to circuit. In other words, the DLCI is what allows the data to be passed to the endpoint nodes outside of the cloud. The DCEs make decisions based on whatever technologies are in use by the telco. Because frame relay is a multiplexing WAN

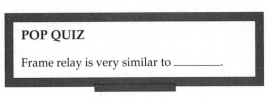

POP QUIZ

Frame relay is very similar to _____.

protocol, there can be multiple logical circuits passing data through the cloud over a single physical circuit.

7.2.7.4   Feckens and Beckens[41]

As much as we all may hate to admit it, network congestion occurs more often than we would like it to. It's just a fact of life in a network. Fortunately, there are a lot of checks and balances in most networks that help to prevent errors and to detect and recover from them when they do occur.

Within the frame relay cloud (the provider's portion of the frame relay environment), there can be thousands upon thousands of transmissions passing

---

[41]These are another pair of fun acronyms similar to catenet (although these are still in use).

through from multiple organizational LANs. All of this data is passing through the same equipment to make its way through the cloud and to a destination. Because of all the end-user data passing through the nodes, congestion does occur.

Frame relay has a couple of functions that help detect congestion and notify the DTEs that congestion is occurring. Additionally, the frame relay header provides an address field that reserves 1 bit for the FECN and one for the BECN. These functions are:

- **Forward explicit congestion notification (FECN)**[42] bit — Within the address field of the frame relay frame header.

- **Backward explicit congestion notification (BECN)**[43] bit — Within the address field of the frame relay frame header.

In addition to the FECN bit and the BECN bit, there is also a bit that is used to indicate if the data is important or not. This field is known as the *discard eligibility (DE)* bit. If the DE bit is "set," the DTE is notifying the DCEs that the frame is low priority and can be discarded if congestion is occurring. This gives the DCEs the capability to prioritize, dropping the data with less importance and only discarding the important data as a last option. The DTEs will retransmit the higher priority data if it gets notification from the DCEs that congestion is occurring.

There are two additional bits in the frame relay frame header that can be set to notify a target node that there is congestion. BECNs are sent to the sending DCEs that there is congestion and FECNs are sent to the target DCEs that there is congestion. Normally, the sending DCE will assume that there are problems if it receives so many BECNs in a certain time period (the number is set by the provider and the subscribing network). It will then cut down on the amount of data it is transmitting[44] or will stop transmitting altogether. When the DTE stops seeing the BECNs, it will return to the way it normally performs.

ACRONYM ALERT

FC — Frame control

---

[42]Pronounced "fecken."

[43]Pronounced "becken."

[44]Normally, a frame relay provider will promise a minimum transmission rate for a virtual circuit. This is known as the committed information rate (CIR). Often, the provider will allow you to exceed the CIR and will try to pass the data on a best-effort basis. Should your edge router start seeing the BECNs repeatedly outside of the standards you have configured, the CIR should be checked and may need to be adjusted. It could be that multiple frames are being received by a router that has a lower CIR and cannot handle the level of traffic at the time (especially if all of the sending routers are exceeding the CIR).

7.2.7.5 Local Management Interface

For the first few years that frame relay was in use, it didn't really have any standards that ensured that the link was up between DTEs and DCEs. Several companies that were leaders in the networking and telecommunication fields banded together to come up with a signaling standard that would work with frame relay to assist in ensuring the link between a DTE and its associated DCE would remain up. What developed was an enhancement known as the *local management interface (LMI)*.

LMI is used to provide link status updates pertaining to PVCs between a DTE and the local DCE. One of the functions performed by LMI is status inquiries that are sent out periodically (normally 10 seconds) to test if a link is up. If the inquiry does not receive a reply, it assumes the link is down. These inquiries are known as *keepalives*. LMI also sends out updates pertaining to the status of all the links in frame relay network, provides information about PVC changes, and ensures that IP multicast is functioning.

7.2.7.6 Frame Relay Frame Format

The standard frame relay frame format is also known as the LMI version of the frame relay frame. Figure 7-31 shows the fields contained within the frame relay frame.

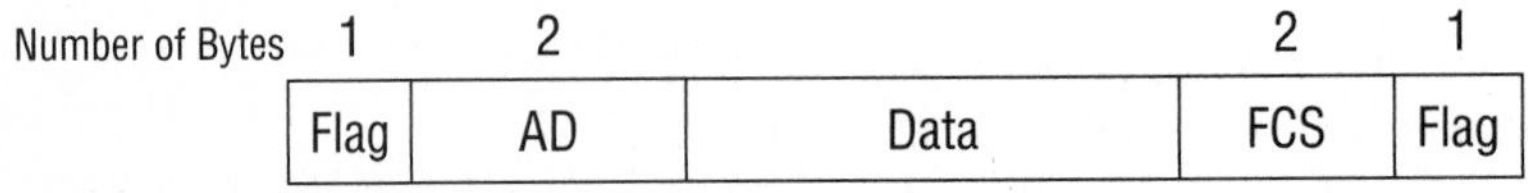

Number of Bytes 1 2 2 1

| Flag | AD | Data | FCS | Flag |

Figure 7-31 Frame Relay frame format

- **Flag** — The frame relay Flag field indicates the start point and end point of the frame.
- **AD** (address) — Included in this field is information pertaining to the DLCI. There are also 3 bits that are included in this field that are for the FECN, BECN, and the DE bit.
- **Data** — The payload!
- **FCS** (frame check sequence) — This field is a checksum algorithm that checksums the frame from the FC field to the end of the Data field. This is where error checking and data integrity are monitored.
- **Flag** — The frame relay Flag field indicates the start point and end point of the frame.

7.2.8   Integrated Services Digital Network

Integrated Services Digital Network (ISDN) is a data transport service that can be used over regular existing telephone lines. The ISDN service enables the telephone line to be digitized, allowing multiple data types to be passed over existing telephone lines. Additionally, ISDN can be used with digital telephone lines.

ISDN is a baseband transmission standard, used to operate over normal copper lines. Broadband ISDN (B-ISDN) was designed to be faster and more reliable than ISDN. B-ISDN operates over fiber optics. As fiber optics are being rolled into more and more residences and businesses, many ISDN users are using the broadband service.

ISDN provides two types of channels to be used for communication in the ISDN environment, the *B channel* and the *D channel*. The B channel is used to carry user data, whereas the D channel is used for signaling between the end user and the ISDN network. The B channel operates at 64 kbps, and the D channel operates between 16 and 64 kbps, depending on the interface rate standard that is being used.

7.2.8.1   *Basic Rate Interface and Primary Rate Interface*

The following two services are used in ISDN to determine bandwidth availability between a source and a destination:

- Basic rate interface (BRI)
- Primary rate interface (PRI)

The BRI service uses two B channels and one D channel.[45] Each B channel operates at 16 kbps. The BRI D channel operates at 16 kbps as well. The PRI service uses 23 B channels[46] and one D channel.[47] Each B channel

> **RANDOM BONUS DEFINITION**
>
> modem — A node used to pass data communication over an analog communications channel.

operates at 16 kbps, whereas the PRI D channel operates at 64 kbps.

7.2.8.2   *ISDN Nodes*

Several node types are used in an ISDN environment. Terminals are a node type that can be either an ISDN terminal type, known as a *terminal equipment*

---

[45]This is referred to as *2B+D*.

[46]PRI in the United States and in Japan includes 23 B channels. Other parts of the world include 30 B channels.

[47]This is referred to as *23B+D*.

type 1 (TE1), or a non-ISDN terminal, known as a *terminal equipment type 2 (TE2)*. The next type of node is called a *terminal adaptor (TA)*, which is used to interface a TE2 with the ISDN network. The next type of node is called a *network termination device type 1 (NT1)* and *network termination device type 2 (NT2)* (or a combination of both). Most ISDN networks will use the NT1.

7.2.8.3 The ISDN Reference Model

ISDN standards span the first three layers of the OSI reference model. At the Physical layer, two different types of frames are used. Which one is used depends on whether the data is flowing from the user node (the terminal) to the ISDN network (TE frame) or from the network to the terminal (NT frame). Figure 7-32 shows the format of the TE frame, and Figure 7-33 shows the format of the NT frame.

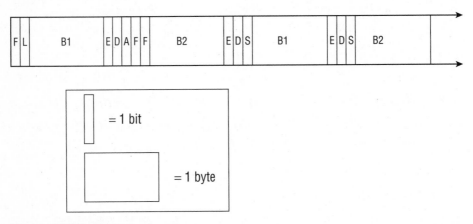

Figure 7-32 The TE frame format

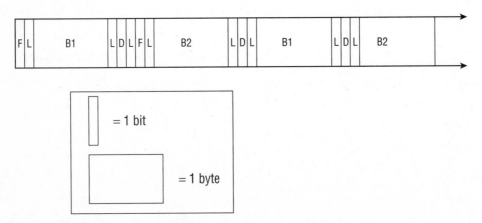

Figure 7-33 The NT frame format

- **F** — Framing bit, marks the beginning of the frame for synchronization.
- **L** — Load balancing bit. These are used to balance the frames signaling.
- **B1** — B1 channel byte. This is B channel data.
- **E** — Echo bit. Echoes D channel data when line congestion is occurring.
- **D** — D channel bit. This is D channel data.
- **A** — Activation bit. Used to activate nodes.
- **B2** — B2 channel byte. This is B channel data.
- **S** — Spare bit.
- **F** — Framing bit. When used, marks the beginning of the frame for synchronization.
- **L** — Load balancing bit. These are used when needed to balance the frames signaling.
- **B1** — B1 channel byte. This is B channel data.
- **D** — D channel bit. This is D channel data.
- **B2** — B2 channel byte. This is B channel data.
- **S** — Spare bit.

The Layer 2 protocol used by ISDN is called the link access procedure D channel (LAPD), which functions like LAPB does for the X.25 protocol. Figure 7-34 shows the LAPD frame format.

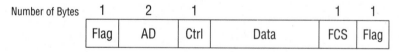

Figure 7-34 The LAPD frame format

- **Flag** — The LAPD Flag field indicates the start point and end point of the frame.
- **AD** (address) — This field identifies whether the frame is carrying a response or a command.
- **CTRL** (control) — This field details which frame type (I-frame, S-frame, or U-frame) is being used, the frame sequence number, and the frame function.
- **Data** — The payload! In LAPD, this is the PLP packet.
- **FCS** (frame check sequence) — This field is a checksum algorithm that checksums the frame from the FC field to the end of the Data field. This is where error checking and data integrity are monitored.

■ **Flag** — The LAPD Flag field indicates the start point and end point of the frame.

Finally, two Layer 3 protocols are used by ISDN: ITU-T and ITU-T I.451. These protocols take care of operations at Layer 3, including setting up sessions, establishing and maintaining connections, gathering information pertaining to remote nodes, and other functions.

> **POP QUIZ**
>
> What are the four endpoint node types used in ATM?

7.2.9   AppleTalk

AppleTalk is a protocol suite developed by the Apple Computer company to be integrated with Macintosh computers to allow users to share resources on a network.

AppleTalk came into existence in the 1980s and was one of the first to implement the client/server network architecture. AppleTalk is a plug-and-play service that doesn't require any intervention on the end user's part to connect to a network. The first version of AppleTalk, known as *AppleTalk Phase 1*, was developed mainly for use in a local network segment. It was able to support a maximum of 135 client nodes and 135 server nodes. AppleTalk Phase 2 was developed to support routing outside of the local segment and could support a total of 253 nodes, regardless of whether they were clients or servers.

The services provided and/or supported by AppleTalk span all the layers in the OSI reference model. Figure 7-35 compares the OSI reference model and the AppleTalk protocols that correspond to each layer.

ACRONYM ALERT

CIST — Common and internal spanning tree

7.2.9.1   AppleTalk Physical and Data Link Layers

AppleTalk depends on the same media access protocols to exchange networking data. Each implementation has to work with the AppleTalk suite. At the Physical layer, AppleTalk data can be passed over fiber, twisted pair, and coaxial cabling. AppleTalk interacts with each implementation of a media access protocol to allow AppleTalk data to be exchanged. Following are some of the protocols used at this layer:

■ **EtherTalk** — Used on Ethernet networks. The protocol that communicates between the network layer and the Physical layer is known as the *EtherTalk Link Access Protocol (ELAP)*.

- **TokenTalk** — Used on Token Ring networks. The protocol that communicates between the Network layer and the Physical layer is known as the *TokenTalk Link Access Protocol (TLAP)*.

- **FDDITalk** — Used on FDDI networks. The protocol that communicates between the Network layer and the Physical layer is known as the FDDITalk Link Access Protocol (FLAP).

- **LocalTalk** — This is the AppleTalk proprietary standard that is included with all Macintosh computers. This standard is supported on Macintosh nodes only. The protocol that communicates between the Network layer and the Physical layer is known as the *LocalTalk Link Access Protocol (LLAP)*.

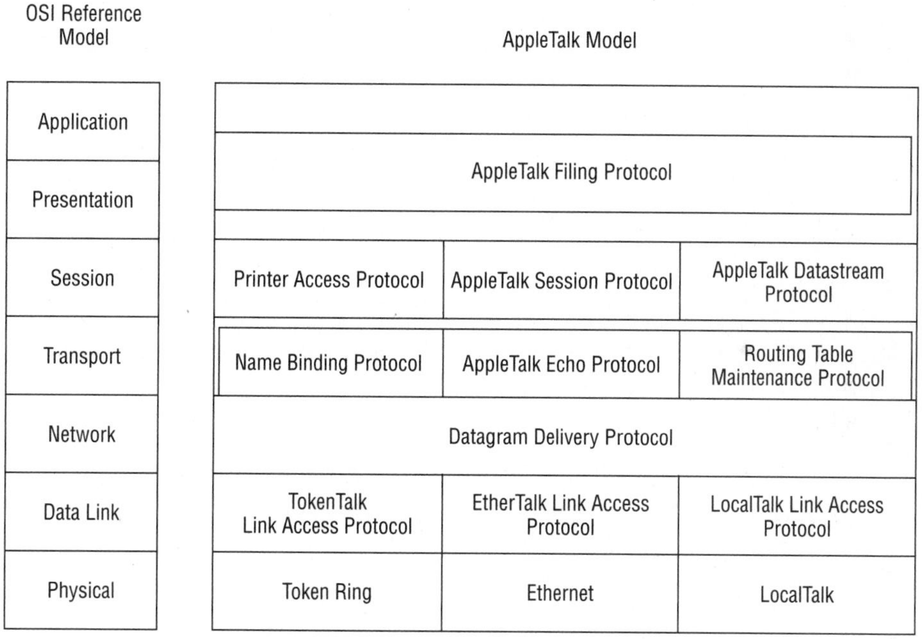

OSI Reference Model	AppleTalk Model		
Application	AppleTalk Filing Protocol		
Presentation			
Session	Printer Access Protocol	AppleTalk Session Protocol	AppleTalk Datastream Protocol
Transport	Name Binding Protocol	AppleTalk Echo Protocol	Routing Table Maintenance Protocol
Network	Datagram Delivery Protocol		
Data Link	TokenTalk Link Access Protocol	EtherTalk Link Access Protocol	LocalTalk Link Access Protocol
Physical	Token Ring	Ethernet	LocalTalk

Figure 7-35 The layers of the AppleTalk model

7.2.9.2   AppleTalk Network Layer

The *Datagram Delivery Protocol (DDP)* is the protocol used by AppleTalk at the Network layer. The purpose of DDP in an AppleTalk infrastructure is to provide end-to-end datagram delivery. DDP uses sockets to identify a logical process on a node and as part of the address that is used in order to exchange datagrams. All the upper layers use sockets as well.

All AppleTalk data is formatted to be exchanged in DDP packets over an AppleTalk network. DDP has two different packet types. The short DDP packet type is not used much anymore. It was developed when AppleTalk was limited to segments only. The extended DDP packet type is what is most commonly used.[48]

Another protocol used at this layer is the *AppleTalk Address Resolution Protocol (AARP)*. Just like the Address Resolution Protocol (ARP) for TCP/IP, AARP maps network addresses to their associated data link addresses.

> **RANDOM BONUS DEFINITION**
>
> Layer 3 switch — A router.

7.2.9.3   AppleTalk Upper Layers

AppleTalk uses several upper layer protocols that were built off of the DDP protocol and therefore use DDP as the protocol of choice when information is being passed down to the lower layers for transport across the network.

Transport layer protocols are used for flow control, circuit management, and error checking, detection, and recovery. The AppleTalk protocols included at this layer are:

- **AppleTalk Echo Protocol (AEP)** — The service provided by this protocol is an echo request or an echo reply.

- **AppleTalk Transaction Protocol (ATP)** — Used to pass transmissions between two sockets.

- **Name Binding Protocol (NBP)** — Maintains and manages the use of host names and socket addresses for nodes within the network.

- **Routing Table Maintenance Protocol (RTMP)** — Used to maintain and manage routing information.

Session layer protocols manage communication sessions between Presentation layer processes. The protocols operating at this layer are:

- **AppleTalk DataStream Protocol (ADSP)** — A connection-oriented protocol that provides a data channel for the host nodes.

- **AppleTalk Session Protocol (ASP)** — Maintains and manages higher level sessions.

- **Printer Access Protocol (PAP)** — Maintains and manages virtual connections to printers, print servers, and other server types.

---

[48]The extended DDP packet is the one most commonly used in new implementations. There is really no good reason to use the short DDP packet, as you need to plan for growth and that packet type limits where your data can be transmitted.

- **Zone Information Protocol (ZIP)** — Manages network numbers and AppleTalk zone names.

The final two layers, the Application and Presentation layers, use the services of the *AppleTalk Filing Protocol (AFP)*[49]. The Presentation layer provides services that are applied to data at the Application layer. Addi-

> **RANDOM BONUS DEFINITION**
>
> internetwork — A group of networks connected to one another through a router.

tionally, the Application layer interacts with Macintosh applications (which the OSI Application layer does not).

7.3   Chapter Exercises

1. True or false: The only type of node that is used on a FDDI ring is a FDDI concentrator.

2. What are the three levels of operation within the X.25 protocol suite?

3. In X.25, _____ are used to pass control data, such as: transmission requests, status reporting, _____ receipt acknowledgements, and termination requests.

4. What are the three main components used by PPP?

5. What is the difference between a DTE and a DCE in an X.25 network?

6. What are the Session layer protocols that are used in the AppleTalk protocol suite?

7. What does the acronym ISDN stand for?

8. What is the frame relay local management interface (LMI) used for?

9. What is a constant bit rate (CBR)?

10. _____ is the foundation protocol of the PPP protocol suite.

7.4   Pop Quiz Answers

1. What was the name of the company that developed ARCnet?

   The Datapoint Corporation developed ARCnet in the late 1970s.

---

[49]AFP is a file sharing protocol.

2. What technology is also known as 1BASE5?

   StarLAN

3. What is the signal called that is passed in Token Ring from one node to the next?

   A token

4. What information is contained in the Destination Address field in a Token Ring frame?

   The Destination Address field contains the 6-byte network address of the node that the frame is destined for.

5. What does the acronym *FDDI* stand for?

   Fiber Distributed Data Interface

6. What are the four main node types in the FDDI environment?

   - Single attached station
   - Single attached concentrator
   - Dual attached station
   - Dual attached concentrator

7. What are DECnet's five phases?

   - DECnet phase I
   - DECnet phase II
   - DECnet phase III
   - DECnet phase IV
   - DECnet phase V

8. Which operating system uses IPX?

   Novell NetWare

9. True or false: IPX is not supported on a Token Ring network.

   False

10. What serial transmission standard was used before PPP came out?

    Serial Link Internet Protocol (SLIP)

11. Which protocol operates at the packet level of the X.25 model?

    Packet Layer Protocol (PLP)

12. What are the three virtual circuit types used in ATM?

    - Permanent virtual circuit (PVC) — This is a static virtual circuit.
    - Soft permanent virtual circuit (SPVC) — This is a dynamic PVC.

- Switched virtual circuit (SVC) — This is an "as needed"[50] virtual circuit.

13. Frame relay is very similar to _____.

    X.25

14. What are the four endpoint node types used in ATM?

    - ATM customer service unit/digital service unit (CSU/DSU)
    - LAN router
    - LAN switch
    - LAN workstation

---

[50]This could also be "on demand."

Part

II

The OSI Layers

In This Part

The Upper Layers

Protocol is everything.
Francois Giuliani[1]

The above quote is truly succinct, a real economy of words. This quote is not only true at the United Nations but also is easily applied to the networking environment. When you think of the mix of various equipment, wiring, networking operating systems, computer operating systems, programs running on servers as multiuser platforms, programs running on local computer workstations (which includes pretty much anything a person can hang off a network segment), the ability to communicate is essential. The United Nations uses translators to ensure that all the representatives from the many varied nations can understand the procedures. A network protocol also acts as a translator between the many subcomponents that we lump together under the word "network."

We would hate to think what a General Assembly meeting of the United Nations would look and sound like without the translators they employ. There is only one word that comes to mind: chaos. How would you ever be able to get anything done? The same goes for networks, except things move much faster than the world's fastest talker can utter even a single word. So protocol is truly everything in the networking world.

[1]Francois Giuliani worked at the United Nations for 25 years. At the time of his departure in March 1996, he was the director of the Media Division of the Department of Public Information (DPI).

This chapter investigates the upper layers of the OSI reference model: the Application layer, the Presentation layer, and the Session layer. We will identify the "translators" being used so that information can flow

> **RANDOM BONUS DEFINITION**
>
> *hardware address* — Synonymous with MAC address, physical address, and unicast address.

smoothly and without error between these layers and eventually be sent over the network media to another network node and the device servicing that node. This is a top-down approach where users attempt to interact with the device they are using to communicate with another device and/or users somewhere over the net.[2]

8.1   Background

Software programs use the upper layers of the OSI reference model to send and receive data over a network. Normally such programs are called applications and although they may interface with the Application layer of the OSI reference model, it does not necessarily need to be the case. In this chapter, "application program" and "Application layer" are not synonymous and refer to different aspects of computer usage.

A computer user purchases an application program and loads it on to his or her computer's hard drive. Basically, programs can be divided into two broad categories: locally run application programs and client/server-based application programs. As the name implies, a locally run application program executes program instructions and all data is maintained within the local computer, so there is never a need to utilize a network connection. A client/server application implies that a client computer and a server need to communicate if the application program is to run successfully. A client/server application in most cases requires a degree of interconnectivity for the application program to communicate with its counterpart server-based program. As this book is concerned with networking, the only application programs that have relevance are application programs that follow the client/server model. Figure 8-1 illustrates a client/server application program scenario.

As you can see in the figure, a client computer communicates over the network with a server. Although they are working in conjunction within a certain application program, they run within their own realms. The server listens on the network, awaiting requests from client computers. When the server receives a request from a client, it fulfills it. The communication between a particular client computer and the server is considered a *session*. Servers only respond to

---

[2]The "net" is in reference to any and all segments of a network, which can include in part or in whole any of the following: local network segment, the local LAN, intranet, or the Internet.

session requests in this environment; they do not initiate the start of session. Once a data transfer to or from the server is complete, it may request to terminate the session. Depending on the server application being run on the server, the server may

POP QUIZ

True or false: The Application layer is where all the application programs you load on your PC are stored.

be capable of maintaining a number of simultaneous sessions with multiple client computers. Server applications that can maintain multiple sessions are usually referred to as *multiuser applications*.

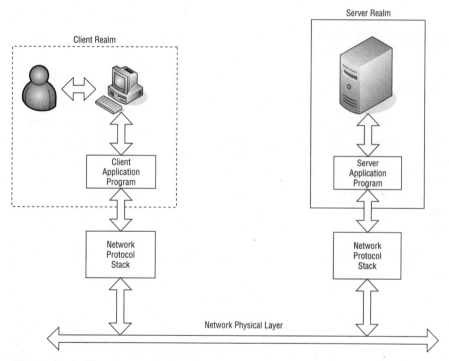

Figure 8-1 A client/server application

The client realm involves not only the client computer and application program, but a user as well. The user initiates requests to the client computer via an input device (usually a keyboard, mouse, or both). The application responds back to the user in graphic images or text displayed on a screen or tone signals played back through the computer's audio system. The application program requires user input in the form of commands and data in order for it to interact with the server application it is working in conjunction with in a particular client/server application.

Although client/server applications work in conjunction with each other, they are autonomous until a session is established between a particular client application workstation and the application server. The server application, in most cases, is con-

ACRONYM ALERT

AARP — AppleTalk Address Resolution Protocol

stantly running on a server that is rarely shut down. For instance, a mail server is always available to receive messages from client workstations, process them, and direct them to another mail server where the recipient of that message has an account. Received messages from other mail servers destined for users on a particular mail server are stored on the server until the mail server is queried by a user to see if there are any messages.

Mail servers or other application servers may also have to perform user authentication to ensure security and user privacy. An example of this would be when users launch a particular application on their client workstation, such as a mail reader. They may be first presented with a dialog message box to enter their user ID and password. Unbeknownst to the users, when they launched the client application it went out over the network and requested to establish a session with the server. The server at that point returned a response that security is required and requested that a user ID and password be provided for the connection to be established and maintained over the length of the session. Users at the client workstation enter their user ID and password, and if it matches the authentication parameters that the mail server is using for authentication, a mail session is opened between the client workstation and the mail server. The simple process of just logging on to a mail server requires interaction of the application program and the network stack[3] to ensure that messages are properly transmitted over the network between the client workstation and the server within a predetermined protocol.

Since TCP/IP (Transmission Control Protocol/Internet Protocol) is the predominant network protocol in use within today's networking world, the remainder of this chapter will refer to the network stack in

POP QUIZ

The predominant networking protocol run over Ethernet networks is _____.

terms of how it relates to the TCP/IP protocol suite. Most, if not all, of today's computer operating systems provide a network stack that is compatible and easily interacts with applications that use TCP/IP to communicate over a network.

---

[3]Usually in reference to the OSI model, "network stack" or simply the "stack" refers to layers within the OSI reference model that, in most cases, have been embedded within the particular operating system running on the computer in use.

8.2 The TCP/IP Model

The TCP/IP model consists of four layers: an Application layer, a Transport layer, an Internet layer, and a Link layer. To accommodate a wide range of application programs that need to communicate over a network structure, encapsulation is performed between the layers to allow data to be moved independently of the application that produced the data. Figure 8-2 illustrates a conceptual view of the TCP/IP network stack.

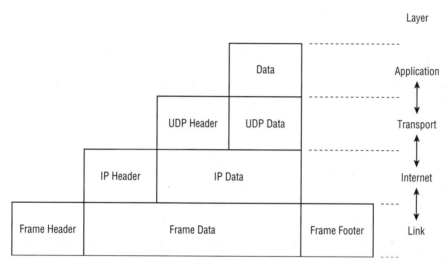

Figure 8-2 The TCP/IP network stack/model

The top level Application layer is the data portion of the network stack. It contains the upper level protocols that allow application programs to encapsulate data so that it can be passed down to the Transport layer. Since the OSI model Presentation layer and Session layer are combined with the OSI model Application layer to make up the TCP/IP network stack's Application layer, any protocols needed within the OSI model for these layers are accomplished via the use of libraries[4] within the TCP/IP model's Application layer.

The TCP/IP model Transport layer maps directly to the Layer 4 Transport layer of the OSI model, and the TCP/IP model Internet layer is usually mapped directly to the OSI model's Network layer. However, the TCP/IP model's Link layer covers both the OSI model's Physical layer and Data Link layer.

Application layer data is passed to the Transport layer, where a UDP header is applied and is framed with the data, as shown in Figure 8-3.

[4]Libraries are collections of protocol routines for various protocol functions.

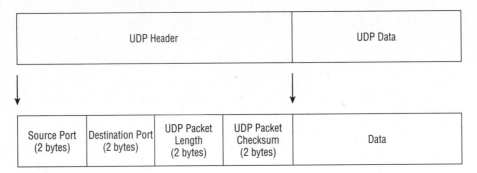

Figure 8-3 A UDP packet

As you can see, there is no address information other than the ports that that are being accessed. Since there is a lack of addressing and control, UDP is referred to as a *connectionless protocol*.[5] With 2 bytes allocated for both the source and destination port addresses, this accommodates up to 65,536 port numbers. However, the lower 1,024 port address values are reserved for defined services and are considered to be the *well-known port values*.[6]

The UDP Packet Length field is 2 bytes in length and contains the number of bytes of the whole packet, including header and data. The UDP Packet Checksum field is also 2 bytes in length and is the checksum of the whole packet, including header and data. Unlike TCP, the Checksum field is optional, which brings into question its use for packet transport over the network. The choice between using UDP and TCP depends on the transport mode selected by the application program developers. A deciding factor may be speed, since UDP does not require further encapsulation and the overall packet size is smaller than TCP by 12 bytes. On a single packet basis, this seems like a small price to pay; however, in applications where large amounts of data are transferred over the network, there can be noticeable performance differences. A software developer may choose not to use UDP where reliability of the transfer is required. UDP has no means of guaranteeing packet delivery. To guarantee delivery requires further encapsulation and the packet is then passed to the Internet layer of the TCP/IP network stack.

> **POP QUIZ**
>
> True or false: UDP is a connection-based protocol.

---

[5]A connectionless protocol means that packets are streamed onto the network without any relation to one another. There is no means to connect packets that may have been fragmented or to determine if packets have been received out of order.

[6]Well-known port addresses are reserved; however, the range above 1024 also has some predetermined services using a high-numbered port. An example would be radius server authentication using port 1812.

At the Internet layer, the UDP packet is encapsulated as data within the IP packet. Figure 8-4 illustrates the applied IP header.

Bit	0-3	4-7	8-15	16-18	19-31
0	Version	Header Length	Type of Service	Total Length	
32	Identification			Flags	Fragment Offset
64	Time to Live		Protocol	Header Checksum	
96	Source Address				
128	Destination Address				
160	Options				
160 or 192 +	**Data**				

Figure 8-4 The IP packet header

You can see that additional information is added to the packet that can affect its delivery over the network. The bit order of the packet delivery begins with bit position 0. Streaming from left to right across the header, the first field encountered is the Version field. Since this packet complies with IP version 4 (IPv4), the value contained in this field is 4.[7]

The next field is the Header Length of the IP header. The value contained in this field is the number of 32-bit words that are contained in the header. This value also indicates the bit position of where the Data field begins. The minimum value for this field is 5. So, in a header containing five 32-bit words, the start of data will begin at bit position 160 (5 × 32 bits = 160 bits). The beginning of the Data field will be pushed back an additional 32 bits if the Options field is present.

The Type of Service field was allocated to provide control over the packet's delivery priority. In the past, this field was not utilized; in recent days,

---

[7]Because this is a 4-bit binary field, the value in binary 4-bit notation would appear as 0100.

it has evolved into a Differentiated Services field (DiffServ). DiffServ provides a method of classifying network traffic for manageability and provides quality of service (QoS) guarantees across an IP network. This

RANDOM BONUS DEFINITION

flow control — A function that prevents a sender of traffic from sending faster than the receiver is capable of receiving.

ability is essential for delivering time-sensitive packets for applications that require real-time performance. An example of a real-time application in wide use today is Voice over IP (VoIP).

The Total Length field contains the value in the number of bytes of the total length of the IP packet datagram, which also includes the header. The minimum value this field can contain is 20, which is the minimum number of bytes in an IP header without any data. Since this is a 16-bit field, the maximum amount of bytes in the datagram is restricted to a theoretical limit of 65,536 bytes. However, most networks do not permit the transfer of super-sized packets without fragmentation. The customary size restriction for TCP/IP on an Ethernet network is 1500 bytes. Larger packets would need to be fragmented and delivered reliably so they can be reconstructed on the receiving network node.

The next three fields, Identification, Flags, and Fragment Offset, are all used when fragmentation of a packet is required. A packet that is too large is broken into fragments, which are placed within a collection of packets to transfer the information within the original unfragmented packet. The Identification field is used to uniquely identify all IP packets that are fragments of a packet that needed to be fragmented before being placed on the network. The Flags field consists of 3 bits. The value of each field may either be a 0 or a 1, where 0 indicates "no flag" being present and 1 indicates "flag bit set." In order of precedence, the most significant bit is reserved and always must be set to 1. The next bit is the do-not-fragment bit. When set, this bit signals that the packet is not to be fragmented. This can lead to packets being dropped if they exceed the overall packet size permitted by a receiving node. The only reason for use of the do-not-fragment flag is that the network node sending the packet knows that the network node that is to receive the packet does not have the capability to reassemble fragmented packets and sets the flag so upstream routers will not fragment the packet. The next flag bit is the more-frames bit, which indicates that more fragment packets are to follow this particular packet. The last packet containing a packet fragment segment will have this bit set to 0 to indicate that no other fragments are to follow this fragment. This bit is always set to 0 for all packets that don't contain fragmented packet segments.[8]

---

[8]If a packet does not contain fragmented packet segments, it is a packet unto itself and is considered an unfragmented packet. Whether to fragment a packet is determined by the amount of data that is be transmitted, since the header is for the most part of fixed length.

The Fragmentation Offset field contains the number of 8-byte blocks that the fragment data is offset from where it was located in the original unfragmented packet. The field is 13 bits long, so the maximum number of offset is 65,528.[9] Since the maximum packet size is fixed at 65,536, the values of the offset, plus the 20 bytes required for the IP header, is greater than the maximum size of a packet. Thirteen bytes are more than adequate for this field.

The Time to Live field is an 8-bit field that indicates how many seconds a packet can live on the Internet. With that many bits, it would equate to 255 seconds as a maximum or four and a quarter minutes. Imagine waiting more than four minutes per packet to see if they had arrived. Needless to say, the reason for the TTL timer is to prevent lost packets from traversing the Internet into infinity if they cannot find a home or until they end up being dropped somewhere along the way. These days this field is not used to display the amount of seconds but is a hop count.[10] As a packet travels across the Internet, each network forwarding device it passes through decrements the TTL field by one before forwarding the packet along to the next network hop. The packet will continue to travel until the packet with a TTL set to zero arrives at the input of a network forwarding device. When a packet with TTL equal to zero is received by a network forwarding device, it will simply not forward the packet and it is dropped.[11] When a packet is dropped, an ICMP (Internet Control Message Protocol) error is sent to the sender alerting it that the packet has been dropped. The typical message is that the TTL has been exceeded, which means the destination was not found. ICMP utilities include `ping` and `traceroute` and use error messages to allow a sender to know if a target address is reachable over the Internet.

The Protocol field is an 8-bit field used to indicate the protocol of the data portion of the IP packet. These are pre-assigned values maintained by the Internet Assigned Numbers Authority (IANA). Some of the most common protocols found in IP headers are a value of 1 for ICMP messages, a value of 6 for TCP messages, and a value of 17 for UDP messages.

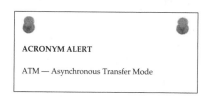

ACRONYM ALERT

ATM — Asynchronous Transfer Mode

The Header Checksum field is a 16-bit field that contains the checksum of the header portion of the IP packet. The data portion carries the checksum of the protocol that is contained within it. When the packet is received, the checksum is calculated and compared to the value contained within the field. If

[9]This values is derived by $(2^{13}-1) \times 8$ bytes per block, or 65,528 bytes.

[10]*Hop count* is a method of counting the hops a packet traverses. As a packet is passed through a network forwarding device (e.g., a router), it is considered as a single hop.

[11]What is meant by "dropped"? Simply that the packet is ignored and not forwarded or analyzed any further. It just ends up in the sky, where all lost packets go. However, network administrators always like to know why a packet is dropped.

there is a checksum mismatch, the packet is dropped. Since the header includes the Time to Live field, which is decremented each time the packet crosses a network hop, the header checksum will need to change if it is to remain valid at the next receiving network node. Because of known decrementing of the TTL field and the possibility that a network forwarding device may fragment the packet before passing it to the next network hop, each network forwarding device must insert the new valid checksum value in order to not create a checksum mismatch at the next receiving network node.

The Source Address field contains 32 bits of address information. The address is represented as four octets. Normally, IP addresses are annotated in what is called *dot-decimal notation*, such as:

```
192.168.16.1
```

Converting each octet into binary is represented as follows:

```
11000000.10101000.00010000.00000001
```

Binary address information in the Source Address field is represented as follows:

```
11000000101010000001000000000001
```

There are times when the source address of a packet is not the address of the sending network node. Various packet-forwarding network devices can perform a NAT function. Figure 8-5 illustrates a user workstation behind a router that is providing a NAT function.

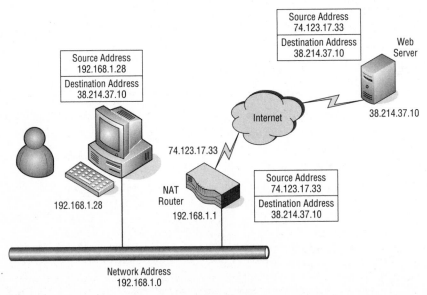

Figure 8-5 A private network behind a NAT router

In the figure, there is a private network[12] with a network address of 192.168.1.0, and on that network is a router with NAT capability of taking packets from a device on the 192.168.1.0 network and routing them out to the Internet. A user workstation at 192.168.1.28 wants to access a web page from a web server over the Internet at 38.214.37.10. Since the NAT router is the default gateway for the 192.168.1.0 network, all traffic that is not destined for the local LAN is sent to it. The user workstation in its TCP/IP settings has the default gateway address of 192.168.1.1, which is the NAT router's local network interface. The user workstation sends a request packet with a destination address of 38.214.37.10 with its own address of 192.168.1.28 in the Source Address field. Since the destination address is not on the local LAN, it is sent to the default gateway at 192.168.1.1.

The NAT router accepts the packet from the workstation at 192.168.1.28 and determines that it is destined to another network device over the Internet. The router replaces the user workstation's IP address with its own public interface[13] address in the Source Address field of the packet. After the address is replaced, it computes a new checksum for the header and inserts it into the checksum field before sending the packet out its public interface at 74.123.17.33.

The packet is routed over the Internet and arrives at the web server residing at the public IP address of 38.214.37.10. The server determines that the request is destined for its

> **RANDOM BONUS DEFINITION**
>
> Fast Ethernet — 100 Mbps Ethernet.

address and notes that the source address is 74.123.17.33. The web server has no knowledge of the user workstation IP address of 192.168.1.28. The web server prepares a response using the public IP address of the NAT router as the destination address.

When the response packet arrives at the NAT router from the web server, it uses its NAT translation table to send the packet to the requesting workstation. It accomplishes this by modifying the destination address to the workstation address of 192.168.1.28 and computing a new checksum for the IP header before sending the packet out its private address interface onto the local LAN. For all intents and purposes, the user workstation believes it is interacting directly with the web server. NAT has some advantages and disadvantages, but for most small local networks it works well and offers

---

[12]Certain network addresses spaces have been determined by the Internet community to remain private. What this really means is that network forwarding devices on the Internet are not to forward any packet with a destination address that falls into the following ranges: 192.168.X.X, 172.16.X.X, and 10.X.X.X, where X denotes any number between 0 and 255.

[13]There are two sides to every router that interfaces a private local LAN network and the Internet. Normally, the interface that is accessible over the Internet is referred to as the *public interface* or *public interface address*.

protection against unsolicited network traffic ever making it through the NAT router to the local private network. If a packet's parameters do not match the translation table's known sessions, the packet is not processed and is dropped.

> **POP QUIZ**
>
> Describe what happens to a packet when it is passed through a NAT-enabled router.

The Destination Address field is pretty much self-explanatory. It is a 32-bit (4-byte) field containing the address information in the same format as the Source Address field. There is no difference in how the destination address is presented. In most circumstances the destination address is not messed with as the source address is with NAT. However, there are instances where the destination address may be translated and that is in special cases involving some sort of NAT router or a firewall. Actually, most routers used for the NAT function on outbound network traffic also have some capability to perform a port forwarding NAT. Notice that the web server in Figure 8-5 is directly connected to the Internet. That is certainly a possibility but is rarely found in today's networking environment because of possible attacks on the server via the Internet. Figure 8-6 illustrates a network that offers services available on the Internet but is protected and hidden from users.

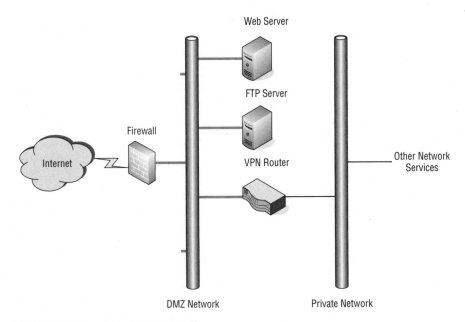

Figure 8-6 Port forwarding NAT

As you can see, the network located behind the firewall is shielded to prevent users on the Internet from accessing these services directly. A firewall may be a network device that is designed as a firewall for the inspection of packets as they are received, or it may be a router running a firewall application on it that provides the packet inspection. In any case, the firewall function requires packet inspection and a determination by the policies put in place by the network administrators of what to do with the received packet. If a packet is received and does not match any of the existing policies, it is dropped.

The network behind the firewall may be a private network, but in this example it is shown as a DMZ[14] network. Connected to this network are services that the Internet community is permitted to reach. In this example, we have a web server, an FTP server, and a VPN router. Obviously, the web server is where web pages can be accessed and is generally used only for queries to obtain information. The FTP server may be only for file downloads but if allowed may also be a place where users can upload files. An example where users from the Internet community at large can upload files to an FTP server is a website that allows user posting on the site or a photo lab site that prints users' digital JPEG files on photographic paper.

In the figure, there is a VPN[15] router between the DMZ network and the private network. This device may be used as a remote access device for users who are remotely located but have permission to use the network service located on the private network. Usually VPN routers require user authentication, which can be performed locally on the VPN router, although it may depend on other authentication servers. For more information on this topic, see Chapter 14, "Network Security."

Back to our lovely red-brick firewall. We said that the firewall is responsible for inspecting the packets and using the policies installed by the network administrators to make a determination on what to do with the packet. To ensure that traffic is routed to the proper services, there must be port forwarding policies in place on the firewall. There are two ways this may be accomplished: either by changing the destination address and forwarding the packet on to the DMZ network, or, if the DMZ network addresses are routable Internet addresses, the packet may be inspected to ensure that only certain traffic is permitted to pass through the firewall. If the DMZ network uses addresses that are classified as nonroutable addresses, the only way traffic can be directed to the servers providing the requested services is by changing the packet's destination address. In this example, the web and FTP services

---

[14]DMZ is the acronym for *demilitarized zone*. In networking parlance, it refers to a network that may have some access by the public at large. The private network is protected by some sort of authentication process to only allow users with the proper credentials to reach the private network.

[15]VPN is the acronym for *virtual private network*. Usually the acronym is applied to the device, but in reality it is not the network in itself. It provides access to the network using security authentication and encryption processes to ensure that the private network is accessed only by those authorized to use its services.

only receive traffic for those particular services. Although these services are shown as separate computers, many services can be supplied by a single server running multiple protocols. In this example, packets directed to port 80 for web services would be directed to the web server, while packets using ports 20 and 21 would be directed to the FTP server. Lastly, VPN requests would be directed to the VPN router, and there are a few VPN protocols that may be used, so for now we will just say any VPN service requests will be directed to it.

The next field in the IP header is the Options field. As the name connotes, this is an optional field that follows the Destination Address field but is not used often. The last field in IP packet is the Data field, which is not part of the IP header so it is not used in the computation of the header checksum. The contents of the Data field are specified within the protocol header and can be any one of the IP protocols. Some of the most common protocols used in an IP packet are ICMP, TCP, UDP, and OSPF. OSPF (Open Shortest Path First) is a routing protocol used to route IP packets over the network.

The last layer of the TCP/IP Model is the Link layer. This is a combination of physical hardware and software to frame the IP packet to transport it over whatever network medium is being used. So frame information depends on the type of network connectivity that is being used. In the case of Ethernet, the IP packet is encapsulated within the Ethernet frame. Figure 8-7 shows Ethernet encapsulation of an IP packet.

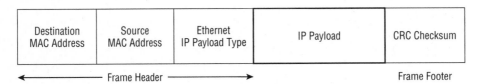

Figure 8-7 Ethernet encapsulation of an IP packet

The Ethernet frame header contains both the MAC (Media Access Control) destination and source addresses, each containing 12 bytes of addressing information. These addresses are unique and are directly associated with the physical network device. The last field in the Ethernet frame header is the Ethernet IP payload type. This is a 2-byte field and indicates the type of IP payload being transmitted by the Ethernet frame. Two of the most common IP payload types are 0x0800 for an IPv4 datagram and 0x0806[16] indicating that the frame is an ARP[17] (Address Resolution Protocol).

---

[16]The numeric representation with an "x" contained within it signifies that the number is a hexadecimal number. Each unit position is 4 binary bits in width. Thus, four hexadecimal numbers would contain 16 binary bits, or 2 bytes. If you still have difficulty grasping the concept of hexadecimal in relation to binary numbers, it is time for a review of number systems.

[17]ARP is a mechanism for a transmitting network node to determine which network node is associated with a particular IP address. The network node assigned that IP address responds with its MAC address.

The Ethernet frame footer contains the CRC checksum for the entire Ethernet frame. It contains 4 bytes of checksum data, which is used to validate that the frame was received correctly by the network node it was for-

warded to. So, if the minimum size of an IP packet is 46 bytes, the minimum size if an Ethernet frame is 64 bytes, with the addition of the 18 bytes of Ethernet header and footer. The maximum size of an IP packet is 1500 bytes, which makes the maximum Ethernet frame allowed onto an Ethernet to be 1518 bytes in total. For large data payloads, fragmentation must be used.

We have worked our way down the TCP/IP model and now it is time to put the frame on the wire. Figure 8-8 conceptually illustrates the relationship between actual network elements and the TCP/IP network stack.

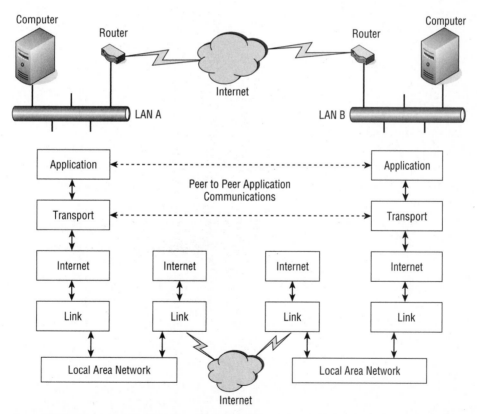

Figure 8-8 The relationship between network elements and the TCP/IP network stack

Two LANs, LAN A and LAN B, have computers that want to communicate with each other using an application program that supports their capability to establish a session and communicate effectively. This is shown as a computer and router connected to each LAN. Each router is connected to the Internet, shown as a cloud since there is an unknown amount of network devices that may be in the path between the router on LAN A and the router on LAN B. The assumption is that if a frame[18] is constructed properly, it can travel across many networks and through many devices in its path to reliably arrive at its predetermined destination.

The application program running on both computers may be aware of the other's network parameters, such as address and type of service, but it does not concern itself with the actual delivery of the data between the two peer computers running the application program. The only concern of the application program running within the TCP/IP's Application layer is preparing the data so it can present it to the Transport layer in anticipation of having the data delivered to the computer residing on the other LAN. So a peer-to-peer application session between two computers over the Internet appears as if they communicate with each other only using the Application layer and the Transport layer of TCP/IP model.

If application programs only concern themselves with getting the data properly packaged for the Transport layer, who does the rest of the actual delivery of the information? As illustrated in Figure 8-8, the lower two layers of the TCP/IP model are the Internet layer and the Link layer, which are directly responsible for reliably transporting the packet of information over the Internet. Since routing devices only need to be aware of addressing information, they only need to use the two lower layers of the model to effect the proper transmission of the information on its journey over the Internet. They are not concerned with data content since routing decisions are made on address and type of service.

The Internet and Link layers are normally part of the operating system and the hardware that is installed on the computer. If we assume an Ethernet-based LAN, then the computer would require an NIC that is capable of providing an Ethernet con-

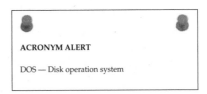

ACRONYM ALERT

DOS — Disk operation system

nection to the LAN. This is what would be Layer 1 or the Physical layer of the OSI reference model. However, it is a portion of the TCP/IP model

---

[18]*Frame* and *packet* are terms that are used interchangeably and are pretty much synonymous. Another term that may be tossed about from time to time is *datagram*. All these terms refer to some sort of encapsulation that includes the data to be transferred along with addressing and type of service being requested. It is how data can traverse the Internet from one computer to another.

Link layer. In order for the operating system to communicate properly with the NIC, device drivers are required that allow the software operating system to configure and control the physical components of the NIC. In a Microsoft Windows environment, this may be transparent to the user due to the capability of the operating system to recognize various pieces of computer hardware and automatically load the appropriate driver to communicate with the installed device. This portion of the TCP/IP model Link layer that includes device drivers maps to the Data Link layer of the OSI reference model.

Once an NIC is installed in a computer and the device drivers are loaded so that the operating system is able to communicate with the device on a physical level,[19] a network operating protocol needs to be bound to the card for it to communicate over the network with another network-connected device. In the case of TCP/IP, this is the address applied to the computer network interface along with its default gateway[20] and the location of at least one DNS server. Most operating systems allow these parameters to be set manually, or the computer requesting the values can apply them automatically from a DHCP server that is servicing that network segment.

Note that the routers illustrated in Figure 8-8 have their Link layers connected to both the LAN and the Internet. In reality these would be two different interfaces and also of differing types of network connectivity. More than likely the router will have an Ethernet interface allowing it to be interconnected to an Ethernet-based LAN. The interface to the Internet is dependent upon the type of service the router is connected to. It may be a point-to-point T1 interface, a FDDI interface, or some other form of high-speed service to the Internet. So a router's Link layer may consist of differing network hardware, device drivers, and Internet layer parameters to effectively transmit a data packet from the LAN to the Internet.

> **POP QUIZ**
>
> What determines the type of framing that is to be used on a particular network segment?

---

[19]Physical level kind of implies actual hardware but includes software that allows the hardware registers be written to for data and control. It is the device driver that makes the translation from hardware-specific elements to the standardized routines within the operating system controlling network-based communications.

[20]Default gateway has been mentioned more than once in this chapter. In a simple network, as illustrated in Figure 8-3, the address applied to the router on the LAN side would be considered to be a default gateway address. Basically, any packet with a destination address that is not located on the local LAN segment is forwarded to the address that is programmed into the default gateway address parameter field.

8.2.1 TCP/IP Application Layer

The Application layer of the TCP/IP model contains the upper level protocols of the TCP/IP protocol suite, such as FTP (File Transport Protocol) and SMTP (Simple Mail Transfer Protocol). Data is encapsu-

> **RANDOM BONUS DEFINITION**
>
> AppleTalk — A protocol suite developed by Apple Computer.

lated and passed to the Transport Control Protocol for actual transmission on the network. The Application layer is dependent upon the lower layers to provide an effective and reliable means of network communications. The Application layer may be aware of the IP addresses and port numbers that are being used by the Transport layer, but it is that layer's responsibility to encapsulate this information as it is passed to the Internet layer below it. Some of the more common Application layer protocols are listed in Table 8-1.

8.2.2 TCP/IP Transport Layer

The two predominant protocols found in the TCP/IP Transport layer are UDP (User Datagram Protocol) and TCP (Transmission Control Protocol). The main difference between these protocols is that UDP does not guarantee delivery, and packets can arrive at the receiving network

> **RANDOM BONUS DEFINITION**
>
> endpoint node — A node that interfaces with the user and the user's communication within a LAN.

node out of order or duplicated, or not arrive at all. UDP is considered an unreliable delivery protocol whereas TCP is considered a reliable delivery protocol. TCP has the capability to detect missing, duplicated, and out of order packets and possesses mechanisms to request a packet be retransmitted if necessary. UDP relies on the use of ports for application-to-application communications. Since the port number is a 16-bit field in the UDP datagram, it can be anything between 0 and 65,535 or $(2^{16}-1)$.[21]

Port numbers may range from 0 to 65,535, but for the most part the first 1024 (0 to 1023 decimal or 0x03FF hexadecimal) are considered to be the well-known ports. The ports from 1024 to 49,151 (0x0400 to 0xBFFF) are registered ports

---

[21] Why would the max port number would be $2^{16}-1$? True, the number 2 raised to the 16th power is equal to 65,536, so that is the maximum number of combinations that can be found when using 16 binary bits. However, one of those combinations is zero, so the −1 from the maximum value for the zero value and you end up the highest numeric value that can be attained with 16 binary bits is 65,535.

with the Internet Corporation for Assigned Names and Numbers (ICANN). Ports 49,152 to 65,535 (0xC000 to 0xFFFF) are considered to be temporary ports that clients can use when they communicate with servers.

Table 8-1 Common Application Layer Protocols

PROTOCOL	PORT(S)	DESCRIPTION
DHCP	67 and 68	Dynamic Host Configuration Protocol provides the means for network clients to obtain an IP address, default gateway IP address, and Domain Name System server addresses.
DNS	53	Domain Name System server requests are used to convert a host name to an IP address so it may be found on the Internet.
FTP	20 and 21	File Transfer Protocol is used to transfer files between an FTP client workstation and an FTP server. Port 20 is for data and port 21 is used for control signaling between server and client.
HTTP	80	Hypertext Transfer Protocol is used to transfer hypertext information over the Internet. The most familiar application use for hypertext information retrieval is a web browser.
IRC	194[22]	Internet Relay Chat is used for group communications over the Internet. Groups are referred to as channels and can also provide direct client-to-client chats and file transfers.
POP3	110	Post Office Protocol version 3 is used to retrieve mail from a mail server by a mail reader application program.
SMTP	25	Simple Mail Transport Protocol is used to send and receive mail messages between mail servers over the Internet.
SNMP	161	Simple Network Management Protocol is used to manage and monitor network devices over the local network and Internet.
Telnet	23	Telecommunications Network protocol is used over local networks and the Internet to establish terminal sessions between a client computer and a server.
NTP	123	Network Time Protocol is used to synchronize time on a network by synchronizing network devices to a time standard found on the local network or over the Internet,
BGP	179	Border Gateway Protocol is the main routing protocol of the Internet. It is responsible for maintaining a table of IP networks and makes routing decisions on path networking policies and rules.
RIP	520	Routing Information Protocol is routing protocol run on local network segments to advertise route gateway addresses within the local network.

[22]IRC runs on the de facto standard port of 6667 and other nearby ports in the range of 6665 to 6669.

HELPFUL HINT

As you'll recall from the discussion on Network Address Translation (NAT,) a device that has NAT capability keeps a translation table. The device uses its own public interface address as the source address, while maintaining a cross-reference to the actual address of the requesting workstation. A technique known as *port mapping* maps the hidden source address to an unused port number. A workstation that requests a page from a web server must access the server using port 80 for the server to respond to the request. When the server receives the request, its only concern is the destination port, which must be port 80. So, what the source port number is makes no difference when servicing the request. The server simply sends the packet back to the requesting IP address, even though it is of a NAT-enabled router and not the actual workstation making the request. When the packet arrives at the NAT-enabled router, it examines the packet and finds that the destination port address correlates to a workstation on its private LAN in its NAT translation table. It modifies the packet with a new destination IP and port address, recalculates a new checksum, and then transmits it on to the private LAN. Therefore, knowing those temporary port addresses are available can come in handy when you're using NAT.

Port 0 is normally reserved, but its use is allowed as a valid source port in transmissions where the transmitting network node does not require a response from the receiving network node, which would be true in a case of a streaming application. Some common UDP network applications that are considered streaming applications are video teleconferencing, gaming, telephone using voice over IP (VoIP), and Trivial File Transfer Protocol (TFTP). Domain Name Services (DNS), an essential component of the Internet for the resolution of IP addresses to domain names, also utilizes UDP for its transmissions.

Whereas UDP is connectionless, TCP is considered a connection-oriented protocol. This means that an end-to-end communication is required with the use of handshaking between client and server. Once the connection is established between the client and server, data can flow across that connection. Servers provide a multitude of services, including web, FTP, and Telnet.

TCP utilizes a three-way handshake in establishing a connection. The server first must bind to a particular service and be available to all connections. This listening on a port is considered to be a passive open. Establishing a connection requires an active open on the server port. To do this the client sends a SYN (synchronization) packet with a random packet sequence number to the server. In response the client's SYN the server replies with a SYN-ACK (acknowledgment) with the initial sequence number received from the client but incremented by one for the next sequence number it is expecting to receive. Also in the packet is the server's initial sequence number. The client then replies back to the server an ACK that contains its initial sequence number incremented by one along with the server's acknowledgment number, which is the server's sequence number incremented by one. After a successful SYN, SYN-ACK, ACK sequence between client and server, a connection[23] is established.

With the use of sequence numbers, it is very easy to determine packet order, duplicate packets, or missing packets. This provides TCP with the capability to provide error-free transmission. Applications requiring a high degree of reliability work best when they use TCP to set up communications over the network between a client and a server running that application program.

HELPFUL HINT

This section noted that certain applications utilize UDP for their transmission of data. An example of this is VoIP. However, telephone conversations are somewhat forgiving for lost audio packets. Voice quality can degrade rapidly when packet loss begins to increase. Depending on bandwidth usage on networks and with the addition of quality of service (QoS) for some traffic, UDP traffic may be affected because of its best-effort delivery method. With VoIP, this is manifested in choppy voice quality and dead air, which some users find intolerable. One way around this issue is further encapsulation, although it does add a degree of overhead to each packet. Some users opt for sending their VoIP data through a tunneling protocol, which is delivered using TCP/IP.

To terminate a TCP connection, the protocol uses a FIN, ACK sequence. When a network node desires to terminate the connection it sends a FIN packet, and the receiving network node sends an ACK in acknowledg-

POP QUIZ

Which TCP/IP model Transport layer protocol is connection based?

ment of receiving the FIN packet. This is considered a half open connection. The network node that has terminated its connection can no longer use the connection for data transmission, but the network node that has not sent its FIN packet can remain open and transmitting data. This sequence of FIN, ACK, FIN, ACK from both nodes is termed a four-way handshake sequence.

Perhaps the most commonly used connection termination sequence is one network node sends a FIN packet and the other network node responds with a FIN-ACK combining the two handshakes into one. The network node that

---

[23]*Connection* is sometimes synonymous with the word *session*, as in client server session. These words are sometimes used interchangeably to represent the SYN, SYN-ACK, ACK sequence.

initiated the termination sequence just responds with an ACK. This type of termination sequence is considered a three-way handshake.

There is a possibility that both network nodes may send a FIN packet simultaneously and also will send their ACK packets at the same time. Since this sequence is done in parallel it is considered a two-termination sequence.

8.2.3 TCP/IP Internet Layer

Some of the common services found at the Internet layer of the TCP/IP model are IP (Internet Protocol), ICMP (Internet Control Message Protocol), and IPSec (Internet Protocol Security). The primary protocol of the Internet layer suite of protocols is IP. Its main purpose is the delivery of packets between network nodes based solely on source and destination addresses since it is a connectionless protocol. Data from the upper layers is encapsulated within the IP datagram for delivery. IP is a best-effort delivery method and has no provision for out of order, duplicate, or missing packets. IP does not guarantee that the data payload has not been corrupted since the checksum it carries is only for the header, ensuring that it is error free. However, this does allow for quick discarding of packets whose headers have been corrupted.

IP is responsible for fragmentation into multiple packets if the data load it receives from the upper layers is too large to send within a single packet. When fragmentation is involved, the IP layer uses flags and offset to aid in the determination of

POP QUIZ

True or false: The TCP/IP model Internet layer IP protocol is a connectionless protocol.

packet sequence and their order. However, IP depends on the upper layers to ensure that the end-to-end integrity of the connection is maintained.

ICMP is another integral protocol of the Internet layer. Its chief responsibility is to send a message to the operating system of a computer when a network error has been detected. These messages usually report that a requested service is not available or the other host could not be reached. Normally ICMP is a

RANDOM BONUS DEFINITION

bottleneck — A point in a data communications path or computer processing flow that limits overall throughput or performance.

single-ended protocol since it not used to transmit messages between network nodes. However, there are some exceptions and the most common of these are the `ping` and `traceroute`[24] commands. These two tools require a reply from a receiving network node. If no reply is received, an error message is displayed.

The `ping` utility is used to determine if a target network node is available over the network. If it replies, the assumption[25] is that the path is good between two network nodes. The `traceroute` utility returns replies from each hop that it

> **POP QUIZ**
>
> What two ICMP applications can be used to verify the presence of an IP address on the Internet or local network?

crosses to reach a particular targeted network node. Usually, it will try to reach a target in a given number of hops. The customary maximum hop count is 30 hops. It is a good indication if the packet is traveling in the right direction or not.

8.2.4   TCP/IP Link Layer

We already mentioned that the TCP/IP model's Link layer maps to the OSI model's Data Link layer and Physical layer. The Physical layer components are the tangible pieces of hardware required to connect a computer to the network. It consists of the cabling, connectors, and NIC, which in most cases is installed in the computer. The hardware pieces are the lowest level of the TCP/IP model and make up the first level of the OSI model.

Normally we do not think of hardware in terms of protocols. However, there are standards and specifications that hardware from different manufacturers must meet to be considered compliant with a standard. An example of this would be the electrical characteristics of cabling used for networking. There are also mechanical considerations such as size and form factor. The interconnection world is large, and manufacturers from all over the globe produce various components that all need to interconnect with products from other networking products manufacturers. So the protocol of the Physical layer is the standards and specifications that define various networking components.

However, we know that the demarcation line between the Physical layer and the Data Link layer of the OSI model is at the Link layer of the TCP/IP model. It is the Network Interface Card.

---

[24] `traceroute` is found mostly in Unix-based systems. In the Microsoft Windows world, the command is `tracert`. This is an accommodation to its predecessor MS-DOS, since commands and filenames could not be longer than eight characters.
[25]The word "assumption" is used here since the fact that a reply is received does not guarantee that the host you desire to reach is actually the host that is replying. There is always a possibility of a duplicate address on a network. You will read more about this in Chapter 16, "Troubleshooting."

An NIC card is a piece of hardware with electrical capabilities of sending intelligent electrical signals to another NIC card on the same network. The intelligence is contained within the bits and order that it places over the network medium, which in a lot of

cases is wire based but may also be either fiber or air, in the case of wireless networking. The NIC contains registers and buffer space where the data and network control signals from the computer operating system are written to while sending packets to or reading packets from the network medium. Figure 8-9 shows a block diagram of a generic NIC.

The diagram in Figure 8-9 is a representation of the basics of any type of NIC card. It is drawn to indicate that the card is capable of full-duplex operation because it contains both send and receive paths that are independent from one another, which would allow for simultaneous receive and transmit capability. To send a frame, the computer operating system needs to communicate with the card. Since these cards are functionally the same, the method used to communicate with a network interface is fixed by the operating system's developer. It is up to the card manufacturer to either manufacture the card so it can be installed in a computer using generic N driver software or provide a tailored driver that would perform this function. Hardware interface software drivers[26] are the link between operating system and the actual network hardware.

Reviewing the block diagram, the computer bus interface component has to adhere to the architecture of the bus structure used within the computer. There have been many bus structures used since the spawning of PCs. In the earlier days, many were proprietary designs. As the industry evolved so did bus standards. One of the earlier standards was S-100, and cards of this type can be found in computer museums and in the cellars of computer aficionados. With IBM's development of the IBM-PC, the bus standard that was rapidly adopted was ISA (Industry Standard Architecture). As computer capabilities began to expand so too did the bus architecture. The next evolution of the bus was the Extended ISA card or, simply, EISA card. Today's bus standard is PCI (Peripheral Component Interconnect). So a network card or any sort of peripheral card needs the capability to be inserted into the internal bus of the computer it is being installed in.

---

[26]*Device driver* is the common name for software that performs the hardware interface to the operating system. It is a piece of software code that allows the addressing and control of a hardware card installed in a computer.

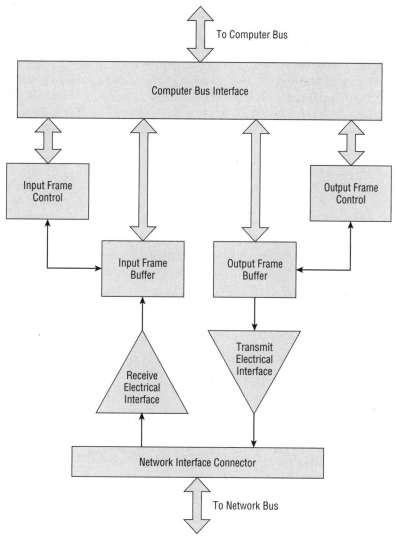

Figure 8-9 A block diagram of a generic NIC

With the network card installed in the computer chassis and the appropriate device driver installed into the computer so that the operating system knows how to communicate with the NIC, the next step is to bind a network protocol to the card so data can be moved to and from the network. Depending on the operating system, differing methods can be used; consult your computer documentation. When all of that is completed, data can be sent and received from the network transparent to the workstation's user.

Outgoing packets from an application program flow down the network stack with each layer encapsulated within the proper protocol. Once the frame that is to be transmitted is assembled and loaded into the output frame buffer, the output frame control prevents any fur-

> **RANDOM BONUS DEFINITION**
>
> collision domain — A set of nodes connecting to a shared medium among which a collision can occur. Stations on the same shared LAN are in the same collision domain.

ther packets from being written into the output buffer until the frame has been completely sent. When the output frame buffer is cleared, the output frame control (through the device driver associated with this card) alerts the operating system that the card is ready to transmit another frame. On the receive side, the card monitors the network medium. When it has received a frame and it is completely in the input frame buffer and passes the checksum validation, the operating system is alerted (again via the device driver for the card) that a frame is ready to be passed up the network stack. As the packet passes through each layer, it is verified and checked as it is de-encapsulated. The input frame control is alerted that the frame is read and that another frame can be received.

The last component to be discussed from the block diagram of the NIC is the connector. Many people are already familiar with the UTP RJ-45 connectors and plugs that are fairly commonplace on PCs, hubs,

> **POP QUIZ**
>
> List what is required for a network card to have full-duplex capability.

switches, and routers. However, depending on the medium being used, the connector will be different and adhere to the standards governing the usage of that type of medium.

8.2.4.1 TCP/IP Link Layer Protocols

The three common protocols residing at the Link layer of the TCP/IP model are ARP (Address Resolution Protocol), RARP (Reverse Address Resolution Protocol), and OSPF (Open Shortest Path First). ARP and RARP are the complement of each other in resolving network addresses. ARP is used to find what hardware MAC address is associated with a particular IP address. It accomplishes this by sending out an ARP request packet as a broadcast to all nodes on its local network segment. The packet contains the IP address that the transmitting network node is seeking. The receiving nodes on the network that do not have the IP address being requested simply ignore the packet. The network node that does have that IP address bound to its network interface responds with its MAC hardware address.

RARP is a protocol that attempts to determine its IP address by broadcasting on the local network segment with its MAC address. It expects a receiving network node to have

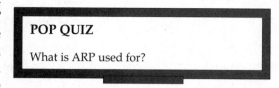

POP QUIZ

What is ARP used for?

an entry in its ARP cache that matches that MAC address with an IP address to transmit back a packet containing the IP address. With DHCP now in wide use, RARP has fallen into disuse. However, DHCP is a TCP/IP model Application layer protocol and does not reside at the Link layer.

OSPF is a dynamic routing protocol used to move packets from network segment to network segment. Two network segments with a router in each that have a path between them can build and interchange route information. Figure 8-10 illustrates a network utilizing OSPF to pass network routing information.

ACRONYM ALERT

RSTP — Rapid Spanning Tree Protocol

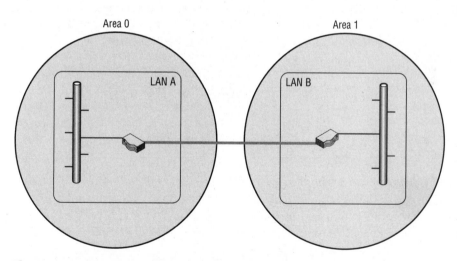

Figure 8-10 OSPF passing network routing information

Notice there are two areas: Area 0 and Area 1. An area is a collection of network segments with routers and other network forwarding devices. For the sake of simplicity, these are shown as two large circles. Within each area there is a router to route traffic from that area to another area. Routers that border a network and pass routing information to another router within another area are called area border routers (ABRs). You will recall in the earlier discussion of routers in this chapter we said they resided within the lower level of the

> **POP QUIZ**
>
> What is OSPF?

TCP/IP model. The OSPF information passed between routers is used to update their routing information tables. The two routers only communicate OSPF information between them and do not pass that information into the network they control. So if a workstation on LAN A wanted to pass data to a server or another workstation on LAN B, it would send the packet to its default gateway. The packet will ultimately end up at the ABR for Area 0 and finding that the targeted address when compared to its learned routes in its routing table is destined for network node in Area 1, forwards the adjacent ABR for Area 1. The information that is used is the Link State Database (LSDB) routing data that is passed between the Area 0 and Area 1 ABR router.

HELPFUL HINT

The OSPF example used is very simplistic. Large networks have multiple areas where one ABR may be interconnected to many other ABR routers. The key to OSPF is to know that the updates exchanged between routers can be found within the router's LSDB. Since this is a dynamic routing protocol, routes may pop up or age out as network nodes are inserted or removed from the network.

8.3   OSI Application Layer

The OSI Application layer resides at Layer 7 at the top of the OSI model. It was mentioned that the TCP/IP Application model directly links to this layer. So the protocols listed in the discussion of the TCP/IP model Application layer are also contained within this layer of the OSI model. This is the layer that is directly responsible for interfacing with the application program a user is using on the computer. The most common use of a computer with Internet access is e-mail. The e-mail protocols residing at this layer are POP (Post Office Protocol), POP3 (Post Office Protocol version 3), and SMTP (Simple Mail Transfer Protocol). POP and POP3 are mail client–based in the form of user e-mail reader programs. SMTP is e-mail server–based and is used to transfer mail from one mail server to another, so this layer is keenly aware of its communication peers. Mail clients know where their mail server is, and mail servers can establish a connection for the transfer of mail between them. Using the example of e-mail at the Application layer, the information the layer is concerned with is the identity of the sender and the identity of the recipient of that message and what application is available to assist in preparing the message to be sent. All e-mail users are pretty familiar with the address format used, e.g., john.doe@his_company.com.

There are two parts to the recipient address: the user name "john.doe" and the domain name "his_company.com". The e-mail is formatted with sender address, recipient address, and message and passed on to the local mail server servicing that

ACRONYM ALERT

MTU — Maximum transmission unit

sender. The mail server is concerned with both the domain name portion of the recipient's address and the recipient's name. The recipient's name is used to identify the local mailbox for that user on the server. The application on the mail server is designed to use SMTP to send and receive mail from other mail servers. Most mail servers run a local post office where local users communicate locally over the local network using either POP or POP3 to retrieve mail from the local mail server. To send mail, users direct their outgoing messages to the SMTP service running on the mail server. Mail clients run POP at the Application layer to read mail and use SMTP to send mail. A mail server also runs two protocols at that layer, SMTP and POP and/or POP3. These protocols rely on the layers below them to actually get the message delivered and alert them when there is a message to pass up from the network.

The Application layer is concerned with any syntax restraints such as the "@" sign in an e-mail message being required as a delimiter between recipient address and domain address. It is also the layer where security is applied for user identification and privacy. If quality of service is being applied to network communications, this is the layer concerned with determining the priority of a packet by its QoS[27] tagging.

NOTE Although there are many devices that are capable of QOS tagging of packets, there is no support for it over the Internet. The Internet is still a best-effort network.

[27]QoS is the acronym for quality of service. We mentioned that the DiffServ field or the Type of Service field of the IP header is used for tagging packets to allow them to be transmitted along the network with a priority determined by how they are tagged.

This chapter covers only a handful of the most familiar Layer 7 protocols. Many more protocols are available, considering that the combination for port numbers is 65,536. Even with some protocols using more than one port, there is still a lot of them. You can obtain information on many protocols by reading their RFCs. RFCs are available over the Internet at www.ietf.org/rfc.html.

> **POP QUIZ**
>
> True or false: The maximum number of protocols the TCP/IP Application layer can have at any one time is two.

8.4 OSI Presentation Layer

The middle layer of the OSI model upper layers is the Presentation layer, which occupies Layer 6 of that model. It has been mentioned that within the TCP/IP model, this OSI layer resides within its top Application layer. In the OSI model, it takes service requests from the Application layer and then issues requests to the Session layer below.

Although we said that this layer resides within the TCP/IP model Application layer, its components are more likely to be found within the computer's operating system. Within this layer, incoming and outgoing data can be translated from one data format to another. This layer also offers the capability for data encryption and compression as well as decrypting and uncompressing data received.

> **POP QUIZ**
>
> True or false: The OSI model Presentation layer maps directly to the Transport layer of the TCP/IP model.

8.5 OSI Session Layer

The lowest layer of the upper layers of the OSI model is Layer 5, the Session layer. Like the OSI model's Application and Presentation layers, it too can be found within the Application layer of the TCP/IP model. True to its name, it is the layer that is responsible for opening, managing, and closing a session between applications. It also provides the capability of restoring a session. It is the layer where authentication and permissions are granted.

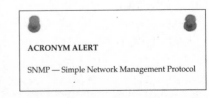

ACRONYM ALERT

SNMP — Simple Network Management Protocol

The Session layer is where TCP SYN handshake sequences are provided for. Although the Session layer is responsible for checkpointing and recovery within the OSI model, it is seldom used by protocols of the Internet Protocol suite. Some of the protocols found within the Session layer are

- **L2F** (Layer 2 Forwarding Protocol) — Used to provide virtual private networks (VPN) over the Internet.

- **L2TP** (Layer 2 Tunneling Protocol) — Used to provide virtual private networks (VPN) over the Internet.

- **NetBIOS** (Network Basic Input/Output System) — In today's networks is usually run over TCP/IP on the local network. It is a naming convention used to identify hosts on a Windows-based network. Although it is run over TCP/IP, its host name is not to be confused with the host domain name a computer may be given to resolve its name to an IP address. Those host names are registered with a DNS server and are not associated at all with a computer's NetBIOS host name, which on larger networks is resolved by a WINS (Windows Internet Name Service) server. In small networks where WINS may not be available, WINS name resolution can be accomplished by editing the LMHOSTS file on the computer to correlate the NetBIOS name to an IP address.

- **PAP** (Password Authentication Protocol) — A simple authentication protocol to allow users access to network services. A major drawback to PAP is that passwords are passed in cleartext and can be easily captured. Since PAP is not secure, network administrators have been making use of CHAP (Challenge Handshake Authentication Protocol), which uses a hashing function to secure the password. MS-CHAP is Microsoft's implementation of CHAP.

- **PPTP** (Point-to-Point Tunneling Protocol) — Provides a means of creating a VPN over the Internet. PPTP uses a standard PPP (Point-to-Point Protocol) session to its peer endpoint using the Generic Routing Encapsulation (GRE) protocol. A second session is then opened using TCP port 1723 to initiate and control the GTE session. Due to the need to have two simultaneous sessions opened, PPTP is not easily passed through a firewall. PPTP has lost favor and is being replaced by the L2TP and IPSec tunneling protocols.

> **RANDOM BONUS DEFINITION**
>
> catenet — A collection of networks connected together at the Data Link layer level.

- **SSH** (Secure Shell) — Allows for the secure exchange of data between two network nodes. It was designed as a replacement for Telnet and other insecure protocols that were used for remote access over the Internet. These shells sent communications in cleartext, and passwords were easily compromised. SSH makes use of public key cryptography for authentication of the remote computer and allows the remote computer to also authenticate the user establishing the session.

The Session layer provides for either half-duplex or full-duplex operation, synchronization points in the message stream, and error checking.

POP QUIZ

At which layer of the TCP/IP model is the OSI Session layer found?

LAST BUT NOT LEAST

As mentioned previously, you are encouraged to review the RFC documentation for any further information on protocols. Be aware, however, that any RFC is subject to variations in interpretation, and one implementation of a protocol may not be identical to another. A network administrator or member of the support staff must always be aware of this when integrating network pieces from different manufacturers. When there are interoperability issues, performance degradation issues, or functional issues, you may have to draw on the RFC to find which way to point the finger.

8.6   Chapter Exercises

1. List in order from highest to lowest the upper layers of the OSI model, also indicating their layer number.

2. An application that runs on a user's workstation and communicates over a network with an appropriate application that is running on a server is considered to be what type of application?

3. Which protocol is considered to be a connection-based protocol?

4. What functionality can be used to disguise addresses from a private address space to be seen on the Internet?

5. List the three private address spaces that may be used and are considered to be not routable over the Internet.

6. Name an Application layer protocol that may be used to perform file transfers over the network.

7. What is the protocol that resolves IP addresses to hardware addresses?

8.7   Pop Quiz Answers

1. True or false: The Application layer is where all the application programs you load on your PC are stored.

   False

2. The predominant networking protocol run over Ethernet networks is

   TCP/IP

3. True or false: UDP is a connection-based protocol.

   False

4. Describe what happens to a packet when it is passed through a NAT-enabled router.

   A technique known as *port mapping* maps the hidden source address to an unused port number. A workstation that requests a page from a web server must access the server using port 80 for the server to respond to the request. When the server receives the request, its only concern is the destination port, which must be port 80. So what the source port number is makes no difference when servicing the request. The server simply sends the packet back to the requesting IP address, even though it is of a NAT-enabled router and not the actual workstation making the request. When the packet arrives at the NAT-enabled router, it examines the packet and finds that the destination port address correlates to a workstation on its private LAN in its NAT translation table. It modifies the packet with a new destination IP and port address, recalculates a new checksum, and then transmits it on to the private LAN. Therefore, knowing those temporary port addresses are available can come in handy when you're using NAT.

5. At which layer of the TCP/IP model can the physical component of a network node be found?

   Layer 1

6. What determines the type of framing that is to be used on a particular network segment?

   The media being used for that network segment.

7. Which TCP/IP model Transport layer protocol is connection based?

   TCP

8. True or false: The TCP/IP model Internet layer IP protocol is a connectionless protocol.

   True

9. What two ICMP applications can be used to verify the presence of an IP address on the Internet or local network?

   ping and/or traceroute

10. List what is required for a network card to have full-duplex capability.

    - input frame control
    - input frame buffer
    - receive circuit
    - output frame control
    - output frame buffer
    - transmit circuit

11. What is ARP used for?

    Address resolution

12. What is OSPF?

    A routing protocol

13. True or false: The maximum number of protocols the TCP/IP Application layer can have at any one time is two.

    False

14. True or false: The OSI model Presentation layer maps directly to the Transport layer of the TCP/IP model.

    True

15. At which layer of the TCP/IP model is the OSI Session layer found?

    Layer 5

The Transport Layer

Transport of the mails, transport of the human voice, transport of flickering pictures — in this century as in others our highest accomplishments still have the single aim of bringing men together.

— Antoine de Saint-Exupéry

The last chapter talked about the upper layers of the OSI reference model. You learned the specific purpose of each layer and how the layers interact with each other. This chapter covers the Transport layer, Layer 4 of the OSI reference model.

The Transport layer is the highest layer of the lower layers of the OSI reference model. The Transport layer sits on top of the Network layer and below the Session layer. This layer is responsible for the end-to-end connection and datagram delivery, as well as congestion control and flow control. The two main protocols that operate at this layer are UDP and TCP, which were discussed in Chapter 5.

The purpose of the Transport layer is to set up connections, maintain connections, shut down connections, and perform error checking.[1] The protocols that operate at this layer are considered either connection-oriented (i.e., TCP) or connectionless (i.e., UDP). Remember that connection-oriented means that the connection must be set up before data can be transmitted, and connectionless means that data can flow without the connection being established first.

---

[1]Error checking and other transport reliability attributes can be handled at this layer, if they are not already performed at the lower layers.

So far this book has explained what the Transport layer is and the services and protocols it provides. This chapter takes a little deeper look into some of the functions that operate at this layer.

RANDOM BONUS DEFINITION

1000BASE-SX — A baseband Ethernet system operating at 1000 Mbps over two multimode optical fibers using shortwave laser optics.

9.1   The Terms and Conditions of Chapter 9

Much like many other chapters in this book, there are some terms you need to have an understanding of, but not necessarily in-depth knowledge. Therefore, we start this chapter off with a few basic Transport layer functions and terms relating to these.

RANDOM BONUS DEFINITION

root port — In the Spanning Tree Protocol, the port through which a designated bridge forwards traffic in the direction of the root bridge.

9.1.1   End-to-End Delivery

The Transport layer provides logical communication between upper layer processes[2] running on different nodes on a network (see Figure 9-1).

Notice in the figure that the lower layer processes are transparent to the Transport layer. The sending node takes the upper layer data and breaks it into smaller segments that are then passed to the lower layers to be encapsulated and trans-

POP QUIZ

True or false: UDP is an example of a connectionless protocol.

ported to a receiving node. The receiving node will cache the data, put the segments back into the message, and pass it to the upper layers to be delivered to the Application layer.

---

[2]Notice this says processes and not nodes. The Network layer provides the logical connection between nodes.

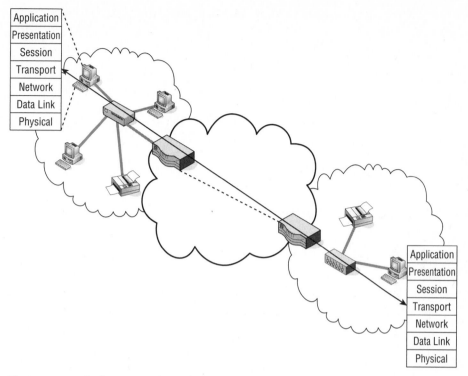

Figure 9-1 Logical Transport layer communications

9.1.2   Standards

Before getting too much further into this chapter, there are a couple of standards that need to be mentioned that deal with the services and operations of functions at the Transport layer. The first of these is the ISO/IEC 8072 standard (Information technology – Open Systems Interconnection – Transport service definition), and the other is the ISO/IEC 8073 standard (Information technology – Open Systems Interconnection – Protocol for providing the connection-mode transport service).

Following is a quick summary of these two standards. The remainder of the chapter covers the information that is defined in the standards.

9.1.2.1   ISO/IEC 8072

The ISO/IEC 8072 standard defines the recommended services provided by the OSI Transport layer while working with the Network layer to serve the needs of protocols used at the Session layer. These are only recommendations or guidelines, and strict adherence is not upheld.[3] Defined in this standard are recommendations for the implementation for the following functions:

- Connection-oriented mode services
- Connectionless-mode services

The main thing to remember about this standard is that it defines the way the Transport layer interoperates with the other OSI layers it works with.

ACRONYM ALERT

BGP — Border Gateway Protocol

9.1.2.2   ISO/IEC 8073

The ISO/IEC 8073 standard sets the recommendations to be followed by nodes (entities) within a network that are utilizing the services of the OSI Transport layer. This standard is also available to future node deployments within an open systems environment. Defined in this standard are recommendations for the following functions:

- The recommendation and scope for classes of procedures that should be taken into account by the nodes when transporting data
- How peer nodes exchange data
- How the nodes exchange information with the transport service
- The manner in which the nodes exchange information with a service provider

9.1.3   This, That, and the Other

This section takes a look at a few other "items of interest" regarding the Transport layer.

9.1.3.1   Types of Transport Service

This is an easy one.[4] There are two types of transport service: connection-oriented and connectionless.

RANDOM BONUS DEFINITION

aggregated link — A set of two or more physical links that appear to higher layer entities as though they were a single, higher capacity link.

---

[3]Keep in mind that all of the functions at each of the layers in the reference model are only recommendations and guidelines that can be followed for conformity sake.
[4]At least we hope it is.

9.1.3.2 Data Units

The following two data units operate at the Transport layer:

- Transport protocol data unit (TPDU)
- Transport service data unit (TSDU)

So, what is the difference between the two types of data units? The *TSDU* is the data that is transmitted to the various layers on both ends of a connection. The *TPDU* is the data that is sent from a protocol on one end to the peer protocol at the other end.

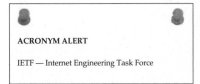

POP QUIZ

TCP is a connection-_____ protocol.

9.1.3.3 Classes of Transport Service

The Transport layer defines the functions of service performed by it within five difference classes of transport service, as shown in Table 9-1.

ACRONYM ALERT

IETF — Internet Engineering Task Force

Table 9-1 Classes of Transport Service

CLASS NAME	CLASS FUNCTION
Class 0	Simple class
Class 1	Basic error recovery class
Class 2	Multiplexing class
Class 3	Error recovery and multiplexing class
Class 4	Error detection and recovery class

9.1.3.4 Types of Network Service

The Transport layer takes into consideration the current error rate status of the connection being used. There are three types of network service used to classify the connection status. The data units are classified into one of the three types based on signal quality:

- **Type A** — A network connection with an acceptable residual error rate as well as an acceptable rate of signal failures.

- **Type B** — A network connection with acceptable residual error rate but an unacceptable rate of signal failures.

- **Type C** — A network connection with an unacceptable residual error rate for the user of the transport service.

9.1.3.5 *Multiplexing*

Multiplexing is the act of grouping several signals into a shared single signal. Multiplexing at the Transport layer is performed between the Transport layer and its adjoining layers. Multiple upper layer users can be multiplexed to share the services of a single Transport layer protocol. The signals are separated by what are known as *transport service access points (TSAP)*. An example of this is shown in Figure 9-2.

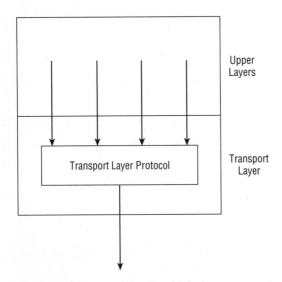

Upper
Layers

Transport Layer Protocol

Transport
Layer

Figure 9-2 An example of multiplexing

Network service multiplexing is also supported at the Transport layer. Multiplexing can occur in both an upward (multiple Transport layer signals to a single network signal) and a downward (multiple network signals to a single transport signal) fashion.

The use of upward multiplexing (see Figure 9-3) is a cost-saving measure that allows multiple Transport layer signals to share a single network signal (a signal purchased from the network provider).

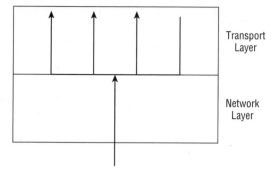

Figure 9-3 Upward multiplexing

Downward multiplexing (see Figure 9-4) is useful when bandwidth and throughput of data are priorities.

RANDOM BONUS DEFINITION

best-effort service — A service provided by an entity where frames or packets are delivered with high probability but with no absolute guarantee.

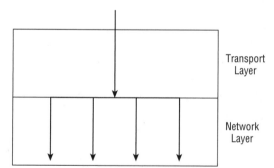

Figure 9-4 Downward multiplexing

AN UNRELATED MOMENT OF PAUSE: WEB ACRONYMS

It isn't just the networking world that uses acronyms. Millions of users are typing away with acronyms that a few years ago didn't exist. A lot of kids out there have added their own, such as POS (parent over shoulder). Jim has already prepared to start running a sniffer if he sees one of his kids using that one — having to warn a pal that the parent is looking in deserves a quick look-see.

Enough rambling. Here is a list of some common web acronyms that you may come across at some point.

(continued)

AN UNRELATED MOMENT OF PAUSE: WEB ACRONYMS *(continued)*

2L8	Too late
AFK	Away from keyboard
AFN	[That's] all for now
AISB	As I said before
B4	Before
B4N	Bye for now
BAK	Back at keyboard
BBL	Be back later
BCNU	Be seeing you
BRB	Be right back
BTW	By the way
CU	See you
CYA	See ya
DL	Download
EZ	Easy
F2F	Face to face
FWIW	For what it's worth
G2G	Gotta go
GMTA	Great minds think alike
HAND	Have a nice day
IC	I see
IDK	I don't know
IK	I know
IKWUM	I know what you mean
IMAO	In my arrogant opinion
IMHO	In my humble opinion
IMO	In my opinion
IYKWIM	If you know what I mean
IYO	In your opinion
IYSWIM	If you see what I mean
JK	Just kidding

(continued)

AN UNRELATED MOMENT OF PAUSE: WEB ACRONYMS *(continued)*

KISS	Keep it simple, stupid
LOL	Laughing out loud
ME2	Me too
NP	No problem
ROTFL	Rolling on the floor laughing
TC	Take care

9.2   Transport Layer Operations

The purpose of the Transport layer is to provide end-to-end delivery of data from one application to another. The Transport layer can deliver data in a reliable or an unreliable fashion. Data flow can be regulated and each end can communicate lost datagram data with the other end. Protocols can operate in a connection-oriented manner as well as a connectionless manner. In the connection-oriented approach, a logical connection between nodes must be established before any data is transmitted. The connectionless approach does not require connection establishment; data is sent as it is received.

> **POP QUIZ**
>
> Which standard defines the way the Transport layer interoperates with the other OSI layers it works with?

In this section, we take a deeper look into the operations for both the connection-oriented as well as the connectionless protocols that are available within the Transport layer.

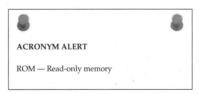

ACRONYM ALERT

ROM — Read-only memory

9.2.1   Connection-Oriented Operations

Connection-oriented protocols require that a logical connection between two nodes is established before any data can be sent. To do this, rules are established that lay out how a connection is set up, maintained, and terminated.

9.2.1.1 Setting Up the Connection

If a node needs to pass data in a connection-oriented environment, a series of messages is passed between the node and the destination node it wants to send the data to. The series of messages is known as the *three-way handshake*, and it works like this:

1. The originating node will send a request known as a SYN[5] to the destination node.

2. The destination node will let the originating node know that it has received the SYN request by sending back a $SYN\text{-}ACK$[6] message.

3. The originating node will respond to the SYN-ACK by sending back an ACK message.

Figure 9-5 shows an example of this.

ACRONYM ALERT

MSTI — Multiple spanning tree instance

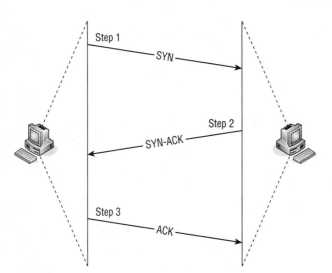

Figure 9-5 An example of a three-way handshake

Don't be fooled into believing this is all that's going on in the connection setup phase. A number of variables are being negotiated during this phase. User node quality of service is matched to any available services that are provided by the Network layer. Some of the services negotiated include

■ Which network services best match requirements set by the user for the connection

[5]SYN stands for synchronize.
[6]ACK stands for acknowledgment.

- Whether multiplexing can (or should) be used
- Datagram size
- Address mapping
- Ability to separate multiple connections
- Inactivity timer information

> **RANDOM BONUS DEFINITION**
>
> optical fiber — A communications medium capable of carrying and directing light signals. Normally extruded or drawn from transparent glass or plastic material.

9.2.1.2 *Maintaining the Connection*

Maintaining the connection is nothing more than ensuring the connection remains stable during the transfer of data between the endpoint nodes. The following activities occur during this phase:

- Segmentation of data
- Reassembly of data
- Splitting data over multiple connections
- Flow control
- Setting the identification parameters for a particular connection between endpoint nodes
- Attending to prioritized datagrams
- TSDU delimiting

9.2.1.3 *Terminating the Connection*

Just like with the connection setup phase, there has to be a way to terminate the connection when the endpoint nodes are finished exchanging data. This phase operates much like the connection establishment phase.

Any node that has an active connection can initiate a connection termination by sending out a *FIN*[7] packet (or by setting a flag in a datagram). The other node can continue receiving data until it sends out a FIN-ACK, acknowledging the request to terminate the session.

> **RANDOM BONUS DEFINITION**
>
> collision detection — The act of detecting when packets collide during transmission.

---

[7]FIN stands for finished.

9.2.2 Connectionless Operations

Connectionless protocols do not require a connection; a transmitting device simply sends data as soon as it has data that is ready to be sent. Protocols that operate in a connectionless manner have a space available in the datagram to identify the source and destination addresses for the endpoint nodes. Connectionless protocols do need an available route to the destination in order to work. This means there must be some type of medium, a data link protocol, and a networking protocol to transmit the data. Other than these, there really is no other requirement.

Protocols that use the connectionless method of transport will often provide error checking and recovery methods, which are lacking in the connectionless environment. Some of these include:

ACRONYM ALERT

SNA — Systems network architecture

- Hop count verification
- Verification of the reassembly of fragmented data
- Datagram priority information and verification
- Datagram size verification

POP QUIZ

How many types of transport service are there?

TIME FOR SOMETHING NICE TO KNOW

Following are some helpful MS-DOS commands that are available with most Windows OS platforms.

◆ To determine whether a remote node is reachable and its connection quality, use the `ping` command.

```
C:\>ping
Usage: ping [-t] [-a] [-n count] [-l size] [-f] [-i TTL] [-v TOS]
       [-r count] [-s count] [[-j host-list] |
       [-k host-list]]
       [-w timeout] destination-list
Options:
  -t       Ping the specified host until stopped.
           To see statistics and continue - type
           Control-Break;
           To stop - type Control-C.
  -a       Resolve addresses to hostnames.
  -n count Number of echo requests to send.
  -l size  Send buffer size.
```

(continued)

TIME FOR SOMETHING NICE TO KNOW *(continued)*

```
     -f        Set Don't Fragment flag in packet.
     -i TTL    Time To Live.
     -v TOS    Type Of Service.
     -r count  Record route for count hops.
     -s count  Timestamp for count hops.
     -j host-list  Loose source route along host-list.
     -k host-list  Strict source route along host-list.
     -w timeout    Timeout in milliseconds to wait for each reply.
```

◆ **To follow the path that is taken by a datagram to a remote node, use the `tracert`[8] command.**

```
C:\>tracert
Usage: tracert [-d] [-h maximum_hops] [-j host-list] [-w timeout]
        target_name
Options:
   -d           Do not resolve addresses to
                hostnames.
   -h maximum_hops   Maximum number of hops to search for
                target.
   -j host-list    Loose source route along host-list.
   -w timeout      Wait timeout milliseconds for each
                reply.
```

◆ **To view and manage the local routing table, use the `route` command.**

```
C:\>route
ROUTE [-f] [-p] [command [destination]
          [MASK netmask] [gateway] [METRIC metric]
          [IF interface]
   -f     Clears the routing tables of all gateway
          entries. If this is used in conjunction with
          one of the commands, the tables are cleared
          prior to running the command.
   -p     When used with the ADD command, makes a route
          persistent across
          boots of the system. By default, routes are
          not preserved
          when the system is restarted. Ignored for all
          other commands,
          which always affect the appropriate
          persistent routes. This option is not
          supported in Windows 95.
command    One of these:
        PRINT    Prints a route
```

(continued)

[8]Tracert stands for trace route.

TIME FOR SOMETHING NICE TO KNOW *(continued)*

```
          ADD      Adds a route
          DELETE   Deletes a route
          CHANGE   Modifies an existing route
destination Specifies the host.
MASK      Specifies that the next parameter is the
      'netmask' value.
netmask   Specifies a subnet mask value for this route
      entry.
          If not specified, it defaults to
          255.255.255.255.
gateway   Specifies gateway.
interface  the interface number for the specified route.
METRIC    specifies the metric, ie. cost for the
      destination.
```

◆ **To view and manage the ARP table, use the `arp` command.**

```
C:\>arp
Displays and modifies the IP-to-Physical address translation
tables used by address resolution protocol (ARP).
ARP -s inet_addr eth_addr [if_addr]
ARP -d inet_addr [if_addr]
ARP -a [inet_addr] [-N if_addr]
  -a      Displays current ARP entries by
          interrogating the current
          protocol data.  If inet_addr is specified,
          the IP and Physical
          addresses for only the specified computer
          are displayed. If more than one network
          interface uses ARP, entries for each ARP
          table are displayed.
  -g      Same as -a.
  inet_addr   Specifies an internet address.
  -N if_addr   Displays the ARP entries for the network
          interface specified by if_addr.
  -d      Deletes the host specified by inet_addr.
          inet_addr may be wildcarded with * to delete
          all hosts.
  -s      Adds the host and associates the Internet
          address inet_addr with the Physical address
          eth_addr. The Physical address is
          given as 6 hexadecimal bytes separated by
          hyphens. The entry is permanent.
  eth_addr   Specifies a physical address.
  if_addr    If present, this specifies the Internet
          address of the interface whose address
          translation table should be modified.
          If not present, the first applicable
          interface will be used.
```

9.3   Transport Layer Protocols

Chapter 5 provided some information on the TCP and UDP Transport layer protocols. Although these are the most popular and most commonly used, the following Transport layer protocols are also in use in some networks today:

- AppleTalk Transaction Protocol (ATP)
- Datagram Congestion Control Protocol (DCCP)
- NetBIOS Extended User Interface (NetBEUI)
- Real-time Transport Protocol (RTP)

These are mentioned only to provide you with the names of a few more Transport layer protocols that you may come across. For the purposes of this book, TCP and UDP are the Transport layer protocols that we will stick with.

ACRONYM ALERT

PPP — Point-to-Point Protocol

9.3.1   A Few More Words about TCP

TCP is a *connection-oriented* protocol. An originating node will contact a destination node to make sure it is available to get the message. Once confirmation is received that it is okay to send data, the transmission begins. TCP is also considered a *reliable* protocol because it has functions built into it that provide for various checks and balances to ensure the integrity of the data being transmitted.

TCP is able to break data down into segments so that smaller chunks of data are lost if there are problems with the transmission. TCP supports acknowledgments for received datagrams, and timers are set for the receipt of an acknowledgment to ensure that data is

RANDOM BONUS DEFINITION

jumbo frame — A frame longer than the maximum frame length allowed by a standard.

received on the destination end. TCP utilizes a checksum to monitor data receipt integrity. TCP also supports datagram reassembly, ensuring that it is put back into the same order it was sent. Finally, TCP supports both congestion control and flow control, allowing a sending node to monitor bandwidth availability as well as whether the receiving node can receive any more data.

TCP uses sequence numbers between nodes to ensure that reliable communication is taking place. Receiving nodes use sequence numbers to put the data back in order when it is received. Sequence numbers are also used to identify problems (lost packets, duplicate packets, etc.) that may occur with a specific packet that had been transmitted. Each end of the connection maintains its own sequence numbers, so data transmission can operate in a full-duplex manner. TCP is known as a *byte-oriented sequencing protocol* because every byte[9] that is being transmitted is assigned a sequence number. The TCP packet is assigned the sequence number of the first byte of the packet. The following packet will get assigned the sequence number of its first byte, and so on. Figure 9-6 provides an example of sequencing.

Figure 9-6 TCP sequencing

In the figure, you can see that data is flowing from one node to another. The receiving node recognizes that it is receiving a packet with a sequence number of 1. As the node receives the packet, the number of bytes in the packet is counted. This will tell the node what packet

> **RANDOM BONUS DEFINITION**
>
> D-compliant — A bridge or switch that complies with IEEE 802.1D.

sequence number is expected next. As you can see, there were 5 bytes[10] in the first packet, so the next packet should start with a sequence number of 6. And that, my friend, is TCP byte sequencing.

TCP also uses acknowledgment numbers that work hand in hand with the sequence numbers. Acknowledgment numbers are simply the sequence numbers in reverse. They are the reply from the destination node that sequence number such-and-such has been

> **POP QUIZ**
>
> The _____ is the data that is transmitted to the various layers on both ends of a connection.

received. Figure 9-7 provides an example of how this works.

---

[9]As opposed to some protocols that assign a sequence number to a whole datagram.
[10]Five-byte TCP segments? Now, that's funny. This number was picked at random for use in the example. TCP segments normally have 512 bytes.

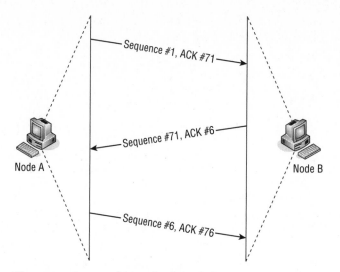

Figure 9-7 Sequencing and acknowledgement

The figure represents communication between a pair of nodes. The originating node sends a packet that is assigned sequence number 1 (because the first byte sequence number is 1) and then sends an acknowledgment of a received datagram. The acknowledgment number is actually the sequence number that the node is expecting next. In the figure, Node A sends a packet to Node B. The packet has a sequence number of 1, and an acknowledgment number of 71. This means that Node A is telling Node B that it has received a packet and the next one it is expecting is sequence number 71. Node B sends a packet with sequence number 71 and the

ACRONYM ALERT

VLAN — Virtual local area network

ACRONYM ALERT

SRAM — Static random-access memory

acknowledgment that packet sequence number 1 was received and the node is ready to receive sequence number 6. Node A then sends the next packet and acknowledges receipt of a previous packet. This process continues until data transmission is no longer required.

9.3.2   The TCP Header Format

The TCP header and the upper layer data are joined to form a TCP segment. The TCP header is where the sequencing number and acknowledgment number are maintained, as well as many other factors needed for proper data delivery. Figure 9-8 shows the format of the TCP header.

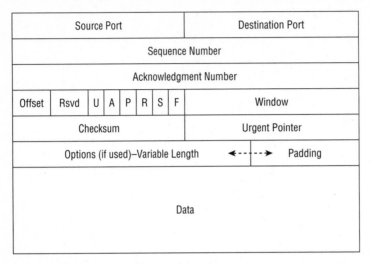

Figure 9-8 The format of the TCP header

- **Source Port** — A 16-bit number that identifies the application that sent the TCP segment.

- **Destination Port** — A 16-bit number that identifies the application the TCP segment is destined for.

- **Sequence Number** — A 32-bit number that identifies the first data byte in the segment.

- **Acknowledgment Number** — A 32-bit number that identifies the next data byte the node expects to receive.

- **Offset** — A field that identifies the length of the TCP header.

- **Rsvd** — An unused field reserved for potential future use.

- **U/A/P/R/S/F** — This field grouping contains the control fields:

  - **U** — Urgent. If this field is set, the destination (receiving) node knows there is urgent data waiting to be sent.

  - **A** — Acknowledgment. This is set when the packet has an acknowledgment for a received datagram.

  - **P** — Push. When this field is set, the receiver needs to deliver the segment to the receiving application ASAP.[11]

---

[11]As soon as possible.

- **R** — Reset. When this is set, it tells the receiving node that the originator is terminating the connection.

- **S** — Synchronize. This field is set at startup when setting sequence numbers.

- **F** — Finished. There will be no more data coming.

- **Window** — A 16-bit number used by TCP for flow control. It indicates the number of available buffers the sending node has.

- **Checksum** — A 16-bit number used for error detection.

- **Urgent Pointer** — This is a 16-bit field. When the Urgent bit is set, there will be a number that points to the sequence number of the data that follows urgent data. This identifies to the destination node that the last byte of urgent data was received.

- **Options** — TCP support options that can be set for the data. This is a variable length field, depending on the option data.

- **Padding** — Padding fills the remainder of the 32-bit field. This is necessary due to the optional and variable length Options field.

- **Data** — The application data: the payload!

> **POP QUIZ**
>
> How many different classes of transport service are there?

9.3.3 A Little More on UDP

UDP is a connectionless protocol. It does not guarantee that data is going to be delivered to a destination. UDP simply transmits data when it has data that is ready to be transmitted. Remember that UDP is usually used to send short bursts of datagrams between nodes where reliability is not a big concern. UDP can get data to a destination quicker, as it avoids the overhead required by all the checks and balances in TCP. Also, because UDP is connectionless, it can support *broadcasting* (sending messages to all nodes within a broadcast domain) and *multicasting* (sending messages to all nodes that are subscribed to the catenet).

> **RANDOM BONUS DEFINITION**
>
> E1 — A T-carrier technology commonly used in Europe, capable of multiplexing 32 DS-0 (64 Kbps) channels for a total data-carrying capacity of 2.048 Mbps.

UDP accepts data (the payload) from the Application layer. It adds a UDP header and passes the header and the payload to the Internet layer. There it is encapsulated into an IP packet and passed on to the Network Interface layer, then is passed over the transmission medium to the destination, where it makes its way up to the Application layer on the destination end of the connection.

UDP segments can be lost along the way. They can also be received out of sequence. This is why UDP is known as a *best-effort protocol*. UDP is beneficial when you need to transmit a lot of data. There is no delay

> **POP QUIZ**
>
> True or false: FIN stands for finished.

with UDP, as there is no need to set up a connection prior to the distribution of the data. If an application needs a method of recovering from errors, the application will handle this task itself. UDP also uses a checksum, which is a method for detecting transmission errors.

9.3.4   The UDP Header Format

The UDP header and the upper layer data are joined to form a UDP segment. The UDP header is simpler than the TCP header due to the overhead required for the connection-orientation used by TCP. Figure 9-9 shows the format of the UDP header.

Source Port	Destination Port
Message Length	Checksum
Data	

Figure 9-9 The format of the UDP header

- **Source Port** — A 16-bit number that identifies the application that sent the UDP segment.
- **Destination Port** — A 16-bit number that identifies the application the UDP segment is destined for.
- **Message Length** — A field that identifies the length of the UDP header.

- **Checksum** — A 16-bit number used for error detection.
- **Data** — The application data: the payload!

POP QUIZ

True or false: The AppleTalk Translucent Protocol is a transport layer protocol.

9.4 The Meaning of Control

In a connection-oriented environment, control of data transmission is important to ensure data delivery. Congestion control and flow control are two mechanisms used. Congestion control is used to avoid congestion on a link by avoiding the oversubscription of the rate that is supported by the link and reducing the rate of datagram transmission when congestion is on the link.

Flow control is a mechanism that an originating node uses to ensure that a destination node can handle the amount of data being transferred.

POP QUIZ

What is a TCP source port?

9.5 Chapter Exercises

1. What are the two ISO/IEC standards that define recommendations for the transport layer?

_____

_____

2. What are the two types of transport service?

_____

_____

3. From the following list, fill in the class function in the table below.

   Multiplexing class

   Error detection and recovery class

   Simple class

   Error recovery and multiplexing class

Basic error recovery class

Class Name	**Class Function**
Class 0	
Class 1	
Class 2	
Class 3	
Class 4	

4. Match the type with the correct description:

   Type _____ Network connections that maintain an unacceptable rate of residual errors

   Type _____ Network connections that maintain both an acceptable rate of signaled errors and residual errors

   Type _____ Network connections that maintain an acceptable rate of residual errors and an unacceptable rate of signaled errors

5. Define *upward multiplexing*.

6. Define *downward multiplexing*.

7. Explain how a three-way handshake works.

8. List four Transport layer protocols.

   _____

   _____

   _____

   _____

9.6   Pop Quiz Answers

1. True or false: UDP is an example of a connectionless protocol.

   True

2. TCP is a *connection-oriented* protocol.

3. Which standard defines the way the Transport layer interoperates with the other OSI layers it works with?

   ISO/IEC 8072

4. How many types of transport service are there?

   Two

5. The *TSDU* is the data that is transmitted to the various layers on both ends of a connection.

6. How many different classes of transport service are there?

   Five

7. True or false: FIN stands for finished.

   True

8. True or false: The AppleTalk Translucent Protocol is a Transport layer protocol.

   False. It is the AppleTalk Transaction Protocol. (Gotcha!)

9. What is a TCP source port?

   The TCP source port is part of the TCP header. It is the 16-bit number that identifies the application that sent the TCP segment.

CHAPTER 10

The Network Layer

It's not what you know but who you know that makes the difference.
— Anonymous

There is not much difference between human networking and computer networking. You can be the most gifted human or the highest powered computer, but lacking the ability to share those resources, you can do nothing as far as the progression of humankind is concerned. The power of information is in its capacity to be shared. Since the evolution of wireless networking, information can be shared not only globally but beyond this world into outer space.[1]

The number of connected computers on the World Wide Web is staggering. Two computers are able to share information between them without concern about how that information is to navigate over the Internet. This is the "who you know that makes the difference" portion of what networking is about. Networking is about being able to route information to a particular computer and receive requested information from that computer without a need to know the path it travels over the Internet.

Think of the Internet as a giant matrix with routing devices at every crossing point to aid in the movement of a packet of information along the cables connecting to the next crossing point. The route a packet of information travels can be different each time another packet of information is sent. The routing device's responsibility is to make sure that the packet will arrive at the destination it is intended for.

---

[1] Amateur Radio on the International Space Station (ARISS) has been experimenting with packet mail from amateur radio operators from around the world to the International Space Station. Although this is not conventional wireless networking, it may be a precursor of things to come when there is a manned base on the moon.

A computer is concerned only with its locally connected default gateway. A *default gateway* is where network traffic is sent when a computer wants to send information to a computer that it knows does not reside on its local network. Every computer and network-connected device has a default gateway set within their network configuration parameters. When information comes in via the Internet, it is accepted by the default gateway and routed on to the local network, directed toward the computer the received data is intended for.

Routing or network traffic forwarding devices need not know every other device that is connected to the Internet. They just need to have a good working relationship with their immediate peers. It is dependent upon networking through these other peer routing devices to know other devices that they also have a working relationship with. It is essential that networks know the right entities to network to.

The Network layer occupies Layer 3 of the OSI model. It receives network requests from the Transport layer and, in turn, issues network requests to the Data Link layer. It is the layer that is responsible for end-to-end information trans-

> **RANDOM BONUS DEFINITION**
>
> mirror port — A switch port configured to reflect the traffic appearing on another of the switch's ports.

fer. The delivery of information is within a *datagram*, also known as a *frame* or *packet*. The Network layer loosely maps to the Internet layer of the TCP/IP model, but the Internet layer deals only with the Internet Protocol (IP), whereas the OSI Network layer encompasses a broader range of both connection-oriented and connectionless network services.

10.1   Network Connection Types

What does a connection-oriented service versus a connectionless network service really mean? All network-enabled devices[2] are connected to a network, right? So they must be connected, right? Well, in the physical sense that is true. However, as far as a network service is concerned, it does make a difference how information is delivered between network nodes. The easy way to differentiate between the two types of network services is that a connected-oriented network service is one where the endpoint network nodes know who a session was established with, whereas in a connectionless network service, the two network nodes do not need to establish a direct connection in order to share information

[2] A "network-enabled" device is simply any computer or packet-forwarding device with the right network interface for the network medium connecting the device, along with the appropriate network software.

10.1.1 Connectionless Network Services

How can two network nodes exchange information if they do not have a connection established between them? This is where connectionless network services come into play. A great example of a connectionless network service is e-mail. E-mail is addressed to a particular user residing in a particular domain. It has no relation to a particular computer or geographical location.

The following is an example of a typical e-mail address:

```
john.doe@hishome.com
```

The recipient of this e-mail is `john.doe` who resides in the network domain of `hishome.com`. This brings in the concept once again of domain names and their relationship to network services. There is a hierarchy to network addressing, and the domain name is the highest level. Figure 10-1 illustrates the network addressing hierarchy.

ACRONYM ALERT

XNS — Xerox Network System

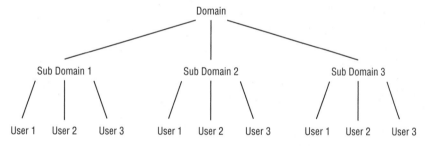

Figure 10-1 The network addressing hierarchy

As shown in Figure 10-1, the top level of addressing is the domain.[3] A domain can contain subdomains that have a varying number of users assigned. For example, the Widget Company has various departments with varying groups of users assigned to those departments. Figure 10-2 could be a method the Widget Company uses to set up their domain.

The Widget Company is a family-owned business founded in the mid-1800s. It prides itself on being wholly American owned and its operations being located only within the geographic boundaries of the United States. Although their products are shipped globally, they support sales and customer service from within the good old USA. Even though they face fierce price cutting from

---

[3]Domains are named by the organization that wants to create a domain for its network infrastructure. Domain names are usually classified with either a company name or some other meaningful words or acronyms for the easy identification of domain ownership.

manufacturers that off-shored their operations, the Widget family of products have maintained their competitive edge due to superior product reliability and what is considered to be best-in-class customer service.

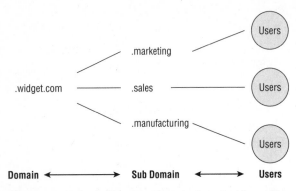

Figure 10-2 The Widget Company's domain hierarchy

The Widget Company wants to create three subdomains for its marketing, sales, and manufacturing departments. These departments have control of various servers that service the users of each department. These users may be either internal or external users over the Internet. The Widget Company domain does not require that all the entities of the domain be located within a single building, city, state, or country. Components that are not only for the overall domain but also for the subdomains may be located in geographically distant locations.[4] However, the network nodes that are part of the domain can still be reached using domain names without the need for absolute address locations. Figure 10-3 illustrates what the overall network topology of Widget Company might look like on a top level network map.

The top level drawing of the Widget Company network shows locations that are solely contained within the United States in various distantly located sites. The various sites are interconnected using the

> **RANDOM BONUS DEFINITION**
>
> link aggregation — The process of combining multiple physical links into a single logical link for use by higher layer link clients.

---

[4]Geographically distant locations can be in the building next door, down the street, in the next town, in the next state, or in the next country. If they are not on the same local network, they are considered to be distant and require special handling to ensure information is transmitted reliably.

Internet as a transportation medium for the domain's network infrastructure. Because these sites are connected over the Internet, they utilize IP for the transmission from site to site.

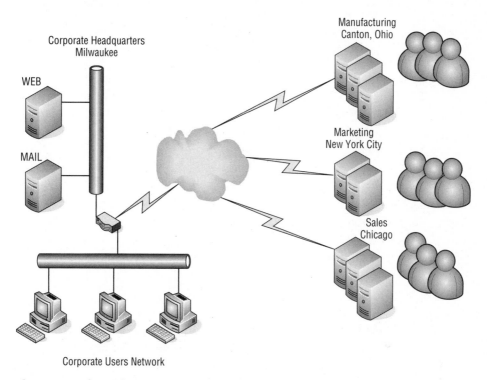

Figure 10-3 The Widget Company's top level network diagram

It was already mentioned that the TCP/IP model's Internet layer is a subset of the OSI model's Network layer. There will be places in this chapter where we discuss the aspects of TCP/IP where it is relevant within the OSI Network layer. The domain aspect can be used for either

ACRONYM ALERT

Telnet — Teletype Network

connection-oriented or connectionless network services. However, the world of TCP/IP uses IP to move information along the world's information highway. To bridge between domain names and IP protocol addresses requires domain name resolution, commonly referred to as DNS (Domain Name System). Further discussion of DNS can be found in Section 10.1.3.

As you can see in Figure 10-3, the corporate offices located in Milwaukee have multiple networks, various computer systems, and a number of servers. This diagram is simplistic in its presentation for a large corporate network, which is far more complex. However, the base principles of network interoperability[5] are fairly similar due to the scalability[6] of networking technologies. The figure shows two servers: a mail server and a web server. The remote offices also have servers located at their sites that are able to pass information from other servers and users located either locally or over the Internet. Using domain names to reach various servers has the following format:

```
Host name.domain name.sub domain name.domain name suffix[7]
```

The mail server named `mail` located at the corporate office would have a domain name that appears as follows:

```
mail.widget.com
```

If the marketing group located in New York City also has a mail server that gathers its mail from the corporate mail server, its name could be:

```
mail.marketing.widget.com
```

Mail shared between users is connectionless[8] because the computer sending the mail does not need a connection directly to the mail server the recipient of the e-mail is connected to. There are differences in e-mail, and perhaps there is some confusion due to the type of e-mail service being used. A local mail program on a computer is capable of creating a mail program entirely independent from any other computer. When it is ready to send the e-mail message, it does so by forwarding the mail to a Simple Mail Transport Protocol (SMTP) server where the user has an account. The message is forwarded by the SMTP server without any further action by the user to aid in the delivery of the message.

---

[5]"Interoperability" is just a fancy name for network node devices to play nice with all the other network node devices connected on the same network.

[6]"Scalability" simply means that networks can start small and grow larger as needed. However, larger networks usually require higher capacity network devices able to handle the amount of information that is to traverse the network within a fixed period of time.

[7]Domain names as illustrated in this example do not have spaces within the name. So, using the above example as a domain name would actually appear as `hostname.domainname.subdomainname.domainnamesuffix`.

[8]A computer connected to its local mail server uses the POP or POP3 protocol to receive mail and SMTP to send mail. These protocols are connection-based because the PC has a direct session with its local mail server. However, mail user to mail user is connectionless because a user-to-user PC session is not needed to send or read mail.

If a user is using web-based mail, the session established by the browser to create the e-mail is a connection-oriented network service. In using web mail, the user establishes a connection to the server serving his or her account to create and forward the message. However, the type

> **RANDOM BONUS DEFINITION**
>
> learning state — A transition state in the Spanning Tree Protocol state machine where a bridge port is learning address-to-port mappings to build its filtering database before entering the forwarding state.

of service is still connectionless since the user is not required to provide any further action to ensure delivery of the e-mail message. This illustrates that even connectionless processes may require some elements of a connection-oriented network service.

SMTP mail servers deliver e-mail to the SMTP mail server servicing a particular domain. Although a user name is attached as part of the message, the SMTP server does not deliver the message to the user. A user must have an account on a mail server in order for the mail to be delivered to that user's post office box. In the case of incorrect spelling of a user name or if a user never had an e-mail account or their account had been deleted, the SMTP server would return the original message with an error header[9] stating the cause for the message not being delivered. The most common reason for return is "user unknown.

E-mail for a user is held on the mail server for a period of time established by the administrator of that server. There are various parameters on most mail servers that allow for a mailbox's size, usually in megabytes, length of time a message is held, and the maximum allowable size of a message. An error message may be returned to an e-mail sender if the recipient is not in compliance with any of the preset parameters. Depending on the mail service provided by the mail server, mail may be read while remaining on a mail server or it may have to be downloaded using the Post Office Protocol (POP or POP3) to the local workstation for reading and any other required action.[10]

To summarize, a connectionless network service has the capability to prepare information for transmittal to another network node without the creation of a real-time connection to that network node in order to complete the transfer of the information being sent.

> **POP QUIZ**
>
> Mail is what type of network service?

---

[9]In computerese, the header is simply the top of the message. In other words, you do not need to read the whole message to see why it was bounced back.

[10]The required action is usually reading the message and either filing it or discarding it. Unfortunately, just like your postal mailbox, your e-mail mailbox also gets a lot of junk mail.

10.1.2 Connection-Oriented Network Services

A connection-oriented network service is exactly what the name implies. A network connection[11] is established between two computers to transfer information from one computer to the other over the Internet. Many client/server application programs are connection-oriented network services. A good example of this would be the interaction between an FTP client and an FTP server.[12] Figure 10-4 illustrates a user residing on a local network at IP address 192.168.2.13 requesting information from a local FTP server whose IP address is 192.168.2.5.

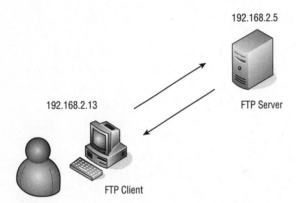

Figure 10-4 An FTP client/server connection-oriented network server

The following portion of the FTP server log illustrates the interaction of the client with the FTP server:

```
Oct 11 20:28:35      Cerberus FTP Server started
Oct 11 20:28:35      Local Host: Rbramant-2

Oct 11 20:28:35      Local Interface 0 located at 192.168.2.5
Oct 11 20:28:35      Listening on Port 21

Oct 11 20:34:39   1  Incoming connection request on interface
                     192.168.2.5
Oct 11 20:34:39   1  Connection request accepted from 192.168.2.13
Oct 11 20:34:52   1  USER anonymous
Oct 11 20:34:52   1  331 User anonymous, password please
Oct 11 20:34:57   1  PASS ***********
```

[11]Although networks use electrical connections for signal transmission, a network connection is when two endpoint network node devices know each other and establish a session that is connected.

[12]Many places within the text server and client are shown and discussed as totally separate network entities. In reality, a computer can be both a server and a client simultaneously for network services.

```
Oct 11 20:34:57  1  230 Password Ok, User logged in
Oct 11 20:34:57  1  Anonymous user ''anonymous'' logged in with
                    password ''guest''
Oct 11 20:35:00  1  PORT 192,168,2,13,19,137
Oct 11 20:35:00  1  200 Port command received
Oct 11 20:35:00  1  LIST
Oct 11 20:35:00  1  150 Opening data connection
Oct 11 20:35:00  1  226 Transfer complete
Oct 11 20:35:08  1  QUIT
Oct 11 20:35:08  1  Connection terminated.
```

You can see that the client initiated the connection to the server. The server forced the client to supply a user ID and a password. The client responded with a user ID and password combination, and is authenticated and allowed to maintain the session with the FTP server.

The FTP client user requested a directory listing from the FTP server. After the listing was received, the user quit the session and thus caused the termination of the connection between the client and the server.

ACRONYM ALERT

STP — Spanning Tree Protocol

A packet capture of this session was performed at the FTP server, as illustrated in Figure 10-5.

Figure 10-5 A packet capture of an FTP session

The FTP session uses the TCP/IP protocol to establish the session and complete the transfer of information from the FTP server to the FTP client. Packet number 7 shows the client requesting a session with the FTP server. Packet 10 is the FTP server acknowledging the session request. Packets 12 through 21 are the packets showing the interaction between the FTP client and FTP server to authenticate the FTP client and establish the FTP session. Packets 22 through 36 are the directory listing request and the transfer of the directory contents information to the FTP client. Packets 37 through 44 are the packets showing that the FTP client is terminating the FTP session and thus terminating the network connection.

An FTP[13] session does involve layers above the Network layer, but FTP helps illustrate the concept of a connection-oriented network service. The two computers establish a connection session and transfer information between them. The Network layer is responsible only for the end-to-end connections and is not involved with the hop-to-hop[14] transfer of the packets over the network.

> **POP QUIZ**
>
> Name the ports used by an FTP client to request an FTP session with an FTP server. Which port is used for data transmission?

WANT TO TRY SOMETHING?

You are encouraged to reproduce the FTP session as illustrated in this section. It requires two computers and software that can be obtained by a free download from the Internet. The FTP session was accomplished by using FTP server software from www.cerberusftp.com and using the ftp command from the command prompt of a Windows XP PC. You can obtain packet capture software for free from www.wireshark.org. The computers can either be on the same network segment or on different segments with network routing devices between the network segments.

10.1.3   Domain Name Services

Many of you are probably familiar with the term URL (uniform resource locator). A typical URL would appear as follows:

```
http://www.mydomainname.com
```

---

[13] The FTP protocol uses two ports for control and data transfer. Control is dedicated to port 21, and port 20 is dedicated to data transfer. An FTP server would listen on port 21 for FTP requests, and the FTP session is negotiated and controlled using this port.

[14] A network hop is any network node a data packet needs to be forwarded through on its journey to the requested destination.

The `http` indicates this is a request for port 80 on a computer with the host name `www` located in the domain `mydomain.com`. In the TCP/IP world, computer addresses take the following form:

```
XXX.XXX.XXX.XXX
```

where `XXX` can be a numeric decimal value between 0 and 255. We are preconditioned to think of URLs as being as follows:

```
prefix.domainname.suffix
```

We are accustomed to seeing .com, .org, .gov, .edu, or .net being used as a suffix, although many others are in use. Also, a country code may be used as the suffix to denote where the domain and host computer are found. So how does one get from a text-based URL name to an IP address? Someone has to take care of it, like the telephone company has with the use of area codes, exchange numbers, and the last four unique digits to reach a particular telephone. So in the case of finding an IP address for a particular computer by its host name, who would have the super-sized host name book that lists every computer connected to the Internet?

Telephones are basically static devices. They are wired into a particular telephone switch with a fixed number. Computers can be moved or exchanged with other computers, and occasionally IP addresses associated with a particular URL can also be changed. So, host-name-to-IP addresses can be pretty dynamic, and a dynamic system is required to maintain the capability to perform host name resolution. There needs to be some form of registration to enable this to occur. There are many companies that sell domain name registration for a fee. But what does that really mean?

> **RANDOM BONUS DEFINITION**
>
> jam — In Ethernet, the process of sending an additional 32 data bits following the detection of a collision to ensure that all parties to the collision properly recognize the event as such.

As with IP addresses, domain names also need to be unique. Domain names must be registered to ensure that they are not duplicated on the Internet. The Internet Assigned Numbers Authority (IANA) is an organization created to establish standard naming for what is called the top level domain (TLD), or root zone. The suffix portion of a URL is the root zone. It is used to parse a host name URL to establish which root zone the host name is a member of. The Internet Network Information Center (InterNIC) is maintained by the Internet Corporation for Assigned Names and Numbers (ICANN) and is responsible for the registration of domain names through registered domain name hosting companies.

When a domain name is registered, it is associated with an IP address and is maintained on a DNS server. Each DNS server needs to know what the designated authoritative name server is in order to receive DNS updates. Although the service is fairly

dynamic, caching[15] is used to save time querying the root name servers each time a request is made for a particular host name. Figure 10-6 illustrates a typical DNS server scenario.

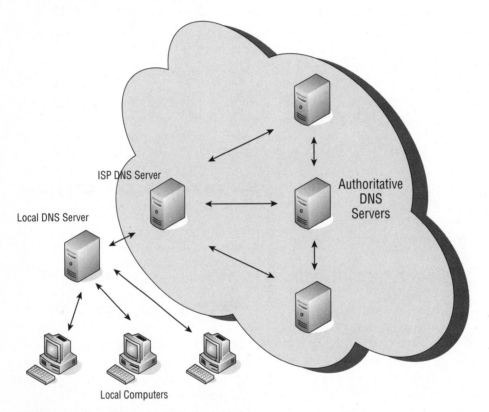

Figure 10-6 A typical DNS server scenario

DNS is part of the TCP/IP protocol suite. The computers on the local network have configured the IP address of the local DNS server into their

---

[15]Caching is the process of saving information for a predetermined amount of time. In DNS, caching can save time for address resolution. However, to ensure that a name resolution stays "fresh," there is usually an expiration time associated with the entry. Old entries are aged out automatically. When a DNS request is made, if it is not in the cache, name resolution needs to be performed. Although under normal circumstances it is completed fairly rapidly, it does take more time than just pulling it up from the local cache storage.

TCP/IP configuration settings. You can verify these settings by issuing an `ipconfig /all` command at the command window of a Windows-based PC. The response would be similar to the following:

```
Ethernet adapter Local Area Connection:

        Connection-specific DNS Suffix  . :
        Description . . . . . . . . . . . : Broadcom NetXtreme
                                            Gigabit Ethernet
        Physical Address. . . . . . . . . : 00-17-08-30-6A-01
        DHCP Enabled. . . . . . . . . . . : Yes
        Autoconfiguration Enabled . . . . : Yes
        IP Address. . . . . . . . . . . . : 192.168.2.5
        Subnet Mask . . . . . . . . . . . : 255.255.255.0
        Default Gateway . . . . . . . . . : 192.168.2.1
        DHCP Server . . . . . . . . . . . : 192.168.2.4
        DNS Servers . . . . . . . . . . . : 192.168.2.1
        Lease Obtained. . . . . . . . . . : Sunday, October 12, 2008
                                            8:08:02 AM
        Lease Expires . . . . . . . . . . : Monday, October 13, 2008
                                            8:08:02 AM
```

In this example, there is only one DNS server, and it is the same as the device that is acting as the default gateway. In this particular setup, the router is capable of running a DNS service, and its DNS servers are the upstream servers at the ISP, as shown in Figure 10-6.

Using the example of a browser attempting to reach a particular URL, if the computer does not have the resolved host name stored in its local DNS cache, it will request it from its assigned DNS server. Figure 10-7 shows a packet capture of a DNS request from a local PC to its local DNS server.

The user is calling the URL www.imagesbybramante.com and, not having the host name cached, it places the request to its local DNS server. If the local DNS server does not have the host name cached, it makes a DNS request to its upstream server and would eventually work its way back to a root authoritative server until the name is resolved. If the name cannot be resolved, an error message is returned. When the name is resolved, it is passed back through the servers until it reaches the computer that made the original request. Figure 10-8 shows a successful host name lookup for the query used in this example.

This has been a top-level discussion of DNS to give you a basic understanding of name resolution in regard to IP. You are encouraged to explore literature dedicated solely to DNS concepts for additional, in-depth information.

POP QUIZ

Name some top-level domain names.

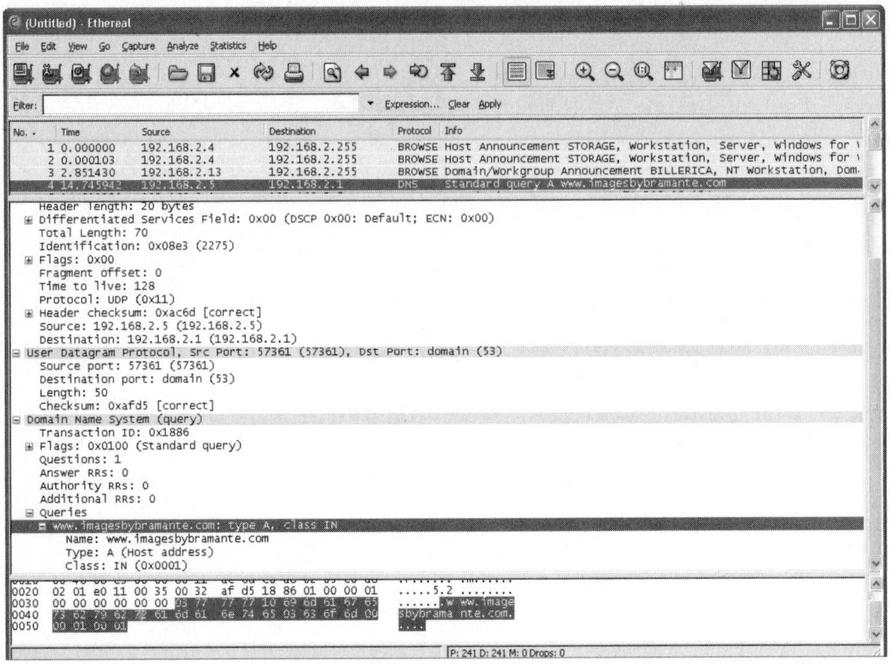

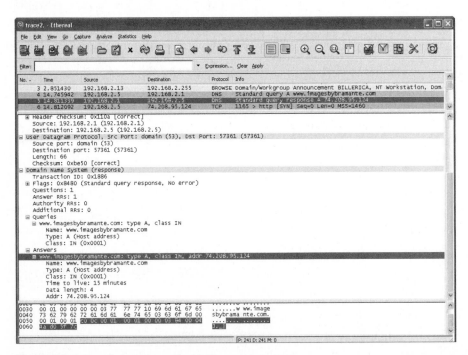

Figure 10-7 A packet capture of a DNS request

Figure 10-8 A packet capture of a DNS response

SOMETHING TO TRY

We suggested earlier that you download a freeware version of Wireshark. It is a useful tool not only for troubleshooting but to give added insight to what is occurring on your computer in terms of network communications. It can be loaded on either a desktop or laptop with your other Windows-based applications. It may be launched prior to opening any application and allowed to capture the packets of that application. This will help build familiarity with the Wireshark application itself and aid in increasing your understanding of TCP/IP and the protocols supported within the TCP/IP protocol suite.

10.2 TCP/IP Network Layer Protocols

The Network layer of the OSI model provides for both connectionless network services and connection-oriented services. It encompasses the protocols of the TCP/IP model's Internet layer. However, the OSI model's Network layer is broader in scope than TCP/IP's Internet

RANDOM BONUS DEFINITION

filtering — The process of inspecting frames received on an input port of a switch and deciding whether to discard or forward them.

layer, and at times, it includes other TCP/IP protocols from its Link layer. Due to this difference, the two layers should not be considered mirror images of each other, although they do have some protocols in common.

10.2.1 Internet Protocol

The Internet Protocol (IP) is primarily a method of moving packets of data across networks comprising various media, seamlessly delivering these packets solely based on the destination address. This is accomplished by encapsulating data from the upper layers into packets[16] in preparation for delivery over the network. IP is a connectionless protocol since packets can be transmitted without the establishment of a circuit to the destination network node. Because IP is a best-effort delivery service, it makes no guarantee that a packet will be delivered. Therefore, data can become corrupted, packets can

---

[16]The word "packet" is synonymous with "datagram" or "frame." These three words are used interchangeably and refer to the structure containing all the pertinent information for the proper construct so that the data can be reliably transmitted and that it can be properly unencapsulated when received at the intended network node.

arrive out of order, duplicate packets can be received, and packets can be lost or discarded.

The mainstay for many years has been Internet Protocol version 4 (IPv4), but due to its limitation of addressing, Internet Protocol version 6 (IPv6) is currently being deployed worldwide. To work around the limited address space of IPv4, the development of Network Address Translation (NAT) helped delay the need to deploy IPv6 any sooner.

10.2.1.1 Internet Protocol Version 4

Because IPv4 utilizes 4 bytes to express an address, it has only 32 bits that can be used for its address. This allows for a maximum combination of addresses that can be supported of 2^{32}, or 4,294,967,296 unique addresses. Since some of the addresses are within reserved address space, the total space is not available as public Internet addresses. IPv4 addresses are mostly expressed in what is referred to as *dot-decimal notation*, for example:

```
192.168.15.85
```

Each dotted section is representative of the decimal value of the byte. So it would look as follows in binary:

```
11000000.10101000.00001111.01010101
```

There is a multitude of variations to express IP addresses, but the dot-decimal notation is the most widely used.

REMEDIAL EXERCISE

For those of you who are not proficient in manipulating numbers between various number systems, try to convert the above dotted binary number to a hexadecimal-dotted notation. Hint: The bits of a byte are equally divided to create two hexadecimal numbers for each dotted binary section. A hexadecimal number is usually represented by 0x<hex valued number>. If you want the answer, wait until you give it an honest try, and then look at the footnote below.[17]

If the upper layers present the TCP/IP Internet layer with data that is too large to transmit within a single packet, the data will be fragmented and transmitted over the network in

POP QUIZ

What is a maximum transmission unit?

---

[17] xC0.0xA0.0x0F.0x55, or in not-dotted notation, 0xC0A00F55

multiple packets. IP performs the fragmentation since it is host dependent, not machine dependent. The maximum transmission unit (MTU) is the number of bytes of data that a particular network medium is capable of handling. It is determined by the largest packet the medium is capable of handling, minus any number of bytes required as a header to transmit the packet over the medium. In the case of Ethernet, which has a maximum packet size of 1500 bytes, the MTU is the maximum packet size minus the number of bytes required for the header. Ethernet normally requires 20 bytes for a header, which provides for an MTU of 1480 bytes. The data is fragmented into the number of packets needed, with each packet tagged indicating it contains a fragment. The receiving network nodes unencapsulate the received fragmented packets and reassemble the data before passing it up to the layer above it.

10.2.1.1.1 Network Address Translation

It was mentioned that Network Address Translation (NAT) was developed to provide a method of using addresses designated as private address space behind a network device, such as a router, that is able to perform the translation from a nonroutable IP address to a publicly known IP address. Table 10-1 shows the reserved addresses for private networking.[18]

Table 10-1 Private Networking Reserved Addresses

ADDRESS RANGE	CIDR	NETWORK CLASS	ADDRESSES
10.0.0.0 to 10.255.255.255	10.0.0.0/8	Single Class A	16,777,216
172.16.0.0 to 172.31.255.255	172.16.0.0/12	16 Contiguous Class B	1,048,576
192.168.0.0 to 192.168.255.255	192.168.0.0/16	Single Class B	65,536

USEFUL NOTE

Generally speaking, the first address of a subnet range ending in 0 is used to designate the network address, and the last address ending in 255 is used to designate the broadcast address of the subnet. It depends on the subnet mask being used whether 0 or 255 is assigned to a host. For example, if the whole

(continued)

---

[18] Although these address ranges are shown to be contiguous, they may be subdivided (subnetted) into smaller subnet ranges within a private network space. Often, these private network classes can be found using class C 24-bit subnet masks of 255.255.255.0 to form smaller network ranges.

USEFUL NOTE *(continued)*

class A subnet of 10.0.0.0 with a subnet mask of 255.0.0.0 is used for a network, then 10.0.0.0 would be the network address and 10.255.255.255 would be the broadcast address for that subnet. This would permit 10.0.1.0, 10.0.1.255, 10.0.2.0, 10.0.2.255, etc., to be used for host addresses. It is important to know the subnet mask that is assigned to a particular IP address range.

USEFUL NOTE #2

The CIDR is the number that indicates the number of mask bits being assigned to a subnet. So, /8 would have a subnet mask of 255.0.0.0, /12 would have a subnet mask of 255.240.0.0, and /16 would have a subnet mask of 255.255.0.0. Have you guessed what the CIDR represents yet? The CIDR indicates the number of bits for the subnet mask starting at the highest significant position and working its way down to the least significant position.[19]

USEFUL NOTE #3

When you see /32 or a subnet mask of 255.255.255.255, it is called a *host route*. This means there is only one network node connected to that address; there is no network, just one device — and that is it. Host routes are used more frequently than you would think, but be aware of this when someone talks of a "slash 32" or "32-bit route."

Figure 10-9 illustrates three separate networks all performing NAT on the 192.168.0.0/16 network address space.

You will notice that the IP addresses assigned to the public interface[20] are addresses that are assigned by an ISP (Internet

ACRONYM ALERT

PHY — Physical layer interface

service provider). These addresses can be either statically or dynamically assigned IP addresses. The type of installation usually dictates how IP address assignment is handled. DSL (digital subscriber line), PPPoE (Point-to-Point Protocol over Ethernet), and dialup network circuits are usually configured to have a dynamically assigned IP address. Dynamically assigned addresses

---

[19]Okay, for the readers who fell asleep during math class: The higher the power of the number, the more significance it has. In our number system, the number to the left of another number has a higher power, thus more significance. The leftmost number is always the most significant number.

[20]A public interface is one that has a publicly routable IP address assigned to it. Private IP addresses cannot be routed over the Internet.

change each time a connection is made. However, the ISP can usually assign a static IP address, if requested to do so.

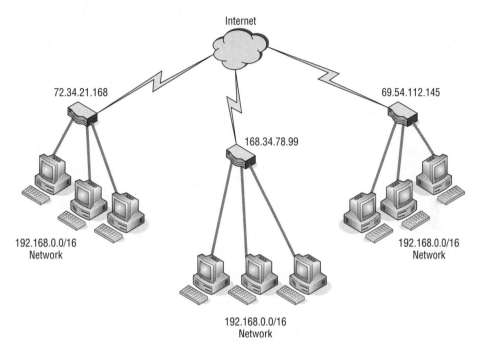

Figure 10-9 A NAT example

Notice that the private IP addresses for all three are in the 192.168.0.0/16 network and that the NAT-enabled router will translate those addresses to its public IP address. The receiving node over the Internet will see the public IP address in the packet's source address. The sending NAT-enabled

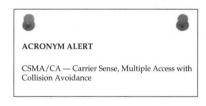

ACRONYM ALERT

CSMA/CA — Carrier Sense, Multiple Access with Collision Avoidance

router keeps a translation table in order to recall which sending workstation on its private IP address space has initiated the session. When the receiving node sends a reply back to the NAT-enabled router, it removes its address from the destination address field of the packet, replaces the IP address from its translation table of the workstation that started the session, and passes the packet into the private network.

Since workstations are on a private IP address space, they are not reachable from the Internet unless a policy to allow this is embedded within the NAT-enabled router. Such policies are called *port forwarding policies*. Usually servers offering web services, e-mail services, or FTP services are located on private networks behind a NAT-enabled router. Figure 10-10 illustrates services being offered to users over the Internet while being located behind a NAT-enabled router on a private IP address space.

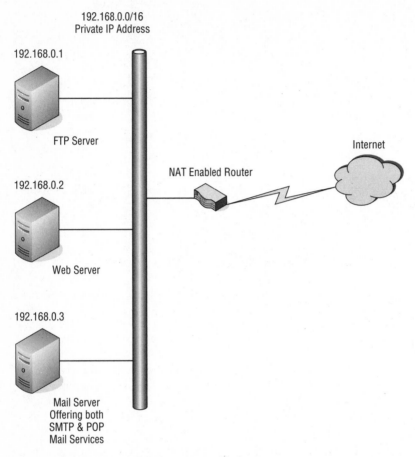

Figure 10-10 Servers behind a NAT-enabled router

Table 10-2 is representative of a NAT port forwarding table a NAT-enabled router would have to accept service requests on its public IP address interface.

When a packet arrives at the public interface with the destination address set to its public IP address and a port service request that matches a port address in the NAT port forwarding table, the packet is modified and passed on to the network, directed toward the server that supplies that service. An example of this is a web page request that arrives at the public IP address of the NAT-enabled server. The NAT-enabled router sees the requested port is port 80, so it replaces its address in the destination field with the IP address of the web server that is at 192.168.0.2, recalculates the checksum for the packet, and passes it on to the private network.

Table 10-2 NAT Port Forwarding Table

SERVICE	PORT	SERVER ADDRESS
SMTP Mail	25	192.168.0.3
POP Mail	109	192.168.0.3
POP3 Mail	110	192.168.0.3
FTP Control	21	192.168.0.1
FTP Data	20	192.168.0.1
HTTP	80	192.168.0.2

NAT does offer some firewall protection since the addresses used on the private IP address are not routed over the Internet. Unsolicited connection requests are dropped by the NAT-enabled router since there is no entry in its NAT translation table. However, when port forwarding policies are enabled within the NAT-enabled router, there is an possibility that one of the servers may be hacked and compromised. A prudent measure would be to have a DMZ (demilitarized zone) by using a router that has multiple private IP address interfaces. Place the servers on one interface isolated by different network addresses and policies. This will prevent the servers from initiating connections into the private network where other users and devices are protected behind the NAT-enabled router.

> **POP QUIZ**
>
> What is the type of address translation that is used to keep track of sessions initiated by a computer on a private network to a service on the Internet?

Due to the development of NAT-enabled devices and the capability to use private network IP address space, the stress of coming up with a new standard to replace IPv4 was lessened. This has allowed the life span of IPv4 to be extended and a gradual transition made to the newer IP address standard IPv6. Although current devices are IPv6-capable, they are still able to be installed and used within the IPv4 environment.

10.2.1.2 Internet Protocol Version 6

The real thrust of moving to IPv6 is the larger address space that it provides, with 128 bits dedicated to address space. The number is so large that it exceeds the national debt, which is pretty hard to do these days. Our scientific calculator claims it is $3.4028 \ e^{38}$, give or take a few addresses. It is so great that each person alive on the face of the earth can have multiple devices using

IP addresses and there would still be addresses left over. Although these numbers are staggering, the real intent of IPv6 is to increase the efficiency of network management and routing. There is a high probability that only a small percentage of the address space will actually be used.

Figure 10-11 illustrates the IPv6 header, which is 40 bytes in total length.

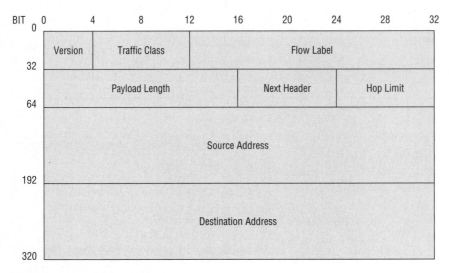

Figure 10-11 The IPv6 header

The first 4 bits are the Version field for IPv6. The next 8 bits are the Traffic Class field, which adds in the control options. The next 20 bits are the Flow Label field, allocated for QoS (quality of service). The Payload Length field indicates the packet length

> **RANDOM BONUS DEFINITION**
>
> encapsulating bridge — A bridge that encapsulates LAN frames.

in bytes. When this field is set to 0, the packet contains a jumbo-sized payload. The Next Header field indicates which encapsulated protocol follows. These protocol values are compatible with the IPv4 protocol field values. The Hop Limit field replaces the TTL (time to live) field of IPv4. Both the Source Address and Destination Address fields contain 128 bits of address data. The standard sized payload can be 65,536 bytes, and if the option is set, the payload can be jumbo-sized.[21] All data fragmentation is controlled by the sending network node since routers will never fragment a packet. However, IPv6 sending network nodes are expected to use a technique known as *path*

---

[21]Techno-geeks like to use jargon and you may hear a variety of words used to describe an entity. A "jumbo-sized" payload merely refers to a payload that is very large.

MTU discovery (PMTUD) to determine the MTU that can be used to send packets over the network.

The address notation used in IPv6 is quite different from that of IPv4. IPv6 addresses consist of eight groups of four hexadecimal numbers, where each field is separated by a colon. For example:

```
113A:00AB:8900:0000:0000:7EA3:0034:3347
```

A shorthand notation would be to reduce the fields containing zeros to just a pair of colons (::). IPv6 address notation has a variety of rules that allow for various methods of displaying the same address. As IPv6 begins to be deployed more widely, there is sure to be a particular notation format that will become the more widely used and accepted format.

POP QUIZ

What is the difference between how IPv4 IP addresses are denoted and how IPv6 IP addresses are denoted?

10.2.2   Internet Control Message Protocol

Internet Control Message Protocol (ICMP) is an essential part of the TCP/IP protocol suite. It provides a means of messaging when a sent datagram is unable to be received by the intended network node. The `ping` and `traceroute` networking tools are also part of this protocol. ICMP error messages are generated in response to detected errors in the IP datagram, routing, or diagnostics. The ICMP protocol suite is part of IPv4, but there is an equivalent to ICMP that is a protocol within IPv6, referred to as ICMPv6. For the most part, computer users are unaware of network problems until a network error message is triggered by ICMP. When a user suspects that a network problem may exist, he or she can use the `ping` and `traceroute`[22] commands to aid in troubleshooting the problem.

10.2.2.1 Ping

The `ping` command within the Microsoft Windows operating system has the following syntax:

```
Microsoft Windows XP [Version 5.1.2600]
(C) Copyright 1985-2001 Microsoft Corp.
```

---

[22]`traceroute` is the normal command for many various operating systems. However, in the Microsoft Windows-based world, the actual command for `traceroute` is truncated to `tracert`.

```
C:\>ping

Usage: ping [-t] [-a] [-n count] [-l size] [-f] [-i TTL] [-v TOS]
            [-r count] [-s count] [[-j host-list] | [-k host-list]]
            [-w timeout] target_name

Options:
    -t              Ping the specified host until stopped.
                    To see statistics and continue - type Control-Break;
                    To stop - type Control-C.
    -a              Resolve addresses to hostnames.
    -n count        Number of echo requests to send.
    -l size         Send buffer size.
    -f              Set Don't Fragment flag in packet.
    -i TTL          Time To Live.
    -v TOS          Type Of Service.
    -r count        Record route for count hops.
    -s count        Timestamp for count hops.
    -j host-list    Loose source route along host-list.
    -k host-list    Strict source route along host-list.
    -w timeout      Timeout in milliseconds to wait for each reply.
```

The most common use of `ping` is to verify that a particular network is available over the network. In the following example, a computer has issued a `ping` command for its default gateway.

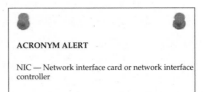

ACRONYM ALERT

NIC — Network interface card or network interface controller

```
C:\>ping 192.168.2.1

Pinging 192.168.2.1 with 32 bytes of data:

Reply from 192.168.2.1: bytes=32 time<1ms TTL=64
Reply from 192.168.2.1: bytes=32 time<1ms TTL=64
Reply from 192.168.2.1: bytes=32 time<1ms TTL=64
Reply from 192.168.2.1: bytes=32 time<1ms TTL=64

Ping statistics for 192.168.2.1:
    Packets: Sent = 4, Received = 4, Lost = 0 (0% loss),
Approximate round trip times in milli-seconds:
    Minimum = 0ms, Maximum = 0ms, Average = 0ms
```

There are many ways to use the `ping` command for troubleshooting various network issues. Chapter 16, "Troubleshooting," will go into greater detail about how this

POP QUIZ

What option would be used to modify the size of a `ping` packet?

tool can be used as an aid in determining what is causing certain network issues.

10.2.2.2 Traceroute

The `traceroute` command is used to trace the path from the sending network node to the receiving network node on a hop-to-hop basis. It reports back on each hop as it is traversed over the network on the path to the destination network node. The following is the syntax for the `traceroute` command for the Microsoft Windows operating system:

```
C:\>tracert

Usage: tracert [-d] [-h maximum_hops] [-j host-list] [-w timeout]
                       target_name

Options:
    -d                       Do not resolve addresses to hostnames.
    -h maximum_hops          Maximum number of hops to search for
                             target.
    -j host-list             Loose source route along host-list.
    -w timeout               Wait timeout milliseconds for each reply.
```

The options are self-explanatory. The `-d` option is often used to save the time that is required to resolve IP addresses to host names for each hop along the path. The following is an example of a successful completion of a `traceroute` command:

> **RANDOM BONUS DEFINITION**
>
> common and internal spanning tree — A collection of the internal spanning trees in a multiple spanning tree region, combined with the common spanning tree that connects MST regions to form a single spanning tree that ensures all LANs in the bridge network are fully connected and loop-free.

```
C:\>tracert www.richardbramante.com

Tracing route to www.richardbramante.com [68.180.151.74]
over a maximum of 30 hops:

  1    <1ms    <1ms    <1ms    192.168.2.1
  2    <1ms    <1ms    <1ms    192.168.0.1
  3    4ms     4ms     4ms     L100.VFTTP-12.BSTNMA.verizon-
                               gni.net [72.74.235.1]
  4    3ms     4ms     4ms     P4-1.LCR-04.BSTNMA.verizon-
                               gni.net [130.81.60.226]
  5    26ms    27ms    27ms    so-7-0-0-0.ASH-PEER-
```

```
                                  RTR2.verizon-gni.net
                                  [130.81.17.179]
    6     28 ms    27 ms    27 ms  130.81.14.98
    7     65 ms    64 ms    64 ms  so-2-0-0.pat2.dax.yahoo.com
                                  [216.115.96.21]
    8     91 ms    92 ms    92 ms  as1.pat2.pao.yahoo.com
                                  [216.115.101.130]
    9     92 ms    92 ms    92 ms  ae1-p151.msr2.sp1.yahoo.com
                                  [216.115.107.79]
    10   100 ms    92 ms    92 ms  ge-1-41.bas-b2.sp1.yahoo.com
                                  [209.131.32.33]
    11    92 ms    94 ms    92 ms  www.richardbramante.com
                                  [68.180.151.74]


Trace complete.
```

If a target node does not allow ICMP, a `traceroute` would not end normally and would appear as follows:

```
C:\>tracert www.wiley.com

Tracing route to www.wiley.com [208.215.179.146]
over a maximum of 30 hops:

    1            <1 ms    <1 ms    <1 ms       192.168.2.1
    2            <1 ms    <1 ms    <1 ms       192.168.0.1
    3      3 ms    4ms      4ms      L100.VFTTP-12.BSTNMA.verizon-
                                     gni.net   [72.74.235.1]
    4      5 ms    4ms      4ms      P4-1.LCR-04.BSTNMA.verizon-
                                     gni.net       [130.81.60.226]
    5              4 ms     4 ms     4 ms       130.81.29.170
    6      8 ms    7ms      7ms      0.so-1-0-0.XL2.BOS4.ALTER.NET
                                     [152.63.16.141]
    7     15ms    14ms     14ms      0.so-7-0-0.XL4.NYC4.ALTER.NET
                                     [152.63.17.97]
    8     13ms    14ms     14ms      0.ge-5-1-0.BR3.NYC4.ALTER.NET
                                     [152.63.3.118]
    9             16 ms    17 ms     17 ms   192.205.34.49
    10            18 ms    17 ms     17 ms      tbr1.n54ny.ip.att.net
                                     [12.122.105.14]
    11            16 ms    17 ms     17 ms      gar3.nw2nj.ip.att.net
                                     [12.122.105.49]
    12            18 ms    17 ms     19 ms   12.88.61.178
    13             *        *        *         Request timed out.
    14             *        *        *         Request timed out.
    15             *        *        *         Request timed out.
    16    ^C
```

The `traceroute` command was truncated with the Ctrl+C key combination to shorten the number of hops, as the command would have continued with "Request timed out" for the default number of 30 hops.

For further testing, the `ping` command was then issued with the following results:

```
C:\>ping www.wiley.com

Pinging www.wiley.com [208.215.179.146] with 32 bytes of data:

Request timed out.
Request timed out.
Request timed out.
Request timed out.

Ping statistics for 208.215.179.146:
    Packets: Sent = 4, Received = 0, Lost = 4 (100% loss),
```

So, it first appears that the target network node is not available, but we know that is not true since our browser displays the following image for that network node address, as shown in Figure 10-12.

Although the `ping` and `traceroute` commands are very useful tools, they are not 100 percent accurate in predicting what is going on in the network. From the above indications it appears that the Wiley website is dropping ICMP packets.

POP QUIZ

What is the default maximum hop count for the `traceroute` command?

10.2.3 Internet Group Management Protocol

Internet Group Management Protocol (IGMP) is a protocol for handling multicast group memberships, which are required in situations with streaming video or multiplayer games. The protocol is used by the client computer to establish a connection to a local multicast[23] router. With the use of local and

[23]Multicast is when you have many users connected to a single service simultaneously. It is analogous to the broadcast of a radio or TV program.

multicast routers, these streaming applications are able to provide service to many multicast clients simultaneously.

Figure 10-12 The Web page for `www.wiley.com`

IGMP-enabled routers check on the users within the group to determine if they have an active session. As long as there is an active group member, the router will continue to forward the multicast to that subnet. If all members are inactive, the packets are simply dropped.[24]

A computer running an IGMP-based application issues an IGMP report packet to join a group. When the router serving that group determines it has one member of the group, it would forward multicast packets to that subnet. Member computers need not inform the IGMP-enabled router when they leave the group. The IGMP-enabled router will perform member queries at fixed intervals to determine if there are any connected IGMP members. If there are, it continues to forward multicast packets to that subnet. The

ACRONYM ALERT

DSAP — Destination service access point

---

[24]"Dropped" is a techno-geek word for a packet not being forwarded. The router just discards the packet to work on the next packet that it receives.

reason for this behavior by the IGMP router is to prevent flooding subnets with multicast packets when there are no connected users from that subnet.

10.2.4 Internet Protocol Security

Internet Protocol Security (IPSec) uses authentication and encryption to establish a secure connection between endpoint network nodes. The terms *VPN* and *tunneling*[25] are used along with IPSec; however, IPSec is

> **RANDOM BONUS DEFINITION**
>
> bit time — The length of time required to transmit 1 bit of information.

the means that permits the use of these capabilities. Tunnels between endpoint VPN devices normally are point-to-point and use a preshared key (PSK) as part of the authentication process. Once authenticated, the endpoints are able to pass traffic between them that is encapsulated using strong encryption[26] to prevent data from being compromised. Figure 10-13 illustrates the use of IPSec endpoint devices as well as IPSec client workstations establishing VPN network connections over the Internet.

In Figure 10-13, Network A and Network B are connected to VPN-enabled routers. These routers use IPSec to establish a peer-to-peer tunnel to allow data to flow between the private internal network of Network A and Network B. Peer-to-peer networks know each other's

ACRONYM ALERT

GARP — Generic Attribute Registration Protocol

statically assigned IP address, and that is part of the security mechanism. The major component of safe data transfer is the use of preshared keys with strong encryption. Depending on the policies established on the VPN routers, users from one network can connect to resources on the remote network the VPN tunnel was established with. Another aspect for consideration when conceptualizing a VPN is determining the permissions that will be allowed for network users. Some users might need access to services on the Internet, whereas users might not require this as part of their jobs. VPN routers act as firewalls and are policy-intensive devices. The normal default state for these

---

[25]*Tunneling* is the term used to describe a virtual protected conduit between two endpoint network nodes. There is no way to actually "build" a real tunnel. The idea is that with strong encryption the packet is undecipherable; thus, it is as if the data stream is traveling within a protected tunnel, unseen to the rest of the Internet. In reality, packets can be snooped, but hacking the real information out of the packet is next to impossible.

[26]Encryption depends on key length. There are two predominant key lengths used within the Data Encryption Standard (DES): 56-bit, referred to as simply DES or single DES, and 128-bit, referred to as triple DES or 3DES.

devices is to allow only tunnel traffic to pass through from one VPN tunnel endpoint to another.

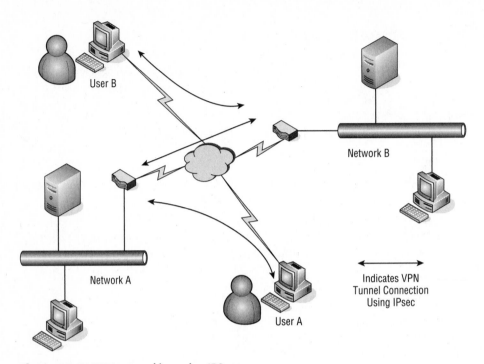

Figure 10-13 VPN networking using IPSec

Remote users using only a computer connected to an Internet access point require a client to be loaded on their PC to establish a VPN tunnel between the computer and a remote VPN router. Once a tunnel session is established, users can launch other applications, which will utilize the connection to gain access to the resources located on the private network protected by the VPN router. The VPN router is capable of setting user policies, either by user or group of users, to limit access to only some of the network's resources. It is also capable of denying remote users the capability to access the private network and then access the remote private network through the established peer-to-peer tunnel.

The use of IPSec to create VPNs using the Internet eliminates the need for direct point-to-point telecommunications between remote network nodes. This is a large cost savings over using directly connected dedicated lines between remote office locations. However, careful planning and thought needs to go

> **POP QUIZ**
>
> Name two components that help make VPNs safe and secure.

into the design of the network, and policies may have to be developed to secure the network from a security breach or the compromise of information as it travels over the Internet.

10.3 Chapter Exercises

1. Name the type of network service being used for each of the following:

   HTTP   _____

   FTP   _____

   Mail   _____

   Telnet   _____

2. A client/server application is considered to be what type of network service?

3. What is a TLD and can you name a few?

4. How is the MTU size determined?

5. What does NAT accomplish?

6. Name two network tools that can troubleshoot a network problem?

   _____

   _____

10.4 Pop Quiz Answers

1. Mail is what type of network service?

   Connectionless

2. Name the ports used by an FTP client to request an FTP session with an FTP server. Which port is used for data transmission?

   Ports 20 and 21. Port 20 is used for data.

3. Name some top level domain names.

   .com, .gov, .edu, .net

4. What is a maximum transmission unit?

   The maximum payload size that can be transmitted without the use of fragmentation.

5. What is the type of address translation that is used to keep track of sessions initiated by a computer on a private network to a service on the Internet?

   Port mapping

6. What is the difference between how IPv4 IP addresses are denoted and how IPv6 IP addresses are denoted?

   Dot-decimal notation versus hexadecimal numbers separated by colons.

7. What option would be used to modify the size of a `ping` packet?

   The `-l` option

8. What is the default maximum hop count for the `traceroute` command?

   30 hops

9. Name two components that help make VPNs safe and secure.

   Authentication and encryption

CHAPTER 11

The Data Link Layer

Power consists in one's capacity to link his will with the purpose of others, to lead by reason and a gift of cooperation.
— Woodrow Wilson

The Data Link layer is Layer 2 of the OSI reference model. This layer allows for direct communication between nodes over the physical channel provided at the lower layer. The communication can be point-to-point (one-to-one communication between two nodes) or point-to-multipoint (one-to-many communication, from one node to many nodes), depending on the nature and configuration of the network.

LAN technology exists primarily at the Data Link and Physical layers of the architecture. The functions performed by a network bridge or switch occur mainly at the Data Link layer. Network switches are able to tremendously enhance the capabilities provided by the Data Link layer. This is true to the point where you have to be careful that the implementation of the features doesn't affect the operations of some protocols within the upper layers.

The generic operation performed at the Data Link layer is the movement of data between nodes within a network over a physical connection. Once the Data Link layer has ensured that a connection is set up, the layer divides data into frames and transmits them to other nodes within a network. The receiving node sends acknowledgments and ensures that the data is received by keeping track of bit patterns in the received frames.

In this chapter, we discuss the Data Link layer. We cover concerns that are experienced in a LAN, as well as some of the mechanisms that are in place to recover from problems. In addition to the operations of this layer, we will discuss the use of switches and bridges in a LAN.

> **RANDOM BONUS DEFINITION**
>
> Layer 2 switch — Synonymous with bridge.

11.1 Concerns of the LAN

Most typical network users do not care about all the protocols and mechanisms that are in use to get their data; they just care that they get it. Because you are not the typical network user, however, you should care how this data gets there. Networks of all sizes produce conditions that are less than optimal, so actions have to be taken to address these needs. If there were no way to control the flow of data, the networking world would be a mess. If you worked in an organization that only used several thousand 10/100 Mbps Ethernet hubs, you would find that the end users would be less than satisfied (especially if you consider the types of data that are flowing in a normal LAN).

What should you concern yourself with in relation to operations at the Data Link layer within a network? This question is the reason this section is in the book. There are a lot of considerations to be aware of if you want to have an understanding of good old Layer 2.

> **POP QUIZ**
>
> The Data Link layer is what layer of the OSI reference model?

In general, the Data Link layer must provide mechanisms for framing, addressing, and detecting errors in data that is being sent to and fro over the physical link. The framing mechanisms provide a way for the frames to be delimited. Node addressing identifies the source and destination for communication on the LAN. Error detection ensures that only good data is received at the destination and then delivered to the upper layers. In some cases, the Data Link layer discards any errors it discovers, or it may employ a recovery mechanism — it all depends on which action it was designed to do.

11.1.1 It Just Is

It's really hard to compare one LAN to another. There really isn't anything typical about any LAN. There are similarities in both design and functionality, but each LAN is unique. This LAN is your LAN, if you will. The concerns of the LAN are fairly typical. There are commonalities that exist in any LAN.[1] The purpose and the expected outcome are the same in any LAN. The purpose of the LAN is to provide the avenue needed for communication of data. The expected outcome is for the LAN to live up to its configured expectations.

No matter what you do, there are some things about a LAN that are a fact.[2] These have remained (and probably always will remain) a constant throughout the lifetime of LANs.

- A LAN consists of multiple nodes that are attached to a single shared medium.

- There are geographical distance limitations.

- Every LAN will have a ceiling on the number of nodes that it supports.

- A LAN cannot survive without error detection, correction, and recovery.

- A LAN needs to support broadcasting and multicasting.

- Like nodes are peers to one another.

- A LAN is administered locally and is not subject to the same rules that are maintained by networks outside of the LAN.

ACRONYM ALERT

DA — Destination address

These are only a few of the things that most LANs have in common. This is an important list for this chapter because these are what the Data Link layer is all about.

11.1.2 Highs and Lows

Another concern for any LAN is to ensure that the highs and lows are met. What do we mean by this? The LAN is there to provide the best possible methods to deliver data over a shared link. This means that the LAN should meet the following expectations:

- **Highs** — This is the portion of data communication that you want more of.

  - **High throughput**[3] — The data throughput is simply the rate of error-free delivery of messages within a network. This includes data

[1] Believe it or not, there are some network administrators who still do not understand that point.
[2] An important thing to remember is that there is technology coming out all the time that not only pushes the limits of the facts of the LAN, but also gives reason for upgrades.
[3] There are other terms that mean the same thing, but some of those have multiple definitions. For instance, when we were determining exactly which term to use, we had originally considered using the term "data rate." Although this would have been perfectly appropriate, it may have been a bit confusing. Data rate is a term that is used to define signaling rate, bit rate, transfer rate, etc. Throughout, we determined, is more specific in this case.

that is transmitted over a physical or wireless channel, switched through a node, or passed through the portals on both sides of the link. The expectation of the LAN is that the data throughput stays at a level as close as possible to the maximum allowable throughput. This is determined by the configuration and design of the network.

- **High total bandwidth**[4] — Bandwidth is the available capacity of the physical or wireless channel, and network nodes provide for the delivery of data messages in the LAN.

- **Lows** — Things that you know will happen, but you don't want to happen.

- **Low delays** — No delays is optimal, but unlikely. There will be peaks and there will be lulls. You can take action to try to stagger network chores (for instance, you can transfer large amounts of data at night so that it does not affect the times when users are all at work). Delays will occur, but the goal is to have as few as possible.

- **Low error rate** — The number of errors in the network needs to stay as low as possible. You can take actions to detect

> **POP QUIZ**
>
> Multiple nodes attached to a single shared medium can define what?

and recover from errors, but you want to be as proactive as possible to prevent them from occurring in the first place.

AN UNRELATED MOMENT OF PAUSE: FUN TECHNICAL TRIVIA!

1. **The Macintosh computer was launched by Apple Computer in 1984, with an ad that played during the Super Bowl. (The Raiders beat the Redskins, 38 to 9.)**

2. **How many approximate lines of code did the following Microsoft OS original releases have?**

   - **Windows 3.1 had over 3 million lines of code.**

(continued)

---

[4]Consider bandwidth as the amount available, and throughput as the actual amount of successful data messages that are transmitted. The throughput normally does not match the bandwidth, as there is other chatter that consumes some of the capacity of the communication channel (Hellos, Acks, etc.). For instance, if the link is a 10 GB Ethernet link, the bandwidth is going to be 10,000 Mbps. The throughput would be the rate of successful messages sent over the link. Of course, this is based on the performance of the network and is variable.

AN UNRELATED MOMENT OF PAUSE: FUN TECHNICAL TRIVIA! *(continued)*

- ■ Windows 95 had over 15 million lines of code.

- ■ Windows 98 had over 18 million lines of code.

- ■ Windows 2000 had over 35 million lines of code.

3. The computer mouse was invented in 1963 by Dr. Douglas C. Engelbart.

4. The term "computer" was first used to describe a mechanical calculating device in 1897.

5. We all know that 8 bits is called a byte, but did you know that 4 bits is called a nibble?

6. The type of keyboard that we are all familiar with is known as the QWERTY keyboard. This name is derived from the first six letters on the top line.

7. Netscape was the most popular Internet browser until Microsoft released Internet Explorer 4.

11.2   Accessing the Medium

We all know that the LAN is made up of nodes connected to one another over a shared medium. We also know that it is called "shared medium" because everyone shares it for transmitting data. It's important to cover a few of the rules that

> **POP QUIZ**
>
> Define *throughput*.

must be upheld in a LAN as far as actually connecting to the network. Sure, we have discussed some of this before, but now is a good time for a refresher!

11.2.1   Rules of Accessing the Medium

The previous section talked about some of the facts of a typical[5] LAN. When dealing with the shared medium, there are some facts as well.

- ■ Within a shared medium, only one node can successfully transmit data at any given time.

---

[5]Typical is used loosely.

- Bandwidth is allocated to support the nodes that are sharing the medium so that each node gets a fair amount of bandwidth, with little to none left over.[6]

- The shared medium should support as much throughput as it is intended to handle.

- The network administrator should ensure that delays are kept to a minimum for data that is transported over a shared medium. A reasonable

> **RANDOM BONUS DEFINITION**
>
> Gigabit Ethernet — 1000 Mbps Ethernet.

amount of waste, overhead, and delay should be taken into account when setting up and maintaining the network, and network monitoring will help you ensure that you meet the goals that you set.

11.2.2   From Tokens to Contention

So, how exactly do you go about ensuring the bandwidth is distributed fairly to the nodes using the shared medium? There are two methods that can be used in a LAN: tokens and contention. When using the token method, a token is passed from node to node. The nodes then pass data among one another in a round-robin fashion. When the contention method is used, the nodes transmit data when they want to. Therefore, it is entirely possible that two stations send data at the same time, causing a collision) to occur (see Figure 11-1).

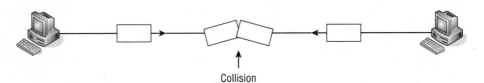

Collision

Figure 11-1 A collision

A collision causes datagrams to be dropped, but it doesn't necessarily mean that the data can't be recovered in some way. There are mechanisms that can

> **POP QUIZ**
>
> Name two methods of ensuring bandwidth is distributed fairly to the nodes that share connectivity within a LAN.

[6]When allocating bandwidth, it is important to use as much as possible. Some will be used by other processes, so a small amount of waste is possible.

be configured to recover from data loss and even prevent conditions that may cause it. Even so, there is a potential for data loss, so you can consider the token method a guarantee, whereas the contention method is more of a probability.

11.2.2.1   Using the Token Method

In Chapter 1 you learned that the token-passing topology consists of a single frame, known as a *token*, that is passed from one station to the next. When a node wants to pass data, it must wait until it receives an empty token. The node can then add its data to the token and pass it along the way. IEEE 802.5 is the official standard for Token Ring, which is the most common LAN token method in use.

A Token Ring topology can be set up physically in either a token ring (Figure 11-2) or a token bus (Figure 11-3) configuration. There is no logical difference between the two methods, as both operate in a token-passing manner.

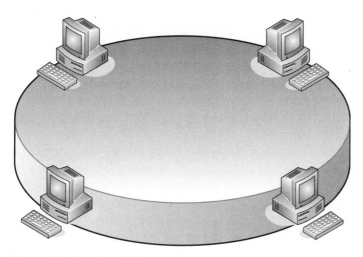

Figure 11-2 A token ring

In a token bus configuration, there is a central node called a media access unit (MAU) or a multistation access unit (MSAU). This device is similar to an Ethernet hub, but it has a computer chip that provides the logical ring that the end nodes are concerned with. The benefit of the token bus is that when a node goes down, the ring can be adjusted so that the other nodes will continue to operate on the network. In a physical ring, if a node goes down, the communication for all nodes goes down as well.

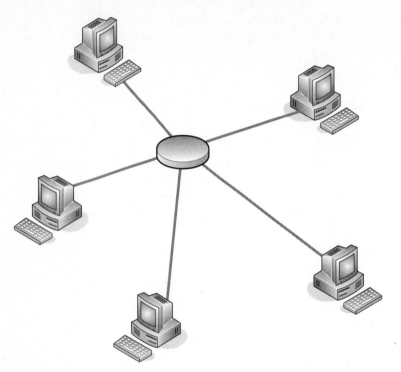

Figure 11-3 A token bus

11.2.2.2 Using the Contention Method

Nodes that use the contention method transmit their data at any time. The first node to get data on the line gets served first. When two nodes transmit at the same time, a collision occurs and the data will be resent. If the network is experiencing a high rate of data at any particular time, there will most likely be a lot of collisions, which will continue until bandwidth availability is restored.

Fortunately, some enterprising individuals came up with a way to sense when there is data being transmitted, thus reducing the number of collisions that can occur. Following are the protocols that are used to ensure that data flow in a contention method environment passes as smoothly as possible:

- **Carrier Sense Multiple Access (CSMA)** — Allows multiple nodes to be attached to a shared network. Prior to transmission, the nodes listen to see if the shared channel is busy and will transmit when they sense that the channel is not busy. "Carrier sense" simply means that a node is listening to see if it can detect an unused channel. If the node senses that there is a busy channel, it will defer transmission of its data until the channel is idle. "Multiple access" defines the fact that there are multiple nodes accessing the shared medium to transmit data.

- **Carrier Sense Multiple Access with Collision Avoidance (CSMA/CA)** — This is an enhanced version of the CSMA protocol in that it adds collision avoidance as a function. In this type of network, collisions are avoided because the station will not transmit data when it senses the channel is busy. The node will listen to the channel for a defined amount of time, and when the node is ready to send data, it will send a jam signal,[7] which lets all the other nodes know that the node is ready to transmit data.

- **Carrier Sense Multiple Access with Collision Detection (CSMA/CD)** — This is an enhanced version of the CSMA protocol in that it adds collision detection as a function. This function allows the transmitting node to monitor the channel for other transmissions. If while transmitting a frame, the node detects a signal coming from another node, it will terminate the transmission, send out a jam signal, and then try to send the frame again.[8] There are different ways for collisions to be detected, depending on the shared medium that is being used. The most popular and most often used CSMA/CD protocol is Ethernet.

11.3   Meet the Sublayers

In order to handle service requests from the network, the Data Link layer is broken into two sublayers: the Logical Link Control (LLC) sublayer and the Media Access Control (MAC) sublayer (see Figure 11-4).

ACRONYM ALERT

DEC — Digital Equipment Corporation

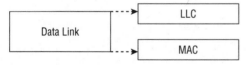

Figure 11-4 The Data Link layer's sublayers

LLC is the upper sublayer and is responsible for flow control, error control, and multiplexing and demultiplexing data transmitted over the MAC sublayer. The LLC sublayer is the sublayer that serves the higher layer client. LLC does

---

[7]A jam signal in CSMA/CD is a message to all other nodes that a collision has occurred and that they should stop transmitting.
[8]A random time interval is set that will determine when a station will try to transmit a frame again.

not have to worry about the design and functions of the LAN, which allows it to buffer these functions so that the higher layer protocols need not worry about the details but can focus on the tasks at hand.

The MAC sublayer is responsible for framing formats and determining which frame is going to be the next to access the shared medium.

11.3.1 Logical Link Control

LLC is a protocol developed by the IEEE 802.2 working group and provides three different types of service:

- **LLC Type 1 (LLC-1)** — Used for connectionless services.

- **LLC Type 2 (LLC-2)** — Used for connection-oriented services.

- **LLC Type 3 (LLC-3)** — Used for acknowledgments in conjunction with connectionless services.

LLC-1 is used for connectionless services. It is a best-effort delivery, providing none of the bells and whistles (for instance, flow control). LLC-1 provides multiplexing services to the upper layers. LLC-2[9] is used for connection-oriented ser-

> **POP QUIZ**
>
> The most popular and most often used CSMA/CD protocol is _____.

vices. Because it serves the connection-oriented operations, it does support the bells and whistles (for example, flow control, error control and recovery, call setup, call management, and call termination). LLC-3, which is seldom used, acknowledges frame delivery in a connectionless environment.[10]

11.3.1.1 LLC Framing

LAN source and destination addresses are determined by the MAC sublayer and will be in the MAC header portion of the frame. The LLC PDU[11] contains the following fields:

- **Destination Service Access Point (DSAP)** — This is used to identify the LLC that is supposed to receive the PDU.

---

[9]Note that nodes that support LLC-2 must also support LLC-1. This is because LLC-2 connections are established from an LLC-1 connectionless session.

[10]LLC-3 is used over LLC-1. This provides you with a bit of reliability without having the overhead of LLC-2. In most LANs you will usually only see LLC-1 and LLC-2. This is because many upper-layer protocols provide for recovery and don't need more than best-effort delivery.

[11]In case you forgot, PDU stands for protocol data unit. The PDU is the entity that all information is transferred in within a network.

- **Source Service Access Point (SSAP)** — This is used to identify the LLC that is supposed to send the PDU.

- **Control** — The Control field provides sequencing data, command information, and responses to requests. Note that any or all of these can be used in any combination.

Figure 11-5 shows the format of the LLC header. The LLC header is either 3 bytes or 4 bytes in length, depending on the version of LLC service type that you are using. The DSAP and SSAP are always 8 bytes in length each, which leaves the control field as the variable length field in the PDU.

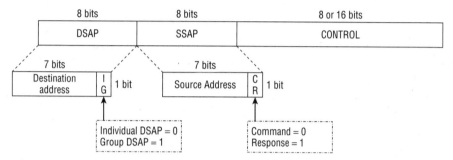

Figure 11-5 An LLC PDU (LLC header)

The DSAP field and the SSAP field are pretty straightforward. The DSAP field is an 8-bit (or 1-byte) field that contains 7 bits for the destination address portion of the field; the additional bit identifies whether it is destined for an individual or group DSAP. The SSAP field is an 8-bit (or 1-byte) field that contains 7 bits for the source address portion of the field; the additional bit identifies whether it is a request or a response to a request.

The Control field is a variable length, depending on what type of LLC you are using, and the type of the frame. The three frame formats you will see are:

- **Informational frame (I-frame)** — Used with LLC-2 only. This type uses a 2-byte (16-bit) field. Its purpose is to send numbered information transfer in LLC-2. Figure 11-6 shows an example of the format of the I-frame format.

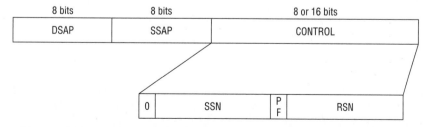

Figure 11-6 The format of the I-frame

- SSN — Sender sequence number
- RSN — Receiver sequence number
- PF — Poll on command frames or Final on response frames

- **Supervisory frame (S-frame)** — Used with LLC-2 only. This type uses a 2-byte (16-bit) field. It is responsible for handling acknowledgments, retransmitting requests, and terminating requests of the I-frames in LLC-2. Figure 11-7 is an example of the format of the I-frame format.

  - S — Supervisory function bits
  - PF — Poll on command frames or Final on response frames
  - RSN — Receiver sequence number

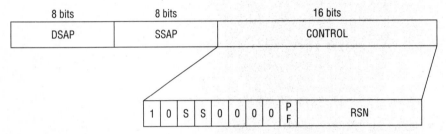

Figure 11-7 The format of the S-frame

- **Unnumbered frame (U-frame)** — Can be used with all LLC types. This type uses a 1-byte (8-bit) field. It is responsible for unsequenced data transfer and may handle some control functions as well (see Figure 11-8).

  - M — Modifier bits
  - PF — Poll on command frames or Final on response frames

> **RANDOM BONUS DEFINITION**
>
> frame — The Data Link layer encapsulation of transmitted or received information.

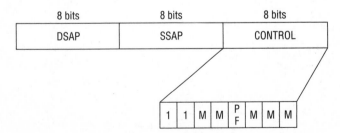

Figure 11-8 The format of the U-frame

11.3.1.2 Subnetwork Access Protocol

The Subnetwork[12] Access Protocol (SNAP) is used in conjunction with LLC-1 for the purpose of upward multiplexing to more upper-layer protocols than what is available with the standard

> **POP QUIZ**
>
> What does DSAP stand for?

LLC 8-bit SAP fields. When SNAP is not in use, the LLC DSAP's 8-bit field provides support of multiplexing to a maximum of 256 clients. Because the DSAP field reserves half its space for group SAPs, you actually can only multiplex to 128 clients.

As far as the PDU goes, the SNAP header is placed directly behind the LLC header in the PDU. If SNAP encapsulation is being used, the DSAP and SSAP fields will be set to 0xAA, which indicates that SNAP is being used and that there is a SNAP header in the PDU. See Figure 11-9 for an example of SNAP encapsulation.

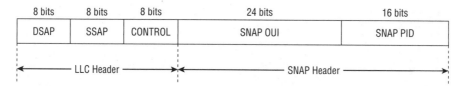

Figure 11-9 SNAP encapsulation

The fields in the SNAP header are as follows:

- **SNAP OUI** — This is a 24-bit field that contains the organizationally unique identifier (OUI). The OUI identifies the organization that the PID is assigned to.

- **SNAP PID** — This is a 16-bit field that contains the protocol identifier (PID), which identifies the upper-layer protocol that the PDU is destined for.

ACRONYM ALERT

EIA — Electronic Industries Association

Here's the clincher: SNAP encapsulation allows you[13] to have up to 65,536 upper-layer protocol identifiers.[14]

---

[12]It's important to note that the term "subnetwork," in the SNAP sense, does not have anything to do with a subnetwork in a TCP/IP sense. This is one of those acronyms that may have actually come before the term. It's nothing more than a way to make SNAP have that fancy ring that we "catenet" lovers like.

[13]In saying you, we are referencing the applicable organization.

[14]This simply blows the 256 (if you are lucky) identifiers out of the water.

A LITTLE MORE ABOUT THE OUI

The OUI is a 24-bit number that can be purchased from the IEEE. The number is unique to an organization (vendor, company, etc.) and serves several purposes. Many protocols reference the OUI (SNAP, for instance). Some even append a few bits to increase the functionality of the OUI. There are a lot of other terms that are used for the OUI. It is also known as a MAC address (more on this in the following section), vendor ID, NIC address, and many more.

Here is a list of a few OUIs that are assigned today. Note that these are globally assigned, which is why they are unique for that particular organization. Also note that often the same company can be assigned multiple OUIs, regardless of the location they are registered to (as in the case of Nortel Networks).

00-00-C0 (hex)	Western Digital Corporation
0000C0 (base 16)	Western Digital Corporation 8105 Irvine Center Drive Irvine, CA 92718 United States
00-0C-41 (hex)	Cisco-Linksys
000C41 (base 16)	Cisco-Linksys 121 Theory Drive Irvine, CA 92612 United States
00-0D-54 (hex)	3Com Ltd.
000D54 (base 16)	3Com Ltd. Peoplebuilding 2 Peoplebuilding Estate Maylands Avenue Hemel Hempstead Hertfordshire HP2 4NW United Kingdom
00-0D-56 (hex)	Dell PCBA Test
000D56 (base 16)	Dell PCBA Test One Dell Way RR5 MS-8545

(continued)

A LITTLE MORE ABOUT THE OUI *(continued)*

	Round Rock, TX 78682 United States
00-0E-40 (hex)	Nortel Networks
000E40 (base 16)	Nortel Networks 8200 Dixie Road Suite 100 Brampton, Ontario L6T 5P6 Canada
00-1F-9A (hex)	Nortel Networks
001F9A (base 16)	Nortel Networks 2221 Lakeside Boulevard Richardson, TX 75082-4399 United States
00-23-0D (hex)	Nortel Networks
00230D (base 16)	Nortel Networks 2221 Lakeside Boulevard Richardson, TX 75082-4399 United States

This list is an example and is only a short list compared to all the OUIs that are registered. If you want to see a complete list, you can view it on the IEEE website (`http://standards.ieee.org`).

11.3.2 The MAC Sublayer

The MAC sublayer is responsible for interfacing between the LLC sublayer and Layer 1, the Physical layer. The MAC sublayer provides access control as well as addressing for the PDU. This sublayer is what makes multipoint communication with a LAN/WAN a reality. This sublayer is also able to operate as a full-duplex logical channel in a LAN. This logical channel supports unicast (point-to-point) services, multicast services (point-to-multipoint), and broadcast (point-to-multipoint) services. All these services are discussed in Section 11.4.

The MAC sublayer uses a MAC address,[15] the address assigned to the node's network adaptor (commonly, a NIC). For channel access, the MAC sublayer employs some control

functions that allow multiple nodes to use the same physical medium. We discuss both the MAC address and the channel access control functions next.

11.3.2.1   The MAC Address

The IEEE 802 MAC address is a 48-bit address that is used to identify the network adaptor for a particular node or interface in the network. The MAC address was originally designed as a permanent address that is unique to the adaptor it is assigned to. Most hardware today allows a MAC address manipulation method known as *MAC spoofing*. That tidbit of trivia is informational, but we won't be going into the details, as it is beyond the scope of this book.

The format of the IEEE 802 MAC address is set up to make it as easy as possible to understand. It consists of six groups of two hexadecimal digits. The groups are separated by either a colon (:) or a hyphen (-). Following is an example of each method:

- 01:00:23:00:bf:00

- 01-00-23-00-bf-00

In these examples, the OUI would be 01:00:23, with the remainder being the NIC-specific identifier. Combined, they make up the MAC address.

MAC addresses can be administered both universally and locally. When the address is administered universally, the MAC address is assigned to the interface by the device's manufacturer. Locally administered

addresses are manipulated by a network administrator for purposes that serve the needs of the LAN.

11.3.2.2   Access Control for the Channel

The MAC sublayer is responsible for ensuring that multiple nodes are able to connect to and share the same physical medium. The groups of protocols that operate and perform this function are known as *multiple access protocols (MAP)*.

---

[15]The MAC address is also referred to as a *physical address*.

These protocols detect and avoid collisions in contention environments and ensure that there are enough resources to set up a logical connection when needed. Remember, earlier in this chapter we said that the most popular contention method used is Ethernet.

11.4   The "ings" — Casting, Detecting, and Addressing

LAN traffic flow is a fairly simple process. There are a lot of standards and configuration options in a LAN that provide a lot of freedom to configure and maintain in an attempt to reach the maximum highs and minimum lows that we discussed in Section 11.1.2. None of this would really mean anything if we didn't have a way of getting the data from the upper layers and making sure it reaches the appropriate process on the other end of the link. Well, we do have a way to do all of this in one very helpful and handy layer — Layer 2!

It is important to keep in mind that some of the "ing" operations occur at other layers of the OSI reference model (upward/downward multiplexing, data link multicasting vs. IP multicasting, etc.). Unless otherwise stated, this section pertains only to the processes at the Data Link layer.

This section covers MAC addressing and end-to-end delivery of data to a single node as well as multiple nodes.

11.4.1   Data Link Addressing

```
Main Entry: ad.dress16
Function: noun, verb, -dresses or -drest, -dress.ing.
1. a direction as to the intended recipient, written on or attached
to a piece of mail.
2. the place or the name of the place where a person, organization, or
the like is located or may be reached: What is your address when you're
in Des Moines?
3. to direct (data) to a specified location in an electronic computer.
```

Directing data is what addressing is all about. At the Data Link layer, this is done by pointing PDUs to the destination MAC address for delivery of a frame within a LAN. The MAC address is the number that is assigned by the manufacturer of a NIC or a network interface. In Figure 11-10, you

ACRONYM ALERT

IC — Integrated circuit

---

[16]*Dictionary.com Unabridged (v 1.1).* Random House, Inc. April 18, 2008.

can see a group of individuals sharing a physical medium. If Bob needs to send anything to Larry, he simply enters the MAC address (01:bb:04:af:00:1f) that is assigned to the NIC card on Larry's PC in the frame and sends it toward Larry's PC.

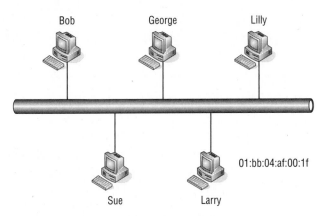

Figure 11-10 Data Link layer frame delivery

That sounds simple, doesn't it? But what we haven't really discussed is how Bob's PC learned the MAC address of Larry's PC. We also need to cover how Larry's PC knows how to get back in touch with Bob's.

It wasn't until the early 1980s' PC boom that there was really a need to formulate addressing that could be learned in a dynamic fashion and could support several hundred nodes. Prior to the PC boom, there were not more than a few nodes in a

> **POP QUIZ**
>
> What does SSAP stand for?

network, and addressing was locally assigned and administered. In a network of only a few nodes, it was easy to maintain networks in this manner. Now, however, with hundreds of nodes communicating with hundreds of networks with hundreds of nodes, there is a real need to have a way to bridge traffic that is easy to administer.

For now, and way into the future, LANs will continue to evolve and expand geographically as well as in technical achievements that are, and will probably remain, a constant.

11.4.1.1 The MAC Address Format

The MAC header of a frame contains the destination and source MAC addresses for the interfaces involved in the communication stream. Figure 11-11 shows the 48 bits that make up the MAC address.

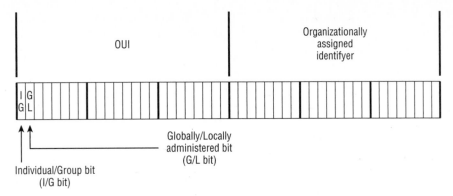

Figure 11-11 The MAC address format

Regardless of whether it is the source or destination address, the format is the same for all but the first bit. When referring to the destination address field, the first bit (the I/G bit) identifies whether the destination target is an individual (unicast) or a group (multicast). The source address field only uses the first bit when using Token Ring or FDDI. When used, it identifies if there is any source routing data in the frame.

The second bit in the source and destination address field indicates whether the address is globally or locally unique. This bit is called the *G/L bit* and it identifies whether the organizational assigned identifier[17] is globally unique (G/L bit set to 0) or locally unique (G/L bit set to 1). If it is a locally unique identifier, then the address is unique only to the LAN.

In any given LAN, there can be a mix of both globally and locally unique addresses. The nodes within that LAN do not have to worry about whether an identifier matches theirs that is in another LAN. This is because LAN-to-LAN communication is handled at the Network layer

> **RANDOM BONUS DEFINITION**
>
> edge switch — A switch that is implemented at the boundary of a VLAN-unaware segment and a VLAN-aware segment of a LAN.

and the IP addressing scheme negates this concern. Nodes within a LAN cannot directly communicate at the Data Link layer with nodes in other LANs. Therefore, it is possible to have a duplicate locally assigned MAC, but they will not be aware of one another.

11.4.1.2 Unicast Addressing

A *unicast address* is simply the address of a particular node's interface within the LAN. The unicast address is the MAC address that is assigned to a device

---

[17]The last 24 bits of the MAC address.

or an interface within the LAN. Unicasting is the act of sending a frame from one source node to a single destination node. Figure 11-12 shows an example of unicasting.

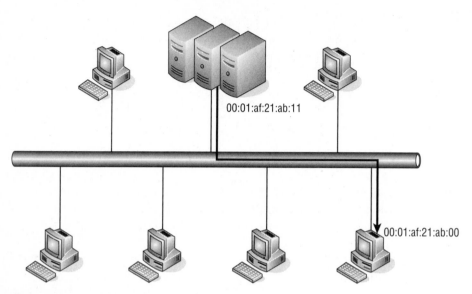

Figure 11-12 Unicasting

The figure shows the server farm sending data to a single node on the LAN. The unicast address of the source is 00:01:af:21:ab:11, which is the MAC address of the interface on the source side of the transmission. The destination unicast address is the MAC address of the interface used by the destination node — in this case, 00:01:af:21:ab:00. All transmitted frames during the session will use the same destination and source unicast addresses.

11.4.1.3   *Multicast Addressing*

Multicasting[18] is the act of sending a message to multiple nodes. Multicasting can be handled at the Layer 3 level (IP multicasting) or at Layer 2 (Ethernet multicasting). This section will focus on Layer 2 multicasting; the Layer 3 multicasting was discussed in Chapter 10.

---

[18]A type of multicast that you might come across in a LAN is the broadcast, which is destined for everyone in the network. Often called the "all F's" MAC address, the broadcast address is always ff:ff:ff:ff:ff:ff. Table 11.2 shows how this address maps to various protocols over Ethernet.

Nodes that participate in a multicast group will be related in some logical fashion.[19] Multicast addresses are group addresses of nodes within a shared internetwork. Multicasting provides the ability for multiple nodes to receive data sent from a single transmission. Figure 11-13 shows an example of multicasting.

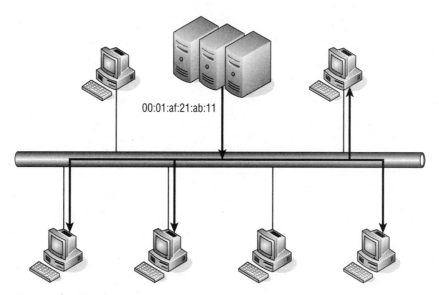

00:01:af:21:ab:11

Figure 11-13 Multicasting

Notice that in the figure not all nodes are receiving the transmission that is being sourced from the server farm. This is because not all of the nodes are in the same multicast group. Also notice that the source address for the originator will be a unicast address.[20]

When a node decides to join a multicast group, it needs to determine if a received frame is a unicast or a multicast frame. NIC cards are configured to recognize when a frame is unicast and when it is not. How is this done? Remember the I/G bit that we

ACRONYM ALERT

LACP — Link Aggregation Control Protocol

discussed in Section 11.4.1.2? This is the bit that identifies if the frame is a unicast (I/G bit set to 0) or multicast (I/G bit set to 1).

---

[19]The multicast will be sent only to those stations that share the function that requires them to receive the message. The stations that are not applicable won't be bothered.
[20]This is because there is only one source node involved.

Table 11-1 shows some well-known multicast MAC addresses that are used by Ethernet.

Table 11-1 Ethernet Multicast MAC Addresses

ADDRESS	TYPE	FUNCTION
01:80:C2:00:00:00	Length field	Spanning tree BPDU
09:00:07:FF:FF:FF	Length field	AppleTalk Multicast
09:00:07:00:00:FC	Length field	AppleTalk Zone Multicast
09:00:2B:00:00:03	8038	DEC LanBridge Hello packet
09:00:2B:00:00:0F	6004	DEC LAT
09:00:2B:00:00:00	8038	DEC LanBridge copy packet
09:00:2B:00:00:01	8038	DEC LanBridge Hello packet
09:00:4EL00:00:02	8137	Novell IPX
AB:00:04:04:00:00	6003	DECnet Phase IV router Hello packets
AB:00:00:03:00:00	6003	DECnet Phase IV end node Hello packets
CF:00:00:00:00:00	0900	Ethernet configuration test

Broadcasting is really nothing more than multicasting to everyone in the LAN. Table 11-2 shows some of the various types and functions performed in the broadcast message.

POP QUIZ

A _____ address is simply the address of a particular node's interface within the LAN.

Table 11-2 Ethernet Broadcast MAC Addresses

ADDRESS	TYPE	FUNCTION
FF:FF:FF:FF:FF:FF	0600	XNS hello packets
FF:FF:FF:FF:FF:FF	0800	IP
FF:FF:FF:FF:FF:FF	0806	ARP
FF:FF:FF:FF:FF:FF	8035	Reverse ARP
FF:FF:FF:FF:FF:FF	809B	Ethertalk

11.4.2 Error Detection

Frames are either fixed-length PDUs (ATM uses a fixed-length PDU) or bit-oriented, which is more common and is what we discuss in this book. Regardless of the frame type, errors can occur in the LAN, and frames can disappear, duplicate, and even become corrupted on their way to a destination.

An error in a length-type frame can cause the frame to terminate and skew the beginning of a new frame. Likewise, a bit can be set incorrectly in a bit-oriented type frame, which can cause duplication and even deletion of the frame. Errors can be caused by numerous reasons, environmental as well as traffic-related. Electrical interference can cause noise on the physical medium, which can corrupt the bits in the frame. Other causes of transmission errors include:

- Signal distortion
- Synchronization issues
- Crosstalk

Errors will occur and there are acceptable error rates that are figured into any LAN design. Excessive errors are not good. Depending on the protocols in use, errors can cause transmission delays, and if not handled correctly, the problem can propagate itself, causing sluggishness and possible outages in the LAN. This is why you need a way to detect and possibly correct errors at the Data Link layer level (as well as some protocols within other layers).

ACRONYM ALERT

TB — Transparent bridge

There are two methods of error detection used at Layer 2, parity check and cyclic redundancy check (CRC):

- **Parity check** — The simplest of the error-checking methods. This method adds a bit to a string of bits to ensure that the total number of 1s in the string is equal to an even or an odd number. For example:

    - **Odd parity** — 01010101 + 1 parity bit = 010101011. Notice that the total number of 1s is an odd number. An

POP QUIZ

What is the Ethernet standard broadcast MAC address?

odd parity bit is always set to 1 if the total number of 1s in the string (before the parity bit is considered) is an even number. By adding 1 to the even number, it ensures that the number is odd, which matches the type of parity in use in this case.

Figure 11-14 shows an example of data transmission using odd parity.

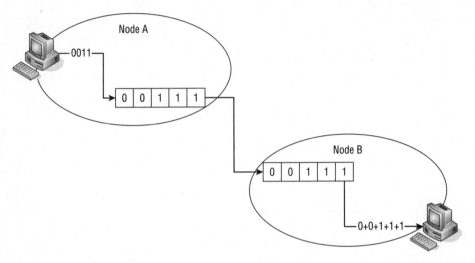

Figure 11-14 Odd parity

In Figure 11-14, node A wants to send the data stream 0011 to node B. Node A computes the value of the data stream $(0+0+1+1)^{21}$ and because odd parity checking is being used, node A turns the parity bit on to 1 before it transmits the data.

Node B then receives the data and computes the overall value (0+0+1+1+1), which is an odd value. Odd Parity is in use, so node B reports a good frame received.

▪ **Even parity** — 01010100 + 1 parity bit = 010101001. Notice that the total number of 1s is an even number. An even parity bit is always set to 1 if the total number of 1s in the string (before the parity bit is considered) is an odd number. By adding 1 to the odd number, it ensures that the number is even, which matches the type of parity in use in this case.

Figure 11-15 shows an example of data transmission using even parity.

[21]When does 1 + 1 = 1? When dealing with binary, when you are either on (1) or off (1).

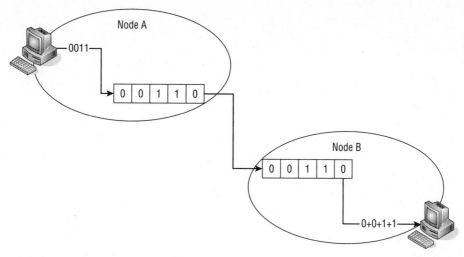

Figure 11-15 Even parity

In Figure 11-15, node A wants to send the data stream 0011 to node B. Node A computes the value of the data stream (0+0+1+1) and because even parity checking is being used, node A does not turn on the parity bit before it transmits the data.

Node B then receives the data and computes the overall value (0+0+1+1+0), which is an even value. Even parity is in use, so node B reports a good frame received.

Finally, let's take a look at the parity check when an error has occurred. Figure 11-16 shows an example of a data stream that is being sent using even parity. Notice that an error occurs before the stream reached the destination. When node B receives the data, it counts the number of 1s and notices that there is an odd number, therefore realizing that an error has occurred.

■ **Cyclic redundancy check (CRC)** — Also known as the *frame check sequence (FCS)*. The CRC is a function used to detect common errors that may occur during data transmission. CRC is a much more complex method of error checking than the parity check method, but it isn't necessarily complicated.

The way the CRC method works is that the node that is transmitting the frame adds a value, known as a *checksum*, to the message that is being transmitted, The receiver uses the CRC method to calculate the checksum on its end and compares it with the checksum that was added by the transmitting node to determine if there was any corruption along the way. Figure 11-17 shows an example of a simple checksum.

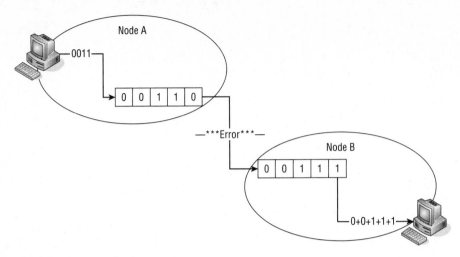

Figure 11-16 A parity error

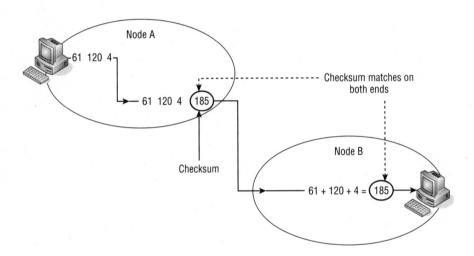

Figure 11-17 A simple checksum

For simplicity sake, this example uses decimal notation. Each decimal number represents a byte of data in a message. This means that there are 256 possibilities in each byte. The checksum algorithm in use simply adds

ACRONYM ALERT

POP — Point of presence or Post Office Protocol

the value of all the bytes and uses the combined value as the checksum. In Figure 11-17, node A is sending the message 61----120----4. Node A adds the total number of bytes and appends the checksum to the message (61 + 120 + 4 = the checksum of 185).

Node B receives the message and adds the value of the bytes in the message (61 + 120 + 4). By adding the total numerical value, node B determines that the checksum should be 185. Once node B determines the value that it thinks it should be, it compares its checksum with the checksum of node A. If there is a match, it knows the message was received intact.

Next, let's take a look at how the simple checksum works when an error occurs. Figure 11-18 shows such an example.

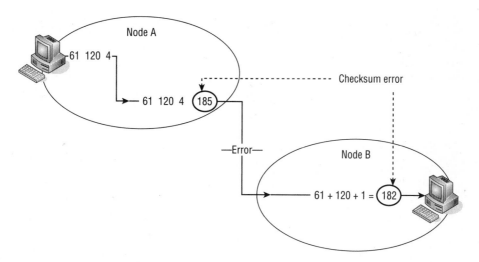

Figure 11-18 Checksum failure

In this example, node A is sending the message 61----120----4. Node A adds the total number of bytes and appends the checksum to the message (61 + 120 + 4 = the check-

RANDOM BONUS DEFINITION

access domain — The collection of nodes that share a network segment among which MAC arbitration can occur.

sum of 185). Notice that somewhere between node A and node B, there is an error that causes the last digit of the message to change from a 4 to a 1.

Node B receives the message and adds the value of the bytes in the message (61 + 120 + 1). By adding the total numerical value, node B determines that the checksum should be 182. Once node B determines the value that it thinks it should be, it compares its checksum with the checksum of node A. In this example, node B recognizes that the message was corrupted (185 does not equal 182), so an error occurs.

The simple checksum used in the example above would not be that reliable. There are too many possibilities of errors occurring with the checksum still intact at the opposite end. For instance:

61 + 120 + 4 = 185

51 + 130 + 4 = 185

60 + 120 + 5 = 185

CRC computes the check-sum by using an algorithm that is basically long division for binary. Additionally, the CRC uses the first 16 bits in the calculation, creat-

POP QUIZ

What is the simplest of all error-checking methods?

ing 65,536 possibilities. (The chances of an erroneous calculation is far less than with the simple example above.) Taking it a step further, the remainder (not the quotient) is what is used as the checksum.

Let's assume that an originator wants to send the first 2 bytes of data used in the example above (61 and 120). Also assume that the CRC divider will be a constant 1-byte divider whose value would equal the decimal number 7. So, now we want to convert these numbers to binary:

61 = 00111101

120 = 01111000

7 = 00000111

Take a look at Figure 11-19, which shows that node A is sending a message to node B.

The message is binary 00111101 01111000. The CRC constant divisor is set to binary 00000111. You want to take the message and divide it by the divider. The remainder is your checksum value.[22]

---

[22]Calculated out (we cheated and used a scientific calculator), the remainder in this case would be binary 00000110 and that is what will be used as the checksum value.

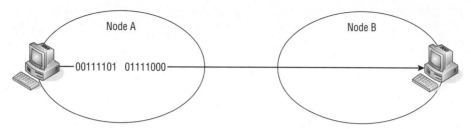

Figure 11-19 The CRC function

CRC algorithms more commonly use a method that closely resembles polynomial arithmetic. Instead of a simple divisor, message value, quotient, and remainder, as you saw in the last example,

> **RANDOM BONUS DEFINITION**
>
> disabled state — A state used in the Spanning Tree Protocol that identifies a bridge port that has been set to not receive or transmit any frames.

these integers are actually seen as polynomials with a binary coefficient. There are many ways to take this even further but are beyond the scope of this book. Really, we could fill pages with the different algorithms that can be used. Therefore, we bring this section to a close. What you really need to understand is that the CRC uses a checksum that can be complex and is used to validate data integrity in a LAN.

Now, all this may sound complicated, but it is fairly simple. To show how simple it is, we want you to take a moment away from the book and relax. Just clear your thoughts and take a break from all of this technical mumbo jumbo and relax. And what better way of relaxing than eating a pizza?

> **AN UNRELATED MOMENT OF PAUSE —**
> **DENISE'S PESTO CHICKEN PIZZA**
>
> If you are a fan of interesting foods, you are bound to love this pizza recipe. It is a super-easy meal to make and well worth the time it takes to make it. Just be careful if you have an allergy to nuts, as pesto contains pine nuts and you may have a reaction.
>
> Note: Delivery is also an option, but they won't have this recipe.
>
> Ingredients:
>
> - Refrigerated pizza dough
> - Pesto sauce
> - Cooked chicken, cubed or shredded
>
> *(continued)*

> **AN UNRELATED MOMENT OF PAUSE —**
> **DENISE'S PESTO CHICKEN PIZZA (continued)**
>
> ▪ **Fresh mozzarella (that doesn't mean shredded!)**
>
> ▪ **Sun-dried tomatoes in oil (rinsed)**
>
> ▪ **Rosemary**
>
> ▪ **Olive oil**
>
> **Directions:**
>
> 1. **Preheat oven to 425°.**
>
> 2. **Roll out the pizza dough, brush on olive oil, and sprinkle with rosemary.**
>
> 3. **Bake for about 5 minutes.**
>
> 4. **Remove the pizza and spread on the pesto, chicken, and sun-dried tomatoes. Top with mozzarella.**
>
> 5. **Bake 10 to 15 minutes, or until the cheese is melted.**

11.4.3   Control of the Flow

Flow control is used to prevent the sender of data from sending more data than the receiver can handle. Without flow control, the sender would not be aware that the receiver can't accept any more data and would continue to send the data, only to have to send it again once they are aware there is a problem.

There are different methods of flow control that can be used. Sometimes it is medium dependant, but there are options that work with higher-layer protocols. The receiving node does not necessarily have to provide feedback when it can or cannot accept more data. Ethernet uses what are known as *PAUSE frames* for flow control.

A PAUSE frame is a message sent by a receiver to the sender, letting the sender know that the receiving node can no longer receive data and that the transmission needs to be paused for a specified period of time. The PAUSE function only works within full-duplex environments.[23]

The PAUSE function has a reserved multicast MAC address of 01-80-C2-00-00-01. This is a MAC address that was set up by the IEEE and is used for the MAC PAUSE frame function.

---

[23]Because this is the most common standard in today's networks, we decided to focus on the PAUSE function in our discussion of flow control. Understand that, from a data link perspective, flow control is a function that prevents a sender from overloading a receiver.

11.5 "Knode" the LAN

We assume that you are all thinking, "What in the heck is *knode*?" A knode is fictional, simply a term that we created as a combination of "know" and "*node*." This may be a bit silly, but it is also good food for thought. Knowing your LAN is every bit as important as having the nodes you need to do what you want in the LAN.

In Chapter 3, "Network Hardware and Transmission Media," we introduced bridges and switches, two types of hardware that operate at the Data Link layer. We are going to finish this chapter by talking about bridge/switch deployment within the LANs. Although only an overview, this section should be a great lead-in to Part III of the book, which deals with network design and implementation. If you are interested in getting a good reference book, Jim's last book,[24] *The All-New Switch Book: The Complete Guide to LAN Switching Technology*, is a comprehensive reference to everything network switching.

So what is different between a bridge and a Layer 2 switch? The answer to this question may surprise you. There is no functional difference between a bridge and a switch. That's right! None! Nada! Zero! Zip! Switch is nothing more than a marketing term that came out in the 1990s. The change was brought about due to the ever-growing LANs. Original bridges could not offer wire speed transmission rates on more than two ports within the bridge. Bridges that could handle the higher rates were still not that reliable and carried a very high price tag.

This all changed when the application-specific integrated circuit (ASIC)[25] was developed. Along with improvements in system memory and higher processor speeds, the ASIC allowed the bridge to be developed, supporting a lot of ports that were capable of concurrent wire

RANDOM BONUS DEFINITION

chassis switch — A switch that is designed in a modular fashion. This type of switch consists of a chassis and multiple plug-in modules.

speed transmissions. The best part was that the cost was less than traditional bridges with the same number of ports per area, but not transmission speeds.

---

[24]This is more than just a shameless plug – it's a really good book.
[25]Pronounced "a sick."

These new devices were introduced to the world and the salespeople of the world decided to call them "switches," and that was where the switch was born.[26] For simplicity sake, we will use the term "bridge" for the remainder of this section. Feel free to substitute the word "switch" if you are so inclined.

Two methods[27] of address-to-port mapping are used:

■ **Source route bridging** — This type of bridging is used in a source-routed internetwork. The path to a destination is determined by the end nodes, not by the bridge itself. An example of an environment that uses source route bridging is Token Ring.

■ **Transparent bridging** — This is the type of bridging that is used in Ethernet (and others).[28] In a transparent bridging environment, the bridge makes the path determinations and the end nodes are not aware of decisions that are being made. They simply throw the data to the bridge and leave the decision making up to it.

ACRONYM ALERT

RISC — Reduced instruction-set computer

Let's take a moment to look at a bridge in a network segment and how the bridge learns and gets the data to and from a set of endpoint nodes. Don't be disappointed if there is not enough meat and potatoes in this section; we will discuss node implementation in further depth in the upcoming parts of this book. As a matter of fact, network design and implementation are up next.

11.5.1   Diary of a Network Bridge

A bridge is a device that operates much like a repeater or a hub, but it makes data forwarding decisions that bridges traffic from one network segment to another. A network segment is simply a group of nodes that are connected to one another via a shared medium (see Figure 11-20).

The only limitations to the number of network segments the bridge can connect would be the number of ports the bridge physically has. In order for a bridge to operate correctly, each node that connects to a segment that is connected to the bridge must have a globally unique MAC address.[29] The bridge will have at least one interface that connects to the network segment

---

[26]The term "switch" is often used when a new product is marketed. Some examples of a node that is called a switch but is nothing like a bridge include Layer 3 switching, routing switch, and application switch.

[27]You may need to run the two types together if you are running a mixed environment. This is supported (thank goodness).

[28]This is also the type that we will focus on (in keeping in line with our focus on Ethernet).

[29]You wouldn't want to introduce confusion when you have the same locally assigned MAC address in a node in two different network segments.

that it knows about, and it will build a table that maps the globally assigned MAC addresses to the port or interface that the bridge has determined the MAC can be reached through.

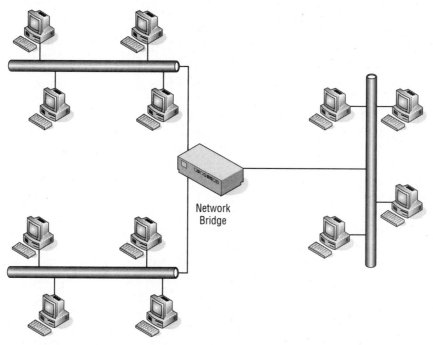

Figure 11-20 A bridge connecting three network segments

The bridge operates in *promiscuous mode*, which means it will take each frame that it receives (regardless of the destination MAC address). The switch then will use information in the frame to make a decision on which segment a MAC address belongs to. In Ethernet, the source and destination MAC address is the information the bridge uses. Figure 11-21 shows an example of two network segments that are able to communicate via an Ethernet bridge. Notice that the bridge has learned the MAC address of each of the nodes and has logged it in the MAC address table, along with the port that it knows it has to go through to reach the MAC.

11.5.1.1   Unicast Operation

Earlier in this chapter, we said that unicasting is the act of sending a frame from one source node to a single destination node. Now let's take a deeper look into what happens in multicast operations. The bridge receives frames on any active interface. The bridge then reviews the frame, looking at the destination and the source MAC addresses. It checks the MAC table to see if it knows the destination and forwards the frame to the destination.[30] The bridge follows the rules of the network protocols that are in use (for instance, the rules of CSMA/CD, flow control, congestion control, waiting for the token, etc.). Another thing that a bridge does when forwarding the frame is to use the source node's MAC address as the outbound interface address, instead of its own. This keeps the bridge transparent to the end nodes and reduces the computations necessary when receiving and retransmitting a frame. Figure 11-22 shows an example of frame forwarding.

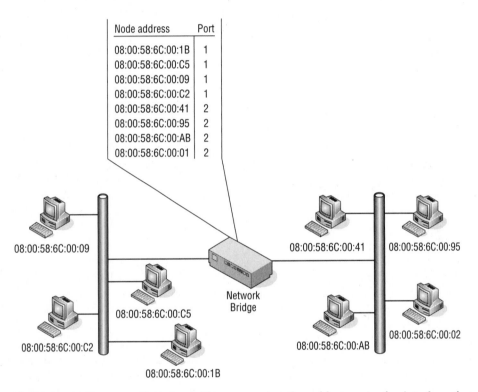

Figure 11-21 The operation of a bridge – mapping the addresses to the interface they belong on

You can see that the source node contains a MAC address of 08:00:58:6C:00:09, and it is sending a frame to MAC address 08:00:58:6C:00:AB. The bridge receives the frame, noting that the destination MAC address is 08:00:58:6C:00:AB. Looking at the address table, the bridge knows that MAC address is reachable via port 3, and the bridge forwards the frame on, leaving itself transparent by identifying itself with the source MAC of the destination.

---

[30]When the bridge sees a source MAC address that it does not currently have in its address table, it will add the information at that point.

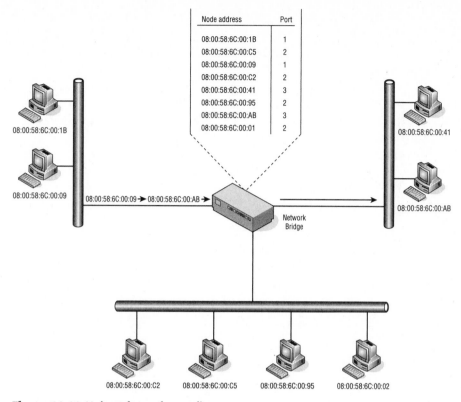

Figure 11-22 Unicast frame forwarding

11.5.1.2 Multicast Operation

When a bridge receives a frame that is destined for a multicast address, the bridge forwards the frame to all the ports except the port on which it is received.[31] In Figure 11-23, the source node that has a MAC address of 08:00:58:6C:00:09 sends a frame to all members of the multicast group. The bridge recognizes that this is a multicast frame and forwards it out to all ports except the port that it received the frame on (in this case, port 1).

11.5.1.3 When the Bridge Just Does Not Know

Sometimes a bridge receives a frame that is destined for a node it does not know about. The bridge is limited in what it can do in these cases. It can

---

[31] This is known as flooding. A couple of things that can be done to cut down on the amount of ports that are flooded to are multicast pruning and virtual LANs (VLANS). These allow the ports in the switch to be separated into groups so that not all are affected when a frame is flooded. This ensures that the multicast traffic only goes out the ports that are part of that multicast group.

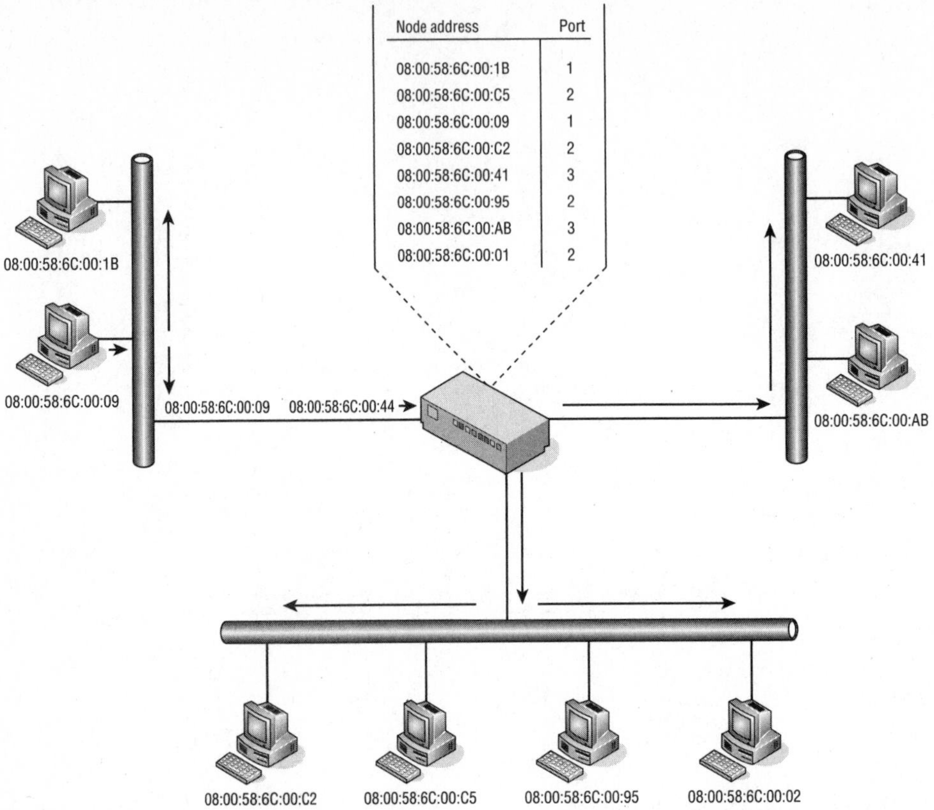

Figure 11-23 Multicast frame forwarding

forward the frame to all ports (except the one it received the frame on), or it can discard the frame.

Figure 11-24 shows node 08:00:58:6C:00:09 sending a frame to node 08:00:58:6C: 00:44. The bridge can't find that MAC address in its table, so it floods the frame out and eventually the frame will arrive at the node via port 3.

RANDOM BONUS DEFINITION

ARP cache — A data structure that provides the current mapping of 32-bit IP addresses to 48-bit MAC addresses.

11.5.2 The Address Table

The bridge would be nothing more than a bulkier rendition of a network hub if it were not for its ability to direct traffic to a proper port for data delivery. The address table is the backbone for the proper operation of a bridge. The

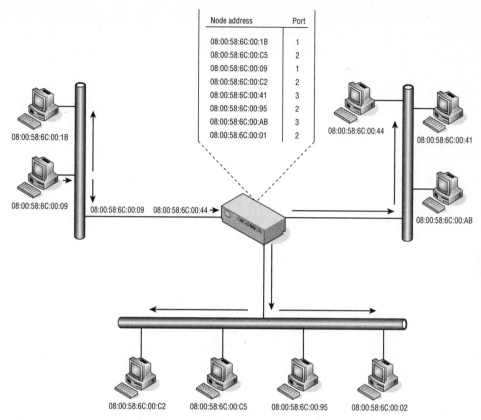

Node address	Port
08:00:58:6C:00:1B	1
08:00:58:6C:00:C5	2
08:00:58:6C:00:09	1
08:00:58:6C:00:C2	2
08:00:58:6C:00:41	3
08:00:58:6C:00:95	2
08:00:58:6C:00:AB	3
08:00:58:6C:00:01	2

Figure 11-24 Unknown destination frame forwarding

address table is built based on the source address of received frames. As we discussed previously, one of the functions of the bridge is to forward and flood frames based on the information in the address table. Another important function is to see if a source address contained in the frame is in the address table, and if not, to add it. If it is, then the port mapping is updated so that the latest destination information is synchronized. Eventually, the bridge will know about every bridge[32] that connects to a shared segment that it interfaces with.

Another important process that needs to occur pertaining to the address table is that the address entries must expire after a period of time. Imagine how big an address table would become if entries were never removed. Additionally, the performance of the bridge could suffer, as the list could become cumbersome to review if too large. When the bridge receives a frame, it checks the address table to see if the source MAC is present. If it is, it flags

[32]And have updated and accurate forwarding information.

the address so that it realizes that the MAC is still active and the information needs to be retained until the address finally does expire.

11.6   Chapter Exercises

1. How is a jam signal used in a CSMA/CD environment?
2. How is a jam signal used in a CSMA/CA environment?
3. An unnumbered frame type is used with which type of LLC?
4. Find the MAC address of your PC's NIC card. Once you have found it, take the OUI and look it up on the IEEE website. What is the information that is listed for that particular OUI?
5. What are the three fields in an LLC PDU, and what do they do?
6. How many bits are in an IEEE 802 MAC address?
7. What are the two error-checking methods used at the Data Link layer?
8. What does full-duplex Ethernet use for flow control?
9. What is the functional difference between a bridge and a Layer 2 switch?

11.7   Pop Quiz Answers

1. The Data Link layer is what layer of the OSI reference model?

   Layer 2

2. Multiple nodes attached to a single shared medium can define what?

   A LAN

3. Define *throughput*.

   Throughput is the average rate of successful messages transmitted over a channel.

4. Name two methods of ensuring bandwidth is distributed fairly to the nodes that share connectivity within a LAN.

   - Token
   - Contention

5. The most popular and most often used CSMA/CD protocol is *Ethernet*.

6. What does DSAP stand for?

   Destination Service Access Point

7. What does SNAP stand for?

   Subnetwork Access Protocol

8. What does SSAP stand for?

   Source Service Access Point

9. A *unicast* address is simply the address of a particular node's interface within the LAN.

10. What is the Ethernet standard broadcast MAC address?

    FF:FF:FF:FF:FF:FF

11. What is the simplest of all error-checking methods?

    Parity check

Network Design and Implementation

In This Part

Design Methodologies

Take a method and try it. If it fails, admit it frankly, and try another. But by all means, try something.

— Franklin D. Roosevelt

Planning and designing a network can be a daunting task. In the early days of data networking, a network consisted of a handful of nodes. Any addressing schemes were normally manually assigned and maintained. This required human intervention any time a node was moved, removed, or changed in any way. This manual intervention was not that bad, however, due to the fact that there were not that many numbers to keep track of.

In today's LANs, this manual addressing would not work. Networks are changing, technology is changing, and LANs have grown to a size that was not foreseeable 20 years ago. In addition, other concerns exist that were not there 20 years ago, including security, the highs and lows[1] of the LAN, and many others.

LANs can be a simple as a handful of nodes in a remote office to as complex as thousands of nodes in a fully meshed routing environment supporting applications that require as much of the highs and lows as can be squeezed out of the LAN any time the application want to do so. LANs are responsible for supporting multiple protocols running over multiple nodes and multiple media types. Many of these node and media types are from different vendors, all of which can potentially be running some proprietary features that may or may not play nice with the nodes, media, and even protocols that are running the LAN.

---

[1]These were discussed in Chapter 11 — high throughput, high total bandwidth, and low error rates and delays.

Sounds challenging, doesn't it?[2] And we haven't even gotten to plans for future growth. What is the organization's five-year plan? Are you installing gear that can be upgraded? How do you know how much gear to plan for without getting more than you need? These are just some of the questions you will need to ask yourself if you are going to design a network.

Planning and designing a data network is complex enough from a LAN perspective, and that is the focus of this chapter. For comparison purposes, we may discuss commonalities between the LAN and networks of smaller and larger size. Proper planning and design of the network can be trial and error at times. Sometimes things just don't do what you want them to.[3] But don't get discouraged. When you encounter problems with a design in the network, follow President Roosevelt's advice.

12.1   Your Task Is to Design a Network

By no means will you be a professional network designer after reading this chapter, but that isn't our intention. As with most of the topics in this book, we are trying to teach you the fundamentals. It's important to understand the difference between a network that was planned and designed carefully and one that was thrown together haphazardly, no matter what you end up doing in a networking career.

Careful planning is essential to ensure that your network will support your organization's needs. So what do you want to consider when you are designing a network?

- What are the needs of the business or organization?

- What should be considered in order to meet current and future needs?

- What are the cost considerations (short and long term)?[4]

These are all important questions to consider. You might want to design the most ultra-fantastic network with all the bells and the whistles, but the budget may not cover it. You might also want to build in some features to make life simpler for you, but that may be beyond the scope of the business model or plan.

ACRONYM ALERT

NFS — Network File System

---

[2]If you like challenge, you would love a job in data networking.
[3]No matter what the salesperson told you.
[4]This would include costs factored in for network maintenance.

12.1.1   Types of Organizational LANs

Following are examples of some of the various network LAN types that are in use. While reading through this list, consider the impact that might occur if these LANs were improperly designed.

- **Hospital LANs** — Life-critical data is delivered to various departments via the computer. Emergency logging is automated. Lives could be in danger if there are any network delays.[5]

- **Banking and financial corporate LANs** — Can you imagine how much money can be lost during the middle of the trading day on Wall Street[6] if the network has delays? What about the delays that could occur in the online trading world? Not to mention all the remote automatic teller machines.

- **Manufacturer LANs** — Production lines in all sorts of different manufacturing environments run with the use of robotics and automation. If there is a data hiccup, thousands of dollars can be lost.

- **Retail LANs** — Retail stores often have a LAN running within them, taking care of inventory and sales along the way. Periodically, the store will connect to the corporate LAN to exchange the data collected. Today, some retail sites run a remote connection into the LAN and are able to provide real-time updates. Imagine the impact if the store is not able to ring sales or communicate as needed with the corporate LAN.

- **Government LANs** — Consider the amount of security that has to be deployed for government LANs. Authentication methods and authorization are of the utmost importance. Consider what might occur if a hacker gains access to a government LAN.[7]

> **POP QUIZ**
>
> Name five businesses or organizations that are not listed above. What do you think the biggest concern would be pertaining to each organizational LAN type?

---

[5]Getting off topic a bit, here is an interesting tidbit of information. There are hopes that one day a doctor can connect to the hospital from home and perform an operation over a video feed with the use of robotics. Won't that be amazing if it ever happens?

[6]Although based on the days that Wall Street had beginning in late September 2008, maybe the network should fail every time that stocks start to tumble. No network ... no trading ... problem solved.

[7]And for any other LAN — security is very important.

And this is just a small list. Name a business type, and there will be some form of network for it. The network itself may not be optimized,[8] but it will most likely be there. What the design of the network for these organizations looks like all depends on the needs of that organization.

12.1.2 Other Things to Consider

Now that we have an idea of the needs of the business, we still have some work to do. The next thing is to ensure that you have a fair balance between what is available to be considered in the network environment (needs vs. wants) and whether the projected business needs limit what technically is available. You don't want to provide more than is needed for the LAN, but you also don't want unreasonable demands driving design decisions.[9] Another important concern for network planners is to not be too cutting edge. You don't want to deploy a brand new switch, new feature, or new code until it has had time to be field tested.[10] Most products undergo a serious amount of testing, but environments are different and new products often introduce new problems that can take time to iron out.

There are also several external factors:

- Consideration needs to be given to WAN interfacing, as well as interfacings with LANs that are within of your realm of control.

- Make sure you know about any government regulations and are in compliance with them.

- What are your competitors using/doing? What network type would you like to have, and who has done it right? What did they do?

ACRONYM ALERT

LSAP — Link service access point

- What is the potential technological growth, and will your proposed design be prepared to support it?

12.1.3 Building the Foundation

Now that you have an idea of the things that need to be considered, you can move on to the planning stage. Before you do so, however, we are going to let you in on a secret. If you have been paying attention to what we have written thus far in the book, guess what? Without knowing it, you already have some of the fundamentals that are necessary to design a network.

---

[8]This can be for several reasons. The network may be outdated, poorly designed, or simply not maintained properly. If you try modeling yourself based on a similar network type, make sure you model your LAN after one that has been operating a while and proved itself successful.

[9]Just because someone wants something to work a certain way does not mean that it can be done.

[10]Keep in mind that you may be able to make some kind of deal if you are willing to test any or all of these.

- You have an understanding of networking concepts.

- You have an understanding of the needs of the organization.

- You have an understanding of the hardware types that operate in a LAN.

- You have an understanding of LAN protocols.

- You know the different types of network topologies that are used in today's LANs.

- You know about LAN protocols and MAC and IP addressing.

> **RANDOM BONUS DEFINITION**
>
> aggregator — The entity that performs the operations required to make multiple physical links function as an aggregated link.

- You know the seven OSI layers and what functions at each layer.

- You know how to make spaghetti and meatballs!

Give yourself a pat on the back. You are ready to start planning the network.

12.2 Let's Start Planning

We just realized that there has not been anything really technical about this chapter so far.[11] You will be surprised at how much nontechnical thought is put into the initial planning stages. Don't worry — there is plenty of technical thought left in the upcoming pages.[12]

We already have established that you have been tasked with planning and designing a network. More than likely, you will be given a team to work with to get this project going.[13] The first task you will want to attack is to develop an action plan and project scope.

12.2.1 Development of Scope

```
Main Entry: scope (skōp)14
Function: noun

1. The range of one's perceptions, thoughts, or actions.
2. Breadth or opportunity to function.
3. The area covered by a given activity or subject.
```

---

[11] Then again, when is cooking up some of Mama Bramante's spaghetti a technical task?
[12] Jim is thinking that a nontechnical book might be fun to write, perhaps *The Networker's Guide to Homebrewing Beer*.
[13] At the very least you should insist on access to someone who knows something when and if you have any questions along the way.
[14] The American Heritage® Dictionary of the English Language, Fourth Edition. Houghton Mifflin Company, 2004.

Developing a project scope is important in the early phases of network design. This is where you gather the information you will need in order to proceed with the project. One of the big considerations is the nature of the organization (the type of network). Do the users only communicate with other users on the network, or is there a need for access to networks outside of your own LAN? Do users need remote access? Do any vendors or customers need access? What applications need to be supported by the network? Finally, it is good to know the budget that is available for the project and the time frame for completion.

The next thing that needs to be addressed is to determine whether the wants and needs are even doable. Is there enough money available to meet the requests? Can the project be completed in the proposed time frame? Will the project's completion keep up with technological growth?

> **RANDOM BONUS DEFINITION**
>
> aging time — This is used in a spanning tree environment — the amount of time a node can be inactive before a dynamic filtering database will remove the node's entry.

Now that the scope has been discussed, and it was determined to probably work, the scope has to be refined even more. The specific services that are to be placed in the LAN need to be determined. Information such as:

- Will the network support voice communications?
- Will the network support data communications?
- Will the network support e-commerce?
- Will the network support video streaming?

After identifying the services, you must determine what the potential traffic flow will be in such a network. What will be required in the future? Some of these can be answered if you are fortunate enough to have a network you can model yours after. Also, if you have a way to test (or get a vendor to help you out), you can possibly get some traffic analysis data that will give you a good idea of what to look for and expect. But the real test is when you go live. The secret is making sure you have enough, but not too much.

Data traffic patterns are subject to variations and fluctuations. Sometimes this is due to a certain time of day or a particular day of the week. Even the weather can affect data flow. Usually the trends point to an event (Friday night backups, Monday morning end node boot-up, etc.), and you just won't know about all of them until you get the network up and running. In the next chapter, we will be discussing ways to baseline.

12.2.2   You Are Not Alone

The great thing about all this is that you are not alone. You can send your scope out to some of the many networking vendors and ask them what they have that will help you do what you

POP QUIZ

Define scope.

want to do. This will get you a lot of information and maybe even some deals along the way. The request for information (RFI) is a standard process used in business to obtain just this type of information from vendors. Once you find what you like, the request for proposal (RFP) is used to seek the best deal.

12.3   A Hierarchical Design Model

There is that word again — *hierarchical*. The hierarchical design model is the most commonly used model in most high-speed LANs today. This model allows for easy expansion. It also makes network management and troubleshooting easier. By breaking nodes in the LAN into three functions, the nodes are able to focus on specific tasks instead of each of them working to perform all tasks. Figure 12-1 shows an example of what we are talking about.

The hierarchical model has the following three different layers, with nodes within each layer performing a specific function:

- Access layer
- Distribution layer
- Core layer

Keep in mind that a model is a recommendation or a guideline more than it is a rule. Sometimes a single node can take care of all the layers itself, sometimes it can't. It's always easier to follow a model, and this one is tried and true.

12.3.1   Access Layer

The access layer is the lowest layer. This is the layer that interfaces with the endpoint nodes. Types of nodes that are found at this layer are wireless access points, hubs, repeaters, bridges, Layer 3 switches, and routers. The access layer is what enables end users to connect to the network. This layer is also responsible for determining when nodes are not allowed access to certain portions of the network.

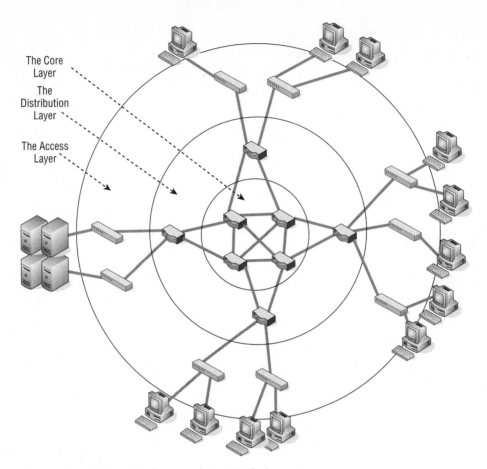

The Core
Layer

The
Distribution
Layer

The Access
Layer

Figure 12-1 A hierarchical approach to LAN design

The access layer can also be the gateway to the LAN for remote users (see Figure 12-2). For this to occur, some form of WAN technology must be used.

Examples of WAN technologies that can be used to connect remote sites to the corporate LAN include:

- Frame Relay
- ISDN
- Leased lines

The access layer can simply be thought of as the endpoint node access to the LAN. It manages the data between the endpoint nodes and the distribution layer. Switched bandwidth and MAC filtering are functions performed at this layer.

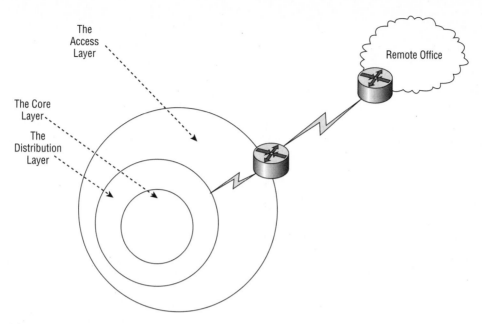

The
Access
Layer

The Core
Layer

The
Distribution
Layer

Remote Office

Figure 12-2 Remote relations to the access layer

12.3.2 Distribution Layer

The distribution layer is the middleman between the access layer and the core layer. Data received from the access layer is sent to the core layer to be routed to the destination. Broadcast domains are separated at this layer with the implementation of virtual LANs (VLANs). Security is also a function that is implemented at this layer.

Network access can be implemented at this layer when policy-based connectivity is required. High-performance Layer 3 switches are implemented at this layer. Guarantees that are required at this layer are high performance, high reliability, high availability, and redundancy.

> **POP QUIZ**
>
> Name three WAN technologies that are used to connect to remote sites.

Policy-based connectivity between the other layers is what you get from the distribution layer. Figure 12-3 provides an example of a method of connecting the three layers together.

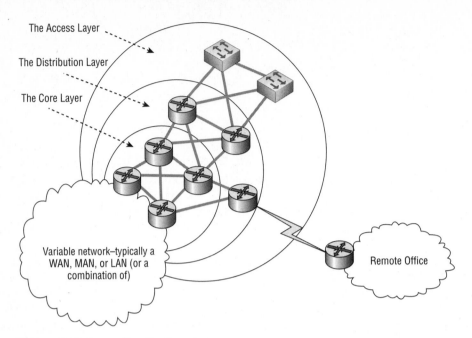

Figure 12-3 Connecting the three layers

Notice that the distribution layer has nodes that aggregate with other nodes in the access and code layers. Additionally, there is a remote connection that is coming from a remote office and accessing the network via the distribution layer.

12.3.3 Core Layer

This is the big daddy layer of this model. The core layer is the backbone of the LAN and often provides connectivity to WANs as well as to Internet services. The core routers[15] are highly available and support redundancy in the connections with the distribution layer nodes. These nodes need to be hefty, as they process data flowing throughout the whole LAN. They have to do that reliably and quickly.

Refer to Figure 12-4 and answer this question: If the drawing represents the physical layout of a network, is this an example of a hierarchical design?

> **POP QUIZ**
>
> What are the layers of the hierarchical design model?

---

[15]When we say routers, we are referring to any node that can provide network layer services. So, a router may be a router, a Layer 3 switch, etc.

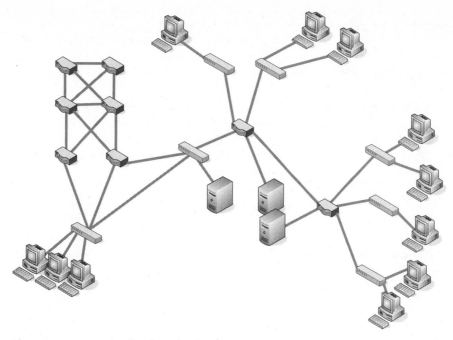

Figure 12-4 An example of a LAN physical layout

The answer to that question is *maybe*. We do not know the logical layout of the network, so it is entirely possible that this figure represents a hierarchical design. Hierarchical in a logical manner, that is; the physical layout is pretty much a moot concern at this point.

AN UNRELATED MOMENT OF PAUSE — BARBECUE CHICKEN NACHOS

We know how easy it can be to get wrapped up in the reading of this book and time can get away from you. Before you know it, you don't have time to make dinner and the last pizza delivery ran 30 minutes ago. This is a super-easy recipe and a really excellent quick fix when you need to fill the void left from skipping dinner.

The layers of the nacho model are as follows:

- ◆ The Determination layer
- ◆ The Preparation layer
- ◆ The Application layer
- ◆ The Thermal layer
- ◆ The Devour layer

(continued)

The Determination Layer

This is the first layer, in which you decide on the toppings that you want on your nachos. Thanks to this handy reference model, you are not confined to the recipe listed here. Anything goes well on nachos, so if you like it, try it out. For this recipe, we have determined that we will be using the following ingredients:

◆ Cheese — Use whatever kind you like (cheddar and/or Monterey jack is good).

◆ Tortilla chips — Any kind will do. We normally use restaurant-style tortilla chips, which make good nacho chips.

◆ Chicken — Chicken breast is the best.

◆ BBQ sauce — At least one bottle of your favorite kind. The ones with the squirt top works well for presentation purposes.

◆ Bacon — One package.

The Preparation Layer

This layer is where you prepare everything that needs to be prepared. Here are the preparation steps:

1. In a bowl, place enough cheese to cover the amount of nachos you plan on eating. You can shred it yourself or buy it preshredded.

2. The chicken can be boiled and then shredded, or sliced and cooked in a pan; the choice is up to you. Don't add a lot of seasoning to the chicken as it cooks, as you will be gaining flavor in your nachos.

3. Fry the bacon and then cut it into small pieces.

The Application Layer

This is where is you put everything together. Apply all your toppings to your nachos in any way you want — it's hard to mess up nachos. This is what we did; it came out yummy and had a nice presentation.

Use a microwave-safe plate or platter. Put a generous handful of tortilla chips (make sure to cover the plate completely). Now put a layer of cheese and about half of your bacon. Make sure to cover the chips completely with the cheese. Now put on another layer of chips. Next, put the chicken, enough cheese to

(continued)

**AN UNRELATED MOMENT OF PAUSE —
BARBECUE CHICKEN NACHOS (continued)**

cover the chips, and the rest of bacon. Make sure that you get some cheese on the chicken, but it does not have to bury the chicken. Finally, squirt the BBQ sauce over the whole thing — be creative. The nachos should be in a heap on the plate, but not flowing off of the plate.

The Thermal Layer

Stick all this in the microwave and cook it for about 30 seconds, then pause for about 5 seconds and then another 30 seconds. Keep your eye on it — when the cheese is melted, they are done.

The Devour Layer

Eat the nachos.

12.3.4   Why Hierarchical?

Some of you probably wondering, "Why hierarchical?" Well, we have been putting a lot of effort into presenting you with a slew of networking information while making the book as enjoyable to read as possible. So when the recipe was written, we thought it might be funny to present it in a hierarchical model. It worked too. Wait — you were not thinking about the recipe at all, were you? What you are really wondering is what the benefits are of a hierarchical model.

Here are just a few:

- **Design replication** — Once you have a working model, you can simply change the addressing schemes and design the next network expansion based on the way the original design was configured.

- **Expandability** — As the network grows, it is very simple to introduce additional nodes into the topology. Future growth planning is a breeze.

- **Redundancy** — Redundancy from the access layer to the core layer is very important in high-speed LANs. When a node fails, you have to have another node picking up the pieces until the node comes back on line.

- **Better performance** — Nodes that operate in the hierarchical model are able to maintain close to wire speed transmissions to all of the nodes it supports.

- **Security** — Access control security is provided at the access layer. The distribution layer can support advanced security that meets the security needs of the LAN.

- **Easy to manage and maintain** — Because of the scalability of the hierarchical design model, the network is easy to manage and maintain. A layered approach to

ACRONYM ALERT

NetBEUI — NetBIOS Extended User Interface

troubleshooting helps you find the source of a network connectivity issue. Additional nodes can be installed fairly simply, and configurations can be built from existing configurations, saving you time and money.[16] Over time, the hierarchical model will pay for itself in money saved due to the ease of maintaining and managing the LAN.

And there you have the hierarchical design model in a nutshell. Now let's take a look at a design model that is used in planning Ethernet segments. The next section covers the 5-4-3-2-1 design reference model.[17] It is a nice model to follow when you are planning a network, as it pulls together many tasks that are needed for basic design principles.

THINGS YOU JUST HAVE TO KNOW

Before we move ahead, here are a couple of terms you need to know.

- ◆ **Collision domain** – A group of nodes, sharing a communication channel, that are all in a group where a collision can occur. These nodes are connected to the same shared medium and are part of the same collision domain. These nodes are not concerned with other collision domains, as they do not have to negotiate for a communication channel bandwidth with them. Collision domains are normally separated by a bridge.

- ◆ **Broadcast domain** – A group of nodes that are all within the same broadcast area. The broadcast domain comprises multiple collision domains. Broadcast domains are normally separated by a node that functions at Layer 3 or higher.

- ◆ **Propagation delay** – The amount of time it takes to transmit a set number of bytes from endpoint to endpoint in a LAN.

- ◆ **Network segment** – A physically related grouping of nodes. Similar in function to a subnet, which is a logical grouping of nodes.

- ◆ **Repeater** – A Layer 1 node that connects network segments.

---

[16]When it works in one segment, it should work in another.
[17]This is also known as the 5-4-3 rule. Either term is fine, as long as you understand the overall concept.

12.4   5-4-3-2-1, Speed Is Not the Big Concern

The rule used for designing a collision domain is known as the *5-4-3-2-1 rule*. This is more of a reference model than it is a rule, providing guidance as to the number of repeaters and network segments that can be on a shared access Ethernet backbone.[18] The 5-4-3-2-1 rule says that between two communication nodes in a shared environment, the following are the maximums that are allowed:

- **5** — This is the total number of segments allowed.
- **4** — This is the number of repeaters used to join the segments together.
- **3** — This is the maximum number of segments that have nodes that are active.
- **2** — This is the maximum number of segments that are not active.
- **1** — This is the number of collision domains.

The 5-4-3-2-1 rule is used in networks that use a tree topology (a combination of a bus and a star topology). The tree topology used groups (segments) that attach to a linear backbone. Figure 12-5 shows an example of this rule.

In a tree topology environment, there can be a maximum of five segments between two communication nodes. Additionally, data can pass through a maximum of four repeaters. Finally, there can be a maximum of three segments that are popu-

> **RANDOM BONUS DEFINITION**
>
> backbone — A network used primarily to interconnect other networks.

> **POP QUIZ**
>
> What is the purpose of a network's access layer?

lated with active nodes. In Figure 12-5, you can see that there are five segments, four repeaters, and no more than three active segments between the source and destination endpoint nodes.

By placing these limits on the collision domain, you are essentially ensuring that the propagation delay is decreased (fewer nodes to pass through). This greatly improves the reliability in the collision domain.

---

[18]Note that this rule only is beneficial in a shared access domain. Switched backbones should consider other methods (most commonly, the hierarchical).

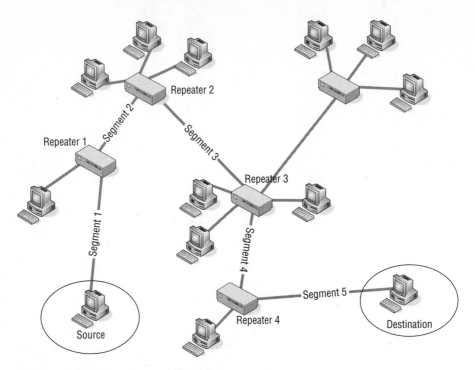

Figure 12-5 The 5-4-3-2-1 rule in action

12.5   Making Determinations

Now that all the preliminary mumbo-jumbo has been taken care of, it's time for you to determine what you will need out of your network. Some things will be contingent on others (for instance, if authentication is going to be used, what will you need to support it?). This is exactly why you will want to review and adjust your plan as you go along.

You have determined the needs and wants of the users of the network. Now you start making determinations on what should be put into the network to support those needs. Be sure to consider potential future growth in your determinations. Some decisions you will make include:

- Which topology are you going to be using?
- Will you be using Ethernet or Token ring?
- How many ports will be needed at each level?
- What is the target transmission speed(s)?
- Which node types are you planning on deploying?

- Which end-user applications will be used?

- Which protocols will need to be supported?

- Will remote access be required?

- Which types of WAN protocol options will be used (if required)?

- What are the security concerns?

ACRONYM ALERT

DDP — Datagram Delivery Protocol

In the next few sections, we will discuss some things you should consider when making these determinations.

12.5.1   Determining Which Topology to Use

Deciding on the network topology really depends on the requirements at each level of the network. More than likely you will be using Ethernet (the most popular shared network protocol), so your biggest decision will be the speed and the actual physical layout of the building in which the network is being installed.

Chapter 1 introduced the topology types in most LANs. The three most popular topology types are the bus, the star, and the ring. Let's take a moment to review these.

12.5.1.1   Bus Network Topology

The bus topology is the most often used topology in LANs. In this topology, the nodes connect to a common shared communication channel, referred to as a *bus*. Figure 12-6 shows an example of a network with a bus network topology.

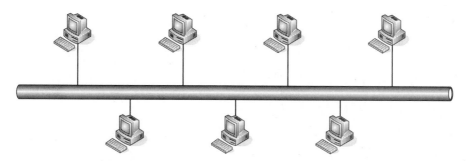

Figure 12-6 The bus topology

So what makes the bus topology the most often implemented?

Advantages:

- It's easy to install.
- It's easy to extend.
- It's less expensive to implement than other topologies.

Disadvantages:

- There is a limitation to the distance a cable can go without a repeater.
- There is a limit to the number of nodes that can be supported.
- The LAN can experience sluggishness in performance when there are heavy traffic loads.
- Security risks exist because all stations can hear what the others are saying on the shared channel.

The cost and ease of use are the biggest reasons for considering the bus network. However, if there are concerns about speed, performance, reliability, or number of supported nodes, another design might need to be considered.

> **RANDOM BONUS DEFINITION**
>
> blocking state — A stable state in the Spanning Tree Protocol in which a bridge port will receive BPDUs but will neither receive nor transmit data frames.

12.5.1.2 Star Network Topology

The star topology can be divided into two categories. It can be a logical star topology or a physical star topology. Figure 12-7 shows an example of a physical star topology where a central bridge or a hub controls the communications to and from attached nodes.

The advantages of a star topology include:

- It offers better performance.
- It's easy to troubleshoot.
- It offers high scalability of the network through the central node.

The disadvantages of a star topology include:

- There is too much dependency on the central node.
- It can be complex to manage.
- Wiring can become cumbersome.

If neither the bus nor the star topology fit your specific needs, you might want to consider implementing a ring topology.

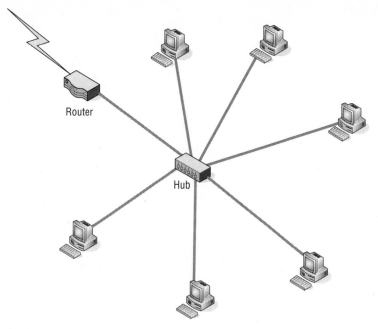

Figure 12-7 The star topology

12.5.1.3 *Ring Network Topology*

The ring topology is used for Token Ring and FDDI LANs. In the ring topology, a frame is passed from node to node until it reaches its destination. Figure 12-8 shows an example of a network with a ring network topology.

The advantages of a ring topology include:

- There is no need to have a mechanism to ensure collision-free datagram passing.

- It can be expanded to cover a greater number of nodes than some of the other topology types.

- It's fairly simple to maintain.

The disadvantages of a ring topology include:

- A failure with one node on the ring can cause an outage to all connected nodes.

- Any maintenance (e.g., adding a node, making a change to a node, removing a node) affects all the nodes that connect to the ring.

- Some of the hardware required to implement a ring is more expensive than Ethernet network cards and nodes.

- Under normal traffic load, a ring is much slower than other topologies.

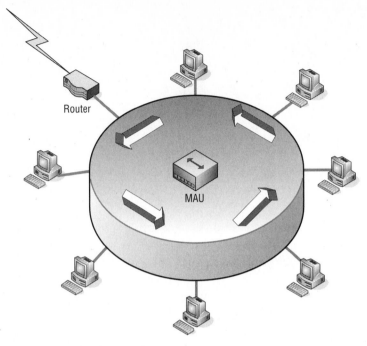

Figure 12-8 The ring topology

Another determination is which nodes to deploy and where to deploy them. The following section discusses some things to consider.

12.5.2 Determining Which Nodes to Use

Traditionally, packet-switched LANs have comprised four main network nodes: concentrators, repeaters, bridges, and routers. For the most part, these traditional nodes are still used and make up various levels of the network. Repeaters and bridges are used heavily in user workgroups, server farms, and in the access layer of hierarchical networks.

ACRONYM ALERT

CST — Common spanning tree

The list of nodes has really grown in the past 20 years. The traditional nodes are still in use, but so many other nodes have been introduced in that time. In addition to the traditional nodes, many networks use Layer 3 switches, Layer 4–7 switches, VPN remote access solutions, etc.

Chapter 3 discussed each of these node types extensively, but here is a quick overview, along with some examples of node deployment.

12.5.2.1 *Traditional Nodes*

The first types of nodes we want to cover are what we will call the *traditional nodes*. These node types are the most often deployed and are found in many home networks. In traditional node networks, each node serves a distinct and specific function. Repeaters and hubs pass data without using any logic at all. Bridges (also known as Layer 2 switches) connect like networks to one another and are able to make correct forwarding decisions. Routers are able to connect different network types to one another and can also make correct forwarding decisions.

Get it? Got it! Good!

12.5.2.1.1 Repeaters

The repeater is a node that simply passes information on. It is used to extend the segment when medium-distance limitations have been reached. Figure 12-9 shows an example of a repeater separating two parts of a network.

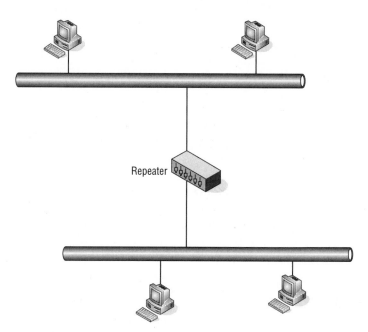

Figure 12-9 A repeater

A repeater amplifies a signal, but that is not its only task. A repeater also filters out any distorted data it has received, and it will not pass that data along. Technically, you can say that the function of the repeater is to amplify good data.

ACRONYM ALERT

ADSP — AppleTalk Data Stream Protocol

12.5.2.1.2   Concentrators

The concentrator used within a LAN is either a hub or an MAU that allows the combination of data transmissions for a group of nodes. Figure 12-10 shows an example of a hub deployed in a LAN.

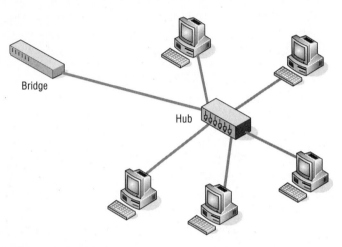

Figure 12-10 A hub

A hub is used to connect segments in a LAN. Hubs have multiple ports, and when data is received on a port, the hub will send the datagram to all of the other ports, so all segments will see all datagrams that are passed through the hub.

An MAU is a type of concentrator that is used to connect nodes within a Token Ring environment. The MAU connects the nodes in a physical star configuration, but the logical operations are Token Ring. The MAU allows the Token Ring to continue operating when a node on the ring breaks. This is much better than the alternative, where a node breaks on a physical ring and the whole ring goes down.

12.5.2.1.3   Bridges

The bridge is a LAN node that operates at Layer 2 of the OSI reference model. The bridge is used to connect different networks to one another. Data received from one network can be forwarded through the bridge to get the data to the correct destination. Figure 12-11 shows an example of bridge deployment.

Bridges are smart enough to know how to send datagrams to a specific port so that not all areas of the network have to receive the data as well. This frees up the other segments to pass data separately, without having to analyze all the datagrams. When a bridge gets the datagram, it passes the data based on the MAC address of the destination node.

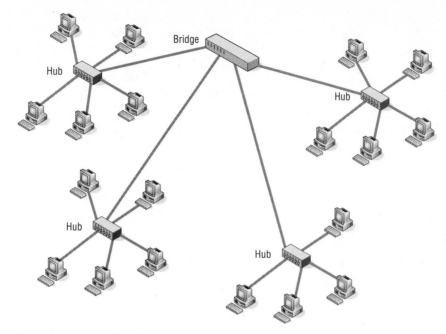

Figure 12-11 A bridge

12.5.2.1.4 Routers

The final node in the traditional node family is the router. Operating at Layer 3, the router is the backbone of most LANs. Routers use IP addresses to route datagrams in a network. Routers support multiple protocols of different types and are

> **RANDOM BONUS DEFINITION**
>
> coaxial cable — A communications medium used in 10BASE5 and 10BASE2 Ethernet systems.

able to separate networks of different types because of this. Figure 12-12 is an example of the placement of a router in a LAN.

Routers are still in use in LANs today, but Layer 3 switches are becoming increasingly more popular. The reason for this is simple. The advanced switches are able to function as a router at a much higher speed due to application-specific integrated circuit (ASIC) technology. Additionally, switching hardware is cheaper to replace than traditional router hardware.

Routers are still used as boundaries between the LAN and the Internet.[19] Figure 12-13 shows an example of this. Routers are also often used for remote connectivity for remote offices.

---

[19]Or other networks that are not controlled by the organization.

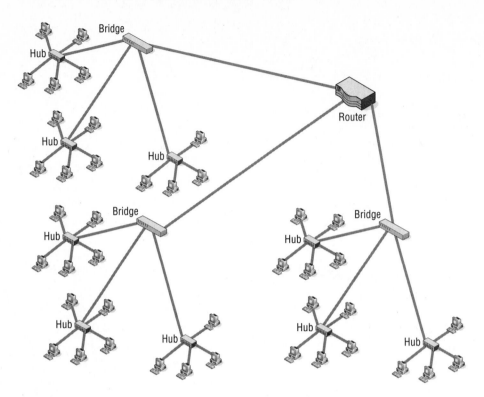

Figure 12-12 A router

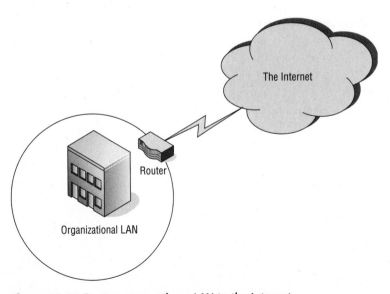

Figure 12-13 Routers connecting a LAN to the Internet

Routers are used to route data between different networks. Routers control the flow of data in and out of the LAN, often working with a firewall solution to limit and/or control data coming into the LAN, as well as data going out from the LAN to the Internet.

12.5.2.2   Node Evolution

```
Main Entry: ev·o·lu·tion[20]
Function: noun.

1. A gradual process in which something changes into a different and
usually more complex or better form.
2. The process of developing.
3. A movement that is part of a set of ordered movements.
4. Mathematics: The extraction of a root of a quantity.
```

Networking never stops growing. As a new product is being introduced, there is another product just around the corner that will replace it. Software upgrades and new program implementations also see the same changes and growth. No longer is a modem the standard for accessing the LAN. No longer do we have to rely on filtering and VLAN techniques to authorize and authenticate. There are a lot of nodes out there that do the trick, and a lot of nodes out there that just plain do it better than traditional nodes.

We already have discussed how the term *Layer 2 switch* replaced the term *bridge*, but it is really just a marketing term. As a matter of fact, it was so well received[21] that almost anything networking is a switch now. In this section, we talk about some other switches that are in a lot

> **RANDOM BONUS DEFINITION**
>
> congestion — The state where the offered network load approaches or exceeds the locally available resources designed to handle that load

of LANs. In addition to the switches, we discuss a bit about VPN and wireless nodes.

12.5.2.2.1 Layer 3 Switches

Layer 3 switches perform the same task as routers and are deployed in high-speed LANs as well as in WANs. The Layer 3 switch is preferred over a router because routing decisions are hardware-based and thus are able to be performed much faster than traditional routers. Layer 3 switches are also able

---

[20]The American Heritage® Dictionary of the English Language, Fourth Edition. Houghton Mifflin Company, 2004.
[21]Well received by the customers or the salespeople. We are not really sure which, but we all know how those sales guys are.

to perform as Layer 2 switches, giving the best of both worlds. They give you the control of data flow that is offered in a routed network and the speed that is offered in a switched environment. Figure 12-14 shows an example of Layer 3 switch deployment.

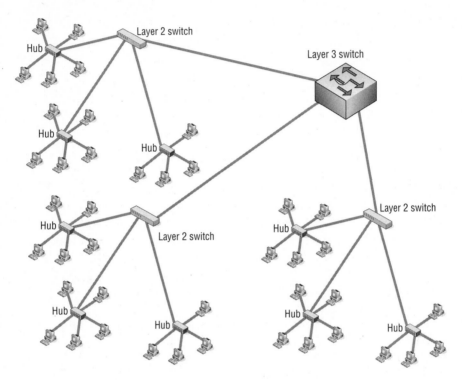

Figure 12-14 A Layer 3 switch deployment

Traditional routers do a great job, but the logic decisions they make are software-based and therefore are a slower process than what is offered by the Layer 3 switches. Layer 3 switches can support the same protocols that are supported by a traditional router and generally cost less than traditional switches.

So what is the hardware feature on the Layer 3 switch? It is the ASIC that makes the Layer 3 switch. A Layer 3 switch can have from one ASIC per chassis up to one ASIC per port.[22]

12.5.2.2.2 Layer 4–7 Switching

Layer 4–7 switching is not traditional Layer 2 switching. Many vendors now market nodes that are able to perform Layer 4–7 functions. It's important to note that even though a node may be labeled a Layer 4–7 switch, multiple

---

[22]This depends on how badly the vendor wants to make sure that you can get wire speed throughput through the device.

vendors use the definition loosely, so it may not really be exactly the same between vendors. Some terms you might come across to describe Layer 4–7 switching include:

- Web switch
- Application switch
- Content switch
- VPN switch

Generally, Layer 4 switches are used to assist in balancing data destined for servers within a network. Layer 4 switches operate at the TCP/UDP level and will make decisions about where to send traffic based on information that is stored at the Transport layer. Not all Layer 4 switches actually do transfers based on that information. Web load balancers are often termed Layer 4 switches, as they are able to forward Layer 2 switches based on the MAC address, but are also able to send some MAC address data to multiple physical ports within the load-balancing switch. Some load balancers are able to monitor load on the server ports and can switch requests that are received to the data port that connects to the server with the lightest load.

As we have said, some of these nodes can function at up to Layer 7 of the OSI model. These are used to load-balance traffic among groups of servers. These servers can provide applications such as HTTP, HTTPS, and many others that use TCP/IP to transport traffic via a specified port.

Layer 4–7 switches use Network Address Translation (NAT), often at wire speed, to provide an avenue to allow multiple clients access to multiple host servers without having to know the exact physical server that is handling the request from the individual client. Some Layer 4–7 switches are also able to provide SSL encryption and decryption services so that the servers don't have to, as well as being able to manage digital certificates.

Layer 4–7 switches provide an excellent service — the almost instant, endless, and secure flow of data to end users. This is certainly an improvement for many users who are beginning to expect instant gratification when connecting to a website. The Layer 4–7 switch may not be for everyone, but it does come in handy when a network needs to have it.

ACRONYM ALERT

MAC — Media Access Control

12.5.2.2.3 Virtual Private Networks

VPN solutions have changed the way that organizations connect to remote sites. Traditionally, site-to-site connectivity was done over leased lines (such as ISDN, dial-up, etc.). As the Internet grew, and technology grew, so did the way that we connect to remote offices. VPN technology allows remote connectivity over a secure tunnel to the organizational LAN, so it will appear as if the remote user or office is actually geographically located within the LAN. Figure 12-15 provides an example of three uses of the VPN solution.

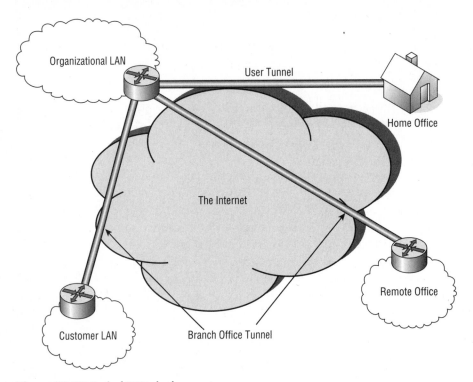

Figure 12-15 Typical VPN deployments

In the figure, you can see that there are three different tunnels going into the corporate LAN. One of these tunnels is a remote user connecting from home through a user tunnel.[23] The other two tunnels connect remote LANs and are known as branch office tunnels. One of the branch office tunnels goes to a remote office for workers in the VPN's organization.[24] The other branch office tunnel is used by customers to connect to the corporate network.[25]

12.5.2.2.4 Wireless Networks

The last topic we will talk about in this node evolution section is wireless networks. Wireless seems to be where networking is really growing. Almost everyone has at least one cell phone, but it does not stop there. You have Bluetooth, infrared, wireless PC connections, etc., almost everywhere you go. We can't tell you the last time we were out and about when there wasn't

---

[23]This type of VPN is also known as a remote access VPN.
[24]This type of VPN is also known as an intranet VPN.
[25]This type of VPN is also known as an extranet VPN.

at least one person using some form of wireless device. Thanks to wireless networks, this is all possible.

IEEE 802.11 is the standard that outlines wireless LAN standards. Another standard, called *wireless IP*, allows mobile devices to remain connected, even when they move into an wireless area that has a different IP scheme than the user has. Basically, this standard allows roaming without losing connectivity.

RANDOM BONUS DEFINITION

dedicated bandwidth — A configuration in which the communications channel attached to a network interface is dedicated for use by a single station and does not have to be shared.

Security is a big concern in wireless networks, so encryption and authorization options need to be considered.

12.5.3 LAN Switching Technology

Layer 2 switches changed what we can do in a network. These LAN switches broke up the transitional shared network and converted it into a switched network. This greatly improved the performance of the LAN as a whole. Figure 12-16 shows an example of a small switched network consisting of the switch (of course) and six end users. If this were a shared network connected by a central hub, all the nodes would have to read all the data transmitted, and the end-user nodes would have to negotiate in order to transmit.

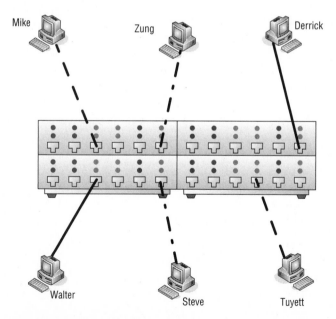

Figure 12-16 A switched network

As you can see, there are a total of six end users. Each user is exchanging data with one other node, but each node is communicating with only one node at a time. Notice that there are three simultaneous active connections (Mike to Tuyett, Zung to Steve, and Derrick to Walter) in the example. Try to do that in a shared network!

12.5.3.1 Switch Types

The way that a switch handles the data it receives depends on whether the switch is a *cut-through* type or a *store and forward* type.

- **Cut through** — In cut-through operations, the switch reads the header of the datagram as it is received on a port. Once the switch determines the port that reaches the destination, the datagram is sent to the port and on to its destination. There is no storing of data in a cut-through environment. There are also no options for error checking or control because the cut-through switch only reads the header for an address and sends the datagram on.

- **Store and forward** — In store and forward operations, the switch stores the data and does error checking on the datagram before it sends the datagram off toward its destination port. Although this makes the transfer of datagrams slower than with a cut-through switch, the data is delivered reliably.

12.5.3.2 By All Means, Be Redundant

A well-designed network will be built with plenty of redundancy throughout. The last thing a network administrator needs is a *single point of failure* anywhere in the network. A single point of failure is a location within the network that does not have a backup link of some sort. In other words, if the link fails, the network that is relying on that link will not be able to reach some or all of the LAN. Figure 12-17 shows an example of a single switch that is used to connect LAN 1 to LAN 2.

Consider what would happen in this example if the switch failed, or if one of the links between a LAN and the switch failed. If there were a failure, LAN-to-LAN communication would not happen. Depending on the problem, it could be several hours before service is restored, and in most businesses, there is a financial impact that could be detrimental.

ACRONYM ALERT

BPDU — Bridge protocol data unit

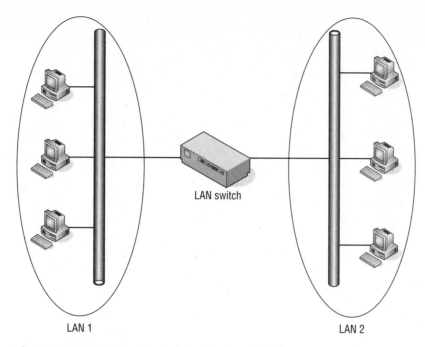

Figure 12-17 A switched network without redundancy

This is why you absolutely want to place redundancy throughout the network. Always have some sort of backup so there is a network convergence to a separate parallel link between endpoints (an example would be the LAN-to-LAN connection in the example we used above). Not only does this improve the reliability of data delivery, but a redundant network in a network diagram also really adds something to the overall picture. Figure 12-18 is an example of a network with redundancy.

So, the problem is resolved, right? Well, technically, yes, the problem of LAN-to-LAN communication being lost when a link goes down is now resolved. But like many solutions in the data world,[26] in resolving one issue, a new issue was introduced. The new issue is a loop, and we discuss it in the next section.

12.5.3.3 I'm Loopy!

We have established that there is a requirement for redundancy if we want our LAN to be reliable. However, in introducing that reliability by adding a second link, we have now created an environment where a loop may occur (see Figure 12-19). We'll now take a different look at the switched network.

---

[26]This includes both public solutions and proprietary solutions.

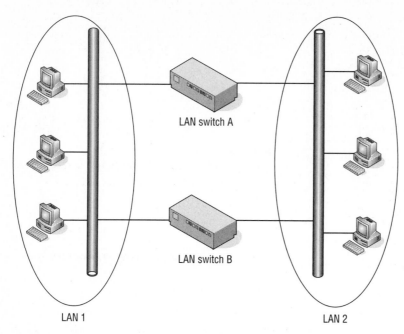

Figure 12-18 A switched network with redundancy

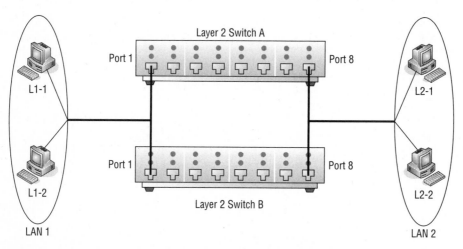

Figure 12-19 A switched network that is vulnerable to a Layer 2 loop

Assume that both switches are aware of all the endpoints. If node L1-1 sends data to node L2-2, that data will be received on port 1 on both switches and will exit out of port 8 on both switches. The data will be sent to the appropriate node, but that node will get two copies of every datagram it receives. Duplication of effort is never desirable[27] and is a big no-no in a LAN.

So, if the redundant solution caused that kind of problem with the unicast traffic, what will happen with multicast traffic?[28] Believe it or not, this is a much bigger problem.

Let's assume that node L1-2 sends out a frame to a multicast address. The frame will be directed to port 1 on both switches. Once received, the frame will be forwarded to port 8 on both switches. This is where it gets fun. We learned that our LAN switch will receive all data received and will forward the multicasts to all other ports except the one it was received on. This means that both switches will receive the frame on port 8 and will forward it to port 1 on both switches. Port 1 will receive the frame, forward it to port 8, and so on. This multicast frame continues in that same loop indefinitely.

> **RANDOM BONUS DEFINITION**
>
> error detection — A procedure used to detect whether received information contains errors.

Pretty bad, isn't it? Now assume something is plugged into every interface on the switch we used in the example, and that every one of them has multiple loops going on. It does not take long for this condition to saturate the bandwidth and overwhelm the resources of the switches involved.

12.5.3.3.1 Darn that Redundancy Anyway

Now that we have determined that a loop is created when a redundant switch is added to the network, we can let you in on a little secret. Redundant switches are not the only thing that might cause a loop within your switched LAN. Here are a few other things that may be the root cause of a loop on the LAN:

- A configuration error within the LAN
- Introducing a duplicate route
- Introducing an additional node into the LAN

LANs can actually become quite complex (if they were not complex from the outset). The more complex a LAN becomes, the more it can create confusion,

---

[27]Remember, your job in designing the network is to ensure performance and reliability. Imagine the extra processing that will occur by not only all of the nodes in the domain, but also the upper-layer tasks that are used.

[28]See if you can answer this yourself before continuing on.

especially if there is incomplete, inaccurate, or missing network documentation. Poor documentation and lack of preparation are leading causes of configuration errors that can lead to a loop in the LAN and can cause disruption in traffic flow, as well as bring portions of the network completely down.

Lack of experience and training is also a problem in many LANs. Sometimes a configuration mistake is made by someone who is not really sure what they are doing.[29] Incorrect provisioning can cause duplicate routes, and duplicate routes can cause loops.

12.5.3.3.2   Loop Resolution

The good news is that there are ways to resolve loops in the LAN and even to prevent them. You can prevent a loop by not making the LAN vulnerable to a loop. In other words, don't do anything that can cause a loop. Although this is the optimal

ACRONYM ALERT

DECnet — Digital Equipment Corporation Network

choice, it really isn't practical in today's LANs.[30] The second option is to implement vendor-specific design solutions that manage and eliminate loops. The problem with this choice is that vendor-specific means vendor-specific.[31] The final option is to implement a protocol designed to control loops in LANs. The *Spanning Tree Protocol* (STP) is just that protocol!

12.5.3.3.3   Spanning Tree

The Spanning Tree Protocol (STP) is based[32] on a protocol that was developed by Digital Equipment Corporation (DEC). Many of DEC's bridges were equipped with their version of the protocol, eradicating loops in the DEC environment. As bridge technology grew, the IEEE eventually set up a task force to develop a public version of this protocol, and STP was born. STP is covered in IEEE 802.1D.

---

[29]When this happens, you can only hope the individual can either fix the issue quickly or be honest about what they did when you are trying to find the solution. Rich and Jim both have network support backgrounds and they can tell stories of troubleshooting issues that would have been resolved a lot faster had the mistake been pointed out early on.

[30]However, it is an open question for some networks where the reliability of data is not the biggest concern. For instance, a mom and pop shop might have a LAN, but really would not suffer if the LAN went down, so the price of redundancy is not worth it.

[31]Although many vendors have proprietary protocols that can interact with another vendor's proprietary protocol, that does not mean they are 100 percent functional in a mixed environment. By implementing a vendor-specific solution, you are effectively tying yourself to that vendor for a while (or will have to wait until the protocol becomes an open standard).

[32]"Based" is the operative word. While the protocols share many similarities, they are not fully interoperable. Therefore, if you are using DEC's version of the protocol, you cannot use the public version in the same network.

Spanning tree[33] uses an algorithm, known as the *spanning tree algorithm*, to make calculations that are used to prevent the dreaded loop. It does this by determining where there are multiple paths to a segment, and then making a calculation that will determine the best bridge to use. Once it determines the best bridge, it will elect that bridge as the *root* bridge. All other bridges in the group will be assigned the title of *designated* bridge when they are participating in forwarding data that the root is sending to a destination. In other words, the designated bridge is the one that is responsible for sending data over the best path. Any bridge that is not the root bridge can be a designated bridge.[34] At the designated-bridge level, there are different port types: the designated port, the root port, and the inactive port. The inactive port can be either a disabled port (a port that is not used) or a port that has been set into a *blocking* status.

Figure 12-20 shows an example of a network containing physical loops (segments A, C, E and segments B, E, D).

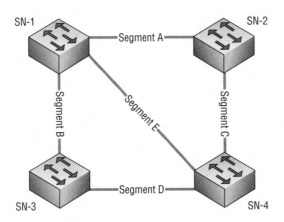

Figure 12-20 A physically looped network

Spanning tree will determine which bridge in the group will be elected to function as the root bridge. The root bridge is always the logical center of the network. The way the root bridge is elected is a process that relies on a data message known as a *bridge protocol data unit* (BPDU).

RANDOM BONUS DEFINITION

globally administered address — A node or interface identifier whose uniqueness is ensured through the use of an assigned organizationally unique identifier (OUI), typically by the manufacturer of the device or interface.

---

[33]A lot of times instead of calling the protocol STP, network professionals just say "spanning tree." We like spanning tree; it flows better.

[34]We should note that as time goes on and changes happen on the network (adding nodes, removing nodes, etc.), each bridge has the potential of being elected as the root bridge at some point in time.

The BPDUs are sent by all the bridges that want to participate[35] in the spanning tree. One of the fields in the BPDU contains the bridge identifier of the sending bridge. Once all BPDUs have been compared, the one with the lowest value will be elected the root bridge. Once the root bridge is selected, designated bridges are used to forward data. The main rule the designated bridge needs to follow is that only one bridge can forward data from the root bridge to the destination nodes. This rule ensures that no loops can occur because only one designated bridge is sending data from the root.

BPDUs are sent by spanning tree nodes to a well-known multicast address. This ensures that everyone in the group will receive the data. Spanning tree will decide which designated bridge it will use to forward a frame and will also decide which designated port to use to forward the data away from the root. Another field that is found in the BPDU is the root path cost. The root path cost is a configurable value that is used to set a priority on a preferred link. The port that is identified as having the lowest path cost will become the designated port and is the port that will be used to forward the frame to its destination. Once the spanning tree has determined the designated port, it will prevent traffic from flowing on other links to that destination by putting the ports on the other links into a *blocking* state.

12.5.3.3.4 Spanning Tree Port States

Every port on a bridge that is participating in spanning tree will have one of five possible *port states* assigned to it. A port state is exactly what it sounds like: it identifies the current state of the port. Each port state is important as it will identify the function the port is performing. These port states are as follows:

- **Disabled** — A port in a disabled state is simply that, disabled. There are many reasons why a port may be disabled. It may be a Physical layer problem, a communication problem, may not be used, etc.

- **Blocking** — A port in a blocking state is an active port that is not being used. Any port that is not a designated port or a root port is going to be in a blocking state. A block port listens for BPDUs to determine if it should become active, but does not participate in frame passing when it is in this state.

- **Listening** — A port in a listening state is not forwarding frames, but is listening to, and sometimes sending, BPDUs.

- **Learning** — A port in a learning state is learning paths to destinations and preparing to forward the frame. This state is used on a port that has not built an address table.[36] A learning port

---

[35] By participate, we mean that the node will use the BPDU to find out about other nodes as well as to receive information that will be used to calculate the spanning tree.

[36] Normally this is due to the port coming up.

will wait a period of time before it starts forwarding frames.[37]
This gives it an opportunity to gather path information.

■ **Forwarding** — This is the port state for the active port that is forwarding frames.

12.5.3.4 Link Aggregation

```
Main Entry: ag·gre·ga·tion (ag-ri-gey-shun)
Function: noun.

1. Several things grouped together or considered as a whole.
2. The act of gathering something together.
```

As networks grow and the end application becomes more complex, there is a real need to increase the capacity of a given link. Link aggregation is a method of increasing the capacity of a channel by allowing multiple physical links to act together as a whole. The parallel links make the endpoint nodes think there is a better performing single channel. Figure 12-21 shows an example of two networks; one is using aggregation and one isn't.

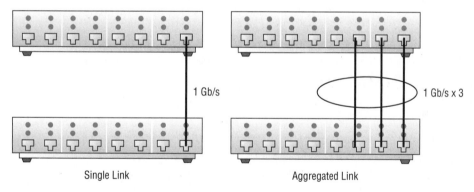

Single Link   Aggregated Link

Figure 12-21 The benefits of link aggregation

The standard that covers link aggregation is IEEE 802.1ad, the Link Aggregation Control Protocol (LACP). Most high-speed LANs can support larger data rates, so it makes sense to use link aggregation. In smaller, lower-speed LANs, aggregation may not make sense due to the restrictions of the environment.[38]

The benefits of link aggregation include:

■ Increased link capacity

■ High link availability

■ Often can be done with existing hardware

---

[37] This is known as "forwarding delay."
[38] Why would you want to aggregate to double your capacity if the network cannot support it?

A few disadvantages of link aggregation include:

- Requires additional interfaces on each end[39]

- Higher potential of configuration errors

- May require device driver updates to ensure compatibility with link aggregation

> **POP QUIZ**
>
> What is forwarding delay?

LACP was introduced in 1999 as a standardized way to aggregate multiple gigabit links in a high-speed LAN. As many LANs already supported some proprietary form of aggregation — for instance, Multi-Link Trunking (MLT) for Nortel and Inter-Switch Link (ISL) trunking for Cisco — for lower-speed networks, it was already well known that these were proprietary and did not work with other vendors' equipment. LACP resolved this for the gigabit world, and things have been growing ever since. Link aggregation has been supported from switch-to-switch, router/server-to-router/server, and switch-to-router/server since it came out, but now many NICs support LACP, allowing aggregation to the end-user level. Although it isn't used everywhere and a lot of LANs still use proprietary standards, we predict that it won't be long for this to be the standard of choice. Of course, at the time of this writing, there are a few proprietary solutions that are under standards review, so who knows what tomorrow will bring?

12.5.3.5 Virtual LANs

Early on in this book, we determined that a LAN is a data network that serves a small geographical area. Most of us think of a group of nodes connected to one another as forming a LAN (in other words, a broadcast domain). Larger organizations have an organizational LAN that is made up of several broadcast domains, the extent of the LAN being the area it covers or a distance-limiting factor. With the LAN, the limits remain for as long as the node exists in the LAN. What we mean by this is that within a LAN, the logical topology is limited to the physical topology as well. Figure 12-22 shows an example of this. You can only adjust those limits by having additional nodes to collect the broadcast domains that may be located within the same area. In addition, a router is required to ensure that broadcast domains are separated, reducing the effectiveness of the router.

---

[39]You may have to buy more equipment, either now or in the future. Not only may you have to purchase more gear now to support this, this also means that you could be consuming empty slots on existing nodes. Although this is great for now, you may have to buy more in the future.

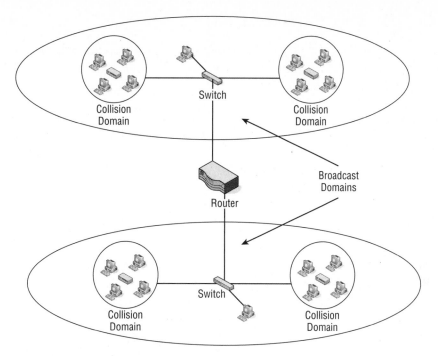

Figure 12-22 A traditional LAN

The virtual LAN (VLAN) was developed to give a LAN bridge the capability to separate these broadcast domains. This not only frees up the router to perform other important functions, but it also allows the network administrator to be flexible in domain configurations. Nodes no longer have to be in the same physical area to participate in a particular broadcast domain. Figure 12-23 shows an example of this. Notice that in each of the VLANs, there are members of each VLAN on each switch. This is a rough example, but the intention is to show that members of VLANs no longer have to be physically together to be in the same broadcast domain.

12.5.3.5.1 Benefits of VLANs

There are a lot of benefits to having VLANs configured in your LAN. Some of these include:

- Better performance. Only VLAN members receive multicasts.
- Members of a group no longer have to physically be located close to the group.
- Administration is easier. Changes to any work area can be done with simple configuration change.

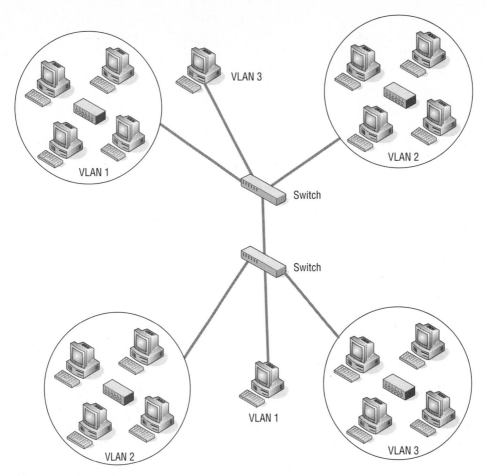

Figure 12-23 A VLAN

- Increased security. Only nodes within a VLAN have access to data.

- No need for a router in order to separate the broadcast domain.

> **RANDOM BONUS DEFINITION**
>
> individual port — A switch port that cannot form an aggregated link with any other port.

12.5.3.5.2   VLAN-Awareness

A node that participates in a VLAN, whether it is a user node or a LAN switch, is known as a *VLAN-aware node/switch*. This simply means that the node is aware of the VLAN rules and is participating in such an environment. VLAN-awareness is the capability to understand that there is an underlying function that allows the mapping of frames to the correct and appropriate destination(s). VLAN-aware switches make forwarding decisions based on the destination address as well as the VLAN to which the frame belongs.

12.5.3.5.3   Tag! You're It!

To determine which VLAN a particular frame is a member of, the VLAN environment uses either implicit tagging or explicit tagging. When the switch receives a frame, it will "tag"[40] the frame with the VLAN identifier where the data came from. This process is known as *explicit tagging* (commonly referred to as *VLAN tagging*, or simply *tagging*). The other type, *implicit tagging*, is a method of mapping an untagged frame to its associated VLAN by inspecting the contents of the frame.

Information that is contained within the explicit tag can be based on MAC address, port, and any other combination of information, but will always contain the VLAN identifier. VLAN tags can be set by a VLAN-aware node, or they can be assigned to a frame when received on a VLAN-aware switch. When a VLAN-aware switch receives an untagged frame, it applies the VLAN mapping rules and forwards the frame with the tagged bit set.

The implicitly tagged frame is a frame that has no tagging at all. Forwarding decisions are made based on the source address, protocol type, network identifiers, etc.[41]

AN UNRELATED MOMENT OF PAUSE — WHAT IS IN THE WORD "TAG"?

In the preceding section, we discussed an implicit tag and an explicit tag. But what other uses are there for the word "tag"? One of the first things that I thought of was the kids' game tag, as in "Tag! You're it!" It wasn't so much me wanting to relive my childhood, but with five kids under my belt, I have spent many weekends playing tag in the backyard.

The next thought when I think of the word "tag" is my two boys, who outgrew tag long ago. Both of them went through a phase where they were constantly squirting Tag body spray on themselves. I thank goodness that the stampede of women you see on the commercials never came charging at the house.

You can call a small label a tag, although I think that "label" is perfectly fine. Tagging a wall means adding your personal graffiti, which some consider art (I have seen some impressive tagging). Your car has a couple of tags on it: a VIN tag, tax tag, license tag, and so on and so forth. There are tags in computer programming, tags on the shelves in the grocery store — as a matter of fact, I don't know that we could get through life without tags. Seriously, try getting through life without seeing that gas is at $4.00 a gallon. Okay, that's a tag we could all do without.

---

[40] A tag is a field inserted into a frame that provides an explicit indication of the VLAN association for that frame.

[41] And any such combination that is predetermined.

12.5.3.5.4   VLAN Types

Membership to a particular VLAN is based on the following criteria:

- **Port-based VLANs** — Port-based VLANs are determined by the ports that are members of a particular VLAN. This is a Layer 1 decision, as no Layer 2 or 3 data is used to make the membership determination.

- **MAC-based VLANs** — MAC-based VLANs are determined by the MAC address of the nodes that are members of the VLAN.

- **Protocol-based VLANs** — Protocol-based VLANs members are determined based on the protocol type in the header of the Layer 2 frame.

- **IP subnet–based VLANs** — IP subnet-based VLAN members are determined by the subnet address contained in the Layer 3 header. This does not mean that a Layer 3 VLAN can route. It cannot. This means there is a Layer 3 subnet address used for the VLAN membership rules.

POP QUIZ

What is implicit tagging?

12.5.4   Determining What Other Determinations Need to Be Determined

This section discusses a few things you should consider in designing a network. Some of the items are good practice talking points and the rest are provided as a vehicle for thought. Some of the determinations are based on decisions particular for your environment. Will you be using SNMP management? Is there a need for secure remote access? How much documentation is appropriate for your network? These are only a few questions that will be answered in this section.

If there is anything missing from this section that you feel is important, blame Rich![42]

12.5.4.1   Talking to a WAN

With any luck, your LAN won't require a connection to a WAN. Individual dialup sessions can be handled by the users on the network, if they require remote connectivity. This is ideal because the number of security issues that you could potentially have is reduced.[43] If this type of LAN works for you, go for it — it will be a gem to maintain in the long run.

---

[42]Just kidding! Jim can't help but give Rich a hard time.

[43]If you are not connected to a WAN, then a hacker has no way in, unless he is already in. The majority of security incidents in corporate LANs can be attributed more to physical (human) carelessness (some examples are losing laptops, leaving areas unsecure, not securing passwords, etc.) than to maliciousness.

The reality is that most of us are going to be working within LANs that do require WAN connectivity, and because of this, there are decisions to be made as to what protocols you want for your LAN-to-WAN connectivity. Examples of options available include:

- Integrated Services Digital Network (ISDN)
- Leased lines
- Synchronous Optical Network (SONET)
- Frame relay
- Asynchronous Transfer Mode (ATM)
- Packet over SONET (POS)
- Point-to-Point Protocol (PPP)
- High-level Data Link Control (HDLC)
- X.25

The protocols and standards used can be determined by you and the service provider. The anticipated bandwidth requirements, type of traffic, costs, and many other items can be (and should be) considered in the

> **POP QUIZ**
>
> What are the four types of VLANs?

decision making. Regardless of the main protocol you choose, it is always a good and effective idea to have a backup plan. For instance, you can use frame relay as a primary method of connecting and have ISDN as a backup. This way, if the frame relay service fails, you can continue to have connectivity.

Connectivity doesn't always stop when you meet the WAN. Often there is a reason for remote offices to connect to the LAN. We have discussed the VPN solution,[44] ISDN, and other services that are in use today. But there are times when you do not need continuous remote access. For instance, a retail store may connect one or two times a day to transmit inventory, sales figures, employee data, etc. In cases like this, a simple dialup connection or satellite link is often used. You and only you can determine what you need.

12.5.4.2 Management and Security

Don't kid yourself. Network security and network management are big business. We will be discussing these topics in later chapters of this book (network security in Chapter 14 and network management in Chapter 15). For the purposes of this chapter, it is important to know a little about both of these as you are determining what other determinations need to be determined.

---

[44]The next best thing to being there!

12.5.4.2.1 Network Security

There is a lot to be said about taking a strong, proactive approach to network security in today's networks. There is a real need to protect the network from not only individuals who are out for a challenge, but also to someone who wants to steal or harm

ACRONYM ALERT

FDDI — Fiber Distributed Data Interface

data in the network. The malicious offender is probably a deeper concern, but either type of security breach can cause harm to the network and to the organization's operation and effectiveness.

Network security is important regardless of whether you are connected to a public network. Without security, your network is vulnerable to an outside (and sometimes even an inside) attack.

Security precautions need to be taken to protect the data that is being transmitted in the network. Here is a list of things to consider:

- Antivirus software is a must for every PC in the network. There are too many viruses and worms that can affect not only that end user's node, but also the entire network. These attacks can be introduced to the network through e-mail, web surfing, and even through a software application loaded from a disk to the end user's nodes.

- A firewall is important, as it will help prevent unauthorized access to the network. Some services that are offered by firewalls are spoofing, encryption and decryption, authentication, filtering, and proxy services. Not all firewalls will offer all of these, so you will need to determine what suits your needs.

- Maintain a strong network authentication procedure. Change passwords often, and control the individuals who can access them.

- Do not discount the importance of physical security. Only authorized individuals should have physical access to network equipment. End users need to understand the importance of not leaving their PCs open and available when they are not at their desks. Passwords need to be protected. Laptops and other mobile gear need to be secure, and users must understand the importance of keeping a good eye on the laptop and the data it contains.

- Utilize network management to keep track of operations within the LAN (more on this in the next section).

Again, we discuss network security further in Chapter 14.

12.5.4.2.2   Network Management

Network management is the process of configuring, monitoring, and maintaining the operations of the entire network. There are two types of network management nodes within a network:

- **Network management agent** — An entity (typically a combination of software and hardware) within a node that is responsible for gathering network management information and reporting it to a network management station as appropriate.

- **Network management station** — A node that communicates with network management agents throughout a network. Typically it comprises a workstation operated by a network administrator, equipped with network management and other relevant applications software.

Security of the network is actually a network management function, but it is such a deep subject that it is often separated from other network management functions. Network management also includes maintaining the reliability of the network as well as keeping track of network overall performance.

We discuss network management in Chapter 15.

12.5.4.3   Choosing Protocols

You have determined what the network will look like and you have also determined the nodes you plan to "roll out." Some of the protocols you will be using in your LAN are determined by

> **POP QUIZ**
>
> What is a network management station?

the types of nodes you have decided on.[45] Some of the major protocols (for instance, RIP vs. OSPF) will be easy to select, just based on the design and the needs of the network. On the other hand, some of the protocols that you will want to implement may be proprietary and not interact well with other protocols. Investigate, test, and then make the determination on what you will implement.

In some cases, the de facto standard may not be the optimum choice, and you may want to implement a protocol based on its current availability. In other words, how widely is it deployed? As we discussed early in this chapter, another rule of thumb is to model your design after another network. Often, you will be able to implement the same protocols.

Complex protocols may have a lot of bells and whistles, but may also be well out of scope for your network. There is a principle in professional communities

---

[45]You would not implement TCP/IP on a Macintosh network.

known as KISS — Keep It Simple, Stupid.[46] Pick your protocols based on need, but follow the KISS principle at all times.

12.5.4.4 *Proactive Thinking*

Throughout the design process, it is important to remain as proactive as possible. Not only do you want to try to figure out traffic patterns and future needs in your design decisions, it is also good to keep in mind that no matter how the network is designed, there will be at least one person at some point who will have a real need to understand the network and whether the performance expectations are being met. Here are a few tips:

- Use the KISS principle as often as possible in everything that you plan for the network. Design the network to be easy to configure, easy to maintain, easy to troubleshoot, easy to replicate, etc.

- Always develop an action plan. Have a logical sequence of steps that you take during the design process and on through implementation (see next chapter). Always have a back-out plan, too. Make sure to leave yourself a way to get things back to where they were working before you tried that last thing.

- Always document everything. Keep a record of IP addressing, node name, protocols running on each slot/port in the LAN, and anything else that you come across that might be important. In some cases, when you can't document, make sure you share. Do not keep node administrative passwords to yourself. Share them with at least one person. The more the network is on paper,[47] the better.

- Following very close to the documentation category, the network diagram is a useful tool to have and keep current. When troubleshooting is necessary, it can save a lot of time if you can point out something that is documented, rather than doing it on the fly.

12.6 Network Implementation

Okay, folks, you have the design of the network determined, you have purchased the equipment, and you have had a test running for several weeks now. Vendors are flying in tomorrow, because it's implementation day! Network implementation is the next stop on the way to the end of this book. We don't know about you, but we can taste that beer already.[48]

---

[46] Although Keep It Simple, Silly, is a bit nicer.
[47] Actually, this will probably be digital, but you get the drift.
[48] That is the beer that we will be drinking when we type the last letter of the book. If you choose to have a beer when you read that last letter, Rich and Jim are hoping that it will be in celebration of a book you enjoyed and not a beer drunk in sadness for the time you wasted. If your opinion is the latter, we hope that those yummy recipes will save us.

In lucky Chapter 13, we will take all the information that you learned in this chapter and put it to use in several different scenarios.

12.7   Chapter Exercises

1. What are the three layers of the hierarchical design model?

2. In this chapter, we listed six benefits of the hierarchical model. List these.

3. This question is actually broken down into questions about the 5-4-3 rule. Refer to Figure 12-24 for these questions.

   (a) Does this network comply with the 5-4-3 rule?

   (b) Identify what A and B represent in the diagram.

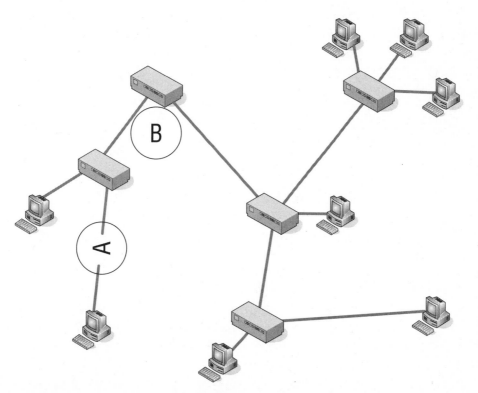

Figure 12-24 An example of the 5-4-3 rule

4. How many possible spanning tree states are there and what are they?

5. In this chapter, we discussed that a spanning tree port can be in a learning state. Why do you think that this is required instead of the port becoming active and just forwarding the frame?

6. A port in a _____ state is one that is _____ paths to destinations and is preparing to forward the frame.

7. What is the purpose of the distribution layer of the hierarchical network?

8. True or false: When the switch receives a frame, it will "tag" the frame with the VLAN identifier from where the data came from. This process is known as implicit tagging.

9. What are the VLAN types we discussed in this chapter?

10. Take a look at Figure 12-25 and then identify the appropriate layer of the hierarchical design model.

The letter A in the example represents the _____ layer.

The letter B in the example represents the _____ layer.

The letter C in the example represents the _____ layer.

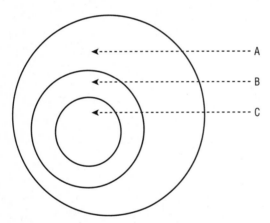

Figure 12-25 The hierarchical model

12.8 Pop Quiz Answers

1. Name five businesses or organizations that are not listed above. What do you think the biggest concern would be pertaining to each organizational LAN type?

   This answer is intended to provoke thought, so there are no right or wrong answers.

2. Define scope.

- The range of one's perceptions, thoughts, or actions
- Breadth or opportunity to function
- The area covered by a given activity or subject

3. Name three WAN technologies that are used to connect to remote sites.

In the chapter, we mentioned frame relay, leased lines, and ISDN. Any protocol or implementation standards used to connect to the remote site are good answers as well.

4. What are the layers of the hierarchical design model?

- Distribution layer
- Core layer
- Access layer

5. What is the purpose of a network's access layer?

This is the layer that interfaces with the endpoint nodes. Types of nodes that are found at this layer are wireless access points, hubs, repeaters, bridges, Layer 3 switches, and routers. The access layer is what allows end users to connect to the network. This layer is also responsible for determining when nodes are not allowed access to certain portions of the network.

6. What is implicit tagging?

Implicit tagging is a method of mapping an untagged frame to its associated VLAN through the inspection of data contained in the frame.

7. What are the four types of VLANs?

- Port-based VLANs
- Protocol-based VLANs
- MAC-based VLANs
- IP subnet–based VLANs

8. What is a network management station?

A network management station is a node that communicates with network management agents throughout a network. Typically it comprises a workstation operated by a network administrator, equipped with network management and other relevant applications software.

9. What is the KISS principle?

Keep It Simple, Stupid

CHAPTER 13

Implementation

First, have a definite, clear, practical idea — a goal, an objective. Second, have the necessary means to achieve your ends — wisdom, money, materials, and methods. Third, adjust all your means to that end.

— Aristotle

Aristotle lived many centuries before the age of computer networking, but his wisdom rings true when it comes to implementing any new network infrastructure. For the most part, organizations have used an evolutionary approach to growing their networks, adding capability when it was needed. As a result, many of today's networks are poorly laid out and maintained, often with little or no documentation.

Many executives like to think of their networks as they do any other utility, such as electrical power, telephone service, etc. There is no mistake about it: corporate networks are part of the ingrained infrastructure in running any type of business.

ACRONYM ALERT

WAN — Wide area network

However, unlike these other utilities, which have large organizations behind them in their support, the network infrastructure is the sole responsibility of the organization that owns it. Unfortunately, they tend to look at it as an overhead function, and when budget cuts are required, it is always the overhead areas that get chopped first. That is all well and good as long as things keep humming along without interruption. But there comes a day when something decides to burp. If there is network equipment stored in accessible closets, you may have the following scenario occur. The janitor thinks he should clean out the back of a closet that has collected a lot of junk along with some portions of the company's network infrastructure. He inadvertently kicks out some cables and plugs them back where he thought they were connected. All of a sudden no one is getting e-mail and the CEO is on the horn trying to find out what is going on. I know this sounds comical and perhaps a bit far-fetched, but we can assure you that it does happen and it can get downright ugly before things are running again.

13.1   Planning

Planning is where you place Aristotle's first line into action: "have a definite, clear, practical idea — a goal, an objective." Good network planning begins with a top-down approach. Today's complex networks evolved from very basic networks and were patched together as more networking capability was needed. This was far from a top-down design. We have seen network installations that would have made Rube Goldberg[1] cringe at the thought of adding his name to its design. Many of these networks became this way primarily by a "if it ain't broke, don't fix it"[2] mentality.

Figure 13-1 illustrates a network planner in the initial planning phase to implement the design approach he decided on using the information provided in Chapter 12 on design methodologies. There is a natural dividing line as far as planning goes;

> **RANDOM BONUS DEFINITION**
>
> 100BASE-TX — A baseband Ethernet system operating at 100 Mbps over two pairs of STP or Category 5 UTP cable.

one side involves a current network infrastructure and the other side a total new design. If this is a totally new design, the planning task only involves how to implement the new network design. If there is a preexisting network, however, several considerations need to be reviewed prior to implementing the new network design. Because the totally new network implementation requires only a subset of a network design that would be required for an older network infrastructure, it will be covered first.

The initial planning phase should consider not only the current network requirements, but also what may be needed in the future, both near-term and long-term. Think of where the growth areas will be and see how that growth can be easily accommodated while growing the network infrastructure in an orderly manner. Remember, you should plan ahead for network growth, rather than cobbling together networking capability as required.

---

[1] Reuben Garret Lucius Goldberg, born July 4, 1883, died December 7, 1970. American cartoonist noted for his cartoons of involved and complex machines, most of them just accomplishing a mundane task in a convoluted manner.

[2] An expression popularized by President Jimmy Carter's advisor Bert Lance.

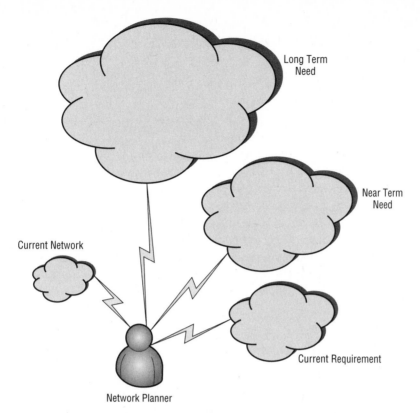

Figure 13-1 The initial planning phase

13.1.1   Totally New Network Planning Phase

As the old saying says, the best-laid plans of mice and men often go awry. The idea is to eliminate as many problems as possible by beginning with a well thought out plan. If you have the opportunity to do a total network design from scratch, there are many variables to consider. The key is to size the network and the network segments so you can meet peak bandwidth requirements without overbuying. Some items involve a recurring cost, whereas others are one-time purchases. Part of the planning entails making appropriate cost estimations. A good place to start is to list both recurring and fixed cost items.

Recurring costs:

- Access fees
- Support contracts (usually billed annually)
- In-house support staff
- Energy needs
- Routine maintenance

One-time costs:

- Hardware
- Cabling
- Initial installation fees

Access fees are the monthly service charges from the telecommunications company for providing access to their network. The rule of thumb is that the more bandwidth required, the higher the cost. Some factors that may help determine which

ACRONYM ALERT

TIA — Telecommunications Industries Association

service to use for access are the services offered and the number of telecommunications companies that are located within the area for your new planned network. If there are multiple telecommunications companies within the area, you should request quotes for the types of services they offer. There may be a one-time installation or hookup fee associated with the service plan you are considering.

13.1.1.1 Initial Planning

The design approach should be completed using a top-down methodology — that is, start with the big picture. However, each phase should entail a document that details what is needed at that level.

We will begin the initial planning phase using a hypothetical[3] example of the Widget Company, which wants to expand their operations west of the Mississippi River. The corporate planners have researched various areas and determined that Denver best suits their needs for their first expansion out of their Midwest region. The first-level network plan may look something like that illustrated in Figure 13-2.

13.1.1.1.1 Office Interconnection Planning

The plan is for a high-speed network between the new West Region office in Denver and the corporate office in Chicago. This is to be a point-to-point connection to provide for the sharing of services located at the corporate offices. The plan entails using a

RANDOM BONUS DEFINITION

application flow — A stream of frames or packets among communicating processes within a set of end nodes.

---

[3]What is being discussed is scalable to any size organization. The required numbers depend on the size of the facility and the number of network users located at this facility.

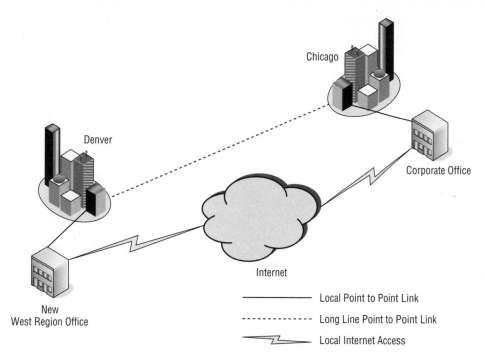

Local Point to Point Link
------------- Long Line Point to Point Link
Local Internet Access

Figure 13-2 The top-level plan for Denver's expansion

carrier to provide those services over its national optical network. However, the plan is to allow the users at the Denver office to also have Internet access locally with a local provider. This Internet access can be used as a redundant path to the corporate office in Chicago, if the need ever arises with a failure in the high-speed optical network. After determining how the offices are to be interconnected, the planning does not end there. Bids will need to be solicited from the optical carriers for services offered and the rate schedule for those services. Also, bids will need to be obtained from local ISPs in the Denver area.

While that bid process is ongoing, other plans can be worked on. You should continue planning both the access to the network from the outside world and the network distribution inside the building. In the Widget Company example, it is determined that a combination server and network services area would also house the access and backbone network distribution equipment. Figure 13-3 illustrates the layout of the combined server and network operations area.

13.1.1.1.2   Network Operations Area

Many companies these days lump computer operations, network operations, and all other telecommunications under the IT (information technology) umbrella. If the company is large enough and the amount of equipment and services offered warrant it, the department could have a number of

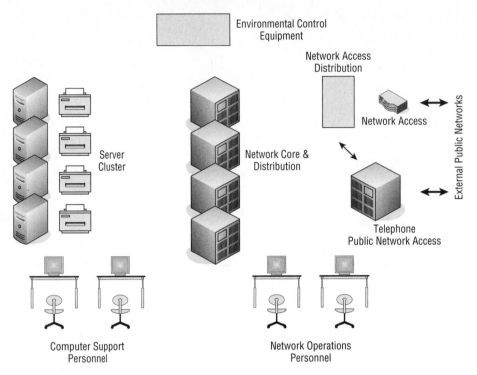

Environmental Control Equipment

Network Access Distribution

Network Access

External Public Networks

Server Cluster

Network Core & Distribution

Network Core & Distribution

Telephone Public Network Access

Computer Support Personnel

Network Operations Personnel

Figure 13-3 The combined server and network operations area

staff to maintain the equipment and support the workforce located at that facility. Sizing and scaling of the support model is proportional; there is no one-size-fits-all approach for each separate installation. Some companies with a corporate office and regional office use a model where much of the IT support is run out of the corporate office, with a smaller staff located at the remote offices performing the hands-on work. Chapter 15 discusses methods of remote network management.

Figure 13-3 shows a single central support area. It is not uncommon to locate core services for IT to save money by not needing more support staff located in different areas of the facility. Once an IT department is set up, the amount of staff required to maintain the on-site equipment and field support calls from the local users for services provided by IT is much lower in the initial implementation phase. If major upgrades to the local network are required, a company can opt to hire contractors or send staff from other locations to assist in the upgrade. Another option is to hire a company to handle the upgrade and pay for the labor that is required directly to that network contractor. Many factors will determine which method would be best, but the overall cost and size are typically the driving forces of the upgrade project. Small upgrades or addition of added network capacity are usually handled by the on-site IT employees.

> **NOTE** On-site IT employee numbers have dwindled due to companies "off-shoring" their support functions. It is a situation that appears monetarily lucrative to those that run the budgets of companies but can be a nightmare at times. Being locally based employees for our entire careers may have jaded us, but it is our opinion that this is a poor way to provide IT services support. It has been our experience that the best run network infrastructures are maintained locally by staff who knew their networks well. It can be difficult for an IT support person on a support call to envision what is going on with a network half a world away. Add to it idiom-based language differences and the frustration level rises to the point of exasperation. The key is knowing what you are paying for when you decide how your IT department is to be staffed.

13.1.1.1.3   Environmental Requirements

There are other considerations to take into account while designing a central area for the computer and network operations for the IT department. One consideration is flooring. There are pros and cons for having a false[4] floor. It can facilitate environmental control of the area by using the space under

ACRONYM ALERT

SPX — Sequenced Packet eXchange

the false floor as the return duct for the HVAC[5] system, and it can be where the power and network cabling can be placed. The major disadvantage is that adding additional cabling at a later date can be difficult since the tiles would need to be lifted to route the cable. A false or raised floor can be more aesthetically appealing than overhead cabling, but it lends itself to an installation that is fairly static. You do not want to use that type of flooring if you anticipate a dynamic work area with many additions and reconfigurations. It is much easier to use overhead cable racks to distribute the network cabling and power buses for the power drops that may be required. These are easily reconfigurable and facilitate changes much more rapidly than routing cables under a floor.

---

[4]A false floor is a raised floor made up of individual panels that are normally two-foot squares. They are laid in over a framework that looks like a giant matrix before the tiles are laid in. Usually, the facility is wired under the flooring before the tiles are placed down.

[5]HVAC stands for heating, ventilation, and air conditioning. When there is a high concentration of computer-related equipment is a fixed area, there is a volume of heat that needs to be dealt with. Most facilities install HVAC systems to control the environment not only for temperature but humidity levels, too. High humidity can cause corrosion, and the last thing you want is something growing on your network connections. Contact corrosion can cause problems that are nasty to diagnose and find.

The environmental control system is usually installed and maintained by an HVAC contractor. However, the sizing of the system requires input from the network planners as to the number of BTUs[6] of heat generated within the area. This will include all the equipment within the area as well as the number of human bodies[7] that will be in the area. The HVAC contractor can use that information to right size[8] the equipment needed, with a fudge factor[9] to compensate for minor growth.

> **RANDOM BONUS DEFINITION**
>
> backoff — The mechanism used in the Ethernet MAC (CSMA/CD) to reschedule a transmission in the event of a collision.

13.1.1.1.4 Network Access Requirements

You may have noticed in Figure 13-3 that the public telephone network access and the network access are in the area dedicated for IT services. It has been decided that this site will use VoIP (Voice over IP) and the telephone sets will be IP-enabled phones. The voice communications will run over the network throughout the facility. So the convergence of the voice and data networks will occur in the IT area. Part of the traffic shaping[10] plan may entail that voice communications between the Denver facility and the Chicago corporate office will go directly from the local phone switch as IP data over the directly connected fiber link.

NOTE The term "convergence" is tossed about heavily in the network world. The simple fact of the matter is, it's becoming an IP world. Any form of data that can be digitized can be transmitted over the network within data packets. However, real-time applications such as voice and video require committed bandwidth rates to guarantee a satisfactory level of service. Humans do not take too well to choppy voice reception or flickering video displays. When planning these services, care must be taken to guarantee the required bandwidth to eliminate these types of issues. Traffic profiling and shaping are essential parts of the planning phase.

---

[6]BTU is the acronym for British Thermal Unit. It is the amount of heat required to heat a pound of water from 60 to 61 degrees while it is sitting at a constant pressure of one atmosphere.

[7]We are talking of live human bodies here. Live bodies generate heat and expel moisture as they breathe. Dead human bodies neither breathe nor generate heat so they need not be counted, but we would not want them around too long either. So although many employers like to work their employees to death, they prefer you to do your dying on your own time.

[8]"Right size" has come to mean many things these days. It usually refers to getting the size right for a particular need. However, it has been hijacked by corporate management as a term to replace "layoff."

[9]"Fudge factor" is a term used to suggest that a number has been tampered with. Here it is used to mean that additional capacity for HVAC equipment is "upped" to compensate for possible future growth.

[10]Traffic shaping is the ability to direct network traffic over segments of a network, depending on bandwidth availability and other policies enforced on the network by the IT staff.

Part of the planning phase is determining levels of access to the network. If it is decided that there will be services available from the Internet, strong consideration needs to go into designing firewalls and DMZ[11] zones. You may want to segment

your network to easily facilitate these DMZ areas. There may be other firewalls that police the traffic flow to and from the network at large. Whenever a network ties into the Internet, there should be a firewall between it and the first router on the Internet. This is to prevent unwanted and unsolicited traffic[12] from finding its way into the local network. A preliminary plan may be similar to that illustrated in Figure 13-4.

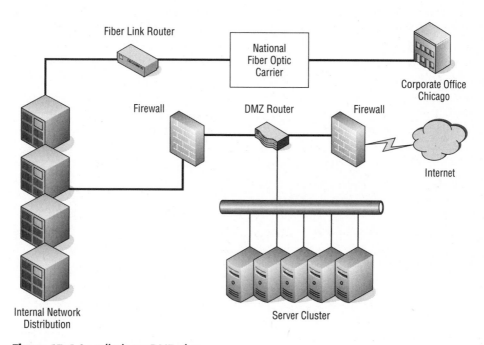

Figure 13-4 A preliminary DMZ plan

[11]DMZ is the acronym for demilitarized zone. It has been adopted by the networking world to mean an area that is not directly connected to any other network segment. It is policed by firewall devices with access policies to prevent a security breach of the network. More on this subject can be found in Chapter 14, "Network Security."

[12]Unsolicited network traffic refers to network traffic originated elsewhere over the Internet that has not been asked for. It may be a possible hack attempt. This type of traffic is generally discarded and not allowed into the network. However, if the location is providing services such as web or FTP to the outside world, the unsolicited network traffic must be allowed through to those services. That is the reason they need to be located within the DMZ.

As mentioned previously, the Chicago corporate office is connected to the Denver office via a fiber link by a service provided by a national fiber carrier. There is no need for a firewall because the two connected net-

RANDOM BONUS DEFINITION

bridge — A networking node that relays frames among its ports based upon Data Link layer information.

works have been secured at both ends of the link. However, since there is another, unsecured path to the Internet, there is a need for a DMZ between the private network and the Internet. You will notice that the DMZ is portioned off with firewalls on both sides that allow for traffic policies to police the traffic flow into and through the DMZ. Policies should be in place to allow users out on the Internet to access services being served by the server cluster in the DMZ. The additional firewall before traffic reaches the internal private network is in place to prevent the possibility of one of the servers being compromised from the Internet and then used for a possible breach of the internal private network. Traffic pattern flow will only allow traffic from the Internet to reach the server cluster and prevent it from accessing the internal private network. Any unsolicited traffic that is originated before the firewall guarding the internal private network will be dropped and not permitted to pass beyond the firewall into the internal private network. Policies have been placed on both firewalls to allow users on the internal private network to access both the server cluster and the Internet since they are originating the network connection.

13.1.1.1.5 Remote User Access

If remote company users need to access the resources on the internal private network, you should consider using a VPN router to allow access through the firewalls. Figure 13-5 shows a typical topology.

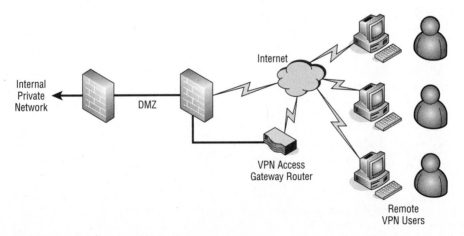

Figure 13-5 A VPN gateway for remote access

The VPN remote users have a VPN client on their PCs that is configured to access the company's VPN access gateway router to permit these users access to the private network and the services that are available to them, as determined by the policies placed

ACRONYM ALERT

RARP — Reverse Address Resolution Protocol

on their user IDs. Companies can restrict the services available to these remote users on an individual basis or group basis. Users are authenticated when they access the VPN access gateway router. Chapter 14 discusses authentication and encryption of VPN connections in greater detail. If users are unable to be authenticated due to invalid credentials, they are not able to gain access to the internal private network. Once users are authenticated, their client is assigned an IP address that is routable through the DMZ firewalls into the internal private network. All policies regarding remote user VPN access must be in place to permit traffic from these users to reach the private network.

Now that we have covered the access to the corporate offices and Internet access for the company-based users, as well as remote users able to log in to the facility in Denver, we are ready to discuss the network distribution within the Denver facility. The Denver facility is a new, four-story building. Users have jacks at their desks to accommodate computer access as well jacks for IP-enabled telephones. To ensure worker productivity, provisions are to be made to let them keep working through minor network failures. The idea is to have redundancy for both the IP phone and the computer network access. Each desk position throughout the facility is to have four Ethernet jack outlet boxes next to it. Figure 13-6 illustrates the Ethernet jack outlet, with two network designations assigned to each pair of jacks.

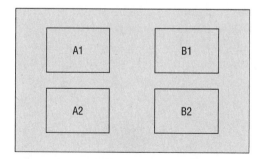

Figure 13-6 The Ethernet jack outlet

13.1.1.1.6   Network Distribution

There are two designations for the networks to be used: A and B. The jacks for each network are labeled 1 and 2. Both the A and B networks are "live" at all times and can be used for load balancing within the network. In the event of a network failure, they can provide a means of network redundancy. This will allow users on the failed network to switch to the

> **RANDOM BONUS DEFINITION**
>
> browser — An application program that provides a graphical user interface to Internet.

remaining operational network if needed. The plan is to have users connect one device (such as their PC) to the A network and the other device (such as an IP-enabled telephone) to the B network. This is just an example of a possible scheme to allow for redundancy and network traffic management. There are a variety of methods to accomplish this and the considerations are primarily cost-based. There is a fine line between true redundancy and overkill. Once it is determined how each desk position on each floor is to be wired, we can consider how the distribution is to be made from the network operations area to the wiring closets on each floor. Each wiring closet is to have two switches that are capable of dividing the local network on a particular floor of the building into separate virtual LANs (VLANs) One switch will be assigned to the A network, and the other will be assigned to the B network. This is illustrated in Figure 13-7.

13.1.1.1.7 Network Backbone Distribution

The distribution of the network backbone from the network operations area to each floor is accomplished using a fiber-optic link to provide a high-speed path for the network traffic coming from each floor. Although the fiber-optic link is illustrated as being daisy-chained from a switch on one floor to another switch on another floor, this does not necessarily have to be the case. The switches more than likely do have that capability and daisy-chaining would certainly reduce the number of fiber optic runs in the wiring closets, but a break in any link can potentially affect more than one floor. Another consideration would be to run direct links from each switch in each of the wiring closets to the switched backbone[13] in the network operations area. The wiring to each floor is Category 5 Ethernet cabling. Usually the cabling runs back to the wiring closet, where it is terminated on a patch panel. This permits easy reconfiguration of network jacks to the network node terminating devices in the wiring closet. Figure 13-8 illustrates the distribution of the Ethernet cabling out from the wiring closet to the devices connected to each network node on the floor.

---

[13]Backbone refers to the distribution of the network out from the core. However, in the day of the multiswitch switched network core, it is difficult to see a "backbone" structure per se. The term today refers to the central distribution out from the core, so a network could have a bunch of backbones.

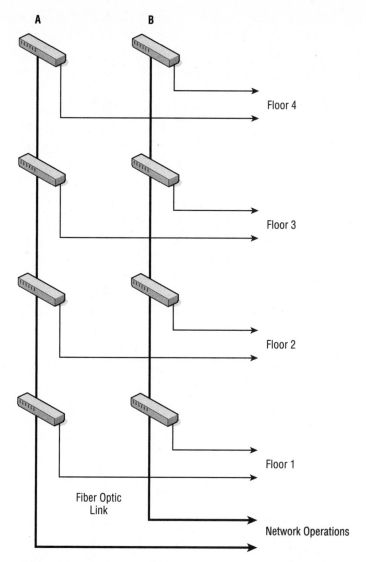

Figure 13-7 The network distribution on separate floors

After being terminated to the patch panel, the network nodes on the floor are connected using patch cables between the RJ-45 Ethernet jacks on the patch panel and the appropriate RJ-45 network jack on one of the network switches located in the wiring closet. Since this is a new installation, it is expected that the wiring closet

ACRONYM ALERT

NOS — Network operating system

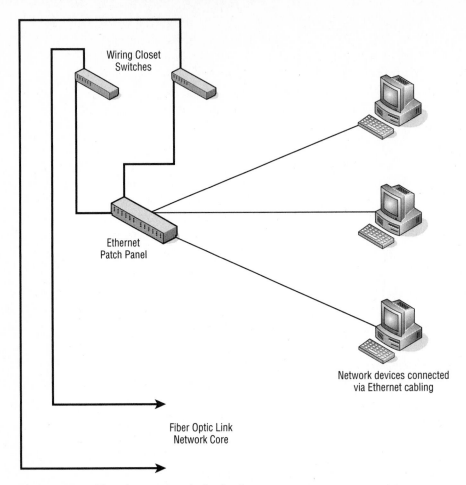

Figure 13-8 Wiring closet network distribution

will be orderly and cables secured and off the floor.[14] Ethernet cables can be bundled and tie-wrapped[15] if needed.

13.1.1.1.8 Wireless Access

So far all the networking that has been discussed is of the wired variety. However, having some wireless network access may be desirable for transient users who may visit the facility and want to use their wireless-enabled laptops.

---

[14]We have seen wiring closet floors with network cable just strewn all over the place and draped onto the floor. The only way to work on anything was to actually walk on the cables. We highly recommend against this type of wiring system. The chances of intermittent and broken connections are tremendous.

[15]Tie wraps are those plastic straps that are ratcheted when pulled tight. They come in various grades, from very small to fairly thick, and various lengths. They are found in many cabling areas and can be easily cut to reconfigure a cable.

The wireless network is capable of being isolated from the wired network and it may not be desirable to have these users plug into the main network. This will minimize the possibility of a virus-infected laptop spreading a harmful virus to the main network. For this installation, you may want to consider a visitors' area, but only allow visiting users access to the Internet, not to other internal network resources. This can be accomplished as illustrated in Figure 13-9.

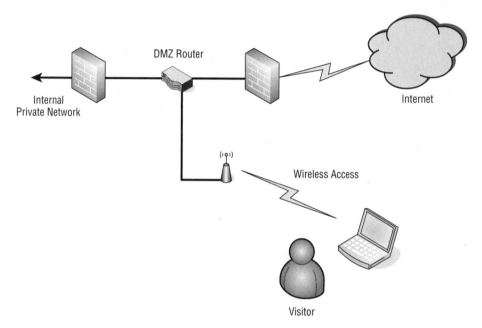

DMZ Router

Internal Private Network

Internet

Wireless Access

Visitor

Figure 13-9 Wireless network access

In this figure, the access point from the visitors' area is routed directly to the router located in the DMZ area. Internet access is allowed as a courtesy to visitors to the Denver facility. The reason for the wireless access point

RANDOM BONUS DEFINITION

collision fragment — The portion of an Ethernet frame that results from a collision.

being wired into the DMZ and not somewhere on the private network is that it could constitute a breach of the private network's security. With the policies on both firewalls, users in the visitors' area are allowed Internet access but are prevented from penetrating the firewall from the DMZ into the private network. Employees from the corporate office visiting the Denver facility will be allowed to connect their laptops to the network from a secured area. Many companies provide "drop in" offices for such visiting employees so that can have access to resources on the private network.

We have now performed the initial planning of the network's design. You have an idea of the overall scope of the project. The project continuously gets refined and developed until the final plan is completed. Each phase through the planning stage must be well documented, and revision control is essential to minimize confusion as the implementation is being rolled out.

13.1.1.2 Finalizing the Plan

The initial planning documentation describes the equipment used and where it should be placed within the facility. Once that has been determined, it is time to lay out the network in regard to addressing and segmentation. We will lay out the VLANs and other subnet segments to be used in various areas of the facility. This is the most critical part of the documentation since it will have major impact on the network's operation and performance.

This example uses the network space 192.168.X.X to define the network. The initial plan of the network layout used IP addressing to specify various segments of the network. An addressing scheme has been devised that uses the third octet of the IP address space to indicate a particular routing switch on any particular floor. Table 13-1 illustrates the IP addressing scheme that is to be used in this network.

Table 13-1 IP Addressing Scheme

FLOOR	SWITCH A	SWITCH B
1	192.168.10.X	192.168.11.X
2	192.168.20.X	192.168.21.X
3	192.168.30.X	192.168.31.X
4	192.168.40.X	192.168.41.X

The tens column indicates the floor, 0 indicates the A switch, and 1 indicates the B switch. This is just an example of how with private IP address space addressing you can parse your network where an IP address can be used as an immediate indicator where traffic may be originating from. Can you think of any advantage of doing something like this?

The first thing that should come to mind is the ability to quickly find a problem just by the IP address of the traffic that is being generated. If there is congestion in the network and a flood of packets are coming from a particular network segment, it can

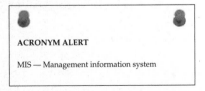

ACRONYM ALERT

MIS — Management information system

be quickly determined by the IP address's third octet. Knowing where the

IP traffic is being originated will aid in rapidly isolating broadcast storms or denial-of-service (DoS) attacks. So careful planning and layout can not only aid with performance, it can also help to troubleshoot network problems.

The final plan should include:

- Complete network diagrams, including IP addresses
- Equipment lists, including their location
- Descriptions of each type of network equipment
- Troubleshooting guides for each type of network equipment
- Lists containing support information for each manufacturer of the network equipment
- A collection location for all warranty statements for all new equipment deployed
- A collection location for all support contracts from the original equipment or other third-party support organizations
- A collection location for all equipment manuals for the network equipment
- Wiring diagrams for each panel deployed about the network
- A collection location for the information dealing with Internet service providers and other telecommunications providers, including data and voice
- A collection location for all license keys that may be required for any of the equipment in the network
- Maintenance/trouble log[16] (used for ongoing support)
- A collection location of all contact information for all staff responsible for the maintenance of the network

The network described in this chapter would have a large amount of documentation associated with it. It may be worthwhile to set aside a portion of the network operations area as a library to collect the hard copy[17] documents as well as files where other information can be kept. The list of finalized documentation is fairly complete, but is not to be construed as everything that needs to be maintained as part of the documentation. Some equipment may come with physical keys, and these too should be collected in an area

---

[16]A maintenance/trouble log can have various forms. It can be a notebook where trouble events are written or it can be a computerized form. A wide variety of software is available for trouble tracking as part of the IT process.

[17]Hard copy refers to documentation in printed form. Many manufacturers are opting for documentation on CD due to the cost of print media. Whatever form the documentation for the equipment is in, it should be properly stored and filed. An index indicating the documentation that is available and its location is extremely helpful.

where documents are safeguarded, cataloged, and under distribution control, noting where each key is used and what equipment it is used with. The documentation and keys (both software-based and physical) should be kept and cataloged where all network support staff can easily find them.

13.1.2 Network Revision Planning

It was said earlier that planning a network upgrade to an existing network is similar to planning the implementation of a complete brand new network. The major difference is keeping portions of the network running and trouble-free while making changes in order to not affect the operation of the company's business. Usually this is accomplished by building a network segment in parallel and verifying its operation prior to making the cutover to the new network segment. Typically, cutovers are planned during off hours. However, if a company is a 24/7 operation, a maintenance window needs to be scheduled for the cutover.

The following sections review just a few of the possible types of network upgrades or expansions that are typically[18] performed. We will primarily discuss access changes, internal network upgrades, and expansions.

> **RANDOM BONUS DEFINITION**
>
> connection-oriented — A communications model in which stations establish a connection before transmitting data

13.1.2.1 Reworking Network Access

What is involved in a change in network access? Primarily, it is the type of pipe[19] coming from the outside. However, when there is a transition in service, there is also a change in the access equipment to accommodate that type of service. This discussion

> **ACRONYM ALERT**
>
> FS — Frame status

uses as an example a small company that currently has Internet services coming in on an ISDN service from the local telecommunications company. The company wants to upgrade to accommodate the increase in Internet traffic required to keep the business growing. Just as you would do in the case of a new installation, they will poll their local telecommunications providers to find a service that fits both their needs and their budget. After a thorough

---

[18]One could argue that there is no typical network upgrade or expansion and we would have to concur. Many variables are involved, so no two upgrades will be exactly alike. However, the planning will be similar.

[19]A pipe is the type of service that is being provided. It could be DSL, cable, T1, fiber optic, etc. It is the carrier that brings the Internet and other telecommunications services to your doorstep.

investigation, the company's IT department settles on a fiber service from the same telecommunications provider they have their ISDN service with. Figure 13-10 illustrates the setup in preparation for the cutover from an ISDN service to a fiber optic service from the same telecommunications provider.

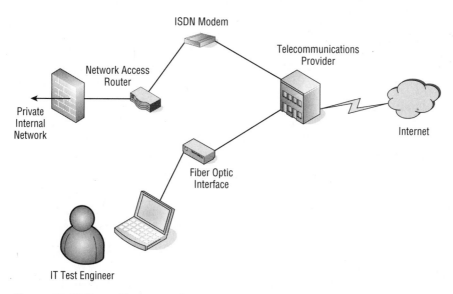

Figure 13-10 Reworking network access

Plans are made to have the telecommunications company bring the fiber cable to the premises of the company while leaving the ISDN service in place. Usually the new service installation includes cabling and the fiber optic interface to convert the fiber signal to Ethernet-compatible signals. Figure 13-10 illustrates that the telecommunications provider has performed its portion of the upgrade of the service. However, instead of cutting over the service on the same day it is delivered and set up, the IT staff wants to first test the reliability of the service provided by the telecommunications provider.

The IT test engineer has connected a crossover cable between his laptop and the Ethernet interface on the fiber optic interface unit. From his laptop, he is able to run a series of tests to verify the operation of the link. He can run burst tests[20] to verify the data throughput of the circuit. Once the IT staff is satisfied that the new access circuit is functioning as expected, they schedule a maintenance window for the circuit cutover. For the scenario of just changing over the service, the cutover is very fast because it only entails removing the Ethernet cable from the network access router to the ISDN modem and connecting it to the fiber optic interface unit.

---

[20]Burst testing is a method of testing the overall throughput of a network link. It generally refers to the ability to generate enough network traffic to stress the link to its maximum bandwidth capability.

Consider a scenario where the company wants to have a redundant access service to the telecommunications provider in case there is a failure of the fiber optic access link. The plan is to keep the ISDN service as a dial-on-demand service. The ISDN service will only attempt to connect to the telecommunications provider's network if it receives traffic on its Ethernet interface. In this type of upgrade, the network access router may have to be either upgraded for an additional Ethernet interface or replaced with a new router. If the router is being replaced, it could be connected to the fiber optic interface and the IT test engineer could run his tests through the router and out over the fiber optic link. The IT engineer can test the routing through the new network by placing a network device on the interface that is to be used to connect the ISDN modem. With the routing policy set as having the preferred route set to the link with the fiber optic interface, a test can be made to see if the secondary route to the ISDN modem takes over routing traffic when the link to the fiber optic interface is disconnected. A secondary test would be to see if the routing will revert back to the primary link with the fiber optic interface when the link has been restored to operation.

After the operation of the equipment and the new fiber optic link have been tested, a maintenance window should be scheduled for the cutover to the new link and network access router configuration.

> **RANDOM BONUS DEFINITION**
>
> cut-through — A mode of switch operation where frames can be forwarded before they are fully received.

13.1.2.2 Upgrading a Network's Core Routers

Changing over the central core routers of a network is a major undertaking. It requires careful planning and implementation that are as thorough as if these were the initial core routers for the network. The criticality of the situation is that you are taking down a working network for an upgrade.

Planning should include designing the new core, documenting the new installation, obtaining the equipment, installing the equipment and bringing it up as a standalone core routing network, and testing it fully to ensure operation before cutting over from the old routing core to the upgraded one. The timetable for this type of upgrade depends on the complexity of the routing core. The size of the core and the number of network nodes involved will determine the amount of time required for the cutover.

Many times when there is a major change in the core routing network, a company may decide to upgrade the entire network behind it. It may involve not only network node devices but all new cabling as well. Many older installations were wired with older Category 3 cabling. With a major upgrade, the decision may be to upgrade the whole network, including wiring and Ethernet jacks.

13.1.2.3 Upgrading the Network's Distribution Components

The network distribution system can include older cabling, Ethernet jacks, and network node devices, such as Ethernet switches and hubs. Usually the upgrade of the network distribution components is not a major impact on the current network

ACRONYM ALERT

IPX — Internetwork Packet eXchange

operations, as a new network distribution fabric[21] can be installed in parallel. This is same process that can be used for an expansion of the network distribution system.

New cabling can be distributed into the areas where the network is either to be expanded or upgraded. With the cabling in place, the Ethernet jacks can be wired in place. Once all the cables are punched down[22] on the patch panel, each run can be tested using Ethernet cable testing tools. With new switches[23] in place in the wiring closet, the patch cables can be placed between them and the patch panel. New cabling, either wire or fiber optic, can be used to terminate each switch back to the network operations area. It, too, will need to be routed over the cable ways between the wiring closet and the network backbone or routing core.

If this process is an upgrade and not a network expansion, it can be done in parallel and users' Ethernet jacks can be moved over to the new network if the IP addressing scheme allows it. To have two parallel networks running and move users from one network to another requires proper routing, as duplicate network addresses would cause routing issues. Planning and documenting the IP addressing scheme is essential to avoid those types of issues.

13.2 Network Supporting Infrastructure

Infrastructure refers to the structural components within a facility in support of the network architecture. Modern buildings make provision for cable ways[24] between floors and from one

RANDOM BONUS DEFINITION

StarLAN — A name for nodes using 1BASE5 Ethernet.

---

[21]The term "fabric" usually refers to the threads of the network that are woven to allow network nodes to be connected into the network. It is at times synonymous with the idea of a woven web, especially when full redundancy is employed.

[22]The term "punched down" refers to the tool used to push the individual wires of the Ethernet cable.

[23]Many times upgrades include new equipment. New switches can replace hubs or older, less-capable switches. For this example, we are using new switches that have been placed in the wiring closet of the area undergoing the network upgrade.

[24]Cable ways is a generic term used to indicate structural devices connected to the walls, floors, and ceiling of a facility to accommodate the orderly distribution of cabling. The amount of cabling that will be supported by a particular cable way will determine its structural strength.

end of a building to another. Cable ways can be seen passing through walls and can be found above false ceilings. Wiring closets are in areas where there are cable ducts to allow the routing of cabling between floors. A wiring closet may have an overhead cable way that looks like a ladder. Cables are routed over the cable way and can be dropped down between the rungs to various areas in the wiring closet.

The network operations area is also part of the facility's infrastructure. Adequate space needs to be set aside for the area, as outlined in the initial planning phase. Another consideration for the network operations area within a facility is security on the physical level. Access to the network operations area should be limited to IT staff to prevent inadvertent disruption of network operation by people who are not responsible for keeping the network operational. This limited access should be not only in the networks operation area but throughout the facility, including the wiring closets and other areas used in support of the network, These areas should be secured behind locked doors.

Infrastructure planning is a process that needs to be done in cooperation between the IT staff and the facility's management team. It is not only about floor space but also includes utilities such as electrical and the HVAC support staff. Network planning and implementation requires the cooperation of many departments along with the IT department.

13.3   Budgeting

Budgeting is an important part of the implementation phase. The company must have the financial resources to pay for a new computer network or an upgrade to an existing network. The initial planning phase perhaps does not need to have the financial numbers up front when the initial plan is kicked off. The initial plan takes a directive on what is needed and starts from there. The IT staff can plan the network and list out the equipment required to complete the task. From that they can get cost estimates to feed into the accounting numbers to see if it is possible to fund the project. The idea is to have as precise as a number as possible so that the budgeting is fairly accurate to prevent coming in grossly over budget. Coming under budget is never an issue; however, coming in over budget could cost someone his or her job.

If the project is large and the burden on the budget is excessive, then in cooperation with financial personnel a new budget can be devised to perform the new network implementation in phases. This will spread the load over several budget periods until the full implementation can be completed.

ACRONYM ALERT

DRP — DECnet Routing Protocol

This is related more for upgrades, because a company would not undertake the design of a new facility and not budget for completion of the facility. The project would not be started for a new facility if the company only had the resources to build only the shell of a building. Companies plan new facilities to allow employees to move in and be productive immediately after project completion

However, upgrading older networks in existing facilities can be done on a piecemeal basis. This will allow for budgeting of the upgrade over several accounting periods, thus easing the financial burden. It would take the following considerations, in order: required infrastructure upgrades, improvement of network access to the outside world, core routing on the backbone, and lastly, the network distribution to the devices that are to be connected to the network throughout the facility. Without an allocated budget a network project is unfunded and possibly would only remain in the planning stage.

13.4 Staging

Staging is the period of time between the final planning phase and when the project begins to get under way. The vendor bidding has been completed during the planning stages and the purchase orders begin to flow out to obtain the needed equipment, infrastructure upgrades, and other contracted network services.

If upgrades are required for infrastructure improvements, they must be completed before the project can move along. Having a set timetable and attempting to stick to it allows for each phase of the overall project to meld into the next phase. If one phase falls behind, the timing for the whole project can be jeopardized. Some portions of the project can be worked in parallel, but infrastructure improvement is not one of them (unless there are separate areas requiring infrastructure improvement, which would allow one area to be completed while another area is being upgraded). If an area requiring infrastructure improvement has not been completed, no other network upgrade activity can take place in that area until the infrastructure improvement has been completed.

Most companies do not maintain construction crews for infrastructure upgrades. These types of improvements are usually completed by subcontractors working under the direction of the company's facility management personnel. Electrical wiring, data cabling, and improvements to HVAC in most cases will be bid out to subcontractors. Contractors winning the bids will need to be under signed contract and have their progress monitored to ensure satisfactory completion of the project.

While the improvement of the network's infrastructure is ongoing, equipment that has been ordered will begin to trickle in. It is best to unpack each box and verify that the

RANDOM BONUS DEFINITION

sniffer — Also known as a protocol analyzer.

piece of equipment is exactly what has been ordered and is fully functional. This may require powering the unit and testing it in some manner. The type of device will dictate the type of testing that can be completed without it being placed within a network. At the least, the unit should be able to link to another network device. In many instances it is not likely that full functionality of the device can be tested as part of a bench test. However, bench testing will help eliminate DOA[25] devices or devices that suffer an infant mortality.[26] If the piece of equipment is unable to be placed within its location, then it can be reboxed and placed in storage until the location is clear for its installation. Pre-testing the equipment will minimize the number of surprises you will encounter. Once the network equipment has been received and the infrastructure improvements have been completed, it is time to move on to the next implementation stage: rolling out the network upgrade.

13.5   Rollout

Rollouts are usually synonymous with network upgrades or expansions. They do not apply to a completely new network in a brand new facility. Although some of the stages are similar, no special considerations are required to work around other company personnel with the possibility of causing network outages, as there is with a network upgrade. With an upgrade of a network in an older facility, where there are company personnel who can be affected, some extra planning is required. Such planning should be performed in conjunction with those who would to be affected to minimize the loss of productivity due to the network upgrade. Much of the network upgrade can happen in the background and in areas where other personnel are unaffected. However, in the areas where personnel are affected, it is best to work out a maintenance window to complete the work. If a work area has daily down time after a shift, this work can be completed in the after-hours time periods.

If a whole network is to be upgraded, the network access and core routing areas, along with wiring closet and network distribution equipment, can be upgraded without interfering directly with company personnel. Of course, cutovers of certain

ACRONYM ALERT

CoS — Class of service

network components can and will affect the whole facility, or at least large portions of the network, but do not require the direct interaction with other company personnel. For those types of cutovers, a maintenance window

---

[25]DOA is dead on arrival. Usually this means the unit did not power on when pulled from the box or perhaps it failed its own self-diagnostic.

[26]Infant mortality is a morbid term and one we prefer not to use. However, it is prevalent in the industry, used to describe a failure of a device shortly after it has been received and powered on.

should be scheduled to be as nonintrusive as possible. Proper notification should be sent out to the whole facility or to those personnel who are to be affected and who will be left without some or all network resources during that period of time.

There are times when a rollout may not go smoothly and either has to delayed and rescheduled or if started, may need to be rolled back due to some impasse that was reached during the maintenance window. Therefore, not only is a careful initial plan required for the rollout but also a contingency plan with a "what-if"[27] clause to deal with all possible combination of events that could occur while the rollout is going on. Plan for the worst-case scenario and you will be covered. Remember, there are always alligators in the swamp, so be prepared to drain the swamp before proceeding and the alligators will have no place to hide.

13.6 Verification

> *Whatever can go wrong, will go wrong.*
> — Murphy's Law[28]

Verification is a kind of nebulous state throughout any network implementation. It is the work done to eliminate as much of Murphy's Law as possible throughout the whole project. As carefully designed as a plan may be, there is always a chance something can go wrong. However, with the proper preparation, these events can be neutralized and dealt with quickly and efficiently.

The verification process should start at the earliest stages of the project. In the early planning stages, you should verify the concepts that are to be implemented into the network design. You should also verify any new products as far as suitability for use within the design. Many times vendors of networking equipment and systems will provide loaners so that their customers can verify a network concept. Part of the evaluation may be a "bake off" between vendors to verify which manufacturer's device or system offers better performance and maintainability.[29]

---

[27] A "what-if" is a decision tree element in a flow chart. A rollout plan can be flowcharted to help you see the possibilities that can occur while the rollout phase is ongoing.

[28] Sometimes attributed to Capt. Edward A. Murphy, Jr., an engineer working on the Air Force MX981 project in 1949 who was testing how much deceleration a human can withstand in a crash.

[29] Maintainability is the state of being able to maintain a piece of equipment while it is installed within the network. Things that may be considered include whether the user interface is easy to use and intuitive or if there are things like air filters that need to be replaced at a certain interval. Other considerations include whether the device has built-in redundancy.

Verification should be performed on every aspect that contributes to the overall success of the project. Have the improvements to the infrastructure been completed and done satisfactorily? Usually this is accomplished with a visual inspection and walkthrough with the contractors who performed the work.

RANDOM BONUS DEFINITION

protocol analyzer — Also known as a sniffer, it can perform packet captures, allowing the datagram to be analyzed. Some of the information that can be seen with this device are source and destination addresses, encapsulation, protocol, and data payload, as well if whether it is a whole packet or a fragment of a larger packet.

In the budgeting phase, after a dollar amount has been approved, there is verification that prices quoted in the planning phases are still valid and that billing for received materials and services is correct and within the set budget. Remember, under budget is good and over budget is bad. If price breaks have been given due to a discount for quantity or a new pricing structure from a vendor, then you are good to go. However, if a situation arises when the cost of the project is going to increase, it is best to put on the brakes and verify why there is a cost increase. You may need to get the financial powers-that-be to buy into the cost increase before proceeding any further with the project.

With the design and budget verified, it is time for the materials and services for which purchase orders have been issued to begin to flow in. We already took care of the infrastructure, so the primary concern is that the correct equipment is being received,

ACRONYM ALERT

CAM — Content-addressable memory

and if installation services also have been contracted, such as power and data cabling, that the work is being performed on time and as expected. Equipment should be logged in as it is received with the recording of dates, time, model, and serial numbers. Many manufacturers provide warranties for their equipment, but it is up to the customer to provide such information to receive warranty service from them.

During the rollout, there needs to be continued verification of where equipment is to be placed and interconnected with the remainder of the network. It is critical that network addresses are programmed correctly and that the equipment is placed in a subnet address it was planned to be placed in. Once the equipment is in place, performance checks should be made to verify the equipment's operation within the network. Normally verification to the end Ethernet jack in any network segment has been verified by the contractors who performed the data cabling. However, verification for end-user performance is normally performed by the IT staff, either in a proactive manner with a new network rollout or in a passive manner.

> **NOTE** A "proactive manner" is one where the IT staff actually asks the end user if everything is working satisfactorily. This can include testing the end user applications that require network interaction.
>
> A "passive manner" is one in which the IT staff performs the rollout of the network project and then sits back and waits for end-user complaints to find the problem areas of the rollout. If there is insufficient staff to perform a full proactive verification of the network, it behooves the IT staff to be selective with whom they verify network operation in a more proactive manner.

There is constant verification of the documentation every time it is used or reviewed for any reason. If there is something that does not appear correct, mark the document and verify if it is correct and how it was intended

RANDOM BONUS DEFINITION

root bridge — The STP bridge with the numerically lowest bridge identifier.

during the planning phase. It is not unusual for there to be minor changes that need to be recorded as the network project implementation is being performed. There may be changes in network addressing, configuration changes performed on equipment, and equipment being replaced. Replacement of pieces of equipment that have not failed is rare; however, there may be times when the equipment does not have a capability that is now required within the network. There needs to be a constant update of any changes within the documentation as the project is going on in order to capture the true state of the network in the event that it varies in any manner from the blueprint that was laid out in the planning phases.

13.7   Documentation

There is nothing more exasperating to any support person than when someone calls seeking help with their network issue but knows squat about it. Okay, perhaps we are being a little harsh here, and you may have inherited a bag of doo-doo from the person

ACRONYM ALERT

ASIC — Application-specific integrated circuit

who had previously held the position you currently hold, but that excuse still sounds pretty lame to the support person on the other end of the support call. The support person is more than willing to work with you, but please provide them with something they can go on. Just because you have a support contract with the vendor does not mean they know everything about how the device is situated in your network.

There are no excuses whatsoever for inadequate documentation if you were present for the implementation of the network project. Unless the network is very static and did not change, the documentation collected and assembled during the various phases of the network implementation should be complete and include all information necessary to support and maintain the network. This would include any network security passwords used on any of the network equipment requiring administrators to supply passwords to obtain control over their operation. Configuration information for each piece of equipment should be saved in both electronic and hard copy form so they can be reviewed if and when it is necessary. Every piece of information that describes your network's layout and operation should be collected and kept for safekeeping in an orderly manner so it can be easily retrieved when it is needed.

If you are a newly appointed network administrator, your first course of action when taking over the control network operation is to review the documentation for the network and a physical inventory of all devices within the network. This is a long and tedious task, but it is best to perform it while not under the gun when the network is burning down. Systematically collecting and cataloging the network you have been placed in charge of will give you a good understanding of your network and the tools to support and maintain it. If no layout plan is available for the network as it currently stands, attempt to draw one up, including the addressing schemes used. There is no substitute for good and thorough documentation.

> **POP QUIZ**
>
> What are the five major phases of a network's implementation?

13.8   The Final Stretch

> *Avoid any action with an unacceptable outcome.*
> — **George E. Nichols, Northrop Project Manager**

The preceding quote is so true. Proper implementation of a network requires care in planning through each phase of the project. This means not only planning for the obvious but the unexpected as well. If all runs to plan, there is no need for contingency plans. However, when stuff hits the fan

> **RANDOM BONUS DEFINITION**
>
> *single-mode fiber* — An optical fiber that allows signals in only one transmission mode.

the absence of contingency plans does make for a very unacceptable outcome. Short-sightedness and attempting to take all the shortcuts possible are actions that will ultimately result in an unacceptable outcome. With thoughtful and careful planning, a

ACRONYM ALERT

AC — Access control

major network implementation can be completed for both the targeted performance and cost within the time period allocated for the project. Think of it as making a fine stew. Plan out the ingredients, have all the ingredients on hand and ready to go, stage the different cooking phases, and let it all simmer. When you are done, you have an outcome that is rewarding and very satisfying.

AN UNRELATED MOMENT OF PAUSE — MOTHER TURBYNE'S STEW

The thought of stew has me hankering to cook up a pot of some fine stew. It is called Mother Turbyne's Stew because the recipe was obtained from my former cube mate, Jamie Turbyne. We shared some fine cuisine over the years from all the fast food eateries available to us while working the second shift. The recipe made its travels among the staff and everyone seems to like it. You can digress from the recipe as presented here to suit your taste. It is also great to freeze up single-sized portions that microwave well to make for a good and wholesome meal on those late nights at work.

Ingredients:

◆ 2 bottles of Guinness beer

◆ 1 to 1 1/2 pounds of stew meat (beef)

◆ 1 medium sized onion

◆ 1 pound baby carrots

◆ 1 pound frozen peas

◆ 2 cloves of garlic

◆ 2 tablespoons of butter

◆ Salt and pepper to taste

◆ Water to bring the stew to a consistency that suits your palate

Preparation:

1. Peel and dice the onion.

2. Add the butter to a four-quart pot and melt over medium heat.

3. Add the diced onions. Cook until they appear translucent. (Do not brown them.)

(continued)

13.9 Chapter Exercise

This exercise can be done as a class project or as a sole contributor project. If is to be part of a class project, the class should be divided into teams consisting of a project manager and a number of associates. It is the duty of the project manager to divide the planning tasks and the implementation phases between the associates.

The project consists of providing network services to a new facility built next door to an adjacent older building that is to be razed for a parking garage after the move to the new building has been completed. This facility will house approximately 500 employees after the move. Business at this facility is expected to grow by 50 percent in the next year, requiring the workforce to be expanded by 20 percent. The long-term goal of the company is for the facility to house 1,000 employees.

---

[30]Other brands of beer have been used successfully. Although there is a distinct difference in taste when going to lighter beers, you are encouraged to experiment on your own. However, this is only if you are of legal drinking age for your area. If not, just add beef broth.

Design a network implementation that will accomplish the immediate and future needs of the company for communication, including both data and other services, such as voice and video conferencing.

Draw out initial plans and some detailed plans showing network segmentation for security and traffic patterns. Detailed drawings may include network addresses and the division of the network using subnets and routing between areas. The entire local network is in the private network space, so pick a designated private IP address space and work from there.

If this book is being used in an instructor-led course, the instructor can provide additional information for the requirements he or she is looking for. It is up to the instructor to select the level of detail that is required

> **RANDOM BONUS DEFINITION**
>
> Q-compliant — A network node that complies with IEEE 802.1Q.

to submit the project on completion. In a class environment, if time is available, the teams can present their project to the class with their reason for the implementation path they selected.

13.10 Pop Quiz Answer

What are the five major phases of a network's implementation?

1. Planning
2. Budgeting
3. Staging
4. Rollout
5. Verification

Managing and Maintaining
the Network

In This Part

Network Security

Uncertainty is the only certainty there is, and knowing how to live with insecurity is the only real security.
— John Allen Paulos

We've all heard the sensational stories of large databases being hacked and people's medical records, charge cards, banking account information, and other sensitive data being compromised and released for anyone with an interest in using that information for some unethical purpose. However, there are breaches of network security that happen daily and may not make the news outlets for all to hear. These are those little quiet events that happen to individuals, listed under the heading of "identity theft." With the Internet, large amounts of data can be collected on any person. The insidious thing about it is there is no warning that you are being tracked or spied upon. There is no way for the individual under scrutiny to know that someone has an interest in who they are and any other information about them that can be garnered from searches on the Internet. With such information, an unscrupulous person can set up a parallel identity and begin assuming that unsuspecting person's life. The stories that eventually come to light in a case of identity theft are when the victims of such a crime have had their lives totally ruined.

Network threats are real and constant. It is unfortunate that so many individuals seek to prey on innocent and trusting people, but it falls upon those entrusted with that information to safeguard it as if it were their own personal data. This chapter explores the various aspects of network security and what it entails.

561

14.1   Elements of Network Security

You cannot become complacent that your network is secure. It takes diligence to ensure that the information entrusted to the network, either stored on mass media or as it is being transmitted over the network, is protected from any compromise. Network security has become a field unto itself, with profes-

> **RANDOM BONUS DEFINITION**
>
> SANS (SysAdmin, Audit, Network, Security) — SANS Institute is a research and educational organization dedicated to training and sharing information with security professionals around the globe.

sional organizations dedicated to maintaining data integrity and security within the computer network environment. These organizations help develop and set standards for the main elements of network security — policies, access control, data integrity, monitoring, and assurance.

14.1.1   Network Security Policies

"Policy" is a pretty broad term in the networking environment. For larger organizations, it is imperative that these policies be written out and maintained in a network usage and security handbook, which all those requiring network access to the organization's network should be aware of. The organization's size, structure, and type of information handled will determine how rigorous and how vigorously applied these network policies are. Policies are usually tailored to fit the needs and functions of the organization for network resource usage.

Consider a simple example of possible network policies using a small family model of Dad, Mom, #1 Son, and #2 Son. #1 Son is a college student who is home only for weekends. His computer is a laptop that was purchased when he entered college. #2 Son is a high school student and needs to be monitored for computer usage, since he tends to let his homework slide. Mom and Dad also want to make sure that their sons are not visiting questionable Internet sites. Mom has a laptop to maintain her social organization's information since being elected its president. Dad is a businessman who has both a home office computer and a laptop. The home network consists of both wireless and wired Ethernet connections to a router connected to the Internet. Figure 14-1 shows a topological diagram of the family's network.

At a family meeting, policies were developed to control network access, monitor content, and ensure data integrity. It was unanimously agreed that each computer will have virus protection software loaded, virus definition files will be maintained on a timely basis, and each computer will be scanned for viruses on a regular basis.

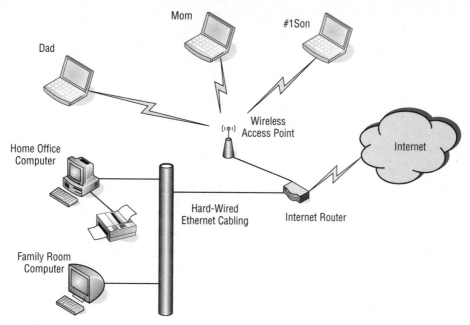

Figure 14-1 A family's network

Computer access for Dad, Mom, and #1 Son is totally unrestricted. #2 Son has been relegated to using the family room computer, which only has access granted to connect to the Internet from 8 AM to 9 PM. At all other times, it can connect to the local

ACRONYM ALERT

SRF — Specifically routed frame

network and use the local resources of the network, such as the shared printer connected to the desktop computer located in Dad's home office. In addition to an Administrator profile, each laptop has a user profile that allows the owner to log on and use the computer either locally or on the home network. The desktop computer in Dad's home office has user profiles for Administrator, Dad, and Mom, with no guest account. The desktop computer in the family room has a user profile for Administrator, Dad, Mom, #1 Son, #2 Son, Local User, and Guest. Dad delegated himself as the network Administrator for all of the household computers.

Basically, overall network control and security was set during the family meeting. Dad had already taken care of some of the more obvious sites he preferred that the boys not visit, but also notified them he would be monitoring their access. #2 Son's Internet connectivity would be controlled and monitored by Mom. She will keep an eye on #2 Son to make sure he does his homework prior to any recreational Internet usage. The family room desktop's Internet access is accomplished by allowing access for that computer's IP address within the time between 8 AM and 9 PM. #2 Son's computer access is controlled by changing his password every day. He is granted a new password on completion of his homework. The Guest user profile password is kept secret by Mom and Dad and will be given to a guest only as necessary. The Local User password is known by all the members of the family, but it only allows use of the local network for access to shared resources on the network, such as the printer. The Local User profile has no Internet access rights.

The reason for the Administrator user profile on each computer is to permit a centralized entity to control every computer's configuration and access privileges to the network. The centralized network entity can enforce network policies on each com-

ACRONYM ALERT

SRF — Source routed frame

puter and user. In this example, Dad is the single entity. In a larger organization, however, there may be a single department given that responsibility, with more than one staff member tasked to perform the enforcement of the organization's network usage and access policies. The larger the organization, the greater the need to formalize and document every policy to avoid confusion and to have uniformity across the organization's network infrastructure.

In larger corporate networks, network policies can be enforced by "pushing"[1] policies down to the computers as they log on to the network. Computers in a corporate environment are usually standardized with as few variations as possible to aid in the supportability of the company's user computer base. It is easier to cookie cutter[2] computer systems than to tailor each one individually. Usually there is an initial software suite of corporate applications that is installed by the IT staff. Depending on the organization and how they enforce their computer and network usage policies, the users of these computers may not be allowed to load additional software without prior authorization. Organizations frown on the loading of rogue[3] software, so if employees require additional software applications beyond the organization's standard software suite, they must seek prior approval.

In our family example, network access is controlled by the computer's user password. All members of the family except #2 Son have control over their own passwords. The homework is #2 Son's token to gain network access for Internet usage. If he needs local access to write reports or print homework,

---

[1]There is no real pushing involved. Network administrators like to use terms that give a sense of direction and control. The idea of pushing is having an application run on a computer that is automatically spawned each time a user logs on to a network. The application connects with a policy server, which sends the updated policies to the computer. In reality, this is two-way communication, so "pushing" is merely a euphuism for the ability to enforce policies remotely on a computer.

[2]*Cookie cutter* is a term used by computer and network administrators to illustrate that it is much easier to replicate the same thing over and over again.

[3]The term *rogue software* refers to unauthorized software.

he can do so by logging on to the shared computer in the family room under the Local User ID and its password. If #2 Son attempts unauthorized Internet access, he will not be granted Internet access for a week.

Dad is both the network and computer administrator for the family and has the ability to program the Internet router to block certain objectionable sites. He had already added objectionable sites to the block access list within the router and has the ability to monitor the sites that are being

ACRONYM ALERT

SAP — Service access point and Service Advertisement Protocol

visited. Periodically, Dad logs on to the router and peruses the accessed site log, looking for URL names that may be for sites with objectionable content. This logging provides Dad a means of monitoring access to the network as well as the address of the computer that is making the connection. From this information Dad can determine if any of the household members are violating the computer and network usage policies.

Because all the laptops use wireless NIC cards for network connectivity, Dad has added a WEP[4] key to the wireless router and on the wireless NIC card configuration for each laptop computer. This is basically a software configuration that identifies a user's laptop to the wireless component of the Internet router by the use of a shared key. The WEP key, Internet router password, and the Administrator passwords are only known to Dad. The only time he would relinquish a pass-

POP QUIZ

Think about your own personal computer network. Do you have any policies in place? Evaluate your current network and find where you think you may need to set up some sort of policy. Think about your place of employment. Do they have a computer network, and if so, do they have policies for its usage? If they have policies, are they adequate in your estimation? Do you see a need for additional policies? If so, list them and why you think these policies are needed.

word to Mom is when there is a network issue and he is not available to perform the task requiring the password. On Dad's return, he will change the password in order to maintain a restriction to the network's resources by using a password revision control. If there is a need to document passwords, this must be safeguarded under lock and key to prevent inadvertent compromise of the network resources protected by these passwords.

---

[4]WEP is an acronym for Wired Equivalent Privacy. This is used by the wireless components within the network for authentication using a shared key. It is used to prevent unintended use of the network.

This simple example illustrates what network security policies entail. They contain every aspect of a network's configuration and maintenance. They also control user access and usage, as well as the content users are allowed to access. Companies with a large number of users may have a generic user policy that covers the more general terms of computer use and network access. However, there may be further policies that depend on locale, right to know, job function, and other variables designated by the company.

> **RANDOM BONUS DEFINITION**
>
> antivirus (AV) software — A computer application that scans computer systems to detect and eliminate computer viruses.

14.1.2 Network Access Control

Network access control is another wide area of concern. The first thought that most people would come up with when asked "What is network access control?" is that it's the use of passwords. But it goes beyond that. When we discuss controlling network access, we are also concerned with the ability of anyone who is unauthorized to have access to any network elements — and this includes physical as well as intellectual information — to alter a network's operation or performance. This means restricting access to where network components may be vulnerable to tampering. It means the security of a facility in its entirety, including the portions of the premises that contain the network components.

> **RANDOM BONUS DEFINITION**
>
> unified threat management (UTM) — A device operating on Layers 2 through 7 that is capable of providing firewall protection as well as filtering content.

14.1.2.1 Network Premises Access Security

There are various ways of securing an organization's premises. They depend on the scope and need of the network to be protected. If a network operation center occupies an entire building, the entire building must be secured to prevent either unintentional or a direct intended act to compromise the network. Since most network breaches are performed by an insider, access to network elements should only be permitted on an as-needed basis. For the most part, restricted access means closed and locked doors, with only those who need access given the right of passage into that network strategic area.

All areas of the network require protection. This is especially true where networking equipment is placed in areas that are mostly unmanned, such as wiring closets and central network distribution points. It is very easy for someone to sit in a wiring closet with a network analyzer and capture traffic from a particular user and lift passwords and other sensitive information. For this reason alone, these areas should be kept under lock and key.

Using actual locks and keys can be cumbersome, but if that is the only means, then it needs to be accomplished until another alternative method to secure the area is realized. If it is feasible, areas should be secured with a combination badge reader and lock release mechanism. This allows for the greatest flexibility while having a means of logging who has entered a restricted area, as well as the time and date they entered. This information can be used if there is ever an investigation of a network event in that particular area. If your organization is unable to have these types of logging and locking devices and the restricted area is under simple lock and key, there needs to be a person in charge of giving out a key while logging in a ledger who borrowed the key, the date and time periods the key was on loan, along with the reason why access was granted.

Network operations should be in an area with restricted access at all times. The only people allowed in that area unescorted are the staff members tasked with the network operation. A badge key system is ideal for securing the area as well as logging who was present at any particular time of the day if the need for that information is ever required. If the network operations area is not a 24/7 facility, the area needs to be secured and monitored during off-shift hours. Monitoring can usually be accomplished as part of the overall security guard activity that goes on after hours.

Most of the security measures are to keep employees not working in the network operations area from tampering with network resources. The intent can be innocent or malicious, but it does not matter which — damage to network elements can have an impact on the ability of a company to do business. It is better to err on the side of being overly cautious or perhaps a bit paranoid.

Network access premises security is not strictly a function of the IT/network operations staff. It partly falls under the facility's management and maintenance, since they are in charge of the building, and the security department, which monitors company assets. The IT/network operations staff may oversee the overall network security, but safeguarding the network and all its elements requires cooperation and assistance from these other departments.

POP QUIZ

While you are at work or at school where there is a network infrastructure, note how their areas are controlled as far as control of access. Do you notice any deficiencies? Do you see areas for improvement? Would you change how the network premises access security is performed?

Although this section is primarily concerned with the physical aspects of the network premises, there needs to be attention on the information maintained within the network operations area. Computer networks can be easily compromised if someone is allowed into sensitive network areas. However, information about the network could point someone with malicious intent toward the areas they are interested in and assist them in targeting those areas. Network diagrams with network addressing should be kept securely and under document control to prevent copies from being taken to plan an attack on the network. Any shared passwords should also be kept under lock and key. A locked file cabinet goes a long way toward preventing easy access to the network.

14.1.2.2   *Network Access Security and Control*

In the earlier example of the family network, network access was primarily controlled by knowing the password to gain access using a user profile. For home and small offices, this type of network authentication may suffice. However, in large networks with a wide range of network services and resources, there is a need to restrict some users to only portions of the network that are required by their function. There is the possibility of multiple authentication services within the same organization. There may be servers within the network that do not rely on network authentication and request a user ID and password from users when they try to gain access to that server.

Figure 14-2 illustrates a small network with an authentication server.

When network users turn on their computers, they are presented with a login dialog window. This login process is twofold. It identifies a user as a particular user with a set user profile for that computer. It also authorizes a user to use the network authentication server for use of the network and the resources connected to it. The services available to the user, after being authenticated that he or she possesses the proper credentials for this network, are print services[5] and access to the Internet.

All network users in the organization have access to e-mail. The e-mail server requires them to log in to their account with a user ID and password. Some users as part of their job function within the organization have access to the application database server, which also requires a user ID/password combination. Keeping separate accounts with separate passwords for each service that requires a login is cumbersome at best. However, there are

---

[5] *Print service* is a general term to express the use of print servers to output print jobs to a bank of network-enabled printers. A print server is a combination queuing/spooling device that stores (buffers) a print job and directs it to a printer designated by the user. Generally, print jobs are serviced in a FIFO (first in, first out) manner. The print server notifies the user on the progress of the print job, displaying error messages if there are any problems with the selected printer.

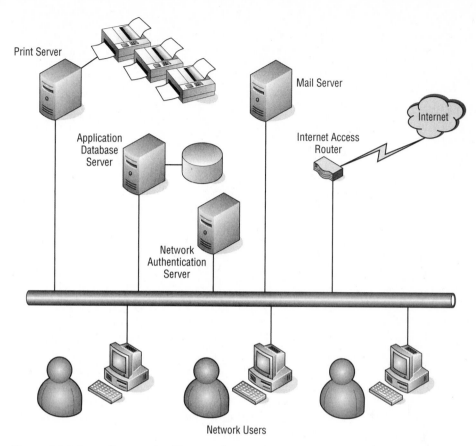

Figure 14-2 A small network with an authentication server

network authentication services that synchronize user passwords with each service they are permitted to use on the network. If access privileges need to be tailored for each separate user, it would become a logistical nightmare to maintain for a network administrator. So a hierarchical approach is used to determine the privileges a user is allowed. Figure 14-3 illustrates a possible hierarchical map.

> **RANDOM BONUS DEFINITION**
>
> network access server (NAS) — A gateway device that protects access to a protected network resource. An additional definition of NAS is *network attached storage*, network-enabled mass storage devices (e.g., hard disks) either singularly or in arrays, that provide increased data reliability through redundancy.

In this figure, users assigned to particular tasks within the organization are placed in groups, with those groups having set privileges for access to certain

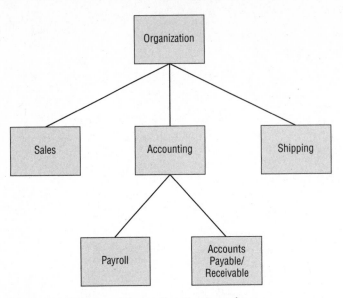

Figure 14-3 A hierarchical authentication schema

network resources. Under the organization umbrella, all users have access to e-mail and print services over the network. However, differentiation between users begins at the group level, where tasks differ for each user.

In this example, the group level has been divided into Sales, Accounting, and Shipping, each with separate functions and particular informational needs, although they all work in the same organization. The Sales group needs to be able to enter sales and

track the progress of orders. The Accounting group is responsible for checking customer credit to permit the continuation of the order process and approve orders to be shipped. The Shipping department processes orders, and when shipped, notes that the orders are completed so that Accounting can process the billing. Although all these groups interact on a particular transaction, they each have separate functions. These functions may be broken out into a particular group of permissions a user has to perform that particular function. The functional separation provides checks and balances throughout the transaction cycle for a particular transaction. It provides accountability for each department and does not allow any one particular user the capability to force a transaction through without assistance from other users in a different department.

In this example of the group hierarchical schema, there are two subgroups within the Accounting group: Payroll and Accounts Payable/Receivable. The reason for this is that payroll is a very important function within any particular organization, and the data handled by that group is confidential and requires more security than other functions within the Accounting department.

It is evident from this example that using the hierarchical approach of groups and users not only organizes users by job function, but also aids in network security by permitting only the services required for each user by their group association. If network permissions need to be changed, they can be performed at the appropriate group level to enforce that change on all users who

RANDOM BONUS DEFINITION

hacker — A person who has evaded network security with the intention of modifying computer software, hardware configuration, and other security measures to either damage their effective operation or compromise them to the point where data theft can be accomplished without the offenders being detected.

are members of that particular group. Further details of network authentication methods will be discussed later in this chapter.

14.1.2.3 Restricting Network Access

Restricting network access for unauthorized users can go a long way toward preventing both theft of services and malicious intent. Malicious intent can fall under a number of different categories. The basic elements include hacking into a network with the intent of making it unusable, altering data to one's advantage, or stealing information to get a competitive edge over an organization. The threat of a network attack is not just from outside but often from within. It is not within the scope of this book to go into the psychological implications or fathom the reasons why a member of an organization would use the network to commit crimes against the organization, but it does happen and not all that infrequently.

Recalling the use of a hierarchical schema to give permissions on a network, a network can be segmented to isolate critical areas and prevent access by those who are unauthorized to use those services. This goes beyond authentication and actually will restrict network access based on network address and type of service being requested. An example of this is illustrated in Figure 14-4.

In this example, the organization has an intranet web server to allow all members of the organization to view information about the organization and the products it offers. To prevent unauthorized changes to this important content, it has been decided

ACRONYM ALERT

OSI — Open Systems Interconnection

to isolate the administration of this server on a network segment of its own. Even though a user ID and password are required to log on to the server

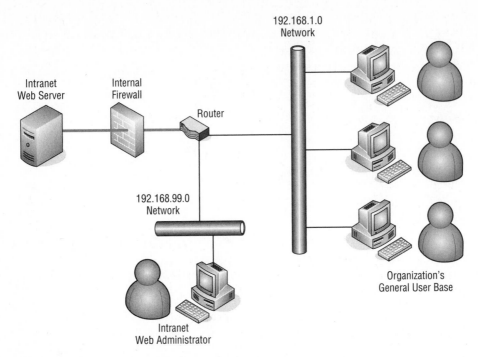

Figure 14-4 Restricting internal network access

for administration purposes, it was thought that extra measures were needed if ever the user ID and password information got into the hands of an unauthorized user. Although it is not illustrated in this figure, the web server is in a secured location where only authorized personnel are allowed. If an unauthorized user is able to gain access to the server room and knows the user ID and password for the server, he or she would be able to access the administration applications on the web server and alter their contents.

A firewall is placed in the path from the intranet web server to analyze the network traffic that is being directed toward it. All users are permitted HTTP port 80 access through the firewall. As long as the traffic is intended for port 80, it will not be

ACRONYM ALERT

VPID — VLAN protocol identifier

restricted. However, if the traffic is requesting a different service from that which is allowed, then those network packets will be discarded[6] by the firewall and never forwarded on to the intranet web server. Notice that the network segments are different for the web administrator and the rest of the organization's user base. For the web server administrator, a policy has been added in

---

[6]"Discarded" is more appropriate than "dropped" when referring to data packets that are not forwarded on by a network-forwarding device. "Dropped" implies an action, when none is really taken.

the firewall to permit any traffic from that safeguarded network to be passed through to the web server. The operative word here is "safeguarded," which implies the web administrator is able to secure not only his or her user ID and password for the web server, but also to prevent unauthorized access to his or her network connection by locking the office when he or she leaves for the day. This prevents access even if his or her user ID and password have been compromised. All precautions are required when it comes to restricting unauthorized network use.

14.1.3   Network Data Integrity

Throughout this book, emphasis has been placed on the ability to pass data over the network without error. So what is network data integrity? It is the guarantee that data sent to an intended network node arrives without alternation. The other part is that if the data being sent is of a sensitive nature, it needs to be safeguarded and not "eavesdropped" upon as it traverses over the network.

One method, as previously mentioned, is to secure the premises and not allow unauthorized personnel into areas where the network could be easily snooped. The other method is to safeguard data with encryption. Encryption encodes the data being transmitted over the network in such a manner that only the two endpoints of the network connection are able to decrypt the data. This was initially performed by sharing a known key[7] between the two endpoints, which was used to encrypt the data that was sent and decrypt the received data to make it readable. Figure 14-5 illustrates an example of sharing a key between two endpoint network nodes.

Rob and Jack want to share sensitive information over the network. The network can include the Internet and any other portions of network, whether public or private. To accomplish this, they decide to encrypt the data before sending it over the network. They settle on an application that allows them to use a shared key between them. This is secure only if they are the only two people who know what the key contains. However, they should not send the key over the same network link. If Rob and Jack are unable to meet privately and the key needs to be carried over a public network, they need to be cautious not to give the people who may be snooping their communications the key along with the encrypted document. It would be better for them to mail the key through the post office than to e-mail it. Or they could simply call each other to pass along the key. The only caveat is that with the convergence of voice and data on the organization's network, if the phone service is one and the same as the data network, then there is no security for Rob calling Jack

---

[7]A shared key is a string of ASCII characters used to encrypt and decrypt data. The key must be known by the entities on both ends of the network connection.

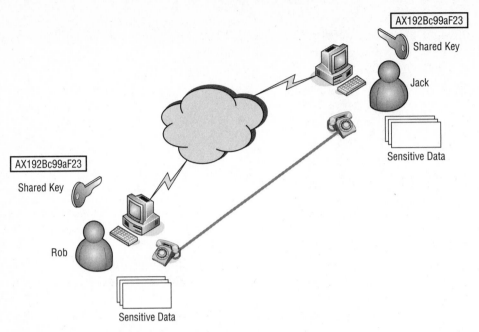

Figure 14-5 Endpoint-to-endpoint encryption using a shared key

over that link to pass along the key. Or Rob and Jack could meet at a bar and pass the key on the back of a cocktail napkin, like a 1940s spy movie.

The advent of VPN technology has removed some of the melodramatic antics about passing a shared key. A VPN can create a virtual data tunnel over a network between endpoints that are secured with encryption while data is being passed

ACRONYM ALERT

MSTP — Multiple Spanning Tree Protocol

between them. The primary reason VPN technology evolved was to use the Internet as a point-to-point carrier for two remote locations. Figure 14-6 illustrates the connection of two networks over a network cloud.

In this example, the network cloud can be an internal network, the Internet, or a combination of both, depending on where the VPN routers are placed in the network. The VPN routers establish an encrypted tunnel between them with the use of a pre-

ACRONYM ALERT

SNMPv2 — Simple Network Management Protocol version 2

shared key and a private key that is known only to the endpoint it belongs to. When the tunnel is established between the two VPN routers, the keys are used to encrypt the data entering the tunnel and decrypt the data as it exits the tunnel. The data is safe between the two VPN routers because of the heavy encryption,

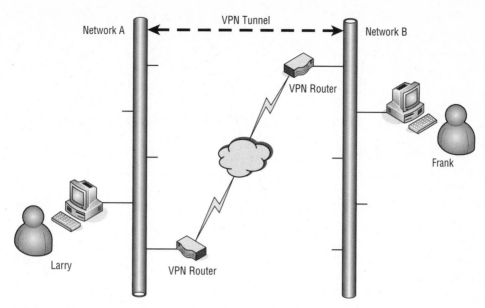

Figure 14-6 A VPN tunnel connecting two networks

but there is still vulnerability once the data has been decrypted and is traveling over the private network.

14.1.4 Network Security Monitoring

Depending on the size of the network, constantly monitoring every node can be overwhelming. However, continuous checking is possible with random checks of certain key areas. The first red flag that should go up is if any of the server logs shows a larger than normal amount of authentication failures. This could be a good clue that someone is attempting to hack into the network. Rest assured that if authorized users forget their password, they will not wait too long before calling the network operations help desk.

Most network administrators generally permit only a single login per user. If a user who has only a single login account tells the help desk that the network authentication server is saying they already have an active session, it is recommended to investigate the reason why before ever increasing a user's account to allow them to have more than one simultaneous active user session. There is a possibility that their user ID and password may have been compromised and another unauthorized user is using their account to gain access to the network.

Administrators should review login data on all servers. They should review the logins to the network authentication server to look for any unusual logins — for instance, if a daytime user is seen to be logging into the network late at night when they have never done so in the past. This can indicate the possibility that a user ID and password have been compromised and that an unauthorized user is gaining access to the network using that account. Unusual activity even by an authorized user may indicate they are attempting to use the network for covert activity.

Calls to the network operations center can also be an indicator that the network is under attack. Of course, there is a possibility that an actual hardware failure may have caused the issue. However, those are usually total outages of portions of the network. Calls such as slow performance or sluggish response from some application servers need to be investigated not as a possible hardware issue but as possible unauthorized network usage. It could be a deliberate act by an individual, or it could be inadvertent and caused by a user receiving a virus on their computer. In any case, a network analyzer should monitor the network traffic on the affected network segments.

Look for what appears to be heavy network traffic flow and determine if it is from a single source or the whole segment. It is possible that a virus has infected multiple computers on a particular segment. There is a possibility that there is a hardware

ACRONYM ALERT

NetBIOS — Network Basic Input/Output System

cause, such as a chattering[8] NIC. You may need to take a divide-and-conquer approach, where you isolate the offending network segment until you can isolate the source of the issue. Sudden changes in performance without any configuration changes on a network could be an indicator of component failure, but usually the issue is not hardware-related. Never ignore users' complaints about network slowness unless you already know the cause. If not, the matter needs to be investigated as quickly as possible to avoid a more catastrophic network event.

14.1.5   Network Security Assurance

A large network needs to be monitored closely on a daily basis. However, assurance is more than investigating issues when they occur. Assurance is a recurring, proactive activity that is accomplished at fixed intervals. The size of the organization's network will determine how often a review of the entire network needs to be done. In the case of multiple installations in various locales, a network security audit can be completed on a rotating basis between the different network areas.

Assuring the network from a security perspective requires full documentation as the network currently exists. The documentation should include

---

[8]*Chattering* is a term used to express that a network card is broadcasting when it should not be. It is constantly beaconing and causing unnecessary traffic flow on the network segment it is connected to.

network diagrams with network address schemes and the physical locations of the equipment and cabling being used. Any deviation from what has been documented as part of the network needs to be investigated. As noted earlier, many if not most network security breaches are caused by personnel employed by the company.

A network assurance security audit should entail the following:

- A list of equipment located in the network segment under audit.
- A network topology diagram showing the network addressing scheme.
- A password list for network servers in the segment.
  - Ensure that all user IDs are active.
  - Ensure that unauthorized users are not on the list.
  - Verify that staff members who have left the company are not on the list.
- Server access logs.
  - Look for suspicious and repetitive logins.
  - Examine what appear to be frequent or out of the ordinary login times.
  - Look for repeated login denials. Are there user IDs that suggest an unauthorized person is trying various user ID combinations? Are these coming from a particular network address?
- Traffic patterns on the network segment under audit.
  - Look for what appears to be unusual traffic flow. Is this traffic legitimate? If so, it may indicate the need to redesign portions of the network segment.

14.2   Network Security Methodologies

There are various methods for ensuring authorized users are permitted access to only those resources they need to perform their function within the organization. This section reviews some of the most widely used authorization methods for network access. The primary authentication methods discussed are Lightweight Directory Access Protocol (LDAP), Remote Authentication Dial-In User Service (RADIUS), and certificates.

> **POP QUIZ**
>
> How often should a network administrator think about their network's security? Give a reason for your selection.

Network protection requires more than just access control; it also includes data integrity. Data traveling to the trusted portions of the network, whether from internal or external sources, can be protected using encryption.[9] The use of data encryption provides the capability for

> **RANDOM BONUS DEFINITION**
>
> managed security service provider (MSSP) — An ISP that provides additional network security management, which may include virus scanning, intrusion detection, and firewall capabilities.

secured tunneling for the creation of virtual private networks (VPNs). The tunnel is created between network nodes that can encode and decode the data that is passed between them.

14.2.1   Authentication

The process of network authentication can be as simple as a user ID[10] and password. However, even with that, users can be restricted by their group association to certain locations or resources within the network. It is the responsibility of the client to properly identify itself to the authentication servers on the network.

14.2.1.1   Lightweight Directory Access Protocol

The use of LDAP emerged from the X.500 directory service. It has gained in popularity as a means of authenticating users for a wide range of network services. It is the model being used for directory services on the Internet. X.500 is the International Standards Organization (ISO) and International Telecommunications Union (ITU) standard that defines how global directories are to be structured. LDAP is used by many suppliers of software for their directory services strategy and has widespread acceptability among the network user base. The standard uses a hierarchical directory structure that is parsed on different levels of categorized information. The customary information used for these categories are elements such as country, state, city, and other locale information.

LDAP uses an Internet identity schema that defines common attributes to define the objects contained within it. Many levels of an LDAP can be defined, and authenticating users depends on the granularity required by the network site.

---

[9]Encryption is using cryptographic means of using "crypto" keys to encode the data so it is not easily readable by anyone that does not have possession of the key.
[10]User ID (identification) is synonymous with username or the prompt that is displayed on some systems as "username."

The most common used elements in LDAP are:

- Users
- Groups
- Filters
- Services

An LDAP directory service is based on a collection of attributes used to define a distinguished name (DN). The intended use of a DN is to define an entry without any ambiguity so that each entry is unique. The entry is defined by a series of attributes,

ACRONYM ALERT

LAT — Local area transport

which are commonly mnemonic strings, such as cn for common name, mail for an e-mail address, etc.

Being a hierarchical, tree-like structure, an LDAP directory's entries are arranged to reflect boundaries that are categorized by geographical, political, or organizational descriptions. An example of this tree-like structure would be starting at the top with the largest entity as country followed by each subgroup (e.g., country/state/organization/department/user).

LDAP uses a special attribute called objectclass to control the required attributes to define an LDAP entry. The objectclass defines the schema rules used for interrogating, maintaining, and updating the LDAP. The primary function of an LDAP server is to respond to service requests for an inquiry by searching the contents of its directory. Since for the most part LDAP data is stored in cleartext,[11] an LDAP server requires the client requesting service to authenticate itself prior to responding to the request for information. Usually the authentication scheme used between an LDAP client and an LDAP server is Password Authentication Protocol (PAP) or Challenge Handshake Authentication Protocol (CHAP). PAP is a point-to-point protocol that uses a simple username and password sent over the network in cleartext for the authentication of an LDAP client requesting LDAP services from the LDAP server. To increase security between an LDAP client and an LDAP server, CHAP can be used. CHAP is also a point-to-point protocol that uses a three-way handshake to validate the identity of the remote client. Both client and server use a hashing algorithm using a shared secret to ensure the validity of the connection. CHAP has security advantages that are more desirable than what PAP offers. However, both client and server must be capable of using that protocol.

Figure 14-7 illustrates a model used between an LDAP client and server.

---

[11]Cleartext is text that is clearly readable and is not encrypted. These files can be usually examined with any text editor.

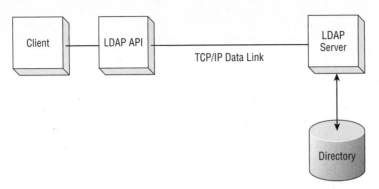

Figure 14-7 An LDAP model

The client can be any device that needs to authenticate users to permit the use of services over a network. The client loads an LDAP application program interface (API) allowing it to open a TCP/IP socket with the LDAP server. Once the server authenticates the client, it permits it to access its directory. A real-world scenario may be similar to what is illustrated in Figure 14-8.

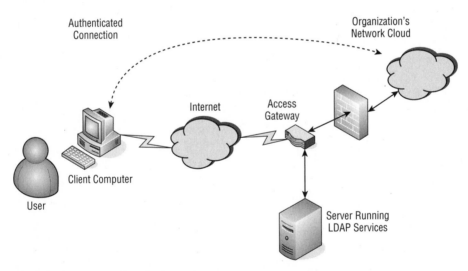

Figure 14-8 User authentication using LDAP

In this figure, a user is attempting to gain access to the organizational network of which he is a member. When the user became a member of the organization, the IT staff responsible for maintaining the LDAP server entered the information regarding this particular user. The information can contain some or all of the following, depending on the schema that is in use: username, full name, department, e-mail address, and filters used to determine access privileges. The user initiates a connection to the device acting as the access gateway.

Upon receipt of the initial contact, the user is required to enter his or her credentials for access. The access gateway device acting as an LDAP client sends the request to the LDAP server it is connected to over the local network. If the access credentials match the database, a response is returned granting access as well as the level of rights that this user is to have on the network. On establishment of the authenticated connection, the remote user is virtually on the organization's network. This illustration is just showing LDAP being used for remote access, but in reality it also can be used for internal services on the network. Multiple servers can have the capability to use the common LDAP database for authentication to the particular services they offer on the network, as shown in Figure 14-9.

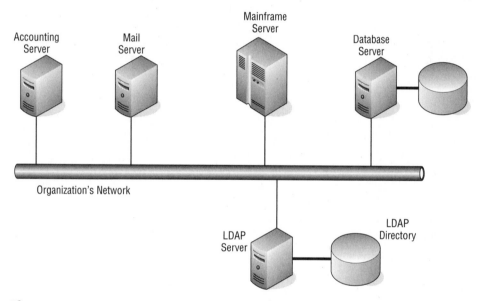

Figure 14-9 An LDAP server servicing multiple clients

As illustrated, there are a number of servers on the network, each of which requires authentication of a user in order to use the services provided by that server. Many servers offer some sort of authentication scheme, but if each server had its own user database, administrators of those servers would be busy ensuring that a particular user has rights to use that server and the level of permissions they are to have on that server. The commonality of having a single LDAP server performing the authentication function service for the network does alleviate the headache of maintaining so many servers. However, the caveat is that with a single LDAP server, there is a single point of failure if that server should go down. Depending on the number of users a site may have, it may be prudent to have an alternative authentication method. One scheme would be to have redundant LDAP servers that synchronize their databases to ensure that user credentials on both LDAP servers are current. If the primary LDAP server were to go down or become unavailable for any reason, the devices requiring LDAP services would switch to the backup LDAP server.

On a smaller network or perhaps due to cost restraints, a redundant LDAP server is not possible. A possible workaround can be accomplished using the internal authentication services of the servers themselves to act as a backup to the LDAP server. This does require additional work on the part of the server administrators, but if needed it can be used if the external LDAP server experiences a failure. The configuration that would be used is to program the servers to first search the external LDAP for authentication requests and if no response is received from that LDAP server to then search the internal authentication database. Using this method takes more effort to maintain, but it would allow the network users to still gain authorized access to the network.

ACRONYM ALERT

GVRP — GARP VLAN Registration Protocol

Figure 14-10 illustrates the flow between the LDAP request and the information returned.

As illustrated, the LDAP client opens a connection over TCP/IP to the LDAP server. After the client is identified and authorized by the LDAP server, the client is bound to the LDAP server and submits an LDAP query. The server continues to return data to the client until the client's query has been satisfied. Upon completion of the query, the LDAP client unbinds from the LDAP server and the TCP/IP connection is closed, indicating the completion of the LDAP transaction.

The following are the basic responses an LDAP client can receive:

- Authenticated
- Denied
- Timeout

When a user is authenticated, the LDAP server returns information about the user, such as group membership, to the client that is requesting the information. Another valid response is that the user is not in the LDAP directory. In the event that a client receives no response, a timeout condition is reached and the LDAP client has two options available: to seek another means of authentication or to deny the user access. A

RANDOM BONUS DEFINITION

firewall — A function using hardware, software, or a combination of the two to detect and prevent unauthorized access to a network.

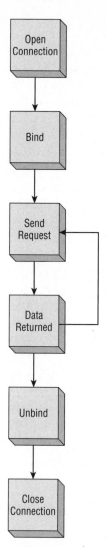

Figure 14-10 The flow of an LDAP request

timeout condition can be reached for many reasons, such as network congestion, a busy server, or simply that the LDAP service on the server has been shut
down. This is the primary reason for having multiple authentication servers
available. Some larger organizations go as far as having redundant sites that
are interconnected but located geographically distant from each other. Redundancy schemes depend on the size of an organization, but no matter how
small the organization, an administrator needs to consider the alternatives
in order to have high availability of the network and its resources for the
user base.

14.2.1.2   *RADIUS*

Like LDAP, RADIUS performs user authentication but also has an accounting component (a RADIUS accounting server) associated with it. Initially, RADIUS authentication and accounting was used by telecommunications companies to authorize subscribers to the network services being offered and as a means of tracking usage for billing purposes.[12] However, RADIUS is not just used by older "legacy" network systems. It has found wide usage in the industry primarily for authentication purposes, although there are organizations that sell information on their online databases based on the amount of time a user remains connected to their service. These organizations use both the authentication and accounting components of a RADIUS server. Interestingly, RADIUS servers or their derivative will remain in use by telecommunications companies for a while to come. They are being used in the cell phone industry to authenticate your calls as well as to keep track of your minutes.

As with an external LDAP server, a RADIUS server provides a centralized user administration service. A RADIUS server can provide authentication services for multiple network devices. These network devices have a RADIUS client embedded within them that can be configured to establish a secure connection with a RADIUS server. The client and server use a shared secret to hash the user password that is being passed from the client to the server. This protects the identity of the user; however, the connection between the client and server is not as secure. The initial connection between the RADIUS client and server is established using either PAP or CHAP, which is less secure since the password being passed between client and server is in cleartext.

When a RADIUS client passes a user's authentication credentials to the RADIUS server, the server will respond with one of the following responses:

- **Access Reject** — The user is denied access to all network resources. Reasons may be invalid credentials, no account on the server, or an account that has been deactivated.

- **Access Challenge** — The user needs to provide additional information. Information requested may be a secondary password, PIN, or token.

- **Access Accept** — The user is granted access.

Once a user is granted access, the RADIUS server returns attributes that have been determined by the information in the user's record contained in the RADIUS server's database.

---

[12]In today's high-bandwidth, constantly connected network world, billing is primarily a monthly flat fee charge dependent upon the type of service that is being subscribed to. But some of us long in the tooth and gray haired guys remember the days of dialup services on 300 baud modems, which were painfully slow and billed by usage. The service type was billed in an increment of hours, such as 25 hours per month, with additional charges for each minute over, which could get pretty expensive. So, yes, the ability to tie accounting to network access was extremely important for those whose revenue was dependent upon it.

The user attributes that can be returned are as follows:

- **Assigned user IP address** — A statically assigned address may be given to a particular user.[13]

- **Assigned IP address pool for the user** — A dynamically assigned address from the address pool this user is assigned to.

- **Maximum connection time** — For connections that are limited by the amount of time they can remain connected.[14]

- **Service level** — These may be in the form of permissions or restrictions on the user's ability to use particular resources on the network.

RADIUS authentication and accounting not only has widespread use among legacy systems, but it can also be found in many installations requiring centralized administration for authentication and accounting purposes. This makes RADIUS the current de facto standard for authentication systems.

RANDOM BONUS DEFINITION

disaster recovery (DR) — A plan to maintain or restore network services after a catastrophic event.

14.2.1.3 Certificates

Digitally signed certificates came into use as a security method of ensuring that the two parties on either end of a connection are who they claim to be. This is to prevent unauthorized (spoofing) users from gaining access to a server pretending to be someone else. This is especially important with the establishment of e-commerce over the Internet. The process binds a user's identity to a publicly encrypted signed key that has been verified and validated by a trusted third-party called a certification authority (CA). The CA registers the certificate, ensuring that the certificate and the relationship between it and the individual user are accurate. Figure 14-11 illustrates the relationship between a user, server, and CA.

---

[13]Particular care is required to avoid duplication when statically assigning user IP addresses. Duplicate addresses on a network can wreak havoc and can be difficult to diagnose unless you get lucky and guess that there may be two different devices responding to requests on a particular IP address. Document well when using statically assigned IP addresses.

[14]Many broadband connections don't use a maximum connection time attribute. However, for services offered by a server, there may be a limited amount of resources, and the number of connections being serviced is a determining factor of the quality of service the server is able to provide. In these instances, this attribute can be used to force log off users that are hanging on the services for long periods of time. The length of time is purely dependent upon the installation site and its operating mode. Many installations allow a maximum of a 24-hour period before a user is given a forced log off.

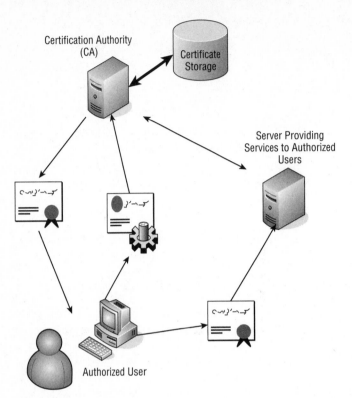

Figure 14-11 The certificate relationship

A user is required to have a signed certificate to gain access to a server over the Internet. The user provides credentials to a CA, which confirms the user's identity and provides the user with a signed certificate. The user then presents the certificate to the server they want to gain access to. Because the certificate is from a trusted CA, the server permits access to the user. The server providing the service can confirm the validity of the certificate by communicating directly with the CA.

The CA is responsible not just for signing certificates to validate a user's identity, but also for administering the certificates it issues. The CA needs to provide storage for issued certificates to provide maintenance of the certificate's validity. If for any reason a certificate has been invalidated, the server must also maintain a certificate revocation list (CRL). The CRL is used to prevent users with invalid credentials from gaining access to a server. Certificates are usually issued with an expiration date, and this too can be a reason for a certificate to be placed on the CRL. Certificate time periods are usually for a number of years, which is set by the certificate issuer.

Certificates are heavily used in web-based applications. Most web browsers can use HTTPS (Hypertext Transfer Protocol Secure). This uses the Secure Socket Layer (SSL), which resides between the HTTP layer and the TCP layer. The user/client creates a secure socket connection to a website/server, taking advantage of public and private key encryption with the use of a digital certificate. SSL has been recently superseded by TLS (Transport Layer Security). TLS 1.2 is defined by RFC 5246, ''The Transport Layer Security (TLS) Protocol Version 1.2.''

TLS is a client/server-based protocol that establishes a stateful connection using a handshake procedure. The handshake is used to negotiate and establish the network security that is used between the client and the server. This handshake interaction is initiated when a client requests a connection to a TLS-enabled server. The client informs the server which ciphers and hash functions it supports. The server then selects the strongest cipher and hash function it supports, and sends a response to the client. In its response, the server returns a digital certificate that verifies its identity, which usually contains its server name, the name of the trusted CA, and its public encryption key.

Upon receipt of the server's digital certificate, the client contacts the trusted CA to verify the certificate's validity before proceeding any further. If the client is satisfied with the server's certificate's authenticity, it generates a random number, which it encrypts with the server's public key, and forwards the encrypted value to the server. The server is the only entity that can decrypt this encrypted number from the client using its private key. The random number is used by both client and server to develop keys to encrypt and decrypt the data that is passed between them. With the completion of the handshake, the secure connection is established and the generated keys are used to encrypt and decrypt the data being passed, until the connection is terminated.

POP QUIZ

Open your browser and examine the certificates in its certificate store. Open a certificate and examine its contents. Note in particular creation and expiration dates. Note the intended uses for this certificate. Does the certificate store contain all the certificates you expected or many more? Can you think of a reason why that is? Note that each browser program may have different ways of displaying the certificate store. An example of this is Apple's Safari browser, where you select Edit ➤ Preferences ➤ Advanced, and then click the Change Settings button for Proxies. Click the Content tab and then in the Certificates section, click the Certificates button to view the certificate store. There are a number of tabs to select the various types of certificates.

If for any reason any part of the handshake process fails, the connection will not be created. The client must attempt to initiate a new handshake sequence when making further attempts to create a secure connection to that particular server.

All browsers have a certificate store associated with them. Usually this can be found under the options for a browser application. An example screen is illustrated in Figure 14-12.

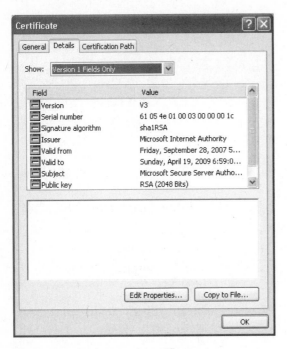

Figure 14-12 A browser's certificate store

14.2.2   Data Integrity

The Internet has provided many positive things. It has spawned whole new businesses with what is called e-commerce. It has allowed people to take communications to new levels. But the flip side is that the hyper-connected world, where information about anything and anyone can be found, has brought out those who have found illicit uses for that information to prey upon unsuspecting users.

The previous section discussed SSL and TLS using certificates to provide proof of identification for authentication. They can also provide an encrypted connection to pass data safely between a user (client) and a server that are directly connected to each other. But what about a remote user who requires services located on the company's intranet? SSL/TLS are client/server-based, which means a connection is established between a user and a particular server. If a user requires many different services on a network, they need to establish a secured connection with each server providing that service.

Tunneling protocols have been developed to allow remote users to work as though they were directly connected to a local network. A conceptual illustration is shown in Figure 14-13.

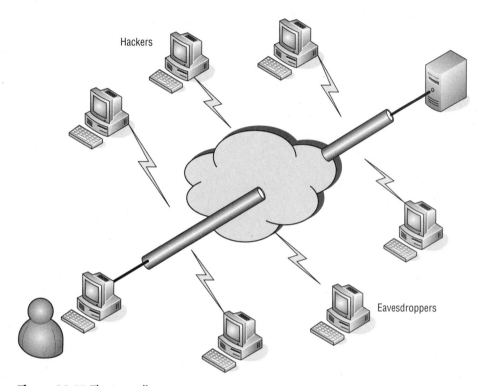

Hackers

Eavesdroppers

Figure 14-13 The tunneling concept

As shown in this figure, a connection between a user and a particular network or server can be under attack not only over the Internet but locally as well. However, if a connection can be tunneled through that hostile environment, the conversation is protected from eavesdroppers or hackers trying to steal a user's identity for later use in an attack on that network or server. With the development of tunneling protocols such as PPTP, L2TP, and IPSec, the concept of the VPN was spawned.

The basic concept of a VPN is that the local network is secure. Earlier in this chapter, we discussed local network security and why it is needed. If the premise is that the endpoint networks are secure, the only way to ensure total network security is to secure the link between the locally secured networks. Tunneling protocols allow organizations with separate, geographically distant networks to connect these local private networks using the Internet as the conduit. Figure 14-14 illustrates this concept.

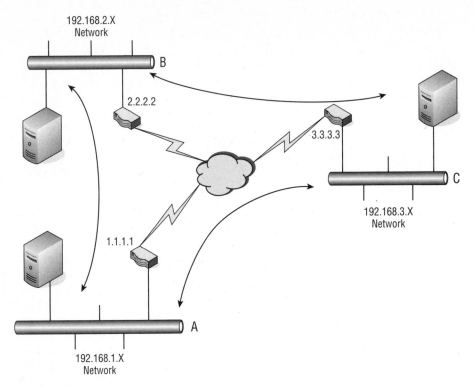

Figure 14-14 The use of the Internet for VPN

This figure shows three private networks: 192.168.1.X, 192.168.2.X, and 192.168.3.X. These are 24-bit mask networks.[15] Each network is connected to the Internet with a VPN-enabled router. The routers require two separate tunnels for each of the two locations they are to be connected to. Although the routers have only one physical connection to the Internet, they are capable of having multiple virtual tunnel connections, as needed. The VPN-enabled router knows the networks that it's connected to, including both the physical connections and the virtual connections.

In this illustration, assume that these routers have only two interfaces: one on the public network (Internet) and the other on the private network (192.168.X.X). Network A's router knows its private network is 192.168.1.0,

---

[15]This is for those who either did not read the earlier chapters or may need a refresher. A subnet mask is made up of four octets having the values of 255, 252, 248, 240, 224, 192, 128, and 0. We will leave it as an exercise for the reader to figure out how we came up with just those numbers and nothing else in between. A 24-bit mask has the first three octets filled, so it would be 255.255.255.0 in decimal dot notation. If 0 is the network address and 255 is the broadcast address for the network, then a 24-bit mask network can have 254 distinct addresses from 1 to 254. If more addresses are needed, it is time to either do some creative subnetting or add routers with additional subnets. Both work and have their respective advantages and disadvantages. If you do not know the differences, it is time for a review of the earlier chapters.

so any packets it receives for this network would be passed into the network and directed to the device that responds to the ARP[16] for that particular IP address. For addresses located on either the 192.168.2.0 or 192.168.3.0 network, the VPN-enabled router knows it must use one of its virtual tunnel routes.

In order to route network traffic over the Internet, actual addresses that are routable over the network need to be used. This illustration is using private IP space addresses, which are not routed, so how does a packet with a destination that is in the private IP address space get routed? This is where encapsulation comes in. The source and destination addresses are the actual physical public addresses of the VPN-enabled routers. So, if a network node on network A wants to send network traffic to network C, the packet is encapsulated within the tunneling protocol and the destination address is set to 3.3.3.3 with a source address of 1.1.1.1. Although these are not the actual addresses of the physical devices that are sending and receiving the data, the VPN-enabled router on the sending node knows that it must encapsulate these addresses, and the receiving VPN-enabled router knows that it must de-encapsulate the packet to ensure its delivery over the private network the router is connected to.

Using encapsulation combined with strong encryption can safeguard and maintain data integrity even while passing the traffic through a hostile environment. If packets are intercepted, the information they contain will not be easily decrypted and thus will not be compromised. Tunneling does not necessarily travel over the Internet, although that is where it is used most frequently. VPN tunnels can be used within an organization's intranet, as well.

> **RANDOM BONUS DEFINITION**
>
> ISDN (integrated services digital network) — A telecommunications standard used for the transmission of voice, data, and video using digital telecommunications over ordinary telephone lines.

14.2.2.1 Point-to-Point Tunneling Protocol

The Point-to-Point Tunneling Protocol (PPTP) does not provide safeguarding of data or perform encryption upon the data it carries. If encryption is required, PPTP depends on the protocol of the data that is being tunneled. PPTP is a peer-to-peer PPP session with generic routing encapsulation (GRE). For the GRE session to be initiated and maintained, a second session is required on TCP port 1723. Due to the need for a second session, PPTP is difficult to pass through a firewall since it uses two separate sessions for tunnel creation.

---

[16]Once again, if you are having a problem with this you better go back for a review. Like, what is Address Resolution Protocol? We ain't telling — you tell us.

The popularity of PPTP, even with its issues with security and its inability to be passed through firewalls, is due to the fact that it was the first tunneling protocol supported in Microsoft's Dialup Networking, initially released with Microsoft's Windows 95 operating system. Authentication to initiate a PPTP tunnel is performed using MS-CHAP or EAP-TLS,[17] which require the use of client certificates. Using a weak password with MS-CHAP is a security risk due to the possibility of the password becoming compromised. EAP-TLS adds further security but requires that clients provide a certificate. Microsoft supports both client and server EAP-TLS implementations in its Windows operating system. The progression path from PPTP VPN tunneling is usually to L2TP or IPSec.

14.2.2.2 Layer 2 Tunneling Protocol

Similar to PPTP, L2TP does not encrypt the data carried within the packet, but depends on the protocol being carried within it to provide encryption and maintain data confidentiality. Although L2TP behaves as a Data Link layer protocol (Layer 2 of the OSI model), it is in reality a Session layer protocol (Layer 5) using UDP port 1701. The entire L2TP packet, including header and data, is transmitted within a UDP datagram.

Because L2TP lacks the capability to maintain confidentiality, it is often deployed with an implementation using IPSec, referred to as *L2TP/IPSec*. L2TP/IPSec negotiates with the IPSec Security Association (ISA) through Internet Key Exchange (IKE). This is accomplished over UDP port 500 using preshared keys, public keys, or certificates for both endpoints of the tunnel. Because L2TP is encapsulated, there is no need to open port 1701 on any firewalls that may be in the path between the endpoints creating the tunnel. The L2TP packet is totally encrypted within the IPSec packet and allows for the secure transport from endpoint to endpoint. In this implementation, IPSec provides for a secure channel within which L2TP can tunnel safely.

14.2.2.3 Internet Protocol Security

IPSec is really a suite of protocols for securing Internet communications, utilizing authentication and encryption within each packet of the data stream between two network nodes. Each endpoint of an IPSec connection negotiates the type of authentication to be used at the start of a session and the form of encryption to be used while the session is maintained. IPSec resides at the Internet layer of the TCP/IP model, which is comparable to the OSI Layer 3 Network layer. Upper level applications above these layers can be protected easily within IPSec, since there is no special design consideration required for its use.

---

[17]EAP-TLS is Extensible Authentication Protocol–Transport Layer Security

IPSec has been embedded into network edge devices such as VPN-enabled routers. Two of these devices can be configured to establish a secure tunnel between them, passing traffic from one protected private network to another. A tunnel of this type is normally referred to as a *peer-to-peer tunnel* since each endpoint of the tunnel is aware of the other endpoint's IP address. In instances where one endpoint is unable to have a static endpoint address, there is a method for tunnel establishment that is referred to as *aggressive mode tunneling*. This is similar to a client connection but allows for the passing of traffic for network addresses that have been defined within the tunnel definition of its security association (SA). At least one endpoint must have a static public address. It is not possible for both ends to be unknown since the IP address is used to provide part of the security for tunnel establishment. The dynamically assigned IP address endpoint knows the peer it is connecting to. The statically assigned IP address endpoint depends on authentication schemes to verify the identity of the aggressive mode peer requesting the connection. Because the dynamically assigned IP address endpoint is not known to the statically assigned IP address endpoint, the tunnel-initiation request has to be started from the dynamically assigned IP address endpoint. Figure 14-15 illustrates an IPSec deployment over multiple sites.

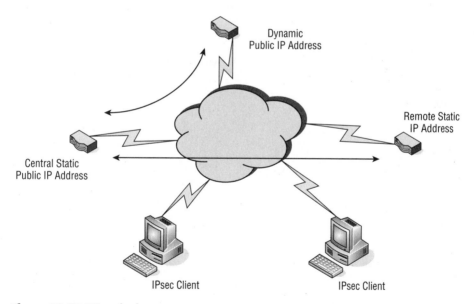

Figure 14-15 IPSec deployment

This figure shows that there is a central site with a statically assigned public endpoint IP address and two other sites to which it has VPN connectivity. One endpoint also has a statically assigned public IP address, and the other endpoint is connected to a service that only allows it to have a dynamically assigned public IP address. These two endpoints know each other and can reach each other because of the statically assigned public IP addresses. Since this is a peer-to-peer connection, either endpoint can initiate a tunnel when there is a need to pass traffic between the two locations. In essence, the tunnel is an on-demand connection. If there is no traffic passing between the endpoints, and if the tunnel idles for a period of time, it can be torn down by a configurable idle timeout setting. Because either end may bring up the tunnel on demand, there is no need for a keepalive[18] to maintain the tunnel in a secure operational state.

The behavior of the aggressive mode tunnel is different from a main mode, peer-to-peer tunnel[19] since the tunnel can be reestablished only from the dynamically assigned public IP address endpoint, sometimes referred to as the *remote endpoint*. If there is an idle timeout and the tunnel is dropped due to inactivity, the central site's statically assigned public IP address endpoint will not be able to bring up the tunnel. If the central site needs to get to portions of the remote network when there is no one at the remote site, a keepalive can be used to allow the tunnel to remain up even when no real traffic is being passed over the tunnel.

Remote users can be located anywhere there is an Internet connection available to connect to any VPN-enabled router on which they have an account. In Figure 14-15, if either IPSec client user has an account on both of the statically assigned public IP address–enabled routers, they can connect to that site with a secure IPSec tunnel. However, there are sometimes special conditions that need to be met if the client is connected on a private network that is using network address translation (NAT) to hide its private IP address space from the Internet. For these conditions, the VPN-enabled router would need to be able to handle "NAT traversal" (NAT-T).[20] There are different schemes for how this is handled and VPN-enabled routers are different in how they handle these scenarios. However, it is something to become familiar with if you do not want to be awakened at 3 AM when the CEO who traveled to Hong Kong is unable to get his e-mail from his hotel room.

---

[18]Keepalive is a mechanism that prevents a tunnel from being shut down due to traffic inactivity between the tunnel endpoints. If a tunnel is idle, there is no certainty that it remains secure. Keepalive traffic maintains the tunnel in an active state and both endpoints are secure in that each is connected to its secured peer.

[19]A peer-to peer tunnel is one where both endpoints have equal capability to initiate and establish a tunnel with its remote endpoint. Both endpoints are aware of the other's IP address.

[20]NAT traversal is when an IPSec client tunnel is created from a private IP address that is not routable over the Internet. How NAT is performed by the router local to the client PC determines how the VPN router that the client is attempting to connect with handles the encapsulation of the returned encrypted packets. There is no set standard on how NAT traversal is accomplished between client and VPN router; it varies from manufacturer to manufacturer.

IPSec tunneling is flexible and fits many VPN schemes. It supports a wide variety of authentication methods and has strong encryption capability. Previously, IPSec used a 56-bit data encryption standard (DES). Now triple DES (3DES) is fairly common. There are IPSec

> **POP QUIZ**
>
> Think of a network that you are aware of and how a VPN solution may be beneficial to the organization. How would you implement the VPN design? What tunneling protocol would you select and why?

clients for many platforms and operating systems, from desktops to laptops to handheld devices. IPSec has been widely deployed and will be with us for some time into the future.

14.3 Chapter Exercises

1. How would you best protect network elements that are located in a remote area away from the network operations center?
2. Name a service that can provide not only user authentication but determine the amount of time a user has been logged in.
3. What is a digital signature associated with?
4. Which tunneling protocol was first supported with Microsoft's Windows 95 operating system?

14.4 Pop Quiz Answers

There are no hard-and-fast answers to these questions. You should use them as an exercise to attune your mind to what it takes to secure a network.

CHAPTER 15

Network Management

*I believe in having each device secured and monitoring each device,
rather than just monitoring holistically on the network,
and then responding in short enough time for damage control.*

— Kevin Mitnick[1]

Network management is a very broad term. It is not a single aspect unto itself but encompasses the entire network operations arena, from the mundane to the cutting edge of network technological advances. It is all-inclusive, from ordering pencils for the network operations staff to buying the latest and greatest piece of networking hardware. In other words, it deals with everything required for the daily operation of the network. It includes the ability to ensure that the network runs smoothly and that the base of network users is content. Remember, there is a direct correlation between the number of calls into the network operations help desk and how well the network is designed, deployed, and maintained. In a perfectly managed network, the help desk telephones simply collect dust. Of course, this is more fantasy than reality, but the idea is to keep the call volume down as much as possible.

The opening quote for this chapter highlights that size of the network does have a bearing on its management. A small office may have a single person who manages everything about the network, so perhaps he or she can have an opportunity to use a holistic approach to network management. However, very large corporate networks have a whole hierarchy of staff, possibly including even a vice president of IT who oversees the entire network operations. The number of network node devices also affects how many

[1]Kevin Mitnick is the author of the book *The Art of Deception*, a convicted computer cracker, and currently a computer security consultant.

support staff are required to maintain the network. Large corporations with networks spread over geographically distant locales may require staffing that appears redundant at times. However, such staffing is required because of the sheer size of the networks and the

> **POP QUIZ**
>
> Think about a network you are familiar with. It may be any network — home, work, school, organization, etc. How would you rate their user to support staff ratio? Give reasons why.

need to mobilize support staff in the shortest amount of time possible. This comes with a cost, so there needs to be a balance between what is ideal and what is practical. Contingency planning can aid in developing required response times and in turn set staffing levels. A totally holistic approach for a very large network is not practical, but cost is always a factor. Each organization has to place a value on its network. Value has to be seen, not implied, and the network staff needs to be aware that many times they are viewed as overhead. A well-managed network can save a company money by minimizing lost productivity; it can also be a driving force in increasing revenues due to speed and availability of resources to increase productivity. Network management is not just a mere casual consideration, it's essential, as it may very well be the foundation on which the modern organization is built.

15.1   Operation

A network operation is the day-to-day operation of network resources. In most instances, the components that make up the network fabric[2] are powered on 24 hours a day, every day of the year, and hopefully are running error-free. Depending on the type of organization, the network it supports will determine whether support staff positions must also be manned on a 24/7 schedule. In an environment where network users (employees) only work a portion of the day, there may not be a need to maintain support staff throughout the 24/7 time period. In these instances, scheduling for support staff should encompass those hours when network users are present. Support staff should be scheduled to arrive before the start of the business day to ensure the network is functional before the network user base starts their workday. Staff members are required to handle end-user calls and respond to these calls if further assistance is required. The main activity of the day-to-day network operation is manning the help desk. Figure 15-1 illustrates a possible network operations help desk implementation.

[2]*Network fabric* refers to cabling and network node devices that forward network traffic, such as routers, switches, and hubs. It does not include endpoints such as PCs and servers not involved in network operation. Servers that provide a network service, such as DNS servers, DHCP servers, print servers, etc., are considered to be part of the overall network fabric.

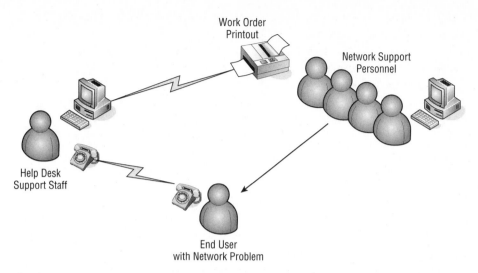

Figure 15-1 A network operations help desk implementation

A successful help desk implementation requires that someone is available to answer the telephone. In small operations, where there is only one person running the whole department, there is still a need to answer the call, no matter where that person may be located. There are a couple of ways this can be done. The first is to have the help desk telephone number be a mobile telephone that is carried at all times. An alternative would be to have a fixed land-line telephone in the network operations area which is the help desk number but is forwarded to a mobile telephone if the phone is not picked up in a certain number of rings. We can already sense the question arising about why bother to have a land-line telephone at all if there is still a mobile telephone in the mix? The answer is that every organization, no matter how small, has aspirations of growing, and with it the network would also need to grow. It would be possible to have the person who is currently heading up the network area eventually add another staff person, even if only on a part-time basis. Then one person can remain in the network operations area while the other is reachable when he or she is out and about in the facility by calling the mobile telephone number. Another possible scenario is that the daytime person is tied to the mobile telephone on a 24-hour basis, with other staff added to maintain and monitor the network during overnight hours. The daytime person should be reachable on an on-call basis.

Larger organizations may have one or more people whose prime responsibility is to answer the help desk telephone calls. This may be a network support person or an operator able to open a service-request ticket for the networking trained staff.

ACRONYM ALERT

VAR — Value-added reseller

In a very large, fast-paced networking organization, the person answering the help desk telephone has the responsibility to triage the call to find out the problem's severity, how the user is affected, the expected response time, and how many other workers in the same area may have been affected. Once all the pertinent information is collected, along with the necessary contact information, a trouble ticket is generated and dispatched to the appropriate network support group for further action.

15.1.1 Help Desk Software

When a call is received, there needs to be some sort of record. Even for a small, low-cost operation, there needs to be at least a spiral-bound notebook designated as the call log. The minimum information includes the date, time, caller, nature of the issue, and whether the issue has been resolved. A step up from the notebook is a spreadsheet that records the same information and perhaps a few more columns for other pertinent information.

The collection of this data is not only used in determining open and closed issues but as a collection of the network's operational history. Recurring issues need to be analyzed to find the root cause and to determine the actions that can be taken to eliminate them. Of course, some software is always better than others. Each has its advantages and disadvantages as far as how it fits into a particular network operations environment. If there is already a help desk or network operations program in use, this may be a situation of living with what you've got. This is especially true if the program has been in use for a long time and is serviceable in that network environment. However, if you are employed in a network environment that has not committed to any particular help desk or network operations program, you can investigate some to integrate into your network support area.

ACRONYM ALERT

MIB — Management Information Base

All help desk programs can open a trouble ticket and follow that ticket through to its resolution. The difference in many is in the database area and their capability to search on issues or generate reports to indicate trends or problem areas. Some programs are fairly inexpensive and a good start. However, it is best to investigate the capability for moving stored network-related information in the event there is a need to migrate to a more sophisticated program in the future. You want to be able to migrate the data to the new software system to provide continuity in the network operations area. Avoid programs that use a compressed, proprietary format and do not provide tools to export the data in a readable and sortable format.

Some programs are single-user applications that are loaded on a local PC. This is fine in a one-person department where future growth may not exist. Attempt to find a program that would easily migrate to a multiuser environment. Client/server applications have client and server components; however, they may require a per-seat license for each user using the client application. Normally, these types of licenses are based on simultaneous connections, so you may not need a license for every staff member who needs access to the program. Make sure there is a firm understanding of the license terms prior to committing to the purchase of the program.

The last consideration is the program's user interface. Is it fairly intuitive, requiring little to no training? The idea is to have a help desk program that increases the productivity of the network support staff, not tie them down with the business of just running the help desk

POP QUIZ

List the minimum information that is needed to generate a trouble ticket or work order for network support.

program. If a program requires leafing through thick manuals for explanation of various functions, it is perhaps best to look in another direction.

15.1.2 Network Operations Staff

In a small, one-person network operations shop, the person needs to wear many hats. Perhaps the person is fairly knowledgeable about all facets of the network environment, but if the network is sophisticated, certain components may need to be supported via support contracts with either the original equipment manufacturer or some other third party with expertise in that particular piece of hardware or software. In larger installations, there may be an entire staff dedicated to different network aspects.

The tasks performed by help desk personnel may be more of a clerical function in a large, high call volume network environment. It would be the responsibility of these staff members to capture as much relevant information as possible and then pass the ticket to a network specialist. In some environments, the call volume may be such that the person answering the telephone at the help desk is expected to perform some minor troubleshooting prior to handing off the ticket for further work by a network specialist. In a shop with a handful of network support staff, the person taking the support call may be expected to manage the issue until it is resolved. There will be times when all the staff is working on issues and no one is available to answer the phone. Calls should be routed to an answering service that relays the messages as soon as a staff member returns to the network operations area.

In large organizations that need to have dedicated expertise in certain areas, the staff can be divided as follows:

- **PC support** — Staff members dedicated to desktop applications and hardware issues related to the computer and the network node it is directly connected to.

- **Server support** — Staff members dedicated to various server-based applications, such as e-mail, authentication servers, domain servers, etc. A server administrator may be dedicated to a single server application.

- **Network support** — Staff members dedicated to the network fabric consisting of network forwarding devices, such as routers, switches, hubs, and related cabling.

- **Telecommunications support** — This function may be broken out into a voice group and a data group. However, with the convergence of voice and data networks, this function can overlap into the network, server, and PC support areas with the use of IP voice-based devices and applications. Data telecommunications staff mostly work with the high-speed network data carriers and the devices locally located to provide a network path to the outside world.

- **User base support** — Staff members dedicated to training users, creating user manuals, and creating and maintaining user accounts, including passwords and network access privileges.

This is a granular description of possible support functions for those organizations that have the ability to divide these functions into separate areas. There are many instances where these functions may overlap or where one support person from one group can help in supplying support to a different group.

15.1.3 Network Monitoring

Monitoring network performance for larger networks is an automated process. There are monitoring stations that monitor not only the health of network devices but also can track traffic patterns through the network. In these types of network environ-

ACRONYM ALERT

WATS — Wide area telecommunications service

ments, network support personnel is dedicated to evaluating the information that is displayed and determining if there is a need for some sort of service on the network. This kind of monitoring is interactive and is normally used in a 24/7 network operations environment to ensure that the network is functioning at optimum performance throughout the day. The networks where this type of monitoring can be found are those that deal with thousands of devices spread not only around a single site but perhaps several sites whose networks are being monitored from a central location.

This type of network monitoring may be too costly for a smaller network installation. However, monitoring can be done on a less grand scale using Simple Network Management Protocol (SNMP). There are low-cost SNMP programs that can be set

ACRONYM ALERT

TAPI — Telephony application programming interface

up on a workstation where the network devices can be polled. These programs poll the devices and query the management information base (MIB).[3] An MIB is a database containing the network objects that provide information on the major elements of the device and its interfaces. The program can simply query and display the retrieved information or in more feature-rich programs, retain the information captured over a fixed interval and display it in a historical graph. So the feature-to-cost ratio would be a deciding factor when selecting a program using SNMP to monitor your network.

Even without SNMP, many devices retain information that can be used to monitor their health. This information can be read using a console connection[4] or Telnet to a management address on the device to retrieve

POP QUIZ

Name the two major types of user interfaces used today in the computer and network areas.

the information. These methods utilize the command-line interface (CLI)[5] of the device to retrieve the requested information. Whereas SNMP for the most part has many standardized MIBs, CLIs can vary from manufacturer to manufacturer, as well as from device to device from the same manufacturer, so there is no standard query. Keeping CLI reference manuals for all the different devices within the network is essential.

Monitoring is a preemptive activity. It is used to provide early warning of network problem areas. It most definitely is capable of reporting network

---

[3]MIB is a collection of object identifiers (OID) to collect information regarding the operation of a network device. There are standard MIB OID values, which every network device supports, and then there are the proprietary MIB OID values, which are designed to query components of a nonstandard device. The MIB database is loaded on an SMNP workstation so it can use the appropriate OID to retrieve the desired information from the network device.

[4]Console connection usually refers to an RS232 serial connection that allows the establishment of a terminal session. This connection can be used to issue commands for either configuring the device or retrieving the requested information. These commands may be of a proprietary nature, depending upon the device. In these cases, the manufacturer's operational manual should be consulted.

[5]Command-line interface (CLI) refers to a line-by-line command set that is a proprietary set of commands designed by the manufacturer to allow the device to be configured or respond to information queries relating to its configuration or operation.

outages as well as network device failures, but its real value is pointing out areas of the network that may need modification to handle increased demand or traffic patterns that can be rerouted for a more even distribution of network bandwidth.

15.2   Administration

The main thrust of network administration is evaluating and allocating network resources and other administrative needs in support of the organization's network. What are the resources? First, it is people — understanding the staffing needs required

ACRONYM ALERT

SOCKS — SOCKet secure server

to maintain a network, scheduling staff members efficiently to carry out the mission of ensuring network maintainability and availability with a minimal amount of downtime. Second, it is relationships with vendors and suppliers, not only for material goods but as resources for their knowledge expertise of the products they market. Third, it is the creation of processes and policies for the smooth operation of the network management group.

15.2.1   Network Management Staff Members

The main topic of discussion in this section is for those network management organizations that have been tasked with the care of a large organization's network. There are natural divisions of labor as far as expertise, with a support hierarchy to coordinate activities to ensure a high level of service to their user base with minimal impact on those users whose productivity is directly related to the availability of network resources.

For smaller network operations with only a handful of staff in support of network resources, this section may seem like overkill. However, networks tend to grow as organizations grow, so this information may be usable as a roadmap to aid in planning that growth. Figure 15-2 illustrates an organizational chart for a hypothetical large network management organization.

In very large companies, it is recognized that the network management organization is an integral part of the organization and that it requires an executive-level employee with the title of VP or director to lead the network management organization. The

ACRONYM ALERT

SMS — System management server

smaller the company, the fewer staff are required. It may be run by a higher-level manager acting as the focal point for the whole department.

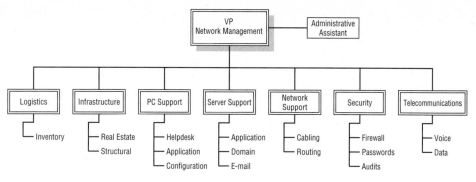

Figure 15-2 A network management organizational chart

15.2.1.1 *Executive Level*

Only a very large organization would have a vice president of network management. The reason for it would be the number of staff positions that are reporting to this position. If a network management organization has a multilevel hierarchy, such as division or group managers with a support structure under them, someone needs to drive the coordination between the various groups. There also may be large purchases for major expansion or upgrades that require contract negotiations. On that level, an executive position is warranted.

This position or office may require additional staff, such as an administrative assistant to coordinate and schedule events. Attached to the position may be an accounting function and a contracts function for managing budgets, accounting for expenditures, and negotiating contracts for equipment and services. The executive position would be able to authorize those expenditures and contracts, and to set staffing levels.

This position is the focal point for all things related to network resources. It is the position that oversees all activities and is responsible for preparing reports to the other members of the executive office. The position requires a skilled management per-

ACRONYM ALERT

RAS — Remote access server

son more than a technocrat. However, he or she must be knowledgeable enough to understand some of the aspects involved with the overall network infrastructure. More technical management is left to the department heads and managers. They are the ones who oversee the day-to-day activity within their respective departments.

15.2.1.2 *Department Heads/Managers*

Department head (or manager) positions should be filled by people who are technically competent in the area they have been placed in charge of. They should have good managerial skills as well as people skills. In a smaller organization, this may be a hands-on position where the department head/manager/supervisor performs some network-related responsibilities as well as oversees the overall

operation of the department. The differing functional areas are broken out for easier identification of their roles and activity level within the organization. In a smaller organization, a department head may wear many hats and cover more than one functional area at the same time.

15.2.1.2.1 Telecommunications Department

This department may have both voice and data responsibilities. It coordinates communication activities not only with internal users, but potentially with remote users as well. The type of telephone service that is in use, POTS[6] or VoIP, will determine how much separation there actually is between the voice and data groups.

The telecommunications department is responsible for interfacing with the long line companies that connect the organization to the outside world. The department also monitors the bandwidth needs of the organization and negotiates contracts and rates with telecommunications providers. Final approval of contracts occurs at the executive level, but the details of the services and support that are to be provided is usually worked out by those that are intimately involved in the daily operations of the telecommunications department.

On the voice side, there is usually a telephone switch that needs to be administered and maintained. The telecommunications department is responsible for the entire circuit, from the switch to the handset of the user base, including assigning telephone

numbers to employees and generating reports about telephone usage and billing.

15.2.1.2.2 Security Department

The security department conducts a broad range of activities that deal with all aspects of network security. It deals with the physical and the abstract. On the physical side, it is tasked with locking down the network to prevent any malicious intent. It is responsible for monitoring the network's security with

---

[6]POTS (plain old telephone service) is the standard convention of analog signals traveling over old low-grade telephone wires. These may be found in older installations where the convergence of the voice and data networks has not yet taken place.

periodic security audits. The department also looks for any vulnerabilities that may exist but have not yet been exploited.

Members of the security department are responsible for developing policies for network usage and for enforcing those policies with monitoring. They are also are in charge of the various firewalls in the network. The group is in control of the traffic that enters and leaves the network. This is accomplished by placing the appropriate policies on the firewall devices to restrict undesirable traffic and permit traffic that is necessary for the performance of the organization's business.

User authentication, including the servers involved, is under the auspices of the group, although parts of this responsibility may be shared with other groups. Ultimately, however, this group is the highest authority on user password control. The

ACRONYM ALERT

PGP — Pretty Good Privacy

group administers the policies that set user permission levels on the network and monitors network usage to ensure it falls within the organization's policies.

15.2.1.2.3 Network Support Group

The network support group is responsible for the distribution of network services over the network fabric. This includes the cabling, wireless access, or whatever network media is being used and the devices placed within the network to facilitate network traffic flow. The group interacts with other network groups to help resolve network-related issues, varying from the network access in the telecommunications group to the PC support group bringing the network to the desktop computer.

The group is in control of the bandwidth distribution across the network, as well as routing policies that control the flow of network traffic. They are responsible for configuring and maintaining all the devices that perform the distribution and routing

ACRONYM ALERT

NMM — Network management module

functions, as well as media that is used. Some large network installations do enough cabling to justify having staff whose sole function is to distribute cable throughout the facility. Smaller organizations subcontract out the cabling function on an as-needed basis. Usually, small runs not requiring a major effort can be carried out directly by the network support staff members. Every network administrator at one time or another has strung a fair amount of CAT 5 cabling.

15.2.1.2.4   Server Support Team

As its name implies, the server support team is responsible for maintaining all servers. These may be specific application servers, such as e-mail, print services, database, etc. The goal is for the servers to function with a minimal amount of downtime. Members of the server support team perform preventive measures, such as running daily backups on all servers that are being strategically used in the conducting of the organization's business.

Access to the servers is normally restricted, even to other members of the network operations group. The reason for this is that the information an organization has and controls is an integral component of its business. The server support group may

ACRONYM ALERT

NOC — Network operations center

work closely with the security group, but it has a major say in any decisions involving the operation of the servers.

If there are network domain servers under the control of the server support group, the group needs to interface with the security, PC support, and network support groups to ensure that users are assigned within the proper domain, subdomains,

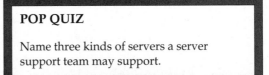

POP QUIZ

Name three kinds of servers a server support team may support.

and groups, and that users can reach all the resources their particular membership allows. The server support group coordinates with the security group to add or remove users as they move into and out of the organization.

15.2.1.2.5   PC Support

The network operations help desk is often the first place a network user calls when experiencing a computer issue, whether network-related or not. For this reason, it may fall within the realm of the PC support staff. In reality, it can be a number manned by a call coordinator function without any particular network technology knowledge other than to determine if the issue is related to software, hardware, or network access. The call can then be directed to a staff member within that particular group for further diagnosis and remedy.

If the help desk is to resolve problems, it needs to be manned by technically competent staff members and requires additional staff, as the possibility of receiving multiple calls simultaneously is a constant reality. It is a balance that needs to be attained and perhaps it can be met with staff members with duties other than help desk–related tasks who can jump in and assist during peak call periods. There is no hard and fast rule of how many user seats per help desk member is ideal. It is not a one-size-fits-all situation.

It benefits the PC support group to have an educated user base, so there may be training personnel assigned to the group whose responsibility is to prepare user-based documentation to facilitate the users in the use of network resources and perhaps other applications. Depending on the organization and the applications used to run the business, there may be multiple application specialists who not only conduct training but who can also troubleshoot issues related to specific applications.

Needless to say, PC support is involved in computer hardware as much it is with application programs. Larger organizations use "corporate builds." These are the base programs that need to be loaded on each computer within the organization. Since a large organization has many users with computers, the ideal situation would be to develop a standard that is a combination of hardware and software given to each user. There are application programs that allow the creation of an image file that contains the base operating system and any other standard applications given to each user, including antivirus, e-mail, and productivity programs such as word-processing, spreadsheet, and database applications. Use of the image file allows for the rapid deployment of standard production PCs. Users requiring additional programs to carry out their functions within the organization would have them loaded on an as-needed basis.

In the area of computer hardware, some organizations depend on support directly from the computer manufacturer. Some go as far as leasing computers from vendors so that they do not own them outright. Usually at the end of the lease, the equipment is returned and the computer is replaced with a more current version. The organization often specifies the software suite image or develops an image and supplies it to the vendor to load on the computers before they are shipped to the organization.

ACRONYM ALERT

JVM — Java Virtual Machine

Members of the PC support group are directly involved in negotiating the technical details of all major computer purchases, but large contracts require final approval at the executive level.

15.2.1.2.6 Infrastructure Group

Users often think of the network as a massive cloud that information flows over. However, the cloud is more solid than its usual representation. In reality, network infrastructure does occupy real estate space. It occupies space not only in closets and offices but also in many different areas throughout the facility it serves. The network operations group may not have real estate staff members as part of its staff. However, there is a need for this function within the group. The staff member performing this function works with facility administrators and real estate management to ensure that the network has the required space and is secured properly.

Planning is required anytime there is a network expansion or change that requires the involvement of other areas of the facility not under the direct control of the network operations group. Network operation staff members need to interface with the people who determine real estate usage. The network staff should map out the space requirements and any other special needs, such as cableway access to support cabling needed within the area.

An infrastructure group as part of the network operations group may only be a reality within very large organizations. However, it is a necessity, and if it's not a group of its own, then one of the functional department heads should assume the role. In all likelihood, it will fall within the network support group.

ACRONYM ALERT

IIS — Internet Information Server

15.2.1.2.7 Logistics Group

The logistics group is responsible for overseeing all the devices deployed in the network, as well as any spare equipment. It is the department responsible for logging the new stock as well as the units that have been returned to the manufacturer for repair (RMA).[7] Various accounting processes are used to keep track of all major components. It is easier if a bar coding process is in place. When a new component is received, its description, serial number, barcode, and date are entered into an inventory database. The date is essential if there is ever a question of warranty. If a company is large enough, it makes sense to have a single department control the flow of materials into and out of the network's facility. If an organization is not large enough, or the volume of goods entering and leaving the network's facility is low, a separate department to handle this activity or function may not be required.

Control of inventory is essential. The PC support group should maintain its own inventory of computer-related materials, as should the server support and network support groups. If the volume is high, a centralized service that performs this func-

ACRONYM ALERT

DDNS — Dynamic Domain Name System

tion for those groups may be warranted. If planned correctly, there can be a savings involved, as well as the elimination of redundant activity.

15.3   Maintenance

Maintenance is a network operations–wide activity. Each area should carry out its prescribed plan of what is considered maintenance. However, the primary activities are as discussed below.

---

[7]RMA (returned materials authorization) is a process used by all manufacturers for the return of materials, whether in warranty or not, for repair or replacement of the failed component.

- **Preventive measures** — This activity can be as simple as performing household-type activities such as making sure that ventilation vents on equipment are free and clear. If there are filters involved, they should be changed at the manufacturer's recommended interval. An occasional survey of all equipment within the network should be taken to ensure that no obstructions block vents or fan intakes. General housekeeping should be performed to eliminate any clutter that may have gathered around equipment. The serviceability of electronic equipment is directly proportional to how well it is kept to its normal operational range. If devices become stressed due to excessive heat, they will eventually fail. Good housekeeping practices can boost the reliability of the network while eliminating unnecessary costs.

- A major preventive measure that often is forgotten is the saving of configuration files related to a piece of equipment. This needs to be done on the initial configuration and any time the unit has been reconfigured. Having the ability to reload a configuration if it is ever lost can save many hours of trying to reconstruct all the configuration information and applied policies by hand. Unfortunately, there are cases when there are no configurations to be had, either in electronic storage or on paper. These are the times the network needs to be reinvented — a most painful task that could cause the loss of network resources not only for hours but for days.

- **Corrective measures** — For the most part, corrective measures deal with a direct failure in the network's operation. They involve troubleshooting, locating the cause of the problem, and eliminating the problem with a correction of some type. It could be as simple as finding a lose connector or as complicated as replacing a major network component. It may also involve finding a workaround to allow network users to continue working, thus eliminating lost productivity due to a network failure. If a workaround can be found, a maintenance window can be arranged for the full repair of the network issue.

- Some network problems occur when a device has lost its configuration. There are many reasons why this happens, such as power surge, etc. However, the impact of the downtime can be reduced with the availability of a configuration backup file. The file can be used to restore the configuration, and in case of an equipment failure the configuration can be quickly moved to a spare unit restoring network operation.

- Corrective measures need not wait for a network problem to occur. It can entail other activities such as taking care of cabling that is exposed in a manner that it may become damaged. It may require a maintenance window to allow for the corrective measure to be taken.

- **Revision-control measures** — Most equipment in the network area has firmware or software programs embedded within it. Like all software, there are revisions that occur due to bug fixes or added features. Manufacturers release updates to software from time to time, but may or may not issue bulletins. It is up to the user base that is utilizing that equipment within their network to keep abreast of any changes that may have taken place. Many times the software is free, and some companies sell maintenance agreements for continued software support after the warranty period has been exceeded. It is best to keep an ongoing relationship with your equipment vendor to ensure that you are made aware of any bug fixes or new features that have been added to the software. Bug fixes are necessary patches, whereas added features are more of a selective choice. If a feature is not needed and your software is running fine in its current configuration, you may be able to save the effort required to upgrade your network device.

15.4   Provisioning

Many people believe that provisioning happens only once, at the initial installation of the network. However, networks tend to change and grow. As a result, they may require some reprovisioning within their life cycle.

> **POP QUIZ**
>
> Performing nightly backups on all network servers is called what type of measure?

This may be adding more bandwidth in certain network segments to facilitate an increase of network traffic, or segmenting networks to isolate elements in order to increase security or improve performance. It could be reprovisioning of a switch to add more VLAN circuits to isolate certain network resources. A VLAN may have experienced network performance issues and upon investigation the network support staff might determine that breaking up the VLAN into multiple segments would increase performance without the need for any additional hardware or bandwidth.

Provisioning of network resources mainly falls upon the network support group. They are in control of the network fabric over which the network flows. However, it is the responsibility of all the network operations groups to identify areas where provisioning may be needed.

Both the initial provisioning and the reprovisioning need to be documented. If there are configuration changes made on a unit, it needs to be backed up and the old configuration file archived. A rule to remember is to never discard the previous running configuration file after making some configuration changes. If in doubt whether a backup of the current running configuration file exists, play it safe and perform a backup before installing any changes on a network device. This will allow for a quick reversal if the new changes do not work or cause other issues. Even if it appears that the new changes are working as planned, it does no harm to archive the previous running configuration file. However, make sure the file name is duly marked that it was the previous running configuration.

ACRONYM ALERT

PKCS — Public Key Cryptography Standard

15.5   Tools

The tools that can be used in the network operations area are many and varied, ranging from generic programs designed to monitor a wide range of network devices to small utility programs that diagnose a specific issue. They may be proprietary and provided by the manufacturer of a device to configure and maintain that device. Some of these tools are graphical (GUI) or others use a command-line interface (CLI). GUIs can be either proprietary or web-based, requiring a web browser for configuration and reporting. Figure 15-3 illustrates a web-based configuration/monitoring tool for a network device.

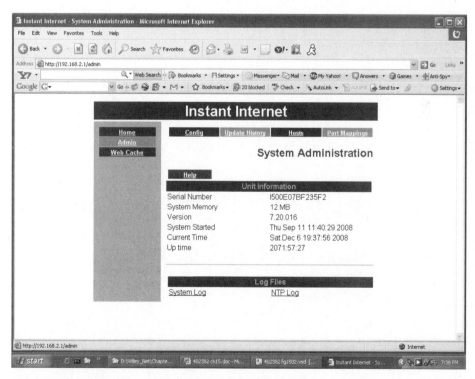

Figure 15-3 A web-based configuration/monitoring tool

The same device also has a proprietary configuration tool, which is also graphical in nature. This user interface is illustrated in Figure 15-4.

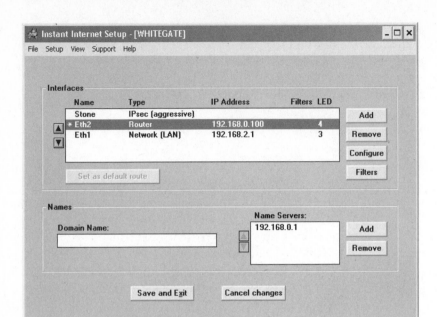

Figure 15-4 A proprietary configuration/monitoring tool

For this particular piece of equipment, the proprietary tool is easier to use than the web-based tool. The implementation depends on how the manufacturer envisions the tool is to be used.

Most equipment manufacturers provide a CLI to configure, provision, and monitor their device. Access to this interface is usually through a console terminal connection or a Telnet session using a TCP/IP connection to one of the Ethernet ports on the device. Figure 15-5 illustrates a typical Telnet session.

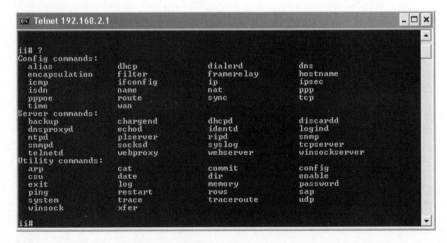

Figure 15-5 A typical Telnet session

Utilities that come with network devices are handy to have and usually a lot easier to use while configuring units, but as far as monitoring one device at a time on a network, they can be formidable at best. SNMP was devised to allow the monitoring

ACRONYM ALERT

SAM — Security accounts manager

of many network devices from many different manufacturers, but it can be used to make configuration changes on the devices as well.

15.5.1   Simple Network Management Protocol

Most of today's network devices are considered to be "managed" devices. Many devices can be managed thanks to the development of SNMP. Devices such as computers, servers, IP telephones, printers, hubs, bridges, routers, wireless access points, remote access devices, and many more all have an imbedded SNMP agent that allows them to be considered "network managed." The SNMP agent is software that answers queries from a network management station (NMS). Each device has a standard MIB and if needed, additional proprietary MIB entries. An MIB is a collection of managed variables within the device that is identified by its object identifier (OID). There are objects for many elements in a device. Each element has its own unique OID. The OID is used to retrieve information on the object or to set an object variable to configure the unit. Figure 15-6 illustrates a network-managed device with an embedded SNMP agent.

A network support staff person is monitoring the network. In normal polling fashion, the device's operational information can be retrieved on an ongoing basis to monitor the overall performance of the network. Network-managed devices can have SNMP traps set for various alert conditions. If a trap setting is reached, the device waits to be polled but sends a trap message to the network management station notifying it of the alert condition on the device. Figure 15-7 illustrates the output from an MIB polling program.

In this figure, the interfaces on the unit are listed with their attributes, which include IP address with subnet mask, MAC address, MTU size, speed, and a description. Notice that all ports are reported, even an AUX console port (a serial RS232 port). Its administrative state is up, but its operational state is down, as there is no connection to that console port. All the Ethernet ports are showing up and operational.

Additional operational information can be obtained from the device, such as the routing table displayed in Figure 15-8.

This figure shows the internal routing table of the device. These are direct routes, which means they were programmed into the device. If a routing protocol were involved, such as RIP or OSPF, those routes obtained from the protocol running on the device would be indicated in the protocol (proto) column.

Network Management Station
Network Managed Device
Network Support Staff
SNMP Embedded Agent
SNMP Agent
OID
OID
OID
OID

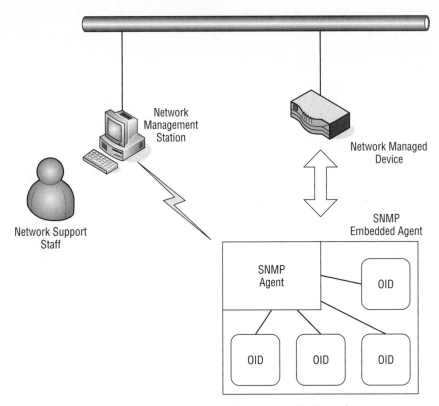

Figure 15-6 A network-managed device with an embedded SNMP agent

Parameters | Interfaces | Addresses | Routing Table | Arp | Gen. Table | Reachability | Traceroute | NSLookup | Ip discovery | MBrowser | Graph
Admin up only
Oper up only
4 entry(s)

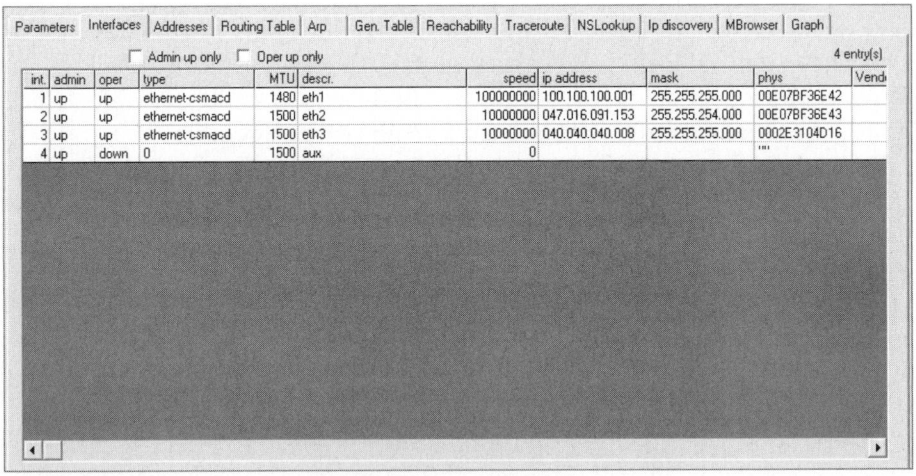

int.	admin	oper	type	MTU	descr.	speed	ip address	mask	phys	Vend
1	up	up	ethernet-csmacd	1480	eth1	100000000	100.100.100.001	255.255.255.000	00E07BF36E42	
2	up	up	ethernet-csmacd	1500	eth2	10000000	047.016.091.153	255.255.254.000	00E07BF36E43	
3	up	up	ethernet-csmacd	1500	eth3	10000000	040.040.040.008	255.255.255.000	0002E3104D16	
4	up	down	0	1500	aux	0			""	

Figure 15-7 The output from an MIB polling program

int.	dest.	next hop	name	metric	mask	type	proto	age	info
2	000.000.000.000	047.016.090.001		1	000.000.000.000	indirect	local	0	.ccil
1	010.000.000.000	100.100.100.050		1	255.255.000.000	indirect	local	0	.ccil
1	010.010.000.000	100.100.100.100		1	255.255.255.000	indirect	local	0	.ccil
1	010.010.010.000	100.100.100.020		1	255.255.255.000	indirect	local	0	.ccil
3	040.040.040.000	040.040.040.008		1	255.255.255.000	direct	local	0	.ccil
3	040.040.040.008	040.040.040.008		1	255.255.255.255	direct	local	0	.ccil
3	040.040.040.255	040.040.040.008		1	255.255.255.255	direct	local	0	.ccil
2	047.016.090.000	047.016.091.153		1	255.255.254.000	direct	local	0	.ccil
2	047.016.091.153	047.016.091.153		1	255.255.255.255	direct	local	0	.ccil
2	047.016.091.255	047.016.091.153		1	255.255.255.255	direct	local	0	.ccil
1	100.100.100.000	100.100.100.001		1	255.255.255.000	direct	local	0	.ccil
1	100.100.100.001	100.100.100.001		1	255.255.255.255	direct	local	0	.ccil
1	100.100.100.255	100.100.100.001		1	255.255.255.255	direct	local	0	.ccil
0	127.000.000.000	127.000.000.001		1	255.000.000.000	direct	local	0	.ccil
1	144.144.143.000	100.100.100.030		1	255.255.255.000	indirect	local	0	.ccil
1	207.031.224.000	100.100.100.030		1	255.255.255.000	indirect	local	0	.ccil
0	224.000.000.000	255.255.255.255		1	240.000.000.000	direct	local	0	.ccil
0	255.255.255.255	255.255.255.255		1	255.255.255.255	direct	local	0	.ccil

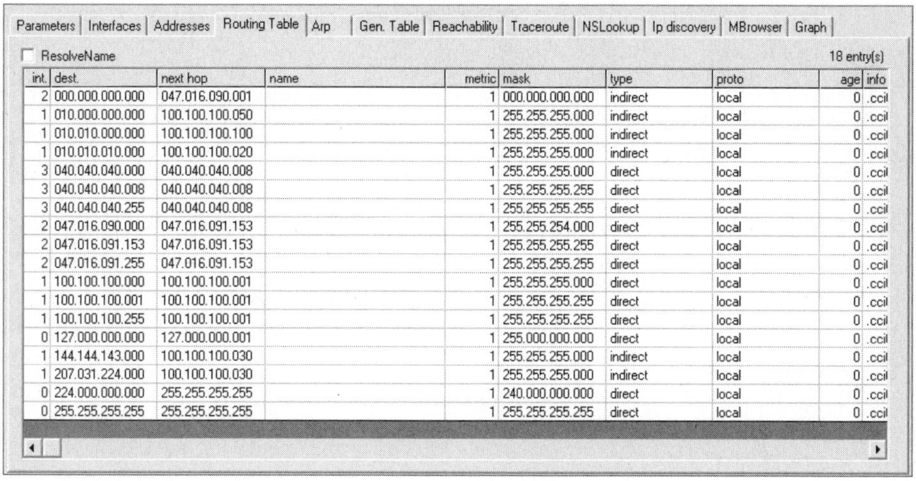

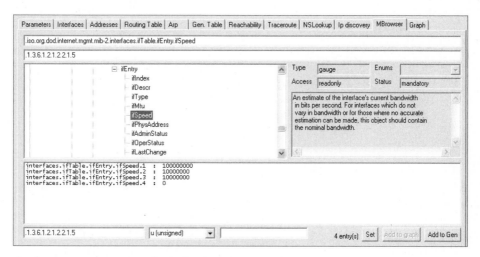

Figure 15-8 MIB program displaying the routing table

An MIB walkthrough can illustrate the OID associated with a particular object. In Figure 15-9, the OID for interface speed has been selected.

Figure 15-9 MIB program displaying interface speed

Notice that the speed of all four interfaces is shown. This differs from Figure 15-7, which showed all the information relating to each interface. To build that table, all the OID entities for each column would need to be gathered for display. However, an OID is unique, and the displayed OID is the interface speed. Notice that the OID description and MIB number are displayed and it is a read-only MIB, so a setting to another value is not allowed.

SNMP uses a community setting to group a number of devices to be monitored within the community. The default community setting is "public," although this can be changed.

POP QUIZ

How is a network device element uniquely categorized within its MIB?

The network management station is able to poll all devices in the community it is monitoring. SNMP traps will be sent to the MNS server that is a member of the community the device is a member of.

A variety of SNMP programs are available, each with varying levels of capability. Standard MIB variables can be read by many different SNMP programs, but the software that reads and sets them may be far different in capability. This is an area a

ACRONYM ALERT

NCC — Network control center

network administrator really needs to comparison shop to get the functions that are desired and the best price-to-performance ratio. Some programs are more glitzy than others, showing all sorts of graphs and histograms. Although they may be attractive, you may be paying extra for information overload. Determine what is valuable for your network and develop a checklist to see which SNMP program has the desired features at the best price.

15.5.2 Packet-Capture Capability

There are times it is difficult to determine what is going on when a network is having traffic problems. Often the only way to do this is to analyze the packets that are entering and leaving a particular network device. Packet-capture devices and programs can return some statistical information when you are investigating traffic patterns or performance issues on a network segment. With the availability of open source packet-capture software, there is no reason not to have this ability, even for a network operations center with a small budget. Even if you are uncomfortable reading through a packet capture to see if you can find a problem, it is useful if you can use the packet capture under the direction of your third-party support organization. Figure 15-10 illustrates a screen of a packet-capture program.

Summary information can be retrieved, and individual packets can be selected, opened, and analyzed. The summary can give you an idea of the performance level of the network segment the packet-capture station is attached to. A packet-capture pro-

ACRONYM ALERT

PDU — Protocol data unit

gram can be a low-cost traffic analyzer that measures network traffic load on a particular segment. Statistical information can also be displayed in graphical form, as shown in Figure 15-11.

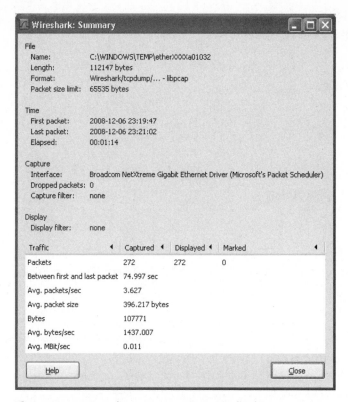

Figure 15-10 A packet-capture program's display

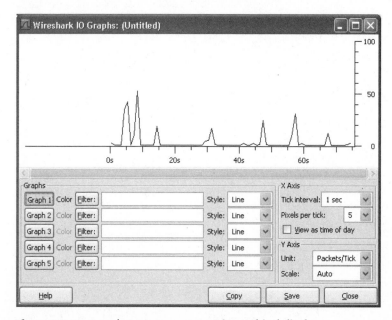

Figure 15-11 A packet-capture program's graphical display

15.6 Chapter Exercises

1. Which protocol can be used to monitor devices on a network?
2. Where would an SNMP agent be found?
3. What would cause an alert to be displayed on an NMS workstation?
4. How would packets on a network be captured and inspected?

15.7 Pop Quiz Answers

1. Think about a network you are familiar with. It may be any network home, work, school, organization, etc. How would you rate their user to support staff ratio? Give reasons why.

   A ratio of 1,000 network users to one support staff member may be considered poor, whereas a 10-to-1 ratio would be considered overkill. At home, it is one to one, because it is your network and you are both the user and support staff. There is no set textbook answer or a one-size-fits-all answer. Staffing levels are set by the dynamics of the organization and how quickly network issues must be resolved.

2. List the minimum information that is needed to generate a trouble ticket or work order for network support.

   Date, time, contact, problem description, severity

3. Name the two major types of user interfaces used today in the computer and network areas.

   GUI (graphical user interface) and CLI (command-line interface)

4. Name three kinds of servers a server support team may support.

   E-mail, print services, database

5. Performing nightly backups on all network servers is called what type of measure?

   Preventive

6. How is a network device element uniquely categorized within its MIB?

   OID (object identifier)

CHAPTER 16

Troubleshooting

Difficulties exist to be surmounted.
— **Ralph Waldo Emerson**

We complete this book with a topic that we all hope we never need to worry about, but all need to know. It is nearly impossible to run a LAN full time with nothing ever going wrong. Even the most carefully designed networks experience "issues." As a matter of fact, when designing your network, you decided on your acceptable level of risk for such issues. Now that your network is operational, it's your actions, both proactive and reactive, that are going to get you out of trouble quickly when problems occur within the LAN.

No two LANs are alike. Even if they are alike in design, operationally they are their own entities. There is no one fix-all for any particular issue within the LAN. The complexities of today's networks (high-speed data transfer, complex end-user application, etc.)[1] complicate the troubleshooting process even more. This is why we find ourselves (us writing and you reading) with this chapter. It's not a troubleshooting bible, but it is a guide that you can use to help you get a feel for 1) what is out there, and 2) a little of what you can expect. We hope it gives you the upper hand when you first approach troubleshooting and serves as a useful reference for you in the future.

The quote used for this section, "Difficulties exist to be surmounted," seemed like a perfect thing to remember when taking on the challenge of an issue that has reared its ugly head. The more that we thought about the quote,

---

[1] According to the NASA Mars Rover update on `http://marsrovers.nasa.gov`, the Mars Rover, *Opportunity*, completed a 7.5 mile journey on the planet Mars that occurred in late September 2008. Think about this. Somewhere in the world (and outside of the world), there was data flowing from here to there that told *Opportunity* exactly where to go and how to get feedback to NASA when it was done.

the more we realized that this really is one of those ideas you should live by. Trouble and difficulty are two of life's guarantees. It is up to us whether we let them overtake the situation. In the network world, we do not have the option of letting the trouble overtake our LAN. That said, let's start surmounting!

16.1   The Little LAN that Cried Wolf

Troubleshooting a LAN can be a seriously tough job to accomplish. Many variables come into play. A specific issue may appear to be one thing and turn out to be something totally different. Sometimes a troubleshooting session can lead to a resolution in a few moments, and other times it may take hours.[2] If the issue is reasonably containable, you can often provide a quick fix without causing too much of an impact for any given set of issues. It's the times when you cannot get a fix in a reasonable amount of time that can cause you to wonder why the heck you even bothered reading this book.[3]

It is never a good thing when a catastrophic event impairs network functionality. Sometimes you may luck out and it will be an issue you have seen or heard of before. Other times, you will end up on a conference call with a team of managers, vendors, and other support staff trying to resolve a LAN problem.

With any luck, you made sure to insist that a robust network management station be installed when you were designing the network. Network management is big business and is well worth the time, money, and effort that are put into deploying one in a LAN. Network management and proactive troubleshooting are optional methods for keeping your LAN up and running. If, for whatever reason, you are unable to do either or both of these, you will eventually come to regret it.

End-user feedback is another way to find out if there are issues in the network. End users can provide invaluable help when you want to isolate an issue and then verify whether a fix worked.[4] Whichever method you use to police your LAN (everything at your disposal, we hope), make sure to establish a specific process to respond to events. You don't want a bunch of unprepared individuals running off to fix an issue with no strategy in mind. If this is the case, a hundred bucks says that you will have more than

[2]Sometimes it can take weeks and possibly even months to reach a full resolution for an issue. These problems are often related to poor design, vendor interoperability issues, or bugs in the code. If you can prove it is an issue with a vendor, you will be able to get them to bend over backwards to get you back up and running. Often there will already be a backup plan, but if not, a temporary resolution will suffice until a permanent solution is developed.

[3]Especially the part that Jim wrote! (Rich just got Jim back for those comments he's been throwing around throughout this book.)

[4]Although you have to fully trust that the end user is giving accurate data.

one individual working on the same issue and possibly heading in opposite directions strategy-wise.[5]

Before we move on in this chapter, let's look at some reasons why a network may begin experiencing problems and at some common feedback you might get when such LAN issues arise.

16.1.1 Feedback

When a problem occurs within your LAN (and remember, it's not *if*, but *when*), you need a notification procedure that alerts you as quickly as possible. After all, you want to narrow down and fix the issue before too many users, services, or applications

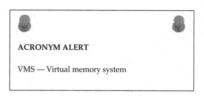

ACRONYM ALERT

VMS — Virtual memory system

are affected. As we have mentioned, you may have a network management station that alerts you during these times, but user feedback is also a great way of identifying a problem.

16.1.1.1 End-User Feedback

Often, the issue may be reported from a single individual, and with any luck, will turn out to be something particular to that one person. That person called in, reported what was occurring, and quickly you have them back up and running. Now it is time for some coffee. Have a great day! Issues that may be reported by an end user include the following:

- Unable to print to a network printer
- Unable to send or receive e-mail
- Unable to access a specific application server
- Unable to be authenticated
- Things on the computer seem a lot slower than usual
- Unable to get on the network

End users are not only useful in notifying you of an issue, they are also helpful in describing what is going on as you attempt to resolve an issue. End users can be walked through different tools that are running on

RANDOM BONUS DEFINITION

10BASE5 — A baseband Ethernet system operating at 10 Mbps over thick coaxial cable.

---

[5]Try to get a couple of bull-headed engineers off their train of thought. Before you know it, they are both making changes and are making matters worse.

their workstation, and you might be surprised how much these tools will tell you.

16.1.1.2 *Management Station Feedback*

As we discussed in Chapter 15, the network management station is a good way of being alerted to issues in the LAN. When an issue occurs that could potentially affect normal data flow, the network management station gives an alert. The alert can be visual (a red node identifier within a GUI) or audio (a "ding" or "beep"). It can also be an alert that sends a message to a phone number, pager, or even an e-mail account (or set of accounts).

The management station can also provide statistical reports. You can review them for anything that seems abnormal. In other words, if you notice a particular port reporting an excessive number of errors, you may want to investigate to determine whether this indicates a problem in the LAN.

16.1.1.3 *Hmm . . .*

It may seem that we are making a big to-do about nothing. We have network management. We designed the network, we know it better than the paper route we had in the seventh grade. Therefore, nothing can happen that we can't overcome in mere moments. Seriously, no sweat. We are done! Or are we?

16.1.2 What Could Possibly Go Wrong?

You know for certain that you took every precaution in the design of your network. It should be reliable and fast . . . very fast. As a matter of fact, you made sure to put in a top-of-the-line network management station with all the bells and whistles. So what could possibly go wrong? The answer to that question is, almost anything. And that is what is so challenging to the network professional. Exactly why is the network having issues? Following is a list of possible issues that you might come across when troubleshooting a problem in your LAN:[6]

- Damaged cables
- Dirty fiber
- Excessive signal attenuation
- Insufficient bandwidth

[6]We are going to let you in on a little secret that those who don't read footnotes may never find out. Pay attention to the items on the list because at the end of the chapter, there is a question that tells you to match each item with the OSI layer it applies to.

- Denial-of-service (DoS) attack
- Electrical interference
- Wireless interference
- Damaged nodes
- Damaged interface
- Dirty interface
- Configuration error
- Authentication issues
- Excessive utilization
- Excessive errors
- VLAN configuration error
- Class-of-service issue
- Quality-of-service issue

ACRONYM ALERT

SSAP — Source service access point

16.1.3 Food for Thought

So far we have reviewed examples of some of the symptoms that you might come across when monitoring and managing the LAN. Without getting too deep into the task of troubleshooting, let's take a look at some of the instant questions that might come to mind when first learning of a network issue.

If you are notified that something is irregular in the LAN, you should ask the following questions:

- How many users are affected?
- Is only one user experiencing the problem or several?
- Is the problem an expected one? If so, do you have an action plan?
- Have you seen the issue before?
- What is the impact to the LAN? In other words, what nodes are affected?
- How many domains are affected?

Understanding the problem is paramount to effective network troubleshooting (as discussed in depth later in this chapter). Without a good understanding of the problem, you may find yourself chasing the wrong trails instead of working toward resolution.[7]

---

[7]Although troubleshooting sometimes is a game of cat and mouse.

"OH NO! I BURNED THE DINNER!"

We have provided you with some excellent recipes to enjoy at some point, but now it is time to take a more serious approach to future dinner plans, so you can proactively be prepared when you happen to burn the dinner. Sure, you may laugh at this thought, and we know that burning the dinner is not something you plan on doing anytime in the near future, but there is a real concern here, and we will tell you why. The concern is that by this point in the book, you are so engrossed in reading that time is flying by. Because of this, it is possible that you may be reading this most excellent book and might, in fact, burn your dinner.

We (Rich and Jim) feel that it is important that we give you some helpful tips on things you can do to be prepared for such quick meal emergencies. By all means, feel free to add any of your own favorites to this (or even to your own) list.

Jim's List of Proactive Staples:

Frozen veggies	Bouillon	Refried beans
Cheddar cheese	Frozen pizza	Ground beef
Canned veggies	Peanut butter	Jelly
Crackers	Ramen	Eggs
Tortillas	Salsa	

Rich's List of Proactive Staples:

Peanut butter	Popcorn	Refried beans
Crackers	Provolone cheese	Salted peanuts
Dried figs	Cranraisins	Cheerios
Oatmeal	Toast	Macaroni and cheese
Franks and beans		

You might also want to consider eating a few leftovers. For a quick and easy meal, throw every leftover in a pot with some water and bouillon and make a nice refrigerator stew. Ramen with some lunch meat or tuna, an egg, and some American cheese makes a really yummy meal. If you can handle the taste and smell of kimchi (a Korean pickled cabbage), you can add that to the ramen, too.

Now, if your meal is for a date, break down and take the person out to dinner. Whatever you do, don't call your mom as a backup for the date. (We are sure she would be more than happy to come over and help, though. Probably with your baby pictures in tow.)

16.2   The Proactive Approach Beats the Reactive Approach Hands Down

It is amazing how many network administrators still take an extremely loose approach to network management. Not that we are here to judge anyone, but it really doesn't make sense in most LANs to take a loose

POP QUIZ

_____ feedback is a great way to be notified of an issue on the LAN.

approach. In at least one[8] of the authors' opinions, proactively troubleshooting your network is one of the most important things you can do to decrease the time it takes to reach a resolution when an issue occurs on the LAN.

16.2.1   Baseline

To know that something is wrong, you have to know what right is (in this scenario, with regard to your LAN). In other words, what is normal? The baseline of the network is defined by the normal behavior of the network. Traffic patterns and protocol behaviors are only a couple of items that can be baselined and used as a comparison when something just does not look right. Here are a few things that you can use to baseline your network:

- **Traffic analyzer** — The traffic analyzer (also known as a network analyzer, packet analyzer, packet sniffer, or just sniffer) is an application or a specialized node used to capture data transmitted on the network. Each packet is captured and can be manipulated and sorted by RFC, protocol, statistics, or whatever specifications are set by the user. The data can be organized and set to graphs or any other form supported by the analyzer and set by the user.

- **Statistical graphing with the management station** — SNMP management stations can usually record statistical data and output the data in reports and graphs. Maintaining such information can prove useful in determining abnormal conditions within the internetwork.

- **Determine thresholds that need to be maintained** — Know your LAN. Test and analyze traffic patterns, traffic capacity limits, overall throughput operation, routing path costs, Physical layer well-being,

---

[8] And I know that the other author would agree with this, even if he doesn't say so.

etc. Keep the results on hand for reference when an issue occurs. Not only can this assist in alerting you of abnormal operations, it can offer proof of the abnormal operations should you need to bring in a vendor for assistance. Understand peak traffic periods, protocol usage statistics, and average throughput. Normal traffic patterns are important in understanding problems that occur in the network and resolving them quickly and effectively.[9]

By having a baseline to compare with, when the end user tells you that things are slower than usual, you will be able to compare the baseline data with real-time data to see if, in fact, the issue resides in the LAN. Baselining is an excellent way of

> **RANDOM BONUS DEFINITION**
>
> campus switch — A switch used within a campus backbone.

reducing the time it takes to find the culprit when there is an issue on the LAN. Keeping a record of captured baseline data is a very important practice to make a habit. You will find that this is helpful not only in reaching a resolution, but also in proving that something is wrong when you start calling vendors for support. Often, you need to have the proof to show to help the vendor help you. In addition, sometimes the vendor won't be able to find an issue if there is no proof the issue exists. By having the baseline data, you have the proof.

16.2.2 Proactive Documentation

Keeping documentation that outlines the physical and logical topology is essential for proactive troubleshooting of the LAN. Even more essential is making sure that this documentation stays current and updated at all times. For instance, it does absolutely no good to maintain network diagrams that do not keep up with the changes that are ever present in the LAN. By documentation, we don't mean you must keep a paper copy of everything you retain; rather, we are suggesting the storage of critical information in either electronic (soft copy) or paper (hard copy) form.

We are offering an overview of some recommended documentation to maintain and have readily available. Like many things in networking, you can look at this information as a reference model. If you don't want to retain any of the information in this section, don't. Feel free to add to this list anything that you feel you need to add. A good saying to live by is, "There is no such thing as too much documentation."

---

[9]This is not meant to infer that you will never reach a resolution without this information. This just makes the job of troubleshooting easier.

Make sure that your baseline documentation is saved and is regularly updated. Make it a habit to change the baseline documentation as changes are introduced into the network. In addition to the baseline documentation, keep good records that pertain to the physical and logical topologies of the network.[10] Keep in mind that even the most impressive network monitoring system is not going to do you any good if you cannot locate a problem node.

At the very least, keep a record of the following:

- A logical topology diagram
- A physical topology diagram
- A spreadsheet or other listing of where user nodes reside
- Documentation that relates to the DMZ
- Documentation that contains information pertaining to nodes outside of the DMZ
- Documentation that outlines the location and node interconnectivity for:
  - Network firewalls
  - Network management stations
  - Mainframe servers
  - Remote access servers
  - Routers
  - Switches
  - Layer 4–7 nodes
  - Wiring closets
  - VLANs
  - VPNs
- Information pertaining to the LAN to WAN connectivity
- Information pertaining to campus-to-campus connectivity
- Documentation listing:
  - Network layer addressing
  - Major node names
  - LAN identification
  - Node serial number
  - Node makes and model names/numbers

---

[10]The topology documentation is especially important for the portions of the network that are related to major host nodes, server nodes, interconnecting nodes, and individual segments within the network.

- Software and hardware version numbers
- Licensing information

- Circuit identification for WAN connections
- Geographical information for nodes listed above, including address and contact name and number
- Node access login information
- Backup copies of:
  - Node configurations
  - System logs
  - System software
- Name and number for support with the ISP
- Name and number for support for the vendors of nodes and application in use within the LAN

Again, these are all simply recommendations. It is entirely up to you what you choose to keep track of. At the very least, keep a record of addressing schemes.[11] It's nice to have if you need a reference point to start troubleshooting from.

> **POP QUIZ**
>
> Name 10 issues that you might have on the LAN.

16.2.3 There Is No Such Thing as Too Much

Establishing a baseline for your network is not the only thing you can do to simplify the task of troubleshooting. You can take a few other proactive steps to help keep the LAN running and get it back to running when you have an issue:

- **Shared knowledge** — It's always good to share what you know. Have discussions with others when you are not sure, and freely offer up any helpful information you may have with anyone who might have a need to know.

- **Proper tools** — Make sure that you and your staff have access to the correct tools. Examples include backup laptops, serial cables, baseline documentation, etc. The staff can only be as effective as their tools allow them to be.

---

[11] Although having just the addressing schemes is really inadequate for today's high-speed LANs

- **Knowledge requirements** — Make sure there is no single point of failure in the network. Make sure that any and all tasks are performed by at least two individuals. This way if someone is on vacation there will be at least one person in the know. Also, make sure that you allow only trained personnel to work on an issue. If this is not an option, make sure they have access to someone who is experienced.[12]

- **Spares** — If it was within your budget when you designed the network, you purchased (we hope) and have network spares on hand. These prevent shipping delays when there is a hardware problem. Be careful when you use network spares; make sure not to do a hardware swap if the issue really isn't the hardware.[13]

Your network is only as effective as you are. If you follow all these proactive recommendations, you can help alleviate some of the pain you might experience when troubleshooting without some of this information.[14]

ACRONYM ALERT

PID — Protocol identifier

16.3   Troubleshooting Tools

When there is a problem on the network, it is important to have access to some important tools that can assist your troubleshooting. Most network nodes have event logs that assist in diagnosing issues with a specific node. In addition, you can refer to MAC address tables in Layer 2 nodes, IP routing tables in Layer 3 nodes, ARP caches, command-line statistics, etc. Because there are many different types of nodes, and the commands to gather such data are vendor-specific, it is nearly impossible to introduce many of these in this book. These are things you will learn and that will be specific to the vendor your organization uses. Fortunately, there are some tools and utilities that are available for you to use, whether built in, downloadable, or otherwise available for purchase.

16.3.1   Helpful TCP/IP Utilities

If you are using a TCP/IP-compatible node, it will most likely include many of the utilities that we discuss in this section. Examples used in this section are

---

[12]Your vendor should have a support staff and/or documentation available. Check with your vendor for details.

[13]Sometimes a hardware swap may appear to fix a problem, but in reality the swap "bounced" the issue, and it may clear up or return depending on what the problem really is.

[14]Not to mention the potential cost to the organization when an issue occurs.

from a Windows-based PC,[15] so be aware that if you are trying to use them on a non-Windows node, the command may differ from what you see here. The result will still be the same, however.

These helpful utilities provide you with commands to determine whether the node that you are issuing the command from is able to reach a destination, verify the correct path is being taken to a destination, verify name-to-address mapping is correct, verify that MAC-to-IP address mapping is correct, and issue tests to other upper-layer protocols.

16.3.1.1 Ping

Ping is an acronym for *packet Internet groper*. The `ping` utility enables you to test whether a destination node is reachable. The `ping` command is most often issued at the beginning of (and several times during) a troubleshooting session. The ping is an ICMP echo request/reply that determines whether a node is reachable and outputs the round-trip time for the process to complete, any packet-loss percentages, and a statistical summary for a given remote node.

The `ping` command is simple to use. Open your command-line window and issue the command `ping`, followed by a DNS name or an IP address. Following is an example of a successful ping to the DNS name yahoo.com:

```
C:\>ping yahoo.com

Pinging yahoo.com [206.190.60.37] with 32 bytes of data:

Reply from 206.190.60.37: bytes=32 time=23ms TTL=50
Reply from 206.190.60.37: bytes=32 time=21ms TTL=50
Reply from 206.190.60.37: bytes=32 time=22ms TTL=50
Reply from 206.190.60.37: bytes=32 time=22ms TTL=50

Ping statistics for 206.190.60.37:
    Packets: Sent = 4, Received = 4, Lost = 0 (0% loss),
Approximate round trip times in milli-seconds:
    Minimum = 21ms, Maximum =  23ms, Average =  22ms
```

Notice that, by default, the `ping` command will send four ICMP requests and will expect four replies. At the end of the session, the statistics are outputted,[16] showing the average success rate, round-trip

> **RANDOM BONUS DEFINITION**
>
> collapsed backbone — A method of interconnecting networks by using a switch or router as a central relay device.

---

[15]Chances are, this is what you will be using in a networking environment.
[16]Also known as *printed*, or *printed on the screen*.

times, etc. So what happens if we issue a command to a node that ping is unable to reach? Following is such an example:

```
C:\>ping testshow.com

Pinging testshow.com [207.215.79.16] with 32 bytes of data:

Request timed out.
Request timed out.
Request timed out.
Request timed out.

Ping statistics for 207.215.79.16:
    Packets: Sent = 4, Received = 0, Lost = 4 (100% loss),
Approximate round trip times in milli-seconds:
    Minimum = 0ms, Maximum =  0ms, Average =  0ms
```

As you can see, we were not able to get even one reply back from the destination node. The responses (*request timed out*) mean that the reply timer expired before a reply was received. If you receive a *request timed out* response, you cannot automatically assume that something is wrong with the remote node. The problem could be anywhere between your PC and the destination node.

Request timed out is a message that indicates that there is no route to the remote node. One of the first things you can do is issue a ping to the interface of your PC (127.0.0.1) to see whether you get a reply. If you do receive a reply, you know that TCP is running and is working on your PC. The next thing you want to do is ping the next hop router, or your default gateway. Continue pinging until your ping fails; doing so will indicate where the issue is occurring.[17]

ACRONYM ALERT

MSB — Most significant bit; most significant byte

You have several options available in most ping utilities. These can assist you in different stages of your troubleshooting session. The options available on a Windows-based PC include the following:

```
Options:
    -t              Ping the specified host until stopped.
                    To see statistics and continue - type Control-Break;
                    To stop - type Control-C.
    -a              Resolve addresses to hostnames.
    -n count        Number of echo requests to send.
    -l size         Send buffer size.
    -f              Set Don't Fragment flag in packet.
    -i TTL          Time To Live.
```

---

[17] Another option is to use the traceroute utility, which we discuss in Section 16.3.1.2.

```
-v TOS          Type Of Service.
-r count        Record route for count hops.
-s count        Timestamp for count hops.
-j host-list    Loose source route along host-list.
-k host-list    Strict source route along host-list.
-w timeout      Timeout in milliseconds to wait for each reply.
```

As you can see, several options are available to help you narrow down a problem in the LAN. An example of what you can do with the command is to issue a permanent ping to a remote destination. You do this by issuing the `ping` command, the identification ID, followed by `-t`. For example, you want to issue a constant ping to the IP address of 10.10.10.1:

```
C:\>ping 10.10.10.1 -t
```

You can use a constant ping when working on an issue between two endpoints within your network, to see if the node comes up and stays up. Also, some VPN tunnel connections require a constant ping through the tunnel, or the connection between the remote site and the corporate site will be dropped and the tunnel will be brought down.

> **POP QUIZ**
>
> Proactive troubleshooting or reactive troubleshooting — which is better?

16.3.1.2 Traceroute

The `traceroute` utility (`tracert` in Windows) enables you to view the sequence of hops that a packet takes to a destination. Each and every router that the packet passes through is listed in the output of the command. This output will continue until the destination is reached, or when the replies are no longer being sent. Following is an example of the `tracert` command from a PC to the `yahoo.com` domain:

```
C:\>tracert yahoo.com

Tracing route to yahoo.com [206.190.60.37]
over a maximum of 30 hops:

  1    1 ms   <10 ms   <10 ms   192.168.1.1
  2    7 ms    7 ms     6 ms    c-3-0-ubr01.boston.cast.net
                                   [43.16.12.1]
  3    9 ms    8 ms     7 ms    ge-1-37-ur01.boston.cast.net
                                   [43.16.12.193]
  4    6 ms    7 ms     6 ms    po-20-ur02.boston.cast.net
                                   [43.16.12.158]
  5    7 ms    7 ms     7 ms    po-24-ur01.boston.cast.net
                                   [43.16.12.161]
```

```
6      9 ms      9 ms      8 ms   po-21-ar01.needham.cast.net
                                    [43.16.12.157]
7     14 ms     13 ms     13 ms   te-3-2-ar01.hartford.cast.net
                                    [43.16.12.62]
8     15 ms     15 ms     15 ms   cr01.newyork.ny.ibone.cast.net
                                    [43.16.12.61]
9     16 ms     18 ms     15 ms   TenGigabitEthernetNYC1.gblx.net
                                    [43.16.12.217]
10    16 ms     15 ms     15 ms   te2-4nyc1.gblx.net [43.16.12.237]
11    24 ms     17 ms     18 ms   NewYork1.Level3.net [44.69.14.13]
12    26 ms     20 ms     32 ms   Washington1.Level3.net [44.69.12.3]
13    29 ms     21 ms     31 ms   Washington1.Level3.net [44.69.14.1]]
14    27 ms     22 ms     20 ms   4.79.228.2
15    23 ms     21 ms     23 ms   ae2-p140.msr1.re1.yahoo.com
                                    [216.115.108.57]
16    22 ms     21 ms     21 ms   ge-9-3.bas-a2.re4.yahoo.com
                                    [216.39.49.7]
17    24 ms     21 ms     22 ms   w2.rc.vip.re4.yahoo.com
                                    [206.190.60.37]

Trace complete.
```

From the responses received, you can see the amount of time it takes for each particular router to respond. If you notice delays, investigate to determine whether the segment that the delay appears in is having issues. Now, let's issue the tracert command to the IP address 207.215.79.16. Notice that this is the same address we used in our failed ping above. You should be able to see this tracert fail at some point during the session:

```
C:\>tracert 207.215.79.16

Tracing route to www.testshow.com [207.215.79.16]
over a maximum of 30 hops:

1      1 ms     <10 ms    <10 ms  192.168.1.1
2      7 ms      7 ms      6 ms   c-3-0-ubr01.boston.cast.net
                                    [43.16.12.1]
3      9 ms      8 ms      7 ms   ge-1-37-ur01.boston.cast.net
                                    [43.16.12.193]
4      6 ms      7 ms      6 ms   po-20-ur02.boston.cast.net
                                    [43.16.12.158]
5      7 ms      7 ms      7 ms   po-24-ur01.boston.cast.net
                                    [43.16.12.161]
6      9 ms      9 ms      8 ms   po-21-ar01.needham.cast.net
                                    [43.16.12.157]
7     14 ms     13 ms     13 ms   te-3-2-ar01.hartford.cast.net
                                    [43.16.12.62]
8     15 ms     15 ms     15 ms   cr01.newyork.ny.ibone.cast.net
                                    [43.16.12.61]
```

```
 9    16ms    18ms    15ms    TenGigabitEthernetNYC1.gblx.net
                               [43.16.12.217]
10    16ms    15ms    15ms    te2-4nyc1.gblx.net [43.16.12.237]
11    24ms    17ms    18ms    NewYork1.Level3.net [44.69.14.13]
12    26ms    20ms    32ms    Washington1.Level3.net [44.69.12.3]
13    29ms    21ms    31ms    Washington1.Level3.net [44.69.14.1]]
14    16ms    16ms    15ms    ex1-tg2-0.eqnwnj.sbcglobal.net
                               [151.164.89.249]
15    *       *       *       Request timed out.
16    *       *       *       Request timed out.
17    *       *       *       Request timed out.
```

As you can see in this example, the last hop that we were able to reach is 151.164.89.249. If you were troubleshooting, you would focus on that router to start with to see why it is not able to reach the destination. It is possible that it

RANDOM BONUS DEFINITION

mirror port — A port configured on a Layer 2 switch used to copy the traffic appearing on another port on the same switch.

can reach the next destination, but the next hop may be filtering ICMP traffic, in which case you would not be able to push the ICMP packet through the node that is blocking that type of traffic.

Here is a test for you. You are doing a tracert and you notice the following:

```
C:\>tracert 207.215.79.16

Tracing route to www.testshow.com [207.215.79.16]
over a maximum of 30 hops:

 1    1ms     <10ms   <10ms   192.168.1.1
 2    7ms     7ms     6ms     c-3-0-ubr01.boston.cast.net
                               [43.16.12.1]
 3    9ms     8ms     7ms     ge-1-37-ur01.boston.cast.net
                               [43.16.12.193]
 4    *       *       *       Request timed out.
 5    7ms     7ms     7ms     po-24-ur01.boston.cast.net
                               [43.16.12.161]
```

Notice that the fourth hop timed out, but the fifth hop didn't. Why do you think this happened?[18]

As with the ping command, you have several options available in most traceroute utilities. These can assist you in different stages of your

---

[18]The answer will be provided at the end of Section 16.3.1.2.

troubleshooting session. The options available on a Windows-based PC include the following:

```
Options:
    -d                      Do not resolve addresses to hostnames.
    -h maximum_hops         Maximum number of hops to search for target.
    -j host-list            Loose source route along host-list.
    -w timeout              Wait timeout milliseconds for each reply.
```

Okay, now getting back to the question at hand: Why did the fourth hop time out, but the fifth hop didn't? This happened because the preferred next hop was not available, so an alternative route was taken.[19]

16.3.1.3 Netstat

By default, the netstat utility displays both incoming and outgoing network connections. These commands prove useful in troubleshooting issues on the network, and when gathering traffic statistics to measure network performance. Following is an example of the netstat command:

```
C:\>netstat

Active Connections

  Proto  Local    Foreign                                      State
         Address  Address
  TCP    PC:1693  PC:1694                                  ESTABLISHED
  TCP    PC:1694  PC:1693                                  ESTABLISHED
  TCP    PC:1663  es.com:http                              ESTABLISHED
  TCP    PC:1671  bs1.ads.vip.ac4.yahoo.com:http             TIME_WAIT
  TCP    PC:1674  jkhiuyg.com:http                         ESTABLISHED
  TCP    PC:1675  a96-17-73-9.deploy.com:http              ESTABLISHED
  TCP    PC:1678  a96-17-72-144.depl.com:http              ESTABLISHED
  TCP    PC:1680  bs1.ads.vip.ac4.yahoo.com:http             TIME_WAIT
  TCP    PC:1683  209.62.185.43:http                       ESTABLISHED
  TCP    PC:1685  bs1.ads.vip.ac4.yahoo.com:http             TIME_WAIT
  TCP    PC:1687  bs1.ads.vip.ac4.yahoo.com:http             TIME_WAIT
  TCP    PC:1690  a96-17-73-27.depogies.com:http           ESTABLISHED
  TCP    PC:1695  a96-17-73-35.deplo.com:http              ESTABLISHED
  TCP    PC:1707  bs1b1.ads.vip.re2.yahoo.com:http           TIME_WAIT
  TCP    PC:1728  8.12.222.126:http                        ESTABLISHED
  TCP    PC:1729  8.12.222.126:http                        ESTABLISHED
  TCP    PC:1735  8.12.222.126:http                         CLOSE_WAIT
  TCP    PC:1737  8.12.222.126:http                         CLOSE_WAIT
```

[19]Thanks to our friend Mr. Redundancy.

TCP	PC:1738	64.236.29.103:http	CLOSE_WAIT
TCP	PC:1739	64.236.29.103:http	CLOSE_WAIT
TCP	PC:1743	209.62.185.43:http	ESTABLISHED
TCP	PC:1746	208.215.179.180:http	ESTABLISHED
TCP	PC:1749	od-in-f166.google.com:http	ESTABLISHED
TCP	PC:1751	66.235.142.3:http	ESTABLISHED
TCP	PC:1752	157.166.226.31:http	CLOSE_WAIT
TCP	PC:1754	157.166.224.32:http	CLOSE_WAIT
TCP	PC:1756	157.166.226.30:http	CLOSE_WAIT

Take a moment to review the data that you can capture with the default `netstat` command:

ACRONYM ALERT

DDR — Double-data rate

- **Protocol** — The first field provided is the Protocol field, which identifies whether the connection is TCP or UDP.

- **Local Address** — This is the name of the local node[20] and the port number that is being used.

- **Foreign Address** — This is the name of the remote node and the port number that the socket is connected to.

- **State** — This field identifies the TCP connection state. Following are the possible TCP states:

  - **LISTEN** — Indicates that the node is waiting for a connection request.

  - **SYN-SENT** — Indicates that a connection request has been sent and TCP is waiting for a matching connection request.

  - **SYN-RECEIVED** — Indicates that TCP is waiting for a confirming connection request acknowledgment after having both sent and received a connection request.

  - **ESTABLISHED** — Indicates that the TCP connection is open. This is the normal state for the data transfer phase of the connection.

  - **FIN-WAIT-1** — Indicates that TCP is waiting for a connection-termination request from the remote TCP. It can also serve as an acknowledgment of a connection termination request.

  - **FIN-WAIT-2** — Indicates that TCP is waiting for a connection termination request from the remote TCP.

  - **CLOSE-WAIT** — Indicates that TCP is waiting for a connection-termination request from the local user.

  - **CLOSING** — Indicates that TCP is waiting for a connection-termination request acknowledgment from the remote TCP.

---

[20]The local node is always the node that you are close to.

- **LAST-ACK** — Indicates that TCP is waiting for an acknowledgment of a connection-termination request previously sent to the remote TCP.

- **TIME-WAIT** — Indicates that TCP is waiting for enough time to pass to be sure that the remote TCP received the acknowledgment of its connection-termination request.

As with the other utilities discussed so far, you have several options available in most `netstat` utilities. These can assist you in different stages of your troubleshooting session. The options available on a Windows-based PC include the following:

```
Options:

-a              Displays all connections and listening ports.
-e              Displays Ethernet statistics. This may be combined
                with the -s option.
-n              Displays addresses and port numbers in numerical
                form.
-p proto        Shows connections for the protocol specified by
                proto; proto may be TCP or UDP. If used with the -s
                option to display per-protocol statistics, proto may
                be TCP, UDP, or IP.
-r              Displays the routing table.
-s              Displays per-protocol statistics. By default,
                statistics are shown for TCP, UDP and IP; the -p
                option may be used to specify a subset of the
                default.
interval        Redisplays selected statistics, pausing interval
                seconds between each display. Press CTRL+C to stop
                redisplaying statistics. If omitted, netstat will
                print the current configuration information once.
```

You can gather so much statistical information from the `netstat` command. Try the command a few times on your PC to get an idea about what you can obtain with this helpful utility.

POP QUIZ

What are two types of topology diagrams that come in handy when troubleshooting an issue within your LAN?

16.3.1.4 Route

You can use the `route` utility to view and manipulate the routing table of a Windows-based node. Note that any Layer 3 node will have this capability.

Following is an example of the `route print` command, which can be used to display the routing table of a PC:

```
C:\>route print
=============================================================

Interface List
0x1 ........................ MS TCP Loopback interface
0x1000003 ...00 10 b5 65 4d 1a ...... NDIS 5.0 driver


=============================================================


=============================================================

Active Routes:
Network          Netmask            Gateway         Interface       Metric
Destination
0.0.0.0          0.0.0.0            192.168.1.1     192.168.1.104    1
127.0.0.0        255.0.0.0          127.0.0.1       127.0.0.1        1
192.168.1.104    255.255.255.255    127.0.0.1       127.0.0.1        1
192.168.1.255    255.255.255.255    192.168.1.104   192.168.1.104    1
255.255.255.255  255.255.255.255    192.168.1.104   192.168.1.104    1
Default Gateway:        192.168.1.1
=============================================================

Persistent Routes:
  None
```

In the routing table, you can see the destination IP addresses, the subnet mask, the gateway, the local interface, and the number of hops to the gateway. Following are the optional flags and commands that can be used with the `route` command for advanced display and configuration options:

```
Options:

    -f          Clears the routing tables of all gateway entries. If
                this is used in conjunction with one of the commands,
                the tables are cleared prior to running the command.
    -p          When used with the ADD command, makes a route
                persistent across boots of the system. By default,
                routes are not preserved when the system is
                restarted. Ignored for all other commands, which
                always affect the appropriate persistent routes. This
                option is not supported in Windows 95.
    command     One of these:
                    PRINT     Prints  a route
                    ADD       Adds     a route
                    DELETE    Deletes a route
                    CHANGE    Modifies an existing route
```

```
destination  Specifies the host.
MASK         Specifies that the next parameter is the 'netmask'
             value.
netmask      Specifies a subnet mask value for this route entry.
             If not specified, it defaults to 255.255.255.255.
gateway      Specifies gateway.
interface    The interface number for the specified route.
METRIC       Specifies the metric, ie. cost for the destination.
```

Let's assume that during troubleshooting you discover that you need to add a default static route to your routing table to reach a remote node. The network you want to reach is the 10.10.10.0 subnet. You know that you have a route to that subnet from the gateway node (192.168.1.1), so you want to set up the static route to the 10.10.10.0 network and the 192.168.1.1 as the default gateway. The syntax is

ACRONYM ALERT

CLNP — Connectionless Network Protocol

```
C:\>route add <IP address> mask <mask> <gateway IP address>
```

So using the addressing that we discussed previously, the following is the input needed to add the static route:

```
C:\>route add 10.10.10.0 mask 255.255.255.0 192.168.1.1
```

To verify that the route was added, check the routing table:

```
C:\>route print
===========================================================

Interface List
0x1 ......................... MS TCP Loopback interface
0x1000003 ...00 10 b5 65 4d 1a ...... NDIS 5.0 driver


===========================================================


===========================================================
Active Routes:
Network          Netmask          Gateway        Interface      Metric
Destination
0.0.0.0          0.0.0.0          192.168.1.1    192.168.1.104  1
10.10.10.0       255.255.255.0    192.168.1.1    192.168.1.104  1
127.0.0.0        255.0.0.0        127.0.0.1      127.0.0.1      1
192.168.1.104    255.255.255.255  127.0.0.1      127.0.0.1      1
192.168.1.255    255.255.255.255  192.168.1.104  192.168.1.104  1
255.255.255.255  255.255.255.255  192.168.1.104  192.168.1.104  1
Default Gateway:       192.168.1.1
===========================================================

Persistent Routes:
  None
```

As you can see, there is now a route to the 10.10.10.0 network. If you were to reboot your PC at this point, the static route will be removed and will have to be re-added. If you want to ensure

> **RANDOM BONUS DEFINITION**
>
> monitored port — A port on a switch that is being mirrored.

that the static route remains until it is manually removed, you need to add the -p flag:

```
C:\>route add 10.10.10.0 mask 255.255.255.0 192.168.1.1 -p
```

16.3.1.5 *Arp*

The arp utility enables you to view and manipulate the ARP table of a Windows-based node. Note that any Layer 3 node will have this capability. Following is an example of the arp -a (to view) command, which can be used to display a PC's routing table:

```
C:\>arp -a

Interface: 19.108.1.14 on Interface 0x1000003
  Internet Address      Physical Address      Type
  19.108.1.1            00-f8-f8-ea-08-bc     dynamic
  19.108.1.102          00-19-ea-f8-36-95     dynamic
```

We want to force our node to learn the route to an IP that is not listed in the ARP table, so we ping the remote node's IP address:

```
C:\>ping 19.108.1.106

Pinging 19.108.1.106 with 32 bytes of data:

Reply from 19.108.1.106: bytes=32 time=23ms TTL=50
Reply from 19.108.1.106: bytes=32 time=23ms TTL=50
Reply from 19.108.1.106: bytes=32 time=23ms TTL=50
Reply from 19.108.1.106: bytes=32 time=23ms TTL=50

Ping statistics for 206.190.60.37:
    Packets: Sent = 4, Received = 4, Lost = 0 (0% loss),
```

Next, we will view the ARP table again:

```
C:\>arp -a

Interface: 19.108.1.14 on Interface 0x1000003
  Internet Address      Physical Address      Type
  19.108.1.1            00-f8-f8-ea-08-bc     dynamic
  19.108.1.102          00-19-ea-f8-36-95     dynamic
  19.108.1.106          00-95-6f-af-84-6d     dynamic
```

The options available on a Windows-based PC include the following:

```
Options:

  -a              Displays current ARP entries by interrogating the
                  current protocol data. If inet_addr is specified,
                  the IP and Physical addresses for only the specified
                  computer are displayed. If more than one network
                  interface uses ARP, entries for each ARP table are
                  displayed.
  -g              Same as -a.
  inet_addr       Specifies an internet address.
  -N if_addr      Displays the ARP entries for the network interface
                  specified by if_addr.
  -d              Deletes the host specified by inet_addr. inet_addr
                  may be wildcarded with * to delete all hosts.
  -s              Adds the host and associates the Internet address
                  inet_addr with the Physical address eth_addr. The
                  Physical address is given as 6 hexadecimal bytes
                  separated by hyphens. The entry is permanent.
  eth_addr        Specifies a physical address.
  if_addr         If present, this specifies the Internet address of
                  the interface whose address translation table should
                  be modified. If not present, the first applicable
                  interface will be used.
```

16.3.1.6   Ipconfig

The ipconfig utility provides the TCP/IP configuration for the PC and enables you to refresh many of the TCP/IP components (such as DNS). ipconfig is the Windows version of this tool, although many operating systems have a similar utility. Examples

ACRONYM ALERT

ASCII — American Standard Code for Information Interchange

of this include the ifconfig command that is used by Unix and some versions of Macintosh operating systems. Following is an example of the ipconfig command:

```
C:\>ipconfig

Windows 2000 IP Configuration

Ethernet adapter Local Area Connection:

        Connection-specific DNS Suffix  . : hs.comcast.net.
        IP Address. . . . . . . . . . . . : 192.168.1.1
        Subnet Mask . . . . . . . . . . . : 255.255.255.0
        Default Gateway . . . . . . . . . : 192.168.1.100
```

As you can see in the above example, the `ipconfig` command provides you with the DNS name pertaining to the ISP connection, node IP address, subnet mask, and the default gateway IP address. A lot of helpful options are available with this command. To view the options, use the `/?` option:

```
C:\>ipconfig /?

Windows 2000 IP Configuration

Ethernet adapter Local Area Connection:

USAGE:
    ipconfig [/? | /all | /release [adapter] | /renew [adapter]
             | /flushdns | /registerdns
             | /showclassid adapter
             | /setclassid adapter [classidtoset] ]

    adapter    Full name or pattern with '*' and '?' to 'match',
               * matches any character, ? matches one character.
    Options
       /?          Display this help message.
       /all        Display full configuration information.
       /release    Release the IP address for the specified
                   adapter.
       /renew      Renew the IP address for the specified adapter.
       /flushdns   Purges the DNS Resolver cache.
       /registerdns Refreshes all DHCP leases and re-registers DNS
                   names
       /displaydns Display the contents of the DNS Resolver Cache.
       /showclassid Displays all the dhcp class IDs allowed for
                   adapter.
       /setclassid Modifies the dhcp class id.

The default is to display only the IP address, subnet mask and
default gateway for each adapter bound to TCP/IP.

For Release and Renew, if no adapter name is specified, then the IP
address leases for all adapters bound to TCP/IP will be released or
renewed.

For SetClassID, if no class id is specified, then the classid is
removed.

Examples:
    > ipconfig                    ... Show information.
    > ipconfig /all               ... Show detailed information
    > ipconfig /renew             ... renew all adapaters
    > ipconfig /renew EL*         ... renew adapters named EL....
    > ipconfig /release *ELINK?21* ... release all matching adapters
```

Many tools are available to help you test and troubleshoot issues in your network.[21] When troubleshooting end-user issues, these tools allow you to relearn IP addressing, DNS information, and DHCP information.

At the beginning of this section, we told you that the `ipconfig` utility will provide you with the TCP/IP settings. To see a detailed list of these settings, just enter the `/all` option:

```
C:\>ipconfig /all

Windows 2000 IP Configuration

        Host Name . . . . . . . . . . . : Widget Net.
        Primary DNS Suffix  . . . . . . :
        Node Type . . . . . . . . . . . : Broadcast
        IP Routing Enabled. . . . . . . : No
        WINS Proxy Enabled. . . . . . . : No
        DNS Suffix Search List. . . . . : hsd1.nh.comcast.net.

Ethernet adapter Local Area Connection:

        Connection-specific DNS Suffix  . : hs.comcast.net.
        Description . . . . . . . . . . : blahblahblah-based
                                          Ethernet Adapter
        Physical Address. . . . . . . . : 1A-10-B5-4D-01-56
        DHCP Enabled. . . . . . . . . . : Yes
        Autoconfiguration Enabled . . . : Yes
        IP Address. . . . . . . . . . . : 192.168.1.1
        Subnet Mask . . . . . . . . . . : 255.255.255.0
        Default Gateway . . . . . . . . : 192.168.1.100
        DHCP Server . . . . . . . . . . : 192.168.1.100
        DNS Servers . . . . . . . . . . : 67.87.71.26
                                          67.87.71.22
                                          67.87.73.16
        Lease Obtained  . . . . . . . . : Sunday, October 19,
                                          2008 4:00:00 PM
        Lease Expires . . . . . . . . . : Monday, October 20,
                                          2008 4:00:00 PM
```

A lot of information is output when you use the `ipconfig /all` command. It is a useful command to view and resolve network connection issues.

---

[21] As well as connection issues with your PC.

This concludes the discussion of TCP/IP utilities in this chapter. We highly recommend that you try as many of these as you can to build a good understanding of how these tools can help you in the future. The next section travels outside of our TCP/IP world and discusses more specialized equipment and processes that assist in network troubleshooting, diagnosis, and resolution.

> **RANDOM BONUS DEFINITION**
>
> LAN segmentation — The practice of dividing a single LAN into a set of multiple LANs.

16.3.2   More Helpful Tools

The TCP/IP utilities that we discussed in the previous section are great tools when troubleshooting Layer 2 and above issues. But what happens when a cable breaks? There are several tools that are handy in troubleshooting Physical layer issues. Following is a list of some of these tools:

- **Volt-ohm meter** — This device is used to measure voltage, current, and resistance.[22] It is used to test electrical continuity through the physical medium. Volt-ohm meters are often called multimeters, which is entirely appropriate. There are two main types of multimeters, analog and digital. Digital multimeters are popular because they are accurate, durable, and may provide additional functionality not supported by an analog multimeter.

  The volt-ohm meter provides basic troubleshooting assistance, but can be helpful in determining whether you have an issue at the Physical layer. As you will find in Section 16.5, you will often start your troubleshooting sessions by looking for Physical layer issues. Having the capability to test the Physical layer at a moment's notice can save valuable time in the long run.

- **Cable tester** — Network cable testers are used to check the integrity of the cabling in the LAN. Cable testers are made for all types of network cabling (STP, UTP, coaxial, and optical fiber), and some cable testers can even choose the type of cabling that will be tested. There are different types of testers out there, and they vary in functionality. Normally, at a minimum, they enable you to test for crosstalk, attenuation, and noise. More advanced testers can test to ensure that the shield used in STP is not damaged, can display MAC address information, and can capture information pertaining to data rates, errors, and collisions.

---

[22]Some volt-ohm meters provide additional functionality to broaden their testing ability.

- **Breakout box** — This is a device used to troubleshoot issues over a serial port. The breakout box is placed between two nodes (for instance, between a router and a CSU). The breakout box monitors the signals and uses LEDs to display information pertaining to the signals.

- **Bit Error Rate Test (BERT) tester** — This device is used to generate a test pattern that the tester and a remote node can use to test the line for errors. Both the tester and the remote side can be set to the same pattern so that the integrity of the test is maintained.

It's not absolutely necessary for you to have any of these tools, but considering the affordability of many of these, it sure makes sense to have them around. You might never use them,[23] but they can prove extremely helpful when you are troubleshooting.

ACRONYM ALERT

FLR — Frame loss rate

16.3.3 Even More Helpful Tools

These are helpful tools that you will find yourself referring to often when troubleshooting, monitoring, and baselining your network. Of course, some of these tools are optional, and some may not be available on every system or network (for instance, some older LAN bridges did not have the capability of generating an event log). If you do have them available, however, by all means use them:

- **Event logs** — Most network nodes have an event log[24] that reports major changes to the status of any particular function of the node. Event logs can be helpful in troubleshooting an issue. In addition, the event log can be set to report catastrophic events. Often, the node will provide a dump of information that can be analyzed by the vendor.

- **Network analyzer** — The network analyzer is used to capture packets that are being transmitted on the LAN. The analyzer will log the data it receives and can analyze the data based on a specified RFC or standard.

  Network analyzers (*sniffers*) can be software based or can be a node running the analyzer software. Sniffers can be configured to capture all the traffic to and from a specified segment, or can be set to capture specific data only (for instance, only ICMP traffic). Sniffers are

---

[23]Scratch that — we all know that if you buy one, you will use it, even if you are just fiddling around.

[24]Many upper-layer nodes provide additional logs, such as security log, radius log, authentication log, hardware log, etc. While these are beyond the scope of this book, they should be reviewed when an applicable issue is occurring.

helpful any time you are having an issue with a portion of the network sending or receiving data. They provide a line-by-line analysis of the packets that were captured.

Sniffers are also helpful in troubleshooting protocol specific issues that may be occurring within the LAN. Intrusion attempts by an unwelcome remote party can be detected with the sniffer.

- **Documentation captures** — When troubleshooting, make sure you keep a copy of everything you do. If you are running commands on the command line, do them through a terminal emulator, such as Windows HyperTerminal. At the very least, capture the following (from all applicable nodes) before you do anything else:
  - Node configurations
  - Event logs (and any other available logs)
  - Status of the interfaces of the node
  - Memory-usage statistics
  - Any vendor-recommended documentation
  - Screenshots that may provide insight to the issue

As you are troubleshooting, capture anything you believe may be important. Any details that may help lead to resolution are recommended. In addition,

> **POP QUIZ**
>
> What does `tracert` do?

if you have a good idea of what the issue is and can capture proof, do so. Document any error messages you encounter. If at some point you need to contact a vendor or another technical support person, you will have a lot of documentation that they can start working with. It is much easier to bring someone up to speed if you have the visual evidence and the troubleshooting performed thus far (and the results).

16.4   A Logical Order

There are various strategies for troubleshooting issues in a LAN. The strategy discussed in this section provides a systematic approach to troubleshooting. There are variations to this troubleshooting model, but they are all geared to work toward the ultimate goal of resolving network issues in a timely manner. Following is an example of a logical model that you can follow to troubleshoot network issues:

1. Define the problem.
2. Consider the possibilities.

3. Determine the issue.

4. Find a possible solution.

5. Test the possible solution.

6. Develop an action plan.

7. Implement the action plan.

8. Monitor the results.

16.4.1   Define the Problem

Before you do anything, you need a good understanding of what the problem is. Sometimes this is a simple step to take, sometimes it isn't. Without fully understanding problem, you will find yourself going around in circles instead of progressing toward resolution.

Narrow down where the problem exists. How many users are affected? What is the overall impact? How many VLANs are down? What range of IPs cannot be reached? These are just a few questions that you should ask when gathering information. It's your opportunity to play detective and investigate. Most organizations have large, high-speed networks that are the core for the daily operations of the business. You need to isolate the problem not only to help you define what it is, but also to keep it from spreading to other segments of the network.

Don't always believe everything you hear. This is not to say that people are lying. A person may make an assumption and provide you more of an opinion than an explanation. You don't have to discount everything you hear. Instead, investigate the issue to confirm whether you

> **RANDOM BONUS DEFINITION**
>
> learning process — The process whereby a bridge builds its filtering database by gleaning address-to-port mappings from received frames.

can see what users are seeing (or saying that they are seeing). Don't take everything you hear to heart, and make sure you keep control over everything that is going on, especially when troubleshooting in a group setting.[25]

16.4.2   Consider the Possibilities

Once you have clearly defined the problem as much as you possibly can, the next step is to start looking at all the things that could be contributing to it. This is when you want to get out all of that baseline information you have

---

[25]This assumes you are the most experienced. If you are not, then have the most experienced person take control of the troubleshooting session, but make sure you keep one person in charge of all the operations. Otherwise, you may find yourself in a position where several members are making changes and not communicating with one another.

been keeping updated and start comparing the baseline data with the current status of the portion of the network you are troubleshooting. What can you determine from this data that is not normal operation? Narrow this down as much as you can.

It's a good possibility that you will never be troubleshooting an issue alone. Complex issues will sometimes require conference calls, and many other technical and nontechnical people will probably join, all hoping to work toward a resolution. Share the known. Share as much as you can. Remember that the more people who have all the facts, the better. When information is withheld (perhaps because someone doesn't want to admit a mistake) is when troubleshooting gets harder.

Once you have determined all the possibilities that may be causing your problem, start narrowing down the list of possibilities by going through them. Take a hard look at each one and see if you can prove whether each is working as intended. If so, you can cross that item off the list. If not, keep it on the list for further evaluation.

16.4.3   Determine the Issue

Now it's time to narrow down your list and go through the remaining items to see whether they can still seriously be considered as culprits of the problem. Continue to gather as much data as you can. Keep a running copy of your command-line sessions. Pull the system logs, get traces, etc. Any data that can be relevant to the issue, grab it. Document, document, document!

Analyze the data. Start with the Physical layer and then move on up the OSI reference model (more on this in Section 16.5). Once you have ruled out the physical medium, continue layer by layer until you determine where the problem lies. Rule out problems with the cables and the interface cards. Next, ensure that data is flowing across the cables. If it is, you will step up to Layer 3: Is information getting passed via the proper route?

The OSI reference model is a great model to follow when troubleshooting. Although some protocols were built without regard to the model, for the most part it is, and probably will forever be, the model to follow.

ACRONYM ALERT

ED — End delimiter

16.4.4   Find a Possible Solution

By this point, you should have a good idea of the issue. Once you have determined what the issue is, try to develop a solution. Make sure to consider all possibilities. Sometimes a problem may be a symptom of another issue. Sometimes more than one solution may be possible. In such cases, decide which is less intrusive and try that one first. Keep a list of other possibilities so you can continue looking into the issue should one proposed solution fail to resolve the issue.

16.4.5 Test the Possible Solution

Once you believe you have a possible solution, try to test it in a lab environment before trying it out in your network. If you don't have a lab to try it out in, you will have to do it on the network. Only in dire circumstances should you work on the network during peak periods.[26] Try to schedule downtime so you can try a solution without affecting too many users.

If you were smart enough to have proposed funds and lucky enough to have received them, you may have enough equipment for a lab. If you do, try to replicate and then test an issue in the lab before rolling the proposed solution out on the network.[27] Doing so provides an opportunity to test the solution, to ensure that the solution works, without negatively affecting the production network.

If you do not have the capability to test the solution, find out if one of the vendors can. If a theorized solution does not resolve the issue in a lab environment, you can work on another solution without any impact to the current network status. Of course, if the network is down and you need to get it back up, you may not have the opportunity to test before putting the testing into action. However, because the network is down, you will have an opportunity to try anything that will get it back up.

16.4.6 Develop an Action Plan

An action plan is one of the most helpful tools you can have available to you when you are implementing a proposed solution to a network problem.[28] Granted, sometimes you might not have the time to build an action plan, but even a verbal action plan is better than making changes without a plan in mind. Action plans should be written in an easy-to-understand manner so that anyone who might be joining the troubleshooting session will have a good idea of what is expected. In addition, the action plan is a great way to coordinate efforts.

The type and amount of data that you include in your action plan depends on what exactly you are working on. The action plan can be as simple as instructions for logging into a node, or as complex as who is involved, where

---

[26]Sometimes you won't have a choice.

[27]The network during troubleshooting sessions is often referred to as the production network. This is to distinguish it from a lab environment or from any question that is not affecting the network.

[28]An action plan is helpful any time you are making a change on the network.

they are involved, steps to be taken, recovery plans, etc. Once an action plan is drawn up, make sure that you have others review it for completeness and sensibility. It wouldn't hurt to have the vendor involved confirm the plan and offer recommendations. Finally, run through the action plan in the lab (if you have one) to see if your action plan resolves the issue.

Again, having an action plan is not a requirement, nor will you always be able to have one. In the long run, though, you will find that the action plan sure makes things smoother.

> **RANDOM BONUS DEFINITION**
>
> local area network — A network that covers a small geographical area.

16.4.7   Implement the Action Plan

It is now time to roll out the action plan. Set up the conference call, notify the appropriate user groups, and implement the action plan. The action plan should be an easy-to-follow document that lays out, in chronological order, the step-by-step troubleshooting procedure, so the implementation phase should run smoothly.

Make sure you have a backup plan so that if anything does go wrong during the change window you have a way to get the network back to where it was before you started the change.

16.4.8   Monitor the Results

Once you have implemented the action plan, it is time to monitor the results. Utilize all tools that you have for the baseline and monitoring so you can gather and compare statistics to ensure the desired effect has been obtained.

Make sure you allow ample time for all the standards and processes running on the node to make the appropriate decisions before panicking that something isn't working. For example, routing updates take time, so you need to allow the appropriate amount of time before you start worrying about something being wrong.

Test to confirm that the problem you are working on is resolved. Also, check other statistics to ensure that no new issues have arisen (in case a change has fixed one problem but introduced another one).

> **POP QUIZ**
>
> What does the command `ipconfig /all` provide for you?

Also be aware that sometimes a fix doesn't work in the production environment, and the troubleshooting process will have to begin again.

16.4.9   Another Fantastic Bonus from the Authors

That's right. Because you might need to have a reference at some point in your networking career,[29] we have included a handy-dandy flowchart to follow (see Figure 16-1).

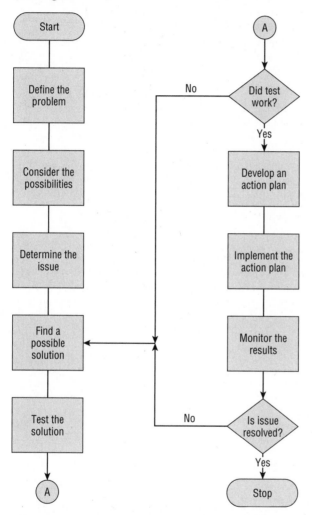

Figure 16-1 The bonus, handy-dandy logical troubleshooting reference flowchart

Continuing on, in the next section we show you how to exploit the OSI reference model when troubleshooting.

ACRONYM ALERT

MAC_PDU — Media Access Control Protocol Data Unit

---

[29]We also realized that we had gone too far into the chapter without a picture for you.

TROUBLESHOOTING TIPS

Keep in mind the following tips and follow them to the best of your ability. These tips will help keep the troubleshooting focus headed in a positive direction:

1. **Troubleshoot methodically.** Make sure that you stay focused on the task at hand and try not to get sidetracked while you are working on issue resolution. It is easy sometimes to get sidetracked when reviewing and troubleshooting the network. Make sure that you test each step completely before moving to the next step. In other words, test the Layer 1 possibilities fully before moving to Layer 2. It doesn't make sense to make sure that a cable is plugged into every interface but the last hop. Be sure that everything along the way is checked and confirmed.

2. **Document! Document! Document!**

3. **Approach every possibility with an open mind.** Don't discount anything just because you have never heard of it before. Review all tests, and retest if you need convincing, but do not ignore or discount any possibility. Also, don't ever assume. Just because you see a symptom that seems like one you have seen before, you can't be sure it is the same until you confirm that fact.

4. **Make sure you research error messages fully.**

5. **Remember that there can always be human error.** Also, humans are not always aware of, or honest about, something they might have done.

6. **Whenever possible, test and replicate an issue.**

7. **Keep anyone who might be affected by the trouble aware that the issue is being worked on. Provide a timeline when possible.**

16.5 Layered Strategy

An effective method of troubleshooting is to follow the OSI reference model (see Figure 16-2). Each layer in the OSI reference model communicates with its peer on the remote node (represented by the dotted line in the figure). Each layer passes data down to the next layer[30] for processing, and each layer provides services to the next-higher layer.

It's important that you understand the functions of each layer[31] and some typical issues that you will see within each layer. As you are trying to diagnose the cause of an issue, you should follow the OSI reference model. In this

---

[30] The exception to this is the Physical layer because that layer doesn't have a lower layer to pass data to.

[31] And by now you should.

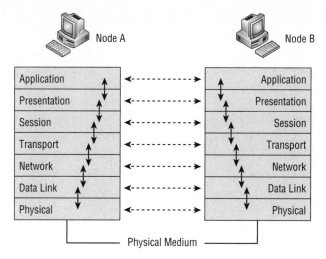

Figure 16-2 The OSI reference model

chapter, we discuss starting at the Physical layer and working your way up,[32] although it really doesn't matter which direction you head. As a matter of fact, you can start at the layer that you suspect is causing the issue and can continue from there. Here is a quick refresher on the roles of the OSI layers:

- **Application layer** — Provides services used by applications (the transfer of files and messages, authentication, name lookups, etc.) within the network.

- **Presentation layer** — Ensures that information received by one host can be read by that host.

- **Session layer** — Sets up, manages, and ends application sessions.

- **Transport layer** — Ensures the transmission of data from one endpoint to another.

- **Network layer** — Provides a path from endpoint to endpoint.

- **Data Link layer** — Provides a way to transport data over a physical link.

- **Physical layer** — Determines the specifications for the operations of the physical links between network devices.

If working from the bottom up, the first layer you check is the Physical layer. Check the cables and the node interfaces to confirm that everything is working correctly. Once you have ruled out the cables and interfaces, check for media access and data encapsulation configurations to ensure that everything

[32]This is because the book is geared toward networking newcomers, and following the OSI reference model from the bottom up makes it easier for a newcomer to work toward a resolution.

is working at the Data Link layer. After the integrity of Layer 2 has been confirmed, check for Network layer issues. Are you having routing problems or problems with addressing in the network? Finally, move on to the upper layers where you verify if the problem is related to memory or buffer issues, authentication, encryption, data compression, etc., all dependent on the layer you are troubleshooting.

As we have stated before, not all standards and protocols follow strict adherence to the OSI reference model. This fact does not change the basic troubleshooting strategy of using the OSI reference model. Regardless of the network issue, the OSI reference model is a good overall base model to follow while troubleshooting.

16.5.1   Common Lower-Layer Issues

Sometimes issues can occur at more than one layer. (For example, you can have a configuration issue in both the Data Link and the Network layer.) Other issues can occur at only one layer of the OSI model (for example, a dirty fiber cable). At

> **RANDOM BONUS DEFINITION**
>
> network — A set of nodes that connect to one another over a shared communication link.

the upper layers, many of the processes can overlap layers, which can make the job of troubleshooting a challenge.

In this section, we discuss common issues that relate to the lower three layers of the OSI reference model.

16.5.1.1   Layer 1

Often a network communication error can be caused by something as simple as a cable not being plugged in. This is why we recommend that one of the first things you do is to check the items that function at the Physical layer. Make sure that your cable is plugged in and that there are no errors (for instance, CRC errors, input/output errors, buffer failures, excessive collisions) accumulating on the interface. Most of these errors can be detected with some simple commands that are run within the command-line interface of a given network node. In addition, most network nodes have LEDs that indicate the status of a given interface. Check with the vendor for the definitions of the LEDs for any particular node.

Common Layer 1 issues that can occur in a network include the following:

- Damaged cables
- Dirty fiber

- Excessive signal attenuation
- Insufficient bandwidth
- Electrical interference
- Wireless interference
- Damaged interface
- Dirty interface

You can find yourself chasing the wrong issue if the Physical layer functions are not checked and verified operational. Just think about it. It makes no sense trying to figure out why you are not able to route to a specific subnet if the problem is as simple as a cable that someone has kicked out.

16.5.1.2 Layer 2

In a given LAN, there are plenty of Layer 2 nodes. Configured correctly, their operation should be transparent to end users, meeting and often exceeding expectations as they perform the function of getting frames from point to point. When a connection issue is occurring and the Physical layer has been ruled out, take a look at the processes operating at Layer 2 to see whether the issue originates or resides at this layer.

So, what will you want to look at? One thing to note is whether you are having an issue with a particular VLAN or are seeing a loop in the network. Then you need to focus on what is occurring at Layer 2 before continuing with your troubleshooting.

Common issues that occur at Layer 2 include the following:

- Configuration error
- Denial-of-service (DoS) attack
- VLAN configuration error
- Class-of-service issue
- Excessive utilization
- Excessive errors
- VLAN issue
- Spanning tree issue
- MAC address table issue
- Hardware compression issue
- Software compression issue
- VRRP issue

In networks where data is transported at both Layer 2 and Layer 3, it is important to ensure that the Layer 2 services are operational before assuming that a routing issue is due to a Layer 3 issue. Make sure that all Layer 2 functions are verified for any IP connectivity issue.

ACRONYM ALERT

PAgP — Port Aggregation Protocol

16.5.1.3   Layer 3

You have determined that the issue does not reside at Layer 1 and Layer 2, so now you want to focus on Layer 3. The simplest way to tell if Layer 3 routing is working is to issue a ping to a remote portion of the LAN. If you are having problems communicating with a particular node or subnet, issue the ping to an IP address of the affected area to see what the results are.

Most routers will provide a command-line interface in which you can issue commands to view the status of your IP interfaces. These show commands will be valuable in reporting the current status of particular interfaces and will assist in narrowing down the source of an issue. Compare the interface information with the information on the remote side of the connection to make sure they match. For the IP interface to be up and operational, the following holds true:

- The interfaces must be on the same IP network.
- The interfaces must have the same IP subnet masking scheme.
- Filters should be checked to make sure that no rules are configured for the interface. If there are rules, they need to be checked to ensure they are correct.
- Make sure that the interface configuration parameters are correct.

If all these items are checked and verified, the issue may reside in other layers, processes, or external to the node. Following are other potential issues that may be occurring at this layer that could be the cause of an IP issue in the network:

- ARP issue
- IP addressing issue
- Configuration error
- Authentication issue
- VLAN configuration error

Keep in mind that for one LAN to communicate with another, there has to be a route to the destination. The route to the destination is either static or dynamic, depending on the environment in which the router is placed. A helpful tool in troubleshooting is the configuration of a static route. Because of this manual configuration capability, network connectivity can often be restored with a static route, at least until the dynamic routing issue is resolved.

Layer 3 nodes (or nodes that provide Layer 3 services) have TCP/IP utilities that enable users to view the routing table, purge the routing table, etc. The routing table, ARP table, and the many `show` commands offered by the nodes are helpful in troubleshooting Layer 3 issues.

> **POP QUIZ**
>
> What are the eight logical steps that we provided in this chapter that you can use to troubleshoot an issue on the LAN?

16.5.2   Thoughts Pertaining to the Upper Layers

If you are able to successfully ping between nodes in different LANs, it is safe to assume that the connectivity issue is not a problem with Layers 1 through 3. If you can get a ping across, but some other things are not working, the problem is in the upper layers. Following are some of the things that you can look at in each layer:

- **Layer 4** — At this layer, focus on whether TCP or UDP is operating as intended. Take a sniffer trace and determine whether acknowledgments are being sent in response to requests. Also, check whether fragmentation is working as intended. Finally, check to see if any filters or QoS parameters may be affecting the flow of data.

- **Layer 5** — Things to look for at this layer include whether the Session layer protocols are receiving errors while trying to communicate. A sniffer trace can be used to determine if the protocols are behaving correctly.

- **Layer 6** — Encryption, formatting, and compression of data occur in this layer. Is data being encrypted/decrypted appropriately? Are encryption configuration settings correct? Are the correct data formats in use?[33] Another concern at this layer is whether a VPN tunnel is operating as it is configured to do.

- **Layer 7** — Are applications working correctly? Sometimes a version of a standard may support new features, and older clients may no longer interoperate with the new versions. Also, end users may still try to connect to a server with the incorrect client, and, of course, the user will not be able to connect.[34]

---

[33]In other words, is the end user viewing the data in the same format as it was sent? Make sure that the end user is using the correct program to view the data.
[34]You just cannot Telnet to a destination when the destination requires SSH.

As you can probably see, there is a method to this madness. Some issues require a bit of thought and investigation, whereas others can become second nature. Following the OSI reference model may or may not

RANDOM BONUS DEFINITION

overprovisioning — A technique of providing more capacity than is actually needed for a given application.

be for you, but it is a tried and true method . . . and methods really do help.

AN UNRELATED MOMENT OF PAUSE

Jim once worked with another engineer who received a phone call from a customer one day. The customer was insistent on getting a field engineer out to his site because the network was having a service-affecting issue. When the engineer arrived, the customer announced that the issue was no longer happening. The field engineer offered to take a look to ensure that the problem was resolved, but the customer kept turning him down.

After a few moments of discussion, the customer reached up on a shelf and produced a router that was no longer serviced by our company. The customer handed the router to the engineer and said, "Well, since you are here, you can help us configure this router." Although we were never able to prove it, we suspect that the customer told a little story to get an engineer on site and then to bully him into configuring the router. If that was the motive, it worked.

After a few years, this customer upgraded their entire LAN. New equipment, with all the latest and greatest (at the time) bells and whistles. With the upgrades, our company recommended that the customer begin training their support engineers on the new gear that would now be supported. The customer didn't think that this training was all that important, so they decided that the engineers would be trained on the job, rather than in a structured training process.

To make matters worse, multiple nontechnical managers took over the implementation phase. The implementation of the network wasn't the smoothest that ever occurred. The problem that ended up happening was that many of the engineers would make changes that would cause an issue, and no one would admit that they had made the change. The fear of being fired in the high-stress environment was very real, so many would not say a thing.

The moral of the story is to listen to others, but make sure you have proof.

16.6 Troubleshooting Examples

There is no way that we could list every possible scenario that you might come across when troubleshooting within your LAN. There are so many different vendors, standards, and configuration possibilities that the task of troubleshooting this week will be far different from what it was five years ago or five years from now. We could go into deep discussion about troubleshooting IPX and you might not ever come across a network running that protocol.

We do think it might be helpful if we run through a few possible situations you might come across in your LAN, and some recommended steps you can take to reach a resolution. We recommend that you follow the command examples we have listed throughout this section.

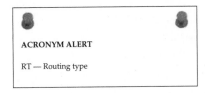

ACRONYM ALERT

RT — Routing type

16.6.1   Example 1: PC Can't Connect

A user on your LAN is not able to connect to the network. The computer comes up, but the user reports that no network connection can be obtained. This is considered a critical issue from the user's standpoint, because she cannot access servers that run applications she needs to do her job.

So far, you know that there is at least one user who is unable to connect to the network. Ask the user if others are affected; if not, you can assume the issue is local to the one user.

Have the user verify that there are LEDs on the network adapter. If there are, have her describe them. Are they blinking or solid? What color are they? Generally, a solid green light means an interface is up and there is a medium (wireless/physical medium) present. A blinking green light normally indicates that there are datagrams being passed through the interface. Any other color or activity indicates abnormal behavior. If the LEDs are not working correctly, have the user ensure that the network cable is properly connected.

If you have checked the interface and the connection and they appear to be intact, but there is still no activity, you can assume that the cable is bad, that the card is bad or is not configured correctly, or that the interface is not receiving a signal from the network for some other reason. Check the network card. Make sure it is inserted into the node correctly and is snug. Check the configuration of the interface and the card and confirm that they are configured correctly and that they match the next hop's interface settings.

Issue a ping to the interface itself. The well-known IP address for a local host interface is always 127.0.0.1. For example:

```
C:\>ping 127.0.0.1

Pinging 127.0.0.1 with 32 bytes of data:

Reply from 127.0.0.1: bytes=32 time<10ms TTL=128
Reply from 127.0.0.1: bytes=32 time<10ms TTL=128
Reply from 127.0.0.1: bytes=32 time<10ms TTL=128
Reply from 127.0.0.1: bytes=32 time<10ms TTL=128
```

```
Ping statistics for 127.0.0.1:
    Packets: Sent = 4, Received = 4, Lost = 0 (0% loss),
Approximate round trip times in milli-seconds:
    Minimum = 0ms, Maximum =  0ms, Average =  0ms
```

The results tell you that your interface is up and your NIC is working as it should. If there had not been four successful replies in the ping test, you could assume that either the NIC is not inserted correctly or that the NIC is failing. Next,

> **POP QUIZ**
>
> What are three common issues you can have at the Physical layer?

check the user's PC to make sure that the correct protocols are set up and are running and that no firewall policies are preventing network connectivity.

If there is nothing local to the user's PC that is preventing her from connecting to the network, it is time to migrate to the broadcast domain to see if issues at that level are causing the problem. Broadcast domain issues can be tricky to diagnose. Thank goodness that VLANs help keep the size of the domain down. Your network topology diagram will be needed when you are having an issue within a VLAN. The topology diagram ensures that you are looking at all possibilities within the VLAN. Otherwise, you will have to rely on memory and will have to explain the topology (possibly multiple times) to others who are assisting in the troubleshooting. Always remember that the logical topology is tougher to troubleshoot than the physical topology.

When an issue arises within the VLAN, the first step is to check all the members in the VLAN to see if there is one in particular that exhibits abnormal behavior. Begin troubleshooting bridges that are in the middle and then move outward. Following logical steps, try to pinpoint the issue:

1. Is there any maintenance going on?

2. Have there been any recent changes that may have created the issue?

3. Verify the configurations of the bridges.

4. Check statistics. Review logs and traces. Utilize `show` and `debug` commands that are available and are applicable.

5. Is this a new configuration? Make sure that all necessary configuration parameters are set correctly.

6. Are the VLANs configured correctly? Make sure that all VLAN rules were followed. Have there been any changes made? Did someone delete a VLAN, or are there other issues going on?

7. Are tagging rules applied correctly?

8. Is a routing issue preventing devices within the VLAN from communicating with other devices?

> **RANDOM BONUS DEFINITION**
>
> port number — A locally assigned, bridge-unique number that identifies each port on the bridge.

Regardless of the variables that apply to your LAN, this section gave you a good baseline strategy to work from when finding the cause of a user connection issue in any given LAN. However, there may be other steps that come into play, depending on the installed protocols, so make sure that you cover anything that may be applicable to your LAN.

16.6.2 Example 2: Reading a Sniffer Trace

Having the ability to read a sniffer trace is a must in any networking career. It is one of the most effective ways to prove an issue exists and what might be happening with a particular process you are analyzing. We use Wireshark version 1.0.4 for the examples in this section. If you have not done so already, we recommend that you download the latest stable version and follow along. (You need to learn how to use a packet analyzer at some point. If for some reason you don't want to use Wireshark, there are a lot of other free options. Wireshark is available at www.wireshark.org/download.html.)[35]

Once you have Wireshark (or some other traffic analyzer) installed on your PC, open it and start a capture.[36] Capture packets on the interface that you are using on your PC. The PC that was used in capturing the examples is a Microsoft Windows platform. The interface that is used on this PC is a NDIS 5.0 NIC (Network Driver Interface Specification, version 5.0), which is the interface architecture included in many Microsoft Windows packages. Make sure the traffic analyzer is set to capture and display the packets in real time so you can watch the packets as they are hitting the interface.

Once the traffic analyzer is running and capturing packets on the interface, we issue a ping command to Rich's website (richardbramante.com):

```
C:\>ping richardbramante.com

Pinging richardbramante.com [68.180.151.74] with 32 bytes of data:

Reply from 68.180.151.74: bytes=32 time=100ms TTL=49
```

---

[35]While you are at it, download the users guide for the software version that you will be using. The users guide is very informative and will explain the features and how to use them.

[36]Because all the basic functions of Wireshark are beyond the scope of this book, we are not going into the details of how to start the capture. The users guide will help you through this. If you are generally quick to learn menu navigation, the process is fairly straightforward.

```
Reply from 68.180.151.74: bytes=32 time=99ms TTL=49
Reply from 68.180.151.74: bytes=32 time=102ms TTL=49
Reply from 68.180.151.74: bytes=32 time=100ms TTL=49

Ping statistics for 68.180.151.74:
    Packets: Sent = 4, Received = 4, Lost = 0 (0% loss),
Approximate round trip times in milli-seconds:
    Minimum = 99ms, Maximum =  102ms, Average =  100ms
```

Now take a look at the example in Figure 16-3. This is a picture of the trace that we captured when issuing the above command. As you can see in the figure, there is a DNS query for richardbramante.com. A DNS response was sent back with the IP address associated with the domain name richardbramante.com. Once the IP address is located, you can see the four successful ICMP echo requests and the corresponding replies to each of this.

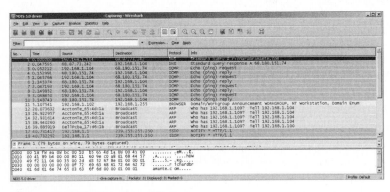

Figure 16-3 Viewing the sniffer trace

Wireshark (and most other analyzers) provides three views to the user. In this description, we used the term *window*, which means a section of the application. You are sure to see what we mean as we go along. The top window of the application shows the list of packets that have been captured, the middle window provides a tree of information for a selected packet, and the bottom window lists the byte information for the packet. Take a look at Figure 16-4 for an example of these windows.

In the example, we highlighted the fourth packet in the trace that we took. This was an ICMP reply packet from source node 68.180.151.74 to the destination node 192.168.1.104. Click on the packet in the upper area of the application to display a tree listing of the details for the fields of the packet. If you can remember the frame format of an ICMP reply, that'll help because this is the data that is provided in each of those fields. The bottom area is the byte information breakdown.

ACRONYM ALERT

SMDS — Switched multimegabit data service

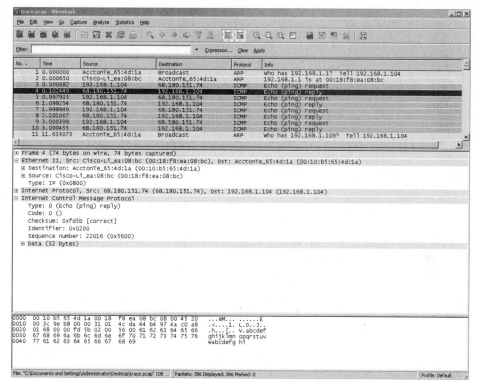

Figure 16-4 Viewing the sniffer trace details

Now that you have had an opportunity to see how a trace is taken and how to break down the information in the packet when you are analyzing/troubleshooting your LAN. Now, we highly recommend that you start another new trace (save your old one for future reference), and this time start multiple processes. Send an e-mail, open an HTTP session, do an FTP, and ping a remote destination (why not richardbramante.com?). While these processes are running, watch the packets processing through the traffic analyzer. This is a great way to better understand the processes of many of the applications used by the users of the LAN.

Another thing you can do is download example traces, which are available in many locations online. These are a good way to learn how to recognize some issues that you may come across. To locate these, just do an Internet search for "packet capture example."

16.6.3 Example 3: Identifying a Broadcast Storm

Network broadcasts and multicasts are a necessary operation for any LAN. If you have baselined your network, you should have a good idea of what is a normal amount of broadcasts or multicasts for your LAN. Therefore, you should notice when you are having more broadcasts than usual. (This condition could be catastrophic if not treated.)

If you are working on a LAN that is starting to run slower than normal,[37] it is a good possibility that you are experiencing a broadcast or multicast storm. Other symptoms of a storm include

- Network operations are timing out.
- Users are not able to connect to the network.
- Users are not able to log on.
- Application access is slow or is not available.
- The network is down.

A network could be experiencing a broadcast storm for several reasons. Hardware may have failed, there may be a configuration error on an interface or a node, spanning tree may have failed, a new application may be causing the issue, a virus or a worm may be attacking the LAN, and many others.

Broadcast storms can be identified in a sniffer trace and via network management systems. Finding the originator can be tricky at times. If the storm is propagating and is affecting multiple areas, you might need to have some coffee and donuts on hand; it's going to be a long night. Once you find the offending interface, you can disable it, and that should calm the storm. A rogue node on the network can be removed after it is located. A worm can be filtered and eventually eradicated with software upgrades and installations. The list goes on and on.

In the case of disabling an interface, you need to track down where the node is located. You can do so with information contained in the trace that you have taken. Some network management applications will also do the tracking for you. Once

> **RANDOM BONUS DEFINITION**
>
> presentation layer — The sixth layer of the seven-layer OSI model

you have located the offending interface, disable it. You can do that through the command line or you can pull out the cable. This can always be reversed, once you are able to clear whatever is causing or contributing to the storm.

16.6.4 Example 4: VPN Client Can't Connect to VPN Server

A VPN client reports that they are unable to connect to the VPN server. They have repeatedly tried to connect and have also tried to reboot their PC, but

---

[37]Jim likes the term *sluggish*.

they are not able to connect. The first thing the user needs to check is whether the VPN client is giving him an error message. If there is one, often it can be looked up at the vendor's website to see what the issue might be.[38] Finally, have the user make sure he has an active connection to the Internet. Has he rebooted his router/modem? Once you have verified that everything is operating correctly on the client side, whether there have been any changes on that end? These changes can be PC modifications, change of service provider, connection setting error, etc. Client issues can be tricky, because the user of the client software often has the capability to manipulate files on the PC. By making changes to their configuration, a conflict may arise that causes issues.

Everything on the client side has been checked and verified that the settings are correct and everything is operating as it should. If the client application allows for local logging, ask the user to set this up so he can log a connection attempt on his end. Also, the VPN server log should be checked for messages pertaining to the user that are on the VPN client side.

Client connection issues can range from a configuration error to a failed authentication attempt. Most of the time, an error will be displayed and should identify the problem that is occurring. If there is no error, check the logs. If you can run a sniffer trace on the client side (and possibly even the public interface of the VPN server), you may be able to see more indications of what the issue may be.

If all else fails, the VPN client software may have to be reloaded on the user's PC. This would have to be accomplished by following the rules of the LAN.[39]

> **POP QUIZ**
>
> What are some Network layer issues that you may come across in a LAN?

16.6.5   Example 5: Two Common LAN Issues

In Section 16.6.1, we introduced a single user's connectivity issue from the application that was running on the user's PC to the VLAN and routing domain that the user belonged to. VLAN issues in a bridged LAN are not the only common issue you might come across. *Duplex mismatching* and *spanning tree loops* are issues that you will come across at some point in your networking career.

In this section, we provide some information on these two issues and some ways to diagnose and resolve the issue. If you have access to a lab, you can

---

[38]Often the error is self-explanatory. For instance, invalid password means that the password is not right.
[39]Hopefully an automatic process or a script has been developed so the installation process is automatic and as transparent to the end user as possible.

easily replicate these issues and take some traces to view the processes and learn how to recognize them.

16.6.5.1 *Duplex Mismatch*

One of the most common issues that arise in an Ethernet LAN is a mismatch in duplex settings. If you have one end set to full-duplex while the other end is set to half-duplex, you will see latency when passing data on that link. It's always a good rule of thumb to run *autonegotiation* on your switch ports that connect to end users. Regardless of what PC they may be using and how it is configured, the switch will be able to recognize and mirror the settings of the other end. When autonegotiation was first introduced as a standard, there were a lot of issues with it working with some bridges that were already installed in networks at the time. Because of this, many network administrators hard-set the duplex settings on nodes in the internetwork. When possible, the settings should be set to 100 MB/full-duplex to ensure maximum performance from the link.

Symptoms that you may see that indicate a duplex mismatch include the following:

- FCS/CRC errors
- Runt datagrams
- Late collisions

The hard-coding of the duplex settings requires that the opposite end is set to the same duplex and speed settings. Although simple in concept, if the network grows, maintaining these settings at both ends might prove a real headache. In addition, if a device is set to autonegotiation, it will not communicate with any device that is not set to autonegotiate. It will recognize the speed of the link, but not the duplex settings.

Because the packets can be sent when you have a duplex mismatch, you cannot rely on a ping test to determine whether a problem exists. When you have a duplex mismatch, data can still be passed over the link, but will have failures when data is being forwarded from both ends of the link. Remember, in TCP many datagrams will send an acknowledgment to the sender, causing traffic to be sent in both directions on the link. The full-duplex side will receive the acknowledgment datagrams, but the half-duplex side will not and will recognize the link as having a series of collisions. This will cause most of the datagrams that were sent by the host on the full-duplex side to be lost. Another symptom you will

ACRONYM ALERT

TC — Topology change

see when there is a duplex mismatch is that the transfer of data is slower than expected when passing large amounts of data (in either direction).

The simplest way to check for duplex mismatches is to look at the configuration settings on both ends of the link.

16.6.5.2 Spanning Tree

A failure in spanning tree usually creates a loop within the area that the spanning tree group covers. The loop is often called a spanning tree loop, although this really does not make sense because spanning tree is there to prevent, not to cause loops. Therefore we should all start referring to it as a *lack of spanning tree loop*. So what does this loop mean? It means there is probably a port within the spanning tree that is forwarding traffic when it shouldn't be. Remember that a port can change from blocking to forwarding when it does not receive a better advertised BPDU from the designated bridge and therefore elects itself as the designated bridge.

Another problem that might be occurring is a duplex mismatch. If there is a duplex mismatch within the spanning tree area, the resulting collisions on the half-duplex side can cause BPDUs to not reach the other bridges and will therefore trigger a loop in your spanning tree. In addition, if the physical medium is reporting errors, this will cause packet corruption, which could cause excessive BPDU loss. Finally, a bridge could get overloaded and run out of resources, preventing it from sending out BPDUs, although this is not as common. Usually, forming and sending the BPDUs is not too resource intensive and will receive a priority over processes that consume resources.

If you experience a loop in your bridged network, you will most likely discover this through system statistics, with a sniffer trace, or because everyone is reporting issues. If you have effectively baselined your network, the network topology diagrams can prove very helpful when troubleshooting the loop. In addition, it helps to know where the root bridge is located in relation to the diagram, and which ports should be blocking, which ones are redundant links, and which are not utilized on the spanning tree. As mentioned previously in this chapter, this information will help you when you are reviewing the traces and the statistics while trying to trace down the problem. This will also assist anyone who may not be familiar with your network.

> **RANDOM BONUS DEFINITION**
>
> Rapid Spanning Tree Protocol (RSTP) — An enhancement to the original Spanning Tree Protocol; provides for a faster convergence when there is a change in the topology of the spanning tree group.

To get out of the loop as soon as possible, disable redundant links (beginning where you suspect most of the looped traffic is occurring). Although this can be time consuming, it will tell you where your problem lies. To disable the link, you can administratively do so or just pull the link and see if the loop dissipates. If the loop does not dissipate, you can put that link back in and move to the next one.

You also want to rely on your system event logs, system statistics, and any traces that you have captured. Some switches also allow options to verbosely log specific events, so you can capture more specific information in your event logs. Another thing to keep in mind when troubleshooting issues in multivendor environments is that some proprietary standards may cause problems with data passing between different vendor bridges. If your environment is such, check with the vendor for any compatibility issues that may exist.

WASN'T THIS BOOK A SNAP?

We know (well, are pretty sure) that you have enjoyed this book, but not as much as you are going to enjoy these cookies if you make them. We recommend that you bake up a couple of batches to munch on while you go over the 200+ bonus questions that follow in the appendixes. This recipe makes about 48 cookies. It was added to this chapter mainly because Jim and Rich have a diet competition going on, and Jim is trying to tempt Rich into baking and eating these cookies. It's also a bonus for you, the reader. Thank you for reading this book. We hope it really was a snap!

Ingredients:

- 1 cup brown sugar, packed
- 1/4 cup molasses
- 3/4 cup vegetable oil
- 1 egg
- 2 cups flour
- 2 tsp. baking soda
- 1/4 tsp. salt
- 1/2 tsp. ground cloves
- 1 tsp. ground ginger
- 1 tsp. ground cinnamon
- 1/3 cup sugar (for decoration)

(continued)

WASN'T THIS BOOK A SNAP? *(continued)*

Preparation steps:

1. Preheat oven to 375 degrees.

2. In a large bowl, mix the brown sugar, oil, molasses, and egg.

3. In a separate bowl, combine the flour, baking soda, salt, cloves, cinnamon, and ginger; stir into the molasses mixture.

4. Roll the dough into 1-1/4 inch balls.

5. Roll each ball in the white sugar and place them on an ungreased cookie sheet, 2 inches apart. Do *not* press the cookies down.

6. Bake for 8 to 10 minutes in the preheated oven. The cookie is done when the center becomes firm.

7. Cool the cookies on wire racks.

16.7   Chapter Exercises

1. For each item in the following list, identify the layer of the OSI reference model that item applies to:

   - Damaged cables
   - Dirty fiber
   - Excessive signal attenuation
   - Insufficient bandwidth
   - Denial-of-service (DoS) attack
   - Electrical interference
   - Wireless interference
   - Damaged interface
   - Dirty interface
   - Configuration errors
   - Authentication issues
   - Excessive utilization
   - Excessive errors
   - VLAN configuration errors
   - Class-of-service issues

2. In the following example, explain why there is a missing hop.

```
C:\>tracert 207.215.79.16

Tracing route to www.testshow.com [207.215.79.16]
over a maximum of 30 hops:

1    1ms   <10ms   <10ms  192.168.1.1
2    7ms    7ms     6ms  c-3-0-ubr01.boston.cast.net
                          [43.16.12.1]
3    9ms    8ms     7ms  ge-1-37-ur01.boston.cast.net
                          [43.16.12.193]
4     *      *       *    Request timed out.
5    7ms    7ms     7ms  po-24-ur01.boston.cast.net
                          [43.16.12.161]
```

3. True or false: The UDP connection state is one of the fields displayed with the `netstat` utility.

4. Network _____ testers are devices used to check the integrity of LAN cabling.

5. List three options that can be used with the `arp` command in Windows, and what each one does.

6. The network analyzer is also known as a _____.

7. What are three ways you can baseline your network? Describe each method.

8. What command in a Windows environment enables you to retrieve detailed information about the current TCP/IP settings of your PC?

9. From your PC, open a traffic analyzer and point it to the interface of your PC. Issue a constant ping to richardbramante.com (`ping richardbramante.com -t`). Next, disable your network connection. What do you notice in your trace?

10. This chapter listed eight quick checks that you can do when you are having issues within a VLAN. What are they?

16.8   Pop Quiz Answers

1. *User* feedback is a great way to be notified of an issue on the LAN.

2. Name 10 issues that you might have on the LAN.

   ▪ Damaged cables

   ▪ Dirty fiber

   ▪ Excessive signal attenuation

   ▪ Insufficient bandwidth

- Denial-of-service (DoS) attack
- Electrical interference
- Wireless interference
- Damaged nodes.
- Damaged interface
- Dirty interface
- Configuration error
- Authentication issues
- Excessive utilization
- Excessive errors
- VLAN configuration error
- Class-of-service issue
- Quality-of-service issue

3. Proactive troubleshooting or reactive troubleshooting — which is better?

   The proactive approach beats the reactive approach hands down!

4. What are two types of topology diagrams that come in handy when troubleshooting an issue within your LAN?

   Logical diagram and physical diagram

5. Name a proactive step you can take to help keep the network running.

   - **Shared knowledge** — It's always good to share what you know. Have discussions with others when you are not sure, and freely offer any helpful information you may have with anyone who might have a need to know.

   - **Proper tools** — Make sure that you and your staff have access to the correct tools. Examples include backup laptops, serial cables, baseline documentation, etc. The staff can only be as effective as their tools allow them to be.

   - **Knowledge requirements** — Make sure there is no single point of failure in the network. Make sure that any and all tasks are performed by at least two individuals. This way if someone is on vacation there will be at least one person in the know. Also, make sure that you allow only trained personnel to work on an issue. If this is not an option, make sure they have access to someone who is experienced.

   - **Spares** — If it was within your budget when you designed the network, you purchased (we hope) and have network spares on hand. These prevent shipping delays when there is a hardware problem. Be careful when you do use network spares; make sure not to do a hardware swap if the issue really isn't the hardware.

6. What does `tracert` do?

   Provides you with a visual view of the sequence of hops that a packet takes to a destination

7. What does the command `ipconfig /all` provide for you?

   A detailed listing of the TCP/IP settings on your PC

8. What are the eight logical steps that we provided in this chapter that you can use to troubleshoot an issue on the LAN?

   1. Define the problem.
   2. Consider the possibilities.
   3. Determine the issue.
   4. Find a possible solution.
   5. Test the possible solution.
   6. Develop an action plan.
   7. Implement the action plan.
   8. Monitor the results.

9. What are three common issues you can have at the Physical layer?

   - Damaged cables
   - Dirty fiber
   - Excessive signal attenuation
   - Insufficient bandwidth
   - Electrical interference
   - Wireless interference
   - Damaged interface
   - Dirty interface

10. What are some Network layer issues that you may come across in a LAN?

    - ARP issues
    - IP addressing issues
    - Configuration errors
    - Authentication issues
    - VLAN configuration errors

Additional Exercises

Chapter 1 — Introduction to Networking

1. What is an Internet service provider? (Section 1.1)

2. *An internet* is often confused with *the* _____, but an internet is not necessarily part of the _____. (Section 1.1)

3. What is an extranet? (Section 1.1)

4. In a client/server network relationship, the _____ stores data that is used by the users of the organizational LAN. (Section 1.1)

5. List three examples of a shared network resource. (Section 1.1)

6. What is a network protocol? (Section 1.1)

7. What is the name of the ARPA subgroup that was set up to focus on research pertaining to anything that related to computing? (Section 1.2)

8. What are the four locations that made up the original ARPANET? (Section 1.2)

9. The Nations Science Foundation Network (NSFNET) was developed originally to allow researchers access to five supercomputers. Where were these supercomputers located? (Section 1.2)

10. A _____ standard is a standard that is developed and owned by a specific vendor. (Section 1.3)

11. What is a de facto standard? (Section 1.3)

12. ANSI is the organization that represents the United States in working with the global community on discussions relating to two important global standards organizations. Name these standards organizations. (Section 1.3)

13. A _____ _____ is a team of IEEE professionals brought together to work on new research activities. (Section 1.3)

14. IEEE 802.3 identifies which IEEE working group? (Section 1.3)

15. IEEE 802.11 is the standard for _____ _____ _____ (Section 1.3)

16. What functions are performed at the presentation layer? (Section 1.4)

17. Network File System (NFS) is a data format that is used at the _____ layer. (Section 1.4)

18. Open Shortest Path First (OSPF) is an example of a _____ layer protocol. (Section 1.4)

19. Point-to-Point Protocol (PPP) is an example of a _____-_____layer protocol. (Section 1.4)

20. What are the reasons why we said that TCP/IP has grown into the "method of choice"? Explain each of the reasons you list. (Section 1.5)

21. Using the terms listed under the table, place them in the appropriate spaces. (Section 1.5)

Diagnostic Utilities	General Purpose Utilities	Services Utilities

```
ipconfig
```
File Transfer Protocol (FTP)

Address Resolution Protocol (ARP)

Remote Copy Protocol (RCP)

TCP/IP print server

Web server

Line Printer Daemon (LPD)

`tracert`

Remote Shell (RSH)

e-mail server

`nslookup`

Line Printer Daemon (LPD)

Trivial File Transfer Protocol (TFTP)

`ping`

File Transfer Protocol server

Telnet

`netstat`

route

DNS

Chapter 2 — LANs, WANs, and MANs

22. A LAN may consist of computers, printers, storage devices, and other shared devices or services available to a group of users within a _____ geographical area. (Section 2.1)

23. What does the term *sneakernet* refer to? (Section 2.1)

24. What are the three main IEEE standards that are primarily associated with traditional LANs? (Section 2.1)

25. The Media Access Control sublayer provides _____ and _____ control. (Section 2.1)

26. What was the name of the company that introduced Token Ring technology? When was it introduced, and what was the operating speed? (Section 2.1)

27. What are the two notable differences between the IBM and IEEE 802.5 specifications for Token Ring? (Section 2.1)

28. True or false: Both IEEE 802.3 and Ethernet are CSMA/CD network standards that are fully compatible with each other. (Section 2.1)

29. Fill out the missing information in the following two tables.
    (Section 2.1)

DB9 Pin Assignment

Signal	Pin
	1
Receive −	
Transmit +	
	5

RJ-45 Pin Assignment

Signal	Pin	Wire Color
		White with orange stripe
Receive −	5	
Transmit +		White with blue stripe
	3	

30. IBM Token Ring used cabling of different types to be used in different
    environments. Connect the appropriate type with its description below.
    (Section 2.1)

    Type 2 _____

    Type 5 _____

    Type 6 _____

    Type 8 _____

    Type 9 _____

    A. This type consists of two parallel pairs. The wires in this cable are
       untwisted and have a maximum length of 50 meters. The primary
       purpose of this wire is to be used in installations requiring the cable
       to run under carpeting

    B. This type consists of multimode fiber optic cable used to extend the
       token ring network and used to interconnect optical repeaters.

    C. This type consists of two shielded twisted pairs. It is considered
       a low cost short distance cable with a maximum length of 45
       meters and is often used for MAU-to-MAU interconnection.

    D. This type is a lower cost alternative to Type 1 cable with a maxi-
       mum length of 65 meters. It consists of two pairs of shielded twisted
       pairs.

E. This type consists of two shielded twisted pairs as can be found in Type 1 cable and four unshielded twisted pairs as can be found in Type 3 cable.

31. Although this protocol is closely related to Token Ring, it is not officially considered as part of the Token Ring family. Name this protocol. (Section 2.1)

32. Define the following bus network terms (Section 2.1):
    - Collision detection
    - Heartbeat
    - Jabber
    - Monitor

33. A star topology is implemented with the use of _____ and UTP cables terminated with _____ plugs. (Section 2.1)

34. Fill in the blanks in the following table (Section 2.1)

Pin	Ethernet	IEEE 802.3
1		
2		
3		
4		
5		
6		
7		
8		
9		
10		
11		
12		
13		
14		
15		

35. What are the two types of duplex? What are the differences? (Section 2.1)

36. Fault _____ is built into the dual-ring FDDI network. (Section 2.2)

37. What is POTS? What is it used for? (Section 2.3)

38. What type of a node is required in order for two LANs to be able to communicate using the ISDN protocol? (Section 2.3)

39. Explain the two most commonly used ISDN services. (Section 2.3)

40. A full T1 line provides _____ channels each with _____ Kbps of bandwidth. (Section 2.3)

Chapter 3 — Network Hardware and Transmission Media

41. Fill in the blanks in the following table. Explain how you converted each one. (Section 3.1)

decimal	binary
0	
1	
2	
3	
4	
5	
6	
7	
8	
9	
10	

42. What is RAM? (Section 3.1)

43. The type of RAM that is used by most PCs today is called _____.(Section 3.1)

44. Define the following: (Section 3.1)

- Read-only memory (ROM)
- Programmable read-only memory (PROM)

- Erasable programmable read-only memory (EPROM)
- Electrically erasable programmable read-only memory (EEPROM)

45. What is the difference between a PDU and an SDU? (Section 3.1)

46. In order for communication to take place between nodes, one end of the connection must be a _____ and the other a _____. (Section 3.1)

47. What are the four IP address network classes? Explain each one. (Section 3.1)

48. The main types of network cables are _____, _____, _____.(Section 3.2)

49. What are the four primary colors of cabling used in twisted pair?

50. True or false: Twisted pair cabling is used in Ethernet and Token Ring networks. (Section 3.2)

51. What are the types of twisted pair cabling? What are the differences in the types? (Section 3.2)

52. What are the two types of fiber optic cabling? Explain each. (Section 3.2)

53. The _____ is a hardware card that allows a PC to participate in passing and receiving data on a network. (Section 3.3)

54. A network _____ is a node that is able to multiplex signals and then transmit them over a single transmission medium. (Section 3.3)

55. What is the name for the node type that is similar to an Ethernet hub, but is used in Token Ring networks? (Section 3.3)

56. What is the name of the Layer 2 device that supports and performs the same basic function of joining network segments within the LAN? (Section 3.3)

57. What is the name of the node that operates at Layer 3 of the OSI reference model? (Section 3.3)

58. A _____is a node that allows the wire speed technologies that are used by Layer 2 and the tools that are needed to route packets at Layer 3. (Section 3.3)

59. Layer _____ switches have the ability to control the flow of data by implementing what is known as _____, which provides for packet queuing into classes of service to ensure that data with a higher priority is attended to before data with a lower priority. (Section 3.3)

60. Name at least three types of network servers that are used in a LAN. (Section 3.3)

Chapter 4 – Operating Systems and Networking Software

61. The portion of a computer that receives data and instructions and manipulates and acts on the received data in a controlled manner is known as what? (Section 4.1)

62. True or false: Data can never be stored on magnetic media because the magnet will erase all data. (Section 4.1)

63. The address space of a node can be determined by taking the number 2 and raising it to the power of the number of address bits that are generated by the CPU. That being said, calculate the following (the first one is done for you: (Section 4.1)

    16 address bits = 2^{16} (65,536)

    20 address bits = _____

    24 address bits = _____

    32 address bits = _____

64. Hard drives are usually mounted within a computer's case but today with USB ports many drives are sold as _____ drives communicating between the drive and computer over the USB port. (Section 4.1)

65. On personal computers input/output connections are in the form of ports dedicated to either _____ or _____ data communications. (Section 4.1)

66. What is the most basic form of an operating system? (Section 4.1)

67. In the world today, there are two main GUI-based operating systems that are in use by most people. What are they? (Section 4.1)

68. As the need for PC connectivity rose, the most common design of network operating systems was the _____ -_____ implementation. (Section 4.2)

69. True or false: One of the early network operating systems, Microsoft Networking, utilized an IPX/SPX protocol stack to provide communications over its network. (Section 4.2)

70. True or false: The problem with TCP/IP networks is that a workstation can only have a single session running at a time with any server on the network. (Section 4.2)

71. What is peer-to-peer networking? (Section 4.2)

72. True or false: To perform peer-to-peer networking, some sort of application program is required. (Section 4.2)

73. List the NetBIOS primitives that are associated with the session service and what each of them does. (Section 4.2)

74. For each of the following statements, give the corresponding operating system name. (Section 4.3)

   A. The operating system that was first developed by AT&T Bell Labs as a multiuser operating system. _____

   B. This operating system was designed more for the desktop environment even though it will run on larger computers. _____

   C. Newer versions of this operating system come with configuration utility programs that assist with the network settings and configuration. _____

   D. This operating system has many similarities and commonalities to Unix. _____

   E. Can be configured with a text editor. _____

   F. This operating system was initially designed to handle many users connected simultaneously and all sitting in front of a character-based terminal. _____

   G. Sun initially developed this operating system for their Sun SPARC workstations. _____

   H. This operating system is a flat file operating system; most of the configuration files are in readable text. _____

   I. This operating system provides strong networking tools to allow it to be interconnected not only to the local LAN but the Internet. _____

Chapter 5 — The TCP/IP Protocol Suite

75. Developers of networking protocols adhere to a _____approach. (Section 5.1)

76. Name the layers of the TCP/IP reference model and list what the responsibility is of each layer. (Section 5.1)

77. What is the name of the protocol that allows for e-mail communications and at which layer does it operate? (Section 5.1)

78. True or false: Secure Shell is an application layer protocol. (Section 5.2)

79. _____ names are names that are assigned to URLs on the Internet. (Section 5.2)

80. Make sure that you have a connection to the Internet, then use the `ping` command to find the IP address for the following domains. Write down your results. (Section 5.2)

    www.cnn.com ＿＿＿＿＿＿

    www.yahoo.com ＿＿＿＿＿＿

    www.wiley.com ＿＿＿＿＿＿

    www.google.com ＿＿＿＿＿＿

    www.richardbramante.com ＿＿＿＿＿＿

81. What does the acronym gTLD stand for? (Section 5.2)

82. What type of organization or business would use the following TLDs? (Section 5.2)

    ▪ .biz

    ▪ .com

    ▪ .edu

    ▪ .gov

    ▪ .jobs

    ▪ .mil

    ▪ .net

    ▪ .org

83. What is the name of the protocol that runs between nodes for the purpose of sharing management information pertaining to the managed system? (Section 5.2)

84. What are the three message types that can be sent from the SNMP manager to the SNMP agents? (Section 5.2)

85. A ＿＿＿＿＿＿ is a database that contains manageable objects and variables of these objects pertaining to a network node, for the purpose of node management within a network. (Section 5.2)

86. The formal language used by SNMP is ＿＿＿＿＿＿(Section 5.2)

87. What is an object identifier (OID)? (Section 5.2)

88. Name some of the improvements that were introduced by SNMPv2. (Section 5.2)

89. Which version of the SNMP protocol is considered the official one? (Section 5.2)

90. What is the name of the protocol that provides the capability for users to access an FTP server and transfer files to and from the server? (Section 5.2)

91. Fill out the correct FTP command in the following table. (Section 5.2)

Command	Function
	Sets the file transfer mode to ASCII.
	Sets the file transfer mode to binary.
	Changes to another directory.
	Terminates a connection.
	Removes a file.
	Places a copy of a file on the remote node onto a specified directory on the local node.
	Used to monitor the file transfer process. For every 1028 bytes received, a # will be placed on the screen.
	Gets a list of available FTP commands.
	Gets information about commands.
	Lists the names of the files in the current directory.
	Used to copy more than one file from the remote node to the local node.
	Makes a new directory.
	Used to copy more than one file from the local node to the remote node.
	Used to copy a file from the local node to the remote node.
	Used to determine the directory path to the current directory.
	Terminates the FTP session.
	Renames a file or directory.
	Removes a directory and any subdirectories, if applicable.

92. True or false: There is no difference between the TFTP and FTP protocols. They have different names because they were developed by different companies, but they are exactly the same in function. (Section 5.2)

93. Using the SMTP protocol, an SMTP client has a total of five message types that are sent to an SMTP server. Following is a list of these message types. Define the purpose of each one. (Section 5.2)

   ▪ HELO
   ▪ MAIL
   ▪ RCPT

- DATA

- QUIT

94. Developed originally by Sun Microsystems, this protocol allows end users access to files that are stored remotely as if the files were local to the end users workstation. What is the name of this protocol? (Section 5.2)

95. What are the three modes of operation used by Telnet clients and servers? (Section 5.2)

96. SSH utilizes _____ _____ _____ which is used to provide cryptographic keys to authenticate remote nodes and users. (Section 5.2)

97. What are the two most popular Transport layer protocols? (Section 5.2)

98. Name at least three Application layer protocols that use TCP. (Section 5.2)

99. Name at least three Application layer protocols that use UDP. (Section 5.2)

100. Name at least five Internet layer protocols. (Section 5.2)

101. What is the name of the protocol that allows for operating system access for diskless nodes? (Section 5.3)

102. Define the following. (Section 5.3)

- Routing protocol

- Routed protocol

- Gateway

- Interior Gateway Protocol (IGP)

- Exterior Gateway Protocol (EGP)

- Static routing

- Dynamic routing

Chapter 6 — Ethernet Concepts

103. What is the speed of the following Ethernet types? (Section 6.1)

- 10BASE-T

- Fast Ethernet

- Gigabyte Ethernet

104. Ethernet nodes using UTP cabling fall into one of two component types. What are those? (Section 6.1)

105. What is a straight-through cable? (Section 6.2)

106. True or false: A straight-through cable can be wired with either the T568A or T568B wiring scheme as long as both ends of the cable are wired exactly the same using the same wiring pin-out. (Section 6.2)

107. A _____ Ethernet cable must have one plug wired with the T568A wiring scheme and the other plug wired following the T568B wiring pin-out. (Section 6.2)

108. What is the major difference between the OSI reference model and the IEEE 802.3 model? (Section 6.3)

109. What is a frame check sequence? (Section 6.4)

110. Define the following. (Section 6.4)

   ▪ Carrier sense

   ▪ Multiple access

   ▪ Collision detection

111. Fill in the missing information in the following table. (Section 6.4)

Half-Duplex Operational Limitations

Parameters	10 Mbps	100 Mbps	1000 Mbps
Minimum frame size			
Maximum collision diameter with UTP cable			100 meters
Maximum collision diameter with repeaters	2500 meters	205 meters	200 meters
Maximum number of repeaters in network path			

112. What is frame bursting, and when was it introduced? (Section 6.4)

113. _____ _____ transmission is the capability of a network node to transmit and receive simultaneously. (Section 6.4)

114. _____ are nodes that are actually considered part of the Physical layer since they are not decision-making devices. They basically provide the interconnectivity on the physical level for network nodes. (Section 6.4)

115. _____ is the capability of a network interface to negotiate the communication parameters to be used between it and the port it is connected to. (Section 6.4)

116. True or false: Network administrators don't have to worry about traffic patterns on the network. (Section 6.5)

117. What does the acronym VLAN stand for? (Section 6.5)

Chapter 7 — Not to Be Forgotten

118. What is the name of the LAN protocol that was once popular in the majority of active LANs and is now used as an embedded standard to serve networks that control technologies such as automation services, transportation, robotics, gaming, and other similar network types? (Section 7.1)

119. _____ technology is, for the most part, the predecessor to what we all know as Ethernet. (Section 7.1)

120. What is the name of the corporation that developed Token Ring technology? (Section 7.1)

121. True or false: Unshielded twisted pair (UTP) cables became the preferred medium used by Token Ring technologies. This is because it was less bulky than shielded twisted pair (STP) cables and was also less expensive than STP. (Section 7.1)

122. What is the name of the first technology that could operate at 100 Mbps? (Section 7.1)

123. What advantages are there in using optical fiber as the primary transmission medium within a network? (Section 7.1)

124. _____ is the FDDI protocol over twisted-pair medium instead of fiber. (Section 7.1)

125. Define the following FDDI node types. (Section 7.1)

    ▪ Single attachment station (SAS)

    ▪ Single attached concentrator (SAC)

    ▪ Dual attachment station (DAS)

    ▪ Dual attached concentrator (DAC)

126. The Digital Equipment Company (Digital) developed and released the first version of the _____protocol in the mid-1970s. (Section 7.2)

127. What are the levels of the XNS model and what layer does each level correspond to on the OSI layered model? (Section 7.2)

128. The _____ protocol is one that is normally found within networks that have nodes that are running the Novell NetWare operating system. (Section 7.2)

129. In order to support multiple protocol datagrams, there are three main components that are used by PPP. What are they? (Section 7.2)

130. The Link Access Procedure, Balanced (LAPB) is the _____ link level protocol that ensures reliable, error-free packet framing and data communication management. (Section 7.2)

131. Match the ATM adaptation layer type to its appropriate function. (Section 7.2)

   AAL1 _____

   AAL2 _____

   AAL3 _____

   AAL4 _____

   AAL5 _____

   A. This AAL type supports both connectionless and connection-oriented data transmission. This AAL type is used to transmit non-SMDS packets.

   B. This AAL type supports VBR transmissions.

   C. This AAL type supports CBR transmissions.

   D. This AAL type supports both connectionless and connection-oriented data transmission. This AAL type is used to transmit switched multimegabit data services (SMDS) packets.

132. AppleTalk is a protocol suite that was developed by the Apple computer company. AppleTalk was developed specifically to be integrated with new _____ computers to allow for resource sharing on a network. (Section 7.2)

133. There are two services used in ISDN to determine bandwidth availability for an end network. These are _____ and _____. (Section 7.2)

Chapter 8 — The Upper Layers

134. The upper layers of the OSI reference model are utilized by _____ _____ to send and receive data over a network. (Section 8.1)

135. True or false: One of the great things about mail servers is that they do not have to perform any authentication, as such authentication is only performed by a RADIUS server. (Section 8.1)

136. The _____ field is an 8-bit field that indicates how many seconds a packet can live on the Internet. (Section 8.2)

137. DMZ is the acronym for what? (Section 8.2)

138. FTP and SMTP are upper-layer protocols that reside within which layer of the TCP/IP model? (Section 8.2)

139. The following table contains some common Application layer protocols. Complete the missing parts of the table. (Section 8.2)

Mnemonic	PORT(s)	Description
DHCP		Dynamic Host Configuration Protocol provides the means for network clients to obtain an IP address, default gateway IP address and Domain Name System server addresses.
FTP		
HTTP	80	
		Simple Network Management Protocol is used to manage and monitor network devices over the local network and Internet.
Telnet		

140. True or false: Port numbers range from 0 to 65,535, but for the most part the first 1024 (0 to 1023 decimal or 0x03FF hexadecimal) are considered to be the well-known ports. (Section 8.2)

141. Explain `traceroute`. (Section 8.2)

142. _____ is a dynamic routing protocol used to move packets from network segment to network segment. (Section 8.2)

143. True or false: Port 0 is normally reserved, but its use is allowed as a valid source port in transmissions where the transmitting network node does not require a response from the receiving network node. (Section 8.2)

Chapter 9 — The Transport Layer

144. What is the standard that defines the recommended services that are provided by the OSI Transport layer while working with the Network layer to serve the needs of protocols that are used at the Session layer? (Section 9.1)

145. What is the standard that sets the recommendations to be followed by nodes (entities) within a network that are utilizing the services of the OSI Transport layer? (Section 9.1)

146. There are two types of transport service. What are they? (Section 9.1)

147. What are the two data units that operate at the Transport layer? (Section 9.1)

148. Match the correct transport service class with its class function. (Section 9.1)

Class 0 _____

Class 1 _____

Class 2 _____

Class 3 _____

Class 4 _____

A. Error recovery and multiplexing class

B. Multiplexing class

C. Simple class

D. Error detection and recovery class

E. Basic error recovery class

149. The purpose of the Transport layer is to provide end-to-end delivery of data from one _____ to another. (Section 9.2)

150. Explain how a three-way handshake works. (Section 9.2)

151. True or false: The term *connectionless* can be misleading as connectionless protocols require a connection before they can transmit data. (Section 9.2)

152. TCP is a _____ protocol, whereas UDP is a _____ protocol. (Section 9.3)

153. In a connection-oriented environment, _____ control and _____ control are two mechanisms that are used to maintain control over the transmission of data. (Section 9.4)

Chapter 10 — The Network Layer

154. SMTP mail servers will deliver e-mail to the _____ _____ server servicing a particular domain. (Section 10.1)

155. `http://www.mydomainname.com` is an example of a _____. (Section 10.1)

156. True or false: Unlike IP addresses, domain names do not have to be unique. (Section 10.1)

157. What protocol is primarily a method of moving packets of data across networks consisting of various mediums, seamlessly delivering these packets solely based on destination address? (Section 10.2)

158. What version of IP allows for 4,294,967,296 unique addresses? (Section 10.2)

159. What would the binary number look like for the IP address 192.168.15.85? (Section 10.2)

160. The real thrust of moving to _____ is the larger address space that it provides with 128 bits dedicated to address space. (Section 10.2)

161. What is the name of the protocol that provides a means of messaging when a sent datagram is not able to be received by a destination node? (Section 10.2)

162. The _____ command is used to trace the path from the sending network node to the receiving network node on a network hop-to-hop basis. (Section 10.2)

163. What is the name of the protocol that makes use of authentication and encryption to establish a secure connection between end point network nodes? (Section 10.2)

Chapter 11 — The Data Link Layer

164. In this chapter, we discussed certain expectations that each LAN should meet. We called them the highs and the lows. What are each of these? Define them. (Section 11.1)

165. A collision causes datagrams to be _____, but it doesn't necessarily mean that the data can't be recovered in some way. (Section 11.2)

166. In a token bus configuration, there is a central node called a _____ or a _____. This device is similar to an Ethernet hub, but it has a computer chip that provides the logical ring that the end nodes are concerned with. (Section 11.2)

167. Define the following. (Section 11.2)

    - Carrier Sense Multiple Access (CSMA)

    - Carrier Sense Multiple Access with Collision Avoidance (CSMA/CA)

    - Carrier Sense Multiple Access with Collision Detection (CSMA/CD)

168. A _____ _____ in CSMA/CD is a message to all other nodes that a collision has occurred and that they should stop transmitting. (Section 11.2)

169. Match the LLC type with the correct answer. (Section 11.3)

LLC Type 1 (LLC-1) _____

LLC Type 2 (LLC-2) _____

LLC Type 3 (LLC-3) _____

A. This LLC type is used for connectionless services.

B. This LLC type is used for connection-oriented services.

C. This LLC type is used for acknowledgments in conjunction with connectionless services.

170. Define the following. (Section 11.3)

■ Destination service access point (DSAP)

■ Source service access point (SSAP)

■ Control

171. The _____ is a protocol that is used in conjunction with LLC-1 for the purpose of upward multiplexing to more upper layer protocols than what is available with the standard LLC 8 bit SAP fields. (Section 11.3)

172. True or false: The LLC sublayer is responsible for interfacing between the MAC sublayer and the Physical layer. (Section 11.3)

173. The IEEE 802 _____ address is a 48-bit address that is used to identify the network adaptor for a particular node or interface in the network. (Section 11.3)

174. What is the name for the portion of a frame that contains the source and destination MAC addresses for interfaces that are involved in a communication stream? (Section 11.4)

175. True or false: Multicasting is the act of sending a message to multiple nodes. (Section 11.4)

176. What is the function of the following well-known MAC addresses? (Section 11.4)

■ 01:80:C2:00:00:00

■ 09:00:4E:00:00:02

■ CF:00:00:00:00:00

■ 09:00:2B:00:00:0F

177. Frames are either _____ _____ or _____ _____ PDUs (Section 11.4)

178. _____ is a function that is used to detect common errors that may occur during data transmission. (Section 11.4)

179. Ethernet uses what are known as _____ frames for flow control within Ethernet LANs. (Section 11.4)

180. Explain the following. (Section 11.5)

   - Source route bridging
   - Transparent bridging

181. True or false: A bridge is a device that operates much like a repeater or a hub, but it makes data forwarding decisions that bridge traffic from one network segment to another. (Section 11.5)

182. True or false: When a bridge receives a frame that is destined for a multicast address, the bridge will forward the frame to all of the ports, including the port on which it is received. (Section 11.5)

Chapter 12 – Design Methodologies

183. Which of the following is _not_ a type of organizational LAN? (Section 12.1)

   - Hospital LANs
   - Banking and financial corporate LANs
   - Manufacturing LANs
   - Retail LANs
   - The Internet

184. What are examples of external considerations that need to be made when designing a network? (Section 12.1)

185. Developing a project _____ is important in the early phases of network design. (Section 12.2)

186. The _____ design models are the most commonly used in most high-speed LANs today. (Section 12.3)

187. In a hierarchical design model, there are three layers. What are they? (Section 12.3)

188. What are three WAN protocols that can be used to connect a LAN to remote sites? (Section 12.3)

189. The _____ layer is the middleman between the access layer and the core. (Section 12.3)

190. The _____ layer is the backbone of the LAN and often provides connectivity to WANs as well as Internet services. (Section 12.3)

191. Explain some of the benefits of using a hierarchical model. (Section 12.3)

192. Specify the maximum allowed in each level of the 5-4-3-2-1 design model. (Section 12.4)

   ▪ _____ is the number of *segments* allowed in total.

   ▪ _____ is the number of *repeaters* used to join the segments together.

   ▪ _____ is the maximum number of segments in total that have nodes that are *active*.

   ▪ _____ is the maximum number of segments in total that are *not active*.

   ▪ _____ is the number of *collision domains*.

193. The _____ topology is the most often used topology in LANs. (Section 12.5)

194. What are the advantages to the bus topology? (Section 12.5)

195. What are the disadvantages to the bus topology? (Section 12.5)

196. What are the advantages to the star topology? (Section 12.5)

197. What are the disadvantages of a star topology? (Section 12.5)

198. What are the advantages of a ring topology? (Section 12.5)

199. What are the disadvantages of a ring topology? (Section 12.5)

200. The _____ topology is used for Token Ring and FDDI LANs. (Section 12.5)

201. The _____ used within a LAN is either a hub or an MAU that allows the combination of data transmissions for a group of nodes. (Section 12.5)

202. The _____, or _____, is a LAN node that operates at Layer 2 of the OSI reference model. (Section 12.5)

203. What is the name of the traditional network node that operates at Layer 3 of the OSI reference model? (Section 12.5)

204. Why is a Layer 3 switch preferred over a traditional router in high-speed LANS? (Section 12.5)

205. List five terms that are used to define a switch that operates at Layers 4-7 of the OSI model. (Section 12.5)

206. Explain what each type of switch does. (Section 12.5)

   ■ Cut-through

   ■ Store and forward

207. Which of the following is a false statement? (Section 12.5)

   ■ A configuration error within the LAN.

   ■ Introduction of a duplicate route.

   ■ A loop only occurs when there is no redundancy built into the network.

   ■ Introducing an additional node into the LAN.

208. What is the name of the public standard protocol that was developed to control loops in a catenet? (Section 12.5)

209. What are the possible port states used by STP? (Section 12.5)

210. The standard that covers link aggregation is _____, the Link Aggregation Control Protocol (LACP). (Section 12.5)

211. What are some benefits of link aggregation? (Section 12.5)

212. What are some disadvantages of link aggregation? (Section 12.5)

213. What are some benefits of creating VLANS within your LAN? (Section 12.5)

214. What are the four types of VLANS? (Section 12.5)

215. What are the two types of network management nodes and what function does each type perform? (Section 12.5)

Chapter 13 — Implementation

216. True or false: Good network planning begins with a top-down approach. (Section 13.1)

217. There is a natural dividing line as far as planning goes; one involves a _____ network infrastructure and the other a totally new design. (Section 13.1)

218. In the chapter, we discussed some fixed costs that you should consider when planning the network. What are these? (Section 13.1)

219. In the chapter, we discussed some recurring costs that you should consider when planning the network. What are these? (Section 13.1)

220. Which is the best answer to the following statement? (Section 13.1)

   Many companies these days lump _____ under the IT (information technology) umbrella.

    A. Computer operations and network operations.

    B. Telecommunication services

    C. Computer operations, network operations, and all other telecommunications

    D. All data communication services

221. What is a false floor? (Section 13.1)

222. What is a DMZ? (Section 13.1)

223. The VPN remote users have a VPN _____ on their PCs which is configured to access the company's VPN access gateway router. (Section 13.1)

224. True or false: The distribution from the network operations area to each floor is accomplished by using redundant STP cabling to provide a high-speed path for the network traffic coming from each floor. (Section 13.1)

225. List the items that should be included in the final documentation of a network. (Section 13.1)

226. _____ refers to the structural components within a facility in support of the network architecture. (Section 13.2)

Chapter 14 — Network Security

227. What does WEP stand for? (Section 14.1)

228. In a networking environment, what is the area that should be restricted and controlled access at all times? (Section 14.1)

229. True or false: The security practices used in a home LAN are sufficient for all large corporate LANs. (Section 14.1)

230. A _____ is placed in the path in front of the Intranet web server to analyze the network traffic that is being directed towards it. (Section 14.1)

231. True or false: Depending upon the size of the network, constantly monitoring every node of a network can be overwhelming. (Section 14.1)

232. True or false: It is bad practice to document the network from a security perspective. (Section 14.1)

233. Name three methods of authentication. (Section 14.2)

234. True or false: The process of network authentication can be simple as a user ID and password. (Section 14.2)

235. What are the four most commonly used elements in an LDAP? (Section 14.2)

236. When a RADIUS client passes a user's authentication credentials to the RADIUS server, the server will respond with one of three responses. What are these responses and what does each mean? (Section 14.2)

237. The use of _____ came into use as a security method used to ensure the entities on opposite ends of a communication channel are who they claim to be. (Section 14.2)

238. _____ is a suite of protocols used for securing Internet communications. (Section 14.2)

Chapter 15 — Network Management

239. True or false: To have a successful help desk implementation, there is a need for someone to pick up the telephone. (Section 15.1)

240. In a large organization, there are usually groups of dedicated individuals who support certain aspects of the network. What are they? (Section 15.1)

241. True or false: Monitoring network performance for larger networks is a manual, time-consuming process. (Section 15.1)

242. In any organization, the security group would have a broad range of activities that deal with all aspects of network _____ (Section 15.2)

243. The _____ support group is responsible for the distribution of network services over the network. (Section 15.2)

244. What is the logistics group responsible for? (Section 15.2)

245. What are three activities that are considered network maintenance? (Section 15.3)

246. The SNMP _____ is software that communicates with a network management station (NMS) to answer queries from the station. (Section 15.5)

247. Each element has its own unique _____, which provides information on the object or is an object that will take a variable setting to configure the unit. (Section 15.5)

248. True or false: Packet capture nodes and programs can return some statistical information if you are investigating

traffic patterns or performance issues on a network segment. (Section 15.5)

249. SNMP uses a _____ setting to group a number of devices to be monitored within the _____. (Section 15.5)

Chapter 16 — Troubleshooting

250. Name at least five of the common LAN issues that we mentioned in the chapter. (Section 16.1)

251. When you are notified of a network issue, what are some of the first questions you should start considering? (Section 16.1)

252. The _____ approach beats the _____ approach. (Section 16.2)

253. Which of the following is a good proactive step you can take to help keep the network from going down and to recover quickly when it does? _____ (Section 16.2)

   ▪ Shared knowledge

   ▪ Proper tools

   ▪ Ensure the proper individuals are trained appropriately

   ▪ Hardware spares

   ▪ All of the above

254. The ping is an ICMP echo request/reply that determines whether a node is _____, the _____ time for the process to complete, any _____ percentages, and a statistical _____ for a given remote node. (Section 16.3)

255. True or false: By default, the `ping` command will send four ICMP requests and will expect four replies. (Section 16.3)

256. The _____ utility by default displays both incoming and outgoing network connections. (Section 16.3)

257. Network cable testers are devices that are used to check the integrity of the _____ in the LAN. (Section 16.3)

258. Name a few things that you should investigate when troubleshooting a node that is having problems. (Section 16.3)

259. What are the steps in the logical, eight-step troubleshooting model that we discussed in the chapter? (Section 16.4)

260. As redundant as it may seem, what are the layers of the OSI reference model, and what is performed at each layer? (Section 16.4)

261. What are some common Layer 1 issues that can occur in a network? (Section 16.5)

262. What are some things that you should look for in each of the following layers? (Section 16.5)

   ▪ Layer 4

   ▪ Layer 5

   ▪ Layer 6

   ▪ Layer 7

263. What are three of the symptoms that indicate a duplex mismatch? (Section 16.7)

264. A failure in spanning tree usually creates a _____ within the area that the spanning tree group covers. (Section 16.7)

265. What are three common ways to find out you have a loop within the LAN? (Section 16.7)

Exercise Answers

Chapter 1 Exercises

1. The network used exclusively by the University of Texas is an example of a *campus area network* (CAN). Note that LAN and MAN are also appropriate responses.

2. What are the names of the layers in the OSI reference model?

   - Layer 7 — Application
   - Layer 6 — Presentation
   - Layer 5 — Session
   - Layer 4 — Transport
   - Layer 3 — Network
   - Layer 2 — Data Link
   - Layer 1 — Physical

3. List at least five applications and/or utilities that use TCP/IP.

   - Telnet
   - FTP

- SMTP
- POP
- SNMP

4. What are the two types of network relationships?

   - Connectionless
   - Connection-oriented

5. Explain the difference between a client/server network relationship and a client/server database system.

   In both cases, the server provides the data requested by a client, but in a database system, the client node has to use its own resources to format and view the data retrieved.

6. What is the 1822 protocol?

   Specifies the method to connect a host computer to an ARPANET router.

7. What are the three types of standards? Do a search on the Internet to see if you can find at least one of each standard type.

   - Proprietary
   - Open
   - De facto

8. The 802.11n standard supports an operating frequency of *2.4 GHz* and *5 GHz*. The maximum data rate for 802.11n is *600 Mbps*. 802.11n reaches a maximum indoor range of *70 meters* and an outdoor range of 250 meters.

9. True or false: The Application layer of the OSI model concerns itself with the application/user interface on a PC.

   True

10. In this chapter, we listed seven reasons why TCP/IP has grown to be the "method of choice." What are these seven reasons?

    - Routing
    - Addressing
    - Name resolution
    - Operates on many types of networks
    - Connection-oriented

- Open standards
- Application support

Chapter 2 Exercises

1. Modem is short for modulator/demodulator.

2. A *LAN (local area network)* is a network where network devices are located within close proximity to each other.

3. CSMA/CD is an acronym for *Carrier Sense Multiple Access with Collision Detection* and is associated with a network using a *bus* network topology.

4. Which network topology allows for orderly network access for the stations connected to that network?

   Token Ring

5. What two standards define a CSMA/CD network?
   - IEEE 802.3
   - Ethernet

6. Name three media types that can be used to interconnect devices located on a LAN.
   - Wire
   - Fiber optic
   - Wireless

7. What is the major characteristic of 10BASE-T cable?

   Unshielded twisted pair (UTP)

8. A personal computer (PC) requires a *network interface card (NIC)* to be connected to a local area network (LAN).

9. FDDI is an acronym for *Fiber Distributed Data Interface*, which is often used to construct citywide networks called *metropolitan area networks (MANs)*.

10. POTS is an acronym for *plain old telephone system*.

11. A dialup service that connects to a digital network is *integrated services digital network (ISDN)*.

12. What technology can be used to create a point-to-point network connection over the Internet?

VPN (virtual private network)

Chapter 3 Exercises

1. Explain what "10 half or 100 full?" means to you, what the difference between 10 half and 100 full is, and list pros and cons of each.

- 10 half is 10Mbps at half-duplex. It is slower and prone to collisions.

- 100 full is 100Mbps at full-duplex. It is faster and not prone to collisions

2. List three types of interfaces and three types of adaptors.

Interfaces:

- The network interface controller (NIC).

- The point at the boundary of a LAN, which connects the LAN to an outside network, is another type of network interface.

- In Layer 3 environments, *interface* is often the term used to describe a network connection and really isn't considered hardware.

Adaptors:

- The network interface controller (NIC)

- Virtual adaptor

- Physical adaptor

3. Why is an NIC card considered both an interface and an adaptor?

The NIC card adapts to the computer, allowing it to have an interface to the network.

4. List three examples of flash memory:

- Memory cards for cell phones

- Memory cards for digital cameras

- Memory cards for video game systems

- PCMCIA type 1 memory cards

- PCMCIA type 2 memory cards

- PCMCIA type 3 memory cards

- Personal computer system BIOS chip

5. List the PDU for each of the OSI layers.

Layer	PDU
Application	Data
Presentation	Data
Session	Data
Transport	Segment
Network	Packet
Data Link	Frame
Physical	Bit

6. What is the difference between volatile and nonvolatile memory?

Volatile memory content is erased when power is removed. Nonvolatile memory retains its contents whether power is on or off.

7. What is the difference between STP and UTP cabling?

STP has a shield around the twisted pairs, whereas UTP has no shield.

8. Explain when you would want to use MMF cables instead of SMF cables. Next, explain in what instances SMF cabling would be preferred over MMF cabling.

SMF cables are thinner than MMF cables. This is because SMF cables are designed to carry a single beam of light. Because there are not multiple beams involved, the SMF cable is more reliable and supports greater distances and a bandwidth much higher than MMF cables. The bulk cost of SMF cabling is much less expensive than the MMF cabling. MMF cabling is made for shorter distances. Unlike SMF, there are multiple beams of light, so the distance and speed is less. Granted, supporting data rates of up to 10 Gbps for distances as far as 300 meters is nothing to sneeze at. Because of the additional modes, MMF cabling is able to carry much more data at any given time.

9. Define *modulation*.

The process of manipulating a waveform to create a signal that sends a message that needs to be communicated. In data communications, modulation is performed by a node that converts a digital signal to an analog signal, in order to be communicated over a phone line.

10. What does a router use to determine the best path to a destination?

Routing table

Chapter 4 Exercises

1. If you have a network-capable PC, try using a few of the network utilities discussed in this chapter.

2. Open a DOS window by running `cmd` from Start ➪ Run and enter the command `ipconfig` and note what is displayed.

3. Issue the command `ipconfig /all` and note what is displayed.

4. If your network allows your PC to access the Internet, execute this command `tracert <insert your favorite website URL>` and hit the Return key. Note the results. You may want to repeat this to other Internet addresses.

5. To display information about all the interfaces on a Unix computer, which command would need to be issued?

   `netstat`

6. What is used on the Internet to find the numeric address of a computer host that resides on the Internet?

   DNS server

7. True or false: Floppy disks are the fastest form of magnetic media.

   False

8. True or false: AT&T is the sole provider for the Unix operating system.

   False

9. Can you name at least one Linux distribution?

   Red Hat, SUSE, Ubuntu

10. If a microprocessor designer wanted to allow his newest chip design to access a greater amount of memory space, what might he do to accomplish this?

   Increase the number of address bits available

Chapter 5 Exercises

1. What are the four layers of the TCP/IP reference model?
   - Network interface layer
   - Internet layer
   - Transport layer
   - Application layer

2. Name four Application layer protocols that we discussed in this chapter.

- DNS (Domain Name System)
- SNMP (Simple Network Management Protocol)
- FTP (File Transfer Protocol)
- TFTP (Trivial File Transfer Protocol)
- SMTP (Simple Mail Transfer Protocol)
- NFS (Network File System)
- TNP (Telecommunications Network Protocol)
- SSH (Secure Shell)

3. Explain the structure of the DNS hierarchy.

DNS names are organized hierarchically, with an unnamed root at the top, then what are known as top-level domain (TLD) names next, followed by second-level domain, and, finally, one or more subdomains.

4. What are the five PDU types that are used by SNMP?

- GetRequest
- GetNextRequest
- SetRequest
- GetResponse
- Trap

5. What is the purpose of FTP?

The File Transfer Protocol (FTP) allows users to access an FTP server and transfer files to and from the server.

6. Why does TFTP not perform many of the functions that FTP does?

TFTP is a simple file transfer protocol designed to transfer boot-up files for diskless nodes.

7. What is a daemon?

A daemon is an application or a process that is running on a server for the purpose of providing client and server access and communication.

8. What are the four control characters used by Telnet for option negotiation and their meanings?

- WILL — Used when the sender wants to enable an option
- WONT — Used when the sender wants to disable an option
- DO — Used when the sender wants the receiver to enable an option

- DON'T — Used when the sender wants the receiver to disable an option

9. TCP is a *connection-oriented* protocol, whereas UDP is a *connectionless* protocol

10. What are the three main reporting functions that we said are performed by ICMP?

    - Error reporting
    - Testing and troubleshooting
    - Informational reporting

Chapter 6 Exercises

1. What does the acronym CSMA/CD mean?

   Carrier Sense Multiple Access with Collision Detection.

2. What form of communications eliminates the need for collision detection?

   Full-duplex

3. When you choose not to configure an Ethernet port's speed and duplex mode what are you relying on?

   Autonegotiation

4. What is needed when setting up VLAN networking?

   The ability to tag frames

5. What is a source address? What is a destination address?

   A source address is the address of the network node that is transmitting the frame. A destination address is the address of the network node that the frame is intended for.

6. What is the maximum number of bytes the Data field can contain in an Ethernet frame? What is the minimum number of data bytes?

   The maximum number of bytes in the Data field is 1500. The minimum number is 46 bytes.

Chapter 7 Exercises

1. True or false: The only type of node that is used on a FDDI ring is a FDDI concentrator.

   False

2. The three levels of operation within the X.25 protocol suite are:

   ■ Physical level

   ■ Link level

   ■ Packet level

3. In X.25, *S-frames* are used to pass control data, such as transmission requests, status reporting, *I-frame* receipt acknowledgements, and termination requests.

4. What are the three main components used by PPP?

   ■ The PPP encapsulation method.

   ■ The PPP link control protocol (LCP)

   ■ The PPP network control protocol (NCP)

5. What is the difference between a DTE and a DCE in an X.25 network?

   The DTE are the user nodes (endpoint nodes), while the DCE is the entry to the cloud (network nodes).

6. What are the Session layer protocols that are used in the AppleTalk protocol suite?

   ■ AppleTalk DataStream Protocol (ADSP) — A connection-oriented protocol that provides a data channel for the host nodes.

   ■ AppleTalk Session Protocol (ASP) — ASP maintains and manages higher level sessions.

   ■ Printer Access Protocol (PAP) — Maintains and manages virtual connections to printers, print servers, and other server types.

   ■ Zone Information Protocol (ZIP) — Used to manage network numbers and AppleTalk zone names.

7. What does the acronym ISDN stand for?

   Integrated services digital network

8. What is the frame relay local management interface (LMI) used for?

   LMI is used to provide link status updates pertaining to PVCs between a DTE and the local DCE. One of the functions performed by LMI is status inquiries that are sent out periodically (normally 10 seconds) to test to see if a link is up. If the inquiry does not receive a reply, it assumes the link is down. These inquiries are known as *keepalives*. LMI will also send out updates pertaining to the status of all the links in a frame relay network, provide information about PVC changes, and ensure that IP multicast is functioning.

9. What is a constant bit rate (CBR)?

A constant bit rate means that the bandwidth required to pass the data is always available.

10. The *Link Control Protocol (LCP)* is the foundation protocol of the PPP protocol suite.

Chapter 8 Exercises

1. List in order from highest to lowest the upper layers of the OSI model, also indicating their layer number.

   ▪ Application Layer — Layer 7

   ▪ Presentation Layer — Layer 6

   ▪ Session Layer — Layer 5

2. An application that runs on a user's workstation and communicates over a network with an appropriate application that is running on a server is considered to be what type of application?

   Client/server

3. Which protocol is considered to be a connection-based protocol?

   TCP (Transmission Control Protocol)

4. What functionality can be used to disguise addresses from a private address space to be seen on the Internet?

   NAT (Network Address Translation)

5. List the three private address spaces that may be used and are considered to be not routable over the Internet.

   ▪ 10.X.X.X

   ▪ 172.16.X.X

   ▪ 192.168.X.X

6. Name an Application layer protocol that can be used to perform file transfers over the network.

   FTP (File Transfer Protocol)

7. What is the protocol that resolves IP addresses to hardware addresses?

   ARP (Address Resolution Protocol)

Chapter 9 Exercises

1. What are the two ISO/IRC standards that define recommendations for the transport layer?

   ISO/IEC 8072 and ISO/IEC 8073

2. What are the two types of transport service?

   - Connectionless
   - Connection-oriented

3. From the following list, fill in the class function in the following table.

   - Multiplexing class
   - Error detection and recovery class
   - Simple class
   - Error recovery and multiplexing class
   - Basic error recovery class

Class Name	Class Function
Class 0	Simple class
Class 1	Basic error recovery class
Class 2	Multiplexing class
Class 3	Error recovery and multiplexing class
Class 4	Error detection and recovery class

4. Match the type with the correct description:

   - Type C — Network connections that maintain an unacceptable rate of residual errors
   - Type A — Network connections that maintain both an acceptable rate of signaled errors and residual errors
   - Type B — Network connections that maintain an acceptable rate of residual errors and an unacceptable rate of signaled errors

5. Define *upward multiplexing*.

   Multiple Transport layer signals to a single network signal

6. Define *downward multiplexing*.

   Multiple network signals to a single transport signal

7. Explain how a three-way handshake works.

   1. The originating node will send a request known as a *SYN* to the destination node.

   2. The destination node will let the originating node know that it has received the SYN request by sending back a *SYN-ACK* message.

   3. The originating node will respond to the SYN-ACK by sending back an *ACK* message.

8. List four Transport layer protocols.

   - ATP (AppleTalk Transaction Protocol)
   - DCCP (Datagram Congestion Control Protocol)
   - NetBEUI
   - RTP (Realtime Transport Protocol)
   - TCP (Transmission Control Protocol)
   - UDP (User Datagram Protocol)

Chapter 10 Exercises

1. Name the type of network service being used for each of the following:
   - HTTP — Connection-oriented
   - FTP — Connection-oriented
   - Mail — Connectionless
   - Telnet — Connection-oriented

2. A client/server application is considered to be what type of network service?

   Connection-oriented

3. What is a TLD and can you name a few?

   TLD is a top-level domain and is usually the suffix of a URL such as .com, .gov, .edu, or .net.

4. How is the MTU size determined?

   MTU is determined by taking the maximum packet size allowed to cross the network medium being used and subtracting the size of the frame's header and the remainder is the maximum payload size or MTU.

5. What does NAT accomplish?

   NAT enables the use of non-routable addresses to be used on a private network that can be used to translate out network requests to the Internet using a public IP address that the requestor's source address has been translated to.

6. Name two network tools that can be used to troubleshoot a network problem.

   `ping` and `traceroute`

Chapter 11 Exercises

1. How is a jam signal used in a CSMA/CD environment?

   A jam signal in CSMA/CD is a message to all other nodes that a collision has occurred and they should stop transmitting.

2. How is a jam signal used in a CSMA/CA environment?

   A jam signal lets all the other nodes know that the node is ready to transmit data.

3. An unnumbered frame type is used with which type of LLC?

   LLC-1, LLC-2, and LLC-3

4. Find the MAC address of your PC's NIC card. Once you have found it, take the OUI and look it up on the IEEE website. What is the information that is listed for that particular OUI?

   User-dependent results

5. What are the three fields in an LLC PDU, and what do they do?

   ▪ Destination Service Access Point (DSAP) — This is used to identify the LLC that is supposed to receive the PDU.

   ▪ Source Service Access Point (SSAP) — This is used to identify the LLC that is supposed to send the PDU.

   ▪ Control — The control field provides sequencing data, command information, and responses to requests. Note that any or all of these can be used in any combination.

6. How many bits are in an IEEE 802 MAC address?

   There are 48 bits in an IEEE 802 MAC address.

7. What are the two error checking methods used at the Data Link layer?

   ▪ Parity checking

   ▪ CRC

8. What does full-duplex Ethernet use for flow control?

   PAUSE frames or the PAUSE function.

9. What is the functional difference between a bridge and a Layer 2 switch?

   There is no functional difference between a bridge and a switch. That's right! None! Nada! Zero! Zip! *Switch* is nothing more than a marketing term that came out in the 1990s.

Chapter 12 Exercises

1. What are the three layers of the hierarchical design model?

   ▪ The access layer

   ▪ The distribution layer

   ▪ The core layer

2. In this chapter, we listed six benefits of the hierarchical model. List these.

   ▪ Easy design replication

   ▪ Easy expandability of the network

   ▪ Provides redundancy

   ▪ Increased network performance

   ▪ Better security

   ▪ Easy to manage and maintain

3. This question is actually broken down into questions about the 5-4-3 rule. Refer to Figure A-1 for these questions.

   a. Does this network comply with the 5-4-3 rule?

   ▪ Yes

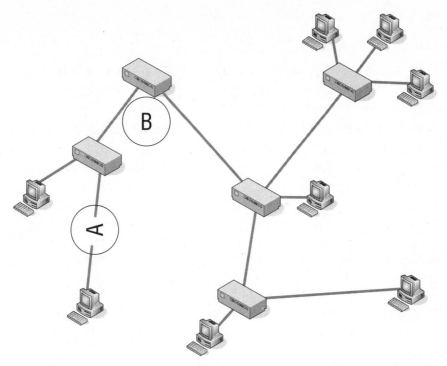

Figure A-1

    b. Identify what A and B represent in the diagram.

- A = Segment
- B = Repeater

4. How many possible spanning tree states are there and what are they?

There are five spanning tree port states:

- Disabled
- Blocking
- Listening
- Learning
- Forwarding

5. In this chapter, we discussed that a spanning tree port can be in a learning state. Why do you think that this is required instead of the port becoming active and just forwarding the frame?

   Having a port wait before forwarding data will prevent the alternative that is offered by the switched default behavior, which is to flood the frame for destinations that the port does not know about.

6. A port in a *learning* state is one that is *learning* paths to destinations and is preparing to forward the frame.

7. What is the purpose of the distribution layer of the hierarchical network?

   The distribution layer is the middleman between the access layer and the core. Data received from the access layer is sent to the core to be routed to the destination. Broadcast domains are separated at this layer with the implementation of virtual LANs (VLANs). Security is also a function that is implemented at this layer.

8. True or false: When the switch receives a frame, it will "tag" the frame with the VLAN identifier from where the data came from. This process is known as *implicit tagging*.

   False

9. What are the VLAN types we discussed in this chapter?

   ▪ Port-based VLANs

   ▪ MAC-based VLANs

   ▪ Protocol-based VLANs

   ▪ IP subnet-based VLANs

10. Take a look at Figure A-2 and then identify the appropriate layer of the hierarchical design model.

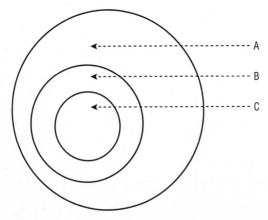

Figure A-2

- The letter *A* in the example represents the *access* layer.
- The letter *B* in the example represents the *distribution* layer.
- The letter *C* in the example represents the *core* layer.

Chapter 13 Exercises

The exercise in the chapter has no right or wrong answers. The important part is that you understand design planning concepts. If Rich and Jim get motivated enough, we will roll out a website with some more exercises. If not, there are many steps that you can take to create your own exercises.

Within Appendix A, there are some more direct questions pertaining to the chapter.

Chapter 14 Exercises

1. How would you best protect network elements that are located in a remote area away from the network operations center?

   Secure the area and keep it under lock and key.

2. Name a service that can provide not only user authentication but determine the amount of time a user has been logged in.

   RADIUS

3. What is a digital signature associated with?

   Certificates

4. Which tunneling protocol was first supported with Microsoft's Windows 95 operating system?

   PPTP

Chapter 15 Exercises

1. Which protocol can be used to monitor devices on a network?

   SNMP — Simple Network Management Protocol

2. Where would an SNMP agent be found?

   Embedded within a network-connected device

3. What would cause an alert to be displayed on an NMS workstation?

   A network-connected device that is being monitored to set an SNMP trap.

4. How would packets on a network be captured and inspected?

   With packet-capturing software loaded on a computer or a packet sniffer device.

Chapter 16 Exercises

1. For each item on the following list, identify the layer of the OSI reference model that item applies to.

   - Damaged cables — Layer 1

   - Dirty fiber — Layer 1

   - Excessive signal attenuation — Layer 1

   - Insufficient bandwidth — Layer 1

   - Denial-of-service (DoS) attack — Layer 2

   - Electrical interference — Layer 1

   - Wireless interference — Layer 1

   - Damaged interface — Layer 1

   - Dirty interface — Layer 1

   - Configuration error — Layer 2, Layer 3

   - Authentication issues — Layer 3

   - Excessive utilization — Layer 2

   - Excessive errors — Layer 2

   - VLAN configuration error — Layer 2, Layer 3

   - Class of Service issue — Layer 2

2. In the following example, explain why there is a missing hop.

```
C:\>tracert 207.215.79.16

Tracing route to www.testshow.com [207.215.79.16]
over a maximum of 30 hops:

1    1ms   <10ms   <10ms 192.168.1.1
2    7ms    7ms     6ms c-3-0-ubr01.boston.cast.net [43.16.12.1]
3    9ms    8ms     7ms ge-1-37-ur01.boston.cast.net [43.16.12.193]
4     *      *       *      Request timed out.
5    7ms    7ms     7ms po-24-ur01.boston.cast.net [43.16.12.161]
```

   In the example, there is a missing hop because the router 43.16.12.193 was unable to reach the preferred next hop and took an alternate path.

3. True or false: The UDP connection state is one of the fields displayed with the `netstat` utility.

   False. UDP is connectionless, so there is no such thing as a connection state. TCP is the connection state that is displayed with the `netstat` command.

4. Network *cable* testers are devices that are used to check the integrity of the cabling in the LAN.

5. List three options that can be used with the `arp` command in windows, and what each one does.

   ▪ `-a` — Displays current ARP entries by interrogating the current protocol data. If `inet_addr` is specified, the IP and physical addresses for only the specified computer are displayed. If more than one network interface uses ARP, entries for each ARP table are displayed.

   ▪ `-g` — Same as `-a`.

   ▪ `inet_addr` — Specifies an Internet address.

   ▪ `-N if_addr` — Displays the ARP entries for the network interface specified by `if_addr`.

   ▪ `-d` — Deletes the host specified by `inet_addr`. `inet_addr` may be wildcarded with * to delete all hosts.

   ▪ `-s` — Adds the host and associates the Internet address `inet_addr` with the physical address `eth_addr`. The physical address is given as 6 hexadecimal bytes separated by hyphens. The entry is permanent.

   ▪ `eth_addr` — Specifies a physical address.

   ▪ `if_addr` — If present, this specifies the Internet address of the interface whose address translation table should be modified. If not present, the first applicable interface will be used.

6. The network analyzer is also known as a *sniffer*.

7. What are three ways you can baseline your network? Explain details for each of these.

   ▪ **Traffic analyzer** — The traffic analyzer (also known as a network analyzer, packet analyzer, packet sniffer, or just sniffer) can be an application or a specialized node that is used to capture data being transmitted on the network. Each packet is captured and can be manipulated and sorted by RFC, protocol, statistics, or whatever specifications are set by the user. The data can be organized and set to graphs or any other form supported by the analyzer and set by the user.

■ **Statistical graphing with the management station** — SNMP management stations usually have the ability to record statistical data and record the data in reports and graphs. Maintaining such information can be useful in determining abnormal conditions within the catenet.

■ **Determine thresholds that need to be maintained** — Know your LAN. Test and analyze traffic patterns, traffic capacity limits, overall throughput operation, routing path costs, Physical layer well-being, etc. Keep the results on hand for reference when an issue occurs. Not only can this assist in alerting you to abnormal operations, it can offer proof of the abnormal operations should you need to bring in a vendor for assistance in troubleshooting an issue. Understanding peak traffic periods, protocol usage statistics, average throughput, and normal traffic patterns is important in understanding problems that occur in the network and resolving them quickly and effectively.

8. What command can be used in a Windows environment that will provide you with detailed information about the current TCP/IP settings of your PC?

   `ipconfig /all`

9. From your PC, open up a traffic analyzer and point it to the interface of your PC. Issue a constant ping to www.richardbramante.com (`ping www.richardbramante.com -t`). Next, disable your network connection. What do you notice in your trace?

   This exercise is mainly for the reader to get a better feel for data collection and process recognition. The main thing we are looking for in the answer to this question is the ARP processes that start when the connection is down, and then the route-learning processes that occur until the connection is recovered.

10. This chapter listed eight quick checks that you can do when you are having issues within a VLAN. What are they?

   ■ Is there any maintenance going on at the time?

   ■ Have there been any recent changes that may have created the issue?

   ■ Verify the configurations of the bridges.

   ■ Check statistics. Review logs and traces. Utilize `show` and `debug` commands that are available and are applicable.

   ■ Is this a new configuration? Make sure that all necessary configuration parameters are set correctly.

- Are the VLANs configured correctly? Make sure that all VLAN rules were followed. Have there been any changes made? Did someone delete a VLAN?
- Are tagging rules applied correctly?
- Is there a routing issue that is preventing devices within the VLAN from communicating with other devices?

Appendix A Exercises

1. What is an Internet service provider (ISP)?

   Internet service providers (ISPs) provide the gateway to the Internet for their customers and information is shared.

2. *An internet* is often confused with *the Internet*, but an internet is not necessarily part of the Internet.

3. What is an extranet?

   An extranet is an intranet that is opened up to allow outside users

4. In a client/server network relationship, the *server* stores data that is used by the users of the organizational LAN.

5. List three examples of a shared network resource.
   - Printers
   - Modem
   - Scanner
   - Data files
   - Applications
   - Storage

6. What is a network protocol?

   A protocol is a standard (or set of standards) that governs the rules to follow for setting up a data connection, communication between endpoints once the connection is set, and transferring data between those endpoints.

7. What is the name of the ARPA subgroup that was set up to focus on research pertaining to anything that related to computing?

   The Information Processing Techniques Office (IPTO)

8. What are the four locations that made up the original ARPANET?
   - Stanford Research Institute

- University of California, Los Angeles
- University of California, Santa Barbara
- University of Utah

9. The National Science Foundation Network (NSFNET) was developed originally to allow researchers access to five supercomputers. Where were these supercomputers located?

- Cornell University
- Pittsburgh Supercomputing Center
- Princeton University
- University of Illinois
- University of California, San Diego

10. A *proprietary* standard is a standard that is developed and owned by a specific vendor.

11. What is a de facto standard?

A de facto standard is a standard that began as a proprietary standard and then grew to a standard that is used by pretty much everyone.

12. ANSI is the organization that represents the United States in working with the global community on discussions relating to two important global standards organizations. Name these standards organizations.

- International Organization for Standardization (ISO)
- International Electrotechnical Commission (IEC)

13. A *working group* is a team of IEEE professionals brought together to work on new research activities.

14. IEEE 802.3 identifies which IEEE working group?

Ethernet Working Group

15. IEEE 802.11 is the standard for *wireless LAN technology*.

16. What functions are performed at the Presentation layer?

- Encryption services
- Decryption services
- Data compression services
- Data decompression services
- Translation services

17. Network File System (NFS) is a data format that is used at the *Session* layer.

18. Open Shortest Path First (OSPF) is an example of a *Network* layer protocol.

19. Point-to-Point Protocol (PPP) is an example of a *Data Link* layer protocol.

20. What are the reasons why we said that TCP/IP has grown into the "method of choice"? Explain each of the reasons you list.

- **Routing** — TCP/IP was designed to route data from node to node of networks of variable sizes and complexities. TCP/IP is not worried about the status of nodes in the network, it is concerned about the networks that it should know about. Various protocols that are within the TCP/IP protocol suite manage data flow between networks.

- **Addressing** — And guess what is built into TCP/IP? That's right, IP. IP provides a way for a node to identify other nodes within a network and deliver data to any endpoint node that it has been made aware of.

- **Name resolution** — TCP/IP provides name resolution as a way to map an IP address (10.10.10.10) to an actual name (`networkz.org`). Can you imagine how tough it would be to remember the IP addresses of all of the websites that you needed to know about? Name resolution really helps.

- **Doesn't discount the lower layers** — Although TCP/IP operates at the upper layers (Layer 3 and above), it does have the ability to operate at the lower levels as well. This means that for most LANs and WLANs, and some MANs and WANs, TCP/IP is able to work with multiple networks of these types and connect them to each other with TCP/IP.

- **Open standards** — TCP/IP was mainstreamed to give different nodes the capability to communicate with one another. The open standards that TCP/IP contains are available to anyone. These standards are determined through the RFC process that we discuss in Section 1.3.9.

- **Talking endpoint to endpoint** — TCP/IP provides a way for one endpoint to speak directly with another endpoint, regardless of any nodes that are in between. It is as if the endpoints were directly connected to one another, even when they are not physically connected to a common network. Thanks to TCP/IP, both the originating and the destination nodes can exchange connection acknowledgements directly with one another.

- **Application support** — TCP/IP provides protocols that provide a commonality among end user applications. Often when an application that utilizes TCP/IP is developed, many of the functions required for the application are already common with any node supporting TCP/IP.

21. Using the terms listed under the table, place them in the appropriate spaces.

Diagnostic Utilities	General Purpose Utilities	Services Utilities
Address Resolution Protocol (ARP)	File Transfer Protocol (FTP)	TCP/IP print server
ipconfig	Line Printer Daemon (LPD)	Web server
Line Printer Daemon (LPD)	Remote Copy Protocol (RCP)	File Transfer Protocol Server
netstat	Remote Shell (RSH)	E-mail server
nslookup	Telnet	Domain name server
ping	Trivial File Transfer Protocol (TFTP)	
route		
tracert		

22. A LAN may consist of computers, printers, storage devices, and other shared devices or services available to a group of users within a *(any term that defines a local or a limited distance is a correct answer)* geographical area.

23. What does the term *sneakernet* refer to?

    The term *sneakernet* refers to the days when data was copied on a floppy disk and then transported by an individual to the destination PC.

24. What are the three main IEEE standards that are primarily associated with traditional LANs?

    - IEEE 802.2 Logical Link Control
    - IEEE 802.3 CSMA/CD Access Method and Physical Layer Specifications
    - IEEE 802.5 Token Ring Access Method and Physical Layer Specifications

25. The Media Access Control sublayer provides *addressing* and *channel* control.

26. What was the name of the company that introduced Token Ring technology? When it was introduced, what was the operating speed?

    When Token Ring was first introduced by IBM it possessed a speed of 4 Mbps, thus not offering any advantage over CSMA/CD networks.

27. What are the two notable differences between the IBM and IEEE 802.5 specifications for Token Ring?

    ▪ The number of nodes on a ring is up to 260 nodes per IBM specification, and the IEEE 802.5 standard limits it to a maximum of 250 nodes.

    ▪ Source routing IBM allows up to 8 fields for route designation when source routing is employed, while the IEEE 802.5 standard allows for a maximum of 14 fields.

28. True or false: Both IEEE 802.3 and Ethernet are CSMA/CD network standards that are fully compatible with each other.

    False — Although both are network standards, the two are not fully compatible with each other.

29. Fill in the missing information in the following two tables.

DB9 Pin Assignment

Signal	Pin
Receive +	1
Receive −	6
Transmit +	9
Transmit −	5

RJ-45 Pin Assignment

Signal	Pin	Wire Color
Receive +	4	White with orange stripe
Receive −	5	Orange with white stripe
Transmit +	6	White with blue stripe
Transmit −	3	Blue with white stripe

30. IBM Token Ring used cabling of different types to be used in different environments. Connect the appropriate type with its description below.

    A. This type consists of two parallel pairs. The wires in this cable are untwisted and have a maximum length of 50 meters. The primary purpose of this wire is to be used in installations requiring the cable to run under carpeting.

    B. This type consists of multimode fiber optic cable used to extend the token ring network and used to interconnect optical repeaters.

    C. This type consists of two shielded twisted pairs. It is considered a low cost short distance cable with a maximum length of 45 meters and is often used for MAU-to-MAU interconnection.

    D. This type is a lower cost alternative to Type 1 cable with a maximum length of 65 meters. It consists of two pairs of shielded twisted pairs.

    E. This type consists of two shielded twisted pairs as can be found in Type 1 cable and four unshielded twisted pairs as can be found in Type 3 cable.

    - Type 2 — E
    - Type 5 — B
    - Type 6 — C
    - Type 8 — A
    - Type 9 — D

31. Although this protocol is closely related to Token Ring, it is not officially considered part of the Token Ring family. Name this protocol.

    Fiber Distributed Data Interface (FDDI)

32. Define the following bus network terms:

    - **Collision detection** — Provided by circuitry designed to detect collisions on the bus network. If a collision is detected, the transceiver notifies the transmitting function that a collision has occurred and then it broadcasts a jamming signal on the network to notify other systems connected to the bus network that a collision has occurred. The LAN is then allowed to settle before the resumption of transmissions on to the bus.

    - **Heartbeat** — Generation of a short signal to inform the main adapter that the transmission was successful and collision free. Although it is specified in the 802.3 standard and the

Ethernet standard, it is rarely used as many adapters confuse this signal with the signal that signifies a collision has occurred.

- **Jabber** — The function that allows the transceiver to cease transmission if the frame being transmitted exceeds the specified limit of 1518 bytes. This helps prevent a malfunctioning system or adapter from flooding the LAN with inappropriate data.

- **Monitor** — This function monitors LAN traffic by prohibiting transmit functions while receive and collision functions are enabled. It does not generate any traffic onto the LAN.

33. A star topology is implemented with the use of *hubs* and UTP cables terminated with *RJ-45* plugs.

34. Fill in the blanks in the following table:

Pin	Ethernet	IEEE 802.3
1	Ground	Ground Control In
2	Collision Detected +	Control In A
3	Transmit +	Data Out A
4	Ground	Data In
5	Receive +	Data In A
6	Voltage	Common
7	Control	Out A
8	Ground	Control Out
9	Collision Detected −	Control In B
10	Transmit −	Data Out B
11	Ground	Data Out
12	Receive −	Data In B
13	Power	
14	Power Ground	
15	Control	Out B

35. What are the two types of duplex? What are the differences?

Duplex is either half duplex or full duplex. The difference between the two is that full-duplex devices are capable of both transmitting and receiving at the same time, whereas half-duplex devices are either in transmit or receive mode but never both simultaneously.

36. Fault *tolerance* is built into the dual-ring FDDI network.

37. What is POTS? What is it used for?

    POTS stands for plain old telephone service. It refers to the use of voice-grade telephone lines to form a point-to-point data connection.

38. What type of a node is required in order for two LANs to be able to communicate using the ISDN protocol?

    LAN-to-LAN connectivity with ISDN can best be accomplished with the use of ISDN routers.

39. Explain the two most commonly used ISDN services.

    - Basic rate — Provides two B channels of 64 Kbps and a single D channel of 16Kbps.

    - Primary rate — Provides 23 B channels of 64 Kbps and a single D channel of 64 Kbps for U.S.- and Japan-based subscribers. Subscribers in Europe and Australia are provided with 30 B channels.

40. A full T1 line provides 24 channels each with *64Kbps* of bandwidth.

41. Fill in the blanks in the following table:

decimal	binary
0	0000
1	0001
2	0010
3	0011
4	0100
5	0101
6	0110
7	0111
8	1000
9	1001
10	1010

42. What is RAM?

    Random access memory (RAM) is memory that is available for data storage and access, regardless of the order in which it is stored. Information stored in RAM is accessible until it is cleared out or the device it is being used on is shut down.

43. The type of RAM that is used by most PCs today is called *dynamic random access memory (DRAM).*

44. Define the following:

- **Read-only memory (ROM)** — Memory that is configured and set by the manufacturer. It contains device systems software that is necessary for the proper operation of the device.

- **Programmable read-only memory (PROM)** — A memory chip that can be written to only once. This will allow someone other than the manufacturer to write data onto the PROM. Just like ROM, the data is there forever. In order to write the data onto the memory chip, a device known as a PROM programmer (PROM burner) is used.

- **Erasable programmable read-only memory (EPROM)** — A memory chip that can be written to and store data that may need to be overwritten at some point. The data on the EPROM is erased by UV light and then can be reprogrammed with a PROM burner.

- **Electrically erasable programmable read-only memory (EEPROM)** — A memory chip that can be written to and store data that may need to be overwritten at some point. The data on the EEPROM is erased by an electrical charge and then can be reprogrammed with a PROM burner.

45. What is the difference between a PDU and an SDU?

The PDU specifies the data that is to be transmitted to the peer layer at the receiving end. The SDU can be considered the PDU payload.

46. In order for communication to take place between nodes, one end of the connection must be a *DCE* and the other a *DTE*.

47. What are the four IP address network classes? Explain each one.

- **Class A** — Class A addresses are identified by a number from 1 to 126 in the first octet. In Class A addresses, the first octet identifies the network and the remaining three octets identify the host. These addresses are normally assigned to larger networks.

- **Class B** — Class B addresses are identified by a number from 128 to 191 in the first octet. In Class B addresses, the first two octets identify the network and the last two identify the host. These addresses are normally assigned to medium size networks.

- **Class C** — Class C addresses are identified by a number from 192 to 223 in the first octet. In Class C addresses, the first three octets identify the network while the last octet identifies the host. These addresses are normally assigned to small to medium size networks.

- **Class D** — Class D addresses are a little different from the other Classes. Class D addresses are used for multicasting. These addresses always begin with the first 4 bits being 1110 and the remaining 29 bits identifying the catenet in which the multicast message is to be sent.

48. The main types of network cables are *twisted pair*, *fiber optic*, and *coaxial*.

49. What are the four primary colors of cabling used in twisted pair?

   ▪ Blue

   ▪ Brown

   ▪ Green

   ▪ Orange

50. True or false: Twisted pair cabling is used in Ethernet and Token Ring networks.

   True

51. What are the types of twisted pair cabling? What are the differences in the types?

   ▪ **UTP (unshielded twisted pair)** — UTP cabling is the type of copper cabling that is used the most in networks today. UTP cables consist of two or more pairs of conductors that are grouped within an outer sleeve. UTP cable is often referred to as Ethernet cable, because Ethernet is the predominant technology that uses UTP cable. UTP cabling is cheap, but does not offer protection from electrical interference. Additionally, bandwidth is limited with UTP in comparison with some of the other cable types.

   ▪ **STP (shielded twisted pair)** — STP cabling is a type of copper cabling that is used in networks where fast data rates are required. STP cables consist of two or more pairs of conductors that are grouped together and then an additional metal shield wraps around the twisted pairs, forming an additional barrier to help protect the cabling. Finally, all of the cables are grouped together and a final outer sleeve is placed over the wiring. STP cables are also referred to as Ethernet cables. STP cables provide additional protection to the internal copper, thus data rates are increased and more reliable. The conductors that are grouped together can be shielded as individual pairs (in other words, each pair will have its own shield), or all pairs can be shielded as a group.

52. What are the two types of fiber optic cabling? Explain each.

   ▪ **Single-mode fiber optical cabling** — SMF cables are thinner than MMF cables. This is because SMF cables are designed to carry a single beam of light. Because there are not multiple beams involved, the SMF cable is more reliable and supports greater distances and a much higher bandwidth than MMF cables. The bulk cost of SMF cabling is much less expensive than MMF cabling.

- **Multi-mode fiber optical cabling** — MMF cabling is made for shorter distances. Unlike SMF, there are multiple beams of light, so the distance and speed are less. Granted, supporting data rates of up to 10 Gbps for distances as far as 300 meters is nothing to sneeze at. Because of the additional modes, MMF cabling is able to carry much more data at any given time.

53. The *network interface controller (NIC)* is a hardware card that allows a PC to participate in passing and receiving data on a network.

54. A network *concentrator* is a node that is able to multiplex signals and then transmit them over a single transmission medium.

55. What is the name for the node type that is similar to a Ethernet hub, but is used in Token Ring networks?

    Media access unit (MAU)

56. What is the name of the Layer 2 device that supports and performs the same basic function of joining network segments within the LAN?

    Layer 2 switch or a bridge

57. What is the name of the node that operates at Layer 3 of the OSI reference model?

    Router

58. A *Layer 3 switch* is a node that allows the wire speed technologies that are used by Layer 2 and the tools that are needed to route packets at Layer 3.

59. *Layer 3* switches have the ability to control the flow of data by implementing what is known as *class of service (COS)*, which provides for packet queuing into classes of service to ensure that data with a higher priority is attended to before data with a lower priority.

60. Name at least three types of network servers that are used in a LAN.

    - Print server
    - File server
    - Network server
    - FTP server
    - Mail server
    - Fax server
    - List server
    - Proxy server

61. The portion of a computer that receives data and instructions and manipulates and acts on the received data in a controlled manner is known as what?

    The central processing unit (CPU)

62. True or false: Data can never be stored on magnetic media because the magnet will erase all data.

    False — The memory storage area can be constructed of various storage nodes anywhere from semiconductor to magnetic media.

63. The address space of a node can be determined by taking the number 2 and raising it to the power of the number of address bits that are generated by the CPU. That being said, calculate the following (the first one is done for you):

    - 16 address bits $= 2^{16}(65,536)$
    - 20 address bits $= 2^{20}(1,048,576)$
    - 24 address bits $= 2^{24}(16, 777,216)$
    - 32 address bits $= 2^{32}(4,294,967,296)$

64. Hard drives are usually mounted within a computer's case, but today, with USB ports, many drives are sold as *external* drives communicating between the drive and computer over the USB port.

65. On personal computers, input/output connections are in the form of ports dedicated to either *serial* or *parallel* data communications.

66. What is the most basic form of an operating system?

    A file manager

67. In the world today, there are two main GUI-based operating systems that are in use by most people. What are they?

    - Microsoft Windows
    - Mac OS X

68. As the need for PC connectivity rose, the most common design of network operating systems was the *client/server* implementation

69. True or false: One of the early network operating systems, Microsoft Networking, utilized an IPX/SPX protocol stack to provide communications over its network.

    False — Novell utilized an IPX/SPX protocol stack to provide communications over its network.

70. True or false: The problem with TCP/IP networks is that a workstation can only have a single session running at a time with any server on the network.

False — The majority of today's networks are TCP/IP-based networks that have a wide range of various applications running over them. A workstation may have multiple sessions to various servers on the network simultaneously.

71. What is peer-to-peer networking?

Peer-to-peer networking is where one computer can share data and resources with another computer.

72. True or false: To perform peer-to-peer networking, some sort of application program is required.

True

73. List the NetBIOS primitives that are associated with the session service and what each of them does.

■ Call — Opens a session to a remote computer using its NetBIOS name

■ Listen — Listens for session requests using NetBIOS name

■ Hang Up — Ends a session that had been previously established

■ Send — Sends a packet to the computer that a session had been established with

■ Send No ACK — Similar to Send but does not require a returned acknowledgement that the packet was received

■ Receive — Waits for the arrival of a packet from a computer a session has been established with

74. For each of the following statements, give the corresponding operating system name. The first one has been completed as an example.

A. The operating system that was first developed by AT&T Bell Labs as a multiuser operating system.

Unix

B. This operating system was designed more for the desktop environment even though it will run on larger computers.

Linux

C. Newer versions of this operating system come with configuration utility programs that assist with the network settings and configuration.

Unix

D. This operating system has many similarities and commonalities to Unix.

Linux and Sun Solaris

E. Can be configured with a text editor.

Linux and Unix

F. This operating system was initially designed to handle many users connected simultaneously and all sitting in front of a character-based terminal.

Unix

G. Sun initially developed this operating system for their Sun SPARC workstations.

Sun Solaris

H. This operating system is a flat file operating system; most of the configuration files are in readable text.

Unix

I. This operating system provides strong networking tools to allow it to be interconnected not only to the local LAN but the Internet.

Sun Solaris

75. Developers of networking protocols adhere to a *layered* approach.

76. Name the layers of the TCP/IP reference model and list what the responsibility is of each layer.

- **Network interface layer** — The network interface layer corresponds to the Physical and Data Link layers of the OSI reference model. This layer is also often referred to as the link layer or the data link layer. The network interface layer is responsible for the device drivers and hardware interfaces that connect a node to the transmission medium.

- **Internet layer** — The Internet layer corresponds to the Network layer of the OSI reference model. This layer is also known as the network layer. The Internet layer is responsible for the delivery of packets through a network. All routing protocols (RIP, OSPF, IP, etc.) are members of this layer. Nodes that perform functions at this layer are responsible for receiving a datagram, determining where to send it, and then forwarding it toward the destination. When a node receives a datagram that is destined for the node, this layer is responsible for determining the forwarding method for information that is in the packet. Finally, this layer contains protocols that send and receive error messages and control messages as required.

- **Transport layer** — The transport layer corresponds to the Transport layer of the OSI reference model. There are two primary protocols that operate at this layer. These are the Transmission Control Protocol (TCP) and the User Datagram Protocol (UDP). This layer serves the application layer and is responsible for data flow between two or more nodes within a network.

■ **Application layer** — The application layer corresponds to the Application, Presentation, and Session layers of the OSI reference model. Users initiate a process that will use an application to access network services. Applications work with protocols at the transport layer in order to pass data in the form needed by the transport protocol chosen. On the receiving end, the data is received by the lower layers and passed up to the application for processing for the destination end user. This layer concerns itself with the details of the application and its process and not so much about the movement of data. This is what separates this upper layer from the lower three.

77. What is the name of the protocol that allows for e-mail communications and at which layer does it operate?

The name of the protocol is the Simple Mail Transfer Protocol (SMTP) and it is an Application layer protocol.

78. True or false: Secure Shell is an Application layer protocol.

True

79. *Domain* names are names that are assigned to URLs on the Internet.

80. Make sure that you have a connection to the Internet, then use the `ping` command to find the IP address for the following domains. Write down your results.

■ www.cnn.com _____

■ www.yahoo.com _____

■ www.wiley.com _____

■ www.google.com _____

■ www.richardbramante.com _____

Because IP addresses can change, the blanks have been left blank. The important thing is that you were able to get an IP address using the `ping` command.

81. What does the acronym gTLD stand for?

Generic top-level domain

82. What type of organization or business would use the following gTLDs?

■ .biz — Restricted for use by businesses

- .com — Intended for use by commercial organizations
- .edu — Post-secondary educational institutions
- .gov — Restricted for use by the United States federal, state, and local governments.
- .jobs — Sites related to employment
- .mil — The United States military
- .net — Miscellaneous
- .org — Miscellaneous organizations

83. What is the name of the protocol that runs between nodes for the purpose of sharing management information pertaining to the managed system?

   The Simple Network Management Protocol (SNMP) is a protocol that runs between an SNMP manager and an SNMP client, also known as an SNMP managed system, for the purpose of sharing management information pertaining to the managed system.

84. What are the three message types that can be sent from the SNMP manager to the SNMP agents?

   - GetRequest
   - GetNextRequest
   - SetRequest

85. A *management information base (MIB)* is a database that contains manageable objects and variables of these objects pertaining to a network node, for the purpose of node management within a network.

86. The formal language used by SNMP is *Abstract Syntax Notation 1 (ASN.1)*.

87. What is an object identifier (OID)?

   An OID is a series of sequential integers that are separated by dots. The OID defines the path to the sought object.

88. Name some of the improvements that were introduced by SNMPv2.

   - Security
   - SNMP manager to SNMP manager communication
   - Improved performance
   - Confidential sessions
   - Additional protocol support
   - Improvements in the way trap PDUs are handled

89. Which version of the SNMP protocol is considered the official one?

    The Simple Network Management Protocol version 3 (SNMPv3) is considered the official standard and is the one that will be developed upon if there are any updates or enhancements needed at some point in the future.

90. What is the name of the protocol that provides the capability for users to access an FTP server and transfer files to and from the server?

    FTP (File Transfer Protocol)

91. Fill in the correct FTP command in the following table.

Command	Function
ascii	Sets the file transfer mode to ASCII.
binary	Sets the file transfer mode to binary.
cd	Changes to another directory.
close	Terminates a connection.
delete	Removes a file.
get	Places a copy of a file on the remote node onto a specified directory on the local node.
hash	Used to monitor the file transfer process. For every 1028 bytes received, a # will be placed on the screen.
help	Gets a list of available FTP commands.
?	Gets information about commands.
ls	Lists the names of the files in the current directory.
mget	Used to copy more than one file from the remote node to the local node.
mkdir	Makes a new directory.
mput	Used to copy more than one file from the local node to the remote node.
put	Used to copy a file from the local node to the remote node.
pwd	Used to determine the directory path to the current directory.
quit	Terminates the FTP session.
rename	Renames a file or directory.
rmdir	Removes a directory and any subdirectories, if applicable.

92. True or false: There is no difference in between the TFTP and FTP protocols. They have different names because they were developed by different companies, but they are exactly the same in function.

    False — TFTP uses UDP while FTP uses TCP. TFTP uses UDP because it is less chatty than the FTP protocol. TFTP does not have all of the functions that are available with FTP. This is because TFTP is a simple file transfer protocol designed to transfer boot-up files for diskless nodes. With TFTP, users are not able to browse directories, make directory changes, list files or directories, and are limited in terms of the files they can access.

93. Using the SMTP protocol, an SMTP client has a total of five message types that are sent to an SMTP server. Following is a list of these message types. Define the purpose of each one.

    ■ HELO — Used by the client to identify itself to the server

    ■ MAIL — Identifies the end user that is sending the message

    ■ RCPT — Identifies the end user that the message is being sent to

    ■ DATA — The contents of the message

    ■ QUIT — Terminates the session

94. Developed originally by Sun Microsystems, this protocol allows end users access to files that are stored remotely as if the files were local to the end user's workstation. What is the name of this protocol?

    NFS (Network File System)

95. What are the three modes of operation used by Telnet clients and servers?

    ■ Half-duplex mode

    ■ Character mode

    ■ Line mode

96. SSH utilizes *public key cryptography*, which is used to provide cryptographic keys to authenticate remote nodes and users.

97. What are the two most popular Transport layer protocols?

    ■ UDP (User Datagram Protocol)

    ■ TCP (Transmission Control Protocol)

98. Name at least three Application layer protocols that use TCP.

    ■ FTP

    ■ Telnet

- SMTP
- DNS
- POP3
- HTTP
- DNS
- IMAP

99. Name at least three Application layer protocols that use UDP.

- DNS
- BOOTP/DHCP
- TFTP
- SNMP
- RIP
- NFS

100. Name at least five Internet layer protocols.

- IP
- IGMP
- ICMP
- ARP
- RIP
- OSPF
- BGP
- IPSec

101. What is the name of the protocol that allows for operating system access for diskless nodes?

BOOTP (Bootstrap Protocol)

102. Define the following:

- **Routing protocol** — Refers to the protocols that perform functions that allow the routing of packets between routers. RIP, OSPF, BGP, etc., are examples of routing protocols. This is sometimes confused with a routed protocol, which is not the same thing.

- **Routed protocol** — Refers to protocols that participate in transmitting data between nodes within a network. Telnet, SNMP, IP, etc., are all examples of a routed protocol. Routed protocols are sometimes incorrectly termed routing protocols.

- **Gateway** — Refers to the entry point for an entity. A computer that provides access to a network area is a gateway. A network that provides access to a network is a gateway. Many applications have gateways that allow information sharing. The node that connects the LAN to the Internet (or any other network type) is a gateway.

- **Interior gateway protocol (IGP)** — A routing protocol that operates within an AS. RIP and OSPF are IGPs.

- **Exterior gateway protocol (EGP)** — BGP is often called an EGP, although the EGP protocol was the predecessor to BGP for IP routing between AS's.

- **Static routing** — Refers to IP routing information that is manually configured on a node by a system administrator.

- **Dynamic routing** — Refers to IP routing information that is learned by the node through a routing protocol, such as RIP.

103. What is the speed of the following Ethernet types?

   - 10BASE-T — 10 Mbps

   - Fast Ethernet — 100 Mbps

   - Gig Ethernet — 1000 Mbps

104. Ethernet nodes using UTP cabling fall into one of two component types. What are those?

   - DTE (data terminal equipment)

   - DCE (data communications equipment)

105. What is a straight-through cable?

   A straight-through cable is a cable where the wire will run to the same number on each end of the cable (i.e., pin 1 on one end would be connected to pin 1 on the other end).

106. True or false: A straight-through cable can be wired with either the T568A or T568B wiring scheme as long as both ends of the cable are wired exactly the same using the same wiring pin-out.

   True

107. A *crossover* Ethernet cable must have one plug wired with the T568A wiring scheme and the other plug wired following the T568B wiring pin-out.

108. What is the major difference between the OSI reference model and the IEEE 802.3 model?

There is a close similarity between the ISO OSI model and IEEE 802.3 model with the difference being at the Data Link layer of the OSI model

109. What is a frame check sequence?

A frame check sequence is a 4-byte field that contains a 32-bit CRC checksum (cyclical redundancy check) value, which is calculated and inserted by the sending network node and is used by the receiving network node to validate the received frame. Both the sending and receiving nodes calculate the CRC value by using the data contained within the Destination Address, Source Address, Frame Length/Type, and Data fields.

110. Define the following:

- **Carrier sense** — All network nodes continuously listen on the network media to determine if there are gaps in frame transmission on the media.

- **Multiple access** — All network nodes are able to transmit any time they determine that the network media is quiet.

- **Collision detection** — When two network nodes transmit at the same time, the data streams from both nodes interfere and a collision occurs. The network nodes involved must be capable of detecting that a collision has occurred while they were attempting to transmit a frame. Upon detecting that a collision occurred at the time they were transmitting a frame, both nodes will cease transmission of the frame and back off. They will wait a period of time determined by the back-off algorithm before again attempting to transmit the frame.

111. Fill in the missing information in the following table:

Half-Duplex Operational Limitations

Parameters	10 Mbps	100 Mbps	1000 Mbps
Minimum frame size	64	64	520
Maximum collision diameter with UTP cable	100 meters	100 meters	100 meters
Maximum collision diameter with repeaters	2500 meters	205 meters	200 meters
Maximum number of repeaters in network path	5	2	1

112. What is frame bursting, and when was it introduced?

    The standard for CSMA/CD Ethernet for Gigabit Ethernet added the capability for frame bursting. Frame bursting is the capability of a Gigabit Ethernet network interface's Media Access Control to transmit a burst of frames without releasing the access to the network media.

113. *Full-duplex* transmission is the capability of a network node to transmit and receive simultaneously.

114. *Hubs* are nodes that are actually considered part of the Physical layer since they are not decision making devices. They basically provide the interconnectivity on the physical level for network nodes.

115. *Autonegotiation* is the capability of a network interface to negotiate the communication parameters to be used between it and the port it is connected to.

116. True or false: Network administrators don't have to worry about traffic patterns on the network.

    False — When administering large network installations it is important to understand the traffic patterns present on the network.

117. What does the acronym VLAN stand for?

    Virtual local area network

118. What is the name of the LAN protocol that was once popular in the majority of active LANs and is now used as an embedded standard to serve networks that control technologies such as automation services, transportation, robotics, gaming, and other similar network types?

    Attached Resource Computer Network (ARCnet)

119. *StarLAN* technology is, for the most part, the predecessor to what we all know as Ethernet.

120. What is the name of the corporation that developed Token Ring technology?

    Token Ring network technology was developed by IBM in the late 1970s.

121. True or false: Unshielded twisted pair (UTP) cables became the preferred medium used by Token Ring technologies. This is because it was less bulky than shielded twisted pair (STP) cables and was also less expensive than STP.

    True — Token Ring originally operated on STP cabling, but converted to UTP cabling in the 1990s. This was greatly appreciated by the networking community as it offered a cheaper and less bulky medium.

122. What is the name of the first technology that could operate at 100 Mbps?

Fiber Distributed Data Interface (FDDI)

123. What advantages are there in using optical fiber as the primary transmission medium within a network?

- Performance
- Greater distances
- Faster transmission speed
- Reliability
- Data security

124. *Copper Distributed Data Interface (CDDI)* is the FDDI protocol over twisted pair medium instead of fiber.

125. Define the following FDDI node types:

- **Single attachment station (SAS)** — Connects to the FDDI ring through a single connector. The connector has an input port and an output port. Data is received on the input port and is sent to the downstream neighbor via the output port. The SAS connects to a concentrator and then to the primary ring only.

- **Single attached concentrator (SAC)** — Like the SAS, the SAC concentrator connects to only the primary ring. The connection is made through another concentrator.

- **Dual attachment station (DAS)** — Connects to the FDDI ring through two connectors (each with an input and an output port). Can connect directly to the ring or through a concentrator.

- **Dual attached concentrator (DAC)** — A concentrator that connects to both rings.

126. The Digital Equipment Company (Digital) developed and released the first version of the *Digital Equipment Company Network (DECnet)* protocol in the mid-1970s.

127. What are the levels of the XNS model and what layer does each level correspond to on the OSI layered model?

- Level 0 — Roughly corresponds to the OSI Layers 1 and 2.
- Level 1 — Roughly corresponds to the OSI Layer 3.
- Level 2 — Roughly corresponds to the OSI Layers 3 and 4.
- Level 3 — Roughly corresponds to the OSI Layers 6 and 7.
- Level 4+ — Roughly corresponds to the OSI Layer 7.

128. The *Internetwork Packet Exchange (IPX)* protocol is one that is normally found within networks that have nodes that are running the Novell NetWare operating system.

129. In order to support multiple protocol datagrams, there are three main components that are used by PPP. What are they?

    - PPP encapsulation method
    - PPP Link Control Protocol (LCP)
    - PPP Network Control Protocol (NCP)

130. The Link Access Procedure, Balanced (LAPB) is the X.25 link-level protocol that ensures reliable, error-free packet framing and data communication management.

131. Match the ATM adaptation layer type to its appropriate function.

    A. This AAL type supports both connectionless and connection-oriented data transmission. This AAL type is used to transmit non-SMDS packets.

    B. This AAL type supports VBR transmissions.

    C. This AAL type supports CBR transmissions.

    D. This AAL type supports both connectionless and connection-oriented data transmission. This AAL type is used to transmit switched multimegabit data services (SMDS) packets.

    - AAL1 — C
    - AAL2 — B
    - AAL3 — D
    - AAL4 — D
    - AAL5 — A

132. AppleTalk is a protocol suite that was developed by the Apple computer company. AppleTalk was developed specifically to be integrated with new *Macintosh* computers to allow for resource sharing on a network.

133. There are two services used in ISDN to determine bandwidth availability for an end network. These are *basic rate interface (BRI)* and *primary rate interface (PRI)*.

134. The upper layers of the OSI reference model are utilized by software programs to send and receive data over a network.

135. True or false: One of the great things about mail servers is that they do not have to perform any authentication, as such authentication is only performed by a RADIUS server.

False — Mail servers may have to perform user authentication to ensure security and user privacy. The determination on whether the mail server will perform such actions is made by the network administrators.

136. The *time-to-live* field is an 8-bit field that indicates how many seconds a packet can live on the Internet.

137. DMZ is the acronym for what?

Demilitarized zone

138. FTP and SMTP are upper-layer protocols that reside within which layer of the TCP/IP model?

The Application layer of the TCP/IP model contains the upper-level protocols of the TCP/IP protocol suite such as FTP (File Transport Protocol) and SMTP (Simple Mail Transfer Protocol).

139. The following table contains some common Application layer protocols. Complete the missing parts of the table.

Mnemonic	Port(s)	Description
DHCP	67 and 68	Dynamic Host Configuration Protocol provides the means for network clients to obtain an IP address, default gateway IP address, and Domain Name System server addresses.
FTP	20 and 21	File Transfer Protocol is used to transfer files between an FTP client workstation and an FTP server. Port 20 is for data and port 21 is used for control signaling between server and client.
HTTP	80	Hypertext Transfer Protocol is used to transfer Hypertext information over the Internet. The most familiar application use for hypertext information retrieval is a web browser.
SNMP	161	Simple Network Management Protocol is used to manage and monitor network devices over the local network and Internet.
Telnet	23	Telecommunications Network Protocol is used over the local network and Internet to establish terminal sessions between a client computer and a server.

140. True or false: Port numbers range from 0 to 65,535, but for the most part the first 1024 (0 to 1023 decimal or 0x03FF hexadecimal) are considered to be the well-known ports.

    True

141. Explain `traceroute`.

    `traceroute` returns replies from each hop that it crosses to reach a particular targeted network node. Usually, it will try to reach a target in a given number of hops. The customary maximum hop count is 30 hops. It is a good indication if the packet is traveling in the right direction.

142. *OSPF* is a dynamic routing protocol used to move packets from network segment to network segment.

143. True or false: Port 0 is normally reserved, but its use is allowed as a valid source port in transmissions where the transmitting network node does not require a response from the receiving network node.

    True

144. What is the standard that defines the recommended services provided by the OSI Transport layer while working with the Network layer to serve the needs of protocols that are used at the Session layer?

    ISO/IEC 8072

145. What is the standard that sets the recommendations to be followed by nodes (entities) within a network that are utilizing the services of the OSI Transport layer?

    ISO/IEC 8073

146. There are two types of transport service. What are they?

    Connection-oriented and connectionless

147. What are the two data units that operate at the Transport layer?

    ▪ Transport protocol data unit (TPDU)
    ▪ Transport service data unit (TSDU)

148. Match the correct transport service class with its class function.

    A. Error recovery and multiplexing class

    B. Multiplexing class

    C. Simple class

    D. Error detection and recovery class

    E. Basic error recovery class

    ▪ Class 0 — C
    ▪ Class 1 — E

- Class 2 — B
- Class 3 — A
- Class 4 — D

149. The purpose of the Transport layer is to provide end-to-end delivery of data from one *application* to another.

150. Explain how a three-way handshake works.

   - Step 1 — The originating node will send a request known as a SYN to the destination node.
   - Step 2 — The destination node will let the originating node know that it has received the SYN request by sending back a SYN-ACK message.
   - Step 3 — The originating node will respond to the SYN-ACK by sending back an ACK message.

151. True or false: The term *connectionless* can be misleading as connectionless protocols require a connection before they can transmit data.

   False — Connectionless protocols do not require a connection; a transmitting device simply sends data as soon as it has data that is ready to be sent.

152. TCP is a *connection-oriented* protocol, whereas UDP is a *connectionless* protocol.

153. In a connection-oriented environment, *congestion* control and *flow* control are two mechanisms that are used to maintain control over the transmission of data.

154. SMTP mail servers will deliver e-mail to the *SMTP mail* server servicing a particular domain.

155. http://www.mydomainname.com is an example of a *URL*.

156. True or false: Unlike IP addresses, domain names do not have to be unique.

   False — As with IP addresses, domain names also need to be unique.

157. What protocol is primarily a method of moving packets of data across networks consisting of various mediums, seamlessly delivering these packets solely based on destination address?

   IP (Internet Protocol)

158. What version of IP allows for 4,294,967,296 unique addresses?

   IPv4

159. What would the binary number look like for the IP address 192.168.15.85?

    11000000.10101000.00001111.01010101

160. The real thrust of moving to *IPv6* is the larger address space that it provides, with 128 bits dedicated to address space.

161. What is the name of the protocol that provides a means of messaging when a sent datagram is not able to be received by a destination node?

    Internet Control Message Protocol, an essential part of the TCP/IP Internet protocol suite.

162. The `traceroute` command is used to trace the path from the sending network node to the receiving network node on a network hop-to-hop basis.

163. What is the name of the protocol that makes use of authentication and encryption to establish a secure connection between endpoint network nodes?

    Internet Protocol Security (IPSec)

164. In this chapter, we discussed certain expectations that each LAN should meet. We called them the highs and the lows. What are these? Define them.

    ▪ **High throughput** — The data throughput is simply the rate of error-free delivery for messages within a network.

    ▪ **High total bandwidth** — Bandwidth is the available capacity of the physical or wireless channel and network nodes provided for the delivery of data messages in the LAN.

    ▪ **Low delays** — No delays is optimal, but unlikely. Delays will occur, but the goal is to have as few as possible.

    ▪ **Low error rate** — The amount of errors that you see in the network needs to stay as low as possible.

165. A collision causes datagrams to be *dropped*, but it doesn't necessarily mean that the data can't be recovered in some way.

166. In a token bus configuration, there is a central node called a *MAU* or a *MSAU*. This device is similar to an Ethernet hub, but it has a computer chip that provides the logical ring that the end nodes are concerned with.

167. Define the following:

    ▪ **Carrier Sense Multiple Access (CSMA)** — Allows multiple nodes to be attached to a shared network. Prior to transmission, the nodes listen to see if the shared channel is busy and transmit when they sense that the channel is not busy. "Carrier sense" simply means that a node is listening to see if it can detect an unused channel. If the node senses that there is a busy channel, it will defer transmission of its data until the channel is idle. "Multiple access" defines the fact that there are multiple nodes accessing the shared medium to transmit data.

▪ **Carrier Sense Multiple Access with Collision Avoidance (CSMA/CA)** — This is an enhanced version of the CSMA protocol in that it adds collision avoidance as a function. In this type of network, collisions are avoided because the station will not transmit data when it senses the channel is busy. The node listens to the channel for a defined amount of time and when the node is ready to send data, it sends a jam signal, which lets all of the other nodes know that the node is ready to transmit data.

▪ **Carrier Sense Multiple Access with Collision Detection (CSMA/CD)** — This is an enhanced version of the CSMA protocol in that it adds collision detection as a function. The collision detection function allows the transmitting node to be able to monitor the channel for other transmissions. If while transmitting a frame the node detects a signal coming from another node, it terminates the transmission, sends out a signal known as a jam signal, and then tries to send the frame again. There are different ways for collisions to be detected, depending on the shared media that is being used. The most popular and most often used CSMA/CD protocol is Ethernet.

168. A *jam signal* in CSMA/CD is a message to all other nodes that a collision has occurred and that they should stop transmitting.

169. Match the LLC type with the correct answer.

   A. This LLC type is used for connectionless services.

   B. This LLC type is used for connection-oriented services.

   C. This LLC type is used for acknowledgments in conjunction with connectionless services.

   ▪ LLC Type 1 (LLC-1) — A

   ▪ LLC Type 2 (LLC-2) — B

   ▪ LLC Type 3 (LLC-3) — C

170. Define the following:

   ▪ **Destination service access point (DSAP)** — This is used to identify the LLC that is supposed to receive the PDU.

- **Source service access point (SSAP)** — This is used to identify the LLC that is supposed to send the PDU.

- **Control** — The control field provides sequencing data, command information, and responses to requests. Note that any or all of these can be used in any combination.

171. The *Subnetwork Access Protocol (SNAP)* is a protocol that is used in conjunction with LLC-1 for the purpose of upward multiplexing to more upper-layer protocols than what is available with the standard LLC 8-bit SAP fields.

172. True or false: The LLC sublayer is responsible for interfacing between the MAC sublayer and the Physical layer.

    False — The MAC sublayer is responsible for interfacing between the LLC sublayer and Layer 1, the Physical layer.

173. The IEEE 802 *MAC* address is a 48-bit address that is used to identify the network adaptor for a particular node or interface in the network.

174. What is the name for the portion of a frame that contains the source and destination MAC addresses for interfaces that are involved in a communication stream?

    The MAC header

175. True or false: Multicasting is the act of sending a message to multiple nodes.

    True

176. What is the function of the following well-known MAC addresses?

    - 01:80:C2:00:00:00 — Spanning tree BPDU

    - 09:00:4E:00:00:02 — Novell IPX

    - CF:00:00:00:00:00 — Ethernet configuration test

    - 09:00:2B:00:00:0F — DEC LAT

177. Frames are either *fixed-length* or *bit-oriented* PDUs

178. *CRC* is a function that is used to detect common errors that may occur during data transmission.

179. Ethernet uses what are known as *PAUSE* frames for flow control within Ethernet LANs.

180. Explain the following:

    - **Source route bridging** — This type of bridging is used in a source-routed catenet. In a source-routed catenet, the path to a destination is determined by the end nodes and not the bridge itself. An example of an environment that uses source route bridging is Token Ring.

- **Transparent bridging** — This is the type of bridging that is used in Ethernet (and others). In a transparent bridging environment, the bridge makes the path determinations and the end nodes are not aware of decisions that are being made. They simply throw the data to the bridge and leave the decision making up to it.

181. True or false: A bridge is a device that operates much like a repeater or a hub, but it makes data forwarding decisions that bridge traffic from one network segment to another.

    True

182. True or false: When a bridge receives a frame that is destined for a multicast address, the bridge will forward the frame to all of the ports, including the port on which it is received.

    False — When a bridge receives a frame that is destined for a multicast address, the bridge will forward the frame to all of the ports *except* the port on which it is received.

183. Which of the following is *not* a type of organizational LAN?

    The Internet

184. What are examples of external considerations that need to be made when designing a network?

    - Consideration needs to be given to WAN interfacing, as well as interfacings with LANs that are within your realm of control.
    - Make sure you know about any government regulations and that you are in compliance with them.
    - What are your competitors using/doing? What network type would you like to have and who out there did it right? What did they do?
    - What potential technological growth is out there, and will your proposed design be prepared to support it?

185. Developing a project *scope* is important in the early phases of network design.

186. The *hierarchical* design models are the most commonly used in most high-speed LANs today.

187. In a hierarchical design model, there are three layers. What are they?

    - The access layer
    - The distribution layer
    - The core layer

188. What are three WAN protocols that can be used to connect a LAN to remote sites?

    - Frame relay

    - ISDN

    - Leased lines

189. The *distribution* layer is the middleman between the access layer and the core.

190. The *core* layer is the backbone of the LAN and often provides connectivity to WANs as well as Internet services.

191. Explain some of the benefits of using a hierarchical model.

    - Design replication — Once you have a working model, you can simply change the addressing schemes and design the next network expansion based on the way the original design was configured.

    - Expandability — As the network grows, it is very simple to introduce additional nodes into the topology. Future growth planning is a breeze.

    - Redundancy — Redundancy from the access layer to the core layer is very important in high speed LANs. When a node fails, you have to have another node picking up the pieces until the node comes back on line.

    - Better performance — Nodes that operate in the hierarchical model are able to maintain close to wire speed transmissions to all of the nodes they support.

    - Security — Access control security is provided at the access layer. The distribution layer can support advanced security that meets the security needs of the LAN

    - Easy to manage and maintain — Because of the scalability of the hierarchical design model, the network is easy to manage and maintain. A layered approach to troubleshooting helps in finding the source or a network connectivity issue. Additional nodes can be installed fairly simply, and configurations can be built from existing configurations, thus saving time and money. Over time, the hierarchical model will pay for itself in money saved due to the ease of maintaining and managing the LAN.

192. Explain the maximum allowed in each level of the 5-4-3-2-1 design model.

    - 5 — This is the number of *segments* allowed in total.

- 4 — This is the number of *repeaters* used to join the segments together.

- 3 — This is the maximum number of segments in total that have nodes that are *active*.

- 2 — This is the maximum number of segments in total that are *not active*.

- 1 — This is the number of *collision domains*.

193. The *bus* topology is the most often used topology in LANs.

194. What are the advantages to the bus topology?

   - Easy to install

   - Easy to extend

   - Less expensive to implement

195. What are the disadvantages to the bus topology?

   - There is a limitation to the distance a cable can go without a repeater.

   - There is a limit to the number of nodes that can be supported.

   - It can experience sluggishness in performance when there are heavy traffic loads.

   - Security risks exist because all stations can hear what the others are saying on the shared channel.

196. What are the advantages to the star topology?

   - Better performance

   - Easy to troubleshoot

   - High scalability of the network through the central node

197. What are the disadvantages of a star topology?

   - Too much dependency on the central node

   - May be complex to manage

   - Wiring may become cumbersome

198. What are the advantages of a ring topology?

   - No need to have a mechanism to ensure collision-free datagram passing

   - Can expand to cover a greater number of nodes than some of the other topology types

   - Fairly simple to maintain

199. What are the disadvantages of a ring topology?

    ▪ A failure with one node on the ring may cause an outage to all connected nodes.

    ▪ Any maintenance (e.g., adding a node, making a change to a node, removing a node) would affect all of the nodes that connect to the ring.

    ▪ Some of the hardware required to implement a ring is more expensive than Ethernet network cards and nodes.

    ▪ Under normal traffic load, a ring is much slower than other topologies.

200. The *ring* topology is used for Token Ring and FDDI LANs.

201. The *concentrator* used within a LAN is either a hub or an MAU that allows the combination of data transmissions for a group of nodes.

202. The *bridge*, or *Layer 2 switch*, is a LAN node that operates at Layer 2 of the OSI reference model.

203. What is the name of the traditional network node that operates at Layer 3 of the OSI reference model?

    A router

204. Why is a Layer 3 switch preferred over a traditional router in high-speed LANs?

    The Layer 3 switch is preferred over a router because routing decisions are hardware based and thus are much faster than those done by traditional routers.

205. List five terms that are used to define a switch that operates at Layer 4-7 of the OSI model.

    ▪ Layer 4-7 switch

    ▪ Web switch

    ▪ Application switch

    ▪ Content switch

    ▪ VPN switch

206. Explain what each type of switch does.

    ▪ Cut-through — In cut-through operations, the switch reads the header of the datagram as it is received on a port. Once the switch determines the port that reaches the destination, the datagram is sent to the port and on to its destination. There is no storing of data in a cut-through environment. There are also no options for error checking or control because the cut-through switch only reads the header for an address and sends the datagram on.

- Store and forward — In store and forward operations, the switch stores the data and does error checking on the datagram before it sends the datagram off toward its destination port. Although this will make the transfer of datagrams slower than with a cut-through switch, the data is delivered reliably.

207. Which of the following is a false statement?

C. A loop only occurs when there is no redundancy built into the network.

208. What is the name of the public standard protocol that was developed to control loops in a catenet?

Spanning Tree Protocol (STP)

209. What are the possible port states used by STP?

- Disabled
- Blocking
- Listening
- Learning
- Forwarding

210. The standard that covers link aggregation is *IEEE 802.1ad*, the Link Aggregation Control Protocol (LACP).

211. What are some benefits of link aggregation?

- Increase link capacity
- High link availability
- Often can be done with existing hardware

212. What are some disadvantages of link aggregation?

- Requires additional interfaces on each end
- Higher potential of configuration errors
- May require device driver updates to ensure compatibility with link aggregation

213. What are some benefits of creating VLANs within your LAN?

- Better performance. Only VLAN members receive multicasts.
- Members of a group no longer have to physically be located close to the group.

- Administration is easier. Changes to any work area can be done with simple configuration change.

- Increased security. Only nodes within a VLAN will have access to data.

- No need for a router in order to separate the broadcast domain.

214. What are the four types of VLANs?

- Port-based VLANs

- MAC-based VLANs

- Protocol-based VLANs

- IP subnet–based VLANs

215. What are the two types of network management nodes and what function does each type perform?

- Network management agent — An entity (typically a combination of software and hardware) within a node that is responsible for gathering network management information and reporting it to a network management station as appropriate.

- Network management station — A node that communicates with network management agents throughout a network. Typically it comprises a workstation operated by a network administrator, equipped with network management and other relevant applications software.

216. True or false: Good network planning begins with a top-down approach.

    True

217. There is a natural dividing line as far as planning goes; one involves a *current* network infrastructure and the other a totally new design.

218. In Chapter 13, we discussed some fixed costs that you should consider when planning the network. What are these?

- Hardware

- Cabling

- Any initial installation fees

219. In Chapter 13, we discussed some recurring costs that you should consider when planning the network. What are these?

- Access fees (monthly telecommunications charges)

- Support contracts (usually billed out annually)

- In-house support staff

- Energy needs
- Routine maintenance

220. Which is the best answer to the following statement?

Many companies these days lump _____ under the IT (Information Technology) umbrella.

C. Computer operations, network operations, and all other telecommunications.

221. What is a false floor?

A false floor is a raised floor made up of individual panels that are normally two-foot squares (two feet on each side). They are installed over a framework that looks like a giant matrix before the tiles are laid in. Usually, the facility is wired under the flooring before the tiles are placed down.

222. What is a DMZ?

DMZ is the acronym for demilitarized zone. It has been adopted by the networking world to mean an area not directly connected to any other network segment.

223. VPN remote users have a VPN *client* on their PCs which is configured to access the company's VPN access gateway router.

224. True or false: The distribution from the network operations area to each floor is accomplished by using redundant STP cabling to provide a high-speed path for the network traffic coming from each floor.

False — The distribution from the network operations area to each floor is accomplished using *a high-speed fiber optic link* to provide a high-speed path for the network traffic coming from each floor.

225. List the items that should be included in the final documentation of a network.

- Complete network diagrams with IP addressing
- Equipment lists with location
- Description of each type of network equipment used in the network
- Troubleshooting guides for each type of network equipment being used in the network
- List containing support information for each manufacturer of the network equipment used within the network
- A collection location for all warranty statements for all new equipment deployed within the network
- A collection location for all support contracts from the original equipment or other third-party support organizations

- A collection location of all equipment manuals for the network equipment deployed in the network

- Wiring diagrams for each panel deployed about the network

- A collection location for the information dealing with Internet service providers and other telecommunications providers, including data and voice

- A collection location for all license keys that may be required for any of the equipment in the network

- Maintenance/trouble log (used for ongoing support)

- A collection location of all contact information for all staff responsible for the maintenance of the network

226. *Infrastructure* refers to the structural components within a facility in support of the network architecture.

227. What does WEP stand for?

   WEP is an acronym for wired equivalent privacy. This is used by the wireless components within the network for authentication using a shared key. It is only used to prevent unintended use of the network from those users not permitted to access the network's resources.

228. In a networking environment, what is the area that should be restricted and controlled access at all times?

   The network operations area

229. True or false: The security practices used in a home LAN are sufficient for all large corporate LANs.

   False — In large networks with a wide range of network services and resources, there is a need to restrict some users to only portions of the network that are required by their function within the organization. There is the possibility of multiple authentication services within the same organization. There may be servers within the network that may not rely on network authentication and request a user ID and password from users when they try to gain access to that server.

230. A *firewall* is placed in the path in front of the Intranet web server to analyze the network traffic that is being directed toward it.

231. True or false: Depending upon the size of the network, constantly monitoring every node of a network can be overwhelming.

   True

232. True or false: It is bad practice to document the network from a security perspective.

False — To ensure the network from a security perspective requires full documentation as the network currently exists. The documentation should include network diagrams with network address schemes being used and the physical locations of the equipment and cabling being used to make up the network.

233. Name three methods of authentication.

- Lightweight Directory Access Protocol (LDAP)
- Remote Authentication Dial In User Service (RADIUS)
- Certificates

234. True or false: The process of network authentication can be simple as a user ID and password.

True

235. What are the four most commonly used elements in an LDAP?

- Users
- Groups
- Filters
- Services

236. When a RADIUS client passes a user's authentication credentials to the RADIUS server, the server will respond with one of three responses. What are these responses and what does each mean?

- Access Reject — User is denied all access to network resources.
- Access Challenge — User needs to provide additional information.
- Access Accept — User is granted access.

237. The use of *digitally signed certificates* came into use as a security method used to ensure the entities on opposite ends of a communication channel are who they claim to be.

238. *IPSec* is a suite of protocols used for securing Internet communications.

239. True or false: To have a successful help desk implementation, there is a need for someone to pick up the telephone.

True

240. In a large organization, there are usually groups of dedicated individuals who support certain aspects of the network. What are they?

- PC support
- Server support
- Network support

- Telecommunications support
- User base support

241. True or false: Monitoring network performance for larger networks is a manual, time-consuming process.

    False — Monitoring network performance for larger networks is an automated process.

242. In any organization, the security group would have a broad range of activities that deal with all aspects of network *security*.

243. The *network* support group is responsible for the distribution of network services over the network.

244. What is the logistics group responsible for?

    Logistics involves overseeing the inventory on hand as spares and accounting for all devices deployed in the network. It is the department responsible for logging of the new incoming stock as well as the units that have been returned to the manufacturer for repair.

245. What are three activities that are considered network maintenance?

- Revision control measures
- Corrective measures
- Preventive measures

246. The SNMP *agent* is software that communicates with a network management station (NMS) to answer queries from the station.

247. Each element has its own unique *OID*, which provides information on the object or is an object that will take a variable setting to configure the unit.

248. True or false: Packet capture nodes and programs can return some statistical information if you are investigating traffic patterns or performance issues on a network segment.

    True

249. SNMP uses a *community* setting to group a number of devices to be monitored within the *community*.

250. Name at least five of the common LAN issues that we mentioned in Chapter 16.

- Damaged cables
- Dirty fiber
- Excessive signal attenuation
- Insufficient bandwidth

- Denial-of-service (DoS) attack
- Electrical interference
- Wireless interference
- Damaged nodes
- Damaged interface
- Dirty interface
- Configuration error
- Authentication issues
- Excessive utilization
- Excessive errors
- VLAN configuration error
- Class-of-service issue
- Quality-of-service issue

251. When you are notified of a network issue, what are some of the first questions you should start considering?

- How many users are affected?
- Is there only one user having the issue, or are there several individuals?
- Is the problem an expected one? If so, do you have an action plan?
- Have you seen the issue before?
- What is the impact to the LAN? In other words, what nodes are affected?
- How many domains are affected?

252. The *proactive* approach beats the *reactive* approach.

253. Which of the following is a good proactive step you can take to help keep the network from going down and to recover quickly when it does?

- Shared knowledge
- Proper tools
- Ensure the proper individuals are trained appropriately
- Hardware spares
- *All of the above*

254. The ping is an ICMP echo request/reply that determines whether a node is *reachable*, the *round-trip* time for the process to complete, any

packet loss percentages, and a statistical *summary* for a given remote node.

255. True or false: By default, the `ping` command will send four ICMP requests and will expect four replies.

True

256. The `netstat` utility by default displays both incoming and outgoing network connections.

257. Network cable testers are devices that are used to check the integrity of the *cabling* in the LAN.

258. Name a few things that you should investigate when troubleshooting a node that is having problems.

- Node configuration(s)
- Event logs (as well as any other logs that may be available)
- Check the status of the interfaces of the node
- Check the memory usage statistics
- Capture any vendor recommended documentation
- Screen shots that may provide insight about the problem

259. What are the steps in the logical, eight-step troubleshooting model that we discussed in Chapter 16?

- Define the problem.
- Consider the possibilities.
- Determine the issue.
- Find a possible solution.
- Test the possible solution.
- Develop an action plan.
- Implement the action plan.
- Monitor the results.

260. As redundant as it may seem, what are the layers of the OSI reference model, and what is performed at each layer?

- Application layer — Provides services used by applications (the transfer of files and messages, authentication, name lookups, etc.) within the network.
- Presentation layer — Ensures that information received by one host can be read by that host.
- Session layer — Sets up, manages, and ends application sessions.

- Transport layer — Ensures the transmission of data from one endpoint to another.

- Network layer — Provides a path from endpoint to endpoint.

- Data Link layer — Provides for a way to transport data over a physical link.

- Physical layer — Determines the specifications for the operations of the physical links between network devices.

261. What are some common Layer 1 issues that can occur in a network?

- Damaged cables

- Dirty fiber

- Excessive signal attenuation

- Insufficient bandwidth

- Electrical interference

- Wireless interference

- Damaged interface

- Dirty interface

- Configuration error

- Denial-of-service (DoS) attack

- VLAN configuration error

- Class-of-service issue

- Excessive utilization

- Excessive errors

- VLAN issue

- Spanning tree issue

- MAC address table issue

- Hardware compression issue

- Software compression issue

- VRRP issue

262. What are some things that you should look for in each of the following layers?

- Layer 4 — At this layer, you want to focus on whether TCP or UDP is operating as intended. Take a sniffer trace and see if there are acknowledgements being sent in response to requests. Also, you will want to check if fragmentation is working as intended. Finally, check if there are any filters or QOS parameters that may be affecting the flow of data.

- Layer 5 — Things to look for at this layer are whether the session layer protocols are receiving errors while trying to communicate. A sniffer trace can be viewed to determine if the protocols are behaving correctly.

- Layer 6 — At this layer, the encryption, formatting, and compression of data occurs. Is data being encrypted and/or decrypted appropriately? Are encryption configuration settings correct? Are the correct data formats in use? Another concern at this layer is whether a VPN tunnel is operating as it is configured to do.

- Layer 7 — Concerns at the final layer are whether applications are working correctly. Sometimes a version of a standard may support new features, and older clients may no longer interoperate with the new versions. Also, end users may still try to connect to a server with the incorrect client and this, of course, will cause the user not to connect.

263. What are three of the symptoms that indicate a duplex mismatch?

- FCS/CRC errors
- Runt datagrams
- Late collisions

264. A failure in spanning tree usually creates a *loop* within the area that the spanning tree group covers.

265. What are three common ways to find out you have a loop within the LAN?

- System statistics
- Sniffer trace
- Because everyone is reporting issues

1BASE5 A baseband Ethernet system operating at 1 Mbps over one pair of UTP cable.

10BASE-T A baseband Ethernet system operating at 10 Mbps over two pairs of Category 3 UTP cable.

100BASE-T Baseband Ethernet transmission of 100 Mbps.

100BASE-TX A baseband Ethernet system operating at 100 Mbps over two pairs of STP or Category 5 UTP cable.

1000BASE-SX A baseband Ethernet system operating at 1000 Mbps over two multimode optical fibers using shortwave laser optics.

access domain A set of nodes among which MAC arbitration can occur.

access point A node that is configured to transmit and receive radio signals in a wireless LAN (WLAN).

access priority The priority used to determine access privileges on a shared LAN segment relative to other nodes that have frames queued.

active monitor A node in a Token Ring LAN that is responsible for handling many boundary conditions and housekeeping functions.

adapter The interface between a node and the network.

address A unique identifier of a node or network interface.

ad hoc A method of allowing wireless nodes to communicate directly with one another.

aggregated link A set of two or more physical links that appear to higher-layer entities as if they were a single higher-capacity link.

aggregator The entity that performs the operations required to make multiple physical links function as an aggregated link.

Address Resolution Protocol (ARP) A protocol that maps the IP address to the MAC address of a node or an interface.

aging process A process used in a spanning tree environment that removes dynamic entries from the filtering database when the associated nodes have been inactive for a specified time.

aging time A process used in a spanning tree environment that specifies the time after which a dynamic filtering database entry will be removed if its associated node has been continuously inactive.

AppleTalk A protocol suite developed by Apple Computer, used in Macintosh computers and other compatible nodes.

application A process or program running on a node.

application flow A stream of frames or packets among communicating processes within a set of end nodes.

Application layer The highest layer of the seven-layer OSI model.

application service provider (ASP) An online business that delivers and manages software over the Internet.

application-based VLAN A VLAN where the association of a frame to a VLAN is determined by application-specific information.

ARP cache   A data structure that provides the current mapping of IP addresses to MAC addresses.

asymmetric digital subscriber line (ADSL)   The most common form of DSL used in home networks. It is popular in home networks because it offers higher bandwidth for download.

Asynchronous Transfer Mode (ATM)   A networking standard that supports high-speed communications for both data and voice transmission.

autonegotiation   A technique used in Ethernet environments that operate over point-to-point links, where the node at each end of the link can learn the capabilities of the node at the other end and automatically configure itself to match the other end.

autosense   A process that allows an interface that supports both traditional and fast Ethernet speeds the capability to automatically sense the medium that is being used.

backbone   A network used primarily to interconnect other networks.

backoff   The mechanism used in the Ethernet MAC (CSMA/CD) to reschedule a transmission in the event of a collision.

backpressure   A technique used to stop a node from sending frames by using the half-duplex MAC mechanisms afforded by the underlying LAN.

bandwidth   The data-carrying capacity of a node or communications channel, usually expressed in bits per second.

baud   An analog signaling unit of measure.

best-effort service   A data delivery service where frames or packets are delivered to a destination with an understanding that delivery of the data is probable but is not guaranteed.

bit   An atomic unit of data representing either a 0 or a 1.

bit stuffing   A technique that provides a unique frame delimiter pattern yet maintains payload data transparency by inserting an extra 0 bit after every occurrence of five 1 bits in the payload data stream.

bit time   The length of time required to transmit 1 bit of information; equal to the reciprocal of the data rate.

blocking   In connectionless networks, a characteristic of a switch, switch fabric, or network interface implying that it is not capable of handling traffic at the maximum frame and/or data arrival rate without having to discard traffic (in the worst case) due to a lack of internal resources.

blocking state   A stable state in the Spanning Tree Protocol in which a bridge port will receive BPDUs but will neither receive nor transmit data frames.

bottleneck   A point in a data communications path or computer processing flow that limits overall throughput or performance.

bridge   An internetworking node that relays frames among its ports based upon Data Link layer information.

bridge port   A network interface on a bridge.

bridge priority   An administratively controlled value that is catenated with the bridge's MAC address to create a bridge identifier.

bridge transit delay   The delay between the receipt of a frame on one port and the forwarding of that frame onto another port of a bridge.

bridged LAN   A collection of networks (typically LANs) interconnected at the Data Link layer using bridges.

broadband   A technique of data transmission that carries multiple data channels over a shared wire.

broadcast address   A well-known multicast address signifying the set of all nodes.

brouter   A node combining the functions of a bridge and a router.

browser   An application program providing a graphical user interface to Internet or intranet services.

buffer   A block of memory used to temporarily store data while it is being processed.

burst mode   A modification to the flow control algorithm originally used in the NetWare (IPX) protocol suite. In burst mode, a node may continue to transmit information even if there are multiple outstanding packets awaiting acknowledgment.

byte   An 8-bit unit of data.

call-back unit   A node that calls a user at a pre-programmed telephone number when a connection is requested to prevent unauthorized access from unknown locations.

campus switch   A switch used within a campus backbone. Campus switches are generally high-performance nodes that aggregate traffic streams from multiple buildings and departments within a site.

canonical format   Synonymous with little-endian format.

carrier sense   In Ethernet, the act of determining whether the shared communications channel is currently in use by another node.

catenet   A collection of networks connected together at the Data Link layer. Also known as a *bridged LAN*.

chassis switch   A switch implemented in a modular fashion, with a base chassis and a set of plug-in blades chosen for a particular application environment.

cheapernet   A slang term for thin-wire coaxial Ethernet (10BASE2).

classification engine   The module within a switch that is responsible for examining incoming frames and classifying them as to VLAN association, priority, and so on.

client   (1) Application software (typically resident in an end-user work node) designed to operate through cooperation and communication with a companion server application (typically resident in a dedicated multitasking computer system). (2) An architectural entity using the services of a lower-layer service provider (for example, a Transport layer entity may be a client of a Network layer service provider).

cluster   A group of nodes that are integrated together to serve a common purpose.

coaxial cable   A communications medium built as a pair of concentric cylindrical conductors.

collapsed backbone   A method of interconnecting networks by using a switch or router as a central relay node.

collector The module within a link aggregator responsible for gathering frames received from multiple, underlying physical links.

collision A simultaneous transmission attempt by two or more nodes on a shared Ethernet LAN.

collision detection The act of detecting a collision.

collision domain The set of nodes among which a collision can occur. Nodes on the same shared LAN are in the same collision domain; nodes in separate collision domains do not contend for use of a common communications channel.

collision fragment The portion of an Ethernet frame that results from a collision. On a properly configured and operating LAN, collision fragments are always shorter than the minimum length of a valid frame.

common and internal spanning tree (CIST) A collection of the internal spanning trees in a multiple spanning tree region, combined with the common spanning tree that connects MST regions to form a single spanning tree that ensures all LANs in the bridge network are fully connected and loop-free.

common spanning tree (CST) A single spanning tree that interconnects multiple MST regions.

communications channel The medium and Physical layer nodes that convey signals among communicating nodes.

communications medium The physical medium used to propagate signals across a communications channel (for example, optical fiber, coaxial cable, twisted pair cable).

configuration message In the Spanning Tree Protocol, a BPDU that carries the information needed to compute and maintain the spanning tree.

congestion The state where the offered network load approaches or exceeds the locally available resources designed to handle that load (for example, link capacity or memory buffers).

connectionless A communications model in which nodes can exchange data without first establishing a connection. In connectionless communications, each frame or packet is handled independently of all others.

connection-oriented   A communications model in which nodes establish a connection before proceeding with data exchange and in which the data constitutes a flow that persists over time.

consultant   A person who borrows your watch, then charges you for the time of day.

conversation   As used in link aggregation, a set of traffic among which ordering must be maintained.

copy port   Synonymous with *mirror port*.

core switch   A VLAN-aware switch that connects exclusively to other VLAN-aware nodes.

crossbar   A common name for a crosspoint matrix switch fabric.

crossover cable   An Ethernet cable that is used to connect nodes of like types to one another for data communication.

crosspoint matrix   A switch fabric designed to provide simultaneous transient connections between any input port and any available output port.

cut-through   A mode of switch operation where frames can be forwarded before they are fully received.

datagram   A frame or a packet, depending on the encapsulation used.

Data Link layer   The second layer of the seven-layer OSI model, responsible for frame delivery across a single link.

data storage density   The quantity of data that can be stored within a data storage medium.

D-compliant   A bridge or switch that complies with IEEE 802.1D.

decapsulation   The process of removing protocol headers and trailers to extract higher-layer protocol information carried in the data payload.

decibel   The standard unit of measurement used for wireless radio signaling.

decoder   The entity within the Physical layer responsible for converting signals received from a communications channel into binary data.

dedicated bandwidth   A configuration in which the communications channel attached to a network interface is dedicated for use by a single node and does not have to be shared.

default port   A switch port configured to be the target destination port for traffic received on other ports and for which the lookup process fails.

default priority   The priority assigned to a received frame when none of the administratively configured policy rules apply to it.

deferral   The mechanism by which a half-duplex Ethernet node withholds its own transmissions when another node is currently using the shared communications channel.

demilitarized zone (DMZ)   Used to help secure LANs from outside attacks.

denial of service   Normally used to refer to a malicious attack on a LAN in an attempt to render a node or group of nodes unusable.

departmental switch   Synonymous with *workgroup switch*.

designated bridge   In the Spanning Tree Protocol, the bridge responsible for forwarding traffic from the direction of the root bridge onto a given link.

designated port   In the Spanning Tree Protocol, a port through which a designated bridge forwards traffic onto a given link in the direction away from the root bridge.

desktop switch   A switch used to connect directly to end user nodes.

driver   The software used to provide an abstraction of the hardware details of a network or peripheral node interface.

dialup   A method of network connectivity that is done between a PC and a network over a standard telephone line.

digital subscriber line   An Internet service that provides home users and small businesses a cost effective ability to access the Internet over normal phone lines at high speeds.

disabled state   A stable state in the Spanning Tree Protocol state machine in which a bridge port will not receive or transmit any frames.

disaster recovery (DR)   A plan to maintain or restore network services after the occurrence of a catastrophic event.

distributed backbone   A shared-bandwidth network used to interconnect other networks, where the backbone communications medium (rather than a central relay node) is used to attach to the lower level networks.

distribution function   The algorithm used by a distributor to assign conversations to particular physical links within an aggregation.

distributor   The module within a link aggregator responsible for assigning frames submitted by higher-layer clients to the individual underlying physical links.

Domain Name System (DNS)   Used to map host names with IP addresses.

download   The act of receiving and storing data from a remote node to a local node.

Dynamic Domain Name System (DDNS)   A system of mapping IP addresses to host names. DDNS works with dynamic IP addresses.

Dynamic Host Configuration Protocol (DHCP)   A network protocol that is used to assign an IP address to nodes when they join the network.

E1   A T-carrier technology commonly used in Europe, capable of multiplexing 32 DS-0 (64 Kbps) channels for a total data-carrying capacity of 2.048 Mbps.

edge switch   A switch located at the boundary between a VLAN-unaware domain and a VLAN-aware domain of a catenet.

egress filter   A qualification function implemented in an output port of a VLAN-aware switch.

egress rule   The rule used to determine whether a frame is transmitted in tagged or untagged format on the output port of a switch. If a frame belonging to a given VLAN is sent tagged, every node that is a member of that VLAN and directly connected to that port must be tag-aware.

encapsulating bridge   A bridge that encapsulates LAN frames for transmission across a backbone.

encapsulation   The process of taking data provided by a higher-layer entity as the payload for a lower-layer entity and applying a header and trailer as appropriate for the protocol in question.

encoder   The entity within the Physical layer responsible for converting binary data into signals appropriate for transmission across the communications channel.

end-of-frame delimiter   A symbol or set of symbols used to indicate the end of the Data Link (or MAC) encapsulation.

end-of-stream delimiter   A symbol or set of symbols used to indicate the end of the Physical layer encapsulation.

enterprise network   The set of LAN, MAN, and/or WAN networks and internetworking nodes comprising the communications infrastructure for a geographically distributed organization.

enterprise switch   A switch used within an enterprise backbone.

error control   A procedure used to recover from detected errors.

error detection   A procedure used to detect whether received information contains errors.

error rate   The ratio of bits (or frames) received in error to the total number of bits (or frames) received.

Ethernet   The popular name for a family of LAN technologies standardized by IEEE 802.3.

explorer frame   In source routing, a frame used either to perform route discovery or to propagate multicast traffic. There are two types of explorer frames: spanning tree explorers and all routes explorers.

extranet   A network that allows access from users that are outside of the controlled LAN.

Fast Ethernet   An Ethernet system operating at 100 Mbps.

fast path   The code thread that is traversed most often and that is usually highly optimized for performance.

fiber optic cable   A network cable designed for high-speed data transfer over long distances. The fiber optic cable consists of multiple glass fibers that are wrapped in an insulated case. Signals within a fiber optic cable are carried over pulses of light.

filtering   The process of inspecting frames received on an input port of a switch and deciding whether to discard or forward them.

filtering database   A data structure within a bridge that provides the mapping from destination address to bridge port (in a D-compliant bridge), or from the combination of destination address and VLAN to bridge port (in a Q-compliant bridge).

firewall   Software and/or hardware used specifically to protect a computer or network from being accessed by unauthorized users.

firmware   Software that is embedded in a node.

flooding   The action of forwarding a frame on to all ports of a switch except the port on which it arrived.

flow control   A mechanism that prevents a sender of traffic from sending faster than the receiver is capable of receiving.

forwarding   The process of taking a frame received on an input port of a switch and transmitting it on one or more output ports.

forwarding delay   A parameter of the Spanning Tree Protocol that defines the delay imposed between transitions from one state to another.

forwarding state   A stable state in the Spanning Tree Protocol in which a bridge port will transmit frames received from other ports as determined by the bridge forwarding algorithm.

fragmentation   A technique whereby a packet is subdivided into smaller packets so that they can be sent through a network with a smaller maximum transmission unit.

frame   The Data Link layer encapsulation of transmitted or received information.

frame check sequence   A block check code used to detect errors in a frame.

frame relay   A Layer 2 protocol that is used to transfer data over a WAN.

full duplex   A mode of communication whereby a node can simultaneously transmit and receive data across a communications channel.

gateway   (1) A node capable of relaying user application information among networks employing different architectures and/or protocol suites. (2) An internetworking node operating at the Transport layer or above. (3) An old term for an IP router. (4) A marketing name for anything that connects anything to anything else.

Gigabit Ethernet   An Ethernet system operating at 1000 Mbps.

gigabits per second (Gbps)   One billion bits per second.

gigahertz (GHz)   The radio signal transmission frequency of one billion cycles per second.

globally administered address   A node or interface identifier whose uniqueness is ensured through the use of an assigned organizationally unique identifier (OUI), typically by the manufacturer of the node or interface.

group address   Synonymous with *multicast address*.

guru   Richard Bramante.

hacker   A person who has evaded network security with the intention of modifying computer software, hardware configuration, and other security measures to either damage their effective operation or compromise them to the point where data theft can be accomplished without them being detected.

half duplex   A mode of communication in which a node can either transmit or receive data across a communications channel.

hardware address   Synonymous with *MAC address*, *physical address*, and *unicast address*.

hash function   An algorithm that distributes items evenly into one of a number of possible buckets in a hash table.

header   A protocol-specific field or fields that precede the encapsulated higher-layer data payload.

hello time   In the Spanning Tree Protocol, the interval between configuration messages as generated by the root bridge.

high-water mark   An indicator that the number of entries or bytes in a queue has risen above a predetermined level.

hop   A unit of measurement used to describe the path between a source and a destination.

hop count   A measure of the number of routers through which a packet has passed.

host   In an IP network, a synonym for *end node*.

hub   (1) A central interconnection node as used in a star-wired topology. (2) A repeater.

implicit tag   A method of mapping an untagged frame to its associated VLAN by inspection of the frame's contents.

individual port   A switch port that cannot form an aggregated link with any other port.

ingress filter   A qualification function implemented in an input port of a VLAN-aware switch.

ingress rule   A rule used to classify a frame as to its VLAN association.

integrated services digital network (ISDN)   A technology that supports the transmission of both data and voice over an existing phone line.

interframe gap   The spacing between time-sequential frames.

internal spanning tree   The spanning tree that has been calculated to run within an MST region.

Internet   A well-known set of networks interconnected by routers using the Internet Protocol (IP).

internet   A set of networks interconnected at the Network layer by routers.

Internet Protocol (IP)   The internetwork protocol used in the Internet, specified in RFC 791.

Internet service provider (ISP) The entity that provides Internet access to homes and businesses.

internetwork A set of networks interconnected at the Network layer by routers.

internetwork protocol The protocol used to move frames from originating source nodes to their ultimate target destinations.

internetworking node A node used to relay frames or packets among a set of networks (for example, a bridge or router).

IP address An address assigned to network nodes in order to transmit data at the Network layer.

IPSec A protocol that implements security in an IP network.

isoEthernet A variant of Ethernet developed by National Semiconductor Corp. (and standardized in IEEE 802.9a) that provides an isochronous communication channel in addition to a 10 Mbps Ethernet LAN.

jabber control A method used to prevent a node from transmitting continuously and thereby disrupting a shared communications channel.

jam In Ethernet, the process of sending an additional 32 data bits following the detection of a collision to ensure that all parties to the collision properly recognize the event as such.

jumbo frame A frame longer than the maximum frame length allowed by a standard.

kilobit (kb) The equivalent of 1000 bits.

kilobits per second (Kbps) One thousand bits per second.

kilobyte (KB) 1024 bytes.

LAN segmentation The practice of dividing a single LAN into a set of multiple LANs interconnected by bridges.

LAN switch A switch that interconnects local area networks.

Layer 2 switch Synonymous with *bridge*.

Layer 3 switch   Synonymous with *router*.

Layer 4 switch   A router that can make routing policy decisions based on Transport layer information (for example, TCP port identifiers) encapsulated within packets.

leaky VLAN   A VLAN that may, under certain boundary conditions, carry frames that do not belong to that VLAN.

learning process   The process whereby a bridge builds its filtering database by gleaning address-to-port mappings from received frames.

learning state   A transition state in the Spanning Tree Protocol state machine where a bridge port is learning address-to-port mappings to build its filtering database before entering the forwarding state.

Lightweight Directory Access Protocol (LDAP)   A protocol that allows the development and management of directories, or databases, that contain information about nodes, personnel, and other aspects of the network.

line driver   An electronic or optical node used to convey line signals onto a physical communications medium.

line receiver   An electronic or optical node used to extract line signals from a physical communications medium.

link aggregation   A process to increase both the capacity and availability of a communications channel.

link cost   A metric assigned to a link, used to compute the spanning tree.

listening state   A transition state in the Spanning Tree Protocol state machine in which a bridge port is listening for BPDUs transmitted by other bridge ports to determine whether it should proceed to the learning state.

load balancing   The practice of allocating traffic across multiple nodes, interfaces, or communications links to evenly distribute offered load and obtain maximum benefit from the available resources.

local area network (LAN)   A network with a relatively small geographical extent.

locally administered address   A node or interface identifier whose uniqueness is established by a network administrator rather than by the manufacturer of the node or interface.

LocalTalk   An Apple Computer–proprietary LAN technology employing CSMA/CA access control at a data rate of 230 Kbps.

low-water mark   An indicator that the number of entries or bytes in a queue has dropped below a predetermined level.

MAC address   A bit string that uniquely identifies one or more nodes or interfaces as the source or destination of transmitted frames. IEEE 802 MAC addresses are 48 bits in length and may be either unicast (source or destination) or multicast (destination only).

MAC address–based VLAN   A catenet where the association of a frame to a VLAN is determined by the source MAC address in the frame.

MAC algorithm   The set of procedures used by the nodes on a LAN to arbitrate for access to the shared communications channel (for example, CSMA/CD, token passing).

managed object   An atomic element of an SNMP MIB with a precisely defined syntax and meaning, representing a characteristic of a managed node.

managed security service provider (MSSP)   An ISP that provides additional network security management, which may include virus scanning, intrusion detection, and firewall capabilities.

maximum transmission unit (MTU)   The maximum size of a unit of data.

Media Access Control (MAC)   The entity or algorithm used to arbitrate for access to a shared communications channel.

megabit (Mb)   One million bits.

megabits per second (Mbps)   One million bits per second.

megabyte (MB)   1024 kilobytes.

megahertz (MHz)   One million cycles per second.

microsegmentation A network configuration model in which each individual node connects to a dedicated port on a switch.

mirror port A switch port configured to reflect the traffic appearing on another one of the switch's ports.

modem A node used to convert digital data to, or from, analog signals for transmission across an analog communications channel.

modulation The process of manipulating a waveform to create a signal that sends a message that needs to be communicated. In data communications, modulation is performed by a node that converts a digital signal to an analog signal, in order to be communicated over a phone line.

monitored port A port on a switch whose traffic is replicated to a mirror port for the purpose of external traffic monitoring.

MTU discovery A process whereby a node can determine the largest frame or packet that can be transferred across a catenet or internetwork without requiring fragmentation.

multicast address A method of identifying a set of one or more nodes as the destination for transmitted data.

multicast pruning A technique whereby traffic is propagated only on those links necessary to deliver it to the nodes listening to a particular multicast address.

multihoming Configuration of multiple network interfaces on a single computer.

multimode fiber An optical fiber that allows signals to propagate in multiple transmission modes simultaneously, ultimately limiting both its bandwidth and maximum extent.

multiple spanning tree bridge A bridge that supports the common spanning tree and at least one multiple spanning tree instance.

multiple spanning tree configuration table A table that maps all VLANs to a common spanning tree or to a multiple spanning tree instance.

multiple spanning tree instance A spanning tree within a multiple spanning tree region.

Multiple Spanning Tree Protocol (MSTP)   The Multiple Spanning Tree Protocol allows for a separate spanning tree for each VLAN group while also blocking redundant links.

multiple spanning tree region   LANs and multiple spanning tree bridges that connect to each other by ports on the multiple spanning tree bridges. Each LAN must designate a common internal spanning tree bridge that must also be a multiple spanning tree bridge. Each connected port must either be a designated port on one of the LANs or a nondesignated port on a multiple spanning tree bridge that connects to one of the LANs.

multiplexing   The act of combining multiple data streams into a single signal and then transmitting the data over a shared medium.

NetWare   A network operating system and related software components developed by Novell.

network   A set of nodes and communication links that allow computers to intercommunicate.

network access server (NAS)   A gateway device protecting access to a protected network resource

Network Address Translation (NAT)   A networking protocol that allows the separation of public and private addresses within a LAN.

network administrator   (1) A person responsible for managing the day-to-day operations of a network. (2) The person blamed for all computing problems, whether they are related to the network or not.

network architecture   A model of the operation and behavior of nodes attached to a network, typically as a series of layered protocol entities.

Network Basic Input/Output System (NetBIOS)   A protocol that provides computer services on a network.

network interface   A subsystem that provides the means for a computer or internetworking node to attach to a communications link.

network interface card (NIC)   A network adapter that provides a hardware interface between an end node and the network.

Network layer   The third layer of the seven-layer OSI model, responsible for routing packets across an internetwork.

network management   The process of configuring, monitoring, controlling, and administering network operation.

network management agent   An entity (typically a combination of software and hardware) within a node that is responsible for gathering network management information and reporting it to a network management node as appropriate.

Network Time Protocol (NTP)   A protocol that is used to synchronize system clocks of nodes in a LAN.

nibble   A 4-bit unit of data (half of a byte).

node   Any device that connects to a LAN.

nonblocking   In connectionless networks, a characteristic of a switch, switch fabric, or network interface implying that it is capable of handling traffic at the maximum frame and data arrival rates without ever having to discard traffic due to a lack of internal resources.

null modem cable   A cable that allows serial port to serial port communication.

one-armed router   A router (typically connected to a VLAN-aware switch) that forwards traffic among multiple logical networks through a single physical interface.

operating system   The software responsible for managing the underlying hardware in a computer.

optical fiber   A network cable designed for high-speed data transfer over long distances. The fiber optic cable consists of multiple glass fibers that are wrapped in an insulated case. Signals within a fiber optic cable are carried over pulses of light.

overprovisioning   A technique of providing more capacity than is actually needed for a given application.

packet   The Network layer encapsulation of transmitted or received information.

patch cable   An Ethernet cable that is used to link nodes that are close to one another. Patch cables are normally made using a stranded sheath, which makes it more pliable and less likely to be broken when transporting them from location to location.

path cost   The sum of the link costs between a given bridge port and the root bridge, used to compute the spanning tree.

pause_time   The parameter of an Ethernet flow control message that indicates the length of time for which a node should cease data transmission.

Physical layer   The lowest layer of the seven-layer OSI model, responsible for transmission and reception of signals across the communications medium.

ping   A utility program used to test for network connectivity by using the Echo Request and Echo Response mechanisms of ICMP.

port   A network interface on a bridge, switch, or node.

port identifier   A value assigned to a port that uniquely identifies it within a switch. The Spanning Tree and Link Aggregation Control Protocols both use port identifiers.

port mirroring   A process whereby one switch port (the mirror port) is configured to reflect the traffic appearing on another one of the switch's ports (the monitored port).

port number   A locally assigned, bridge-unique number identifying each port on the bridge.

port priority   An administratively controlled value that is catenated with a port number to create a port identifier.

port-based VLAN   A catenet where the association of a frame to a VLAN is determined by the switch port on which the frame arrived.

preamble   A frame field used to allow a receiver to properly synchronize its clock before decoding incoming data.

Presentation layer   The sixth layer of the seven-layer OSI model, responsible for converting information between a local format and a common network format.

priority   The principle whereby preferential treatment is given to certain network nodes, applications, or traffic over others.

priority regeneration   A technique used in a VLAN-aware switch to map locally significant, natively signaled user priority levels into globally significant values.

priority tag   A tag adhering to the syntax of IEEE 802.1Q, but used solely to indicate frame priority as opposed to a VLAN association.

promiscuous mode   A mode of operation of a network interface in which it receives all traffic regardless of destination address.

protocol   A set of behavioral algorithms, message formats, and message semantics used to support communications between entities across a network.

protocol analyzer   A network management tool that is used to parse and decode frames for the purpose of monitoring and/or isolating faults in a network.

protocol stack   A set of layered protocol entities that implement a given network architecture.

protocol-based VLAN   A catenet in which the association of a frame with a VLAN is determined by the Network layer protocol encapsulated by the frame.

Q-compliant   A bridge or switch that complies with IEEE 802.1Q.

quality of service (QoS)   A collection of networking techniques that are used to provide data delivery guarantees with predictable results.

Rapid Spanning Tree Protocol (RSTP)   An enhancement to the original Spanning Tree Protocol; provides for a faster convergence when there is a change in the topology of the spanning tree group.

reassembly   The process of reconstructing a packet from its fragments.

relay entity   The architectural abstraction within an internetworking node that transfers data among the ports of the node.

remote bridge   A bridge that has at least one port connected to a WAN link to allow a catenet to span geographically dispersed LANs.

repeater   A node used to interconnect LAN segments at the Physical layer.

ring number   A locally assigned, catenet-unique value identifying each ring in a source-routed catenet.

RMON probe   A node capable of passively monitoring network traffic, gathering statistics related to that traffic, and reporting it to a network management node using SNMP.

root bridge   In the Spanning Tree Protocol, the bridge in the catenet with the numerically lowest value for its bridge identifier.

root port   In the Spanning Tree Protocol, the port through which a designated bridge forwards traffic in the direction of the root bridge.

route descriptor   A catenation of a ring number and a bridge number within the routing information field of a source-routed frame.

route discovery   The process of determining the available route(s) between a pair of nodes in a source-routed catenet.

router   An intermediate node operating as a Network layer relay node.

routing   The process of relaying packets between networks.

segment   A subset of a larger network.

serial cable   A cable that connects to a serial port and allows for bi-direction data flow between a node and a PC or an external modem.

serial port   A port that connects to a serial cable and allows for bi-direction data flow between a node and a PC or an external modem.

server   (1) Application software designed to operate with a companion client application. 2) An architectural entity providing services to a higher-layer client.

Session layer   The fifth layer of the seven-layer OSI model, responsible for process-to-process communication.

shared bandwidth   A characteristic of a communications channel in which the available capacity is shared among all the attached nodes.

shared bus   A type of switch fabric that uses a common communications channel as the mechanism for frame exchange among the switch ports.

shared media   A physical communications medium that supports the connection of multiple nodes, each of which may transmit and/or receive information across the common communications channel.

shared memory   A type of switch fabric that uses a common memory pool as the mechanism for frame exchange among the switch ports.

singlemode fiber   An optical fiber that allows signals to propagate in only one transmission mode.

sink   The ultimate destination of a frame or packet on a network. A sink absorbs and removes the frame or packet from the network, as opposed to relaying or forwarding it to another link.

sniffer   A network analyzer.

source   The original sender of a frame or packet on a network. A source generates new frames that may be forwarded by internetworking nodes, and which are absorbed by the ultimate destination.

source pruning   A technique used within multicast pruning in which the source of a multicast stream is turned off if it is known that there are no nodes currently listening to the stream.

source routing   A method of bridging where the path through the catenet is determined by the communicating end nodes rather than the bridges, and frames carry explicit routing information. Used exclusively in Token Ring and some FDDI LANs.

source routing bridge   A bridge used in a source-routed catenet.

spanning forest   A set of multiple spanning trees in a single catenet. Traffic for any given VLAN propagates over a single spanning tree in the forest.

spanning tree   A loop-free topology used to ensure that frames are neither replicated nor resequenced when bridged among nodes in a catenet.

Spanning Tree Protocol (STP)   A protocol used by bridges to determine, establish, and maintain a loop-free topology that includes every reachable link in a catenet.

stackable switch   A switch equipped with a means of connection to other similar switches such that the set of interconnected switches can be configured and managed as if it were a single switch.

standing request   A method of switch fabric arbitration where an input port requests the use of a specified output port and is notified at a later time when that request can be granted.

start-of-frame delimiter (SFD)   A symbol or set of symbols used to indicate the beginning of the Data Link (or MAC) encapsulation.

start-of-stream delimiter (SSD)   A symbol or set of symbols used to indicate the beginning of the Physical layer encapsulation.

store-and-forward   A mode of switch operation where frames are completely received before they are forwarded on to any of the output ports of the node.

straight-through cable   A twisted pair cable that is wired for normal DTE-to-DCE communications.

stream   The Physical layer encapsulation of transmitted or received information.

strict priority   A method of priority scheduling where higher priority traffic is always processed before lower priority traffic.

subnet mask   A 32-bit field that, when logically with an IP address, produces the network portion of that address. The bits of a subnet mask are set to 1 for those bits that correspond to the network portion of the associated IP address and to 0 otherwise.

subnet-based VLAN   A catenet where the association of a frame to a VLAN is determined by the network portion of the IP source address contained within the frame.

switch   Synonymous with *internetworking node*.

switch fabric   The mechanism used to transfer frames from the input ports of a switch to its output ports.

switch mirroring   A process whereby one switch port is configured to reflect the traffic appearing on all other ports of the switch.

switched LAN   A LAN characterized by the use of a switching hub rather than a repeater hub as the central node.

switching hub   A switch used as a central interconnection node in a star-wired topology.

symbol   An encoded bit or group of bits. A symbol is the atomic unit of data at the Physical layer of the OSI model.

T1   A T-carrier technology capable of multiplexing 24 DS-0 (64 kbps) channels, for a total data-carrying capacity of 1.536 Mbps.

tag-aware domain   A region of a virtual bridged network in which all nodes are tag-aware.

tag-awareness   A property of a node that supports and can use VLAN tags.

tagged frame   A frame that includes a VLAN tag.

task force   A subcommittee within an IEEE 802 working group that is responsible for the development of a particular standard or standards.

throughput   A measure of the rate of data transfer between communicating nodes, typically in bits per second.

time-to-live (TTL)   A field within an IP packet used for lifetime control. Routers decrement the TTL field; packets can be discarded if the value ever reaches 0.

token   A mechanism used to administer access control among nodes on a token bus or Token Ring LAN. Under normal conditions, only the node in possession of the token may transmit frames.

token bus   A LAN whose MAC algorithm uses token passing among nodes on a logical bus topology.

token domain   The access domain of a LAN using a token-passing MAC (for example, token bus or Token Ring). See also *access domain*.

token reservation   A mechanism that allows nodes to arbitrate for the future use of a token at a given priority level.

Token Ring   A LAN whose MAC algorithm uses token passing among nodes on a logical ring topology.

token-passing   A method of arbitrating access to a shared LAN where control is passed among the attached nodes through the use of a token.

topology   The physical or logical layout of a network.

topology change   An event that evokes recomputation of the spanning tree in a catenet.

trailer   A protocol-specific field or fields that follow the encapsulated higher-layer data payload.

translational bridge   A transparent bridge that interconnects LANs that use different frame formats.

transparent bridging   A method of bridging in which the path through the catenet is determined by the bridges themselves and nodes can communicate without any knowledge of the presence or action of those bridges.

Transport layer   The fourth layer of the seven-layer OSI model, which typically provides reliable end-to-end message delivery across the underlying potentially unreliable network.

trap   An unsolicited message sent from a network management agent to a network management node, usually to signal a significant event.

trunk   A common name for an aggregated link.

tunnel   A node used to encapsulate one protocol within another, often at the same layer of their respective architectures.

twisted pair   A communications medium consisting of two helically intertwined copper conductors.

type encapsulation   The Ethernet frame format in which the Length/Type field identifies the protocol type of the encapsulated data rather than its length.

unified threat management   A device that operates on Layers 2 through 7 and is capable of providing firewall along with the ability of performing content filtering.

unmanaged switch   A switch that does not support any remote network management capability.

untagged frame   A frame that does not include a VLAN tag.

uplink port   A switch port designed to connect to a backbone switch or network. An uplink port often supports a higher data rate than the attachment ports of the switch.

upload   The act of sending data from a local node to a remote node.

user priority   The priority associated with the application submitting a frame. User priority is carried end-to-end across a catenet.

virtual bridged network   A catenet that comprises one or more VLAN-aware nodes, allowing the definition, creation, and maintenance of virtual LANs.

virtual LAN (VLAN)   A subset of the nodes, applications, and/or links within a catenet, as defined by their logical relationship rather than their physical connectivity.

VLAN association rule   An algorithm used to map a frame to the VLAN to which it belongs.

VLAN tag   A field inserted into a frame that provides an explicit indication of the VLAN association for that frame.

VLAN-awareness   A property of a node that supports and can use VLAN capabilities within a catenet.

wide area network (WAN)   A network with far-reaching geographical extent. Typically, the links comprising WANs are owned by, and leased from, common carriers, which imposes a recurring cost as a function of distance and/or data rate.

wire speed   The maximum frame and data arrival rate possible on a given network interface. Wire speed on a 100 Mbps Ethernet implies rates of 100 million bits per second and 148,809.5 frames per second.

wireless fidelity (WiFi)   A term that describes certain types of 802.11 WLANs.

wiring closet   A room used to house and interconnect network and/or telecommunications equipment. Hubs, switches, and routers are typically installed in wiring closets.

workgroup switch   A switch used within a single department or workgroup.

working group   A group formed by interested members of an organization. The working group can have open meetings, as well as communication through Internet forums and mailing lists. The working group works on issues relating to standards and standards development.

Worldwide Interoperability for Microwave Access (WiMAX [IEEE 802.16]) A task force responsible for the IEEE 802.16 standards for broadband wireless access networks.

X.25   A suite of protocols, used in packet-switched networks, that encompasses Layers 1 through 3 of the OSI reference model

zone   A set of logically related nodes within an AppleTalk internetwork. Nodes in the same zone can communicate as a single workgroup regardless of whether they are on the same or different networks. An AppleTalk zone constitutes a Network layer VLAN.

AAL1: ATM adaptation layer 1

AAL2: ATM adaptation layer 2

AAL5: ATM adaptation layer 5

AARP: AppleTalk Address Resolution Protocol

ABR: Available bit rate

AC: Access control

AC: Alternating current

ACK: Acknowledgment

ADSL: Asymmetric digital subscriber line

ADSP: AppleTalk Data Stream Protocol

AFP: AppleTalk Filing Protocol

AIM: AOL Instant Messenger

ALG: Application layer gateway

AN: Access network

ANSI: American National Standards Institute

AP: Access point

API : Application program interface

APIPA: Automatic private IP address

ARB: All routes broadcast

ARCnet: Attached Resource Computer network

ARE: All routes explorer

ARP: Address Resolution Protocol

ASCII: American Standard Code for Information Interchange

ASIC: Application-specific integrated circuit

ASN.1: Abstract Syntax Notation 1

ASP: AppleTalk Session Protocol

ATC: ATM transfer capability

ATM: Asynchronous Transfer Mode

ATM MPE: ATM Transfer Capability

ATP: AppleTalk Transaction Protocol

AURP: AppleTalk Update-based Routing Protocol

BER: Bit error rate

BERT: Bit error rate test

BGP: Border Gateway Protocol

BGP4: BGP version 4

BOOTP: Bootstrap Protocol

BPDU: Bridge protocol data unit

bps: Bits per second

Bps: Bytes per second

BRI: Basic rate interface

CAM: Content-addressable memory

CAT5: Category 5 cable

CATV: Community antenna television

CBR: Constant bit rate

CCITT: International Consultative Committee for Telephone and Telegraph

CCD: Clear channel data

CDDI: Copper distributed data interface

CFI: Canonical format indicator

CIDR: Classless interdomain routing

CIST: Common and internal spanning tree

CLNP: Connectionless Network Protocol

CMIP: Common Management Interface Protocol

CMT: Connection management

CMTS: Cable modem termination system

COAX: Coaxial cable

CODEC: Coder/decoder

CoS: Class of service

CPU: Central processing unit

CRC: Cyclic redundancy check

CSMA/CA: Carrier Sense Multiple Access with Collision Avoidance

CSMA/CD: Carrier Sense Multiple Access with Collision Detection

CST: Common spanning tree

CTD: Cell transfer delay

DA: Destination address

dB: Decibel

DBR: Deterministic bit rate

DC: Direct current

DDNS: Dynamic Domain Name System

DDP: Datagram Delivery Protocol

DDR: Double-data rate

DEC: Digital Equipment Corporation

DECnet: Digital Equipment Corporation Network Architecture

DEUNA: Digital Ethernet UNIBUS Network Adapter

DHCP: Dynamic Host Configuration Protocol

DiffServ: Differentiated services

DIX: Digital–Intel–Xerox

DMA: Direct memory access

DMS: Digital multiplex switch

DMZ: Demilitarized zone

DNS: Domain Name System

DOS: Disk Operation System

DoS: Denial of service

DPM: Downtime performance measure

DPNSS: Digital private network signaling system

DPT: Dynamic packet trunking

DQDB: Distributed queue dual bus

DRAM: Dynamic random access memory

DRP: DECnet Routing Protocol

DSAP: Destination service access point

DSCP: DiffServe code point

DSL: Digital subscriber line

DSP: Digital signal processing

DSLAM: Digital subscriber line access multiplexer

DSPVC: Dynamic soft permanent virtual circuit

DSVD: Digital simultaneous voice and data

DTMF: Dual-tone multi-frequency

DTR: Data terminal ready

DTR: Dedicated Token Ring

DWDM: Dense wavelength division multiplexing

E-RIF: Embedded routing information field

ECC: Error-correcting code

ECL: Emitter-coupled logic

ECMP: Equal cost multipath

ECS: Encryption control signal

ED: End delimiter

EEPROM: Electrically erasable programmable read-only memory

EIA: Electronic Industries Association

EMI: Electromagnetic interference

FC: Frame control

FCS: Frame check sequence

FDDI: Fiber distributed data interface

FE: Fast Ethernet

FIFO: First in/first out

FIRE: Flexible intelligent routing engine

FLR: Frame loss rate

FOIRL: Fiber-optic inter-repeater link

FPGA: Field-programmable gate array

FR: Frame relay

FS: Frame status

FTP: File Transfer Protocol

GARP: Generic Attribute Registration Protocol

Gbps: Gigabits per second

GE: Gigabit Ethernet

GHz: Gigahertz

GigE: Gigabit Ethernet

GMRP: GARP Multicast Registration Protocol

GQOS: Guaranteed quality of service

GVRP: GARP VLAN Registration Protocol

GW: Gateway

HDLC: High-level data link control

HDSL: High (bit-rate) digital subscriber line

HILI: High-level interface

HTTP: Hypertext Transfer Protocol

Hz: Hertz

IAD: Integrated access device

IANA: Internet Assigned Number Authority

IBM: International Business Machines

IC: Integrated circuit

ICMP: Internet Control Message Protocol

IEEE: Institute of Electrical and Electronics Engineers

IETF: Internet Engineering Task Force

IFG: Interframe gap

I/O: Input/output

IP: Internet Protocol

IPX: Internetwork Packet eXchange

ISDN: Integrated Services Digital Network

ISIS: Intermediate system to intermediate system

ISO: International Organization for Standardization

ISP: Internet service provider

IST: Internal spanning tree

ITU: International Telecommunications Union

IVL: Independent VLAN learning

Kbps: Kilobits per second

LACP: Link Aggregation Control Protocol

LAN: Local area network

LAT: Local area transport

LDAP: Lightweight Directory Access Protocol

LDP: Label Distribution Protocol

LE: Local exchange

LED: Light-emitting diode

LEN: Line equipment number

LER: Label edge router

LF: Largest frame

LFI: Link fragmentation and interleaving

LFSR: Linear feedback shift register

LLC: Logical link control

LLQ: Low latency queuing

LRU: Least recently used

LSAP: Link service access point

LSB: Least significant bit

LSB: Least significant byte

LVDS: Low-voltage differential signaling

MAC: Media Access Control

MAC_PDU: Media Access Control protocol data unit

MAN: Metropolitan area network

MAP: Manufacturing automation protocol

Mbps: Megabits per second

MDA: Media dependent adapter

MDM: Multiservice data manager

MF: Multifrequency

MG: Media gateway

MGCP: Media Gateway Control Protocol

MIB: Management information base

MIPPS: Micro integrated project planning system

MIS: Management information system

MLT: Multilink trunk

MM: Multiple mode

MOP: Maintenance-Oriented Protocol

MP: Media proxy

MP: Multipoint procession

MPEG: Motion Picture Experts Group

MPLS: Multi-protocol label switching

ms: Milliseconds

MST: Multiple spanning tree

MSTI: Multiple spanning tree instance

MSTP: Multiple Spanning Tree Protocol

MTBF: Mean time between failures

MTP: Message Transfer Protocol

MTU: Maximum transmission unit

NAT: Network Address Translation

NBP: Name Binding Protocol

NCC: Network control center

NCFI: Non-canonical format indicator

NCP: NetWare Core Protocol

NCS: Network call signaling

NE: Network element

NetBEUI: NetBIOS Extended User Interface

NetBIOS: Network Basic Input/Output System

NFS: Network File System

NGRB: Networking Guru Rich Bramante

NIC: Network interface controller

NMI: Network management interface

NOC: Network operations center

NOS: Network operating system

NSAP: Network service access point

ns: Nanoseconds

NTP: Network Time Protocol

OC-3: Optical carrier level 3

OC-12: Optical carrier level 12

OC-48: Optical carrier level 48

OC-192: Optical carrier level 192

opcode: Operation code

OS: Operating system

OSI: Open Systems Interconnect

OSPF: Open shortest path first

OUI: Organizationally unique identifier

PAgP: Port Aggregation Protocol

PAN: Personal area network

PAR: Positive acknowledgment and retransmission

PAR: Project authorization request

PATRICIA: Practical Algorithm to Retrieve Information Coded in Alphanumeric

PBN: Packet-based network

PC: Personal computer

PCB: Printed circuit board

PCI: Peripheral component interconnect

PCM: Pulse code modulation

PCR: Peak cell rate

PDU: Protocol data unit

PHB: Per-hop behavior

PHY: Physical layer interface

PID: Protocol identifier

PL_PDU: Physical layer protocol data unit

PNNI: Private network to network interface

POP: Point of presence

POP: Post Office Protocol

POS: Packet over SONET

PPP: Point-to-Point Protocol

PRI: Primary rate interface

ps: Picoseconds

PSTN: Public switched telephone network

PVC: Permanent virtual circuit

PVID: Port VLAN identifier

QoS: Quality of service

RAM: Random access memory

RARP: Reverse Address Resolution Protocol

RAS: Remote access server

RBGoN: Rich Bramante, Guru of Networking

RDRAM: Rambus Dynamic Random Access Memory

RED: Random early discard

RED: Random early detect

RFC: Request for Comments

RII: Routing information indicator

RIP: Routing Information Protocol

RISC: Reduced instruction-set computer

RMON: Remote monitor

ROM: Read-only memory

RPSU: Redundant power supply unit

RSTP: Rapid Spanning Tree Protocol

RSVP: Resource Reservation Protocol

RT: Routing type

RTCP: Real-Time Control Protocol

RTP: Real-Time Transport Protocol

RTTP: Real-Time Transport Protocol

RTMP: Routing Table Maintenance Protocol

SA: Source address

SAP: Service access point

SAP: Service Advertisement Protocol

SD: Start delimiter

SDH: Synchronous digital hierarchy

SDU: Service data unit

SFD: Start-of-frame delimiter

SG: Signaling gateway

SGMP: Simple Gateway Management Protocol

SGRAM: Synchronous graphic random access memory

SIP: Session Initiation Protocol

SM: Single mode

SMDS: Switched multimegabit data service

SMT: Station management

SMTP: Simple Mail Transport Protocol

SNA: Systems network architecture

SNAP: Sub-Network Access Protocol

SNMP: Simple Network Management Protocol

SNMPv2: Simple Network Management Protocol version 2

SNMPv3: Simple Network Management Protocol version 3

SOHO: Small office/home office

SONET: Synchronous Optical Network

SPF: Single point of failure

SPVC: Soft permanent virtual circuit

SPX: Sequenced Packet eXchange

SR-TB: Source routing-to-transparent bridge

SRAM: Static random access memory

SRB: Source routing bridge

SRF: Specifically routed frame

SRF: Source routed frame

SRT: Source route/transparent bridge

SSAP: Source service access point

SSE: Silicon switching engine

SSRAM: Synchronous static random access memory

STE: Spanning tree explorer

STP: Spanning Tree Protocol

STUN: Simple traversal of UDP over NAT

SVC: Switched virtual circuit

SVL: Shared VLAN learning

SVoIP: Switched Voice over IP

TAG: Technical Action Group

TB: Transparent bridge

Tbps: Terabits per second

TC: Topology change

TCI: Tag control information

TCP: Transmission Control Protocol

TDM: Time division multiplexing

Telnet: Telecommunication network

TFTP: Trivial FTP

TIA: Telecommunications Industries Association

TLV: Type-length-value

TOS: Type of service

TP-4: Transport Protocol Class 4

TP-PMD: Twisted-pair physical medium dependent sublayer

TREN: Token Ring encapsulation

TSAP: Transport layer service access point

TTL: Time to live

TXI: Transmit immediate

UDP: User Datagram Protocol

UI: User interface

UNI: User to network interface

UPS: Uninterruptible power supply

UTP: Unshielded twisted pair

UUI: User-to-user interface

VAX: Virtual address extensions

VBR: Variable bit rate

VC: Virtual channel

VLAN: Virtual local area network

VMS: Virtual memory system

VoATM: Voice over ATM

VoIP: Voice over IP

VoP: Voice over Packet

VPID: VLAN protocol identifier

VPN: Virtual private network

VRRP: Virtual Router Redundancy Protocol

WAN: Wide area network

WDM: Wavelength-division multiplexer

WFQ: Weighted fair queuing

WG: Working group

XIJI: Extended LAN interface interconnect

XNS: Xerox Network System

XTP: Express Transport Protocol

ZIP: Zone Information Protocol

Index